READING AS THE ANGELS READ

Speculation and Politics in Dante's Banquet

MARIA LUISA ARDIZZONE

Reading as the Angels Read

Speculation and Politics in Dante's Banquet

UNIVERSITY OF TORONTO PRESS
Toronto Buffalo London

Toronto Buffalo London
www.utppublishing.com

ISBN 978-1-4426-3706-1

Toronto Italian Studies

Library and Archives Canada Cataloguing in Publication

Ardizzone, Maria Luisa, author
Reading as the angels read: speculation and politics in Dante's Banquet / Maria Luisa Ardizzone.

Includes bibliographical references and index.
ISBN 978-1-4426-3706-1 (bound)

1. Dante Alighieri, 1265–1321. Convivio. 2. Politics in literature. I. Title.

PQ4310.C4A74 2016 851′.1 C2015-906560-7

University of Toronto Press acknowledges the financial assistance to its publishing program of the Canada Council for the Arts and the Ontario Arts Council, an agency of the Government of Ontario.

To Franca Ghitti
To her "Other Alphabets"
In memoriam

Laudent nomen tuum, laudent te supercaelestes populi angelorum tuorum, qui non opus habent suspicere firmamentum hoc et legendo cognoscere verbum tuum. Vident enim faciem tuam semper. Et ibi legunt sine syllabis temporum quid velit aeterna voluntas tua. Legunt, eligunt, diligunt; semper legunt et numquam praeterit quod legunt.eligendo enim et diligendo legunt ipsam incommutabilitatem consilii tui. Non clauditur codex eorum nec plicatur liber eorum, quia tu ipse illis hoc es et es in aeternum.

Let them praise thy name – this super-celestial society, thy angels, who have no need to look up at this firmament or to gain a knowledge of thy Word by reading it – let them praise thee. For they always behold thy face and read therein, without any syllables in time, what thy eternal will intends. They read, they choose, they love. They are always reading, and what they read never passes away. For by choosing and by loving they read the very immutability of thy counsel. Their book is never closed, nor is the scroll folded up, because thou thyself art this to them, and art this to them eternally. (Aurelii Augustinii, *Confessionum libri XIII*, XIII, XV)

Contents

Preface

This book proposes a rereading of the *Convivio*, the doctrinal work that Dante left uncompleted and withdrew from circulation. Divided into five chapters that are preceded by an introduction, the book focuses on the first three treatises, discusses the fourth treatise, and, starting with the introduction, tries to reconstruct the cultural and philosophical background that provides the motivation for the *Convivio*. Although respectful of previous historical readings, the book uses both well-known and recently discovered documents to introduce an innovative interpretation of the work, stressing its cognitive goal and tracing its attempt to establish a theory of earthly human happiness, in which perfect knowledge is the natural basis of a well-organized political community.

Written in the years of exile, conceived as a commentary on a few canzoni written in Dante's Florentine years, the *Convivio*, according to what we read in the first treatise, was intended to consist of fifteen treatises commenting on fourteen canzoni, plus an introduction. Reserved at first for a select few who were allowed to have access to the rare manuscript of the work, the *Convivio* started to be read in Florence in the 1330s by a a small circle of Dante's admirers. The rarity of its circulation in those years can be connected with another peculiarity: Dante, in his work, does not mention the vernacular treatise (Azzetta 2005, 2009). It is, however, also true that both in the *De vulgari eloquentia* and in the *Commedia* he openly recalls the first two canzoni of the *Convivio*. A careful reading and understanding of Dante's work makes manifest that, although not openly recalled, the contents of this book were a crucial reference point for Dante, not only in a work like *De vulgari* (almost composed at the same time as a part of the *Banquet*) but also in the *Monarchia* and *Commedia*. That the *Convivio* holds the key for a better understanding of Dante's problematic discourse about the human being's essence is well known. That the Convivio introduces the problematic issue of human earthly happiness as being at once theoretical and political is among the results of my reading that this study attempts to establish .

I first became interested in the *Convivio* while I was working on Ezra Pound and his idea of Paradise in the *Cantos*. The plan for this book, however, was conceived after I completed my work on Guido Cavalcanti. The idea of rereading Dante's *opus* conceived as a whole is part of what moved me and motivated my work. A first part of my rereading of Dante in this perspective appeared in Italian in 2011 in *Dante: Il paradigma intellettuale: Un'inventio degli anni fiorentini.* The book explored the *Vita nova* and the first two canzoni on which the *Convivio* comments, showing a continuity/discontinuity between the prosimetrum and the two canzoni themselves. Focusing on the intellectual as the new model on which to shape the contents and the rhetoric of Dante's writing, my work attempted to follow the formation of Dante's paradigm, identifying in such organization, a pathway of reflection that opens to the *Convivio.*

Many people have contributed to my book in different ways over the course of the years: colleagues, students, and friends. I recall here – citing Dante's definition used for Guido Cavalcanti – only my three "first friends." To all of them I owe a great debt of gratitude for having enlarged my knowledge and having strongly contributed to my intellectual life. I recall Mary de Rachewiltz and our years of study and research in Pound's library in Brunnenburg, starting in the early 1980s when we were working on Ezra Pound's Italian edition of *Cantos.* I recall Vanni Scheiwiller, the editor and intellectual who introduced me with great generosity to Milano cultural life, tradition, and *milieu,* sharing with me his friends, library, and archives.

I recall Franca Ghitti, the great Italian artist whose work and life have deeply influenced my ethical and intellectual choices. To Franca Ghitti, the "first" of my "first friends," to her "Other Alphabets," through which she reformulated the idea and language of sculpture, disclosing a new world, this study is dedicated.

Maria Luisa Ardizzone
New York, May 2015

I owe a debt of gratitude to Peter Kalkavage for his years of editorial assistance, for having improved my English text, and for reading what I have written with learned passion and intelligence.

READING AS THE ANGELS READ

Speculation and Politics in Dante's Banquet

Introduction

The image of circles rotating around a point – which is represented in *Paradiso* 28 as the relation between God and the angels, moved by the desire of their own origin – has to be considered as the visualized result of a long tradition of searching for the perfect model of knowing. The angels contemplate, and are figured as, circles moving around a centre, which is their origin. This centre is the highest object of love and desire. The axis of representation is an absolute relational being. The angels have a vision of God; they are able to see Him, and it is because they are able to see Him that they can have intellection of Him, and it is because they have intellection of Him that they can desire and love Him.

Dante here offers a formal principle of his poetics. He represents in image the abstract entity called *theoria* – that is, the vision of the highest intellectual being – as formulated in the angelology of Pseudo-Dionysius and his commentators, read in relation to Aristotle's *Metaphysics*. Angelic *theoria* works as a paradigm that establishes a cognitive principle expressed in terms of likeness and desire; that is, the angelic hierarchies represented as circles desire to be similar to the point they seek: "Così veloci seguono i suoi vimi, / per somigliarsi al punto quanto ponno; / e posson quanto a veder son soblimi" (They follow the ties of love with such rapidity because they are as like the Point as creatures can be, a power dependent on their vision) (*Paradiso* 28, 100–2).

The Aristotelian tradition is linked with Neoplatonism, and the return to the origin is basic in such representation. This desire for likeness on the part of the angelic intelligences is expressed here in geometrical terms, as a tending to become a point, because the origin of their circular being is a point. The angels manifest the coincidence between love, as the desire for one's origin, and intelligence, as the sublime vision of an originating principle.

Similitude is a form of homology that generates the desire for perfection. This figuration, in which perfection is proper to the point, makes clear that the angelic intelligences in their perfect desire experience a tension or tending towards a principle of unification that depends on the divine conceived as being One. This procures to them a deifying unity and the highest knowledge at once. The mathematical language of geometry works appropriately.

The movement of the angels according to Pseudo-Dionysius – described as circular, spiraling, and rectilinear, which includes the "anagogy," or going up – is basic in this representation, which captures the meaning of love for the perfect One, a love that is also knowledge. Love and knowledge are one and the same thing, and *intelligere* implies at once the One as object of both *intus legere* and the activity of *legere* (*lego as colligere*); the two meanings are interdependent. These verses, in fact, visualize this twofold sense, synchronically suggesting the hierarchies of the beings who share it. This representation or poetic figure causes us to reflect on various meanings as they move from Greek into Latin, and, subsequently, into the vernacular. Words like *intelligere* (*noein*) – to have intellection of the One (*ennoein*) – or *henosis* or *unum facere* (unification), are part of the tradition that establishes the natural impulse of all created beings towards the One.

Because the logical subject of these passages is the angelic orders responsible for the movement of the heavens, the angels' desire to become one implies that the tension towards the One on the part of the many beings is a natural, divine law inscribed in the universe. The search for unity expressed in this language of desire implies not only a tension towards the One but also a unifying link among those who live according to this higher law of intelligence and love. According to Pseudo-Dionysius, the angels form societies, and their organization as a society is ruled by their impulse towards the One. *Paradiso* 28 presents two kinds of visualizations. The first is the movement, as we have seen, of the angels around their centre, which is God. The second is the movement of the heavens around their centre, the earth. This visualization suggests different relations in the two orders between the centre and the periphery. In the first, perfection is in the centre, and a relation of proximity and centripetal attraction is therefore proper to the dimension of angel-intelligences. This is reversed in the heavenly hierarchy, where the principle that presides over the relation is that of distance from the centre, which is the earth. The idea here is that magnitude is considered as a value, but only in the world of physics. To this value is opposed the point, which is the minimal geometrical element or absence of magnitude, which Dante uses to represent both the smallest dimension and the infinite, according to what we read in the *Convivio* (II.13.26–27). Here, Dante's image points to a dialectical interaction that inverts values. Magnitude, in the system of the heavens, implies sublimity. The system of intellectual beings obliges us to invert this perspective. The sublime point is a minimal unity able to evoke the infinite. The world of physics is thus surpassed by a metaphysical value, to which the category of measurement is not applicable. The genuinely infinite does not coincide with what is infinitely big but, on the contrary, denies the category of magnitude and measurement. The relation between the two circular worlds, one physical and the other intellectual, which works as a model of the earthly physical world, is established in virtue of a sublime appetite, which, in thinking the same perfect being, desires and moves.

The interaction takes us back to what the point – the One – asks us to consider.

It is in the intellectual dimension that the tension towards the One takes place. The angelic hierarchies that enjoy the greatest degree of the sublime vision find their appropriate image in progressive smaller circles. Basic to this figuration is the idea of the divine as a form of energy that both radiates outwards and attracts as a unifying principle. God as One is both the principle of intelligence and the absolute logical and ethical value.

The terminology used in these canti, which indicates the angelic intelligence as substances (separated, of course), recapitulates contents already introduced in the *Convivio*, at first in *Voi ch'ntendendo il terzo ciel movete*, and later in *Amor che ne la mente mi ragiona*. The divine here, in this canzone, is suggested as performing a reflexive activity. It refers to a God who thinks Himself and, in thinking, creates noetic beings. This view is a product of late antiquity and the medieval reshaping of the Platonic theory of ideas. The theory is refuted by Aristotle in his *Metaphysics* but re-emerges in a tradition that we may identify as Neoplatonic and that was accepted in the thirteenth century by Bonaventure, Albert the Great, and Thomas Aquinas, among others. Dante appropriates this theory in his *Convivio*, where he depicts the new lady as a divine idea (*Amor che ne la mente mi ragiona*, v. 72) – that is, as the object of contemplation by both intelligences and human beings. The lady, as we read in the canzone, who is one but also loved by many, produces in virtue of it a *de facto* community naturally unified by contemplation and love. The *Convivio*'s third treatise establishes that this contemplative activity in human beings is *discontinuata* (discontinuous). *Paradiso* 29 will indirectly reiterate this view when it asserts that the angel-intelligences do not experience a contemplation that is *intercisa*, since they do not change their object of contemplation and their object does not undergo change.

In any case, what emerges from this line of thinking in the *Convivio* is that the divine, regarded as the intellectual apex of noetic beings, creates a hierarchy in which the value is intellectual. This value in the *Convivio*'s third treatise appears to be proper to both the angel-intelligences and to the intellectual soul of the human beings (though to a different degree). This creates a hierarchy of likeness in the cosmos, which Dante represents and discusses in his doctrinal treatise in order to figure out an earthly happiness that he shapes by freely drawing from different sources and *auctoritates*.

Paradiso 28 thus works as the model of a knowing identified with love that creates a unity of intellectual beings who are able to contemplate, in concert with one another, the same Being. The intellectual activity of these beings is precisely what allows them to move the heavens, thus granting life and generation in the sublunary world. This perhaps embodies the ideal condition for social life, in which association derives from what has the power of associating, and this is the One. The love for the *donna gentile* in the *Convivio* creates, as we will see, a *de facto* community: the lady is one and is loved by the many. And because love and knowledge are coincident in relation to her, this love makes manifest that a knowing subject who is at once one and plural is involved in such activity. This is one of the crucial issues that this book is proposing – an issue that is understandable in light of the methodology this study utilizes, in which the three canzoni and the prose text that commentates them are read following the natural continuity that Dante has organized.

Recalling this content is of help in confirming the importance of supernatural vision as a point of arrival for a path Dante had followed since the time he was writing his doctrinal vernacular treatise, or rather since the canzoni *Voi ch'ntendendo il terzo ciel movete* and *Amor che ne la mente mi ragiona*. Establishing the intellectual as a paradigm for both the angel-intelligences and the human being, Dante, starting in his Florentine years, constructs an edifice in which theological and philosophical contents are organized to create a new idea of human beings, which he expresses in the vernacular in order to offer a new awareness to those who have no access to Latin authorities. What comes on the scene is a new value: the intellectual. This is an old value, traditionally enrooted and linked to God in the medieval culture, but it is now proposed as new because it implies a plurality of beings that living together the experience of the highest knowledge creates *de facto* a kind of society. The invention of the *donna gentile* seems to be coincident with this new value.

Such invention must be read in continuity with the intellectual as paradigm, which Dante started to build in his Florentine years and continued in the first years of his exile. Because God is the highest intellectual being, the *intellectualitas* itself is determinant for the contents of the book and its rhetoric, as well as for the aspirations and desires partially shared by the separate substances, angelic hierarchies and human beings. This is what the *Convivio* tells its reader by creating a perfect abstract narration as derived from the nature of the characters he selects for his plot. The love for a lady – a divine idea depicted as a being that is one but is desired by many – is an abstract representation that furnishes the groundwork for a notion of community based on common intellection and the common desire to know. What makes *de facto* a community is a common natural essence and goal. Social communities work because of it. In light of this, contemplation and politics come to be closely related. Dante here rethinks old philosophical contents while appropriating new ones.

1. *Panis Angelicus*: Inventing the *Panis Humanus*

By choosing to write the *Convivio* in the vernacular, Dante was bringing into his text an ensemble of learning and problematic contents that were part of the Latin tradition. The *Convivio* included in itself the awareness of, and perhaps the exercise of, translating them. To explain his choice, Dante asserted that it was not his aim to speak only to grammarians, or to the learned. He was attempting, on the contrary, to enlarge the virtual circle of his readers, including in it those who participated in civic life and were not literati. The *Convivio* is therefore a work of popularization, in which an important role is given to the activity of synthesis and translation of texts Dante selects for his banquet of learning. At the beginning, the reader is introduced to what will be the central theme of the *Convivio*: human knowledge. Dante links this to the incipit of Aristotle's *Metaphysics*: "Tutti gli uomini naturalmente desiderano di sapere" (All men by nature desire to know). After a few lines, this knowledge is placed in relation with that of angels and defined as the "bread of angels," a metaphor taken from Psalm 77. This aspect of Dante's method makes clear that he intends to take into account theological learning and philosophical learning. Aristotle's *Metaphysics*, rethought through texts like the anonymous *Liber de causis*, Pseudo-Dyonisius's works, such as that on the angelic hierarchies or on *De Divinis nominibus*, and the commentaries on them, read in relation to Aristotle's *Nicomachean Ethics* and its medieval commentaries, is essential to understanding the doctrinal treatise. The poet informs his readers that he intends to collect what will fall from the table of those people who sit at the banquet of learning, where one may eat the "bread of angels." But he, the poet, who sits only at the feet of those learned people, collecting the crumbs that fall down, will organize a general banquet of contents that he had already partially introduced in previous years. It is important for us to understand, however, that these intellectual crumbs aim at constructing an organic, living whole. A kind of abstract architecture takes form, in which internal spaces continuously intersect and interact, like infinite logical associations. Introducing crumbs of the bread of angels, Dante sends his readers back to the so-called doctrinal canzoni, which he wrote when he was still living in Florence. He gives us only fragments of a discourse, apparently made of scattered pieces, that nevertheless has its own internal goal of unity:

> Oh beati quelli pochi che seggiono a quella mensa dove lo pane delli angeli si manuca! e miseri quelli che colle pecore hanno comune cibo! ... E io adunque, che non seggio alla beata mensa, ma, fuggito della pastura del vulgo, a' piedi di colouro che seggiono ricolgo di quello che da loro cade, e conosco la misera vita di quelli che dietro m'ho lasciati, per la dolcezza ch'io sento in quello che a poco a poco ricolgo, misericordievolemente mosso, non me dimenticando, per li miseri alcuna cosa ho riservata, la quale alli occhi loro, già è più tempo, ho dimostrata; e in ciò li ho fatti maggiormente vogliosi.

> Blessed are the few who sit at the table where the bread of the angels is eaten, and most unfortunate those who share the food of sheep! ... Therefore I who do not sit at the blessed table, but, having fled the pasture of the common herd, gather up a part of what falls to the feet of those who do sit there, and who know the unfortunate life of those

> I have left behind, for the sweetness that I taste in what I gather up piece by piece, and moved by compassion, though not forgetting myself, have set aside for those who are unfortunate something that I placed before their eyes some time ago, by which I have increased their desire. (I.7–11)

More suggested than explicit, from the beginning of the treatise there enters a relation between the bread of angels and that which human beings may also share. This happens in a way that accords with human imperfection. According to Psalm 77:25, *panis angelorum manducavit homo*, but the poet will introduce a barley bread that is accessible to human beings because it is in vernacular. Augustine, identifying the bread of angels with the *verbum*, and the *verbum* being coincident with the ideas in the mind of God, allows us to understand the incipit of the *Convivio*. All men desire to know God and his ideas, but this goal can be reached also by eating and sharing the barley bread; the contemplation of the divine is not just for the *sapientes*, not just for those learned in Latin. *Panis angelorum* can also be a human bread that illiterate human beings can taste and share.

The initial quotation from Aristotle's *Metaphysics*, once it is related to the bread of angels, points the way to a clear perspective; the *Convivio* seems to concern itself with the earthly contemplation of the divine being. The love for the gentle lady, in a transposed transumptive mode, heralds a new idea about the human condition and human desire. The idea involves a new learning that Dante rereads in connection with the old one. Theology and philosophy, which for Dante are not terms of opposition, are brought together on the same page. He seems to treat them as different linguistic formulations of the same crucial questions and content, the desire to know being the highest goal of the human being.

From the opening pages, the *Convivio*'s reader is called to make links, to establish relations, to fill empty spaces. Dante thus challenges the reader to contribute to the building of the work. The first point to be evaluated, in the first treatise, is Dante's introduction of another bread as a metaphor for his commentaries on several canzoni that he had composed in his Florentine years. Food was the metaphor for the poetry itself; that is, for the canzoni, the prose will comment. Without the bread, we read, the canzoni have a "shadow of obscurity," so that the reader is able to evaluate only their beauty rather than their goodness (first treatise).

If beauty is in relation to obscurity, Dante seems to return to a principle he had established in his *Vita nuova*, starting with the canzone

Donne che'avete intelletto d'amore. There, the poetic language was used in the context of a methodology in which the difficult played a major role. Dante's precedent here is Augustine, who in the *De Doctrina Christiana* indicated the difficulty of understanding biblical tropes as an intellectual, sweet, formative exercise. The continuity with the *Vita nuova* in the *Convivio* is thus programmatically announced. It is not only a narrative continuity but also, and importantly, a rhetorical one. Both are works written in the vernacular that combine poetry and prose. But the way of discussion in the *Convivio* will be more "virile," as befitting Dante's increased maturity. Its author was moved to write the canzoni, as we read, by virtue and not by passion. In addition, the *Convivio* intends to reveal the true meaning of the canzoni, which no one can perceive unless he or she is introduced to it, because it is hidden beneath the figure of allegory. This will bring true delight to the ear as well as useful instruction concerning both this mode of speaking and the mode of understanding the writings of others. What is indicated here is of central importance: in the *Convivio*, the food is the poetic text, necessarily followed by the commentary as bread. Thanks to such bread – that is, *buon udire* – the commentary will be a kind of training towards the "subtle" (*sottile*) as a way of speaking, or as a way of reading and understanding the writings of others.

The use of the vernacular fits with this training. The words cited above introduce us to the relation that is put forth in the commentary for the understanding of a text as an exercise of the reader's intelligence. It thus becomes immediately evident that the rustic bread is regarded as capable of furnishing a kind of knowledge that is related to the "bread of angels." The angelic bread immediately introduces the angel, identifying Him through the food that nourished Him, the contemplation of the divine being, and his thinking. But the angel also provides the human being with a model that he can imitate. Dante himself will contribute to this idea when he puts forth the intellectual activity of the human soul as similar to that of the angels. This theme enters with the first two canzoni on which the doctrinal treatise intends to comment.

2. Reading the *Convivio*

Since contemplation is possible for both angels and humans, the different modes of this activity are crucial to the *Convivio*, a work in which the centre of discourse seems not to be fixed but rather changes according to the perspectives its author assumes and the varying objects of inquiry as they arise. Each time a centre reveals itself, there is a point of convergence for different lines of thought that appear problematic.

The multiplicity of viewpoints derives from this fact. As the angels *circumvolunt* the divine being, so too readers of the *Convivio* will move their minds, circling around a point to which the text draws their attention. This multiplication of centres is part of the training towards the absolute intellectual being. The coincidence between God as the absolute intellectual being and the activity of intelligence aimed at knowing Him is a crucial content of Dante's reflection. The finding of multiple centres is one of the new aspects that this work proposes and obliges us to recognize. Similitude and dissimilitude mark the pathways of the treatise right from the beginning: "All human beings naturally desire to know." Assuming the desire for the "bread of angels," to which human beings aspire despite their mortality, the *Convivio* offers its rustic bread in a language that is itself still experimental and fragmented. Like the angels, the human being has a similitude to the divine being. The relationship between the angel-intelligence and human intellect is one of the pathways the *Convivio* invites us to consider, starting from the first chapters of the treatise where we read about the bread of angels, suggested to be related to barley bread. This "bread" is rustic because it is expressed in the vernacular. But it also points to a relationship with the angelic bread that human beings can also eat.

According to this reading, which has, however, been neglected, Dante in the *Convivio* turns the page of what he had already written. He constructs his work through a continuity/discontinuity with the contents established in the canzone *Donne ch'avete intelletto d'amore* and in the prose of the *Vita nuova,* which he appropriates and makes more powerful in the first two canzoni in the *Convivio.* This knot of relations suggests and confirms that the nature of the new love for the so-called gentle lady was, since its beginning, a transumptive way to introduce new contents in which Aristotelian learning plays a major role – in particular, Aristotle's *Nicomachean Ethics* with its inner link with the *Metaphysics,* as established in book 10. According to our reading, the *Convivio* explicitly embraces the intellectual contemplation of book 10 of the *Nicomachean Ethics,* stressing in addition a social-political awareness. The *luce nuova* and *sole nuovo* of *Convivio* I.13 seems to herald a turning of the page and a new beginning, and the use of vernacular contributes to making it manifest.

A new sense of history penetrates the *Convivio*; an attempt to rethink and reshape the role human beings play in space and time is what the doctrinal treatise aims at. The ideal reader of *Convivio* is someone that has to be educated about such new values. The reader's intellectual identity is not already shaped but has to be created, and the book should greatly contribute to this. The sense of a new historical beginning marks the doctrinal treatise, which the choice of the vernacular eloquently introduces.

In the thirteenth century, new social classes, new democratic institutions, the vernacular languages, and new ways of thinking about human nature produced the expectation of a new beginning, in which movements like Franciscanism and the rise of universities in the twelfth century competed to inaugurate. At that time, the old social categories (*bellatores, oratores, laboratores*) had disappeared, and cities required an intellectual who was not just an academic clergyman but rather a thinker, organically connected to his society. The criticism of Alain De Libera (1991b), of what has been proposed by Jacques Le Goff (1985) – that is, the coincidence in the Middle Ages between the academic professor and the intellectual man – finds in the *Convivio* an exemplary text that reverses Le Goff's outmoded interpretive categories. De Libera speaks of the crisis of the university and of the deprofessionalization of the intellectuals. The *Convivio* confirms this view, insofar as it testifies to the birth of an intellectual class not tied to the universities. A man of the city, living in exile and mostly travelling, Dante has experience of the *vita activa* and intends to link the new learning with political life. Latini Brunetto's *Tresor* is of course crucial in such perspective, but has to be seen in a wider context. It is from this standpoint that he proceeds when, before the exile, since the 1290s, he projects the cognitive problem onto a cosmic dimension and proposes the celestial contemplation of the angel-intelligences and movers of the heavens as the model that unites contemplation and action. The first verse of *Voi ch'ntendendo il terzo ciel movete* introduces this in an unequivocal way.

The awareness of a new society characteristic of his age inspires Dante to fashion cultural tools for a reading public ignorant of Latin but committed to participating in the political life of the *civitas*. For them, the *Convivio* condenses a learning that is both ancient and modern, philosophical and theological, as well as scientific, by introducing a new method that organizes its contents as a collection of a few theses introduced by the poetic texts and subsequently discussed in the commentaries. Written in prose in the years of Dante's exile (probably between 1303 and 1308), but organized as a commentary on the three canzoni (according to the text we have received) written by him in his Florentine years (the 1290s), the *Convivio* aims at creating a cultural and civic consciousness for modern laymen. For them, Dante refashions and summarizes traditions of late antiquity and of the Middle Ages, asserting that *theoria*, or contemplation, is the highest virtue to which human beings can aspire and that earthly happiness is indeed possible, albeit imperfect.

The *Convivio* uses new texts and new translations to structure a paradigm of contemplation on the angelic model. Linking the *theoria* of Aristotle's *Nicomachean Ethics* with contents derived from the anonymous *Liber de causis* and from the intersection of angelology with the *Metaphysics*, Dante focuses on the intrinsic unity and continuity between contemplation and action. The angel-intelligences, conceived as intellectual beings capable of contemplating God and thereby moving the heavens, guarantee the continuity of creation and the life of the sublunary world. They appear to furnish the paradigm for new intellectuals, who, in virtue of *theoria*, or contemplation, will be able to influence and shape the life of the city. The intellectual, therefore, is not only devoted to pure speculation, but he is also one who, by virtue of this speculation, is able to operate in the *civitas* or *polis* and to shape its life. The *Convivio* in this way is seen to acquire an ethical-political goal.

Dante thus creates a new category for the intellectual-philosophers. Conceiving them as men of political action, he offers them the paradigm of the angel-intelligences as movers of the heavens and furnishes them with a learning that is organically related to the promotion of a new society. Rhetoric is the first science that is introduced, creating a link (still to be understood) between the heaven of Venus and its movers in the prose of the *Convivio*'s second treatise. The importance of rhetoric in the *Convivio* remains an unwritten chapter. Dante will link this science to those derived from the new organization of learning based on a model derived from Greek-Arabic culture. In such a link he will reshape the concept of rhetoric as well as that of poetry. Both disciplines will be conceived, according to a line of thought initiated by Alfarabi, as sciences of civil discourse; that is, they will be conceived as part of politics and will work in the city. The link between the love for the gentle lady and a social-political awareness that this love makes manifest is one of the contents that our reading evaluates. How what we call society starts to be, seems to be one of the true foci of Dante's thinking. Dante seems to put forth a simple question: Why is a human being a political animal? The answer in the *Convivio* includes a reflection on what creates naturally a link among human beings. Such a natural link, according to Dante, is not just biological but is also intellectual: human beings think together, and because of this they are a *de facto* society. This seems to be the true sense of the love for the *donna gentile*; the discourse about the gentle lady is thus intertwined with a civil awareness. It is this love that makes manifest that a human community is naturally formed in virtue of such love, which the third treatise will define also as friendship. The origin of human society seems to be not just biologically motivated but also intellectual. The *Monarchy* will return on this issue, confirming it.

In Brunetto's *Tresor*, the role that is given to politics, thought of as an architectural science, and the most important of sciences, was no doubt of great importance. In light of it, Dante not only rethinks the political value of rhetoric and its political goal but also considers, in the footstep of Aristotle, ethics as part of politics. This link with ethics is part of the picture and crucial to the proper understanding of the manifold contents of the *Convivio*. Ethics in fact implies a political awareness, and earthly happiness appears to be both ethical and political at once. The polemic against the avid grammarian (first treatise), the choice of cultural parameters that he freely draws from that of the universities, the celestial example as a paradigm for the sublunar world, and the interaction with models of thought coming from the Greco-Arabic synthesis: all these are fundamental to Dante's writing. They are also fundamental to a rereading of the *Convivio* that underscores the importance of the speculative activity for the practical life.

To establish this discussion and its contents, the reader must follow Dante's path from the canzoni to the commentaries. A crucial content of the canzoni is the introduction of the love for the *donna gentile* as the result of a speculative activity proposed in opposition to the activity of the memory tied to Beatrice (second treatise). The *donna gentile* is put forth as a divine idea contemplated by both pure intelligences (intellects) and human beings. This is indicated through the collective name, *gente* (third treatise). The prose commentary will highlight the importance of these themes by creating a field of relations and a strong continuity between the literal and the allegorical commentaries.

Taking the angels and their contemplation of the separate substances or divine ideas as the model, Dante appropriates some theories, maybe to the point of heterodoxy, with the purpose of establishing the value of what pertains to human earthly life. Happiness, if based on Aristotelian theory or contemplation, implies the human being's likeness to God and His contemplative activity. This content takes Dante along different paths. He associates Aristotelian and Neoplatonic elements in order to introduce at first the theory of contemplation of the separate substances in life as possible for human beings. In doing so, Dante appropriates debates of his own time. These are documented for us both in many philosophical texts and in a series of articles that were condemned in the thirteenth century, the most famous and incisive of which are the Parisian condemnations of 1270 and 1277. In the *Convivio*, as I underline, these articles are not recalled but may be retraced in an indirect way. Dante appears to read, with great freedom. Texts of philosophers and theologians such us Augustine, Severinus Boethius, Aquinas, Bonaventure, Albert the Great, Siger of Brabant, and Boethius of Dacia are part of works useful to understanding his discourse. Many contents that were condemned were discussed by some of the thinkers just mentioned. In addition, this study evaluates a few recently published documents – mostly anonymous and written in the late thirteenth century or early fourteenth century, such as, for instance, the *Questiones in Metaphysica* (Fioravanti 1991) – in the attempt to better evaluate whether and how the *Convivio* is involved in the line of thinking usually associated with so-called intellectual happiness (third treatise).

My reading concentrates on the vocabulary and contexts that the terminological choices reveal on the page. This study evaluates the continuity that the *Convivio* aims at establishing among different cultural fields and linguistic formulations. I emphasize in particular that, as Dante creates a new way to appropriate the learning belonging to different cultural areas, he intends not to synthesize them but rather to bring them to the same page, as nuclei for the reader's reflection. Thus, elements of a theological-biblical matrix are not connected with philosophical elements, but rather brought near. The goal seems to be not reconciliation or synthesis but rather an awareness that historically different linguistic formulations may arise from the same questions or problems.

The unfinished *Convivio* testifies to a tension that exists among fragments within a complex thought. The method that Dante declares – that of picking up philosophical crumbs and considering them as fragments of a construction yet to be made – shows that he writes with his tradition lying in the dust – that is, in ashes – signalling his awareness of the transitional character of cultural forms. This awareness leads him to employ both the Neoplatonic and theological traditions, linking them with the manifold forms of Aristotelianism. In the century that rediscovers Aristotle, Dante moves between biblical texts, Platonic and Neoplatonic contents, and Aristotelian texts, and rereads them in light of the debates of his time, but in a most personal way. He constructs a thinking organized in blocks. He solidifies them in a new linguistic form marked by a transumptive rhetorical mode, whereby a thing is said and much remains to be understood. The task of decodification is left to the reader, who must establish new relations not explicitly exposed in the text. The importance assigned to poetry – to its peculiar language, and to the so-called allegory of poets – must be considered as recalling the fragment which introduces Orpheus (II.1.4). Orpheus here is not the Orpheus who descends to the realm of the dead, but the Orpheus who is able to tame the beasts and move trees and stones. The mythical poet, with his chant, makes cruel hearts grow tender and humble, and, as the text explains, bends to his will those who neglect knowledge and art, as well as those who have no rational life whatsoever and are almost like stones. It seems that the myth is used to suggest a civil awareness reminiscent of Cicero's *De inventione*, which attributes to rhetoric the responsibility of civilizing primitive human beings. Dante, however, stresses the role of poetry in this. He starts to ground the importance of poetry for the associated life of human beings. Brunetto's model, as it appears in his *Rhetoric*, is assumed here, but is rethought and expanded.

Although it uses ancient and medieval learning, the *Convivio* is a project for a modern sense of the present, in which the value of *civitas* is strengthened. Written for its contemporaneous readers, the *Convivio* appears to us today as a work full of a sense of posterity. It postulates the future reader who will be aware of the culture that Dante anticipates. Dante writes, therefore, not just with his tradition in ashes (as indicated above) but also with his contemporary world fated in turn to become dust. He offers and anticipates cultural parameters that his age maybe does not share, does not accept, or is not ready to understand.

The priority of the future is introduced as an interpretive parameter that also evaluates the geographical places in which the *Convivio* takes its form: not only the Florence of the *philosophantes* (the city where he wrote the first two canzoni and perhaps also the third), but also other cities where secular thought had already blossomed; not only Bologna, as is usually recognized, but also Padua and Verona. With them penetrates the dimension of the north, and such dimension has a pre-humanistic fragrance. The prose of the *Convivio* offers us a form of knowledge that is both secular and theological, and which ends up drawing a new sense of human nature and goal. An earthly story projected onto the cosmic dimension does not create a devaluation of what belongs to time; rather, it introduces a cosmic dimension into the temporal and human.

My reading underlines how Dante's banquet of learning is the result of the poet's effort to escape from the idea of a monolithic organized system. The bread of the angels, the metaphor with which the *Convivio* begins, becomes edible only if we can taste this bread as "crumbs" that are both biblical-theological and philosophical. The crumbs, which we are told fall down from the table of wise men, are often unrecognizable fragments that Dante takes from the great systems of thought and inserts into his text. It is not the great systems themselves that combine to produce the structure of the *Convivio*, but rather the perception of the fragments – of the *briciole* (crumbs), as Dante calls them. These are collected so that the reader may consider and articulate them.

In virtue of this loose system, the discourse on speculation assumes various forms. It includes an inquiry into the nature of human language, the new awareness of poetry as an intellectual language, and the modern-ancient use of the poetical figures and of rhetoric. But first of all, it implies a new sense of learning thought in relation to politics, an awareness that penetrates not just from Aristotle but also from the field of rhetoric and law.

An important aspect of my reading derives from the strong continuity I establish between the poetry and the prose of Dante's text. This continuity takes us back to the contents and problematic perspectives that the canzoni had already anticipated in an obscure way. The strong relationship between the contents of the texts of poetry and of the commentaries is responsible for the understanding and the reading this study proposes.

By discussing Dante's new love for the so-called gentle lady, and distinguishing the literal term (gentle lady) from the allegorical (philosophy), thereby distinguishing the love for the new woman from the love of philosophy, my reading evaluates Dante's discourse on human knowledge, which takes place in the canzoni themselves and, afterwards, in the two commentaries dedicated to them. The continuity of the contents and meanings proposed in the first two canzoni is crucially important. In this reading, we see the deliberate ambiguity that Dante builds into the text.

The reading underlines how the problem of knowledge emerges in relation to ethics, and how ethics for Dante, as for Aristotle, necessarily implies politics. To accomplish this end, the *Convivio* adopts a subtle language that uses inductive and deductive reasoning, both in the literal commentary and in the allegory, in which the sense and meaning of the letter is to be understood in relation to the allegorical sense that confirms and enlarges the literal meaning. Among the themes introduced, one of the most important is, as already noted, that the love for the new lady is projected into the cosmological dimension. Cosmology and knowledge are of course related. Moreover, it is suggested that politics and cosmology should also be related.

Here we find the convergence of different lines of thought. The methodological doubt that this investigation signals, which Dante does not usually declare but which is perceptible, becomes a prevailing element of the *Convivio*. Dante apparently wants to strengthen the new contents discussed by confronting fundamental biblical-theological themes with those of the philosophical tradition. That learning has a political goal, in the sense that is functional to life in the city, and implies the importance of an earthly perspective. The love for the gentle lady heralds a new sense and value of time in which a new spatial dimension enters as a territory virtually open to investigation and intellectual dominion. Projected inside the universe, which is described as a celestial machine, this love introduces a new landscape, a new geographical sense of the relationship between earth and heaven. The human being lives not just on the earth but in a spatial intellectual dimension; he or she has an interior conversation with the angel-motors of the heavens and compares his or her intellectual power with that of the pure intellects. It is his love for the gentle lady that creates such new and challenging perspectives.

The identity of the gentle lady is difficult to comprehend. I discuss her initially without immediately identifying her with philosophy, as is usually done in the commentaries. This allows me to grasp the relation between philosophy and divine wisdom, from which the true identity of "human philosophy" emerges. Crumbs of thought that are apparently unconnected establish the possibility that man can contemplate a separate substance in his earthly life. The relationship between the angel-intelligences and other separated substances are part of the discussion. Because of it, such love approaches human beings and heaven in this life. These contents are offered to the reader using a carefully organized methodology.

A discourse on method must thus evaluate not only the two different linguistic forms Dante uses to discuss his contents, and the diachronicity on which they are constructed but also the temporal and geographical distance between Dante's composition of the poetry and that of his prose. Dante's experiences and his new meetings of the first six years of his exile were no doubt important in the writing of the *Convivio* – a work that was planned as a commentary to fourteen canzoni that were written previously, as we read in the first treatise. But first were the discussions of *philosophantes* crucially important in establishing a new model of learning and a new idea about human life goals. In the *Convivio*, the love for philosophy has not just the meaning of introducing a secular sense of learning; rather, it introduces the intellectual power of human beings, similar to the angel-intelligences in their speculative activity and thus, like them, able to influence earthly life. The highest activity remains speculation, but from speculation derives action. The canzone *Voi ch'intendendo il terzo ciel movete* thus establishes a new working-in-progress paradigm.

But in the *Convivio*, a founding stone is the attention to the formation of a new society. What comes on the scene as new is the awareness of a civic life and community, whose members require cultural training. Attention to civic life was already active in the *Vita nuova*, where Beatrice's death was not a just private loss – it was also a loss for the city. The *Lamentations of Jeremiah* that Dante quotes in the *Vita nuova* (XXX.1) refer not to Florence alone but more broadly to what Augustine called the City of Man.

The *Convivio*, on the one hand, openly provides a paradigm for intellectuals; on the other, it requires that the reader understand the relationship that establishes the social-political context for these intellectuals. The important role played by Aristotle's *Politics*, mediated by its inner link with Aristotle's *Nicomachean Ethics*, is part of the picture, as is the link that connects ethics and politics with metaphysics. Therefore, among the aims of the treatise must be included the identification and formation of a new kind of reader. This reader, though not equipped with Latin, must be aware of a true sense of human life and the importance of earthly happiness. The multiplication of perspectives that the *Convivio* offers, and the multiple relations among them, introduce the sense of an infinite relational universe nevertheless conceived of as spatially finite. This is a contribution offered to a reader whom the *Convivio* seeks to produce. To establish the identity of Dante's ideal reader, we must do more than look at a real or already existing reader. We must thus think of someone yet to be made, a reader who is educated in the very act of reading the work itself. This formative role may in part explain why the *Convivio* was left unfinished when Dante started to write the *Commedia*. By that time, Dante no doubt entrusted the formation of the reader to the poetry of that work.

3. A Modern Idea of Learning: Crumbs of Philosophy

From what has been said so far, it is clear that the structure of the *Convivio* anticipates a modern idea of learning. According to this idea, it is not any single system of thought that dictates the philosophical structure of this work, but rather a plurality of contents derived from different systems. I have already touched on the Platonic theory of archetypes that enters into the text, proposing that the forms of things live in the mind of God. The divine thinking is one of the foci of the *Convivio,* and the bread of angels, taken from the Psalms, in Augustine, was read as the ability on the part of angels to contemplate the divine ideas. Augustine, who affirms this in his commentary on the Gospel of John, draws on a line of thinking that anticipates ideas in Dante's own age, especially those of Bonaventure, Aquinas, and Albert the Great. Aquinas, in a work entitled *De Ideis,* reformulated authoritatively in the thirteenth century a content that was active in Neoplatonism, especially in Latin Neoplatonism. Bonaventure, for his part, was drawing not only on this Augustinian line but also on the theory of ideas, which was criticized by Aristotle, discussed by the saint in the *Hexaemeron,* judging this lack to be a point of weakness in the system itself. This took place in the 1270s, when Bonaventure assumed his well-known position against the diffusion of radical Aristotelian thinking, which was decisive in the condemnation in that decade. Thus, the *Convivio,* in recalling the "bread of angels," was both inviting its reader to evaluate the meaning of divine *sapientia* and also drawing attention to the archetypes or ideas. This is operative in the text, even though it is not openly enunciated. It is certainly a turning point that is central to Dante's doctrinal vernacular treatise.

The relationship between the *panis angelicus* and the *panis humanus,* which I introduced above, indicates a content that is problematic. The divine ideas could be visible not only to the angels but perhaps also to human beings, who could participate, however imperfectly, in an ideal and purely intellectual world. The *Convivio* traces the relationship between the angelic vision of the divine ideas and the theory of the human intellect. This relationship is one of the foci of the *Convivio,* which the reader may follow in the second and third treatise.

Reading as the Angels Read is divided into five chapters that explore and attempt to trace a discussion of the human intellect by reading the four treatises of the *Convivio,* but mostly focusing on the second and third treatises, in which the making of the theory of human intellection is organized. On this basis, this book develops a thematic reading of the doctrinal treatise, devoting more space to those sections in which the discourse is on intellection or where Dante introduces elements that cooperate to organize this issue. The different space that my text devotes to the various treatises depends on what drives my study. Thus the fourth treatise is discussed in relation to this issue. In the reading, however, other elements are evaluated in order to understand how the new topic that is introduced – the notion of true nobility – has the purpose of indirectly reshaping his previous ideas about human intellectual power. The discussion of this treatise, on my reading, confirms that the love for the *donna gentile* is Dante's way of introducing and discussing the nature and power of the human intellect.

This topic was first traced in the two canzoni *Voi che'ntendendo il terzo ciel movete* and *Amor che ne la mente mi ragiona*. The invention of the *donna gentile* (ever since the canzoni, we propose) aims at establishing the nature of the human mind. Dante engages in a transumptive way of suggesting this true nature. The being of the beloved throws light on the essence of the mind that loves her. His focus on knowledge is constructed through induction and deductions. We have seen that he organizes a complex framework in which central themes are the knowledge of the angel-intelligences and the theory of ideas in the mind of God. The inquiry into the number of movers of the heavens (second treatise) is, in our reading, strategic in establishing a line of thinking that aims at showing the identity of the gentle lady in the third treatise. From this derives the main content of this treatise. Here my reading focuses on the strategies of writing that Dante activates, for instance, the shifting of the logical subject. The intent, as I propose, is to establish the nature of the mind that loves and that contemplates the *donna gentile*. This contemplative human activity, as I mentioned in the first section of this introduction, is suggested as common to humankind and is also defined as "discontinuous." It is difficult to deny that this idea was influenced in some way by a thinking derived from Averroes and his theory of a common intellect. However, the *Convivio* shows that Dante does not accept the materialistic structure to which the theory of the intellect is related in the field of Averroism. Moreover, he does not share theories about the death of the individual soul that are connected with this philosophical line. Instead, the crucial idea is that human beings think best when they think together. This content, according to my previous study, was anticipated in Dante's Florentine years and continues to evolve in the *Convivio* and the *Monarchia*.

4. A Method of Reading

The method of reading that has taken form in my exploration partially follows the one I employed in my *Dante, Il paradigma intellettuale* (2011). In keeping with this method, the first two canzoni have been read for the first time in their internal narrative continuity. The meanings that derive from this reading allow us to establish another continuity: that between the first two canzoni and the contents of the prose text. Thus the first outcome of this reading is the evaluation of a line of great interest in which all events constitute an intellectual narrative. That is, the *Convivio* organizes a kind of abstract narrative in which events and characters are intellectual events and intellectual beings. The reader is invited to follow a narration in which angels, separate substances, mind, and cosmology all interact. By following how this interaction is organized, and what motivates it, the reader may grasp what my study assumes to be the main line of the doctrinal treatise. This study puts forth the view that the true centre of the book, traditionally read as an encyclopedia of learning, is a discussion of human intellectual power in its inner natural link with political life within a community.

The first chapter of this study, "Introducing a Cosmic Intellectual Dimension," discusses how the love for the *donna gentile* is the result of a heavenly event influenced by Venus's movers or angel-intelligences. According to the canzone, a spirit provided with speech comes from that heaven and produces in the one who says "I" a contemplative relation with a new lady who leads to a further series of intellectual events. The identity of the lady as a separate substance and a divine idea, which the second canzone reveals, paves the way for a comprehension of the intellectual nature of this new love. This introduces the key theme of the identity of the thinking subject discussed in my chapters 3 and 4. Within this scheme that is active in the two canzoni, the prose organizes a momentous discourse that seeks to establish the limits and power of the human mind.

My reading of the commentary on the first canzone points out how a fragmented narration introduces a discourse about two different loves (that of Beatrice and that of the new lady) proposed in an irreducible dialectical opposition. The text organizes what is defined as the two *diversitadi* as mutually conflicting thoughts that contend within the character that says "I." Dante's enigmatic speech introduces a discourse about the human soul and the different nature of the sensitive and intellective soul. The reading proposes that the two ladies and two loves battling within the first person narrator are transumptive ways of discussing the nature of the human soul. It shows that Dante's writing is pervaded by an ethics of doubt. A turning of the page takes place when the discourse about knowledge that is related to the *donna gentile* is built, but not through the activation of Aristotelian process, which starts from the sensitive soul and its imaginative activity; rather, in a peremptory way that risks generating confusion in the reader, Dante changes his mode of representation. Now the core of the discourse is speculation, which is shared by both heavenly intelligences and human beings. The latter, however, speculate in a specifically different way. The prose text of the third treatise indicates this fact through its emphasis on the discontinuous (III.13.7). Moreover, the canzone *Amor che ne la mente mi ragiona* introduces the same idea with a *quando* (v. 26) that anticipates the *non sempre* (III.13.3), which Dante offers as an explanation in the commentary on the poem. But the crucial issue in the second treatise is the discussion of the number of intelligences. Dante here appeals to book 12 of Aristotle's *Metaphysics*. He integrates it with Aquinas's *De substantiis separatis*. Because the number of intelligences is infinite and does not coincide with the movers of the heavens, the *donna gentile* is confirmed (as anticipated in the canzone) as a separate substance and a divine idea that performs a contemplative divine activity (chapter 2, "Loving a Divine Idea").

This introduces the important discourse on the divine ideas, which raises the following important question: Can human beings know this divine idea in their mortal lives? This theme in Dante's age was judged to be heterodox and condemned but was accepted by Albert the Great. Indeed, it is fundamental to the theory of so-called intellectual happiness that Albert assumes is possible in mortal life. My reading then proceeds to discuss this theory with reference to various texts devoted to the topic.

By developing contents related to the theory of the ideas in the mind of God, chapter 2, in its final part, explores the meaning of Dante's identification of the various heavens with the sciences. The discussion includes the inter-relational character of these sciences, and the extent to which the *cognominatio angelorum* plays a role and influences Dante's understanding. The chapter introduces what I call a Trinitarian logic. This opens a pathway in which the discussion of contemplation implies that a relation between two beings, or orders of being, always includes a third that makes manifest the relation itself. Here Dante follows, it seems, Bonaventure's *Hexaemeron*, on which he draws freely. He discusses angelic contemplation as organizing for every order a plural contemplation of the three persons of the Trinity, seen in their unity and mutual relations.

This works as a model for the contemplation of the *donna gentile*, because we are told that she is contemplated by the intellects. This suggests that a third being (in the canzone, "*amore*") should manifest this relation, whose nature is indicated by that of the loved object. Of course, this line of thinking is suggested and needs to be retraced. The reader lacks the elements that can assist his understanding. This representation, however, introduces a logic of relations that applies to the system of sciences. This system in the *Convivio* employs a threefold relation that connects the intelligences, heavens, and sciences, where theology is put forth as the highest science. This way of proceeding draws on a debate within theology itself. Dante's method is that of identifying the different heavenly spheres and the various sciences ("Dico che per cielo io intendo la scienza"; II.13.2), entrusting the intelligences with a process of mediation. That is, he makes them beings capable of mediating a learning whose aim is God, because it derives from Him.

The second chapter of this book closes by briefly touching on the relation between the divine ideas that are infinite and the ideas of the so-called *possibili* that are identified with the "possibles" of the divine thoughts that cannot be limited to what human beings know or establish as fields of knowledge or sciences. So the "possibles" of learning are infinite in the same way as are the divine ideas. A universe that is finite, in other words, possesses a dimension of the infinite. This is another field of reflection that is only suggested by the text, but is not developed or organized. Such lines of thinking, which do not lead the reader to a meaning but are merely suggestive, are among the most unrivalled experiences of reading the *Convivio*.

Chapter 3, "Reading with *Suspicio*," which is constructed around the logical-rhetorical figure of *suspicio*, allows us to formulate a series of hypotheses. These find confirmation in Dante's discussion of philosophy, the meaning of which must be understood in relation to the sources he employs and connects. Chapter 3 discusses the theory of intellectual happiness. Dante uses fragments from Severinus Boethius to introduce philosophy as being in the mind of both God and human beings. What is interesting is that he goes back to Boethius to introduce tenets that are close to theses condemned in Dante's age. The result suggests a theory that implies the eternity of philosophy. But the *Convivio* does not deal with the implications of this theory, as they occur in the philosophy of Averroes and his followers.

In its second section, my third chapter follows the way in which Dante organizes the construction of the identity of the thinking subject in relation to the love for the gentle lady. We discern in the text a shifting between an individual subject, unable to reach a high level of knowledge, and another subject expressed through a verbal form that is impersonal. This points to the possibility of a plural subject that is able to contemplate the gentle lady. The subject, which is conceived of as both a thinking subject and a political subject, seems to anticipate the *Humanitas* or *Universitas* of the *Monarchia*.

Chapter 4, "Community and Intellectual Happiness," follows Dante's introduction of the field of *honestum* and the link between the *summum bonum* and *honestum* as the common good. This opens up many possible routes for investigating the coincidence between the highest knowledge and political or communal happiness. The relation between virtue and the common good, read through Aristotle and Cicero, establishes a common good that belongs to the earth, though its model is in the heavens. *Ius* and justice are in the world of history, but their model appears to be heavenly.

But the main result of the theory of intellect in the *Convivio* is reached only when the reader understands Dante's attempt to link the notion of intellect suggested as one and common to the theory of *logos-verbum*. This theory had been active ever since the *Vita nuova*. But in the *Convivio* it appears in relation to the *donna gentile* in the allegorical commentary of the third treatise, which identifies *philosophia* and *sapientia*. To connect the *verbum-logos* with the theory of the common intellect – that is, two milestones of medieval culture as the result of two different traditions – is one of the greatest contributions of the vernacular treatise. These two traditions in Dante appear to be confronted but not unified. They must be considered in their inner closeness and distance at once, a distance that needs to be preserved.

Because the differences are crucial, we may follow Dante's treatment of them in terms of a logic of relations, without any attempt to unify them. This is the powerful contribution of the third treatise. The common reason, *logos*, or intellect, is, according to Dante, the basis of human *conviventia*. The love for the *donna gentile* manifests a de facto *communitas*, in which intellectual identity is common. This activity is basic to our life in space and time. The third treatise thus appears to fulfil the meaning of the first lines of the vernacular treatise: "All men by nature desire to know" (*Tutti li uomini naturalmente desiderano di sapere*). Here what must be stressed is the quantifier "*tutti*."

The *Monarchia* will make a crucial addition that only human *universitas* can attain the best earthly knowledge and happiness. Moreover, the possible intellect is more effectively actualized in a community of individuals – that is, in human beings thinking in concert. That this idea begins to evolve in the *Convivio* is a thesis of my study and is discussed primarily in chapters 3 and 4.

Book 10 of the *Nicomachean Ethics*, in its internal relation to the *Metaphysics*, is important to this end. According to Aristotle, *theoria* is the highest knowledge. The object of this knowing makes us similar to God. E. Gilson's claim about the supremacy of the *Nicomachean Ethics* in the *Convivio* is here superseded (E. Gilson 1972). In chapter 4, I discuss this content by introducing both Alfarabi's *De scientiis* and Aquinas's *Proemium* to the *Metaphysics*. According to Aquinas, metaphysics is a science with three heads. As a transphysics, it is located after the physics, but as the science of the First Being, it is above ethics, because ethics aims at metaphysics, as we learn from book 10 of the *Nicomachean Ethics*. Finally, according to Aquinas, metaphysics is coincident with theology and is one of its parts. Thus, when the *Convivio* locates theology as the highest science, it includes metaphysics as the science of the First Being.

Human happiness is the goal of the *Convivio*. The first three treatises allow the reader to understand the kind of happiness Dante seeks to establish. Intellectual happiness is the true aim of the first three treatises, which Dante shapes in an itinerary marked by doubts and uncertainties and superb new intuitions. True virtue will be the intellectual highest virtue of the *Nicomachean Ethics*, the virtue that the love for the lady activates. The identity of the human mind that the love for the gentle lady reveals is the true centre of Dante's discussion. That this knowledge is possible only for communal human thinking coincides with the invention in the third treatise of a thinking subject that is both one and many. This subject becomes the true protagonist of a new historical-political dimension that Dante's *Convivio* heralds, along with a new sense of human life (chapter 4).

The fifth treatise (*Syllogism and Censura: The Moralization of Nobility and the End of Intellectual and Political Aristocracy*), which comments on the third canzone, *Le dolci rime d'amor ch'io solia*, introduces a break and motivates it. A discontinuity enters: the focus is no longer the gentle lady, but rather nobility, which is proposed as tied to philosophy and indirectly related to the discourse on intellection. My reading stresses the extent to which the discourse on nobility in the canzone is conceived as a criticism of wealth and materialism and organized as a kind of refutation. This criticism returns in the prose, which in a synthetic but powerful way introduces in philosophical terms the doubt about the theory of the origin of prime matter (chapter 5). The fourth treatise makes comprehensible the pathway that leads to a kind of contemplation that is conceived in a different way from that treated above and is defined through theological elements. My reading points out how in the fourth treatise Dante exercises a kind of *censura* with respect to the previous treatises. This *censura* is focused for the most part on remaking the discourse on human intellect. Such remaking is the beginning of a rethinking that is powerful and which remains more within the borders of orthodoxy. Dante introduces as his aim the fight *contra gli erranti*. This aim drives his discussion of nobility. Reading the canzone, we may easily understand that the word "nobility" is the correlative of the intellect that God bestows on human beings. The ways of this bestowing are explained in the prose. But the canzone first requires a basic understanding of two things: one is why the discussion of nobility is linked to a quotation from Aquinas' *Summa contra Gentiles* (as he will explain in the commentary); the other is the controversial topic that is confronted here. I briefly discuss these in an attempt to show how Dante links nobility and intellection, and how this link manifests a reshaping of the theory of intellect introduced in the previous treatises, in particular the third (chapter 5).

5. Traces of Politics in the *Convivio*

Before concluding, I return to the title of this volume (*Reading as the Angels Read*), and in particular to its subtitle (*Speculation and Politics in Dante's Banquet*). I do so in order to point out the sense in which the word "politics" is used here, when it is said that the *Convivio* implies a political content, which the title relates to speculation.

Politics in the *Convivio* is thought of as the natural condition of human beings. It consists at first in their participation in the life of the community. In this sense, politics is not about the various kinds of regimes, but belongs to the awareness of social life and its importance. Of course, the fourth treatise will introduce the political institution of the Empire, which will be treated later in Dante's Latin political work. But before writing the *Monarchia*, Dante was, since his first work, aware of the community and city in which he was living. The *Vita nuova* shows such awareness in many ways. It offers the picture of a community living in the small city of Florence, which the death of Beatrice will transform in the world-city of Jeremiah's *Lamentations*.

The fact that the character who speaks in the first person tells his readers that because of the death of Beatrice he writes to the princes of the world (*scrissi a li principi de la terra*) announces that the private story implies a political meaning. Here, politics implies the sense of a community deprived of its *logos*, which Beatrice represents (Ardizzone 2011). The *Convivio* and the partially synchronous *De vulgari eloquentia* are built on an awareness of politics. What is particular or individual is conceived of as being part of a larger community, and the *koine* is both linguistic and political.

Politics in the *Convivio* grows on the margins but affects the various centres of the work. It embraces every individual action, including the cognitive. The sense of citizenship, and the awareness that cognition may create a possible common intellectual life for citizens, is linked to the fact that human individuals cannot live alone and actualize themselves, but are determined in relation to the social and historical situation. Society and state are *in interiore hominis* but also *inter homines*. The political essence of the *Convivio* takes form right from the first line – "all men naturally desire to know" – in which the "all" or "*tutti*" must be evaluated. This phrase, taken – as already said – from the opening of Aristotle's *Metaphysics*, in Dante indicates a community that is universal but also peculiar to those who live according to reason and whose aim is knowledge.

Dante's sense of politics, however, does not start with the universal *polis*. On the contrary, his sense of *civitas* is grounded on a realistic perspective. The *Vita nuova* shows that the sense of the smaller communities that make up the city is part of the landscape in which Dante's love story takes place. The *libello* offers the picture of a *milieu* made of meetings and conversations that qualify small social groups in society. Teodolinda Barolini (2009, 2014) has pointed out in her work on Dante's *Rime* the sense of social groups as something new. She focuses on the *brigata*, for instance, as a group composed of men and women, and points to the theme of friendship, which implies not only a philosophy of friendship but also a social history. A sociology of *brigata*, she writes, is evident in several of the sonnets. Many texts that have been read as texts of love's ideology are documents of moments of social life. Barolini's discussion can be fruitfully linked to a study by Michaud Quantin, who has explored, in relation to vocabulary, the beginning of a new sense of communal life. He studies, for instance, the appearance of the word *societas* and distinguishes between natural societies and those legally recognized. Before being legally recognized, small living entities were formed, whose rise was a reaction to feudalism and a fight against centralization (Michaud-Quantin 1970). These were the antecedents of the subsequent small entities legally recognized, which includes the *vicinie* that the *Convivio* introduces in its last treatise (Ardizzone 2013). But, as Barolini shows, Dante and, after him, Boccaccio did have the sense of small societies that naturally formed within the larger society. The above-mentioned *brigata,* for example, is a natural community composed of women or of men, or of both, in which we have a sense of society as a living body.

Individual life, which takes place in a network of social relations, is linked in the *Convivio* to the theme of speculation. This is established in a circular relation that proceeds from speculation to action, and from action to speculation. This speculation enters through the angels' metaphorical ability to read inside the mind of God. The speculation of angels in its turn links speculation and action in the world of time. The angelic desire to see into the mind of God (and by reading in that book, according to Augustine, they *semper* contemplate the divine ideas) must be related to new notions as these derive from the meeting of the old theological learning with the philosophy of Aristotle. This contemplation in the framework encompasses action. In fact, it is because the angel-intelligences look at the perfect intellectual models that are in the mind of God, thus contemplating his ideas, that they are able to move the heavens and promote generation and life in the world of history and time. The key words in the fragment from the *Confessions* quoted as an epigraph in the opening of this study are *eligere* and *diligere. Legere,* and the object of this *legere,* is indicated as *verbum.* In Augustine, this coincides with the ideas in the mind of God, identified also as the *panis angelorum,* which the *Convivio* recalls in its beginning.

The classical thought revives and evolves in Dante. The state is a natural formation that derives from the political nature of the individual. Dante will make a crucial addition that the intellectual activity of the human being is more powerful – and more natural, as well – when it is common. In the same way that the political human being lives in *interiore hominis* and *inter homines,* the intellectual activity lives in *interiore hominis* and among human beings. A sort of natural law thus presides over human life. The biological and the intellectual both aim at the same purpose, which is social and political. In this respect, the *Convivio* represents the Ur-phase of the project of the *Monarchia.* The intellectual reader to be formed by the *Convivio* lives in the *civitas.* The *Monarchia* will conceive this *civitas* as one and global. This will imply not only that human beings think best when they think together but also that the highest form of intellectual life cannot take place in a single city but in the city that coincides with the world. Aristotle's *Politics* opens by asserting that the *polis* is coincident with community, which is the most sovereign good of all, since the city encompasses all the other communities. Aristotle's claim, as well as that of Aquinas, is that the city exists by nature. Dante's discussion of intellect, as it begins to take form in the *Convivio*, seems to derive from the naturalness of the city and thus from the consideration that the human being is by nature a civic political animal. This suggests that the individual qua individual is an incomplete entity (Pungle 2013, 36). Aristotle's idea is that human beings are political animals because of their *logos*. Politics is actualized in human rationality but also in the community. The relation between being a political being and a rational one can be found within the *Convivio*, where the love-friendship for the *donna gentile*, in a highly transumptive way, heralds this awareness. The link between the discourse on intellection and the theory of *logos* that emerges in the last section of the third treatise, is discussed in these terms in my study.

Part of politics can be assumed to be the variant that the third treatise introduces when Dante's love for the *donna gentile* is stressed as friendship. The love for the *donna gentile* is the love for the absolute good, and the *bios theoretikos* is foundational. In Aristotle, the moral virtues have as their final goal contemplation. This implies that the moral norm is interior and is a tendency towards a likeness to God. Historical readers have interpreted this as the desire to know God (Fioravanti 2014).

The love for the *donna gentile* does not conceal its meaning. The awareness that the moral is a tendency towards a perfect good adds a value that is objective and is the foundation of moral life. Moral duty is the choice of actions and balanced acquisitions that drive towards the contemplation of the *donna gentile*. In light of this, Dante does not refer only to love when he speaks of his relation to the *donna gentile*, but speaks also of friendship. This suggests a link with books 8–9 of the *Nicomachean Ethics*, which are dedicated to a discussion of friendship. But this friendship is nuanced in Dante. He projects it into an ideal sphere. It is like a latent platonic dimension that derives from the fact that the *donna gentile* is shaped within a platonic framework: the canzone *Amor che ne la mente mi ragiona* presents her in fact as a divine idea. In the *Nicomachean Ethics*, friendship includes the various forms of human relation in the city. But in Dante, the friendship for the *donna gentile* functions also as an hypostasis. The model of perfect friendship is conceived as being the basis of a true love. Moreover, it seems that this relation is the archetype of every true human bond. The friendship of the *donna gentil*e is a great addition to Dante's love for her. The difference may seem slight at first, but it bears traces of the platonic *philia*, which considers that the foundation of friendship is the moral principle of *agathon*, the good as absolute.

This idealistic dimension is also historical: it leads the individual to be *civis*. *Paradiso* 8, the canto devoted to the heaven of Venus, will recall the canzone *Voi ch'intendendo il terzo ciel movete*. In fact, this heaven, which presents different forms of love, seems to suggest that the proto-form of love is friendship. This friendship is the permanent medium through which Dante introduces different forms of love. The idea at work here may also be that true friendship is the archetype for all forms of *conviventia*. This would update the ideal love of the *Vita nuova* by showing the persistence of a reflection that the *Convivio* has already put forth: the thought that the love and friendship of an idea implies a larger discourse on the essence of human beings. Friendship is the perfect proto-form of love. The love for the *donna gentile* must pass through this discussion. The ruler of this behaviour is *nous*. Such love implies and is aimed at the Good, which is intellectual, but may be also social. Dante indicates this object of love as the *honestum* ("da questo amore nasce la vera e perfetta amistade de l'onesto tratta"; and from this love springs the true and perfect friendship, derived from what is honest; III.3.11). This word *onesto, honestum* refers here to an object that is beautiful because it is intellectual and a common good (chapter 3).

In parallel with what Aristotle's *Politics* says about the individual as an imperfect being unable to live for himself, the addition in reference to the love-friendship for the *donna gentile* is that the act of intellection as well cannot take place in its most perfect form in the individual as such. In *Paradiso* 8, the friendship with Carlo Martello works mostly perhaps as an invention, but in light of the recalled canzone *Voi che'intendendo il terzo ciel movete*, it seems to introduce the celestial intellectuals as paradigm. It was within the goal of the highest good, proper to the angel-intelligences, here rethought as a model including a political common good, that the friendship between Dante and the Prince takes its meaning. Cosmology and politics appear intertwined, and the *Convivio* shapes the first intuition of a content that the *Paradiso* will propose in various ways.

The *Convivio* opens a multitude of new perspectives and ends by leaving open a series of questions in many cases never formulated in such a way before. The formation of the reader is never abandoned through the four treatises. We know, however, that for a long time such a reader remained only an ideal one. In recent years, new studies, like those of Arduini (2008, 2010, 2012) and Azzetta (2006, 2010), allow us to follow the *fortuna* of the doctrinal work from its beginning, after the death of Dante, to its diffusion in the Quattrocento until the sixteenth century (S.A. Gilson 2009).

It is the modern reader of the *Convivio*, however, who adds a new level of understanding of the work when he or she considers that this doctrinal and largely enigmatic book is no doubt the product of unrepeatable historical conditions. The *Convivio*, its language and logic, and the way in which learning is organized, cannot be detached from the edifice of medieval culture, from its platonic-Christian, Aristotelian thinking as active in the debates of the thirteenth century and in the first decades of the fourteenth, which, in their turn, were thought of as irremediably destined to be superseded by new visions and new models of learning. What emerges is a new, earthly sense of human life. The history of the *fortune* of the book is in part coincident with the evolving awareness of a modern sense of what it means to be a human being.

1 Introducing a Cosmic Intellectual Dimension: The Dialectical Nature of Human Being

The first two canzoni that Dante commentates in the *Convivio* were written in the years in which the poet was completing the *Vita nova* and in particular its prose text. In a previous study, I have proposed a reading and interpretation of the first two canzoni showing a continuity with the language and themes that the *libello* has focused on – a continuity that implies, however, a discontinuity, because the canzoni bring on the page new contents and a break with the love that the *Vita nuova* has proposed. Such discontinuity in *Voi che 'ntendendo il terzo ciel movete* was openly announced because of the entrance of a new lady and a new love. Using a language highly rhetorically organized, the gentle lady introduced a new thought as it derived from the reading of new books and from new meetings, to be identified, according to what we read in the prose of the *Convivio*, with Dante's frequentation with the so-called *philosophantes*. With philosophy, we are told, Dante attempted to console himself over the loss of Beatrice. The new thought enters since the first line of *Voi che 'ntendendo il terzo ciel movete*, the hendecasyllable that condenses a synthesis of a Neoplatonic and Aristotelian thinking that envoys the reader to the theories discussed by the *philosophantes*. This is a term that in the thirteenth century did imply a specific meaning – that is, intellectuals who were discussing new theories and establishing a link between the substances separated of Aristotle's *Metaphysics* and the angel-intelligences of Pseudo-Dionysius (Michaud-Quantin 1974).

Thus the first verse of the canzone announces the entrance of a hot topic that contrasts with the most traditional learning of *Vita nuova*, introducing the readers to a new pathway. The *Convivio* will of course be the result of such a pathway, but it is the canzoni that open, at first, the door to the new contents. That such contents were updating old intellectual interests and inclinations in Dante, as testified in the *Vita nuova* and in its *ornatus* of praise, has been my claim in *Dante. Il Paradigma intellettuale* (2011).

In this chapter, I intend to stress at first the inner link between the poetry and the prose text, showing to what extent understanding the *Convivio* requires the comprehension of the contents Dante introduced in *Voi ch'intendendo il terzo ciel movete* and *Amor che ne la mente mi ragiona*. Dante organizes them with a strong intellectual structure that the treatise does not explain. The prose text, however, introduces a series of topics that organize a network crucially important to the readers of the treatise. Dante did not insert in the *Convivio* the text of the canzoni, according to what is given in the modern edition of the treatise; rather, he was just quoting them fragment by fragment. This implies, as De Robertis (2005) notes, that the canzoni were well known and already in circulation since the years they were written. The reproduction of the canzoni at the beginning of the second to fourth treatises was an initiative of the first editors of the treatise. Thus my reading of the canzoni as an antecedent to the *Convivio* goes along with Dante's idea. The verse texts are actually the pre-texts of the contents Dante will discuss, but such pre-texts work as foundational of the new topics he will introduce. I use the word "foundational" in order to stress the results of my previous reading: the two canzoni contain the themes that the prose will discuss, and to understand the *Convivio* requires a preliminary reading and understanding of the canzoni. In them we find a thought that we may define in part tendentially heterodox, and in part such assumed to be in Dante's age.

It is such strong content that presides over the exposition of the prose text of the *Convivio*. Scattered in its form, proposing crumbs of a philosophical thought given in vernacular for people not learned and unable to understand Latin, the *Convivio* tells its readers that the canzoni are the main course of the banquet of learning Dante organizes during his exile. To define the *Convivio* as an encyclopedia of learning does not do justice to the true nature of the treatise – not because the work does not include a learning already circulating, that the treatise selects and reorganizes, but because its essential aim is not to furnish such encyclopedia. Rather, such learning – or more accurately, learnings – presented as crumbs or scattered fragments were introduced to give to the readers a new awareness. It is this awareness that is the true goal of the work. The love for the *donna gentile* is a discourse about the individual human being considered in himself, on the one hand, and in relation to the community, and, as such, part of the *humanitas*, on the other, as he will write years later. The political nature of the work – an aspect that this book introduces and that has, until now, never taken into consideration – comes out at first from the canzoni, and it is in their reading that the meaning of the work acquires its own first shape. The political nature of the treatise is organized following the natural link between speculation and praxis, and this can be grasped just if the reader is aware of the meaning of the first two canzoni. *Subtilitas* and high rhetorical awareness challenge the reader. Perhaps one of the strong inventions of the work is the creation of a logical subject that is plural and singular at once. Moreover, it is the recurrent shifting of the logical subject which shows the subtleties of the treatise and Dante's ability to link logic and grammar to express a content not yet pronounced in vernacular in this way and that penetrates to modify the idea of the thinking subject itself.

It is with the introduction of this main content that Dante challenges himself and his readers. For this invention, Dante draws from many sources and does appeal to different traditions and cultures. My reading tries to reconstruct this background and Dante's attempt to use different sources in order to shape his idea of the human being and his goal. Rethinking philosophical contents as derived from Aristotelianism and Neoplatonism, and linking them to those derived from the theological tradition, the *Convivio* heralds the beginning of a new society and of a new sense and goal of human being. The love for the *donna gentile*, introduced in the *Vita nuova* as a psychological content, has to be followed in its parabolas as the consummate rhetorical ability of her inventor makes it. On the back, there is the old Latin tradition and also a more recent Aristotelian tradition that Dante knows as debated in its Latin pronunciation, and both seem to wait to enter into the new dimension that the vernacular and the society that uses it creates. The print age in the fifteenth century marked the beginning of a new era.

The construction of the vernacular was the expression of a new era, too. The awareness of the new vernacular language – and its construction as a grammatical language encompassing what, until that point, was expressed in Latin – we know is an enterprise to which Dante has greatly contributed, and such construction implies in him the deep sense of a new society. The *De vulgari eloquentia* is the document of it. But it has to be seen in its continuity as testified in Dante's work. Dante's utilization of vernacular starts from *Vita nuova*; the *libello* and the love for Beatrice are the beginning of a new sensibility that encompasses old texts and contents but creates the fresco of a new sense of culture.

The *Convivio* continues such a pathway. The love for the *donna gentile* makes powerful such awareness. The canzoni are the turning of the page. But it is the new page that needs to be understood. The sense of the treatise cannot be grasped if the reader is deprived of such awareness.

To introduce the reader to the first treatise, I summarize here the main contents of the first two canzoni.[1] The first canzone[2] of the *Convivio* introduces the angelic choir of the Thrones, linking it to the heaven of Venus, the third heaven, and, as Dante will explain in the text in prose, with the science of rhetoric.

An initial reading tends to highlight the significance of the second treatise looking at the three different levels of understanding of the text as they take shape in the two different temporal phases: the poetic text, situating itself in the years that are partially coincident with the writing of the *Vita nuova,* and the later prose text, considered to have been written in the first years of exile.

This inquiry does not pursue the possible continuity between the *donna gentile* of the *Vita nuova* and that of the *Convivio,* but rather to what degree the so-called *ornatus* of praise may create a link between *Donne ch'avete intelletto d'amore* and *Voi che 'ntendendo il terzo ciel movete.* This perspective supports that trail upon which we embarked considering, according to the indication of *Purgatorio* 24, *Donne ch'avete* as a model of Dantean *stil novo,* and we have reread that poem, seeking in it the semantics of praise as propaedeutic of a refoundational methodology of the discourse of poetry. It is intended, therefore, to evaluate *in primis* the text of the canzone, which the temporal hiatus that detaches it from the prose text allows. To be read side by side, in turn, and in relation to the commentary beginning with the literal one, the identity of the *donna gentile* is sought in these two texts. In other words, her identity is sought without making it coincide on this level with philosophy, but isolating from it its first denomination, that of "*donna gentile,*" with respect to the second, proper to the allegorical commentary, where her new name, *filosofia* (philosophy), only apparently expresses in terms of scholasticism the portmanteau complex of the *donna gentile.* In reality, it confirms and reinforces the meanings that emerge from the canzoni and from the literal commentary reconsidering them along different lines of thought. The way I have chosen to read is motivated also by the fact that it is a relationship and level of understanding of the text that is largely disregarded. It is also to be considered that the text in prose in some key passages that will be dealt with is corrupt and therefore difficult to read. I further mention that the second treatise programmatically signalled the importance of the literal commentary: "Sempre lo litterale dee andare innanzi, sì come quello ne la cui sentenza li altri sono inchiusi, e sanza lo quale sarebbe impossibile ed inrazionale intendere a li altri e massimamente a lo allegorico" (The literal sense must always be accorded primacy, as the one in whose meaning all others are contained, and without which it would be impossible and irrational to attend to the other senses, especially the allegorical; II.1.8).

The letter, furthermore, was considered the base of the understanding of a text, for example, in a work of high circulation like Hugo of Saint Victor's *Didascalicon* (1939) or *De studio legendi*.[3] To this aim, the author of the *Convivio* recalled one of the basic principles common in the Middle Ages and which he tells us he derives from Aristotle's physics – that is, that it is natural to proceed from that which we know best to that which we do not know (II.1.13–14).

To be pointed out immediately is that the relationship that is proposed with the canzone *Donne ch'avete* from the *Vita nuova* consists in more than the apostrophe for which De Robertis,[4] in his commentary, provides the genealogy and lineage. It is rather that *novo* (novelty) (already heralded in *Donne ch'avete intelletto d'amore*, where the new was realized in the *ornatus* of the praise) that opens up here to a further inflection of that newness. As is known, the first canzone proposes the emergence of a new love as a new power capable of putting the old one for Beatrice to flight. The field of meanings is introduced by "un ragionar che è nel cuore" (a reasoning taking place in the heart)[5] that indicates how the discourse of love is created in the encounter between the heart – "il segreto interiore" (one's private inner being) – and reason. The entrance of the intelligence-choir of Thrones that presides over and generates the movement of the heaven of Venus, associated with rhetoric as will be seen in the commentary, along with their influence on human beings, are the speech's referent.[6]

What is useful in reconstructing the relational method that is introduced here comes from what we read in the opening of the first chapter. Dante introduces his *modus*, expounding a literal sense and an allegorical sense. He puts them in relation where the literal sense is the base, foundation, and principle for knowledge based on proof, and his method will be that of departing from things known towards the unknown, and therefore from the literal sense towards the allegorical. This way of knowing is defined here as "naturalmente innata" ("natural to us from birth"; II.1.14). Therefore, two temporal phases are composed and face each other in the second book of the *Convivio*. The text of the canzone in hendecasyllable – canzone *illustre* (illustrious) – is written, it seems, between 1293 and 1294 (Petrocchi 1983), while the commentary is much later (between 1303 and 1307–8). These are two temporal phases that are also two directions of understanding the text, and that therefore are to be seen in their relational nature, but also – to be taken into account as far as it is true – in their difference.

The focus of this canzone is found initially putting the text in relation to *Donne ch'avete* and considering the radicalization that occurs, since the speech no longer takes place with women gifted with intellection of love, but with the angelic intelligences. I recall that my reading of that canzone of the *Vita nuova* saw in the praise the entrance of an *ornatus* that has individuated the intellectual as the centre of meaning. The praise that linked the intellectual beings, angels and humans, was the exponent of a mental language and introduced anagogy, the intellectual activity of ascension in which God was thought of as the intellectual being par excellence. The contribution that Guinizzelli's poetry had provided for this strong intuition has already been indicated in my previous work, and the linguistic resolution that took shape from it has also been pointed out. Praise in Dante became, then, not only the exponent of an intellectual language qualified to express desire for Beatrice on the part of intellectual-spiritual beings (angels and saints), but a language which human beings also practiced, therefore suggesting and introducing a *similitudo,* which spoke of a similarity between the intellectual essence of the angels and that of human beings in that they are united by such laudatory activity.[7] And so, what arose from this, it is suggested, was the relationship between the women who have an understanding of love and love as an intellectual being, and Beatrice as a being to be put in relation to the intellectual creatures, and therefore the *dire* (speaking of) with these women, as an intellectual discourse according to the modes explored in my previous study (Ardizzone 2011, 39–79). But we have also seen how praise involved the linguistic nature of human beings as the centre of deep reflection already in that canzone (*Donne ch'avete*) and that the prose in some way made it explicit in its value as an instinctive and natural manner: My tongue spoke as if moved by itself, Dante tells us, and says "Donne ch'avete intelletto d'amore." If this digression is posed here again it is because the first canzone commentated in the *Convivio* suggests a continuity with those meanings.

In the praise, which also had a tradition in the *Laudari* (books of praise) that Dante echoes in those optative, vocative, or desiderative forms within which it falls but which was also sought by him in its philosophical valence, he found a language of tension towards the divine characteristic of the angels and he applied it or, better, transferred it onto Beatrice.[8] The tension towards the divine from the part of intellectual beings, which expresses itself as praise – taken up, it seems, from Thomas Aquinas and Gregory the Great – was used to express desire for Beatrice both on the part of the angels and saints and on the part of whoever was writing in the first person. Activating this *modus*, the canzone was built upon speech creating a parallel between that celestial *clamare* (entreating), representative of an intellectual desire, and the desire of the "I" for Beatrice where the sensual aspects of love fell, while what emerged was the conquest of a level where the intellectual and the natural came to set themselves in relation to each other. The exponent of this was the linguistic-mental level made explicit as praise, and an important aspect of my reading was to note that the word *lode* or *loda* (praise) opens radially towards a set of meanings where praise also appeared as the result of an *impositio nominis*.

The continuity that the first canzone of the *Convivio* manifests with the canzone *Donne ch'avete* is what is therefore to be considered immediately and, within the limits of such a problematic, the relationship between the text and literal commentary is to be gathered from it at first. Praise, therefore, in the inflection that Dante makes of it, aware of the background of praise and of its use in the *Duecento*, resumes its vocative linguistic mode.[9] This vocative recurs in the first verse of *Voi che 'ntendendo il terzo ciel movete*, bringing its rhetorical and philosophical significance up to date. The exordium of the canzone, because the vocative form is repeated, creates *in primis*, then, a continuity with *Donne ch'avete* that is partially stylistic and, above all, of thought. It authorizes us to seek a continuity between the *Vita nuova* and the *Convivio* that does not find its place within the problematic of the *donna gentile* and its (hypothetical) before in the *libello* (little book) and then in the *Convivio*. Instead, we are to reconsider the continuity of the choice for what is interior and intellectual as it takes shape, beginning with *Donne ch'avete*, and as it evolves in the first canzone that will enter in the vernacular treatise, delineating also new facets that reinforce those already anticipated in the *libello*.

Moving on to *Voi che 'ntendendo*, let us consider how this line of thought proves itself and evolves. The first level of meaning, as it comes to us from the canzone itself – which the *Convivio* recalls and reproduces in fragments, and which brings us to think, as already said, that the poetic text already had its own independent circulation (De Robertis 2005) – introduces a series of relationships which the commentary then reinforces in turn. Staying with the poetic text, then, here in brief is the content of the first canzone of the *Convivio*: the sad soul which experienced the sweet thought of Beatrice is put to flight, and instead, a new power penetrates, and that virtue – which inspires the speaker to look at a new lady, and in particular, at the eyes of this lady, bearer of *salute* (bliss; 24), or salvation – dominates him. In confrontation with that new power, the old, humble thought of an angelic lady who is crowned in heaven is destroyed. The bewilderment of the soul changed the poet's life, generating fear, but the words of the *spiritello* of love nevertheless usher in the qualities of this new lady: "pietosa e umile, / saggia e cortese nella sua grandezza" (compassionate and humble ... wise and courteous in her greatness; 46–7). The canzone, we read, is for the few and this is to be understood. Appropriately – we point out – the "voi" of *Donne ch'avete* is echoed along with the apostrophe already generally present in other poetic compositions.[10] But what is fundamental is that the canzone binds the new content to a *dire* that is addressed to the intelligences of the third heaven as ideal referents by virtue of its peculiar newness: "udite il ragionar ch'è nel mio core, / ch'i nol so dire altrui, sì mi par novo" (hear the reasoning taking place in my heart: I know of no one else to whom I can relate it, so novel does it seem to me; 2–3).

The reasoning taking place in the heart is, in fact, placed at the core, as is therefore the "dire" which is an internal *locutio* and is addressed to the angels precisely for being of an intellectual sort. This will be made explicit where it will be explained at the level of commentary that "udite" means to understand with the intellect. Among the intelligences, the speech is directed to those of the third heaven since, he explains, it is to their mediation that he owes his state, from the rays of their star the spirit which disputes with the soul originate: "El ciel che segue lo vostro valore, / gentili creature che voi siete / mi tragge ne lo stato ov'io mi trovo" (it is the heaven that responds to your power, noble creatures that you are, which draws me into the state in which I find myself; 3–5).[11] The exchange in the heart, and so the internal word, is once again the propulsive centre of meaning where the new seems to identify itself:

Io vi dirò del cor la novitate,
come l'anima trista piange in lui,
e come uno spirto contro lei favella,
che vien pe' raggi della vostra stella.

> I shall speak to you of the novel condition of my heart, how there my sad soul weeps, and how a spirit, which comes from the rays of your star, disputes with her. (10–13)

A problematic continuity is set, then, between this canzone, and the *modus laudis*. This continuity confirms itself where one considers the meaning of what is narrated: the overcoming of the thought of love for Beatrice by virtue of a new thought which brings the narrator to look at a new lady. From this new thought then proceeds a new type of love whose identity, we will see, emerges where one sets out to consider the new lady in her relationship with the new thought in the canzone inspired by a "spirito" (spirit; 12) – "Questi mi face una donna guardare" (This newcomer makes me look at a woman; 23) – and where the fundamental event is the speculative nucleus which penetrates to denote the being of such a new thought. The mode in which such speculation is proposed is essential in order to grasp the new that enters the canzone.

A difficult point of *Voi che 'ntendendo il terzo ciel movete* to be understood is the kind of influence that the angelic intelligences exercise on human beings and on the origin of such power and influence, and it is in light of this that the whole speech that is expounded acquires a precise and important significance. What Dante will indicate later in the commentary as "donna gentile" is to be seen in relation to this preliminary assumption.[12]

Dante takes to the extreme an idea already introduced in *Donne ch'avete*, where Beatrice is recalled by the angels and saints, speakers in the canzone of an intellectual language, and because of that qualified to introduce the new intellectual level that Dante intends to bring into his speaking. The *Convivio*, one of its levels, is essentially built upon a before; it continues a process of intellectualization of love that began already with *Donne ch'avete*. Love for the lady in the *Convivio* is nonetheless heralded as a radical turning of the page with respect to the circle of references on which the discourse on love was built in the language of vernacular poetry. It is true therefore that Dante had already intended in the *Vita nuova* to reinforce and carry to the extreme in an intellectual key his love story for Beatrice, but from what we read, in *Voi che 'ntendendo il terzo ciel movete*, we are attending to a new turning of the page, and the new page which results remains up to now to be understood at least in its internal and intertextual dynamics. If in the poetic text the climax is in a transformation that occurs in the sad soul to which the old love is confined and in the characterization of a new thought of love, it will be in the combined reading of the poetic text and the prose text that the sense of the discourse will acquire further meaning. Let us start, then, from the poetic text and see who the agents and interlocutors are.

1. The Canzone: *Voi che 'ntendendo il terzo ciel movete*

The intelligences that move the third heaven, the heaven of Venus, will, in the commentary, be identified by Dante with the Thrones but are not here made explicit as such. They are the addressees of the first-person speech, since his new state is inspired by the "cielo che segue" (heaven which responds to) their "valore" (power), that is, which the intelligences move. The speech of the author of the canzone is directed to them, expressed with a "ragionar" that is in his "core" (heart). The recounting speaks of the "novitate" (novelty) in his heart, and of "cuore" (heart) which, he will write in the commentary, is "one's private inner being" and therefore internal (II.6.2). Here are the other agents: the sad soul, and the spirit that disputes with her (the soul) and which comes from the rays of the star of Venus. In the second stanza, called forth as well is a pleasing thought that made its way to the feet of our Lord where it saw a lady in glory, a thought that was already proposed as superior to the soul – indeed the soul declared, "Io me 'n vo' gire" (I, too, wish to make my way there; 19). Such a thought produced a sweet inner speech – "parlav' a mme sì dolcemente" (it would speak to me of her so sweetly; 18) – and this brought about the soul's inclination to flee. The new being expressed with "chi" – "Or apparisce *chi* lo fa fuggire" (Now *one* appears *who* causes it to flee; 20, emphasis added) – which puts the old thought to flight, holds sway over the first-person narrator with such power: "che 'l cor ne trema che di fuori appare" (that the trembling of my heart is reflected in my external bearing; 22) (to be noted here are the traces again of an old language of love – Cavalcantian traces I mean to say – but the speech seems to want to set itself forth in an alternative way).

This "chi" (one who), which appears inspired by a spirit that comes from the rays of the star of Venus and is proposed, in the prose of the commentary, as a being that is part of the intellectual sphere, brings him to look at a lady and in particular at her eyes, and his words are the repeated words of this "chi": "Chi veder vuol la salute, faccia che gli occhi d'esta donna miri" (Anyone who would see bliss, gaze into the eyes of this lady; 24–5). Now salvation comes from this lady and from her eyes, while in the past Beatrice was the lady of salvation.

The new spirit-thought destroys the humble thought that spoke of Beatrice, angel now crowned in heaven: "Trova contraro tal che lo distrugge / l'umil pensero, che parlar mi sole / d'un'angela che 'n cielo è coronata" (The humble thought which used to speak to me of an angel crowned in heaven finds in this one a fatal adversary; 27–9). This is the direct speech of the soul that grieves and laments the flight of the old thought –"questo piatoso che m'ha consolata" (this compassionate one who has consoled me; 32) – therefore the memory of Beatrice, and that, always with the direct speech quoted in the text, commentates the new event that involves the eyes of the narrator of the event: "Qual ora fu che tal donna gli vide! / perché non credeano a me di lei?" (I rue the hour that this lady saw them! Why would they not heed what I said of her?; 34–5). It is always the soul's *locutio* which informs us that "negli occhi di costei de' star colui che le mie pari ancide'" (in the eyes of this lady lies "the one who kills all such as me"; 36–7). The narrator adds that it was not sufficient that I (the soul) was aware of this and so attempted to refrain from them (my eyes) looking at that lady, because I have been defeated all the same because of her: "E non mi valse ch'io ne fossi accorta / che non mirasser tal, ch'io ne son morta" (But it did me no good to be aware of this: they went straight ahead and gazed on her, and have thereby caused my death; 38–9). We should note the eye-to-eye correspondence that occurs between the first-person reasoner and the lady on one side, and the wise clarification inserted there where the soul relates that the eyes that look at the lady are not the eyes of the soul, but those of the first-person speaker. It is in that clarification that we find the nature of the dialectical relationship between the *anima memoriale* (the part of the soul related to memory) and the new lady: "Io dicea: 'Ben ne li occhi di costei / de' star colui che le mie pari ancide!'" (I told them: "Without a doubt, in her eyes must lie the one who kills all such as me"; 36–7). It is the soul that is speaking. What is asserted here is important: it is not that which is indicated as the soul that experiences the activity of speculation, but the first-person speaker, and without the mediation of the soul. The play of the *prosopopoeia*, difficult and complex because of the various voices that intervene, forms, block by block, a mosaic that appeals to the intelligence of the reader and in which the event that is narrated acquires its meaning – that is, the act itself of speculation and intellectual knowledge does not occur by way of the encounter between the *anima* (soul) and the new thought inspired by the heavenly spirit. Instead, it is suggested that this takes shape from the relationship of the gaze between the new lady, at which the heavenly spirit inspires looking, and the eyes of the speaker. The first meaning to consider is that the *anima memoriale* is told as in opposition to the speculative activity. To this is linked the entrance of the new lady and the incipit of the speculative activity as the overcoming of that activity of memory which tied the speaker to the thought of Beatrice.

Much of what is said remains undefined and requires the reader's intervention; for example, who the "colui" (the one; 37) is, who is in the eyes of this lady, and who seems to have killed the *anima memoriale* (even if it is clear that it deals with something tied to the area of the thought, a new thought, as will emerge from the commentary). Furthermore, what is the contrast between what is indicated as the soul and what the new lady is intended to mean?

We should also note the entrance of a new voice: it is that of a "spiritello d'amor gentile" (a noble, fresh spirit of love; 42). Words given to a spirit only apparently resume Cavalcantian modes, and in fact Dante makes an adjectival form already used ("noble," related to a spirit) his own and he leads us immediately into the intellectual sphere.

However, in order to understand the genealogy of "gentile" (noble) linked here to "spirito" (spirit), we must go back over the Guinizzellian trail that is resumed and reinforced. In Dante, this trail finds its place in the intellectual sphere where the outcome of the mediation of intelligent beings implies a specific meaning. "Gentile," in fact, is not more coincident with the historical notion of nobility, as already largely demonstrated by "Al cor gentil rempaira sempre amore." This in Dante is confirmed where nobility is said of a being that is proposed as intellectual. In fact, the "noble" spirit (gentile; 42) is that which comes from the rays of the star, as stated in lines 12 and 13 and, as we will read in the commentary, the rays mediate divine light.

Fundamental to understand is what is set forth beginning with the first verse: the relationship between the heavens and the intelligences which move them, a relationship which was a chapter of the philosophical-scientific thought of the time and was shaped in the encounter between philosophical and theological content to which the angels-intelligences actually belong. In the relationship between the heaven and the intellectual movers, however, Dante seems to underline – we will see it in the commentary – the prominence of the intellectual action responsible for the movement of the heavens.[13] Also to be considered, therefore, is an idea that Aquinas, for example, and Saint Bonaventure also had put into focus and which discusses the theory of the astral influence and its material consequences. This idea, according to a study by Litt (1963),[14] saw pre-eminence in intellectual action – that is, in that of the angel-intelligences, over the physical one of the heavens – a pre-eminence which nevertheless was also central in a text that had already entered into the *curricula studiorum*, that *Liber de causis* which the *Convivio* will draw on openly and in different ways in the prose text.[15] In the canzone, meanwhile, it is said that the "spirito" originated from the rays of the star and, according to Bonaventure for example, the influence of the intelligences is light which comes from the absolute source of light. This explanation coincides with the one that Dante will provide in the commentary. This poses, then, a distinction by which it is not to be read that the heavenly body would influence human beings according to a materialistic theory of love operated by the influence of heaven. The contest makes the will to connote the discourse of love in a new way, unequivocal only if the opposing contexts are individuated. It is evident, in fact, that the mode of proposing love and the relationship with the heavenly sphere is not meant to recall that materialism that Guido Cavalcanti, and the culture of which he was a bearer, had constructed, making love descend, as in "Donna me prega," from the influence of Mars. Introducing what he indicates as "new," the author of the canzone seems to refer not so much to his own evolution, but above all to what is different from what his fellow poet-friends had written. Waiting, then, to better identify the reasons for such novelty, let us continue our reading. The commentary, in fact, will offer further elements for an awareness of the turn pursued:

> Poi li ho chiamati a udire quello che dire voglio, assegno due ragioni per che io convenevolmente deggio loro parlare. L'una si è la novitade de la mia condizione, la quale per non essere da li altri uomini esperta, non sarebbe così da loro intesa come da colore che intendono il loro effetti ne la loro operazione.[16]

> After calling them to hear what I have to say, I give two reasons why it is only they whom I may fittingly address. One is the novelty of my condition: since other human beings lack experience of it, it would not be understood by them as it is by those who, in understanding their own operation, understand the effects they cause. (II.6.3)

The influence exercised by the intellectual souls or heavenly intelligences on the sublunar world is the first level of meaning to be kept in mind. This, for example, was discussed by Siger in his commentary on the *De causis*,[17] proposition 4 therein (see Marlasca 1972b). The answer was that the heavenly intelligences flow their *bonitates* into the lower souls – at least, so reports Siger, who nonetheless was also inclined towards a materialistic reading.[18] But in the cited text, a nuance of meaning comes which belongs to a series of details that lead us to suspect that the canzone meant to introduce the discourse on human intellection according to modes in which the encounter with the intellectual sphere, thought of as separate and nonetheless attainable, becomes the fundamental centre of reflection. The relationship of similarity between human beings and purely intelligent substances is therefore a content to keep in mind.

The adjective "gentile" (noble) attributed to "spirito" (spirit), then, is introduced in order to re-establish the discourse of spirits and therefore also that of the heavenly influences. On the margins of Dante's discourse there is in fact one of the subjects of the great debate – attested to by the Parisian condemnations, and in particular by that of 1277 – on astral influence, which held that heavenly bodies influence human bodies while their spiritual movers influence souls by way of spiritual power that is, however, effected through the body. This prohibited subject was actually a position that Aquinas seemed to share at least in part.[19] Essentially, the heavens neither influence nor determine the intellectual life of human beings, but the mover-intelligences can influence it since they mediate the first being; the type of influence is debated also in this case.[20] The *Liber de causis*,[21] however, and, in particular, its rereading by Albertus Magnus, is a text to refer to in order to understand the line of thought that attracts the still-young poet. Human beings receive from above a spirit-thought which allows them to see an intellectual form; this seems to be the departure point of the canzone. Human intellectual activity comes to be by virtue of an influence that originates externally. An intellectual being is mediated by the angel-intelligences.

We should take note to reinforce the internal coherence of the poetic text, that is, that the intelligences in verse 5 are indicated as "gentili creature" (noble creatures), to which the "spiritel d'amore gentile" (noble, fresh spirit of love; 42), passing through the "spirto che vien pe i raggi de la vostra stella" (spirit which comes from the rays of your star; 12–13), is linked. Notably, this spirit that "favella" (speaks) reconfirms the relationship between the field of intellection and that of *loquere* already attested to in what we have identified as the field of praise in Dante's *Vita nuova*.

The commentary will be more explicit, and if Aquinas called the angels "spiritual creatures" (*De spiritualibus creaturis*), Dante also calls them spiritual (i.e., intellectual) creatures; in the literal explanation, "spirito," he writes, means thought; it is thought. A novelty that takes shape, then, and that the author underscores, is that, from a physical or corporeal being, from a very subtle corporality – the pneumatic spirit of medical science, of which Cavalcantian texts were an important point of reference in the field of poetry – we move here to consider the spirit an intellectual being. We should note that the adjective "gentile" (noble) attributed to "spirito," as in "spiritel d'amore gentile" (noble spirit of love; 42), refers us back to Cavalcantian texts still important at the height of the drafting of the two canzoni, but only as a dialectical assumption. "Spirit" clearly goes through an open re-semanticization, which contrasts medical knowledge and natural philosophical knowledge, privileging the assumption of that tradition which links *spiritus* to *nous* and of which Chenu gave brief and effective recognition in one of his contributions to medieval lexicographical studies.[22] We will return further on to consider the use of such terminology. But it remains to be established what this spirit, which in the text in verse comes from the rays of the star, is in terms of the theory of knowledge.

I believe that the first conclusion could be synthesized thus: a heavenly being descends into the sublunar sphere and generates intellection in the first-person speaker, but that intellectual activity excludes in its coming into being what is given in an activity of memory. The new lady signals the entrance of the vision of a being that allows speculation, but this does not happen in Aristotelian terms, by virtue of the abstraction of the phantasm kept in memory and therefore located in the sensitive soul – that is, by means of the agent intellect which works to activate the possible. I am using an Aristotelian terminology here, only in order to point out its non-exposition and essentially the voids and unsaid elements that this textuality, if taken on, nonetheless compels us to utter. We have the intervention of a heavenly being that certainly could carry out the role of an intellect – light which comes from the principle of light – but on some level, the novelty announced is that here the spirit is introduced as being capable of promoting speculative activity that does not seem to pass through a process that includes the sensitive *anima memoriale*. We will see, however, that not everything coincides in this interpretation and the areas of uncertainty are to be taken into consideration because they signal what was perhaps the uncertainty characteristic of Dante, who in those years was still in dialogue, on the one hand, with a knowledge that was Augustinian at its base and, on the other, with the world that Cavalcanti represented. Dante was nonetheless already critical of that manner of conceiving of the discourse on love, and therefore on human beings, and the poetic manner itself which Cavalcanti's discourse ossified.

Let us continue our reading and refer the words of the noble spirit: "[Anima] Tu non sè morta, ma sè ismarrita" ([Soul] You are not dead, but bewildered; 40). The soul which is said to be lost, in this context, could mean that the direction taken, regret and memory, had to be overcome, but in more general terms, means that the seat of this new love is no longer the sensitive soul. It must be noted nonetheless that the word "pensiero" or "penser" (thought), "soave penser" (pleasing thought; 15), or "l'umil penser" (humble thought; 28), used as a synonym of *memory* and *regret*, in the poetic text already gives *memory* a nuance of meaning that differentiates it from the Aristotelian theory of the internal senses. What seems to follow is that it is the topos of love, linked to the sensitive soul and which Dante had already circumscribed and indirectly refused in *Donne ch'avete intelletto d'amore*, that reappears, but here qualified to introduce the identity between intellectual activity and the new love. The first question that one asks oneself is the following: in the canzone, is the subject of the "dire" (speaking of) the dialectic that opposes one lady to another? Is such opposition meant to introduce a discourse of a cognitive nature? And other questions follow: Is the transformation that is told – "quella bella donna ... ha transmutata in tanto la tua vita" (that beautiful lady ... has so deeply transformed your life; 43–4) – the figure of a new way of conceiving of love? Does it imply a cognitive operation that takes form in the text? And, does what the poetic text and what the commentary tell us induce the same meaning?

Let us begin with the fact that in the canzone an awareness emerges and it is the core of Dante's discourse: that in the individual there exist two different ways of relating to love. In the text, they break down into the emergence of two nuclei and positions, both of which are active and characteristic of human beings. It is necessary to be immersed in and aware of the debates that intersect in order to understand why the closed and doctrinal character of the canzone is unavoidable and why Dante initiates a comment on this, and to understand how, by virtue of the commentary itself, the poem reveals itself to be a discourse about intellection and an instrument of intellection.

Even if the soul is afraid, it is afraid of the intellectual dimension that it perceives as a new and transformative tension: "ché quella bella donna che tu senti, / ha transmutata in tanto la tua vita, / che nn'ha paura, sì se' fatta vile" (for that beautiful lady whose power you feel has so deeply transformed your life that you go in fear of her, so base have you become; 43–5). The new type of love for the new lady is of course told as being the experience of the same subject who has lived that for Beatrice. Proposed in terms of a dialectical opposition, such experience tells us something about the subject himself.

Let us go on to read the verse that follows: "e pensa di chiamarla donna, omai" (and resolve to call her your lady henceforth; 48). Here, "donna" (lady) stands in for *domina* (domination, dominion), and it is an invitation to the soul itself to overcome the subjective level of memory for a new intellectual one, which the soul can attain. The soul, if it will avoid deceits – the illusions of its fragility, since it is still tied to the sensitive level – will be capable of seeing such wonders that it could not but be handmaid to this love. So the soul – memory in its two-headed identity, sensitive and mental together – becomes handmaid of a love whose being is purely intellectual. The dialectic that we have indicated seems to find a synthesis here. At this point, a fundamental articulation of the text in question is whether human beings can attain these two cognitive levels, and there emerges that the canzone tends to focus on two ways in which the essence of human beings manifests itself, which are made to correspond to two different ladies. If the two ways are related to one another, in order to go beyond theories in which love was in some way tied to a soul closed within a cognitive circuit linked to subjective experience, it is also true and unavoidable that the canzone suggests to us the existence of two ladies, since it wants, through two different types of love, to make explicit two essences which present themselves in opposition (even if the appeal that we find is at the moment of interaction): "pensa di chiamarla donna omai!" (resolve to call her your lady henceforth!; 48). The commentary, in turn, will follow this line, but in the commentary the genesis of the new love reveals something that it was not possible to read in the poetic text.

For the moment, let us return to the canzone and let us note that it is to be read correctly interpreting the first verse at the opening: "Voi che 'ntendendo il terzo ciel movete." We cannot limit ourselves, as in De Robertis's (1988) commentary to the Vasoli edition of the *Convivio*, to explaining that the heaven is moved through intelligence, but we must understand the relationship between intelligence and the divine.

It is from the divine, in fact, that the separate substance or intelligence receives that power which allows it to move the heavens. There is an entire tradition, both Aristotelian and Neoplatonic, that penetrates Dante's vocabulary. *Intendere* (to understand; to intend) implies also *tendere verso* (to tend/aim towards), that is, desire and intellection; it is through this explanation that we understand how the angels move the heavens,[23] that is, owing to desire for the first cause. *Intelligere* is possible where there is *omousia*; the angel-intelligences are *omoiosis*; that is, they resemble, even if imperfectly, the divine. As such, in similitude they tend (within *intendere* there is *intentio*)[24] and understand (*intendono*) and, in the tension towards the divine, they operate the movement of the heavens by virtue of *intentio*.[25] At the basis of this verse there is, therefore, a Neoplatonic-Dionysian-Proclian knowledge arrived at also by virtue of the *De causis*, which Dante could know both through direct reading and also in the commentaries of Albert and Aquinas (though Siger and Giles of Rome, for instance, also comment on the *De causis*). This knowledge is retraced in the variously commentated books 4 and 5 of Pseudo-Dionysian's *De divinis nominibus*.[26] Also to be considered are the commentaries on Aristotle's *Metaphysics*, book 12 (still 11 for Albert), and the commentaries on Dionysius's *De coelesti hierarchia*, or Aristotle's *De coelo*, made by those who, like Aquinas, reconciled Aristotle and Dionysius.

This verse, then – the first of the canzone that is also fundamental to understanding the sense of the general discourse of the *Convivio* (which *Paradiso*, in particular cantos 28–9, will resume – refers us back to the *De causis*, proposition 3 in Aquinas's commentary, or is in the steps of Albertus's work which this predicate transfers to human beings.[27] Here is the text from the *De causis*:

> Omnis anima nobilis habet tres operationes, nam ex operationibus eius est operatio animalis et operatio intelligibilis et operatio divina. Operatio autem divina est quoniam ipsa praeparat naturam cum virtute quae est in ipsa a causa prima. Eius autem operatio intelligibilis est quoniam ipsa scit res per virtutem intelligentiae quae est in ipsa. Operatio autem animalis est quoniam ipsa movet corpus primum et omnia corpora naturalia, quoniam ipsa est causa motus corporum et causa operationis naturae.

> Every noble soul has three operations; for among its works there is a vital operation, an intellectual operation, and a divine operation. Now its operation is divine because it prepares nature by the power that is in it from

> the first cause. Now its operation is intellectual because it knows things by the power of the Intelligence that is in it. Now its operation is vital because it moves the first body and all natural bodies, since it is the cause of the movement of bodies and of the operation of nature.[28] (*Super librum de causis Expositio* 2002, 17)

Proposition 18, in Aquinas's commentary, also announces the same or similar content:

> Res omnes habent essentiam per ens primum, et res vivae omnes sunt motae per essentiam suam propter vitam primam, et res intelligibiles omnes habent scientiam propter intelligentiam primam.
>
> All things [are] beings [*entia*] because of the first being, all things are self-moving because of the first life, and all intelligible things have knowledge because of the first intelligences. (Ibid.)

Here, the criterion is that of participation, as Aquinas explains in his commentary[29] and elsewhere. In truth, the entire discourse of the canzone involves that activity that is indicated as speculative and which is at the base of the intelligences' being and operation. The text is to be understood, therefore, as placing itself on speculative terrain. If understanding (*intendere*) involves the return to the cause, reflection is like a reflected ray, something that returns upward, which is to say, to the primary principle. This happens in the same act of intelligence. Proclus's *Elementatio theologica*, translated by William of Moerbeke (also known as Guillelmo de Morbecca, whose translation Aquinas used while reading the *De causis*), according to the propositions that Aquinas recalls; in his commentary on proposition 15 of the *De causis*,[30] he assumes that this act involved desire for one's own essence, a meaning implied by *return* as *revertere* in Latin and *epistrophe* in the Greek of Proclus. The return, however, was to something primary that the terminology establishes, since the *strophe* (to turn) is the root of *epistrophe*.[31] This act in the intelligences is carried out through an intellectual movement that in Pseudo-Dionysius is indicated as circular, straight, and oblique – or helicoidal – a winding around one's own centre that is also a climb, a winding climb therefore, of which one of the causes is resemblance. The criterion of resemblance is fundamental since angelic intelligence is an exemplum – that is, an image of that which is higher (Aquinas, *Super Librum de causis expositio* 2002, commentary, 21).[32] *Intendere* therefore presupposes, as Dante uses it, a *tendere verso*, an act of appetition that also involves a tending towards the self, since its resemblance to the first cause is in its essence. Since this intelligence is derived from the first cause, however, the return to the self in the intelligences involves an intelligence of the first being. Central here is that proposition of the *De causis* that we have already cited, which says that every noble soul, thanks to the power that it receives from the first cause, can carry out three operations. This relational complexity is at the basis of influencing and understanding.

Each of these intelligences is thus both capable of knowing itself, and what is above it and proceeds from it (Aquinas's comment on the *De causis*, propositions 3; 15). The implicit constitutive principles of this first verse are two: one is the notion of the first cause that involves that of influencing, and the other is that of resemblance and desire. From this proceeds the movement of the heavens, with the remark in the *Convivio* that the heavens are given as passive, while in *Paradiso* the heavens are matter and form, a point which we cannot discuss here.[33]

Without this Neoplatonic and Neoaristotelian base (that is, the new Aristotle, here the one of the *Metaphysics* who is encountered in the commentary with the Pseudo-Dionysian and Proclian-causistic line, which is aware, in turn, of the Aristotelian position), not even the discourse that takes place in the poetry is comprehensible. The intelligences are given the discourse on love and the internal battle because Dante wants to underscore the intellectual nature of the new love. The resemblance, by virtue of intellection between angel-intelligences and human beings, is the centre of attention. The state of the speaker, we read, is affected by the heaven that the intelligence moves: "El ciel che segue lo vostro valore, / gentili creature che voi siete, / mi tragge nello stato ov'io mi trovo" (it is the heaven that responds to your power, noble creatures that you are, which draws me into the state in which I find myself; 4–6). That state is made explicit when we read what is announced as the novel condition of his heart (10) and then how the sad soul weeps (11) and how a spirit which comes from the rays of the star disputes with her (13). The resemblance between human beings and angels is suggested; the angel-intelligences resemble the divine according to the *De causis* (see again, for example, Aquinas's proposition 3, and Pseudo-Dionysius),[34] the human intellectual soul being placed in a nonetheless inferior hierarchy. The accent is therefore not only on the influence that the intelligences exercise, in which a distinction is set between what comes from the rays of the star, which is a speaking spirit, and what comes from the influence of the heavens.[35] In parallel – unsaid but strongly inferred – a meaning seems to be the focal point which emerges only if the first verse is understood: the angels move the heavens by way of *intelligere* (understanding through intellect) and the movement comes from the relationship between the intelligences and the absolute intellectual being. Therefore, the vision characteristic of the intelligences seems to be the model to which the speaker looks when he introduces the new love, the new thought, the new lady: "Questi mi face una donna guardare" (This newcomer makes me look at a woman; 23). There is, therefore, not only a dialectic between old love and new, but also between vision and memory. The vision heralds the vision of an absolutely intellectual being – the meaning suggested by the context and the relationships that exist in this.

Love, *pronominatio* for human knowledge, introduces, according to the modes already put into focus in particular by Cavalcanti, the discourse on the ontology of human beings, and that ontology takes its place here, and is its novelty, in a resemblance with the intelligences and their operations. The enigmatic identity of the new lady slips in. To skim through that enigmaticness is part of what the text itself will indicate as a difficult way of speaking, and in underground relationship with the canzone's beauty itself, that it is characteristic of the mind to be able to understand. In the final verses we also read that the novelty "diletta mia novella" (my beloved fresh and fair; 60) is precisely in a type of beauty difficult to grasp, and that essentially the difficult and the intellectual belong both to what is said and to the way itself of saying it.

A reader who here uses tools that have revealed themselves to be suited to reading Cavalcantian poetry will not gain much. The attempt of the text seems to be that of changing perspective. The memory introduced, which could tempt us into a deciphering linked to theories on the internal senses, signals a track that will not lead to predictable developments. At the centre of the canzone, there is not the sensitive soul, which was already central in the Cavalcantian discourse, but the intellectual mode assigned to the powerful and cosmological image of the intelligences, beings here put forth as reflective and as such capable of carrying out a mover activity of the heavens and an intellectual power and influence. Neither, however, is the point, even if it is centrally placed, that intellection is characteristic of human beings; in fact, the two loves hypostatized as two thoughts and two ladies come to represent two human modes in and of themselves in a problematic relationship, a relationship that the speaking subject experiences and presents as dialectical and nevertheless as possible for human beings. Yet the relationship between the intellective level and the level related to memory appears to be the first centre of reflection that the canzone imposes for consideration. Of the relationship between intellectual vision and memory, it is said that they are opposite ways of relating to the two ladies. But it is also to be considered that the logical subject who experiences the dimension of memory is indicated as the soul, and that the only relationship to proceed between this soul and the new lady is given to us where the new lady sees the eyes of the first-person speaker and this is registered as the defeat of the soul: "Degli occhi miei dice questa affannata: / 'Qual ora fu che tal donna gli vide!'" (Of my eyes this wearied one says: "I rue the hour that this lady saw them!"; 33–4). The defeat of the soul is a point to understand. The field of speculation is introduced and the *anima memoriale* stands out by virtue of this lady set in a dialectical relationship with speculative activity. However, it is also to be considered that this lady whom the first-person speaker looks at is proposed as a vision provoked by a spirit that comes from the rays of the star and therefore by a being belonging to the celestial sphere. We are also told, however, that the *anima memoriale* must become handmaid to that lady immediately set forth as the inspirer of speculative activity. There are tenuous traces that bring us to think that, in the canzone, its author attempts on his own and with a non-Aristotelian language to expound a problem of cognitive order in which is put forth the overcoming of the *anima memoriale* for a higher form of knowledge, which emphasizes speculation. The entrance of a new thought-being, which, be aware, comes from the celestial sphere and is an *additum* being, is the first unavoidable content that is proposed. If this is true, a focus of the text's meaning is born on the margins of a thought that the second half of the thirteenth century had debated in various forms. Love is a phenomenon that brings us back to an essence and, therefore, to establish the ontology of human being. This seems to be the centre of a discourse of cognitive nature and around which are radially arranged other subjects that already provide here a relational plot that the prose will reintroduce and develop much later.

The conversive and intellectual movement that marks the incipit of the canzone – in which is set the relationship between *intelligere* and moving, between *intelligere* and the order of the cosmos, between contemplation and action – remains the most evident trace of the importance that intellectual knowledge assumes therein, perhaps postulated as a model of human knowledge. The resemblance with the knowledge of the angel- intelligences is suggested even if the modes of that resemblance are not made explicit. The angels' object of contemplation and desire in their understanding is what could function as a strong connection, but here this is not said; it will be the prose that introduces this content, and the text of the second canzone written before that of the prose – "Amor che ne la mente mi ragiona" (Love which discourses to me in my mind) – which we will discuss in the second part of this book.

Let us sum up, then: If the account ("ragionar") is given to the intelligences of the third heaven, which in the *Convivio* are the Thrones – according to the organization Dante follows of Gregory the Great's *Moralia in Job* or Brunetto's *Tresor* and not Dionysius, as will be clarified in canto 29 of *Paradiso* – and the Thrones move and preside here over the heaven of Venus, the first and essential level of understanding of the text is suggested where "udite" (hear; 2) is explained as "intendere per intelletto" (to understand with the intellect; II.6.2) and "cuore" (heart; 2) is explained with "segreto dentro" (one's private inner being; II.6.6). This is to be read as a reflection of Neoplatonic and Christian tradition and therefore of the notion that the human soul is the fundamental content on which this dialogue is structured. What emerges is that the tradition put into focus by Augustine and his readers comes to link *il ragionar* (thinking, reasoning) with the heart, and internal human *verbum* to the intellectual mediatory being of a "spirito che favella" (spirit which disputes; 12) that indeed comes from the rays of the star of Venus. The internal *verbum*, identified by Aquinas as the intellectual principle (see Lonergan 1967, Ardizzone 2011), is therefore suggested as a centre of meaning in the text of the poem. That in this canzone also, as already in *Donne ch'avete*, the stylistic texture is built on a *sermocinatio*, and that such *sermocinatio* is spoken by beings that are either of memory or are absolutely intellectual, exposes a continuity between the two texts, but also a difference where the tension is what makes the dialectical nature of the discourse emerge.

Dante, who identified the intellectual sphere, which is also what connotes the novelty of the "dire" (speaking of), now introduces the reasoning of his heart and therefore the battle between two opposite thoughts in his mind. The dialectical process is the signal of a methodological awareness.

The object of the narration is the encounter that takes shape in the reasoning of the heart between a new spirit which "favella" (disputes; 12) and an old thought or soul. The encounter introduces the contrast between a love inspired from above, which brings him to look at a new lady and the love for Beatrice. We have an internal dialogue, the heart reasons, but to say it, to put it into poetry, is difficult and the new mode is narrated to the intelligences because it can be understood only by those who influenced it, mediating the celestial being.

It is fundamental to understand in what this novelty consists:

> Io vi dirò del cor la novitate,
> come l'anima trista piange in lui,
> e come un spirto contro lei favella,
> che vien pe' raggi della vostra stella.

> I shall speak to you of the novel condition of my heart, how there my sad soul weeps, and how a spirit, which comes from the rays of your star, disputes with her. (10–13)

The contrast between the soul and the spirit (this is what introduces the novelty), is announced: what is indicated as the sad soul is put to flight by a spirit. This spirit is not the equivalent of the Cavalcantian spirit, as already said, but is thought – its corresponding equivalent in Greek would connect *nous* and *pneuma*[36] and by that connection it comes to be part of the intellectual series. This spirit is the result of the rays coming from Venus, "raggi de la vostra stella" (rays of your star; 13); the intelligences of this heaven are responsible for the influence that comes from the rays of the star and the rays of the star are light, intellectual light. It is to them that the spirit addresses its speech not only because its condition comes from them, but because what Dante is attempting to establish is an intellectual speech. The continuity with the problematic of *Donne ch'avete* is evident just as is evident that the solution remains the one indicated in that canzone: the agents involved are those who indicate the existence of an intellectual language, just as Severinus Boethius, in dealing with the categories, had established that whether characteristic of the divine or of the physical world, the involved beings are those who indicate their statute (see de Libera 1999, 66–7). The linguistic aspect, then, is always central; the logical subject and centre of the canzone's meaning is the "dire" (speaking of), with a sampling of discourses, and it is a "dire" where the novelty of the heart is that of one's private, inner being. So the speaking of expresses an intellectual tension of the language itself, while the spirit is indicated as "gentile" (gentle), as a synonym of "noble" according to the *De causis*, since noble is that which is nearest the divine, and therefore intellectual.

The novelty is to be understood. The language of love frees itself from the connotation of what pertains to the sensitive, and of which regret and memory seem to be a part, and this soul, because it is still anchored to experience and subjective memory, is guided towards its own overcoming and directed towards transcending itself. The new word is determined by a condition generated by the intellectual influence that comes from the intelligences that move the heaven of Venus, and which, much later, the commentary will associate with the science of rhetoric.

We are talking, then, about knowledge. A relationship between the vision of the intelligences and human knowledge slips in – their influence is spoken of as mediation of celestial light, and in the internal speech, the continuity between the internal narrating "I" and the intelligences themselves is suggested.[37] The notable fact is that a new poetic word comes from that construction and the pleasing thought of the past – which ascended up to the divine, contemplated Beatrice in her glory, spoke to him inside, and involved his poetry of regret after the death of Beatrice – is put to flight by this new spirit that is also suggested as being involved in speaking activity: "favella" (disputes; 12). An entire Cavalcantian track is retravelled and seems taken up again, but is actually erased. Apparently the field of flight – "come si fugge / questo piatoso che m'ha consolata!" (how he flees, this compassionate one who has consoled me!; 31–32) – recalls celebrated Cavalcantian passages of which it resumes the verdict but inspires from it a new meaning. Now the *anima memoriale* is put to flight by he who holds sway over it with a new power (between *vis* and *valor*). What is crucial to understand is that speech which is entrusted to the noble spirit of love: "Tu non sè morta, ma sè ismarrita" (You are not dead, but bewildered; 40). The soul is not dead, the soul does not die, although it may become bewildered. Contemplation, consideration, and speculation place themselves along the cognitive scale at a higher level than what pertains to memory.

It has been said that "spirito" stands for mind, intelligence, and thought,[38] and the soul that can find itself suggests that the sensitive part of the soul, the *anima memoriale* can find herself where she recognizes the superiority of the new thought of love that is characteristic of the intellectual dimension of human beings. And, in fact, this spirit, coming from the rays of the star that brings the speaker to look at a new lady and at her eyes, bearers of salvation, is a speaking spirit: "Questi mi face una donna guardare, / e dice: 'Chi veder vuol la salute, / faccia che gli occhi d'esta donna miri'" (This newcomer makes me look at a woman, saying: "If anyone wishes to discover fulfilment, let him gaze into the eyes of this lady"; 23–5). As a consequence of the fact that the beings involved in the new event are promoted by an intellectual being, we must think that the eye is equivalent to the mental eye, according to a distinction characteristic of ancient and medieval culture. Dante himself, in the first book of the *Convivio*, will discuss the spiritual eye according to a methodology that disseminates reactants throughout the text that offer a system of referents which however remains open. Nonetheless, the position of the author is not always coherent in the poetic text, as, for example, when he writes "che 'l cor ne trema che di fuori appare" (that the trembling of my heart is reflected in my external bearing; 22), or "sed e' non teme angoscia di sospiri" (provided, though, that he is not afraid to endure the anguish of sighing; 26), which are typical ways of expressing love as passion. The attempt, however, is to give shape to a different meaning and to use an old language but giving it a new value insofar as the referents of the speech itself are declared and that seems to be formulated on the basis of a strong awareness on Dante's part of the agents introduced to the speaking.

In this sense, let us again consider the representation of the soul as weeping. The words of the soul under the metaphor of weariness announce, on the one hand, that this new lady is in opposition to the old thought, which the soul lived on. What is then put forth is the relationship between eyes and eyes – not the eyes of the soul, but those of the speaker: "Qual ora fu che tal donna li vide!" (I rue the hour that this lady saw them!; 34) – and so the awareness of a new language qualified to express a new content penetrates into the old theme of love. There, where there is an abdication of the soul's reasons and of its cry, and with the sense of novelty that Dante inspires, the necessity of a new reading becomes possible. So, among the speakers of direct discourse – "Io dicea: 'Ben ne li occhi di costei / de' star colui che le mie pari ancide!'" (I told them: "Without a doubt, in her eyes must lie the one who kills all such as me"; 36–7) – it is still the soul; the one who kills is a new type of love that kills the old one and therefore the *anima memoriale*, but the elaborated death of the soul, clarified as bewilderment, is here the beginning of a new order of things that in the poetic text is traced not without some uncertainty, which the commentary then, *in primis* the literal one, will aim to discreetly dispel. The choice of commenting on this canzone is nonetheless understandable. We can see, in fact, that the one who gives the identikit of the new condition is the noble spirit inserted here in a speaking act where the speaking function is bound to the intellectual one, to the new condition, and to the texture of the canzone. Since this spirit, then, another novelty, comes from the light of the star, a relationship between nobility and intelligence is suggested; it is intellectual excellence – that is, excellence tied to the intellect – that gives meaning to the word "gentilezza" (nobility). Here are the words of a noble spirit that provide the diagnosis for the soul's condition: it is not dead, it is only bewildered. What, then, is the path that the soul must travel? The new lady is frightening because the *anima memoriale* cannot confront her. (This is a fundamental suture point: what does it mean that the *anima memoriale* cannot confront her?) It is by again turning to cognitive theories, Aristotelian in origin, that one can begin to understand the poetic text, and, in fact, the entire canzone forces consideration of this area of meanings that are similar to those confronted by Cavalcanti, but which open up to an answer that opposes Cavalcanti's contents and his language bounded to physicality or corporality.

To understand the position that the author assumes in this text, it behooves us to follow him step by step. It will not be in reading it through the prefabricated structure of some cognitive theory, whether heterodox or not, that one will understand this canzone, in which the first invention is precisely in having introduced two ladies to represent the dialectical tension of the discourse as metaphorical of the duality or of the two spheres of existence to which the canzone means to give voice. It is in duality that we have the trace of Cavalcanti's mark, even if Dante's tension is clearly that of carrying out a transfusion, attempting to resume that content and guide it towards other outcomes.

The verb "mirare" (to see; 46) keeps the speculative area active. The language signals that tension, the "optima digna" of the *De vulgari eloquentia*, are already individuated. The vocabulary, the skillful use of adjectives, brings us into a new dimension; this lady, humble like Beatrice, is also "cortese," therefore noble, and this suggests a resemblance with the intelligences that, in the *De causis* and in Dionysius's *De divinis nominibus*, are noble because they resemble the divine. Nobility becomes intellectual excellence, where "intellectual" implies resemblance to beings classified as purely intellectual. The characteristics of the new love that already open up to what will later be clarified about the "donna gentile" (noble lady) can be defined beginning with this: it is inspired by an intellectual being and guides us within parameters where internal word, eye, and its reflectiveness and thought are part of a whole, intellectual knowledge and its complexity is at centre. What is to be understood is to what the dialectical tension between intellection and memory opens up and what synthesis is outlined, if one is outlined.

In Cavalcanti, "Donna me prega," the sphere of "consideranza" (contemplation; 27) was detached from the sensitive sphere; possible intellect existed in that intellectual dimension, but human beings were anchored to their sensitivity. Here, what is actually being said is that "consideranza" (although the term does not appear) is characteristic of human beings who share it with the angel-intelligences, and it is influenced by them in the mediation of an intellectual light that comes from the divine.

Here, we are approaching what is the central discourse of the *Convivio*: human knowledge and intellectual power as correlatives of the appropriate aim of human beings which also opens up the relationship between knowledge and action.

The process that follows, which seems to me possible to reconstruct, is worthy of note. The problem that is posed and that takes shape immediately in the canzone through the invention of she who the commentary will indicate as "donna gentile" is the human being as an intellectual being whose form is the intellectual. (From her introduction, it is to be underscored that "donna gentile" is a *transumptio, nominatio,* or *pronominatio* and therefore also one of those mythopoetic inventions that the Middle Ages called *integumentum.*)

An interesting aspect emerges where one considers that this new being, or new lady, only later called "donna gentile," comes to perhaps figuratively identify something up until that moment unsaid in that way. In fact, if "gentile" is the same as "nobile," and "noble" means "resembling the divine" in the territory in which it is set, the relationship with the noble souls and, that is, the intelligences of the *De causis,* is born. The entrance of the new dimension that she introduces means that this lady in some way correlates with the world of the intelligences. She is not the Guinizzellian lady-angel, but the aim of the Bolognese judge is part of a background that the canzone draws from and it is in continuity with what *Donne ch'avete* had also put into focus. But the Guinizzellian background is not enough to explain what is already being put into action here. It will be *Amor che ne la mente mi ragiona* (Love, which discourses to me in my mind) that introduces the elements qualified to clarify that a new knowledge penetrates into the continuity with the past, and this opens up a rift that the intrusion of a new textuality makes inevitable.

The canzone is difficult and closed and the envoi makes that peculiarity explicit as an invitation to the reader to penetrate the meaning that runs under the words. It is therefore to be considered that in *Voi che 'ntendendo il terzo ciel movete* the declared undertaking was to make *venustas* (beauty) coincide with a *modus intelligentiae* that was appropriate for the mind to understand. The novelty of the canzone, stated in the closing, is exactly in this exercise of intelligence that the canzone requires; in declaring the difficulty of the text, the envoi places the novelty and beauty of the text itself in that difficulty:

> Canzone, io credo che saranno radi
> color che tua ragione intendan bene,
> tanto la parli faticosa e forte.
> Onde, se per ventura elli addivene
> che tu dinanzi da persone vadi
> che non ti paian d'essa bene accorte,
> allor ti priego che ti riconforte,
> dicendo lor, diletta mia novella:
> "Ponete mente almen com'io sono bella!"

> Canzone, I cannot but believe that they will be rare who properly grasp your meaning, so exacting and difficult are you in what you say. So if you chance to come into the company of those who seem to you not quite to understand your meaning, then I exhort you, my beloved fresh and fair, to take heart and say to them: "At least recognize how beautiful I am!" (53–61)

"Bella" and "novella," set in rhyming position, both are in relation to "mente" (mind; 61)[39] and "Ponete mente" (recognize; 61). The novelty coincides with the intellectual beauty that is both a *modus scribendi* and a content. The intellectual beauty that we have already considered for "Donne ch'avete intelletto d'amore" returns and the verb *intendere* ("intendan," or [they who] grasp; understand) reaffirms the internal relationship between the "dire" in verse and the understanding of the angels ("Voi che 'ntendendo") and the appeal to their understanding that the canzone's first line expresses. The relationship that takes shape is an appeal to the reader formulated in continuity with the appeal to the intelligences: "però vi priego che lo mi 'intendiate" (and so I beg you to understand what I say; 9). While it indirectly confirms the discourse on the resemblance between the intelligences and human beings, it formulates poetry as an intellectual language delegated to speech both with intellectual beings that are angel-intelligences and with human beings suggested as being participants in that intellectuality. If the understanding of the angels involves the moving of the heavens, the beauty of the poetic text also seems to delineate itself as both an intellectual and motive activity.

At the level of personal history, the first book will tell us that the *Convivio* does not deviate from the event of the *Vita nuova* and that, rather, it is for the motive of clarifying that Dante, as we read, wrote up the commentary on the two canzoni that needed explanation. Poetry itself came to suggest itself as a new way of telling or relating, but what did this novelty consist in? In *Donne ch'avete*, the *sermocinatio* of intellectual beings was followed by that of love, alluding to the new identity that is meant to be given to love and at the same time connoting the very nature of *locutio* in the intellectual. In *Voi che 'ntendendo il terzo ciel movete*, the attempt at establishing the new content of poetry in an intellectual seeing (*visio, video*) connected love with an intellectual reality on the one hand and, at the same time, connected *venustas* (beauty) to the intellectual and, therefore, to what the mind was capable of understanding. That direction and meaning were indicated in the apostrophe to the angel-intelligences. The vocative case was its equivalent and established a relationship between this "dire" and praise; I recall that in *Donne ch'avete* the locution that the angel said in the divine mind was vocative, as were the locutions of the laud books. The "ragionar" (reasoning) in the heart, however, and what becomes the object of the narration in this canzone addressed to the angel-intelligences tells us that the internal word is the crucial point of this discourse that is given in a thinking that is also a seeing and therefore a significant point is again in the internal *verbum*, in Augustinian terms, the enigma of a divine resemblance (and as such common to all intellectual beings). The intellectual seeing in the poetic text is what penetrates in order to overcome the old way of loving tied to the *anima memoriale*, and it sets itself forth in continuity with the internal *verbum*, suggesting an identity between internal word and intellectual vision. The exchange in the heart is difficult and that difficulty is in its novelty. It is a novelty of the heart and therefore of the internal plexus. These are elements that we have already proposed, but less explicit is that the novelty resides in the will to connote that way as intellectual. This is suggested by the fact that it is addressed to the angelic intelligences and by the initial claim of submission to those beings and to the intellectual influence that they exercise, by virtue of their understanding and moving of the heavens, on human beings: "El ciel che segue lo vostro valore, / gentili creature che voi sete, / mi tragge ne lo stato ov'io mi trovo" (It is the heaven that responds to your power, noble creatures that you are, which draws me into the state in which I find myself; 4–6), where the "state" is a mental or intellectual state. Internal language and intellectual vision emerge as centres of meaning where the meaning is in their relationship.

The reconsideration of theories tied to material influences is evident. Dante is aware of a culture that builds the identity of human beings on the material and sensitive even if it is difficult at this chronological level, coinciding with the canzone, to establish if the text of "Donna me prega," a clear referent of this knowledge, had already been written. But the reasoning of "Donna me prega," built on the material and sensitive identity of human beings and played out on a language of physics, is in stark contrast with the reasoning of this canzone, built on a language where internal speech and the nature of the discourse itself stress the intellectual level to which it means to give voice as revealing of the true nature of human beings. The high style of the *De vulgari eloquentia*, the sublimation is put into action.

Not only is the overcoming, but not abdication, of the *anima memoriale* then narrated, but poetry appropriates, attempts to make its own, the visual interior thinking, mediating the Augustinian base with a peripatetic awareness. The encounter in Dante between an old textuality and a new one, and the attempt to think these lines of thought through and in continuity, is part of a method which the canzone ends up introducing into the text.[40]

We will return to this, but what is now pressing to underscore is that in this phase poetry bears witness to an intellectual level that is its beauty in a correlation between the recounting of a new intellectual way of loving and the passage to the intellectual sphere. If we consider the line that, from the Sicilians, arrives at Cavalcanti, the novelty that reveals itself is that Dante invents a new way of conceiving poetry. We saw that in the opening of the *Convivio* he asserts that the content of the canzoni and their allegory are to be explained because in no way does he mean to deviate from what was written in the *Vita nuova*. We see, then, how the *pane rustico* (rustic bread) is introduced, along with the commentary with the purpose of explaining what the closed nature of the texts does not allow us to understand.

The *Convivio* assigns its motive to an intellectual level, the essence of which it is necessary to explain. The poetic mode fixes itself as intellectual and its beauty is in this intellectual type of pulchritude, whose rhetorical basis will be given in the *De vulgari eloquentia*. The first novelty here is in the founding of a transumptive discourse, evident where the personal story, Beatrice, is changed (*transunta*) into *anima memoriale* while the new lady (*transume*) represents the intellectual soul. Furthermore, another figure, *prosopopoeia*, that can be considered still part of the complex figure of *transumptio*, enters when the word is given to the soul and the spirits. So it would seem that the model that is carefully avoided in the texture of the poetic text is the model of "natural dimostramento" (natural demonstration) of Dante's first friend, just as for his "ragionamento" (reasoning) he does not ask for an expert in natural philosophy, but chooses as interlocutors the beings who are capable of hearing and therefore understanding by way of the intellect the difficult (*difficilis*) meaning which the poem encloses. The widening of the potential circle of readers is evident, just as must appear evident the supremacy of intellectual values over the expert ones of natural philosophy.[41] The criticism of the materialistic culture characteristic of medical doctors, which will find its theorist in Petrarch, is actually written by Dante before the poet of Arezzo. In the intellectual, the *fictivus* (figure) does not only fix itself as fundamental, but it also becomes an integral part of the formative and educational project, the importance of which is to be considered since poetry, in the *Convivio*, is suggested as being part of civil conversation, and civil conversation is part of politics To read a text of poetry requires the use of the mind and it is proper for the mind to grasp the type of beauty characteristic of poetic language, and therefore of tropes, which is an intellectual beauty.[42] The notable fact is the awareness and continuity that is set among the interior word and intellectual vision and the poetic text itself, its language entrusted to what the *De vulgari eloquentia* will define as *volgare illustre* by virtue of vocabulary, structure, and content (see Ardizzone 2013).

One level of the novelty is also indebted to his first friend and not only because he is outlined in dialogue with his poetic modes and modes of thought, but above all if we consider how a cognitive event actually takes shape in the canzone just as the same type of event took shape in "Donna me prega," but also in other texts. For example, ballad 26 in Cavalcanti (1986) was the account of an event that was of a cognitive type. In fact, the word "salute" (salvation) there signalled the cognitive act, "la salute tua è apparita" (Your salvation has appeared), coinciding with the speculative activity and the genesis of the abstract form (for this I refer to Ardizzone 2002, 17–46). But returning to Dante and to the canzone under discussion, we see that the first event is signalled when a relationship of sight is established between the eyes of the lady and the eyes of the character who says "I": "Chi veder vuol la salute, / faccia che gli occhi d'esta donna miri" (If anyone wishes to discover fulfilment, let him gaze into the eyes of this lady; 24–5). The second event, favoured over the first on the level of intelligibility, occurs when the soul laments that the eyes of the lady exclude the *anima memoriale*:

> L'anima piange, sì ancor len dole,
> e dice: "Oh lassa a me, come si fugge
> questo piatoso che m'ha consolata!"
> De li occhi miei dice questa affannata:
> "Qual ora fu che tal donna li vide!
> e perché non credeano a me di lei?"

> The soul laments, so keenly does it sorrow still over that thought, and exclaims: "What sorrow is mine: how she flees, this compassionate one who has consoled me!" Of my eyes this wearied one says: "I rue the hour that this lady saw them! why would they not heed what I said of her?" (30–5)

Until this passage, the speaker is the soul, and its *locutio* is narrated by the first-person narrator, but what is the soul saying with "perché non credeano a me di lei"? It is simply and basically saying that it was not on the peculiarities characteristic of the sensitive soul and the *anima memoriale* that one relied in order to attain intellectual knowledge. Let us see what follows: "Io dicea: 'Ben negli occhi di costei / de' star colui che le mie pari ancide!' E non mi valse ch'io ne fossi accorta / che non mirasser tal, ch'io ne son morta" (I told them: "Without a doubt, in her eyes must lie the one who kills all such as me." But it did me no good to be aware of this: they went straight ahead and gazed on her, and have thereby caused my death; 36–9).

The difficult passages say something that is certainly intuitable, here qualified to identify the sensitive soul's *locutio*, so that what is indicated as the death of the soul by virtue of eyes involves the overcoming of the sensitive soul and the entrance into a new dimension where what is proper of the sensitive soul is transcended to initiate an intellectual process. That overcoming occurs by virtue of speculation – the Aristotelian subplot is suggested. Even if the text avoids the terminology of such a subplot, it is alluded to if we consider that the spirit that comes from above and that brings the character who says "I" to look at the lady inspires a speculative activity, and the lady that sees the eyes of the "I" aims to suggest the phase of intellection or speculation that occurs through the direct vision of a substance that is inspired through the mediation of the intelligences. But the subplot requires then that we decipher the insertions towards the purpose of understanding why intellection does not occur through abstraction of the image preserved in memory but by virtue of the new being. Further on in the text it is outlined that the sensitive soul, if it will become handmaid to the new lady, will be able to see wonders. These wonders involve a different way of knowing, no longer determined by the sphere of the senses and memory. The prose, in the section dedicated to the allegorical commentary, will explain that to see wonders means to know the causes of the wonders themselves (II.15.11), and the text recalled there will be Aristotle's *Metaphysics*. In the difficulty of identifying the discourse according to an Aristotelian mode, it seems that either because of a lack of skill or because of the will to reconsider the theme of human knowledge in a different perspective, what emerges is the giving voice to, on the one hand, a dialectical contrast and, on the other, further on, to an alluded-to *coniunctio*. In fact, to become "ancella" (handmaid) uses an expression taken from the annunciation but it introduces a topical mode of the radical texts that state that the sensitive soul is "propter intellectivam." The new lady enters, then, with the problematic duty of comprehension; she could be the *transumptive mode* to speak of the vision of a separate form that the intellect allows, bearing in mind that in the heterodox field both the possible and the agent are separate substances at times identified. But whatever the most probable explanation is, it is evident that the two ladies come to represent two different ways that are both proper of human beings: one represents the *anima memoriale*, tied in some way to the sensitive sphere but superior to it at the same time and not identifiable with Aristotelian memory; the other, a separate being that it is possible to consider.

The stanza that follows would seem to clarify some points of doubt for the reader, and here, skillfully inspired by the noble, fresh spirit of love, the passing or overcoming of the condition of memory is suggested where the new lady that the soul "sente" (feels) has transformed its life so that the soul goes in fear of her, so that it has become base. The meaning that can be drawn is that bewilderment is a transformation in which the *anima memoriale* can no longer exist according to the motives of its own experience and subjectivity, but here is the exhortation: "mira" (see her), and so on. And call her your lady. So the sensitive soul is exhorted to choose the new lady to rule, and the meaning that comes from this is that the intellectual faculty is higher than that of memory – it is superior to it – but it also tells us about a relationship between the two, the nature of which is difficult to ascertain. Here, the word "amore" – "Amor, segnor verace, / ecco l'ancella tua; fa' che tti piace" (Love, true lord, behold your handmaid; your will be done; 51–2) – enters as the relationship between two beings, one of which ends up being subjected to the other, but as will be clarified in the prose text, by choice and consent. Love will return in the next canzone but here its meaning is that the *anima memoriale* becomes handmaid to the intellectual. "Love" here stands for intellectual knowledge. It seems that this canzone is giving voice to a certainty: on the one hand, to be human is to be intellectual, and therefore to be endowed with a resemblance to purely intellectual beings; on the other, there is the problematic relationship between the individual sphere of memory and the intellectual. The suggested resemblance with the angel-intelligences who *intendono* (have intellection) – which implies the vision of the divine being, desire, and therefore the movement of the heavens – seems to be the reference, qualified to explain that, by virtue of their mediation, and therefore thanks to the spirit mediated by them for human beings, the possibility is granted of looking at a being that allows their speculation. What one would expect is that such speculative activity would occur through the abstraction that the agent intellect operates on the phantasms, which then allows the actualization of the possible intellect. But this is not actually said. "Love" is charged with meaning, where it suggests the relationship between a being (soul) related to memory and a separate one.

In this reconstruction we can identify the intellect with the spirit that comes from above, and from the origin of light, and therefore from God, according to a theory of Augustinian foundation, widely diffused in Bonaventure and also in Albert. It is indisputable that here the intellect does not bring one to the abstraction of the image preserved by memory, but to look at a new lady, the separate nature of which, it is suggested here, allows intellection. Comparisons with Cavalcanti's most important canzone are possible where, also in Cavalcanti, the intellect was suggested as being separate and whose activity is suggested to be *consideranza* (contemplation). In Cavalcanti also, memory remained anchored to its sensitivity. For us, however, it is arduous to establish both that "Donna me prega" had already been written, and therefore also that this canzone is responding to Cavalcanti. On the contrary, the philosophical uncertainties which are experienced in the reading here could be a signal that that great theoretical text was not yet written – or, also, that those points that appear to us to be uncertainties are actually the traces of the attempt at mediating different pieces of knowledge, as if a circle of references were to be reconsidered in another perspective, as determined by the intrusion of a new textuality.

In any case, the fact that the spirit of celestial provenance is a speaking spirit ("favella," or disputes) confirms this plurality of registers and brings us, for example, into the Thomistic and Augustinian field. In fact, it is Aquinas who makes the internal *verbum* the equivalent of the intellect (Lonergan 1967, 183–220). The difficult point of the canzone's meaning, however, is that intellection takes shape by virtue of a being external to human beings. To what philosophical textuality is this love-knowledge turning for *auctoritates*? The most problematic passages to resolve are in the different responses that seem incompatible amongst themselves: in one we read, "questi mi face una donna guardare" (this newcomer makes me look at a woman; 23), where the eyes of the mind are those that look; the other passage is where it is revealed that the *anima memoriale* seems to experience an intellectual *trasmutatio* while remaining within the motifs of the sensitive – "quella bella donna che tu senti" (that beautiful lady whose power you feel; 43). The sensitive soul detached from the intellectual and anchored and limited to its sensitivity suggests that intellectual knowledge is possible by virtue of a separate being or form. The vision of a separate being as the inspirer of intellection, in which the *anima intellectualis* is contrasted with the sensitive soul, would seem to give voice to the so-called theory of the philosophers who, against the thought of theologians, held that two souls were active in human beings (Van Steenberghen 1977, 341) and that the human soul was a compound and not a simple entity. Such a reading was in contrast with that of the theologians, who held that one single soul was the cause of all of man's activities thanks to its three powers and operations. Does the poetic text seem to bear this not-new philosophical notion in mind? It was on this notion that Albert had built one of his theories that contradicts it, but Cavalcanti's discourse in his most important canzone was built, or will be built, on the different and antithetical natures of the sensitive and intellectual souls.

In *Voi che 'ntendendo il terzo ciel movete*, perhaps the general position of the philosophers did not penetrate; rather, the particular support for and rereading of that theory as was given by Albert, in a work in which what was already set forth in his *De anima* was summarized. Albert's emanationist noetics, in which the intellectual soul and its knowledge flows in it from the divine light, is a trail to be considered. According to Albert's reconstruction, it would be from the divine light that both the possible intellect and the agent intellect flow. There is in the soul a constant flow of light that, through the mediating agent intellect, progressively actualizes in the soul the potential intelligibles that the soul possesses as possible intellect. I am going to cite, then, some fragments of this work. For example, in chapter1.5 of the *De origine et natura animae rationalis*, we read that, on the basis of what was said in the third book of the *De anima* and in the *De intellectu et intellegibili*, is it easy to find what the origin and the nature of the rational soul is, since it is not the act of any body, a corporeal form, or a power operating in a body. By virtue of this, it is impossible that it is generated by qualities or forms that are in the human seed, or that it derives from the same seed, but, the separate intellect being the first mover in nature, the rational soul is a resemblance of the light of the agent-intellect because it is generated from that.[43] Further on, recalling his *De animalibus*, he explains that the intellect in conceiving of the nature of the rational soul penetrates from the exterior, not because the intellect causes it from outside nature, but because it draws it out from its light and not from some material cause.[44]

The intellectual nature of human beings penetrates, therefore, from an extrinsic cause, and it is intellectual light that comes from the cause of light, and Albert explains that the nature of the soul comes in part from the inside and in part from the outside. In fact, the vegetative and sensitive souls are drawn from matter and matter would not be capable of generating its form were it not informed by the universal intellect that acts in the works of generation. This theory, that then culminates in that *inchoatio* that Dante will introduce in the fourth book, could actually be the background responsible for the exposition of the different identities of the intellectual soul and the sensitive soul, both functions of human beings, but different in nature, one being intellectual and the other material.[45] Let us further note that if we identify the speaking spirit in the text of the canzone with the intellect, then it seems that *locutio* and intelligence come together in human beings from the cause of light, according to a mode that will be confirmed in the *De vulgari eloquentia*, book 1, and in *Purgatorio* 25.61, where in the *locutio* (*fante* belongs to the area of *for, fari, parlare*), the passage from animality to the intellectual nature of man will be individuated.

Returning to the text of Albert, what remains to be considered is chapter 8, where Albert confronts and responds to the query on the nature of the soul and if the soul is simple or compound. The answer is that the soul is compound; what does Albert mean with this term? Not that it is composed of matter and form, but simply of two causes, of which one is intellect in itself, and therefore agent intellect, and the other is from that which is intellectual, and therefore the possible intellect. It is proper to intellectual nature to know the separate substances.[46]

The other question that we have formulated receives its answer in Albert's theory on the origin of the soul that, by virtue of his idea that the intellectual cannot be drawn from or generated by matter (as we read in the first quotation), rejects the theory of an agent-intellect that is produced by way of progressive abstractions. His *De anima* rejects this *modus* in many passages, in which there emerges nonetheless the dual nature of the possible intellect qualified to contemplate both separate substances and entities abstracted from matter.[47] Such a theory in Albert approaches the paradigm of human intellectual modelled on that of separate substances or separate intelligences, a mode Albert thinks is possible to the human beings in our mortal life.[48]

Certainly, in the text of the canzone, not only is no clear trace of the language of Albert, but the way in which the dialectic between the two ladies is presented recalls at first the so-called thought of the philosophers, who saw two opposing and irreducible natures in human beings, a thought that actually comes from those thinkers that Albert himself does not accept, as we read in his *De origine et natura animae rationalis*.

Yet memory treated as activity in its own way suggests that an Augustinian-Bonaventurian pre-structure comes to meet a new textuality that leads Dante to write a canzone where multiple relationships take shape and make that pre-structure more important that what has been said. If we see that the treatment of memory in the canzone is irreducible to that of Cavalcanti in "Donna me prega," then the referents are not just in the Pseudo-Dionysius; rather, they are in the encounter with the *De causis* and the importance of the intellectual, which all seem to draw like lines of reflection, and these are what offer Dante the alternative, according to which he can reconsider his real or fictivus event in cognitive terms and in terms of an absolute dialectic with his first friend.

Now, if this is true, then in the canzone takes place the meeting between a causistic, Dionysian, and maybe Albertian universe that is going to be grafted onto a preceding line. In the meeting, the readjustment includes the passage from a memory understood in an Aristotelian sense towards one understood in an Augustinian sense.

The text offers us a cross-section of the two live realities, but the problematic point is the following: Do these two realities enter into relation with one another? And what type of relationship is established? If the life of the soul is transformed (*trasmutata*), it is clear that we are informed of a cognitive relationship, but the subject of the intellectual activity is not the sensitive soul that remains strictly in its dimension of *sentire* (feeling). Yet it seems that we have the trace of a relationship between the sensitive soul and the intellectual soul. It is evident that the intellect is an external being and that it does not come about by way of abstraction from the elements. This thought certainly returns to positions that go back to Averroes, but Albert also follows the commentator where he does not accept the theory of the *eductio* of the intellect from the elements. Albert's point, which in some ways is similar to that of Averroes (*De anima* 3.5; 397, 311–17), is that the vegetative and sensitive souls can be drawn from the elements and from the seed, but the intellectual soul cannot have the same origin – it would be as though to deny the divine and intellectual nature of human beings. This subject seems to be close to what the canzone offers us: intellect penetrates the soul from the exterior, and the theory of *eductio formarum* cannot be applied to human intellect (*De anima*, 1.2.13; 54, 78–81).

However, it has been said that everything in the canzone does not agree with this reconstruction. The first element of discord emerges where the *anima memoriale* is proposed as a thought that is represented as ascending heavenward. With this the *anima memoriale* brings us back to an Augustinian line resumed by Bonaventure where memory and intellection are in relation with each other according to a non-Aristotelian path; by virtue of this, the theory of the intellect as light that comes from the cause of light could also come at first from an Augustinian-Bonaventurian line. The speaking spirit, however, which is the figure of the possible intellect of divine provenance, leads us back in its turn to the theory of the intellect as internal *verbum* which was a Thomistic synthesis of Augustinian content. In other words, what emerges as an interesting aspect is the re-use in an Aristotelian awareness of *substratum* (substrate) already utilized by Dante.

The canzone seems constructed as the result of a suture between an Augustinian and Bonaventurian *stratum* (already characteristic of the Dante of the *Vita nuova*) and an awareness of a new line of thought that he encounters and that offers him a new framework within which fragments of previous thought get stuck and remain. But the sutures in some cases let the stitches show. In any case, in the canzone the traces of a probably Albertian mediation help us and maybe helped its author to link an Augustinian thought with a peripatetic field.[49] It is not to be overlooked, however, how conceiving of this intellect as separate was also in line with a position testified to by "Donna me prega," where the possible intellect was assumed to be separate, whose activity is *consideranza* (contemplation) and therefore contemplation of a separate substance.

Dante's canzone, however, signals different awarenesses with respect to those of Cavalcanti. The essential fact is that the canzone is constructed in opposition to a thought that postulates the identity of human beings in the sensitive soul. The intellectual nature of human beings is the crucial point of attention. The attraction for theories that are borderline heterodox passes through this antecedent, nevertheless we can add that in this text it is not a matter of heterodoxy but rather of syncretism and attraction for contents verifiable in Albert, who assimilates subjects from Arabic peripateticisim, but who rejects the dangerous centre that comes from a thinking that establishes the unicity of human possible intellect.[50] In 1294, then, or thereafter, our analysis signals and confirms the importance that the intellectual nature of human beings assumes. The field in which Dante attempts to enter is not what may be termed Cavalcantian heterodoxy. On the contrary – it seems that the canzone is written to oppose positions like those to which "Donna me prega" testified, or would testify, where love was a metaphor or, better, *denominatio* in order to demonstrate the material nature of human beings dominated by passion and appetites of the sensitive soul. The choice of the intellectual in Dante appears therefore not only in continuity with choices already made at the time of the *Vita nuova*, but it also opposes the territory investigated and circumscribed by Cavalcanti. Already a privileged interlocutor in the *libello*, it opposes the culture that identifies the discourse on human beings with the world of physics and biology. Dante's *contra medicos* becomes an interlinearity to be recognized – it is not assigned to a specific text, but the canzoni seem to delimit a portion of its territory.

In any case, we pass now to the commentary in order to consider our interpretation in the light of the prose text, and yet considering that the latter, written, as noted, many years later, could introduce different meanings. Whether "Donna me prega" was already written or not, the canzone signals the taking shape of a problematic that does not seem unaware of the debate in which Cavalcanti was a subtle actor and also a critic. What emerges is the realization of an opposing way of representing human beings and, in this, the recourse to other *auctoritates* where the syncretism that is active is responsible for the reader's out-of-place feeling.

2. The Invention of the *donna* as *gentile*

One aspect that has been discussed is that the canzone, through a *sermocinatio* – that is, the introduction of multiple direct discourses uttered by different beings – put into focus the crisis of a love identified in the *anima memoriale* and tied to subjective experiences, against which there emerged a new female identity that opened up to the discourse of intellection. The canzone in our reading proves itself to be doctrinal and its focus is the theory of human knowledge. On these premises the commentary still develops a doctrinal discourse of extraordinary novelty not only because it is laid out in vulgar forms but, and above all, for the way in which Dante, resuming one of the crucial points of the discourse of his time, developed it in prose in personal ways and synthesis. It is indeed in the prose that the invention of the *donna gentile* (i.e., the utilization of the adjective "gentile") takes shape.

The invention of the *donna* as *gentile* in the *Convivio* (in the *denominatio* that characterizes her here) takes shape in the commentary on the first canzone and therefore in the second book of the work. But that invention passes through a precise inflection that witnesses the definition of two levels of comprehension of the text itself, which is one canzone: the literal one and the allegorical one. It is to be considered that it is the commentary above all that brings us towards dimensions that were up until that moment unthinkable. The *Convivio*, its prose, determines a role for poetry that the poetic texts that the *Convivio* recalls do not reveal. Dante's method that is sanctioned in the *De vulgari eloquentia*, and of which the *Convivio* is evidence, while it makes the *modus poeticus* the highest language and the one on which prose is to be modelled, establishes at the same time his own poetic mode. That mode chooses the tropic and difficult, but referential (i.e., that which is possible to explain in prose), as established in chapter 25 of the *Vita nuova*. If the prose model is the poetic, and the poetic is *fictivus*, *fictio* as fabula and figure together, it will be up to the prose to elucidate the levels of meaning of the *fictivus*, and that elucidation occurs recalling authors, creating contexts, and inserting pre-selected passages within a referential line qualified to open them up. The outcome aspires to bind together intelligence and knowledge, promoting a chain of associations that the mind of the reader must be capable of grasping. Behind this, there is an entire antique and medieval tradition that associates knowing and *exercitium*, the difficult and the intellectual, the spiritual as *exercitium*, that Dante connects with both new and old outcomes of the rhetorical-poetical tradition (see Hadot 2005; Emery 2007).

We must reflect, then, that in beginning the commentary, about ten years after the writing of the poetic texts, Dante is concerned with establishing the statute of those texts as allegorical already in the first chapter where we find the possibility of laying the commentary out according to the four senses: the literal or *fictivus*, the allegorical another, and then the moral and the anagogical. Rivers of ink have been poured out on that point, but what interests us is the taking shape in that passage of a relationship between the fictitious, what is tied to the narrative fabula, and the trope-figures. The invention of the *donna gentile* is fabula and trope at the same time. I mean to say not only that the figurative speech is the stemma of the poetic text but also that what Dante indicates as literal commentary actually builds itself on the *fictivus* and includes *narratio* and figurae. Among the figurae is *transumptio* (mother of all the ornaments according to Boncompagno da Signa), within which texts like Boncompagno's *Rhetorica novissima* and the *Poetriae* include various tropes, *pronominatio* among them.[51] The *donna gentile* is a *pronominatio* if we consider what already emerges from the poetic text. In this text, in fact, the problematic discourse on human knowledge is transferred onto her. Human knowledge, its power and limit, are pronounced as love for the gentle lady. Such love introduces the theme of the goal of the individual and his search for happiness in time and space.

To notice in this the structural importance of the *fictivus* means to connect the commentary and the poetry to the awareness of the nature of poetic language, intellectual since it is figurative, and of which the story itself, or fabula, is a projection. The definition of the *stil novo* that Dante will formulate is not extraneous to the meanings that are put into focus here.

The discourse on the tropes as a language of intellection that runs throughout ancient culture is transmitted to the Middle Ages by Augustine in particular. His theoretical discourse on the use of the tropes as it takes shape in his *De trinitate* (book 15, 9–11) and *De doctrina christiana* is to be considered fundamental for that line of thought that considers the tropes as difficult and intellectual language and, in their difficultness, sweet.[52] To also be considered is how and to what extent the *Poetriae* connected the discourse on tropes to *intelligere* (Faral 1962) as an appropriate mode for the intellectual discourse because it is based on the function of understanding through the intellect. Dante finds a language in which the rhetorical-poetical figure presides over both what he calls the literal sense and what he calls the allegorical sense, and from this use the anagogical sense follows, as does that which is indicated as moral.[53] What the *De vulgari eloquentia* will theorize about poetry as a model for prose is actually here in the *Convivio* taking parallel shape. In the literal and the *fictivus*, we should consider, therefore, the *integumentum* and how this is articulated in tropes. The written prose, which recognizes the primacy of poetry and which uses a language of tropes, joins both that part of the commentary that is indicated as literal and the allegorical. The *Convivio* constructs the difficult as intellectual and the intellectual as beautiful, and intellectual beauty is anagogical in and of itself. Augustine had written a fundamental theoretical page where, commenting on Paolo di Tarso, he had associated tropes and speculation. It was Augustine again who introduced the beautiful as intellectual and the difficult as an exercise and ladder to the divine (Ardizzone 2011, chaps. 1 and 2).

The coincidence between the mode of tropes and the discourse that the *donna gentile* introduces in the prose text relies on what the *Poetriae*, that is, the poetics of the thirteenth century, called *ornatus difficilis* and that the *Convivio* appears to use as *sermo* consistent with the content that is proposing. The beauty of the difficult and, accordingly, the *ornatus difficilis*, is actually part of both the poetic text and the prose text. The construction of an illustrious prose – in accordance with what the *De vulgari eloquentia* theorizes for poetry – is what the *Convivio* realizes as *sermo* consistent with its own content.

Let us briefly return to *Voi che 'ntendendo il terzo ciel movete*. We have seen that in the second stanza of the canzone, the sweetness of the speech of the internal thought that followed Beatrice in heaven was put to flight by a new spirit, which forces the speaker to look at a new lady and to look at the eyes of this lady; as we subsequently learn, in the eyes of this lady there is a new type of love that kills the *anima memoriale*. Dante offers us a few words that, in context, act as signals of a meaning that goes beyond the words themselves. When he says that seeing "la salute" (salvation; 24) is possible when one looks at the lady's eyes we are facing a discourse of speculation where the eyes are mirrors: "faccia che li occhi d'esta donna miri" (let him gaze into the eyes of this lady; 25). "Miri" (gaze into) does not just mean to "look at," but to see that the looking at each other between these eyes involves the reflective mirror qualities of the eye. It also means an activity of mirroring or reflecting, of looking and admiring. It is evident that the new love, though brought by the spirit and indicated as "colui che le mie pari ancide" (the one who kills all such as me; 37), is located in the eyes of the new lady that act as mirrors. According to a widely circulating theory, the nature of the mirror is that of showing an image; an eye that looks at another eye sees itself in a mirror and it is a reciprocal seeing – whoever looks at is looked at by the looked herself. Such seeing actually unveils a form of speculation (Rachel is a figure of this in *Purgatorio*), and in linking itself to the discourse on love, the field of speculation operates a transfusion where it faces a physical-biological line that it opposes.[54] But in order to understand what Dante was putting into action at the time of writing the poetic text, and what he then resumes in the years in which he writes up the commentary (that is, more or less ten years later), we must reread the commentary and precisely that section where, after having reintroduced the *donna gentile* of the *Vita nuova* who appeared to his eyes and who, we are told, took over some place in his mind, it is explained to us that two opposing thoughts were battling within the first-person narrator. One thought was that nourished by the new image, and the other was that one tied to Beatrice. What interests us in particular, however, is that fragment in which it is explained to us that the *donna gentile* (her thought in the mind of the speaker) was nourished by his sight, which is in front of him, and Beatrice, who is behind him, in memory therefore, according to a theory on the internal senses that offers us the first key to reading this passage.[55] Dante's readers have no doubts about the fact that Beatrice and the *donna gentile* are two different ladies. Criticism has not called the two different identities into question and it cannot be said that this is an error of perspective. Dante wanted to present us with the struggle between two different loves that he hypostatized in the two women. It is nonetheless unavoidable that the prose text reveals something that in the poetic text was absent or much more concealed.

The prose text confirms that the two ladies – Beatrice and she who is called *donna gentile* – are ways through which Dante problematizes the human nature identity. The struggle between the two kinds of love that the second treatise proposes nevertheless opens up to the reader the possibility of seeing the suggested relationship per opposition between the two figures, as a relationship that confirms an issue related to human knowledge, and this is understandable to whoever possesses some rudiments of the medieval theory of knowledge. The new lady and her vision, and her eyes that look at his eyes, are certainly the signs of it – they would seem to act as referents for this meaning. In this case, the vision of the *donna gentile* would be *pronominatio* for the vision of an intellectual form that the mind contemplates. This is suggested because, by virtue of celestial influence and therefore of an intellectual agent, this vision is activated; the phantasm placed in memory represents instead the highest part of the sensitive soul. Such a reading is confirmed in the commentary. In this case, the *donna gentile* would be the name that is attributed to the new being that the mind is able to contemplate as a result of an event caused by the heavens.

Yet everything does not converge in this reconstruction, and the tortured text of these prose passages seems to be an example of the torment in the thought and pen of Dante himself that passes into his transcribers.

3. Reading Samples

I begin by citing the part of the literal commentary that is useful for getting closer to a different and more complex meaning. In particular, I am going to isolate three fragments: the first fragment is found at II.2.1, the second at II.7.1, and the third at II.8.1. Probably also the digression on the immortality of the soul that is debated, beginning with II.8.7, can be used to understand what we are dealing with here. I will cite, then, the text of the *Convivio* as set by Ageno (1995), pointing out where useful the version used by Vasoli (1988) and the possible variations between the two. I will also keep in mind the more recent edition of Giorgio Inglese (2004) that at times goes back to the critical edition of the *Convivio* accomplished by Simonelli (1966). I begin, then, citing the following paragraph:

> Cominciando adunque, dico che la stella di Venere due fiate rivolta era in quello suo cerchio che la fa parere serotina e matutina, secondo diversi tempi, appresso lo trapassamento di quella Beatrice beata che vive in cielo con li angeli e in terra con la mia anima, quando quella gentile donna, cui feci menzione ne la fine de la Vita Nuova, parve primamente, accompagnata d'Amore, a li occhi miei e prese luogo alcuno ne la mia mente. E sì come è ragionato per me ne lo allegato libello, più da sua gentilezza che da mia elezione venne ch'io ad essere suo consentisse; ché passionata di tanta misericordia si dimostrava sopra la mia vedovata vita, che li spiriti de li occhi miei a lei si fero massimamente amici. E così fatto, dentro [me] lei poi fero tale, che lo mio beneplacito fu contento a disposarsi a quella imagine.

> I may begin, then, by saying that after the passing away of the blessed Beatrice, who lives in heaven with the angels and on earth with my soul, the star of Venus has completed two revolutions in that circle of hers which brings her into view in the evening or in the morning, according to the time of year, when that noble lady of whom I made mention at the end of *The New Life* first appeared before my eyes accompanied by Love, and made a certain place for herself in my mind. As I recount in that little book, it came about, rather as a result of her nobility than of my choice, that I consented to be hers, for she showed herself to be moved by such deep compassion for my widowed life that the spirits of my eyes made themselves her friends above all else. Having become so, they then formed such an impression of her within me that my will was drawn to find its happiness in putting itself at the disposal of that image. (II.2.1–2)

The subject of this passage is known; what is of interest to me is underscoring the beings involved and the chronology. Two years after the death of Beatrice, Dante writes, a noble lady appears who comes to occupy a place in his "mente" (mind). While Beatrice lives in heaven with the angels and on earth with his soul, the new lady is called noble and occupies a place in his mind. The adjective *gentile* (noble) that he here takes up again from the *Vita nuova* is in any case to be compared with a probable new awareness which emerges from the canzone where that occurrence comes to be indirectly put in relation to the entrance of a spirit-being that, it is said, was an intellectual being.

What is narrated takes up again, as noted, the encounter with the *donna gentile* of the *Vita nuova* and tells us that, more by her nobility than by his choice, the spirits of his eyes became her friends above all else, and his will was happy to put itself at the disposal of that image. Dante then affirms that love, in order to grow and become perfect, needs time and nourishment from thoughts, especially if, as in this case, there are contrasting thoughts, so that in order that the new love were perfect it was necessary to set up a conflict between the thought that nourished it and the opposite one, which kept the citadel of his mind for the glorious Beatrice. Here is the passage:

> Ma però che non subitamente nasce amore e fassi grande e viene perfetto, ma vuole tempo alcuno e nutrimento di pensieri, massimamente là dove sono pensieri contrari che lo 'mpediscano, convenne, prima che questo nuovo amore fosse perfetto, molta battaglia intra lo pensiero del suo nutrimento e quello che li era contraro, lo quel per quella gloriosa

> Beatrice tenea ancora la rocca de la mia mente. Però che l'uno era soccorso de la parte [de la vista] dinanzi continuamente, e l'altro de la parte de la memoria di dietro.

> However, it is not in an instant that love is born and grows and reaches perfection: it requires a certain passage of time, and nourishment from thoughts, especially where contrary thoughts hinder its progress. So before this new love could become perfect, a great struggle had to take place between the thought that nourished it and the thought that opposed it, that is, the thought that still held the citadel of my mind on behalf of the glorious Beatrice. Since one drew help continually from what lay before, that is, from sight of that lady, while the other drew its help from what lay behind, that is, from my memory. (II.2.3)[56]

What takes place is therefore explained as a battle between two contrasting thoughts, one of which drew help from sight (and therefore from the eyes of the first person that looked at the eyes of the lady) that is continually in front – "dinanzi" (what lay before) – and the other of which drew help from memory – from behind. What is of interest to me to underscore is that the struggle is presented as put into action through sight, but it is a mental sight from which the nourishment came to the (new) thought, while memory is here indicated as "rocca de la mente" (citadel of the mind). Let us continue:

> E lo soccorso dinanzi ciascuno ie crescea, che far non potea l'altro, [te] men[d]o quello, che impediva in alcuno modo, a dare indietro, il volto; per che a me parve sì mirabile, e anche duro a sofferire, che io nol potei sostenere.

> And since the help drawn from what lay before grew with each passing day, something made it impossible for the other by the new thought, which completely prevented any backward look – all this seemed so astonishing to me, and such a painful experience, that I was unable to endure it. (II.2.4)

Here, a variation is to be pointed out as given in the text of Inglese: instead of "[te]men[d]o," it reads "coment[e]."[57] Beyond these corrupt passages, however, we are nonetheless able to construct a sense that variations do not alter much.

The mental vision essentially hinders and generates the difficulty in turning his face back, which means, in context, that looking back, in its primary meaning, means to return to the past. Feeling this situation to be hard and almost like an exclamation and almost excusing himself – "de la varietade, ne la quale parea me avere manco di fortezza" (the change newly occurring within me, which seemed to imply a want of strength on my part; II.2.5) – he turns his voice "in quella parte onde procedeva la vittoria del nuovo pensiero, ch'era virtuosissimo sì come vertù celestiale; e cominciai a dire: *Voi che 'ntendendo il terzo ciel movete*" (to the quarter whence flowed the victory of the new thought, which had all the strength of a power drawn from the heavens. I began with the words: *You who move the third heaven by understanding*; II.2.6).

An aspect to underscore is that Beatrice is indicated as occupying the "citadel of the mind." This phrase, "rocca de la mente," would seem to translate "apex mentis," but in any case a thought related to memory is represented here and therefore memory would appear as the highest of the internal senses according to an Aristotelian knowledge, while the *donna gentile*, meanwhile, is proposed as a "pensiero" (thought) of a different type whose image his "beneplacito," that is, his free will, "fu contento a disposarsi" (was drawn to find its happiness in putting itself at the disposal of that image; II.2.2). However, because this text comments on a canzone that tells us that the new love is the fruit of the intelligences' influence, the intellectual series becomes enriched by a new element since the angelic intelligences influence the intellectual part of human beings. Indeed, in the above-cited fragment we read that the "nuovo pensiero" (new thought) "era virtuosissimo sì come vertù celestiale" (had all the strength of a power drawn from the heavens). This thought is therefore not only influenced by the intelligences, but in the commentary we are told that its power is similar to that of the intelligences. We have, in other words, on the one hand, the affirmation of human intellectual power as mediated by celestial influence, but, on the other, it is said that it is similar to the intellectual power of the intelligences and the intelligences understand the divine through the intellect (*intelligono*) because they see the separate forms or substances and therefore the ideas-forms. The meaning of the word "vertù," pointed out here for its ambiguity that places it between valor and *vis* (power), tells us that in human beings there exists a power that is similar to celestial power, and celestial power brings us back to the intellectual power that presides over the movement of the heavens. That power in the angel-intelligences, as we noted above, is composed of a contemplating and a moving, where the moving is the effect of the contemplating. The background that feeds this passage, that reaffirms and enlarges content already introduced in the poetic text, is to be understood because it seems to bring us back to a line of thought that saw in the operationality of the intelligences a model of human intellectual operation. The *De causis* that characterizes the power that the intelligences derive from God as *virtus* is part of a thought that Dante probably wants to activate. Celestial influence therefore becomes part of that intellectual paradigm that Dante is introducing, but the influence is also mediation and the resemblance between the new thought and the celestial power suggests that the first-person speaker shares that form of contemplation which is characteristic of angel-intelligences, who see or contemplate separate forms in the divine mind. In note 29, I have cited Aquinas's commentary on proposition 3 of the *De causis*, where, on the one hand, the theory of the angelic vision of separate substances is explained, and on the other, it is said that souls, through angelic mediation, become participants in the illumination coming from God. What is actually suggested here, however, is that the new thought is a form of contemplation similar to the power of heavenly beings and, for that reason, a power of contemplating a separate substance. On this basis, and as confirmation of what is already written in the canzone, the commentary explains that the old thought coinciding with the memory of Beatrice is associated with the *anima memoriale*, which in the field of aristotelianism we know is the apex of the sensitive soul – Dante defines it as the "rocca de la mente," which recalls Cavalcanti's "cassar de la mente" in his first sonnet to Dante as we read it in the *Vita nova* (sonnet 37). The new thought is instead part of an intellectual reality. They are two entities that the text tells us are in battle and the battle exists because both place themselves in relation to the same individual. In other words, they are two functions and two powers that relate to him, but one, the one related to memory, is clearly an activity proper to the sensitive soul, while the second comes from the mediation of separate beings. In the same way, the new lady is a being that the individual looks at, but she is an intellectual vision, while Beatrice is situated inside his memory. In II.6.7 (171), it is again clarified that the spirit is nothing but a thought, a "frequente pensiero" (recurring thought), and that what takes place is the struggle between two thoughts. Dante distinguishes between the new thought, whose aim is "commendare e abbellire" (to commend … and show how attractive she [the new lady] is; II.6.7), while the other thought pertains to the soul, "non è altro che un altro pensiero, accompagnato di consentimento, che, repugnando a questo, commenda e abbellisce la memoria di quella gloriosa Beatrice" ([which] here refers specifically to another thought coupled with consent which, in opposition to the first thought, commends the memory of that glorious lady Beatrice and shows how attractive she is; II.6.7–8). It is clear that we are again in the field of praise bestowed upon two beings proposed as different – *commendare* (to praise) and *lodare* (to commend) – of which Dante calls one thought "anima" (soul), which depends upon memory, and the other "spirito" (spirit), which comes here from the heaven.

He further introduces an important distinction in defining the intellectual field: "Dico anche che questo spirito viene per li raggi de la stella" (I also say that this spirit is due to the rays of the star; II.6.9). Since, as we read, "li raggi di ciascuno cielo sono la via per la quale discende la loro vertude in queste cose di qua giù" (the rays from all of the heavens are the means whereby the power of the heavens flows down into things here on earth; II.6.9), and since the rays are no other than light that comes from the cause of light through the air until it reaches the illuminated thing – light being only in the star, and the rest of heaven being diaphanous, that is, transparent – it comes from this that "questo spirito, cioè questo pensiero" (this spirit [that is, this thought]; II.6.9) only comes from the star, from its rays, and not from the entire heaven. What is meant here is that the pre-eminence in the heavens' influence is assigned and prizes the intellectual way, the rays being light that comes from the cause itself of light, God being represented as light and the absolute intellectual being.

Rather than the pre-eminence of a physical influence, what is underscored is the intellectual nature of celestial influence; in fact, Dante adds that, by virtue of the nobility of its movers (i.e., the movers of the star), the star itself has a lot of influence on human souls and on other things (according to Litt [1963], this is Aquinas's typical position). However, the theory on the angel-intelligences, mediators of divine light, leads us back to the theory of divine illumination in human beings that is called agent-intellect in the Aristotelian century, and that Bonaventure, for example, following the Augustinian path, thinks of as illumination. It is thought of in the same way by Albert and Aquinas. If we consider this context, however, then what is proposed is to be reconsidered.

It is true that the novelty of the discourse is in the tension towards the overcoming of the affective-sensitive sphere. Memory and regret – consent to memory and the regret of a human being – are placed as an opposition of what is announced as a thought coming from the star that seems to be put forth as *consideranza* (contemplation). Since the star is Venus, not only is the intellectual nature of this love introduced, but love goes on to reveal something about the nature of the being who loves.

A difficult meaning is also to be grasped on that operational level that the text proposes both when Dante writes that "vostra" (your; of you who move the third heaven) operation – that is "vostra" revolution – is what drew him into his current condition, and when the text puts forth an identity between *intelligere* and "muovere" – that is, producing a movement, in a passage in which the verb *intendere* (to understand) implies intellection and sublime appetition. This identity is then reiterated in chapter 6, where *intendere* means "to move with the intellect alone," as said above, and the verb "intendendo" (understanding; 54) is reaffirmed in a context of not clear meaning when he writes "'ntendendo li loro effetti ne la loro operazione" ([those who] understand the effects they cause through [their own operation]; II.6.3) and, therefore that "la novitade" (novelty) of his condition would not be understood by other human beings since they have not experienced it but by "coloro che 'ntendono li loro effetti ne la loro operazione" (by those who understand their own effects in virtue of their operation; II.6.3).

This is an obscure passage, certainly, but the first level of meaning that comes from it is that these intelligences have intellection and move (*intendono*) and they therefore act because they understand through the intellect. However, it also comes that their activity is composed both of intellection and by the movement that derives from it. In other words, the movement of the heavens is an operation performed by intellectual beings who, in virtue of an intellectual activity, make it. This introduces an intellectual level that is operational and produces another operation, in a synchronous way, but in which the relationship between the intellectual and the operational or active, or between intellection and operation or activity, is to be noted because it is here, in the mediation of the *De causis*, that a resemblance between the understanding of the intelligences and that of humans is suggested.

Transferred onto human beings, however, as it seems to be, this implies that intellection occurs through the vision of an external being or separate substance – that intellectual vision occurs by virtue of a contemplative operation, and that this operation is able to cause another operational activity, although its nature is not given. Let us go on to consider the meaning of this assertion that not only is the human soul a compound (this we had already identified as a possible meaning), but that its intellectual operation occurs by virtue of contemplation of an external being. The separate nature of the intellectual seems to be suggested, as does, therefore, the being and essence of the *donna gentile*, whom the first-person speaker looks at with the eyes of the mind. This kind of meaning, put in relation to the *intelligere* of the angel-intelligences, is what we are asked to understand.

The other fragment useful for what we are pointing out is the passage that we find at II.8. Dante announces in the literal commentary, in chapter 7, that he is moving on to deal with the second part of the canzone; he returns to the battle he is experiencing and he again confronts the "diversitadi" (differences) that are combating in him. He further puts forth an interesting distinction where he first clarifies that things have to be called (*denominatio*) by the ultimate nobility of their form – that is, by what in them is most noble – and that therefore when it is affirmed that human beings live, what is meant is their most noble activity, and that is the use of reason, "che è sua speziale vita e atto de la sua più nobile parte" (which is the life specific to him and the activity of his most noble part; II.7.3).

On this basis, Dante explains the meaning of the first verses of the second stanza of the canzone. He indicates that the thought of Beatrice was a contemplative thought – that is to say that in thinking, the I "contemplava lo regno de' beati" (contemplate[d] the kingdom of the blessed; II.7.5). He adds, "Ed è da sapere, che qui si dice 'pensiero' e non 'anima', di quello che salia a vedere quella beata, perché era spezial pensiero a quello atto" (I should explain that I use the word "thought" here, and not "soul," of what ascended to see that blessed one, because this was a specific thought consisting of that particular act; II.7.8). As clarification and distinction, he further declares, "L'anima s'intende, come detto è nel precedente capitolo, per lo generale pensiero, col consentimento" (As I explained in the preceding chapter, "soul" refers to the generic thought coupled with consent; II.7.8). This point that Dante underscores and that pushed the soul to leave is indicated as the root of a difference, a difference that would seem to be between a sweetness of thought that brought him to desire to reach Beatrice, and a new one that now appears and makes it flee; Dante introduces a new thought that puts the other one to flight, and this thought is powerful in taking it over and in winning over the entire soul. The power of this new thought inspires him to look at the eyes of this lady (II.7). These are the premises that induce the reader to find a series of associations where the level of the soul appears transcended towards a thought that is given as the overcoming of oneself: soul, memory, contemplating thought, and a new one that makes the previous flee since it is more virtuous, where virtue implies a more powerful intellectual value – "E dico 'fuggire', per mostrare quello essere contrario, ché naturalmente l'uno contrario fugge l'altro, e quello che fugge mostra per difetto di vertù di fuggire" (I use the word "flee" to indicate that the old thought is contrary to the new, for one contrary naturally flees the other, and the one which flees shows that it does so through a lack of strength; II.7.9).

The section that follows (II.8.1–2) announces the desire to open judgment on that part in which different thoughts contend in him. Dante asserts the appropriateness of saying last that which the sayer chiefly aims at, and thus he will speak before of the soul (first it is worth telling on behalf of the soul, that is, on behalf of the old thought, and then of the other), which means that the new thought is that at which the sayer chiefly aims. Since he holds to reasoning more of "quello che l'opera di costoro a cu'io parlo fa, che quello che essa disfà, ragionevole fu prima dire e ragionare la condizione de la parte che si corrompea, e poi quella de l'altra che si generava" (what the activity of those whom I address brings into existence than what it brings to an end, the reasonable thing to do was first to recount and discuss the condition of what was being terminated, and thereafter that of what was being generated; II.8.3), what follows is the discourse that I quote and that he himself expresses as doubt:

> Con ciò sia cosa che amore sia effetto di queste intelligenze, a cu' io parlo, e quello di prima fosse amore così come questo di poi, perché la loro vertù corrompe l'uno e l'altro genera? con ciò sia cosa che innanzi dovrebbe quello salvare, per la ragione che ciascuna cagione amo lo suo effetto e, amando quello, salva quell'altro.
>
> If love is indeed the effect brought about by these Intelligences whom I address, and the former effect was love no less than the latter, why does their power terminate the one and generate the other? It should rather preserve the former for every cause loves the effect it produces, and while loving that effect preserves any other which it has already produced. (II.8.4)

The answer that Dante provides is the following: "lo effetto di costoro è amore" (the effect brought about by those beings is certainly love; II.8.5). This effect cannot be conserved, however, except in those "subietti che sono sottoposti a la loro circulazione, esso [amore] transmutano di quella parte che è fuori di loro podestade in quella che v'è dentro, cioè de l'anima partita d'esta vita in quella ch'è in essa" (subjects as lie within their revolution, they transfer love from what lies outside their power to what lies within it, that is, from the soul that has departed from this life to one living in this life; II.8.5). Essentially, changing the love object is motivated here as the result of Beatrice's death because the angel-intelligences have powers over what is subject to their revolution – that is, subject to the heavens moved by them. It is a complex and even cryptic passage. The first obscure point is signalled where it is asserted that the intelligences cause love but they cannot save it, except in those subjects who are subjected to their revolution. This is a passage that is unravelled, underscoring that the theory of generation and corruption is not expounded here, but the power that the intelligences have over human souls is suggested. This is a crucial point, also because a language is used that brings us back to an Aristotelian theory of generation and corruption (which implies the heavens' influence), but in order to dispel the theory.

Dante formulated a similar and at the same time different discourse in a letter to Cino da Pistoia, datable between 1305 and 1306, that is in reference to a sonnet also addressed to Cino. The letter is quoted in my note as it is in Epistle III, and to be pointed out initially is the basic consideration that what is characteristic of the laws of physics (i.e., generation and corruption), appears used here in this passage of the *Convivio*, at least at the terminological level, in reference to the intelligences and the heavens. The reader nonetheless knows that the physical world is the world of necessity and the world of the intelligences and intellectual reality are not subject to it. That which is caused by the intelligences cannot be subordinated to any form of necessity. So this discourse appears as a concealed speaking, a kind of sophism where one part is true and another is false, and whose aim is to inspire knowledge. It would also be one of those subtle speeches that Alain de Lille discusses and that Augustine had already considered in his *De doctrina cristiana*.[58]

Indeed, what Dante writes here has been generally accepted or, better, it did not induce suspicion in his readers. His discourse would seem to be a faultless one, but actually this is not so. It is evident that he wants to compare two types of love; if they are both love, why does the new love corrupt the previous one? Since they (intelligences) cause love, they should then, because they love the second love, save the first one. The concealed speaking seems to want to inspire us to set a distinction between the first and the second love, a distinction that Dante himself suggests when he distinguishes between the old thought of Beatrice and the new thought. But the answer introduces further obscurity even if it is apparently put forth as clarifying. Dante asserts, in fact, that this doubt can be easily answered: it is true that the effect of these intelligences is love, but they cannot save it except in those beings who are subjected to their revolution. Therefore they change (transmute), transform, and carry out a shift from the part that is outside of their power to the part that falls under their power. The shift is from the love for a soul that is no longer in this life to the soul that is in life. Here, the obscurity means at the same time that that love that is located in memory, dictated by the sensitive soul, does not fall under the angelic power that presides over the intellectual. If this is true, what is meant to be suggested is that intellectual heavenly influence acts on a living mind, so if the thought of Beatrice represents the sensitive soul, one meaning that can be deduced from this is that the intelligences act on human intellect and therefore the love for the new lady is nothing other than a way to introduce the intellect as something that is given only to human beings and because they are living.[59]

In the traditional discourse on the heavens' influences, it is clear instead that the heavens act on physics. Therefore, a meaning to grasp here is in the pre-eminence of intellectual action as introduced beginning with the poetic text. The other resolute point is to understand that both Beatrice and the new lady are, we remember, names or *pronominatio* for the sensitive and intellectual activity of human beings, and the action of the intelligences finds expression in the new love, and therefore on the first-person narrator. It does not make sense, then, that Beatrice, since dead, would not be subject to the intelligences and she is therefore substituted by the living *donna gentile*. What is meant here is simple and at the same time complex: a love nourished by these intelligences can no longer be located in the *anima memoriale*, but so that the intellectual activity occurs, a new level of human beings, that is, their intellectual function, must come into play. But what are we talking about? If Beatrice is the name for the activity of memory, and therefore for the sensitive soul, and the *donna gentile* is represented as what allows speculation, it is clear that to say that the intelligences cannot act on what is dead means that the intelligences cannot exercise their action on the sensitive soul, because Beatrice was located in the activity of memory. In the metonymic and transposing game, then, the *donna gentile* represents an intellectual being shown in a difference, here unresolvable, with the sensitive soul. Not only this, but there is also the implicit criticism of that cognitive path that holds that human beings are subject to the heavens' influence – a stigmatized discourse in Dante's age, but in medical science and natural philosophy this is a fundamental subject, linked to that of astral influence as it is testified to by the poetry of Cavalcanti.

What is necessary, we read, is precisely the *transmutatio* – the same that nature performs when it transmutes into a new human *form* its preservation from father to son, since it cannot perpetually preserve its effect in the father (II.8). He adds, "Dico 'effetto', in quanto *l'anima col corpo, congiunti,* sono effetto di quella; ché [l'anima poi che] è partita, perpetualmente dura in natura più che umana" (I use the term "effect" to indicate that *the soul and the body joined together* are the effect caused by human nature, for when the soul leaves the body it lives on forever in a nature higher than human; II.8.6, emphasis added). The question to be asked is how the word "natura" (nature) is being used here. To be noted here is the verbal form "congiunti" (together, joined) that generates *suspicio* both for the context within which the discourse is articulated and for the cultural time in which it is placed. The *coniunctio* indeed implied that the intellectual soul was not an act or form of the body, but united them through an accidental *coniunctio,* and by virtue of the abstraction of phantasms. It involved the *genus* difference between sensitive and intellectual considered a separate being. Essentially, here the intelligences or separate substances seem to be introduced in order to demarcate the separateness between the sensitive and intellectual.

The *donna gentile* represents the vision of a separate being. The text is lightly corrupted here and there, and for that reason we cannot be certain of the exact way in which Dante develops the reasoning. The fact that it is maintained that the intelligences act only on what is living – and this creates the necessity of substituting Beatrice, dead by now, with a new being that is that of the *donna gentile* – seems dictated by an intention that appears clear only to those who are equipped with doctrine. Indeed, Dante seems to fail here what he proposed where he addressed an audience of non-specialists. Here, he is speaking in a concealed way and, above all, he creates one of those logical mechanisms that allow only those who are knowing to discover the meaning of what it says. Let us see, then: it is true that the intelligences influence the sublunar world, but in the context in question they act on the mind of the first-person narrator and not on the object of that love. In fact, Dante already wrote that this love proceeds as the effect of the intelligences as secondary and mediating causes of the divine according to subjects that he takes up from the *De causis* as mediated by its commentators and not.

If we look at the specific context, we notice that in giving this answer or explanation, the text changes the terms of the discourse of influence; his discourse is not aimed at the relationship between the heavens and generation and corruption, but at how the influence is attested to as an intellectual influence. In fact, it is on him, on his intellectual soul, that the intelligences, as mediating beings, act, but in the transposed discourse the problem becomes this: the intelligences cannot activate such acts on the sensitive soul, and thus on the related memory.[60]

This section of chapter 8, then, deliberately introduces a faulty argument, or paralogism, or better, it introduces a proposition whose value as truth is uncertain according to those sophismatic practices characteristic of Dante's age that give proof here of his penchant for the logical modes, many examples of which we will find in the fourth treatise of the *Convivio* and in the *Monarchia*.[61] At this point, the references to relate are two. One is the absence of a relationship between memory and the new vision of the subject's eyes that could suggest speculation as being the result of the abstraction of the form kept in memory. Here, the abstractive process is the fulcrum of meaning that the text allows us to verify as absent, according to a theory of knowledge that is Aristotelian in origin, in which knowledge occurs through the abstraction of the phantasm and of which there is no trace here. This authorizes seeing in the *donna gentile* the being that allows an intellection or, better, to take up an expression used in the canzone, "ché quella bella donna, che tu senti, / ha *transmutata* in tanto la tua vita" (for that beautiful lady whose power you feel has so deeply *transmuted* your life; 43–4) – a *transmutatio* from a love tied to the sensitive soul to one for a separate substance. To this is related the activity of naming that makes it exist; to give names in Boethius's *Isagoge* (*PL*, 64) means to name things unnamed until that moment. We know also that the *nominatio* was part of the *transumptio* both in the *Poetriae* and in the texts of the *modernorum* logicians. Dante's method is that of contaminating the rhetorical field and the logical one. The first initial aspect is to reconsider the resuming of the event of the *donna gentile* of the *Vita nuova*, and that continuity that was so sought-after at the level of plot, or of narrated events, has instead to be considered as the evolution of lines of thought. Actually, such resumption has the function here of creating that *integumentum* or mythopoetic fiction that actually allows the author to introduce into the language of love a being surely belonging to the intellectual field, and this brings in the problematic relation between the *anima memoriale* and the act of intellection.[62] The point for Dante, already aware of the

Aristotelian discourse on the soul, is to suggest the shift from the sensitive soul and its apex located in memory to an intellectual knowledge of which the *donna gentile* is the figure. That, however, did not develop in the canzone as the result of a process of abstraction, just as it did not develop through abstraction in the prose that we have commented on. We will see, however, that the meaning of *donna gentile* develops in becoming, is inclusive, and goes beyond this connotation. It seems that in the commentary, Dante also inserts certain passages of difficult meaning on purpose so that the reader is pushed to look for the true sense of the discourse that the *fictivus* proposes and of which the *donna gentile* appears, on her level, to be a figure and guarantee. If the literal sense is to be understood, it actually develops from a meaning that emerges from a small series of transpositions that the allegorical then reproposes in another form. Already, from the literal commentary, from an enigmatic and trope-based discourse we can arrive at a philosophical meaning. Essentially, in what Dante calls "literal commentary," the meaning is to be sought operating precisely on two planes and following them simultaneously where one thing is said and another meant. That complexity will escape those who do not know to go beyond the literal sense, as will the sources that Dante goes back to. The reader has to proceed with the awareness that literal interpretation is the foundation for the reading. From it we derive the crucial meanings, and what is indicated as allegorical sense builds itself upon these meanings.

Returning to what seemed to be a suggested interpretation that involved and required abstraction and that would have meant the mode through which human beings arrive at intellection, which was dealt with in the first pages of this section, it is to be considered that the meaning in that case would be that the *donna gentile* was nothing other than an intellectual way of knowing Beatrice. The new love would have been like a speaking of the overcoming of that which pertains to the sensitive soul and a speculative act. Was the *donna gentile* already from that point tied to, or suggested as being in relation to, the possible intellect? Does Dante talk about the new love in order to give a new meaning to the old one? In what, then, does the new consist? Rereading the text, we notice that it was actually precisely against this interpretation that the fragments we have cited are structured. Further on Dante uses physical forms to talk about an order that is not physical. The terminology of generation and corruption, for example, is properly used; this terminology in fact refers to the Aristotelian work *De generatione et corruptione*. There is, in fact, no doubt that this work is part of Aristotelian physics – physics operated by the heavens – but here in the discourse that we have followed until now, the privileged centre is on intellectual beings. But we know also that the angels intelligences influence the world of physics. This is not a clear cover (*integumentum*) that perhaps should serve as a signal along with the other that the intelligences cannot exercise their intellectual influence on what is dead and that therefore they cannot act on the sensitive soul of which the thought of memory tied to Beatrice is the figure. The intelligences mediate the divine from him derives *vita et intelligere*. The different natures of the sensitive soul and of the intellectual soul are what it is required to understand. However, if the *integumentum* was not already used in reference to generation, it however is active in the *comparatio* with the transmuting from father to son – "Si come la natura umana transmuta, ne la forma umana, la sua conservazione di padre in figlio, perché non può in esso padre perpetualmente [quel]lo suo effetto conservare" (Just as human nature transfers from father to son the task of preserving itself in the human form because it cannot preserve its effect in the father himself forever; II.8.6) – the correlative meaning that emerges from that *transmutatio* is that the human species, because transmutation does not perish. In transferring it to the theme of love, the intelligences perform the *transmutatio* towards the end of being able to continue to exercise their power. We should note that the term "nature" and the power of intelligences are in some ways correlated, but in opposition. We should also note that the term "nature," which has two frequencies – the first, human nature that transmutes the human form and presides over its preservation, and the second, which "dura in natura più che umana" (lives on forever in a nature higher than human; II.8.6) – can be understood if this last use of "nature" is read as a synonym of "form." Form is *species*, but *species* has a complex semantics in medieval Latin: it can mean the human species or also the intellectual species or form. In such a combination, it is to be noted that one parallel is imposed between the survival of the human species in the *transmutatio* and the lasting power of the intelligences that look for exercise their power.

The first sense is clear: the soul that suffers, rather than suffering and longing to die, will be able to save itself, thanks to the intervention of the intelligences of heaven carrying out that *transmutatio* that makes it gets or better reaches the preservation of the intellectual species or form – that is, arrive at the species as in the natural order nature does its preservation from father to son. It is thus the human species ("form") that is preserved, and here the intelligences with their mediatory influences is the species or "form" that allow to be loved. That it is possible to preserve it emerges from the fact that the soul, once it is divided from the body, lasts in perpetuity in its intellectual form. "In a nature higher than human" means that the intellectual soul perpetually lasts in its more-than-human – that is, purely intellectual – nature or form. Here the meaning occurs where Dante uses the word "natura" (form) in the meaning of "species": "natura più che umana" (a nature higher than human). Here nature means "form." Because of this, the physical order and the intellectual order also present themselves as correlative but separate and opposite. The suggestion is that not the individual but the species is preserved for what belongs to the human species. If this reading is true, it is an Averroistic nuance that probably penetrates here.

This passage seems to present itself as a kind of sophismatic procedure but with the goal of furnishing instruction. The terminology in fact uses "form" ("ne la forma umana"; II.8.6) with the meaning of species or genre. The *sub-intendue* needs a reader able to familiarize himself with a specific terminology.

Transmutatio (to transmute) therefore involves a change in form; the parallel that is put forth is between a human form and one higher than human form – the earthly and corporeal and material is transcended in order to attain intellectual knowledge that is here proposed as occurring by celestial intervention to promote love for an intellectual being. Love and knowledge appear thus to be identical.

Obviously the fundamental question remains open: how, according to these fragments read alongside the poetic text, does human knowledge happen? The Aristotelian terminology avoided in the canzone, but reconstructible in the commentary, requires considering the identity of the *donna gentile* as is proposed in the commentary. Here, it is a matter of intellectual knowledge, certainly; but does such knowledge occur through abstraction of phantasms by means of the intellect or does it occur through the vision of a separate form? And still, what does it mean to combine the discourse on cognitive *transmutatio* to the one on human *transmutatio* from father to son? It is an ambiguous discourse, especially if we consider that Dante carries it out in relation to the survival of the soul and we see that indeed here he asserts that it is the species that survives. This is a discourse perhaps marked by the position typical of radicalism that held that it is not the individual that lives on, not the individual intellect that survives, but precisely the species – in fact, the theory of the intellect considered as one for the human beings postulated the eternity of the species and the death of the individual soul. Here, Dante is talking to us about the continuity of the species, but it is probably an intentionally ambiguous discourse. The ambiguity proves itself, in fact, where, moving on to deal with the immortality of the soul, which he forcefully affirms, he writes that we believe in life after death because we are comforted by the philosophers and by all the other wise writers. He places Aristotle among the philosophers, but it is noted that the Stagirite is obviously not interested in immortality unless we go back to that passage of the *De anima* 3.5 where one reads that intellect is perpetual and incorruptible and separate. Recalling this passage, we have to be aware that it was on this passage that the discussion about intellect arose since antiquity, and later, Averroes had based himself to establish his thesis of the separate and unique and eternal intellect. It is also true that the so-called orthodox readings – and this is valid for all those of Aquinas – commented on this passage differently.

So it seems that the event of the *donna gentile* resumed from the *Vita nuova* is useful for the genesis of one of the most tortured and nonetheless important passages of Dante's work. The narrative part in the *Convivio* that I am talking about here is the fiction that covers a lofty and difficult truth. However, the decoding of the canzone already inspired this meaning where the second lady was the *fictio* for speaking and initiating a discourse on human speculation. Perhaps the brief note on the soul here is therefore like a corollary to what is said. The digression on the immortality of the soul is in fact indirectly tied to our opportunity for intellectual knowledge because it is by virtue of our intellectual nature that human beings live on in perpetual form; Dante takes up again what was first said at II.8.6: "perpetualmente dura" (lives on forever). He further opposes the most stupid, most base, and most pernicious bestiality of whoever believes that after this life there is no other life, and he turns to the authority of the philosophers, mentioning Aristotle, Cicero, and so on. Of Cicero, he recalls the *De senectute* (the book on old age), in which, however, the theory of the eternity of the soul is Platonic, and therefore living on occurs in correlation to pre-existence. Then he introduces another distinction: we are the most perfect among the animals but if we live without this hope of another life, as some do, we are entirely mortal like brute animals, and therefore what differentiates us from the animals is this that is indicated as hope. This means that having that hope comes from human reason. Thus our living depends on a mental state; this is very different and also, however, close to what we read in *Paradiso* 24, where "fede è sustanza di cose spate / e argomento de le non parventi" (faith is the substance of things hoped for / the evidence of things that are not seen; 64–5).[63] He then adds that the truest doctrine of Christ ascertains the eternity of the soul. This doctrine, he adds, makes it certain above all other reasons, however, that this was given to us by "quello ... che la nostra immortalitade vede e misura" (he ... who himself sees and measures our immortality; II.8.15). From this it follows that we can have a partial knowledge of these truths that he expresses as "seeing with a shadow of obscurity," because we are a mixture of mortal and immortal (II.8.16), but we can have an idea of it through faith and this is most perfect. It seems to me here that, rather than a Thomistic position, as elaborated by the historical readers of the treatise, the most evident trace leads us towards Siger's method, which emerges in the works in which are expounded more or less radical theories. He is looking for a very personal *conciliatio* between the truths of reason and those of faith, and this brings him to expound both the doctrine of the philosophers and the subjects of the truths of faith. What he states is that knowledge through faith is superior to that through reason. This position is traceable, for example, in Siger's *De anima intellectiva*, where the detachment from more radical and absolute positions, like those expounded in his *In tertium*, is evident. Thus, if in speaking about the survival of the soul the authorities are the philosophers – and not just Aristotle but also Cicero, who holds that the soul lives on because it pre-exists according to a Platonic way of thinking about the human soul, a theory which returns in *Paradiso* 4 (49–54) only to be refuted – and if he recalls the Stoics, about which he does not have clear ideas, because he bases himself on Albert, who identifies the Stoics with the Platonists (see de Libera 1990a) the discourse ends up being less ambiguous. The reference to Christ is more interesting still because it signals the attempt at an agreement that is methodological to say the least, and not only has its illustrious prehistory in Siger but also because Dante will return to this various times in the *Convivio*, suggesting the attempt at, or personal search for, not synthesis, but a relational point of view. The fact, then, that in addition he advances as argument that if a thing is thinkable that thing exists, brings us back instead to a different methodology that is a method introduced by Anselm (*Proslogion*: If a thing that is perfect is thinkable, it exists).

Summarizing what has been said, at the centre here is placed, as a novelty, the love for an intellectual being – a love mediated by intellectual beings, displayed in alterity with the love for Beatrice, described as a love lived by the sensitive soul. The transumptive mode ends up being deliberately used to create, in continuity with the poetic text, a prose where speaking is "faticosa e forte" (exacting and difficult; 55), whose *ornatus* resides in what the poetry itself announced, and where the beauty, that is such because it speaks to the mind, requires thought – "Ponente mente almen com'io sono bella!" (At least recognize how beautiful I am!; 61) – and identifies its own novelty in that peculiarity – "diletta mia novella" (my beloved newness ; 60). Chapter 11 confirms this reading for us. Let us see how he explains its meaning. The envoi (or "tornata"), he writes, he put forth to say something as the canzone's ornament (therefore *ornatus*). A distinction follows between that which is beautiful and that which is good in a sermon, and he asserts that goodness is in *sententia* and beauty is in the ornament of the words. They are both generators of delight, but it is goodness, and therefore meaning, that is especially delightful. But such goodness in the canzone is difficult to grasp because the people who speak in it are various and many distinctions are required, while beauty, he says, is easy to see. For this reason it seems necessary to him, then, that the reader direct more attention to beauty than to goodness. Then, having clarified that the intentions of the words of the canzone go to humans even if they are addressed to the canzone, he reaffirms that few are those who can understand the canzone, and the reason is that it speaks difficultly, and about this he already said that his verdict is that it is difficult because it is new. To see its beauty calls for not only the sight of the eyes but also that of the mind, comprehensible where the construction that – he says – pertains to grammarians (it is tied to the rhetorical order and musical harmony) brings us back to that *ornatus difficilis* of which the *De vulgari eloquentia* traced the identikit identifying it in the transumptive mode (*De vulgari eloquentia*, 2.6). In that identity between mental vision as intellection and poetical rhetorical construction the canon that the *De vulgari eloquentia* theorized more or less in the same years takes its shape.

4. Trajectories of Doubt

But there is another trajectory that is to be followed and that rises from a doubt: up to what point is this Aristotelian frame we have suggested authorized? Aristotelian frequencies are not absent from the prose text, but up to what point are we authorized to put forth that line of thought as the interpretive key? In the canzone there is very little that is Aristotelian, aside from the open call to the moving angels of the heavens, which is Aristotelian-causistic in origin; traces of Aristotelianism can neither be read in the term "anima" (soul) that is not connoted in an Aristotelian way, nor in the word "memoria" (memory). Aristotelian elements are introduced instead in the commentary and, for example, "memoria" placed in the rear part of the mind induces us to read within this circle of references the placement of the *donna gentile* in the front part of the mind, but it is to be added that the usable elements are few, even if they are essential.

Nonetheless, it is worthwhile to return to this section and follow another interpretive trail to use as a counter-proof, and that can be found starting from the relation that it is possible to place between memory and vision. We will now return to the second chapter to better understand that relation that Dante places between the memory of Beatrice and the new seen being. We will turn back to the theory of the internal senses, but in order to notice that this variously discussed theory cannot provide us with an answer except in part. Yet knowledge of these theories inspires not an answer but a *suspicio*. It is known that in the theory of the internal senses circulating in the culture of Dante's time,[64] common sense and imagination are in the anterior part of the head, *cognitio* in the middle, and memory in the posterior. According to the idea that Dante wants to focus on here, if what is introduced with the new lady is a new thought, it could comprise an activity of reflection that makes us see reflected in imagination the image that is in memory, which the text, however, proposes as a thought. This is already said in the canzone – "soave penser" (pleasing thought; 15) – and is underscored in the literal comment, "qui si dice 'pensiero' e non 'anima', di quello che salia a vedere quella beata, perché era spezial pensiero a quello atto" (I use the word "thought" here, and not "soul," of what ascended to see that blessed one, because this was a specific thought consisting of that particular act; II.7.8). He writes, however, again in the commentary, that the new thought makes the old one cease, that they are opposing, that it is powerful to take it, and that its effect is that it makes him look at a lady:

> Poi quando dico: *Or apparisce che lo fa fuggire,* narro la radice de l'altra diversitade, dicendo, sì come questo pensiero di sopra suol esser vita di me, così un altro apparisce che fa quello cessare. E dico "fuggire," per mostrare quello essere contrario, ché naturalmente l'uno contrario fugge l'altro, e quello che fugge mostra per difetto di vertù di fuggire. ... Sussequentemente mostro

> la potenza di questo pensiero nuovo per suo effetto, dicendo che esso mi fa mirare una donna, e dicemi parole di lusinghe, cioè ragiona dinanzi a li occhi del mio intelligibile affetto per meglio inducermi, promettendomi che la vista de li occhi suoi è sua salute.
>
> When I then say: *Now one appears who causes it to flee,* I describe the root of the other conflicting thought, recounting that just as the thought spoken of above used to be life for me, so another appears who puts an end to that thought. I use the word "flee" to indicate that the old thought is contrary to the new, for one contrary naturally flees the other, and the one which flees shows that it does so through a lack of strength … I then indicate the power of this new thought by describing its effect: it makes me gaze at a woman, and speaks alluringly to me, that is, it discourses before the eyes of my intellectual desire in order to draw me more strongly, by promising me that this desire will find its fulfilment in the sight of her eyes. (II.7.9; II.7.11)

At this point, then, the elements that had induced me to read an opposition between the sensitive soul and the intellectual soul in the poetic text begin to show themselves skillfully confirmed in the prose. Again in the commentary, he also writes that the new thought did not allow him to turn his face back:

> Però che l'uno era soccorso de la parte [de la vista] dinanzi continuamente, e l'altro de la parte de la memoria di dietro. E lo soccorso dinanzi ciascuno die crescea, che far non potea, l'altro, [te]men[d]o quello, che impediva in alcuno modo, a dare indietro, il volto
>
> Since one drew help continually from what lay before, that is, from sight of that lady, while the other drew its help from what lay behind, that is, from my memory, and since the help drawn from what lay before grew with each passing day, something made impossible for the other by the new thought, which completely prevented any backward look. (II.2.4)

Here, it seems to me that the text, however partially corrupt, is providing another element that the reader must be capable of deciphering. Since it is known that turning back means *revertere,* and *revertere* to memory involves a form of reflection, it seems to me that he is suggesting here that the cognitive intellectual act does not occur through a *revertere* that would imply the abstraction of the image preserved in memory. Since, therefore, it is pointed out that this occurs, we must think that the new lady matters in the commentary and involves a thought that, perhaps already sketched out in the text of the canzone, is strengthened here. Carrying on, we indeed find other elements of *suspicio*[65] where the new thought is defined as "virtuossisimo sì come vertù celestiale" (which had all the strength of a power drawn from the heavens; II.2.5), where celestial power, decoded for what that expression involves in time's culture and debate, is that of the separate substances, and therefore purely intellectual. The *donna gentile* is a figure of intellectual knowledge, but our intellectual knowledge can occur where we know through abstraction the images provided to us by the senses. However, that way was put in doubt in the passages just indicated, because the power of the new lady did not allow this kind of activity in the character who speaks. The problematic point, then, is this: is the new thought meant to mean that looking at the lady involves the contemplation of a being or a separate substance? If the contemplation of the gentle lady does involve abstraction from the sensible we are within a sort of parameter, but if, instead, the new contemplation is that of a separate substance in life , we are in line with a thought that is partially close to that indicated as heterodox. It will be seen in the next chapter that Albert accepts, however, some contents of this thought without the consequences that come from it in the field of radical Aristotelianism. Certainly, however, not only is what was sketched out in the poetic text reaffirmed, but actually the constant *suspicio* that this reading activates ends up drawing out of the reader that the text does not provide the elements necessary for an interpretation of it. Actually, and this will be returned to, it will be what the second canzone brings to the page that allows us to understand the traces dispersed in the second treatise. Paying attention to the fact that at the time of the commentary on the first canzone the second was already written (at least, it is held so with good reason), its content was therefore already active in the mind of its writer. A strong continuity is also placed between the prose of the second treatise and the third, since it is this that allows us in large part to understand or, better, to place in a cognitive and philosophical ambit what, in the second treatise, is put forth in an obscure, or perhaps at least in part philosophically uncertain, way.

Also, the specification regarding the "spirito" (spirit) which comes from the rays of the star indicates that the spirit that comes from the star is light and this is to be reconsidered in relation to the fact that the separate substances are separate and are light, as Averroes, for example, in the commentary of *De anima* (p. 400) indicates the possible intellect as "novus genus," which is light (II.6.9). We find a similar reference in a text of unorthodox belief like Giacomo da Pistoia's *Quaestio de felicitate* (Kristeller 1955). However, the eloquent spirit in the canzone seemed to express an intellectual function that inspires the author to look at the new lady (that distinction is reaffirmed here in the prose), and her eyes in motion, therefore setting a speculative relationship from which the sensitive soul related to memory seems to be excluded. In the prose, the spirit is "uno frequente pensiero" (a recurrent thought) that brings him to "commendare e abbellire [la nuova donna]" (commend this new lady and show how attractive she is; II.6.7). If we go back to the paradigm of praise as the interior language appropriate for a discourse about intellectual beings, which pertains to the intellectuality of the speaker, it seems that the new thought is a form of *consideranza* (contemplation) obtained not by way of *continuatio* but by way of an intellectual vision determined by an external and intellectual being, which also seems to suggest what the philosophical thought of the time called intellectual happiness. An element to be considered is the adjective "frequente" (recurrent) attributed to the thought: "dico che questo [spirito] non è altro che uno frequente pensiero" (I should explain that "spirit" here refers specifically to a recurrent thought; II.6.7). This perhaps can induce *suspicio* and signal a meaning, since the spirit-light expounded as a separate being, as is said, if it is directly referred to the lady, makes us think that in relation to the fact that she is a separate being, human beings do not always experience intellectual activity but only when they are able to contemplate that separate being as we will read in the third treatise. Actually in the prose text, the attempt at identifying the heavenly spirit is traceable and thought in terms that do not allow us to arrive at the concept of intellect, nor distinguish what, in terms of Aristotelianism, was called possible intellect and agent intellect, both thought of as separate within radical and Averroist thinking (Van Steenberghen. 1977; Aquinas 1976). In fact, the new love that develops from an intellectual impulse, given by an external entity or through the vision of an intellectual being that comes from outside, suggests elements of separateness, but it is not possible to say more, reading the sections that we selected.

Yet the fact that this new thought is an act of its most noble part, that is, rational, as we read in the second treatise (II.7.4), and does not include, it seems, a relationship with the body – against Aquinas, for example, who strongly establishes that the intellect is the act of the body – signals again an element of possible separateness. The word "diversitadi" leads us to another sign of separateness; do the two "diversitadi" (conflicting thoughts; II.7.2) allude to the two different and irreducible souls (sensitive and intellectual) of radical philosophical thought? In other words, while the poetry was more nuanced or less open, the prose irrefutably puts forth the two entities as different and opposed.

Obviously the commentators' glosses on the *Convivio* that led the vision of the new lady back to imaginative activity are misleading (see, for instance, Busnelli-Vandelli 1964; Vasoli 1988; Ageno-Brambilla 1995). Once again, it is to be reconsidered that if, as one reads, the speaker cannot speak about the new love to any but the angel-intelligences, it is because this love is similar to the way of loving characteristic of those contemplating substances. In the angels-intelligence, to love is to see and what they see are the separate substances that are divine ideas; this, however, is not said here. The reader who searches for a meaning has to be aware of such a lacuna – that is, of a space that the writing does not fill, a white space to be evaluated as a kind of strategy in writing. Through it the reader is pushed to trace texts to be referred to. The theory of ideas in the mind of God is a crucial content of medieval philosophy that enters in the *Convivio* but is not properly understood.

This tension towards putting forth a parallel between the vision of the angel-intelligences and that of human beings is one of the difficult points of the *Convivio*, as will be evident especially when the second canzone and the third treatise are read.

A most suspect passage, however, is the one where the text speaks of generation and corruption, which has already been dealt with (II.8.3). Even if the language used either is the fruit of unskillfulness – they are in fact topical Aristotelian words – or involves a materialistic penchant that, if applied to the fact that the thought that becomes corrupted is a metaphor for the sensitive soul, it involves a series of suspect deductions, among which is the corruption of the sensitive soul (a thing peacefully shared, however). But if the intellectual function is induced by the external and is separate, does it belong *de facto* to the individual? What is deduced from this? If one of the difficult points of heterodox thought held that what is separate can be intellected only from a separate being, would the difficult and trope-based discourse be strongly suspected of introducing subjects at risk for the so-called orthodox credo? The distinction and the answer nonetheless requires passing through the Albertian filter, the Sigerian one, and Thomisian one as well, and we will do so with the next treatise, postulating a continuity between the two treatises in prose that brings us back to that between the two canzoni, as it has already been anticipated.

5. Other Doubts: Memory and Speculation

Another aspect to take into account is to reconsider the canzone and its commentary, and the elements that permit us to place this text in a set of references that are not purely Aristotelian. If that reconsideration makes sense, it is because it reconfirms our reading and at the same time brings us to think that its writing is close to the cultural parameters of the *Vita nuova*, and therefore Augustine and Bonaventure (rather than Aristotle) who return again but in relation to a new line of knowing. Bonaventure, especially, and his Augustinian basis, although reconsidered in a perspective that includes a knowledge of Aristotle yet without fully adopting Aristotelian philosophy, seems to be the perspective by which we can reconsider the canzone in its bonds between memory and speculation. In fact, *Voi che 'ntendendo il terzo ciel movete* introduces the element of speculation in ways that do not follow Aristotelian parameters as put forth in the *De anima*.

To begin, let us return to the Aristotelian theory of knowledge as given in *De anima*, and consider how going back to it does not help us to understand, *in primis* because the new lady does not belong to the imaginative sphere that, in Aristotle, is part of the functions of the sensitive soul. It is true that Aristotle establishes the relation between vision and imagination, but that is the vision of a sensible being.[66] It is also true that his *De anima* tells us that the mind does not think without images linking imagination and cognitive activity, but in his theory one cannot leave sensation out of the consideration of knowledge.

Indeed, it is always Aristotle who, after having distinguished thought and sensation, and after having introduced the intellect as a separate being in no way mixed with the corporeal, explains that in our dianoetic activity images take the place of sensations, and therefore the mind does not ever think without a mental image, just as we, in order to think, need mental images, and thought in its activity thinks of the forms (*eide*) that are the mental images. But since images are generated by sensations, and from those of sight in particular, our mental knowledge would also not exist without sensation or sensitive knowledge (*aistesis*). We must have some mental picture, then, of what we think in order to think, and mental images are similar to the perceived objects with exception made for the fact that they are without matter (3.8, 431a–432a).

The *De memoria et reminiscentia* (*Parva naturalia*) reiterates that thinking is not possible without an image. In thinking, the same phenomenon happens as in drawing a figure; memory is not without an image, memory belongs to that part of the soul in which there is also imagination, which is an affection of the common sense. It is clear that the affection produced in the heart must be conceived like a drawing.

It is evident that in the canzone this type of knowledge is not called up. We read that the first-person narrator is divided between two ladies, also defined as thoughts – one is of memory and the other is proposed as a visual one. One represents a past experience and the other a current experience. They are two thoughts that the canzone proposes to us, of which one is made explicit as such; the other is introduced by a "chi" whose identity it is entrusted to the reader to reconstruct.

In the prose text, then, the new sight (and its object, the lady) put in dialectical relation to memory suggests more than a trace of a cognitive theory, even if it is undoubted that the new sight cannot be propaedeutic of a passage to an imaginative activity as opposed to memory. It is significant not only to discard this, but if we want to remain within the parameters of the internal senses, also Aristotelian in origin, then, reading some treatises that use this theory so widespread, Dante's discourse becomes clearer. It is true that the parts of the reception of sense, and of the formation of the image, are in the front of the brain and the part of the activity of memory is behind, but to know speculatively means to see in front because the image that is behind is reflected. In fact, at the centre of the brain there is the site of *cognitio*. This was a common thought and studied by the Arabs. We find it summarized with clarity in the treatise of Hunain Ibn Is Haq that makes the common theory of the Aristotelian tradition explicit – a theory which returns, for example, in Albert.[67]

As Averroes himself had noted, however, the internal senses belong to the sensitive soul while the intent, both in the canzone and in the prose text, was to connote the thought linked to the new lady as an intellectual experience, not by chance inspired by a heavenly spirit who "favella" (speaks; 12). In the prose sections that we have recalled, Dante tells us that his words rise from the anterior part, so in the part linked to the new vision and so from the new thought, and since the core of the novelty is exactly in this intellectual seeing, intellectual seems to be the nature of its word. Essentially, not only is the nature of the vision intellectual, but in the canzone a continuity is clearly set between new thought and new word. Yet both of the two ladies are linked to thought and both of the thoughts are shown in relation to speech (*dire*) and the frequencies of *dire/parlare* weave the text of the canzone itself. Let us see a few of their occurrences: "dire altrui" (no one else to whom I can relate it; 3); "parlare della vita" (putting into words my experience; 7); "Io vi dirò" (I shall speak to you; 10); "favella" (speaks; 12); "parlava a mme" (it would speak to me; 18); "l'anima dicea" (my soul would say; 19); "e dice" (saying; 24); "dice" (says; 33); "Io dicea" (I told them; 36); "dice uno spiritel" (replies a … spirit"; 42); "tu dirai" (you will say; 51); "la parli" (what you say; 55); and "dicendo" (saying; 60). It is clearly a matter of *sermocinatio*, and it occurs through contrast between a *dire* that expresses memory of the past and the new intellectual vision where the eyes are those of the mind. Both postulate an equivalency between *dire* as poetic word and *dire* as internal word and thought. The new thought that enters inspires a speculative thought. The new vision opposes the *anima memoriale*, and the frequencies of the seeing link the new thought to an intellectual vision. The *dire* that is always linked to the inner word and that occurs between the memory of the past and intellectual vision is an unequivocal meaning and links internal thinking, inner word, memory and intellectual vision. In fact, it is the mind that can grasp the beauty of the canzone, and that beauty announces the individuation of an intellectual beauty. The continuity with subjects characteristic of the *Vita nuova* is evident as it is evident, reading the poetic text in relation to the commentary, that the disruptive event had to be the entrance of a new textuality and of a new learning, essentially Aristotelian, but which Dante tries to recompose in a perspective of continuity with, or built upon, an Augustinian learning. The point to consider is that, already in the canzone, the new lady, later the *donna gentile* of the *Convivio*, proposes narrative material of the *Vita nuova* and makes something else of it. By virtue of that new thought, for example, Beatrice is no longer put forth as an absolute but becomes a relative, and in fact, what is now the absolute becomes what is determined by the mediation of the angel-intelligences. When we read in the prose that the intent of its author is to not deviate from what was said in the *libello*, we understand that the continuity has to be understood through the turning point to which a new learning gives new shape.

In fact, this new lady that in the poetic text is proposed in relation to speculation seems on the one hand to suggest in the commentary that such speculation is nothing but a way to express the dianoetic or reflexive activity that brings what is behind back in front, but as an abstract form. There are two possible interpretations: (1) the *donna gentile* would be what allows that speculative activity, and looking at the lady therefore means thinking by virtue of the possible intellect that would be coincident with the heavenly spirit that allows contemplation; or (2) this spirit would allow the speaker to see the form kept in memory, which is behind, in a new way, or that memory behind is reflected in front by virtue of the median mirror – that is, the site of *cognitio* or *cogitation* – and sets what is in memory in front thanks to the reflection that takes place in the middle part of the mind, which is the part of *cogitatio* and that could function as a mirror. I believe, however, that the thing is resolved thinking that the eyes which are mirrored in other eyes bring in front that which is behind and make it abstract; that is, the mirror that is inside the mind is expressed externally as *speculatio*, eyes as mirrors in the eye as a synonym of the capacity to transform into an abstract being what is connoted of that sensible that is active in the phase of memory.

The fact that such speculative activity occurs by virtue of an *additum* being – the heavenly being – that intervenes points out to us that it is not possible to resolve the discourse within the theory of the internal senses. The internal senses do not guarantee intellection and Averroes was aware of this (*De anima* 3.6; see also de Libera 1999, 95). If this is a possible trajectory, what is actually to be considered is, on the one hand, the link between the commentary to the first canzone and the text of the second canzone and its subjects. It is here that readers may orient themselves because new contents are unavoidably set forth. In this, in fact, as one of the centres of the discourse, we find the problematic issue of the vision in life of the separate substances to which the *donna gentile* belongs, as we will learn reading *Amor che ne la mente mi ragiona*.

What now requires examination is that trace of memory in the canzone *Voi che 'ntendendo il terzo ciel movete* that is not linked to the internal senses, as the prose will suggest, but is intellectual in origin.

If we want to find the traces of intellectual memory in Dante's discourse, a text to look at is that of Bonaventure, and by virtue of this text the memory of Beatrice would send us back to a set of relationships qualified to construct intellection.

It is a text that allows us to get to the heart – that is, it brings us closer to Dante's thought – and I do not mean that this is necessarily a source for Dante. One finds in Bonaventure a text that, it is hypothesized, Dante could have known in the years in which he frequented the *philosophantes* of the Florentine convents and among the others, the Franciscan one of Santa Croce. I am talking about a fundamental text on speculation, the *Itinerarium mentis in Deum,* and I would also like to recall, as a methodology common to cognitive theories in the Middle Ages, that another work by Bonaventure entitled *Quaestiones disputatae de scientia Christi.* In this work, what is repeated is that truly knowing something means knowing its essential truth. To know something means to know its eternal truth. In 4.32, this type of knowledge is put into relation with the Aristotelian language and the notions of possible intellect and agent intellect. Bonaventure also makes it explicit that in our condition as wayfarers, we cannot see God but see by way of enigmas or *in speculo,* but he also writes that all that which each intelligent soul learns, it learns by means of something superior to it (130). This brings him to also assert that if agent intellect is intelligent in act it is so by means of something superior to it, and that is God. In another passage (138), he explains that, also in this condition as wayfarers, intellectual knowledge requires eternal reason as normative and driving – not by itself, however, but along with created reason and therefore imperfectly. Still, we find the Pauline term "enigma" used (142) – that is, we cannot know eternal truths except through images and enigmas. I cite this paragraph because it explains the Dantean path as fundamental to a reasoning which is constructed through enigmas. So, since certain knowledge belongs to the rational spirit, because it is an image of God, in it the spirit attains the eternal reasons. However, since in our condition as pilgrims on Earth the spirit does not fully conform to God, it does not attain them in a clear, full, and distinct way.

A bit further on, he writes that since the soul is not a perfect image of God, according to itself, it attains, along with the eternal reasons, the similitudes abstracted from the sensible image as reasons distinct and characteristic of knowledge without which, as long as we are pilgrims on Earth, we cannot know the light of eternal reason unless we are provided with a special revelation (as happens to those who are enraptured in ecstasy or in the revelations of God to some prophets; 142–4). If the last part does not belong to the *Convivio,* but can be pertinent to the *Commedia,* enraptured in ecstasy or vision, the part useful for the *Convivio,* I mean here, is the first and therefore the problem of how true knowledge is possible for human beings. This happens, according to Bonaventure's response, because we have in us a principle of resemblance, and because of that principle we can imperfectly attain the eternal reasons in this life. This text contains a response to the cognitive problem that does not act according to Aristotelianism but silently embraces Aristotelianism and other cognitive ways. In the passage on the agent intellect, Bonaventure declares that it is characteristic of human beings, but through divine intervention (128). I have proposed this fragment from Bonaventure because, in the invention of the new lady in the canzone, it seems that Dante means to draw on that type of culture discreetly Aristotelian, but inscribed into an Augustinian tradition as in Bonaventure. In relation to this text of Bonaventure's, in other words, human knowledge is not sought just through an abstractive Aristotelian method, but its certainty is based on the presence in the mind of eternal reason, which is given through illumination.[68] But it is Bonaventure's text that appears to be important for the discourse on memory in the context we have recalled and that appears to be important also for that methodology which seems at least in part to be congenial to Dante. So, then, it is not Aristotle but a language and line of Bonaventure which obviously draws on the Augustinian ones. But important is that in Bonaventure there is the trace, either explicit or implied, of Aristotelian knowledge and what derived from him, which makes it so that in Bonaventure answers to problems are found that are resolved differently in Aristotle. I cite some passages, bearing in mind that the object of Bonaventure's discourse in this part of the *Itinerarium* is not the knowledge of human beings but how it is possible to know God in his vestiges in this sensible world. Bonaventure liberally uses Aristotelian modes that intersect with a line of Augustinian-Platonic authority. It is through the five senses, he writes, that knowledge of all the things that exist in the sensible world enters. Citing a passage that we find in Aristotelian physics and, that is, in establishing the motion of bodies, "omne, quod movetur, ab alio movetur"(everything that is moved is moved by something else; 2.3); the text introduces our inclination for knowing the spiritual movers that move bodies, as through the effects the causes are known. Bonaventure reaffirms that the sensible world enters through the act of learning in the soul ("per apprehensionem"; 2.4), but sensible things enter not through substance but through images of likeness (species). He then offers in specific language the route that the perceived object follows up until the generation of the "specie" (species).[69] Then, we are at 2.5 (516), where he adds that the *delectatio* or pleasure follows that act of learning and after perception and delight judgment rises: what is judged is why it gives pleasure and the reason for the delight that the object provokes in the sense. Let us see what the judgment is: "Diiudicatio igitur est actio, que speciem sensibilem sensibiliter per sensum acceptam introire facit depurando et abstrahendo in potentiam intellectivam." (Judgment is an action which allows the entrance of a sensible form entered through sense making it pure and making it abstract and intellectual). Aristotle, in turn, had said in the *De anima* that the act of judgment involves both intellection and perception. The point to which the Franciscan returns, however, is still the *diiudicatio,* which in the most excellent and immediate way "ducit nos in aeternam veritatem" (drives us to the eternal truth). Judgment, we read, occurs by way of reason that abstracts from place, from time, and from mutability (and so from dimension, succession, and change) in an invariable, uncircumscribable, and interminable way since nothing is entirely unchangeable and without end, etc., except just that which is eternal. That which is eternal, furthermore, is God or is in God. So, if that which we judge with utmost certainty we judge by way of those laws, then it is clear that God is the reason for all things and therefore, further, those laws by means of which we judge with certainty around sensible things, being infallible and indubitable to the intellect that learns them, are indelible in memory which recalls them as present. It is necessary that they are unchangeable – not made, not created, but eternally existing in the eternal art from which, through which, and according to which all things that have a form are formed, and therefore, they cannot be judged if not in reference to that eternal art, like the being that holds supremacy of form in all things and like the rule that governs all of them, through which our mind judges all that which enters it through the senses.[70]

I would link to such passage, not as a source but as methodology, the shift from the memory of Beatrice towards the new love (II.2), which the prose indicates happens through and with the consent (II.6.8) that implies the judgment in the assent and which would be, then, the way through which from a private, localized story one arrives at judgment of the being linked to its sensible being. Obviously, what is to be noted in the passage, the original of which is given in a note, is that Bonaventure takes his distance from the abstractive Aristotelian mode and finds that, in judgment, human activity gets to participate in divine light. This mode occurs by virtue of those laws through which the act of judgment, which he calls divine laws, occurs, in which human beings participate where they are capable of abstracting from space, time, and from that which is changeable. These laws enter into play in the act of judgment. Such laws are inscribed in the mind, not as subjects but as a cognitive method that goes beyond sensible knowledge. If the conclusion to point is at 13 (524), it is that "invisibilia dei a creatura mundi per ea que facta sunt intellecta, conspiciuntur" (the divine invisible things are seen by creatures through mirrors, i.e., in the speculation of created things).

We have the crucial point in chapter 3, where Bonaventure examines how we can know God through His image signed inside our natural powers "naturalibus potentiis insignitam" (528).

We come back to ourselves, he writes, in our mind "et conari debemus per speculum videre deum" (we have to attempt to see God through mirrors). A passage of a certain Augustinian derivation begins: the mind loves itself, it could not love itself if it did not know itself, and it could not know itself if it did not have a memory of itself. However, the following observation is more useful to our goal: we understand nothing with intelligence that is not present in our memory ("quia nihil capimus per intelligentiam, quod non sit presens apud nostram memoriam"; 3.1; 527). This passage, mindful of Augustine, is also part of an Aristotelian line and from that, he writes, you understand not with carnal eyes but with those of reason that the soul has three faculties. Consider the operations and behaviours of these three faculties and you will be capable of seeing God *per imaginem*, through yourself in mirrors and in enigma "et videre poteris Deum per te tamquam per imaginem quod est videre per *speculum in aenigmate*" (1 Corinthians 13:12).

However, the fragment of the most importance for what we are developing had to be in that way of conceiving memory on the Augustinian base as proper to Bonaventure, which thinks memory as a cognitive stronghold of human beings. Memory remembers not only the past and present but also some simple and eternal principles (528), he explains, since it retains past things remembering them, present ones perceiving them, and future ones foreseeing them. It remembers, for example, principles and axioms of the sciences as eternal and eternally, since it cannot forget them until it will use reason and it does not learn them as new things but it recognizes them as innate truths. Right from the act of remembering temporal things, that is, past, present, and future things, memory reveals itself to be an image of eternity, whose invisible present extends through all times. "From the second operation, however, it results that memory must be informed not only by images of the sensible world but also from above, receiving simple forms that cannot enter through the door of the sense and through images of sensible objects. In addition, it has a perpetual light always present and in that it remembers the eternal truths."[71]

He concludes on this basis and these premises that "Sic per operationem memoriae apparet quod ipsa anima est imago dei et similitudo adeo sibi praesens et eum habens presens" (The operation of memory reveals that the soul is the image of God and his likeness). The soul, therefore divine image, can participate in God both in act and power. Memory, however, does not know only through what enters through the doors of the senses and through images, but remembers "suscipiendo et in se habendo simplices formas" because it has in itself simple forms. Essentially, what he indicated as an act of judgment on perceived beings implies presence in the soul and the use of simple forms that the human being receives from above.

We have here second thoughts on the notion of memory reconsidered by virtue of an external divine action that penetrates to give memory its cognitive value. Bonaventure continues considering also intellectual knowledge in relation to the being in itself: you cannot know a particular thing without knowing the being in itself.

The word used by Bonaventure is "intellect as a cognitive act" beginning with 3.3, and the discourse continues up to asserting that human intellect is joined to eternal truth and we can see the truth if we are not hindered by concupiscence and phantasms that are placed between us and the ray of truth. In order to arrive at the fragment on memory very important in my discussion, then, I underline that according to Bonaventure, it is necessary to pass through the crucial act of elective power that is founded on counsel, judgment, and desire, and all three of these activities are set in relation to the divine. Judgment which is based on a law that is superior to it and the mind that judges is noticed through it because it brings it (i.e., the notion of the highest Good) inside imprinted ("impressa notio summi beni") and so the mind in its deliberating applies divine laws. Desire is also part of the same casuistry, and indeed that which we love most attracts us. Therefore, it is only the supreme good: that God's creatures can love nothing if not for desire for Him and they err when they accept as truth simulacra and effigies. This part is concluded not only by asserting that memory, with its operations, guides us to eternity, intelligence to truth, and elective power to the supreme good, but we further find in paragraph 5 another concise and important fragment when, on an Augustinian track, he writes that considering the order, origin, and custom of these three powers, we are guided to the most blessed Trinity. Indeed, he continues, from memory rises intelligence, which is its offspring since we know when the image of the thing that is in memory *penetrates the intellectual acumen becoming thought*, from memory and from intelligence radiates love as the bond between one and the other. These three powers – that is, the mind that generates, thought, and love – correspond in the soul to memory, intelligence, and will. It is important to give Bonaventure's Latin text:

> Nam ex memoria ortur intelligentia ut ipsius proles, quia tunc intellegimus, cum similitudo, quae est in memoria, resultat in acie intellectus, quae nihil alius est quam verbum; ex memoria et intelligentia spiratur amor tamquam nexus amborum. Haec tria, scilicet *mens generans*, verbum et amor, sunt in anima ...

> From memory is generated the intelligence as its own offspring. We have in fact intellection when the similitude that is in memory penetrates in the intellect, which is the verb, therefore from memory and intellect is generated love as the link between them. Thus the generative mind, the word, and love are in the soul. (*Itinerarium*, 3.5; 534)

The word "nexus" – that is, "knot" or "link" – does not escape us, and it also cannot escape us that intellectual knowledge that is given not by an Aristotelian path can however show an awareness of Aristotle's texts. The semantics of the term "memory" also cannot escape us, and its complexity, if seen in relation to this text, evolves on an Augustinian position which is developed, for example, in the *De trinitate* and also in the *Confessions*.

The relevant fact to note is that in the commentary on the poetry, the overcoming of the memory occurs in the moment in which we have consent, and here a new being is introduced that Dante proposes as intellectual. In the paragraph shifting to the intellectual operations, he suggests that the new being could be exactly the offspring or intelligence called, by way of *pronominatio, donna gentile* (II.2.1).

Essentially, the second book of the *Convivio* does not allow us to establish who the *donna gentile* is but *cum ombra* in the shadow, and in enigmas, we are introduced to her certainly intellectual and certainly transmuting dimension. A method is proposed through her introduction in order to move on from an Augustinian memory, memory as *mens*. The *donna gentile* seems to testify that passage; she promotes a new thought, follows an act of consent, and it implies a will, but *in primis* it is the angelic influence that promotes the new thought and is a mediator of divine light. It is certainly to be considered that the canzone introduces these themes. When we read that the reasoning is new and that the canzone speaks strongly and difficultly, we are inspired to think that there is a difficult nucleus proposed in this text. I believe that that nucleus is in the transformation of the theme of love that becomes localized in the intellectual soul where the new lady absolves the propaedeutic function of representing the intellectual human soul and its victory over the sensitive soul and over the subjective personalization of love and the opening up to a new way to consider love. It has already been said that this is actually set in continuity with *Donne ch'avete* and with other lines already present in the *Vita nuova*. However, the commentary introduces an entire new problematic that developed what was implicit and yet traced perhaps along a discreetly Aristotelian base.

If, as has been proposed, the canzone means to demonstrate the cognitive genesis that occurs in the human soul by virtue of a principle that comes from God, an intellectual being, which generates the internal transformation, of which Dante offers us a cross section, the first observation to make regards his careful avoidance of Aristotelian language in that description.

The recognition itself that we have made, on the other hand, merits a comment because only with difficulty could we find a sure basis or source for this interpretation of ours. Certainly, memory, situated behind, is part of all the theories linked to Arisotelianism, and so on, but the *donna gentile*, put forth as a figure of the being that allows speculative activity made possible by the intervention of a divine spirit, directs us towards understanding this new figure, proposed as a "visum principium" (Rachel's activity is so explained by Bonaventure in the *De mysterio trinitatis*, book 7; 486 [a seen principle]). Dante introduces the image of eyes that see eyes of the new lady, which makes us think that he introduces a path that is non-Aristotelian, but aware of Aristotelianism, setting into motion a discreetly Platonic-Augustinian solution at least along that line. Perhaps in taking Bonaventure up again, the genesis of the intellectual process develops through the activity of judgment. The laws that we use in judging are innate in us, so from sensible learning through judgment will we arrive at an intellectual knowledge. The words "consentimento" (consent; II.6.8–II.7.8) and "beneplacito" (will; II.2.2) refer us back to the area of judgment and will. In the canzone, this is said to be determined by the light that comes from the stars, the intelligences, mediators of divine light. By virtue of that mediation the speaker looks at this lady: "Questi mi face una donna guardare" (This newcomer makes me look at a lady; 23). Loving this lady involves an intellectual knowledge of a being loved through speculation and transmutation of the old love. The activity of memory, from sensible memory to *mens*, is part of the reactants. The commentary establishes that we deal with two different thoughts proposed in a dialectical relation. We know no more from the text and it is part of the method that Dante establishes to not say any more; after all, for this reconstruction we have firmly avoided digressions. The sense that is drawn from this, however, is that the lady is at the same time the result of speculation and the promoter of speculation, but of a speculation that is also inspired from above, and therefore what promotes speculation itself comes from above (angel-intelligences, rays of light, a spirit gifted of speech, God). It is therefore possible to assimilate what we have selected and discussed into the intellectual process. In fact, Dante wants to offer the cross section of a speculative or intellectual knowing that is made possible by principles that are inside us, but we must be able to activate that intellectual process by virtue of divine intervention. There is the shift from the *anima memoriale* immersed in regret, memory of Beatrice, to the intellectual soul until the consent to which the arrow of our attention is moved as if put in relation to memory.

Certainly, between the first and the second canzone of the *Convivio*, in light of what has been said, we may anticipate that a continuity is put forth. The word *verbum*, in fact, was in Bonaventure on an Augustinian base and was identified with intellectual knowledge. When "cum," the image that is in memory, is reflected in the intellectual acumen "tunc intellegimus," then we have intellection ("cum similitudo, quae est in memoria, resultat in acie intellectus, quae nihil aliud est quam verbum, tunc intellegimus").[72] It is evident that "cum" has temporal value in its relation to "tunc," just as the word *verbum*, which includes (as in the *logos)* the meaning of an expressible thought (*sermo* and *ratio*). The genesis of the verb proceeding from those connections, beyond any other consideration, tells us that the inner verbum occurs in an intellectual process.

It is said that Bonaventure's basis is in Augustine's *De trinitate*; the complexity of Augustine's discourse is such that Bonaventure appears to be an ingenious simplifier of it. However, if we go to book 9 of the *De trinitate*, at the opening 9.1, we find a passage that repudiates this reconstruction that I am attempting to propose here. A different reading in light of such Augustinian passage can be given. In fact, Augustine cites a passage of Paul's letter (Philippians 3:13–15) that he summarizes saying that perfection is *intentio*, "non aliud quam ea quae retro sunt oblivisci, et in ea quae ante sunt extendi secundum intentionem" (intention is just to forget things that are part of the past and to incline towards the things that are in front of us). The source of this passage seems to be Plotinus *Enneads*, 3.7.11. In this fragment, *intentio* is the concentration of the soul that unifies itself. But this theory is actually not different from what Dante does with the *donna gentile* where what is in memory, which is regret and division (*distensio*), or dispersion in the Augustinian sense, is overcome in a single principle or new thought, as Dante clarifies in the commentary, that unites the *animus* whose struggle between different thoughts is revealed in the loss of internal unity or, in Augustinian terms, in the *distensio* (or dispersion). In the last paragraph of the allegorical commentary of the second treatise, the first-person narrator tells us that he had overcome the contradiction.

What is indicated signals that perhaps at first glance a knowledge of Augustinian derivation as taken up again by Bonaventure had to be like a trace present in the canzone that was certainly in continuity with what was present in the *Vita nuova*. This knowing is encountered, and the canzone clearly points it out with a new textuality. The intrusion of a new textuality had to have a disruptive effect and, already from this point, an important aspect is signalled, and that is the attempt to reconsider, reconciling where possible, those different lines of thought and language. The commentary is a document of it. This will remain a characteristic of the method that brings Dante to attempt to reconsider on his own the different subjects of those bodies of knowledge: more than border lines, the *Convivio* points out the border crossings within apparently different territories that its author sees in relation to each other. In any case, the new knowledge is clearly revealed where the discourse of the angel-intelligences enters and with it their function as mediatory creatures of the divine being. Linked to this track there also seems to be that strong appeal of a philosophical thought that brings him to reconsider human knowledge in terms apparently conflicting as is proposed, according to a philosophical theological thought and one more clearly philosophical.

2 Loving a Divine Idea: A Cognitive and Educational Process

1. Loving a Divine Idea

The discussion about the second treatise cannot be concluded without recalling some nuclei of discourse that are inserted into the text and apparently tied to Dante's desire to provide an encyclopedic knowledge for his readers. My interpretation will show a sense of continuity with the main theme traced in the first part of the second treatise. The passage that I am going to read regards at first the brief discussion about the intelligences. The query that the text poses regards their number and whether or not this coincides with that of the angelic choruses moving the heavenly spheres. It is a problem that the author of the *Convivio* faces after having introduced the discourse about the heavens (II.3) and their number. The query, little valued by his readers, actually not only makes evident the continuity of a discourse constructed through joints, but, if understood, also allows us to enter into the meaning of what is indicated as *donna gentile*. The mode of the joints, in turn, signals the development of a method.

With regard to the number of the heavens – nine – it is known that Dante here draws on Ptolemy and refutes Aristotle's opinion. But we know that he adds another heaven that he indicates as the heaven that Catholics propose and that is called the Empyrean, "che è a dire cielo di fiamma o vero luminoso" (meaning the heaven of flame or of light; II.3.8).

The characteristic of this heaven is its immobility, "per avere in sé, secondo ciascuna parte, ciò che la sua materia vuole" (because it possesses in its every part the perfection required by its matter; II.3.8). And this heaven is the cause of the "quasi incomprensibile" (almost beyond comprehension; II.3.10) movement of the Primum Mobile because it would like to be joined, in every one of its parts, with the Empyrean heaven: "quieto e pacifico è lo luogo di quella somma Deitade che sola [sé] compiutamente vede" (restfulness and peace are the marks of this dwelling-place of that most high Godhead who alone fully sees Himself; II.3.10).

The description of this heaven continues and what we read here is part of a body of meanings that are of great importance. Indeed, God who sees only Himself recalls the way in which Aristotle describes the divine substance of the *Metaphysics*: he who thinks himself and exercises his reflexive activity (*Metaphysics* 12).[1] The part that follows introduces another subject: "Questo," which we read is "è lo soprano edificio del mondo, nel quale tutto il mondo s'inchiude, e di fuori dal quale nulla è; ed esso non è in luogo ma formato fu solo ne la prima Mente, la quale li Greci dicono Protonoè" (This is the heaven that crowns the universe: in it the whole universe is contained, and outside of it nothing exists; it does not itself exist within any place, but rather was formed only within the primal mind, or Protonoe as the Greeks call it; II.3.11).

To define the Empyrean as "edificio del mondo [che] non è in luogo," (the heaven that crowns the universe [that] does not itself exist within any place), implies a meaning as it emerges from the root "edificare" (to build; to found), and so the Empyrean is already immediately suggested as being in relation to creation which, however, takes its shape not *in loco* but in the primal mind. In Cicero, for example, on a Platonic basis we find "edificare" the world – "edificare mundum" – as production. So the world that "s'inchiude" (is contained), that "fu formato" (was formed) and therefore had or took shape in the mind of God, suggests a link with the models and archetypes of Platonic origin, and in fact God is indicated here as *nous* or primal mind. The Aristotelian God who thinks Himself is therefore linked here to Middle/Neoplatonic and Christian tradition and creates by generating the archetypes of things that His mind produces thinking. Thomas Aquinas, in the *Summa theologica*, also uses the verb *edificare* in a context linked to the divine ideas (*De ideis* 1.15). The motion, too, of the Primum Mobile, which the *Convivio* introduces as endowed with "velocissimo movimento; ché per lo ferventissimo appetito [...] in quello si rivolve con tanto desiderio, che la sua velocitade è quasi incomprensibile" (utmost speed, for [...] there burns an ardent longing [...] it revolves inside that heaven with a desire so intense that its speed is almost beyond comprehension; II.3.9), is to be seen in this relationship. The Seraphims, in fact, are the order that presides over that heaven and are moved by most ardent desire for what they contemplate. What they contemplate are the divine ideas and the divine ideas are the archetypes of creation. A text that has to be introduced at this point is Thomas Aquinas's *De substantiis separatis* where we read about the motion of the Primum Mobile and where this theory of ideas in the divine mind is like the fabric that supports the whole.[2] Also in this the appetite of the Primum Mobile is told as an intellectual appetite of the first motor, the first mobile being a body animated by intellectual creatures who hunger for or desire the divine being. In his edition of the *Convivio*, Vasoli (1988) rightly reminds us of how this attributing of appetite to the Primum Mobile was not really widespread. But essentially in this description we have the coexistence of two dimensions, one of which is physical and the other is intellectual. The heavens, the first nine in the *Convivio*'s, are part of the physical but their motion is the fruit of an intelligence acted upon by the intellectual desire which is characteristic of the intelligences. Returning to the Empyrean, we wonder where does this theory come from that Dante recalls and which suggests a relationship between the Empyrean and the theory of ideas in the divine mind? We will see that in the third treatise Dante will cite Severinus Boethius for the ideas in the divine mind, a theory largely used by Albertus Magnus too. But for the link between the Empyrean and the divine ideas we must draw in part on Nardi (1930, 1944) who gave us an important exegesis on the Empyrean and in which is mentioned the relationship with what was indicated as the "anima del mondo" (soul of the world) and therefore the Empyrean as the place of the divine ideas or archetypes (see also E. Gilson 1974). However, Nardi does not introduce into the reading of the *Convivio* this content that we find only mentioned in his essay on the Empyrean. In Epistle 13 the Empyrean returns with modalities that confirm the Empyrean as the place of archetypes[3] where we read that it is "causativus e formativus" in comparison with "formabilis" (13.25). And in *Paradiso* we know that the Empyrean coincides with the divine mind (Luce e amor; Light and love; 27.112): "ciel ch'è pura luce:/ luce intellettuali piena d'amore" (the Heaven of pure light, / light intellectual, full of love; 30.39–41).[4]

If the divine ideas are in the mind of God, they constitute God's thoughts. The angel-intelligences understand through the intellect (*intelligono*); *intelligere* is exactly the angels' power of seeing God's ideas. It is a tradition that Dante seems to already have in mind when in the first book of the *Convivio* he introduces the bread of the angels, which is precisely the *verbum*, and the *verbum* is divine *sapientia*, identified by Augustine with the ideas that exist in the mind of God and that are the archetypes, the ideal models of creation (as cited in *Evangelum Johannis*, P.L. 35). Introducing this theme, the *Convivio* suggested a parallel and a distinction between angelic speculation, which speculates seeing the forms and ideas of creation in the divine mirror, and human speculation. The *De vulgari*, in continuity, began considering from the linguistic-verbal point of view the difference between the angel-intelligences and human beings. At the centre of this dissimilar similitude, there was the relationship between language and concept where the angelic one was precisely the angels' seeing in the divine mirror that was suggested as the great collector of communication and where *intelligere* means to see (*De vulgari eloquentia* 1.2.3–4).[5] It would be interesting to consider if and how the path of the divine ideas penetrates, also, and directly in the Latin treatise that Dante *grosso modo* writes contemporaneously with a part of the first three books of the *Convivio*. We saw that Augustine and his commentary on the Gospel of John, as well as his *Quaestio de ideisi*, were basic texts for Dante. Among others that have written on the divine ideas was Thomas Aquinas, in the *De veritate* and *Summa theologica* in particular, setting them in relation with angelic knowledge. It is by going back to these texts that it is possible to establish the continuity of a thought from which Dante draws. And now, at this point in the *Convivio*, Dante returns to the angels, and not just on a biblical-Augustinian basis but fortified by knowledge that is central to the culture of his time, which has already been introduced by explaining the first verse of the first canzone that the *Convivio* comments on. It is the prose of the second treatise, in chapter 4, that introduces a discussion on the angel-intelligences on which it is useful to linger. Displaying a series of *auctoritates*, the way in which the discourse is confronted, demonstrates that the text proceeds using and bringing on the page different lines of thought with a subtle strategy. It is a method that Dante adopts with determination; the *Convivio* demonstrates that while the contexts from which the author draws what he deals with are reconstructible, the terminology that he uses to construct his discourse is not always coincident with those withdrawals.

Let us start with the section that he dedicates to introducing the angel-intelligences, movers of the heavens, substances separate from matter, that is, intelligences "le quali la volgare gente chiamano Angeli" (popularly known as Angels; II.4.2). Dante takes Aristotle's opinion (*Metaphysics* 12) into consideration, which linked the intelligences to the heavens and put forth as many intelligences as there were revolutions in the heavens and no more: "e non più: dicendo che l'altre sarebbero state etternalmente indarno, sanza operazione" (their reasoning was that any other intelligences would live an eternally purposeless existence, since they would lack any activity; II.4.3). He then introduces the conception of others, and he names Plato, "che puosero non solamente tante Intelligenze quanti sono li movimenti del cielo, ma eziandio quante sono le spezie de le cose" ([who] held that there were not simply as many intelligences as there were movements of the heavens, but that there were in addition as many as there were particular species of things; II.4.4). He attributes to this line of thought the responsibility for this theory that holds that the angels are generators of the heavens as those species are generators of other things and each one is the example of its species. He adds that Plato calls them "idee" (ideas) and that these are "forme e nature universali" (forms or universal natures; II.4.5). He writes:

> Li gentili li chiamano Dei e Dee, avvegna che non così filosoficamente intendessero quelle come Plato, e adoravano le loro immagini, e faceano loro grandissimi templi: sì come a Giuno [...] Le quali cose e oppinioni manifesta la testimonianza de' poeti ... anco si manifesta in molti nomi antichi rimasi o per nomi o per sopranomi a lochi e antichi edifici, come può bene ritrovare chi vuole.
>
> The pagans call them gods and goddesses, although they lacked this philosophical conception of them which Plato possessed: they worshipped their images, and erected immense temples to them, as to Jupiter [...] Clear evidence of such behaviour and of such views is found in the writings of the poets [...] clear evidence of such matters is also found in the many ancient names which survive as the names or nicknames of places and ancient buildings, as anyone who wishes can readily verify. (II.4.6–7)

He poses, then, a further consideration when he says that "per ragione umana queste oppinioni di sopra fossero fornite" (the opinions just given were derived from human reasoning) and yet actually "la veritade ancora per loro veduta non fue" (they still did not give an accurate account); that is, the account regarding these substances was not found, "e per difetto di ragione e per difetto d'ammaestramento" (due as much to a failure in reasoning as to a lack of instruction; II.4.8). The conclusion that he arrives at is rather lapidary: "pur per ragione veder si può in molto maggiore numero esser le creature sopra dette, che non sono li effetti" (for by its own powers reason can determine that the creatures spoken of above exist in far greater number than the effects; II.4.8).

The meaning of this passage, in order to be understood, must consider that here not only are the angel-intelligences dealt with but so are the separate substances, which do not have mover operations. In Thomas Aquinas's *De substantiis separatis*,[6] these substances that do not have motor functions are introduced in relation to celestial motors, that is, the motors of the heavens, but as their aims. In chapter 2 of his treatise we read, in fact, that both the Primum Mobile and every heavenly body are moved by their own (intellectual) soul and each one has its own desired separate being which is the aim of its own motion. This is a motive for which there are many separate substances that are in no way motors of the heavenly bodies, and there are many others of them that function as movers of heavenly bodies.[7]

Thomas Aquinas attributes this thought to Aristotle[8] and then summarizes the philosopher's position: thus between us and the supreme God nothing is set but a double order of intellectual substances, that is, the separate substances that are the aim of heavenly motors, and the souls of the spheres that move through hunger and desire.[9] And again in the same chapter he affirms that we cannot know the number, power, and disposition of the separate substances from the number of the heavenly movements.[10] He concludes by saying that it is not necessary that the near aim, that is, nearer than the supreme heaven, is the supreme immaterial substance, which is the supreme God, but it is more likely that between the primal immaterial substance and the heavenly bodies there are many orders of immaterial substances, of which the inferior is arranged to the superior as to its near aim. It is indeed necessary that every thing is in proportion to its near aim and it is then unlikely that a corporeal substance is oriented towards the supreme immaterial substance as to its near aim.[11] Essentially what is deduced in this passage is that the intelligences' intellectual appetite that moves the heavens is aimed at the desire for separate substances which are of a superior order and these are the object of the movers' desire. Here Aquinas recalls Avicenna who sustained that the first cause is not the immediate aim of heavenly movements but some first intelligence.[12] Aquinas's text is more explicit further on, for example in chapter 14 (cited in the first note on the *De substantiis*) where he confronts the theme of divine knowledge whose substance is his *intelligere* and who understands (*intellige*) everything through intellect, understanding (*intelligendo*) also himself through intellect because his existence is universal and a source principle of existence. And even more explicitly in chapter 16: the angels' intellects are participants in the intelligible species either, according to the Platonists, of ideas or of the first substance which is God. The intelligible species of divine intellect, through which He knows everything, is nothing other than its substance, which is also His *intelligere* and from which it is deduced that nothing is superior to divine intellect. So the intelligible species arrive at the angels' intellect from this intellect, while they arrive at human intellect from sensible things by virtue of the action of the agent intellect.[13] Dante does not recall this text; rather, his discourse for justifying his hypothesis is that, given that they (the intelligences) are held by everyone to be most perfect and blessed, it would be irrational to think that they have less than we humans who enjoy the blessedness of civil life and of contemplative life. But since the angels' intellect is single and those who have the blessedness of contemplation have a more divine way of being, we must hold that to the angels, beyond the office of moving the heavens, is given also that of pure contemplation. But since their intellect is single and perpetual and those who have the office of governing cannot have anything else, it is suitable that there be others outside of this function that only exist in speculation (*Convivio* II.4.11).

So what he sustains is that some angels have intellect that performs as movers functions and others have intellect that performs a contemplative function.[14] And so, he writes, since they have one single intellect it is deduced that some have active intellect and others have only speculative intellect. This is the kind of perfection that God gave to many and "[p]er che si conchiude che troppo maggior numero sia quello di quelle creature che li effetti non dimostrano" ([t]he conclusion follows that these creatures exist in far greater number than those for whom we have evidence from the effects produced by them; II.4.12–13). A following passage points out Dante's uncertainty. Recalling Aristotle, he writes:

> E non è contra quello che par dire Aristotile nel decimo de l'Etica, che a le sustanze separate convegna pure la speculativa vita. Come pure la speculativa convegna loro, pure a la speculazione di certe segue la circulazione del cielo, che è del mondo governo; lo quale è quasi una ordinata civilitade, intesa ne la speculazione de li motori.

> This does not contradict what Aristotle seems to say in book 10 of the *Ethics*, that the contemplative life alone is worthy of substances which are independent of matter. For if we grant that the contemplative life alone is worthy of them, then it is simply from the contemplative activity of some of these beings that the circling movement of the heavens derives, which is what governs the universe; and the heavens are like a well-ordered society, whose exemplar is perceived by the contemplative activity of the beings that move them. (II.4.13)

Here, "pure" has the meaning of "solo" (only) in the first two instances and of "tuttavia" (however), or also "solo," in the third.

This passage, with respect to the "ordinata civilitade" (well-ordered society) attributed to the angels, would seem to depend on Dionysian textuality. Roques (1996), in his study on the Dionysian universe, indicates thearchy as a form of monarchy; Dante alludes to the celestial world as a well-ordered society whose order is understood in the movers' speculation and so the centre as the vertex towards which the intelligences aim.[15] Actually a cornerstone text is Aristotle's *Nicomachean Ethics* which deals with the two forms of happiness appropriate for human beings and puts forth a distinction between the happiness of the active life and of the contemplative life (*Nicomachean Ethics* 10 1177a, 12–1179a, 32).

If it is certainly interesting to think about the angel-intelligences in terms of *civitas* and therefore as a unit that inspires the division of tasks, then what emerges is Dante's looking at the celestial as a model for the *civitas* of the sublunar world. But an important point, and one disregarded by readers, is that in this passage Dante uses *auctoritates* towards the end of establishing that other separate substances exist that do not coincide with those that move the heavens. Thus we may see that the paradigm of the Platonic ideas, like that of the divine ideas, is not mentioned by chance. So recalling Aristotle and the passage of the *Nicomachean Ethics* (10 8, 1178b, 20–3), where it is affirmed that the speculative life is proper to the separate substances, and adding that the revolution of heaven follows only the speculation of certain ones, serves him in order to establish some separate substances that are not identifiable with the function of the heavenly movers. In confirmation of this truth and of the innumerable number of these creatures, he first asserts that in us there is some light of their essence (II.4.17), then, reaffirmed that the ancients did not see the truth of these spiritual creatures, he observes that we were, instead, "ammaestrati da [...] Cristo" (instructed by [...] Christ; II.5.2).

The way in which this passage is conceived informs us that "noi semo di ciò ammaestrati da colui che venne da quello, da colui che le fece, da colui che le conserva, cioè da lo Imperadore de l'universo, che è Cristo, [...] uomo vero [...] per che ci recò vita. 'Lo qual fu luce che allumina noi ne le tenebre', sì come dice Ioanni Evangelista" (we, however, have been instructed on the realm of the spiritual creatures by him who came here from there, by him who made these creatures, by him who conserves them in being, that is, by the Emperor of the universe, Christ himself; [...] truly a man, who [...] brought us to life. "He was a light that illumines us who dwell in darkness," as John the Evangelist says; II.5.2–3). As already pointed out, the trace of a relationship between Christ-*verbum* and the divine ideas in the Gospel of John that Dante recalls here as testimony resumes Augustine's thesis identifying the *verbum* and divine ideas. Certainly in Augustine we have a rather interesting gloss in relation to what we are discussing, in which "tutto in lui era vita" (in him was life; John 1:4) is read as life is the ideas that exist in the mind of God. In John 1:18 we read, "vita est lux" (life is light), and Augustine writes: by this life humankind is illuminated, the human soul illuminated by life means that this life is the life of humankind (*Commentarium* 1, 16, 17, 18, 19).

It is the Augustinian thesis that seems to penetrate here where through Christ a relationship between the divine ideas and the illumination that human beings receive is suggested, a thesis also taken up by Aquinas in his commentary on the Gospel of John.[16] Not only in this passage of the *Convivio* is it asserted that those creatures are in very great number but also a varied textuality is recalled to give further evidence of those theses, evidence which ends up activating the method of interaction between a Platonic tradition and a Platonic-Christian tradition. The source par excellence, which is the *De causis*, is not made explicit, while Pseudo-Dionysius is not recalled in chapter 5 of the treatise, a chapter in which the discourse on angelic contemplation is introduced.[17] Aquinas also expressed himself on the number of intelligences as was seen in his *De substantiis separatis*, while the thesis of the plurality of the ideas in the divine mind is read in his *Summa theologica* (1, q.15, 2),[18] and in his *De substantiis separatis* a relationship between divine thought and the divine ideas or causes or archetypes of things is suggested and confirmed.[19]

Since these angel-intelligences are many more than what we know and since there are separate substances not put in charge of being motors, the naming of these remains open. Setting a relationship between angel-intelligences and ideas in the divine mind is probably a suggestion that also comes to Dante from the *De causis*, from proposition 3 which, in Aquinas's commentary, recalls the Platonic conception of many gods, but in order to condemn it. In this, Aquinas appeals to Dionysius who had all the gods come together in God. In any case the method of reading that the text imposes on us is to be understood. Actually, the sense of chapter 4 is captured where it is set forth in relation to the preceding chapter and where not only the relationship between the heavens and the motors is considered but also the relationship between the heavens and the being of the Empyrean. In particular that between the Empyrean and the divine conceived as the primal mind which relates to the theory of the archetype-ideas. These chapters are revealed to be important because they allow us to understand the method through which the *Convivio* is structured. That method contaminates different bodies of knowledge and looks inquiringly into different subjects in an attempt to rethink them.

The point on which we must now concentrate is the following: what encourages Dante to take up the plurality of the separate substances, asserting that their number is higher than that of the heavens' movers or motors? Aquinas's position and the relationship with the doctrine of ideas in the divine mind is to be confronted with what is readable in the entire tradition that takes up this theory that is so widespread.[20] But it is also probative in this case to recall, for example, Albertus Magnus and his commentary on the *De causis*. Here, the theory of archetypes in the divine mind is recurring and variously attributed both to the Stoics and to Plato and the Platonists. See, for example, book 2, treatise 1, chapter 20 (85): "Plato in lumine intellectus universaliter agentis formas ideales rerum posuit, ex quibus sicut ex quodam sigilli res materiales imprimuntur" (Plato in the light of the universal agent intellect placed the ideal forms of things from which material things are imprinted as seals).

To this theory is linked the theory that the heavens do not create but act because they are moved by the intelligences and they operate not as creator-beings but, as both Albert and Aquinas write, "per viam formam et informationis" and, that is, by virtue of the intelligences and in their looking at the models (forma) and informing the world of generation and corruption about them. It seems, then, that the idea of a number of separate substances higher than that of the movers can occur on the trail of a plural textuality. Consider Albert's commentary on the *De causis* and his notion of "influere" and "processio" as the multiplication of forms and ideas (see book 2 in particular, or also treatise 1, chapter 23, 87–9):

all the intelligences influence thanks to the first cause, but not all in the same way. And the conclusion informs us: "Iam ergo ostensum est propter quid intellegibiles formae factae sunt multae" (Thus it is explained why the intellectual forms are many).

Another example (182, 23) makes us understand how linked ideas in the mind of God are to the notion that the intellect proceeds as the first principle in all living things.[21] But the question remains open as to why Dante is interested in establishing that there are separate substances that are not responsible for moving activity. Especially if in some way this fits well with what we faced in the first part of this chapter as the problematic posing of human knowledge in relation to the invention of the *donna gentile*. If the basis can be the tradition of the idea-forms that originate from divine thought, it remains to be established if and how this passage can be in some way tied to that strong line that the vernacular treatise seems to construct and that regards the problematic issue of human knowledge. The second canzone, already written, expounded on subjects in some way ascribable to this line. Essentially, there is no trace here of a precise motive that this specification leads to unless we consider that Dante does need this in order to leave the knowable and utterable open, according to Aquinas's reconstruction that links the ideas in the divine mind to the theory of the possibles that the divine mind thinks. According to Aquinas, in fact, the ideas in divine mind cannot be limited to what we recognize in creation (Wippel 1993, 36–7; 46–8).[22] Whether or not this is in Dante's mind, he nonetheless assumes it *in primis* as poet, and as poet he introduces the nominative potential and so renames or names anew something that he intends to bring to the page; and by that new *nominatio*, he makes something knowable to us.

Yet, if the first canzone in that passage where he talks about a "spirit" that comes from the star as the mediator of divine light is read in the Albertian perspective of the commentary on the *De causis* about God as *dator formarum* (which is cited above, forms of which the intellect is part), it would signal for us the problematic assumption of a point: the relationship between the existence of separate substances and human knowledge.[23] But Aquinas's position from the *De substantiis separatis*, that the divine ideas are infinite and that there are separate substances without operation, opens the field of the possibles (see Wippel 1993, 36–7; 45–7), and of the possibles as unnamed, which is a trace whose imprint seems to remain in Dante's mind.

The naming, *donna gentile*, that resumes the old name-figure of the *Vita nuova* but gives it new meaning does not seem to be ignorant of such perspective. Besides, the ancients, as we read in the book and as confirmed by the poets, had given many names (II.4). When Dante writes that "pur per ragione veder si può in molto maggiore numero esser le creature sopra dette, che non sono li effetti" (for by its own powers reason can determine that the creatures spoken of above exist in far greater number than the effects; II.4.8), he tells us that separate beings exist to which we cannot get back by virtue of effects and which we neither know nor name, and he opens the road to our comprehension of the new naming that allows adding to what was already taken stock of, the new being. The *Convivio* will actually name that being in more than one way, and by virtue of that naming what is inferred are the levels of being that the *donna gentile* pronounces and puts into relation. To understand the Dantean path, we must remember once more that Severinus Boethius in his *Isagoge* had postulated that a new name is made to correspond to a new, shown reality (*PL* 64). We must remember that to impose names and create names (*onomatopoeia*) was part of rhetorical-poetical *nominatio,* which in the so-called *Poetriae* was part of the complex figure of *transumptio. Transumptio* brings us back not only to the rhetorical-poetical field but also to that of logic, and specifically to that logic indicated as *logica modernorum* (De Rjik 1962) to which Pietro Ispano does belong. As is known, Ispano is one of the Wise whom Dante met in the heaven of the Sun in Paradise. The intersection between a problem of cognitive order and the logical-rhetorical-poetical instrumentation put into action towards that aim is part of the reactants that intervene to make the reading of this section of the text complex.

The relationship that is a continuity between the divine ideas and the theory of the *De causis* is also to be considered in Albertus Magnus's reading of God as *dator formarum,* and this is to be linked to what the poetic text already introduced, and so the angelic mediation of what proceeds from God, and so, as we already read, what is indicated as intellect. Let us underscore that what Dante indicates as "new," is new *in primis* because it is expressed in the vernacular. It resumes philosophical notions and, by virtue of these, rethinks the cognitive field in relation to the Ptolemaic-Aristotelian cosmology and to the new syntheses elaborated by philosophers. The philosophical perspective is put forth in relation to a theological brand of knowing. Chapters 3 through 5 of the second treatise are symptomatic of that methodology; they seem constructed like blocks offered to the readers, so that readers think about them in relation to each other.[24]

Above I introduced the theory of the names of the angel-intelligences in Pseudo-Dionysius that involves a relationship between name, function, and the ontology of their being,[25] but the perspective that introduces separate substances, which are not limitable to the number of the movers, induces us to seek what the name attributed in the prose to the new lady, *donna gentile*, can mean here. The second canzone, already written as we know, had openly suggested that the new *donna* is an idea in the divine mind ("costei pensò Chi mosse l'universo"; he thought of her who set the universe in motion; 72) that the intelligences look at ("Ogn' Intelletto di lassù la mira"; Every intellect there on high gazes on her; 23); she is presented, therefore as a separate substance and a divine idea. On this subject, it is necessary to reaffirm that the method that was followed of avoiding having to identify the *donna gentile* with philosophy, which is another *nominatio*, supports us for establishing the relationship that runs between this chapter and the lady's name. Before being "philosophy," she is, in fact, *donna gentile*, and here we already have a form of transumptio (*transumere*); to understand it means to consider the process that Dante follows when he gives her a cognitive-philosophical identity. The tension towards putting forth a comparison between the intellection of human beings and the intellection appropriate for the intelligences seems then to indirectly return and to construct the focus of the discourse. If this is true, we are in the ambit of what type of reflection? The necessity of overcoming the fictional barriers of the chapter division and also of the division in treatises becomes pressing; in order to understand, it is actually necessary to activate the horizontal reading strategy (a term not casually related to the horizon): within this ideal plan and hypothetical line continuities are traceable, for example, between this chapter and the second canzone that will enter in the next treatise. These help us to understand the identity of the *donna gentile*. Let us return to the point. We have already discussed the existence of separate substances not coinciding with the movers, but that human beings can contemplate separate substances in life was a burning subject, as documented by the Parisian prohibitions. I have suggested in part the sources of that thought and problematic, so it is not so much what is said and expounded that is interesting in and of itself but rather the background that this theory lets us glimpse. In the meantime, let us remember that according to the fragment of the *De substantiis separatis*, angelic knowledge and human knowledge differ precisely in this, and so while the angel-intelligences see the separate forms or divine ideas, human beings know forms that are abstract but not separate in and of themselves, so says Thomas Aquinas.

That the angel-intelligences contemplate these ideas without motor function is a theory that we have already considered; but that a contemplation similar to that of the angels, and therefore of a separate form, is also possible for human beings is a subject that, held to be heterodox by some, had found propitious terrain in Albert's text, which can take us within a structure of useful references. In his *De anima,* the Coloniese had dedicated, for example, a chapter to the knowledge of a substance separate from the part of human beings.[26]

Essentially, Albert wonders, besides the knowledge of abstract images if it is possible for the human intellect to have knowledge of of separate substances? If it is up to the possible intellect to understand (*intelligere*) separate beings through the intellect, then it does not always receive from phantasms and from things that have magnitude but is joined sometimes to the separate intelligence conceived as an intelligible form. The answer sounds positive: human beings can know both separate substances and abstract beings, the possibile intellect can know both of them, and because that can happen in this first way, a superior happiness and a divine way of being is allowed to the human beings. At the conclusion of this passage, Albert refers to Alfarabi and to what Alfarabi himself calls contemplative happiness (*De anima* 1968, 3.3.6).

So this trace would bring us to think that if human beings contemplate a separate substance as form, the *donna gentile* would be a *nominatio* in some way linked to a philosophical type of intellectual happiness, and what would be drawn from this is that human beings can share a cognitive mode that is characteristic of the angels-intelligences. But we may see that this theory, generally held to be paradigmatic of a heterodox thought, is actually taken up by Albert, even if the modes of that contemplation as expounded by Albert on the one hand or by other philosophers on the other are built upon key and visible differences. Indeed, when we observe the documents, we can see that what emerges is how the crux that these different positions create achieves results that are often irreconciliable among themselves, where a vaster problematic is considered to which the theory of the intellect considered as one is linked. This is a position opposed not only by Aquinas but also by Albert and taken up instead by Siger, even if with various distinctions in the evolution of his work.

These are the relationships, some of which are expounded and others which work as a subtext, that create the texture of this part of the *Convivio.* It is what the text sought and suggested about the plurality of the separate substances that allows in the third treatise, beginning with the canzone *Amor che ne la mente mi ragiona,* to put the *donna gentile* forth as a separate substance but also as a divine idea to which Dante gives name and function. The *donna gentile* is, on the one hand, suggested as a product of divine contemplation and thus of divine thought that thinks himself ("costei pensò Chi mosse l'universo"; he thought of her who set the universe in motion; see Wippel 1993, 3–10); this content, Middle Platonic and Neoplatonic in origin, was also in the work of Thomas Aquinas. On the other hand, she is the object of contemplation on the part of the intellect but – as we will see – that contemplation of this idea-form, in some sections of the *Convivio,* is also possible for human beings (even if the modes of that contemplation are given with a closed and often contradictory language, perhaps the fruit of strong uncertainties). This contemplation from the part of human beings is not retraceable, of course, in Aquinas's text but in Albert's. The *donna gentile,* as the product of a thought that thinks himself, belongs to the divine, and in the prose of the third book of the *Convivio* we will read, in fact, that she is a prototype and is in the mind of God; here, indeed, she is said to be the archetypal form of the human soul that is in the divine mind. A divine idea, then, and a separate substance. What is said indicates a relationship with the vocabulary that is methodological, the ideas are the perfect models of the sensible because they are archetypal forms of creation in the divine mind, they are God's thoughts, in part named and in part to be named, obviously in an infinite process.[27] Such infinite possibles correspond to the infinite potentiality of names, to nominate implies a cognitive-logical activity that is also proper to poetry and to prose for Dante to be written as poetry.

The reading of this part of the *Convivio* brings the seal of Nardi's contribution that certainly had the credit of introducing the discourse of the separate substances but ended up by dissipating its meaning. What especially mattered to Nardi was demonstrating that Dante was indebted to Averroes (see Nardi 1960, 47–61). What is now pressing for me here is to establish the basis of Dante's discourse on idea-gods, not only in light of the texts recalled by Nardi and reproposed by Vasoli himself but also going on to consider that great line of medieval thought which brought Platonic ideas in the mind of God and made them God's ideas or perfect archetype-forms of things, linking it to the theory of the intelligibles. It is a theory that penetrates through what Chenu (1999) called eastern *lumen,* but that includes not only the work of Pseudo-Dionysius but also the *De causis* which enters in its link with Proclus and his *Elementatio theologica*. We also find it, then, in Albert, and in the *De causis* as commentated by Aquinas, and in the version commentated by Siger who refers in part to Aquinas. In both, this theory is tied to the existence of a hierarchy of beings as derived from the One or First Cause, which takes up Neoplatonic postulations as Saffrey (2002), editor of the *De causis* in Aquinas's commentary, showed in his studies. The importance of Aquinas's reading depends on the fact that he reads the *De causis* alongside Proclus's *Elementatio theologica*, already translated by Guillelmo de Morbecca (1992) but also alongside the Pseudo-Dionysius's *De divinis nominibus* to which Aquinas himself dedicates a commentary. He attributes to Plato theories that are Proclus's. In Aquinas's reading, then, the Platonists believed that the god-forms or divine forms are intelligible in and of themselves and are the object of intellection on the part of an order of subordinate gods that are divine intellects, and below those beings there is another order of supersensible reality which are the souls and, below these, the bodies. Let us see in fragments, then, Aquinas's commentary text on proposition 3:

> Ad cuius evidentiam sciendum est quod Plato posuit universales rerum formas separatas per se subsistentes. Et, quia huiusmodi formae universales universalem quamdam causalitatem, secundum ipsum, habent supra particularia entia quae ipsas participant, ideo omnes huiusmodi formas sic subsistentes *deos vocabat*; nam hoc nomen Deus universalem quamdam providentiam et causalitatem importat. Inter has autem formas hunc ordinem ponebat quod quanto aliqua forma est universalior, tanto est magis simplex et prior causa; participatur enim a posterioribus formis [...] Et, quia huiusmodi formae quas deos dicebant sunt secundum se intelligibiles, intellectus autem fit actu intelligens per speciem intelligibilem, sub ordine deorum, id est praedictarum formarum, posuerunt ordinem intellectuum qui participant formas praedictas ad hoc quod sint intelligentes, inter quas formas est etiam intellectus idealis. Sed intellectus praedicti participant praedictas formas secundum modum immobilem, in quantum intelligunt eas. Unde sub ordine intellectuum ponebant tertium ordinem animarum quae mediantibus intellectibus participant formas praedictas secundum motum, in quantum scilicet sunt principia corporalium motuum per quos superiores formae participantur in materia corporali. Et sic quartus ordo rerum est ordo corporum ...

> To make this clear we ought to realize that Plato maintained that the universal forms of things were separate and per se subsistens. Because according to him, such universal forms have a certain universal causality over particular beings that participate in them, he consequently calls all

> such forms subsisting in this way "gods." For the word "god"implies a certain universal providence and causality.
>
> Furthermore among these forms he articulates this order: the more universal any form is,the more simple and prior cause it is, for it is participated by later forms [...] Forms of this kind which they call "gods" are intelligible in themselves,but an intellect becomes intelligent in act through an intelligible species.Thus they placed below the order of gods, i.e. of forms menioned above, an order of intellects that participate these forms in order to be intelligent; and the ideal intellect is among these forms. But the intellects mentioned above participate in these forms in an immobile way insofar as they understand them. Thus they placed under the order of intellects a third order, that of souls,which with the mediation of intellects, participate in these forms trhough motion insofar as they are the principles of corporeal motions through which corporeal matter participates the higher forms. And so the fourth order of things is that of bodies ... (Aquinas, *Super Librum De causis*, 2002, 18–19)

Dante seems to be aware of this text but his discussion sounds different. He introduces therefore the postulate of the infinite numbers of substances separate assuming that some of them enjoy the contemplative life and some the duty of being movers of the heavens. The conclusion is that the number of the separate substance is more that the effects can show. Here is Dante's text in *Convivio* II.4.1–13:

> Poi ch'è mostrato nel precedente capitolo quale è questo terzo cielo e come in sé medesimo è disposto, resta di mostrare chi sono questi che 'l muovono. È adunque da sapere primamente che li movitori di quelli [cieli] sono sustanze separate da materia, cioè intelligenze, le quali la volgare gente chiamano Angeli. E di queste creature, sì come de li cieli, diversi diversamente hanno sentito, avvegna che la veritade sia trovata. Furono certi filosofi, de' quali pare essere Aristotile ne la sua Metafisica (avvegna che nel primo di Cielo incidentemente paia sentire altrimenti), che credettero solamente essere tante queste, quante circulazioni fossero ne li cieli, e non più: dicendo che l'altre sarebbero state etternalmente indarno, sanza operazione; ch'era impossibile, con ciò sia cosa che loro essere sia loro operazione. Altri furono, sì come Plato, uomo eccellentissimo, che puosero non solamente tante Intelligenze quanti sono li movimenti del cielo, ma eziandio quante sono le spezie de le cose (cioè le maniere de le cose): sì come è una spezie tutti li uomini, e un'altra tutto l'oro, e un'altra tutte le larghezze, e così di tutte. E volsero che sì come le Intelligenze de li cieli

sono generatrici de l'altre cose ed essempli, ciascuna de la sua spezie; e chiamale Plato "idee," che tanto è a dire quanto forme e nature universali. Li gentili le chiamano Dei o Dee, avvegna che non così filosoficamente intendessero quelle come Plato, e adoravano le loro imagini, e faceano loro grandissimi templi: sì come a Giuno, la quale dissero dea di potenza; sì come a Pallade o vero Minerva, la quale dissero dea di sapienza; sì come a Vulcano, lo quale dissero dio del fuoco, ed a Cerere, la quale dissero dea de la biada. Le quali cose e oppinioni manifesta la testimonianza de' poeti, che ritraggono in parte alcuna lo modo de' gentili e ne li sacrifici e ne la loro fede; e anco si manifesta in molti nomi antichi rimasi o per nomi o per sopranomi a lochi e antichi edifici, come può bene ritrovare chi vuole.E avvegna che per ragione umana queste oppinioni di sopra fossero fornite, e per esperienza non lieve, la veritade ancora per loro veduta non fue, e per difetto di ragione e per difetto d'ammaestramento; ché pur per ragione veder si può in molto maggiore numero esser le creature sopra dette, che non sono li effetti che [per] li uomini si possono intendere. E l'una ragione è questa. Nessuno dubita, né filosofo né gentile né giudeo né cristiano né alcuna setta, ch'elle non siano piene di tutta beatitudine, o tutte o la maggior parte, e che quelle beate non siano in perfettissimo stato. Onde, con ciò sia cosa che quella che è qui l'umana natura non pur una beatitudine abbia, ma due, sì com'è quella della vita civile e quella della contemplativa, inrazionale sarebbe se noi vedemo quelle avere [la] beatitudine della vita attiva, cioè civile, nel governare del mondo, e non avessero quella della contemplativa, la quale è più eccellente e più divina. E con ciò sia cosa che quella che ha la beatitudine del governare non possa l'altra avere, perché lo 'ntelletto loro è uno e perpetuo, conviene essere altre fuori di questo ministerio, che solamente vivano speculando. E perché questa vita è più divina, e quanto la cosa è più divina è più di Dio simigliante, [e tanto è da Dio più amata quanto è più di Dio simigliante], manifesto è che questa vita è da Dio più amata: e se ella è più amata, più l'è la sua beatanza stata larga: e se più l'è stata larga, più viventi [Dio] l'ha dato che all'attiva. Per che si conchiude che troppo maggiore numero sia quello di quelle creature che li effetti non dimostrano.E non è contra quello che pare dire Aristotile nel decimo dell'Etica, che alle sustanze separate convegna pure la speculativa vita. Come pure la speculativa convegna loro, pure alla speculazione di certe segue la circulazione del cielo, che è del mondo governo; lo quale è quasi una ordinata civilitade, intesa nella speculazione delli motori.

Now that in the preceding chapter it has been shown what this third heaven is and how it is ordered in itself, it remains to show who they are who move it. And so we must first know that its movers are substances separate from matter, namely intelligences, which the common people call angels. Although the truth is now known, different people have held different opinions about these creatures as they have about the heavens.

There were certain philosophers, among whom seems to be Aristotle in his *Metaphysics* (although in the first book on *Heaven* he appears incidentally to think otherwise), who believed that there were only as many of these beings as there were circular movements in the heavens, and no more, saying that any others would have existed in vain for eternity and have lacked all activity, which would be impossible since their being consists of their activity.

There were others, like Plato, a most eminent man, who maintained that there are not only as many intelligences as there are movements in heaven but also as many as there are species of things, just as there is one species for all men, another for all gold, another for all dimensions, and so on.

They held that just as the intelligences of the heavens brought them into being, each its own, so other intelligences brought into being all other things and exemplars, each its own species; and Plato called them "ideas," which is as much as to say universal forms and natures.The pagans call them gods and goddesses, although they did not think of them in a philosophical sense as did Plato, and they venerated images of them and built great temples to them, as, for example, to Juno whom they called the goddess of power, to Pallas or Minerva whom they called the goddess of wisdom, to Vulcan whom they called the god of fire, or to Ceres whom they called the goddess of grain.

These matters and opinions are made evident by the testimony of the poets, who depict in various places the custom of the pagans both in their sacrifices and in their creed, and they are also manifest in the many ancient names which survive as names or surnames of places and of ancient buildings, as anyone who wishes can easily discover. Although the above-mentioned opinions were the product of human reason and no scant observation, they nevertheless did not perceive the truth because of both a deficiency of reason and a lack of instruction; for even by reason alone it can be perceived that the creatures mentioned above are of far greater number than are the effects which men can apprehend.

One reason is this: no one, whether philosopher, pagan, Jew, Christian, or member of any sect, doubts that they are full of all blessedness, either all or the greater part of them, or that these blessed ones are in the most perfect state of being.Consequently, since human nature as it exists here has not only one blessedness but two, namely, that of the civil life and

> that of the contemplative life, it would be illogical for us to find that these beings have the blessedness of the active (that is, of the civil) life, in governing the world, and not that of the contemplative life, which is more excellent and more divine. And since the one that has the blessedness of governing cannot have the other because their intellect is one and perpetual, there must be others outside this ministry who live by contemplation alone. Because this life is more divine, and the more divine a thing is the more it is like God, it is manifest that this life is more loved by God; and if it is more loved, the more has its blessedness been bountiful; and if it has been more bountiful, the more living beings has he given to it than to the other. We conclude from this that the number of these creatures is much greater than the effects reveal.This does not run counter to what Aristotle seems to say in the tenth book of *Ethics*, namely, that the contemplative life alone befits separate substances. Although the contemplative life alone befits them, to the contemplative life of just a certain number of them falls the circular movement of the heaven, which is the governing of the world, which is a kind of civil order conceived within the contemplation of its movers.

Dante uses a knowledge that comes to him, it seems, from Aristotle's *Metaphysics* and that he compares with passages from Aquinas's commentary on proposition 3 of the *De causis*, but actually he uses these texts directing them towards a subject that it is not possible to find in these. It is only in reading the second canzone, which at that time was already written, that we realize there is a subject outlined in it towards which the commentary on the first canzone is aimed. A point seems to emerge: the hierarchy that Aquinas, on the basis of Proclus, proposes is the background against which an important subject of the second canzone is formulated. In this, the existence of an intellectual hierarchy in the cosmos is put forth as the subtext towards which important lines in the prose text of the second book aim.

We are therefore forced to go outside the prose text in order to understand it and to go back to the text in verse. It is by virtue of this that both Albert's position, which has already been mentioned, and that of Siger end up being useful for understanding the prose text. Siger also, in his commentary on the *De causis*, deals with the theory of the number of movers in ways that recall Aquinas's theory, but with the turn towards a different discourse which opens up to the theory of the separate and unique human intellect. A problem that Siger sets forth is whether or not those separate substances are eternal. In his *Les*

Quaestiones super librum De causis (1972b), question 13 puts forth the query of whether heaven is animated ("Utrum coelum sit animatum") and so deals with the number of movers (the lemma and comment on this *quaestio* are also to be considered). Question 17 discusses, in turn, whether there are several ideas or only one (Utrum sint plures ideas vel una tantum) and this *quaestio* is to be related to question 23: "Utrum sint aliquae intelligentiae non habentes ordinem ad motum in caelestibus" (Whether there are intelligences that are not ordered to move the heavens). [28]

In question 13, then, while he is talking about the motion of the heavens animated by the intelligences, he also discusses the notion of intelligence that connects to the problem of what eternity is – "Quid sit eternitas" – also already faced in Quaestio 8. In the lemma and commentary on question 13, Siger examines proposition 3 of the *De causis* – "Omnis anima nobilis habet tres operationes; nam ex operationibus eius est operatio animalis et operatio intelligibilis et operatio divina" (Every noble soul has three operations, from its operations we have an animal operation, an intellectual operation, and a divine operation) – and, attributing the root of some propositions to Plato, he offers a hierarchy that seems to take up that of Aquinas. In this hierarchy, the highest level puts forth the separate forms of things as the first in the order of things, which he calls gods. Below these there is the order of the intelligences which through the participation of the gods or through the act of the intelligibles become intelligences in act. Below the order of the intelligences, he sets that of the noble souls, and below the noble souls, those which through movement reveal the ideal forms in matter. Below the order of the souls there is the order of bodies, and in the order of the superior intelligences he spoke of or pronounced not so much the intelligences but the divine intelligences. The intelligences of inferior order are only intelligences and similarly in the order of souls and in the order of bodies (for noble souls here he means the superior soul in the order of the souls, and these are the souls of the heavens). At that point he poses the question about the ideas and the separate forms that Plato had introduced and proposes to respond, then, to five queries: "ideo querendum est hic de ideis et formis separatis quas Plato ponebat." What interests us in this context is the third, "utrum quaelibet idea sit deus aliquis," and the fourth, which inquires if there are several ideas or one: "Utrum sint plures ideae vel una." And the fifth: whether a form separate from matter and a material form joined to matter and its perfection can be of the same reason and of the same species, "Utrum forma separata a materia e forma materialis materiae coniuncta et eius perfectio possint esse eiusdem rationis et eiusdem speciei" (Siger 1972b, 71).

So Siger's answer reports that the first cause is God and since the ideas are first causes of the things that are in its genus, every idea is in its way some kind of god. But against this there is that nothing caused is a god: "Nihil causatum deus est." And since every idea – except one single one, that which is most universal – is caused, none of them, except the most universal, can be a god. In the *solutio* he concludes thus: it is necessary to say that since He imagined the ideas, each one of them is in God in some way. Plato puts ideas forth as the first order of things and says each one of them is like a god because it is the first cause of the things of its genus. Siger links, therefore, idea-gods to causality and so, as will be seen, to the theory of creation that the Brabantian philosopher faces in a personal way. Question 17 responds to the fourth query – whether there are several ideas or one only ("Utrum sint plures ideae vel una tantum") – thus: the answer is that there are as many ideas as there are species of things but there is only one idea that is the mover of everything and that is the first cause. Question 18 responds to what was the fifth query and so whether a form separate from matter and a material form joined to matter can be of the same reason or species; the answer is that the one being material and corruptible and the other separate and incorruptible, they are different for what belongs their genre as is said in the book 10 of *Metaphysics* ... what is naturally separate and what is not separate from matter cannot be of one and the same species: "Forma separata est incorruptibilis, materialis autem corruptibilis. Sed corruptibili et incorruptibile differunt genere, ut dicitur *decimo Metaphysicae* [...] 'separatum a materia de natura sua e non separatum non possunt esse unius speciei.'" Here, an observation is added that recalls one of the articles of the Parisian condemnation of 1277: "Ergo in specie talis forma non potest esse pluralitas in numero" (Thus such form according to its species cannot be plural in number; Siger 1972b, 80–1).

And in questions 23 – "utrum sint aliquae intelligentiae non habentes ordinem ad motum in caelestibus" – we read, instead, a thesis that more or less reminds us of Aquinas's,[29] Found reaffirmed here are the subjects that Siger had already expounded in part in the *commentum* to questions 12 and 13. But what appears in Siger is that the discourse on the number of the movers is nourished by a background where the crux was not only the number of the mover intelligences but also the problem of their eternity, and the theory of the ideas as first causes after the first cause. Another point, that is important, is that a separate form is unique in species, that is, for the human species there is just one separate form. From this Siger will proceed in order to explain the nature of human intellect which he confronts in the propositions that follow, up to the twenty-seventh, which in a direct way poses the central query on human intellect and whether or not it is one for all human beings: "Utrum intellectus multiplicetur multiplicatione hominum aut sit unus in omnibus" (Whether the intellect is multiplied according to the multiplication of human beings or is just one for all human beings). The twenty-eighth, meanwhile, discusses a key point: "utrum essentia causae primae intelligatur ab intellectu nostro" (whether our intellect can have intellection of the essence of the first cause; Siger 1972b, 108, 117). We must add that not only is there no trace of this problematic issue in Aquinas but also that his commentary immediately eliminates every temptation where he recalls Pseudo-Dionysius's position on the many gods he made come together in the one God, which we have already considered.

Dante, here, does not absolutely follow the theory that is in Siger; his point, at which he is aiming, is that having established the existence of separate substances that do not coincide with the angel-intelligences (we read in chapter 4 that "per ragione veder si può in molto maggiore numero esser le creature sopra dette, che non sono li effetti" [for by its own powers reason can determine that the creatures spoken of above exist in far greater number than the effects]; II.4.8), he proceeds by opening the discourse on the being and essence of the *donna gentile*. But actually it is possible to intuit something more where we link this line of discourse with the second canzone, *Amor che ne la mente mi ragiona*.

Because if we follow the order of the discourse as put forth in the second treatise and we read the fifth chapter after the fourth, another path is created and, in fact, the sequence brings us to think that Dante is taking up the position that Aquinas underscored as being proper to Dionysius: that all gods led back to one as cited above. The contemplation of the angel-intelligences in chapter 5 is put forth as contemplation of the Trinity and stated as plural by virtue of a plural relationality, but built on the fact that the One is one and trine and so among the nine orders and the One- trine are created a series of relations. This is a chapter of great importance and fascination which becomes stronger in the continuity retaken from and evaded in the fourth chapter, because here in the fifth Dante is able to make that trace of the Platonic imprint, so important for the Pseudo-Dionysius even if he does not recall it, shine through.[30] Actually the chapter signals the awareness both of the

De Hierarchia angelica and of the *De divinis nominibus*. The Trinitarian entity refers us back to the thought of the One, one and trine at once, that implies, in Neoplatonic terms, *processio* and *reditus*, while the angelic namings are nothing but the namings of a multifariousness which, by creation, proceeds from the first cause. Here, the names of the hierarchy are exposed, which by virtue of contemplation, which involves *reditus*, open up to new relationships to which, however, a name is not given. According to a useful study by Kenelm Foster, the text which Dante goes back to here is a passage of the *Hexaemeron* of Bonaventure, who was obviously aware of Dionysius, and Bonaventure's method is that of multiplying the relations and giving a name to the relations themselves.[31] In any case, the two chapters, chapters 4 and 5, are an important trace of a method. I cite a fragment from chapter 5:

> Per che manifesto è a noi quelle creature [essere] in lunghissimo numero; per che la sua sposa e secretaria Santa Ecclesia – de la quale dice Salomone: "Chi è questa che ascende del diserto, piena di quelle cose che dilettano, appoggiata sopra l'amico suo?" – dice, crede e predica quelle nobilissime creature quasi innumerabili. E partele per tre gerarchie, che è a dire tre principati santi o vero divini, e ciascuna gerarchia ha tre ordini; sì che nove ordini di creature spirituali la Chiesa tiene e afferma. Lo primo è quello de li Angeli, lo secondo de li Arcangeli, lo terzo de li Troni; e questi tre ordini fanno la prima gerarchia: non prima quanto a nobilitade, non a creazione (ché più sono l'altre nobili e tutte furono insieme create), ma prima quanto al nostro salire a loro altezza. Poi sono le Dominazioni; appresso le Virtuti; poi li Principati: e questi fanno la seconda gerarchia. Sopra questi sono le Potestati e li Cherubini, e sopra tutti sono li Serafini: e questi fanno la terza gerarchia. Ed è potissima ragione de la loro speculazione e lo numero in che sono le gerarchie e quello in che sono li ordini. Ché con ciò sia cosa che la Maestà divina sia in tre persone, che hanno una sustanza, di loro si puote triplicemente contemplare. Ché si può contemplare de la potenza somma del Padre; la quale mira la prima gerarchia, cioè quella che è prima per nobilitade e che ultima noi annoveriamo. E puotesi contemplare la somma sapienza del Figliuolo; e questa mira la seconda gerarchia. E puotesi contemplare la somma e ferventissima caritade de lo Spirito Santo; e questa mira l'ultima gerarchia, la quale, più propinqua, a noi porge de li doni che essa riceve. E con ciò sia cosa che ciascuna persona ne la divina Trinitade triplicemente si possa considerare, sono in ciascuna gerarchia tre ordini che diversamente contemplano. Puotesi considerare lo Padre, non avendo rispetto se non ad esso; e questa contemplazione fanno li Serafini,

che veggiono più de la Prima Cagione che nulla angelica natura. Puotesi considerare lo Padre secondo che ha relazione al Figlio, cioè come da lui si parte e come con lui sé unisce; e questo contemplano li Cherubini. Puotesi ancora considerare lo Padre secondo che da lui procede lo Spirito Santo, e come da lui si parte e come con lui sé unisce; e questa contemplazione fanno le Potestadi. E per questo modo si puote speculare del Figlio e de lo Spirito Santo: per che convengono essere nove maniere di spiriti contemplativi, a mirare ne la luce che sola sé medesima vede compiutamente.

That is why it is clear to us that these creatures exist in immense numbers; this is why his spouse and confidant, Holy Church – Solomon says of the Church: "Who is this coming up from the wilderness, rich in all that brings delight, leaning on her beloved?" – states, believes, and preaches that those most noble creatures exist in virtually countless numbers. She divides them into three hierarchies, that is, into three holy or divine principalities, each hierarchy itself having three orders; in fine, the Church holds and affirms that there are nine orders of spiritual creatures.

The first is that of the Angels, the second that of the Archangels, and the third that of the Thrones; these three orders comprise the first hierarchy – not first in respect either of nobility or of creation, for the others are certainly more noble than they and all were created together, but first in respect of our movement upwards toward their level of being. Then come the Dominations, followed in turn by the Virtues and the Principalities; these comprise the second hierarchy. Above these come the Powers and the Cherubim, and highest of all, the Seraphim; these comprise the third hierarchy. Both the number of the hierarchies and the number of the orders enable us with great confidence to give an account of their contemplation. For since the divine Majesty exists in three persons who constitute a single substantial being, the contemplation of these persons can take three forms. The supreme power of the Father can be contemplated; on this the first hierarchy gazes, that is, the hierarchy is first in nobility and last reckoning from our position. The supreme wisdom of the Son can be contemplated; on this the second hierarchy gazes. The supreme and burning love of the Holy Spirit can be contemplated; on this the lowest hierarchy gazes, the hierarchy which, being closest to us, offers us a share of the gifts it receives. Since, further, each person of the divine Trinity can be considered in three ways, each hierarchy contains three orders which contemplate in different ways. The Father can be considered simply with respect to himself; this is the contemplation proper to the Seraphim, who see the First Cause more fully than any other angelic nature. The Father can be considered in terms of his relationship to

> the Son, that is, with respect to how the Son comes forth from him and how he is united to him; this the Cherubim contemplate. Again the Father can be considered in terms of the procession of the Holy Spirit from him, with respect both to how the Spirit comes forth from him and how he is united to him; this is the contemplation proper to the Powers. Both the Son and the Holy Spirit can be contemplated in a similar way. There must, therefore, be nine kinds of contemplative spirits who gaze into that light which alone sees itself completely. (II.5.5–11)

The correspondence between the Trinity and the ternary structure of the hierarchies creates a path within the path. To the plurality of the gods, Neoplatonic in origin, is contrasted the plurality of the, named, angelic hierarchies, and that plurality is multiplied in the plurality of the relations that are posed, but to which no name is attributed.[32] When shortly after he will link the angelic orders to the heavens then there are two names: that of the angelic order and the heavenly one, and they seem to postulate a third name. This will enter later where the various sciences will be introduced. What emerges is that new relationships and new names are put forth and those relationships are sciences or bodies of knowledge.

If we instead follow another path complementary to this one, but one not identifiable with the first, then what is said in chapter 4 continues and takes up subjects readable in the second canzone. In this one point is the contemplative activity of which this *donna gentile* is the object on the part of the intellects ("Ogn' Intelletto di lassù la mira"; Every intellect there on high gazes on her; 23) and which will become the object of discussion in the third treatise. The word "intelletto" (intellect), on this basis, is to be reconsidered and, for good reason, we can hold that it does not coincide only with the intellect of the angel-intelligences. What seems to emerge in any case is the will to not follow the Aristotelian predicate, and so not only the number exceeds that of the movers of the heavens but also their idleness is a useful point for establishing the criterion of contemplation and the existence of separate substances as beings purely contemplating of a universe of ideas or gods that Aquinas calls "formas separatas per se subsistentes" and that are "secundum se intelligibiles" (and that are intelligible in themselves).[33] And, as we saw, Siger follows him. Looking always to Aquinas's explanation, we understand that it is because the intellect becomes intelligent in act by virtue of an intelligible species below the order of gods (i.e., of the above-mentioned forms), that an order of intellects are put forth that participate in the said forms towards the aim of being intelligent. Yet these intellects participate in the above-mentioned forms in an immobile way because they understand them by way of the intellect. Below the order of the intellects a third order of souls is placed which, mediating the intellects, participate in the aforementioned forms according to movement, since, that is, they are principles of the movement of bodies by means of which superior forms are participated in by corporeal forms and these are the angel-intelligences.

It is actually thanks to Aquinas that we are able to understand what this section of the treatise is putting into being. Essentially, the discussion of this fourth chapter of the second book allows us to establish a connection by virtue of which the theory of ideas in the divine mind, as suggested in the third chapter, is linked to a theory descending from the *De causis* and introduced in chapter 4. This connection is grasped looking at Aquinas's commentary on the *De causis*, proposition 3, because it is Aquinas who reads the *De causis* in light of Proclus and Dionysius.[34] By virtue of this, a third connection is established that we can understand because having initially hypothesized a continuity between the first two canzoni, in the second canzone, *Amor che ne la mente mi ragiona*, we already traced the presence of a theme that suggests the identity of the *donna gentile* as being a separate substance and a divine idea that "[o]gni Intelletto [...] mira" (Every intellect [...] gazes on).[35] Yet the finality of this discourse that in Siger introduces the theory of the single human intellect, in Dante, at least in this treatise, does not appear unless we go yet again to look for a relationships with the content of *Amor che ne la mente mi ragiona* because there Siger's line would seem present for the author of the canzone perhaps also as a dialectical term. Actually the method that emerges is created by a continuous pursuit of establishing relationships, thus Neoplatonic and Christian syntheses are resumed and prepare other syntheses.

Returning, then, to the theory of the separate substances that are non-coinciding with the heaven's movers, we can say that not only was that theory emergent from a complex terrain and an expression of the encounter between Aristotle and Middle/Neoplatonism, but in the thirteenth century it was opening and opening up to a different problem, of which Siger's work seems to be an eloquent expression. It is not only in this commentary on the *De causis*, which is considered a work not among Siger's most radical, that the *quaestio* of the separate intellect, single in its species, is posed. Siger had, in fact, posed the same problem in the *Quaestiones in Tertium De Anima*, a text that reveals a more openly radical position where a peremptory question is posed: "Utrum sit intellectus unus in omnibus" (Whether there is just one intellect in all human beings; question 9, 25). The first point to examine, and which is part of what he will discuss again in his commentary on the *De causis*, is that the relationship with the celestial movers is recalled here as well (question 2). Not only is it posed that the intellect is made eternal just as the world is eternal (this is Siger's theory, according to which the world is at the same time eternal and created), but it is stated that the intellect is the mover of the human species, it is one and is made eternal, and it is not multiplied by the multiplication of individuals (Et intellectus, quod intellectus est motor humanae speciei, est unum factum eternum, non multiplicatum multiplicationi individuali; *In tertium*, question 2, 6). And in the same *quaestio* it is noted that what is eternal in the future is also in the past (omne aeternum ex parte post, scilicet in futuro, aeternum est in praeterito; *In tertium* 4). Again (5) it is said that what is immediately made by the first cause is not new and, Siger writes, is made eternal, and for this Aristotle puts forth that the world was eternal, because it was made without any mediation by the first cause"quia erat factus immediate a causa prima" (question 2, 6).

Essentially, it is in following Siger's discourse that we realize that the discourse on the number of the separate substances, whether coinciding or not with the number of motors, is certainly indicating a contention between an Aristotelian position – only movers – and one, defined as Platonic, which postulates the existence of separate substances not coinciding with the movers. Actually in postulating the existence of separate substances, surreptitiously linked to the theme of the eternity of separate substances, it was the discourse on human intellect and on the modes or mode of humans' knowledge that was introduced. In chapter 4 of the second treatise this discourse is not traceable. But reading this chapter in continuity with some passages of *Amor che ne la mente mi ragiona*, some relationships can be anticipated. If in the canzone it is said "costei pensò Chi mosse l'universo" (He thought of her who set the universe in motion; 72), then the *donna gentile* could belong to the order of the idea-gods of Proclian authority and in Aquinas's mediation. But there is still something to underscore in order to understand and that is that in Aquinas it penetrates, on the basis of the *De causis*, that in that hierarchy the intellect and the intelligible, the thinking and the thought are identified (the *vous* and the *voeton*)[36] and that, therefore, the intellection of these beings (i.e., they are intelligible) is possible by virtue of an order of intellects subordinate to these, which understand by way of intellect: "intellectus fit actu intelligens per speciem intellegibilem." If divine ideas are eternal, a subject about which there are no uncertainties because God never thinks anything new, the *donna gentile* is linked to the statute of the eternity of separate substances, she is a form to be intellected. Putting the *donna gentile* in relation with divine ideas, Dante penetrates, then, into an ambiguous terrain. Obviously that ambiguity does not emerge except from the relationality that his discourse comes to construct. Where he pronounces with Aquinas the theory of divine ideas the danger is not signalled and that the divine ideas are eternal is peacefully accepted and shared. Actually it is only the field of relations that can suggest what the meaning is that this part of the text means to put into focus. The relationships are in and of themselves expressions of a method.

In fact, returning to the *Convivio*, the tortured passages suggest to us Dante's effort in posing a parallel between human beings and angel-intelligences, but it also opens up to an important turning point which is understood when, going forward, we will examine not only the relationship between the *donna gentile* and the separate substances but also the theory of the possible intellect contemplating a separate substance and considered by some thinkers as a separate substance.

That human beings are capable of contemplating a separate substance is a theory that we find in Albertus Magnus's notion of *intellectus adeptus*. Siger, in turn, pointed this subject out in question 13 of the *In tertium* when he asked: "Utrum intellectus possibilis agentem intelligat" and his answer was positive: "Propter hoc dico quod intellectus possibilis ipsum (agentem) potest et limpide intueri" (*In tertium* 45). And the notion that it is possible for human intellect to contemplate a separate form is recurring in Siger, but we saw that Albert's also postulates this notion although with strong differences with respect to Siger, differences that Albert makes explicit in that text of his on intellect, *De intellectu et intelligibile*, and also in his *De origine animae*, to which we will return in the following chapter.

The notion that seems to emerge if we link the fourth chapter of this second treatise to what is read in the second canzone is that such a separate substance is eternal and, in fact, the divine ideas are eternal. Furthermore, it emerges that the lady-separate substance is the object of contemplation on the part of the intellects, which gaze on her. It remains thus to establish what the word "intelletto" (intellect) involves as we will do in the next chaper of this study.

In conclusion, in the sections where the angels are on the one hand associated with and at the same time distinguished from the separate substances – ideas, held to be infinite (in part because separate substances without moving operations come to be thought in relation to the hierarchy of the intelligences contemplating the ideas that live like archetypes in the divine mind) – what emerges from those associations is that to contemplate, as from the text of the *Convivio*, involves understanding by way of intellect (*intelligere*). That intellect becomes intelligent in act by virtue of an intelligible species that it contemplates. Then, when we read in the canzone that "[o]gni Intelletto di là su la mira" (every intellect there on high gazes on her), intelligences dedicated to the speculation of a form or species or separate substance are being spoken about. And we read, in the second canzone, "costei pensò Chi mosse l'universo" (he thought of her who set the universe in motion); we deduce that that form or species is an idea or a god in an equivalency between Platonic *deos* and ideas in the divine mind as suggested in the fourth chapter of the second treatise, which sutures elements and different traditions that are, in part, contiguous.[37]

The introduction, then, of a plurality of substances separate from matter, finds its philosophical reason where subjects that the *Convivio* will introduce in the third book are anticipated. These are subjects that nonetheless were already in the author's mind as the canzone *Amor che ne la mente mi ragiona* that the third book will comment on testifies,[38] but which the second book already brings to the page yet without making the sequence towards which it guides explicitly. The continuity between chapter 4 and chapter 5 indicates a methodology not to be disregarded. The causistic universe of Proclian descent is considered in relation to the Dionysian one, the problem of the relationship between the Platonic and Neoplatonic One and the multiple many, is linked to angelic contemplation and the angels are announcers of the divine. *Manentia*, *processio*, and *reditus* are the referential subcategories. The Trinitarian essence of the divine is central in the fifth chapter and by virtue of that essence there is the contemplative activity that realizes a multiplicity of relations where the first model is divine contemplation. Bonaventure's text built those relations and multiplied them in the link between the hierarchies and the divine thought, in its turn, in self-relation as identity and difference.[39]

It is on this relational texture that the other important fragment or embedment in this second treatise can be reconsidered where the sciences are introduced, expounded in an identity with the heavens to be understood, therefore to be also considered, according to the thought of the time as we will see, in relation to *sciens*. And *sciens* refers us back to the angel-intelligences put in charge of the movement of the heavenly body.

2. Method and Strabismus

In closing this chapter, the method that I used and that resumes that characteristic of the author of the *Convivio* is to be underscored. In order to understand the set of motives, uncertainties, and contradictions or failures often more apparent than real that cross through this second treatise, it is to be considered that the strabismus[40] that our reading put into action was determined by the author's strategy. The subjects that had penetrated the canzoni and that later will penetrate the commentaries impose the recognition of moving on a double track. In the second book, while he is commenting on the first canzone, Dante is aware of those subjects that he posed in the second canzone that make him follow a method in which, in a problematic way, subjects draw near each other that in a chronological and poetic order had already entered, but which in the order of the prose writing will be made explicit later.

The speech with the angels and that which is called the theory of the intelligences' influence was already expounded, starting in the canzone *Voi che 'ntendendo il terzo ciel movete* and moving within complex coordinates. Here, according to my reading, it seems that the angel-intelligences mediate a divine form or separate substance, model, or archetype-idea that is perhaps equivalent to the intellect according to positions characteristic of, *in primis*, Albert, commentator on the *De causis*.[41] It is, however, only in the intersecting reading of the two poetic texts that it was possible to integrate this reading and in particular keeping the essential meaning of the second canzone in mind where, knowing how to read it, the new lady is stated as a separate substance. This is an awareness that actually came to determine some intersections in the commentary, however, without it being stated. By virtue of that strabismus of reading, I have introduced here what seems to reveal itself as the identity of the *donna gentile*: the separate form that the possible intellect sees and that in Albertian terms involves seeing a separate form, it is the same in Sigerian terms. Intellection by virtue of the vision of a separate form, this is the same *modus* of intellectual knowledge that we can find in Aquinas's text attributed to the order of intellects that become intelligent through *speciem intelligibilem*. This was also

Siger's position in the *De causis* and in other works, but in Albert's and Siger's position it is clear that human beings can have the same kind of intelligere, even if different conclusions then follow from this. Close to Siger is what is stated by a now canonized text of heterodox Aristotelianism, for example, Giacomo da Pistoia's text on intellectual happiness where happiness is dealt with as contemplation of a separate substance defined as *novus genus*. That way of putting human knowledge forth is formulated on ways of conceiving human intellect that are common, in part, to various philosophers and are, in part, essentially different. To these text-testimonies of a thought partially indebted to Arabic Peripateticism can be added a new testimony and it is the one published by Fioravanti in 1991, which I will cite in the next chapter, whose similarity to Boethius of Dacia's *De summo bono* is underscored by Fioravanti (1991) himself. But in Dante the new lady is realized through different notions and withdrawals in which Albert's thought that takes up from Avicenna the theory of God as *dator formarum* also plays a strong role. Albert, in turn, links this theory to the recurring theory of ideas in the divine mind that resumed and updated the Platonism of ideas as archetypal forms which endured in part in the *De causis* commented on by Siger. This commentary, it has already been said, appears in turn to have been influenced by the reading of Aquinas's commentary that kept the Latin Moerbekian traslation of Proclus's *Elementatio theologica* in mind in writing it up.[42]

While the allegorical commentary will confirm this reading of ours, a point that is worth underscoring is that the theory of the plurality of separate substances, the Thomistic base which this part of the *Convivio* appears to be aware of, is actually useful for Dante in order to formulate the theory of the *donna gentile* as species-form, which the intellects look at in the second canzone and which the first person narrator looks at in the first. Before moving on to deal with what develops from these premises, it is necessary to underscore that Dante's method is not that of using theological texts to feign and veil heterodoxy[43] (nor is it that used by his readers) who deduce an orthodox position where a source orthodox is recognized.[44] Actually, it seems that Dante uses various pieces to formulate a new whole. The *Convivio* demonstrates that the contexts are what express the complexity of meaning; for instance if he quotes for an Aristotelian text Moerbeke's translation or Aquinas's commentary this does not mean that Dante's position identifies with Thomistic thought. Starting from the first line, "tutti li uomini naturalmente desiderano di sapere" (all men naturally desire to possess knowledge; I.1.1), for example, Dante creates his own subjects that derive in this case, as is known, from Aristotle's *Metaphysics* and that can also derive both from Aquinas or from other commentators of this text, but also from questions debated in different areas. For example, we find this question discussed in texts indexed as Averroist and attributed to the fifteenth century where the passage is posed as a *quaestio* (Kuksewicz 1965, 282),[45] but it is a citation that we also find in Bonaventure's *De trinitate,* and this is also a point Siger discusses in his *Quaestiones in Metaphysicam* (1983). Foster indicated the source of the quotation from the *Metaphysics* that opens the *Convivio* in Aquinas. Actually, the dimension that the *Convivio* imposes on us for consideration is no longer or not only that of the source one, but that of the horizon one, where it allows us to construct an inside and an outside and inside there are texts and judgments that are offered for the new construction, perhaps also an orality of debate converges in it, which Dante had to experiment with in the encounters of his exile years. In any case, whether he follows Aquinas because he cites from him or whether he follows other traces, the *Convivio* demonstrates that the contention that opposes Nardi to Busnelli and Vandelli, then for certain verses reaffirmed in other readings, does not hold up as a hypothesis of reading. Just as the dialectic between orthodoxy and its opposite is not the referential structure but is to be considered point by point. The theory that Dante lives a corruptive love for philosophy, a deviance from which then comes repentance – a thesis loved by Dante scholars of the 1900s especially after the resounding rediscovery of Sigerian thought – is not capable of responding to the queries that the *Convivio* leaves open and opens. One of these to be evaluated is the tension towards the relationship that Dante looks for establishing among theories that are far and in some cases opposite. A logic of relations seems to preside to his methodology within which he reformulates or will rethink subjects. An example of that method is for example the notion of human intellect considered in front of the theory of the *logos,* among the most interesting and disregarded, which we will introduce in the next chapter. But an another aspect to consider is that a slow reading, for example, suggests that there are subjects in the doctrinal treatise that Dante will never abdicate; Dante's *Paradiso* proposes syntheses that in light of the *Convivio* are to be rethought.

I think that at this point we can follow the trace already signalled and put forth a further relationship onto which the reading opens that has been proposed between chapters 3, 4, and 5 of the second treatise. The inner link we have retraced between a causistic-Proclian-universe and a Dionysian and a Bonaventurian one that uses different bodies of knowledge comes to a Trinitarian idea that is very strong and able of activating a universe of plural relationships that suggest a methodological and logical awareness. The antique and medieval tie, Neoplatonic and Christian, between the One and the many, the One and the plural, enters here to establish a foundational content that Dante will articulate in a personal way. In a culture where the syllogism is the highest form of knowledge, the *Convivio* makes the one-trine dimension of the first being penetrate. The theory of the heavens as sciences, which we will discuss in the last part of this chapter, perhaps connects to this. We must then go on to look at that part of the treatise that the *Convivio* indicates to us as allegorical commentary. It is here that Dante relates to us, according to an "esposizione allegorica e vera" (allegorical and true exposition; II.12.1) and opposed to that which he defines as "fittizia" (fictitious), how his love for philosophy was born. He gives us a definition of philosophy that follows that in which philosophy was said to be "donna di questi autori, di queste scienze e di questi libri" (the lady of these authors, these disciplines and these books; II.12.5) and "somma cosa" (something of supreme importance). Now (II.12.9) philosophy is said to be "donna" (lady), "figlia di Dio" (daughter of God), "regina di tutto" (queen of all creation), "nobilissima e bellissima filosofia" (most noble and beautiful philosophy), and these are the definitions that return in the last chapter of this second treatise that he synthesizes thus: "E così, in fine di questo secondo trattato, dico e affermo che la donna di cu' io innamorai appresso lo primo amore fu la bellissima e onestissima figlia de lo imperadore de lo universo, a la quale Pittagora pose nome Filosofia" (And so I shall end this second book by forthrightly declaring that the lady whom I loved after my first love was the most beautiful and most honourable daughter of the emperor of the universe, to whom Pythagoras gave the name of Philosophy; II.15.12).

We must consider that "figlia" (daughter) implies the same process of eternal procreating that is characteristic of the doctrine of the *verbum*, in any case, philosophy, daughter of God, brings us towards that theory of the ideas in the mind of God, called *sapientia* by Augustine, which the commentary on the Gospel of John tells us is divine widsom. In the medieval tradition, divine *sapientia* is the word and the word refers to the divine ideas. If this is true, the *donna gentile*, daughter of the emperor of the universe, is, in continuity, the allegorical form of that activity of divine thought or divine *sapientia*, which are the ideas or archetypes with which God created the world and with which the world continues to be created in the mediation of the intelligences and the heavens.

The relationship that emerges is that philosophy is a divine activity that is also human; at the centre of the discourse, relocated, are pieces of a whole already made explicit but dispersed and others not already stated are made explicit. If Lady Philosophy is the daughter of God, and "daughter" implies eternal procreating as divine thought, Lady Philosophy is to be associated with the *verbum* or the bread of angels with which the doctrinal work opens, the relationship that is posed is the following: the angel-intelligences are eager for their bread which is the *verbum*-divine ideas that they know through the species and that it is possible for them to contemplate since they possess them through *viam imaginis* (resemblance). So, if human beings have philosophy as their lady perhaps they share something that belongs to the angelic-intelligences and is related to the divine thought. And yet pieces are missing from this reconstruction that would allow us to see the mosaic in its entirety. The first urgent thing to place in order to understand is set in the third treatise where the word "philosophy" will be opened in its etymology and read on a Pythagorean basis as the love of wisdom, and this allows the assembly of the various pieces. Indeed, God loves philosophy since thinking Himself he generates *ab eterno* His ideas, the divine love for philosophy which is his reflexive activity, from Augustine reader of Neoplatonic texts on divine wisdom onward, coincides with the divine ideas. The fact that human beings also have philosophy as their lady, then, brings us towards other currents that have been indicated but that are not clearly expressed in the text, and here it is that once again we are forced to look at this text and at the same time elsewhere, proving that such strabismus is a methodological tool the text imposes on us.

In fact, it is proven that this work imposes a reading in which the visible axes are displaced. The understanding of the text occurs through stratifications that are also the result of a gestural expressiveness that is at the same time mental and corporeal as dictated by the necessity of going forward and backward where, in returning to what has already been read, it is the understanding of what comes after that allows an understanding of what was said before. It is as if the temporal order was disregarded in the generation of an intellectual simultaneity that is outlined as an *optimum* difficult to attain. Actually, what the allegorical commentary calls philosophy is not understood if the memory of what the text first called "nuova donna" (new lady) and *donna gentile* in the litteral commentary is lost. In the second canzone, *Amor che ne la mente mi ragiona*, we will read that that lady is gazed on by the intelligences and is thought by human beings (in an identity between thinking and seeing which has already been underlined); looking at that lady had been an upsetting event as early as the first canzone. But if in the allegorical commentary of the second treatise, philosophy is the most beautiful and most honourable daughter of God, a piece that is missing is the one that opens up to philosophy from *philos-sophos*, a fundamental connection for the pivotal meaning. That is, where binding is the fact that divine love for *sofia* is His thought, and divine thought is reflexive and contemplates *ab eterno* and generates *ab eterno* thinking His ideas. Divine idea, then, but now it remains to make explicit what the love is that human beings nurture for philosophy. Notions coming from the *De causis* link up here with subjects from the Aristotelian *Metaphysics*. So it is the second canzone that introduces subjects that the third treatise will then discuss in continuity with the theory of the infinite ideas in the divine mind. In closing, then, what was was already said is synthesized and Dante writes: "E così, in fine di questo secondo trattato, dico e affermo che la donna di cu' io innamorai appresso lo primo amore fu la bellissima e onestissima figlia de lo imperadore de lo universo, a la quale Pittagora pose nome Filosofia" (And so I shall end this second book by forthrightly declaring that the lady whom I loved after my first love was the most beautiful and most honourable daughter of the emperor of the universe, to whom Pythagoras gave the name of Philosophy"; II.15.12). So, the filial relationship of philosophy with the divine being is reaffirmed and Pythagoras is recalled as the imposer of the name: "a la quale Pittagora pose nome Filosofia" (to whom Pythagoras gave the name of Philosophy). In the next treatise we will read that philosophy is the love of wisdom and the circuit will make itself evident. Human beings, like angels, love divine wisdom, which in the first treatise is the bread of the angels or *verbum*, and divine wisdom is the divine ideas, archetypes of the creation that God generates *ab eterno* thinking Himself. The *donna gentile* identified with philosophy manifests her eternity, and love for philosophy is nothing but love for a separate and eternal substance. Divine ideas are eternal; the repronunciation in the Christian-Neoplatonic key is not able to not reveal the suspect origin of that position. Dante, however, rethinks it side by side with the theory of the *verbum*; it is possible also for humans to manducate the bread of the angels, so says the biblical source. And the bread of the angels is precisely the divine ideas, and divine ideas are the *verbum*, so says Anselm and Bonaventure and Aquinas and before them Augustine, and also Philo had dealt with the theory of the *logos* in relation to the divine ideas (see Woolfson 1948; Gersh 1986; Dillon 1996). But if this is true and if this theory says that the *donna gentile* is a separate substance, the true point to be investigated is whether or not the discourse on the single common intellect is hidden inside the love for her. It seems that Dante's point is to find a relationship between the theory of the intellect, archetype of the human soul in the divine mind, and the theory of the *verbum*.

The *donna gentile* as philosophy and love of *sapientia* expresses the tension towards creating a parallel among angelic contemplation and human contemplation and divine contemplation. The resemblance with angel-intelligences also remains in the tension towards the *verbum*, but the way in which this tension of ours is satisfied in this life, if it is, is one of the obscure and difficult paragraphs to decipher in the discourse of the *Convivio*, not because it is not traceable but because Dante poses it in relation to a series of subjects that penetrate to modify the meaning and to reformulate that notion. At the centre there is the discourse on the nature and finality of human beings that the *Convivio* will indicate in the third treatise. While the so-called Platonic hierarchy helps us to understand, other pieces are missing, some of which will be arranged further on, and among these are the relationships that are posed with the Aristotelian *Nicomachean Ethics* and *Metaphysics* and their commentaries. The intellectual universe conceived as in continual expansion, that modifies itself constantly hinders a crystallization of the subjects in the reader's mind.

If the physical universe is finite, the intellectual is put forth in its infinity and part of this is the incessant chain of modifications in meaning. The space of human thought is outlined in a continual becoming and is infinite in its relations and modifications. The Trinitarian model and the angelic contemplation that are realized in a multiplication of relations are outlined as paradigmatic and perhaps can act as the keystone of the methodology that this part of the vernacular treatise puts into being. Contemplation of the divine being, one and trine, from nine orders that contemplate the Trinitarian relationships generating, in turn, other relationships, gives shapes to a plural, dynamic, hierarchical, and relational universe that is intellectual.

3. Another Piece of the Mosaic

Let us go back one moment. That the theory of the separate substances was useful in order to put forth a complex and finalized discourse is confirmed for us if we go on to read chapter 9 of the second treatise. There we find a passage where that tension signals the necessity for a synthesis, here is the cryptic fragment where it is elaborated for us that the human soul, the logical subject, could enter by virtue of disposition into relation with the new lady as a good inclined towards perfection:

> Però che dice che alcuna volta, di questa donna ragionando, dicesse: Ne li occhi di costei dovrebbe esser virtù sopra me, se ella avesse aperta la via di venire; e questo dice quivi: *Io dicea: Ben ne li occhi di costei.* E ben si dee credere che l'anima mia conoscea la sua disposizione atta a ricevere l'atto di questa donna, e però ne temea; ché l'atto de l'agente si prende nel disposto paziente, sì come dice lo Filosofo nel secondo de l'Anima.

> It declares that it would say from time to time, speaking of this lady: "In her eyes there would certainly be a power I could not withstand, were the way left open for her." It says this at the words: *I told them: "Without a doubt, in her eyes ..."* There should not be the slightest doubt that my soul recognized that its disposition was such as to be readily affected by the influence of this lady, and that for this reason it went in fear of her, for the influence of any agent produces its effect in a subject which is disposed to receive it, as the Philosopher says in *On the Soul*. (II.9.6–7)

This passage comments on a cryptic fragment of the canzone (verse 36), as has already been seen in the first part of this chapter of ours, in the meantime we should note the anaphora of "atto" (influence) that returns twice in the same period, to which "atta" (such as [to be readily affected]) is added but with a variation of meaning between "atta"/"adatta" (such as/suited [to be readily affected]) and "atto"/"azione" (influence/action). What counts is nonetheless the intuited possible relationship between the soul and this being of an exquisite intellectual nature, a relationship that allows satisfying what seems posed as a cognitive theory. The lines that follow state in the deciphering of the commentary that the sensitive soul's reasons are overcome by the intellectual event in a passage that is nonetheless not very clear: "colui che le mie pari ancide" (the one who kills all such as me; 37) seems to suggest that the victory of intellection overcomes the reasons of the *anima memoriale*. But the premise to these passages is in the event that took shape shortly above where we read "[p]erò quando dico *che tal donna li vide*, è tanto a dire quanto che li occhi suoi e li miei si guardaro" (so when I say that this *lady saw them* this is the same as saying that her eyes and mine looked into each other; II.9.5). The speculative act takes shape here in the encounter between a heavenly being mediated by the intelligences of the third heaven and the eyes of the narrator. Speculation seems to be linked to intellectual vision. How, then, does the act of intellection happen and what is the role of the *anima memoriale*? Here, in the prose text, the exclusion of the soul appears to emerge as the exclusion of individual and subjective reasons of memory in the triumph of speculation. And chapter 10 continues on this line; here is the incipit of the chapter:

> Dimostrata è la sentenza di quella parte ne la qual parla l'anima cioè l'antico pensiero che si corruppe. Ora seguentemente si dee mostrare la sentenza de la parte ne la qual parla lo pensiero nuovo avverso; e questa parte si contiene tutta nel verso che comincia: *Tu non se' morta*. La qual parte, a bene intendere, si vuole in due partire: che ne la prima [lo pensiero avverso riprende l'anima di viltade; e appresso comanda quello che far dee quest'anima di viltade; e appresso comanda quello che far dee quest'anima ripresa, cioè ne la seconda] parte, che comincia: *Mira quant'ell'è pietosa*.
>
> Dice adunque, continuandosi a l'ultime sue parole: Non è vero che tu sie morta; ma la cagione per che morta ti pare essere, sì è uno smarrimento nel quale se' caduta vilmente per questa donna che è apparita: – e qui è da notare che, sì come dice Boezio ne la Consolazione, "ogni subito movimento di cose non avviene sanza alcuno discorrimento d'animo" –; e questo vuol dire lo riprendere di questo pensiero. Lo quale si chiama "spiritello d'amore" a dare a intendere che lo consentimento mio piegava inver di lui; e così si può questo intendere maggiormente, e conoscere la sua vittoria, quando dice già "anima nostra," facendosi familiare di quella.

> I have made clear the meaning of that part in which the soul speaks, the old thought which is being destroyed. It is time now to proceed to clarify the meaning of the part in which its adversary speaks, the new thought; this part is entirely contained in the stanza beginning: *You are not dead*. This part will be better understood if it is recognized that it has two subdivisions: in the first the opposing thought reproaches the soul with being base; then in the second it tells this soul which has been reproached what it must do, beginning with the words: *See how compassionate ... she is*.
>
> Taking up the final words of the soul, it says: it is not true that you are dead; what makes you think that you are is a bewilderment into which

you have basely lapsed because of this lady who has appeared. It should be noted here that, as Boethius says in his *Consolation*, "no sudden change in one's circumstances occurs without the mind undergoing a certain disorientation" – this is what is meant by the reproach made by the new thought. This thought is called "a fresh spirit of love" in order to indicate that my power of consent was inclining in its favour; this is further and more clearly indicated, and this thought's victory signalled in advance, when even at this stage it uses the words "our soul," assuming a friendship with it). (II.10.1–4)

The expression "anima ripresa" in the first instance means "reproached" or "blamed," "riprende l'anima di viltade [...] e appresso comanda quello che far dee quest'anima ripresa" (reproaches the soul with being base [...] then [...] it tells this soul which has been reproached what it must do; II.10.2), but in the second it opens up and implies speculation, "comanda quello che far dee quest'anima ripresa per venire lei a sé" (it tells this soul which has been reproached what it must do to regain its self-possession; II.10.5) – and so "mira" (see) implies an exhortation to speculation.

A fragment follows that would seem to be a diversion:

Poi, com'è detto, comanda quello che far dee quest'anima ripresa per venir lei a sé, e lei dice: *Mira quant'ell'è pietosa e umile;* ché sono proprio rimedio a la temenza, de la qual parea l'anima passionata, due cose, e sono queste che, massimamente congiunte, fanno de la persona bene sperare, e massimamente la pietade, la quale fa risplendere ogni altra bontade col lume suo. Per che Virgilio, d'Enea parlando, in sua maggiore loda pietoso lo chiama. E non è pietade quella che crede la volgar gente, cioè dolersi de l'altrui male, anzi è questo uno suo speziale effetto, che si chiama misericordia ed è passione; ma pietade non è passione, anzi è una nobile disposizione d'animo, apparecchiata di ricevere amore, misericordia e altre caritative passioni. Poi dice: Mira anco quanto è *saggia e cortese ne la sua grandezza*. Or dice tre cose, le quali, secondo quelle che per noi acquistar si possono, massimamente fanno la persona piacente. Dice "saggia": or che è più bello in donna che savere? Dico "cortese": nulla cosa sta più bene in donna che cortesia. E non siano li miseri volgari anche di questo vocabulo ingannati.

Then, as was noted, it tells this soul which has been reproached what it must do to regain its self-possession. It says to her: *See how compassionate*

> *and humble she is*, for there are two qualities which are the proper remedy for fear, which is the emotion that clearly has overwhelmed the soul. These are the qualities just mentioned, which, particularly in combination, give assurance of a person's good will; this is especially true of compassion, which makes every other good quality radiant with its light. That is why the greatest tribute which Virgil pays to Aeneas is to call him compassionate. Nor is compassion what the common people understand by this word, namely, commiserating with someone in his misfortune; this is, rather, one of its particular effects, called pity, which is an emotion evoked in us. Compassion, however, is not an emotion evoked in us, but a noble disposition of mind, receptive to love, pity, and other kindly emotions.
>
> It continues: See, too, *how wise and courteous* she is *in her greatness*. Here, speaking of those qualities which we human beings can acquire by our own efforts, it singles out three which most draw us to a person. It speaks of her being "wise": now what is more attractive in a woman than widsom? It speaks of her being "courteous": nothing more becomes a woman than courtesy. And the wretched common people should not remain in ignorance about the meaning of this word either. (II.10.5–7)

Here, the adjectives that in the canzone were aimed at defining the new lady as "pietosa e umile" (compassionate and humble; 46), accompanied by "saggia e cortese" (wise and courteous; 47), explain this last "cortese" (courteous), drawing it near to "cortesia e onestade è tutt' uno" (human goodness; II.10.8), and here the intellectual value of *cortese* is to be considered side by side with the fact that *nobile* is tranformed into *intellettuale* by virtue of the *De causis*, and *onesto* is, beginning with Cicero, beauty as intellectual value (Ardizzone 2011). He explains thus: "La grandezza temporale, de la quale qui s'intende, massimamente sta bene accompagnata con le due predette bontadi, però ch'ell'apre lume che mostra lo bene" (Social greatness, which is what is referred to here, most becomes a person when it is accompanied by the other two good qualities just spoken of because it sheds a light that brings into [...] relief [...] goodness; II.10.9). Therefore, he says, goodness is an intellectual value and power that is not possibile without that light. Without anticipating subjects here that will be reproposed in the next treatises, the new intellectual value stated in the adjectivation that links *saggia* to *cortese* introduces a third element that acts as the connection; the honesty is the moral field that is linked and that emerges in relation to a vocabulary aimed at making the intellectual emerge as the effect of coincidence between good and beauty. *Pietosa*, in turn, is related to Virgil and the *Aeneid*: "Per che Virgilio, d'Enea parlando, in sua maggiore loda pietoso lo chiama" (That is why the greatest tribute which Virgil pays to Aeneas is to call him compassionate; II.10.5).

The whole that is composed preannounces the tragic and a tragic new. What was written in the *De vulgari* is complementary to a thought that is delineated here and will be delineated with more clarity in the third treatise. At the conclusion of this passage, the soul elects that new lady "domina," which means the victory of intellectual values and the verb "contenterà" is introduced.

> Poi sussequentemente impone a lei, cioè a l'anima mia, che chiami omai costei sua donna, promettendo a lei che di ciò assai si contenterà, quando ella sarà de le sue adornezze accorta; e questo dice quivi: *Ché se tu non t'inganni, tu vedrai.*

> It goes on to instruct her (that is, my soul) to call that woman her lady from now on, promising her that this will bring her great happiness, when she becomes aware of the lady's manifold beauty; it says this at the words: *For, if you banish self-deceit, you will witness.* (II.10.11)

The intellectual values of the new lady are at the centre, the soul will have to abdicate its own motives if it will want to find *contentezza* (happiness). What is suggested in chapters 9 and 10 will become clearer if we read the allegorical commentary and if we read chapter 15 in particular. Here "adornezze" (manifold beauty) is explained as seeing "le cagioni" (the causes) of things. First we read that the eyes of this lady are her demonstrations which straight in the eyes of the intellect cause the soul liberated from conditions or other limitations to fall in love (II.15.4). Then he announces "ché per lei si vedranno li adornamenti de li miracoli" (that through the lady will be witnessed the beauty of things that arouse wonder; II.15.11), and he then explains that the beauty of the wonders consists in seeing the causes of things, "le quali ella dimostra" (and these she reveals; II.15.11).

The lady's beauty is in her intellectual identity but that intellectual identity is explained as seeing "le cagioni" (the causes) of things and the causes of things are the idea-archetypes and that identity unequivocally links the new lady to the divine ideas. Not only does "contentezza" announce the field of an intellectual happiness but also that happiness consists in seeing separate substances or idea-archetypes. The discord between the two thoughts and the two ladies is concluded therefore with the submission to intellection that allow a knowledge that promises to attain *contentamento* (happiness, satisfaction) in the knowledge of causes or, as we read in *Metaphysics* 1, knowing the first causes. Philosophy or wisdom is knowing the most universal causes. The crux of the debate is that that this knowledge is divine science and not human, according to Aquinas (see *Metaphysics* book 1); while of an entirely different opinion are those who consider the contemplation of separate substances possible for human beings in life, which is the equivalent of *sapientia* or *philosophia* as Aquinas explains (third treatise, *Metaphysicorum* 18–19). The *Convivio* had opened up precisely on the knowledge of the *Metaphysics* and that knowledge is the science of the causes and principles, and Aquinas writes that that science is divine, but Dante, we can see, is attributing it to human beings. Boethius of Dacia's *De summo bono* was put forth on a similar line just like the already recalled new text published by Fioravanti (1991). In both the desire for knowledge that can satisfy human beings is the knowledge of an uncreated being:

> Nihil complet desiderium hominis nisi ens increatum, ergo illud summe desiderat [...] Intellectus (sciens) habens cognitionem de aliqua re, sciens rem istam habere aliam causam naturaliter inclinatur ad istam causam rei quia non potest cognoscere rem nisi per causam; sed omnis res citra Primum habet causam primam; ergo intellectus naturaliter inclinatur ad causam primam.

> Only the uncreated being can satisfy the human being's desire ... the intellect being a knowing being has cognition of something, and because it knows that this thing has a cause naturally inclines toward this cause because the intellect can know things just trhough their cause, but every thing with the exception of the First has a first cause thus the intellect is inclined toward the first cause. (Fioravanti 1991, 280)

And here is the full fragment of chapter 15 in which after having identified love for the lady as philosophical study, the beauty of the lady is deciphered as the beauty of things that arouse wonder: "annunzia che per lei si vedranno li adornamenti de li miracoli: e vero dice, ché li adornamenti de le maraviglie è vedere le cagioni di quelle; le quali ella dimostra, sì come nel principio de la Metafisica pare sentire lo Filosofo, dicendo che, per questi adornamenti vedere, cominciaro li uomini ad innamorare di questa donna" (it proclaims that through the lady will be witnessed the beauty of things that arouse wonder: this is no less the truth, for the beauty of wonderful things consists in seeing the causes of those things, and these she reveals; this seems to be the Philosopher's view at the beginning of the *Metaphysics,* where he says that it is through seeing such beauty that men are drawn to love this woman; II.15.11). This fragment confirms for us not only that philosophy is here assumed as the science of the causes and principles, identifying it with the *Metaphysics* as *prima scientia,* but also that that philosophy which is characteristic of the divine being is possible for human beings. Since God, eternal being, conceives eternal and intellectual beings, the new lady is delineated in relation of identity to separate and eternal beings and we will see that only what is separate and eternal can attain that knowledge. The human mind's notion, represented as in love with the new lady in the canzone *Amor che nella mente mi ragiona,* is thus what is needed to be explorend. We will discuss this issue in the next chapter.

The intellectual universe that the *Convivio* discloses arrives here at the end of the second treatise, and here my inquiring and reading and rereading undertaken in various ways and by various paths comes to a stop. It remains to underscore only how the *adornationes* of the *donna gentile* coincide with the *adornationes* of the text that deals with them; understanding the metonymic and transumptive game allows us to relish the text and to share the intellectual as value. To see wonders involves the knowledge or vision of separate beings.

The conclusion that philosophy is the daughter of God and so divine filiation involves ideas and confirms her being and essence as a separate substance and object of love and study which the *Convivio* considers to be the drive of human beings. The similarity to what is read both in Giacomo da Pistoia and in Boethius of Dacia is linked to what is expounded – that through study one arrives at philosophy and philosophy involves the contemplation of separate beings – and makes us better understand relationality as the viaduct for reading the *Convivio.* The multiple inlays of Dante's mosaic are made by withdrawing fragments from different texts, and the citations or sources if identified are not proof of orthodox thought or vice versa. Actually, the *Convivio* cites from different texts perhaps available to its author in the moment in which he writes and he makes them all come together towards a thought that aims to be put into focus through variations and diversions and tacit complementarities. On this basis, before closing, let us go on to reread one of the best known passages of the treatise – the one where we are informed that by "cielo" (heaven), the author means "scienza" (knowledge): "Dico che per cielo io intendo la scienza e per cieli le scienze" (By "heaven" I mean knowledge, and by "heavens," the various sciences; II.13.2).

4. The Heavens Are Sciences

In order to understand what the text suggests but does not make explicit, a notion of Neoplatonic provenance common to and shared by thinkers like Thomas Aquinas and Albertus Magnus is to be introduced. This notion sustains that in the world of the intelligible *sciens et scitum*, that is, the knower and the known, are identified with each other.[46] From the texts that we used to read and interpret the query on the number of movers, we deduced a theory in circulation which came from Neoplatonic sources. By virtue of that theory – the angel-intelligences look at other separate substances which they speculate – not only is the existence of separate substances that do not coincide with the number of heavenly movers deduced but also these actually know and contemplate an intellectual being contemplating, in his turn, the divine, and they mediate the divine being. They mediate it because they see; they know the ideas in the divine mind. In that hierarchy, it is clear that the angel-intelligences are *scientes*, and this is readable both in the *De causis* and the Pseudo-Dionysius, as well as in Albertus Magnus, Thomas Aquinas, and Siger de Brabant. Let us go on, then, to reread chapter 13 of the allegorical commentary that begins by taking up again the first verse of the canzone *Voi che 'ntendendo il terzo ciel movete*:

> A vedere quello che per lo terzo cielo s'intende, prima si vuol vedere che per questo solo vocabulo "cielo" io voglio dire; e poi si vedrà come e perché questo terzo cielo ci fu mestiere. Dico che per cielo io intendo la scienza e per cieli le scienze, per tre similitudini che li cieli hanno con le scienze massimamente; e per l'ordine e numero in che paiono convenire, sì come trattando quello vocabulo, cioè "terzo," si vedrà.La prima similitudine si è la rivoluzione de l'uno e de l'altro intorno a uno suo immobile.

> To understand what is meant by the third heaven the reader must first understand what I mean by the word "heaven" itself; he will then understand how and why it was necessary to make reference to this third heaven. By "heaven" I mean knowledge, and by "heavens" the various sciences, and I do so on the basis both of three principal similarities between the heavens and the sciences, and of the order and number found in each group which are clearly alike, as will be seen when I come to discuss the other word "third." The first similarity is that each member of both groups revolves around something immobile within it. (II.13.1–3)

Here a homology is put forth between bodies of knowledge and the structure of the universe, just as a resemblance is put forth between the method of the sciences and the movement of heaven that turns around its centre. He explains thus:

> La prima similitudine si è la revoluzione de l'uno e de l'altro intorno a uno suo immobile. Ché ciascuno cielo mobile si volge intorno al suo centro, lo quale, quanto per lo suo movimento, non si muove; e così ciascuna scienza si muove intorno al suo subietto, lo quale essa non muove, però che nulla scienza dimostra lo proprio subietto, ma suppone quello.

> The first similarity is that each member of both groups revolves around something immobile within it: each moving heaven revolves around its centre, which is not itself affected by that movement; likewise each science turns around its subject without affecting the subject itself, since every science takes as given the existence of its own subject and does not seek to prove it. (II.13.3)

The second similitude depends on illuminating and indeed "ciascuno cielo illumina le cose visibili" (every heaven sheds light on things that can be perceived by the eyes), just as "ciascuna scienza illumina le intelligibili" (every science sheds light on the things that can be perceived by the intellect; II.13.4).

The third similitude, then, regards what is indicated as "inducere perfezione ne le disposte cose" (bring[ing] about perfection in things disposed to receive it; II.13.5). Here is the fragment:

> E la terza similitudini si è lo inducere perfezione ne le disposte cose. De la quale induzione, quanto a la prima perfezione, cioè de la generazione sustanziale, tutti li filosofi concordano che li cieli siano cagione, avvegna che diversamente questo pongano: quali da li motori, sì come Plato, Avicenna e Algazel; quali da esse stelle, spezialmente l'anime umane, sì come Socrate, e anche Plato e Dionisio Academico; e quali da vertude celestiale che è nel calore naturale del seme, sì come Aristotile e li altri Peripatetici. Così de la induzione de la perfezione seconda le scienze sono cagione in noi; per l'abito de le quali potemo la veritade speculare, che è ultima perfezione nostra, sì come dice lo Filosofo nel sesto de l'Etica, quando dice che 'l vero è lo bene de lo intelletto. Per queste, con altre similitudini molte, si può la scienza "cielo" chiamare.

> The third similarity is that they bring about perfection in things disposed to receive it. All philosophers agree that the heavens are the causes which bring about the first perfection, that is, the generation of substances, even though they give different accounts of how this effect is produced by them. (Some say that it is brought about by the beings which move the heavens; this is the opinion of Plato, Avicenna, and Algazel. Others say that it is brought about by the stars themselves, particularly in the case of human souls; this is the opinion of Socrates, and of Plato and Dionysius the Academic. Others say that it is brought about by a heavenly power operative in the natural heat of the seed; this is the opinion of Aristotle and the other Peripatetics.) Likewise, the various sciences are what bring about the second perfection in us: through mastery of them we can contemplate the truth, this being our highest perfection, as Aristotle indicates in the *Ethics* [Book VI], when he says that the truth is the good which fulfils the intellect. On account of these similarities, and many others, the term "heaven" may be used to signify knowledge. (II.13.5–6)

As is readable in this passage, the theory of the influence of the heavens, responsible for the generation of the substance of things, is evoked and different theories are also recalled of who saw that generation flow from the heavens and who saw it flow from the intelligences and who sees it generate from the stars (this is valid in particular for souls). Let it be of who holds, like Aristotle, that they came from the heavenly power that acts on the human seed. On these passages, for the interpretation of which many have been helpful (not only Nardi but also Vasoli in his notes on the *Convivio*), I will not linger. The one aspect that it is useful to underscore is that here the meaning of "generazione sustanziale" (generation of substances; II.13.5) is essential for understanding what he is talking about. The "generazione sustanziale," in fact, regards the bringing about of the form or intellectual substance, which in the canzone was expressed through the heavenly spirit. So the form of the substance here is human intellect inspired through the mediation of the angel-intelligences. In relation to this, what is of great interest to put into focus immediately is what the text indicates as "perfezione seconda" (second perfection; II.13.6). Let us return to the text:

> Così de la induzione de la perfezione seconda le scienze sono cagione in noi; per l'abito de le quali potemo la veritade speculare, che è ultima perfezione nostra, sì come dice lo Filosofo nel sesto de l'Etica, quando dice che 'l vero è lo bene de lo intelletto. Per queste, con altre similitudini molte, si può la scienza "cielo" chiamare.

> Likewise, the various sciences are what bring about the second perfection in us: through mastery of them we can contemplate the truth, this being our highest perfection, as Aristotle indicates in the *Ethics* [Book VI], when he says that the truth is the good which fulfils the intellect. On account of these similarities, and many others, the term "heaven" may be used to signify knowledge. (II.13.6)

The word "induzione" (bring[ing] in) comes from the Latin *inducere*. What is reaffirmed here is not only the concept of influence but also, unsaid and put forth in continuity with what we read, the role of the intelligences that mediate the divine also emerges. Here, the divine is wisdom as is implict in the word "philosophy," according to the explanation that the text will provide only in the third treatise. Yet this meaning is already active and chapter 12, where the commentary indicated as allegorical begins, opens up for us, at least in part, this way of understanding the text. It opens it up to us by degrees. At the centre of the chapter, in fact, the mind is put forth which, after Beatrice's death, attempts to find consolation in reading and in reading a book that – he tells us – not many knew. The book was that of Boethius, *De consolatione philosophiae*, and also that other by Cicero, the *De amicizia*. Actually, in reading these texts, what the character who says "I" finds is that philosophy, which is the lady of these authors of those sciences and those books, was someone of supreme importance.

The discovery and frequenting of the *philosophantes* follows, but the part that interests us here is the one in which he begins, starting from the canzone, to show his condition "sotto figura" (II.12.8). This "figura" is necessary because the new love could not be revealed in vernacular rhyme since such rhyme was not capable of bearing the gentle lady, nor was the audience well disposed since it was entirely inspired to believe that his former state was that of love (but not his current condition). He begins the canzone and informs us that now, in this part dedicated to the allegorical commentary, he will give us not the fictitious sense but what the canzone "intende" (means). To be noted here is a not casual identity between the intelligences' understanding and the true meaning of the canzone suggested through the verb "intendere" (to understand), and where what is expounded is not only the activity of *intelligere* as common but also the relationship with the so-called allegorical level which is to be understood, that is, understood through intellect (*intelligere*; and in which one thing is said and another has to be understood [*intelletta*]). For a study like ours, dedicated to underscoring the exercise of reading as *intelligere* and in which some not renounceable modes of an ancient-medieval thought are presupposed – which we dated back in the Christian tradition to Augustine and his invention of the difficult as an intellectual value and exercise and from which an entire tradition derives – chapter 12 becomes an important link of transition. In the meanwhile, in reading it we see that it opens up to a meaning of philosophy as it is understood in the *curricula studiorum* and, that is, as an organic set of disciplines. But reading imposes for consideration here that philosophy is equivalent to divine wisdom and is characteristic of the divine being who gives himself in an activity of thought described as philosophical which, then, human beings, through love for philosophy, participate in, in their way. If divine love for philosophy involves love for wisdom, and wisdom is the divine ideas, the god who thinks himself is put forth as the model for human beings, and contemplation of the divine ideas becomes the focus of philosophical activity. Study will be able to reach a knowledge that is codified as philosophical. The second perfection is possible because the first perfection or "generazione sustanziale" (generation of substances) has given human beings a being whose nature is that of understanding and understanding implies the return to the first cause. Love for philosophy translates the intellectual being and essence of human beings.

Study, according to the hierarchy of the sciences given in the *Convivio*, which includes the old arts of trivium and quadrivium together with the new Aristotelian sciences in addition (and so physics and metaphysics placed in the same heaven, and then ethics,and then theology), will be able to reach a knowledge codified as theological at the highest level. In taking care to understand, it is useful for us that there is that distinction taken up by Thomas Aquinas, which put metaphysics forth as a three-headed science: transphysics (which the *Convivio*, in fact, places after physics), theology or divine science, and prima philosophia (first philosophy). Here is a fragment from the proem to Aquinas's *Metaphysics*:

> Secundum igitur tria praedicta, ex quibus perfectio huius scientiae attenditur, sortitur tria nomina. Dicitur enim scientia divina sive theologia, inquantum praedictas substantias considerat. Metaphysica, inquantum considerat ens et ea quae consequuntur ipsum. Haec enim transphysica inveniuntur in via resolutionis, sicut magis communia post minus communia. Dicitur autem prima philosophia, inquantum primas rerum causas

considerat. Sic igitur patet quid sit subiectum huius scientiae, et qualiter se habeat ad alias scientias, et quo nominetur.[47]

This is a knowledge that for Aquinas (commentary on the *Metaphysics*) is only divine but that for Dante can be the object of human knowledge. It was seen above how the wonders of the new lady were her beauty and, that is, the knowledge of the causes and principles. Actually, it is this thought that the allegorical commentary introduces. If this is true, the activity of study as proposed by Giacomo da Pistoia (*Quaestio de felicitate*, 1955), which guides us to its highest level, to the knowledge of a separate substance, is actually repronounced through the resumption of the educational canon. And Dante tells us that the sciences inspire the second perfection in us, and so education, and through familiarity with these (*habitus*), we can speculate on truth, "che è ultima perfezione nostra, sì come dice lo Filosofo nel sesto de l'Etica, quando dice che 'l vero è lo bene de lo intelletto" (this being our highest perfection, as Aristotle indicates in the *Ethics* [Book 6], when he says that the truth is the Good which fulfils the intellect; II.13.6). Here we are at a passage of the *Ethics* to which Dante will return in the third book, but it is clear that the true that coincides with the good as the aim of an intellectual activity or power makes the curricular educational program coincide with the highest knowledge characteristic of the *Metaphysics*, which is knowledge of the first being and knowledge of the universal causes and principles that we discussed as beings that belong to the divine thought.

If the highest science is theology, and in Aristotelian terms theology and metaphysics are linked, ethics is not contrasted with this content where the aim of ethics is metaphysics and the divine knowledge works as the model. But here in Dante's text the discourse plays out on the theory of influence, and if the heavens are sciences because they are moved by an intellectual being and *sciens*, the question that is posed is the following: What is human science and how is it possible to arrive at that science?

The meaning of this passage is not just that one arrives at the heavens by philosophical means as was elaborated. Rather, it is how our knowledge is similar to the intelligences' knowing. Dante seems to tell us two things: on the one hand, human beings can conquer knowledge with their intellectual forces, and on the other hand, the angels-intelligences that mediate divine light make us the ideal for that conquest. At the same time, it is the angelic paradigm that is constructed as a point of reference, and it is its science that occurs through the contemplation of a divine idea.

Does our intellectual essence seem to come from above, mediated by the intelligences and by sciences? In what sense can it be asserted that the heavens are sciences?

The relationship between the heavens and the sciences was already in twelfth-century works like that of Alain de Lille's *Anticlaudianus* or Restoro d'Arezzo's *La composizione del mondo*. Our discourse, though, deals with considering the resumption of this subject that Dante formulates when he asserts "dico che per cielo io intendo la scienza e per cieli le scienze" (by "heaven" I mean knowledge, and by "heavens" the various sciences; II.13.2), in light of the relationship between the angel-intelligences and divine wisdom.

In fact, the theory of the heavens defined as sciences (chapter 13) brings us back once again to the role of the intelligences, mediators of the divine, according to the modes that come to Dante from the *De causis* and where once again the theory of divine *sapientia* returns to what the being that has *scientia* corresponds. The angelic intellect, as a relational being between the divine being and heaven, is, as such, qualified to put into practice the archetypes that it sees in the divine mind as a second cause and at the same time it works in transmitting the sciences or the corpus of knowledges.

There are degrees of awareness that must be conquered in order to understand how in this part of the *Convivio* a mode already used and retraceable in other texts is taken up in order to direct it towards a resemanticization that is possible by virtue of the role assigned to the angel-intelligences. The idea that knowledge comes from God is a Platonic trace that is found, for example, in Marziano Capella's *Nozze di Mercurio e Filologia*. The same mode appears in Bonaventure's *De Reductione artium ad theologiam*.[48] But the heavens as sciences seem to testify to or suggest a method that penetrates in Dante and in his vocabulary, and it is that of giving a name, science, that implies here a unit made of two, heaven as *scientia* is such by virtue of *sciens*, which is the angelic intelligence, as mover, and by the heavenly body. It is in Albertus Magnus that the notion of heaven moved by a mover is recalled and the motion is attributed to the *science* of the mover itself. I am going, therefore, to cite some useful passages in Albertus Magnus's commentary on the *De causis* (93), and also look at the *De causis* in Thomas Aquinas's commentary on proposition 18 and at Siger's commentary on the *De causis*.

Let us then read first proposition 18 as it is in Aquinas's text: "Res omnes habent essentiam per ens primum, et res vivae omnes sunt motae per essentiam suam propter vitam primam, et res intelligibiles omnes habent scientiam propter intelligentiam primam" (All things have their essence thanks to the first being, and all living things are moved thanks to the first life and all things that are intelligible have knowledge thanks to the first intelligence). The explanation reports that the first intelligence gives *scientia* to its caused effects and each true science is not without intelligence and intelligence is the first being that has science and lets science flow: "Intelligentia dat causatis suis scientiam, quod est quia omnis scientia vera non est nisi intelligentia et intelligentia est primum sciens quod est et est influens scientiam super reliquia scientia" (The intellectual being gives to what it causes science, this is why every true science is together with intelligence,and intelligence is the first knowing being and influences science on other knowing beings) (100). But also to be considered are proposition 23, where it is reaffirmed that "proprietas intelligentiae est scientia" (it is proper to the intellectual being to have science), and proposition 31, where heaven is given as passive (in the *Convivio* the heavens are passive) and moved by intelligence and is defined as *medium*, mediator.[49]

We also find proposition 18 commented on in Albertus Magnus's commentary on *De causis* book 2, treatise 3.12: "Qualiter omnia intellectiva sciunt per intelligentia primam" (in which way all intellectual beings have knowledge in virtue the first intelligence) (149). Albert's position that holds that the first intelligence is the agent intellect universally acting on the intelligences that is then received in a different way is a mode that seems to generate reflection in Dante. And, again, in Albert (151), a useful synthesis is read where it is reaffirmed that the first intelligence is an intellectual being, and it is pure intellectuality: *intellectualitas.*

If the scientia of intellectual beings derive from the first intelligence, then the sciences in Dante are plural but they all come from a single being. When in the *Convivio* we read "[d]ico che per cielo io intendo la scienza e per cieli le scienze" ([b]y "heaven" I mean knowledge, and by "heavens" the various sciences; II.13.2), we can consider that if science is a human linguistic formulation received through angelic mediation, the principle on which this knowledge is founded and that Dante illustrates in the *Convivio* is essential for establishing the type of logic that presides over it. The angel-intelligences, according to the hierarchy recalled above, contemplate other intelligences and those purely contemplative intelligences are the divine ideas and the divine ideas are the *verbum*. Angelic knowledge is, therefore, the knowledge of the causes of things; science is knowing the first causes-ideas, and human beings also aim at that knowledge.

We also know that in the *Convivio*, the angel-intelligences contemplate the Trinity and contemplate it in its inner contemplarive relationships; the character of angelic knowledge seems to preside over the names of the angelic hierarchies. Their names imply the kind of contemplation of divine essence they do. For instance, in this treatise, Dante links the hierarchy of Thrones to the heaven of Venus and the science proper to this hierarchy is rhetoric. But because according to Gregory the Great and the Pseudo-Dyonisius, Thrones contemplate God as justice, it is justice that the *sciens* reads in God. Dante uses the hierarchy established by Gregory the Great (it was also in Brunetto) because he wants to tie Venus and rhetoric to the divine. Linking rhetoric to divine suggests that rhetoric is related to the field of the archetypes that are in the mind of God. This is a content we will read in the *Monarchia*. The angel-intelligences are *scientes*, the movement of the third heaven is the result of what they see. They inspire a higly intellectual speech; it tells the experience of contemplating a new lady. The word love implies here a personal and collective experience such as the speculation of the gentle lady will organize. What enters here is a universe of plural relations and in those a strong new meaning is given to rhetoric. Linguistic science, par excellence, is the science of civil conversation in which the science of government derives from God as the principle of justice. But much more can be read in such relations if we rethink the contents of the canzone in continuity with the prose. Speech and intelligence in the human being seem to be unified, as we read in the canzone, and the love for the new lady implies this background that is coincident with what we read in the *De vulgari eloquentia* about the origin of human language. There, God was the giver of a form from which came the result of speech and intelligence. In the prose of *Convivio*, the link between divine justice and rhetoric is also suggested, and again this sends us back to contents that the *De vulgari eloquentia* has already introduced and that we will touch on in the next chapter when we speak about the *honestum*.

The angelic hierarchies' contemplation as described in chapter 5 of this treatise, and which I have discussed above, goes on to incidentally suggest the relational character of the sciences based on the relation of the Trinity. For example, the grammar, linked to the heaven of the moon and said to be infinite, proposes the infinity of the possible constructions of the *gramma*. Grammar as the science at the basis of various learnings must be capable of pronouncing them and must be conceived as a discipline open to all the various possibilities. But Aquinas, who puts the *scientes* between eternity and time, suggests that the sciences are at the same time eternal and in a state of becoming. If God's ideas are infinite and eternal, then the linguistic modes are infinite and, in fact, grammar should be capable of pronouncing them.

But the mediators of this grammatical infinity are the intelligences of the lowest hierarchy that in the organization chart of the *Convivio* contemplate a one and trine God. The meaning of this relationship involves a logic that puts into a strong relationship between the three sciences of the trivium as linguistic disciplines according to modes that were explored and put into practice in the curricula. The sciences constructed as *processio* – linguistic universes emerging from the divine mind and penetrating the world trhough the mediation of the *scientes* and aiming towards God (the *reditus)* in virtue of the *sciens* – requires that we understand who is the subject who can realize such return. It is the concept of *sciens* that may need to be enlarged in light of the entrance of the new lady.

The concept of heaven includes, therefore, its synonym, science, which is actually the knowledge that the intelligence sees in God, mirroring itself, since the species it possesses. The supremacy of intellectual values through heavenly influence is here confirmed. But if the heaven-sciences are linguistic universes of an infinite potentiality, such are the ideas in the divine mind according to Aquinas (Wippel 1993), they seem to be the actuals of the possibles. As is known, in *Paradiso*, the sciences disappear and only the heavens remain. The *donna gentile* as philosophy (which is activated in different linguistic beings) would be, on the allegorical level, divine wisdom or a representation of the divine ideas.

Philosophy and the desire to know, taken up from the incipit of the *Metaphysics* and on which the *Convivio* opened, coincide. Human beings aim at the knowledge of the causes and principles (and the causes are separate substances) here in this life, but the discourse of the *Convivio* contains other hypotheses, other temptations and inflections. See, for example, how in chapter 14 a different thing is said from what we read in chapters 9 and 10 where it is affirmed that metaphysics deals with the first substances, "le quali noi non potemo simigliantemente intendere se non per li loro effetti" (which similarly we cannot know except through their effects; II.14.8).

In concluding this section, I want to underline here what the names of the angelic hierarchies imply in Dante's culture. In general, it is assumed that the names of the angels are set in relation to God. Iin Dionysius's *De caelesti hierarchia* (in Migne 1879, *PL* Vol. 122, chap. 4) it reads, "quod significet angelorum cognominatio" (which is the meaning of the names ofangels) (1046), and this idea is also found in Albertus Magnus's commentary (79): "praeterea nomina eorum imponuntur secundum immediate deo assistere [...] quae omnia dicunt relationem ad inferius, videtur, quod non debeant dici angeli" (their names are given according to their relation to God ... all names that say a relation with inferior beings cannot be called angels). In Albert's *Super Dionysium De caelesti hierarchia* (66), we read that t the names of angels make manifest the divine illumination.[50] In Dionysius, again, we read that angels are *scientia*.

This passage of the *Convivio*, then, apparently neutral, is to be read in its strong relationship to the discourse of what the intellects see and the discource of the idea-form-gods or ideas, but it also opens and suggests that if the *scientiae* in angelic mediation enter in time and in becoming, but are of divine origin, human beings, where they look for philosophy, seek those plural knowledges that philosophy as the love of *sapientia* gathers. They seek them aiming at the highest possibility of seeing the principles and causes. They therefore identify love for science with tension towards the divine, divine ideas, and divine wisdom that the word "philosophy" (*philos sophos*) expresses. It is true that in the second book this meaning is not yet made explicit. Essentially, knowledge as structured by the *curricula studiorum* has at its highest level theology, which in the recurrent distinction is divided between metaphysics and theology. Metaphysics is at the same time divine science, the science of the causes and principles, and first philosophy, as knowledge of the first being. Actually, in order to construct this chain of deductions, I used a definition of philosophy (love of wisdom) that the *Convivio* does not offer in the second book but in the third. In doing so, we anticipated a synthesis that the text does not want taking shape in the second book. The significance of this postponing, however, is evident. Philosophical knowledge leads to knowledge of separate substances. Said in other terms, human beings' fulfillment occurs in knowledge and culminates in the highest knowledge. The significance of the educational system is in the ascending and aims at reaching perfection. Philosophical knowledge, in its ascending being and essence, and in the shift from one science to another, is an activity that leads us to speculation. But if the heavens are sciences, by virtue of the *sciens*, which is an angel-intelligence, human beings also participate in their way in that perfection through the sciences up to the highest science that allows us to know the causes of things (*Metaphysics*). Furthermore, if the true is the good that fulfills the intellect, it will be the tension towards this true that the sciences allow. Ethics aim at metaphysics in its meaning of the science of the causes and principles. It is at this point that the being and essence of the *donna gentile* reveal themselves or should reveal themselves as a separate substance without motor operation and thus be assimilable to the divine ideas. But actually, various pieces are missing to arrive at that synthesis. The axes of vision relocated in our proceeding as readers were determined to reach that meaning, but that meaning will be given in its entirety in the third book.

The theory that the heavens are sciences because they are moved by the intellectual being that is *sciens* and that sees the idea-archetypes of creation in the divine mind opens up to another possibility, that of the intelligences, mediators of the divine ideas in creation and co-audience to creation. The theory of creation through *intelligentia*, which the *De causis* expounds, is suggested within this chapter that opens up to the heavens as sciences: If they mediate ideas or archetypes or causes of things, their task is also that of second causes. Here, not only is a theory of influence suggested but also that of creation, perhaps of its continuation in time that occurs with the collaboration of the angel-intelligences. This is a knowledge that comes from the *De causis* (see D'Ancona Costa 1995) and about which more can be said after reading the third book.[51] It is worth, in the meantime, recalling that the philosophical study that was introduced as possible for human beings is suggested as a divine and angelic activity in which human beings can participate. This leads us towards positions and subjects that the Parisian prohibition of 1277 had already stigmatized, and if the censor had already expressed himself on the condemnation of the philosophy, other positions condemned in Paris in 1277 (which we reproduce in a note) are in relation to what this part of the *Convivio* discusses.[52]

3 Reading with *Suspicio*: Mind and Philosophy. A Philosophical Discussion about Mind

TREATISE III, PART 1

1. The Canzone: Amor che ne la mente mi ragiona

In the opening of this chapter, I will briefly summarize the contents that the canzone *Amor che ne la mente mi ragiona* introduces in the doctrinal treatise. Like *Voi che'ntendendo il terzo ciel movete,* the text will be read following Dante's methods and in its independence from the prose commentary. *Amor che ne la mente mi ragiona* was in fact written during the Florentine years, and probably close to the time in which Dante wrote the first canzone (*Voi che 'ntendendo il terzo ciel movete*), on which the second treatise of *Convivio* will comment. The continuity the poet organizes between the two canzoni is an important element in any attempt to understand the meaning of each poem. An essential preliminary consideration shapes our reading of the treatise: the true meaning of the *Convivio* cannot be reached by isolating the prose from the poems. As in *Voi che 'ntendendo il terzo ciel movete,* the focus of the canzone is the love for the new lady, love and intellection are one and the same thing, and this love aims at discussing and establishing human intellectual power. The canzone is not only doctrinal but also highly organized rhetorically. The complex figure of *transumptio,* the *ornatus difficilis* of the thirteenth-century *Poetriae,* shapes the language of *Amor che ne la mente mi ragiona,* in which one thing is said but another must be understood. Dante, in addition, identifies the canzone as praise. Praise and the transumptive mode, traditionally part of the theological tradition, inaugurate a discourse partially in conflict with theology. Boncompagno da Signa's *Rhetorica novissima* and Alanus of Lille's *Regulae caelestis iuris* are texts useful to understanding how Dante works with tradition in order to reshape it. Another traditional element is the opening of the canzone, in which the connection between love and the interior word harks back to contents Dante introduced in his first book, the *Vita nuova*. Among the contents of *Amor che ne la mente mi ragiona*, the following are the most important:

1. Love is represented as a relation between the mind and the lady, where mind is proposed as an activity of reasoning and desiring: "Amor che nella mente mi ragiona / della mia donna disiosamente" (Love, that speaks to me within my mind with fervent desire of my lady).

2. The interior word is proposed as having an obscure relation with the intellectual activity: "Lo suo parlar sì dolcemente sona / che l'anima ch' ascolta e che lo sente / dice" (His speech is filled with sounds so sweet / That then my soul, which hears and feels him, says). The suggestion is that the canzone's discourse is about human thinking that is shaped by the interior word and establishing a kind of equation between interior word and intellectual cognition.

3. A likeness is introduced between the being of the new lady and the divine thinking. The *donna gentile* is represented as part of God's thought and in an obscure relation to the origin of the universe: "costei pensò Chi mosse l'universo" (She has been thought by Him who set the universe in motion; 72). The language of praise, which is used, intends to introduce the readers to the divine identity of the gentle lady.

4. The *donna gentile* is proposed as an idea in the mind of God. She is contemplated by both the heavenly intellects and the human mind.

As an idea that is divine and a separate substance, according to what we read, she receives the divine light as the angel who sees Him – "In lei discende la Virtù divina / si come face in angel che L vede" (Into her descends celestial power as it does into an angel that sees him; 37–8) – and is contemplated by heavenly intellects – "Ogn' Intelletto di lassu la mira" (Every intelligence admires her from above, 23). That she is contemplated by such intellects suggests that Dante is introducing contents of Neoplatonic derivation that Aquinas discusses in two of his latest works: the commentary on the *Liber de causis* and the *De substantiis separatis*. In light of both these works, the identity of the new lady can be delineated in terms of the contents she brings on the page.

What is in play here is a discourse about the identity of the human mind. This mind is linked to the lady through love and is represented as part of the intellectual beings that are privileged to have a relation with her. In this light, the human mind seems to be the true focus of the canzone. The love for the new lady aims at unveiling the mind's cognitive power.

The continuity established with the first canzone, once understood, is of great help. In *Voi che 'ntendendo il terzo ciel movete,* it was a celestial spirit mediated by the intelligences of the third heaven and described as gifted with the activity of speech that originated the love-speculation for the new lady. The notion of human mind seems to be introduced here following a pathway that can be defined as Albertine. For example, Albert's commentary on the *Liber de causis*, where God is proposed as the giver of forms, appears to be an appropriate reference. In the canzone, a spirit-form that comes from the third heaven creates in the character who says "I" an intellectual desire towards a form or separate substance or divine idea. It is in virtue of this form and of the kind of desire it creates that we may define the nature of such love as intellectual, while the nature of the mind that loves seems suggested as similar to that of the intellects or separate substances.

Proceeding in our reading, we see that the second canzone approaches diverse fields in order to construct a new whole. An Augustinian area (interior word) lives close to a Neoplatonic one (a form given, the ideas in the mind of God), and both are organized in an Aristotelian context. Pivotal readings here are not only those by Augustine but also the *Liber de causis* in the commentary of Albert the Great and Aquinas, and, as mentioned above, Aquinas's *De substatiis separatis*. In addition, Aristotelian contents can be referred to Albert, Aquinas, and perhaps Siger of Brabant. Different linguistic formulations seem to be used to give an answer to the same problematic issue – namely, the power and limits of human knowledge. Especially impressive is Dante's purpose of rethinking and organizing different lines of thought. The author, in fact, seems to ascertain how very different lines of thought are directed to the same goal through different traditions and linguistic formulations: truth can be sought in different ways.

The problematic issue of human knowledge is at stake here. The word "intellect," which appears throughout the canzone, requires investigation, starting from its relation to the word "soul." The break between soul and intellect announced in a trasumptive mode in *Voi che 'ntendendo il terzo ciel movete* is reiterated in this canzone. The soul laments her inability to understand the interior word of love, a word previously introduced as the result of the intellectual tie between the mind and the lady. The word "soul," linked to both "sentire" and intellectual "listening," shows the double nature of the human being as at once sensitive and intellectual: Lo suo parlar sì dolcemente sona, / che l'anima ch'ascolta e che lo sente" (His speech is filled with sounds so sweet that then my soul, which hears and feels him, says; 5–6).[1]

The canzone introduces praise, which is programmatically addressed to the lady: "Però, se lle mie rime avran difetto / ch'entraron nella lode di costei" (And so if fault is found to mar my verse which undertakes the praise of her; 14–15). According to Aquinas, who resumes an old medieval tradition, praise is identified as an intellectual language proper to the angels when they speak to God (*Summa theologia* 1.107.1). Because of it, praise here confirms the identity of the lady as related to the divine being.[2] That a human being can use the language of praise in this context reiterates the intellectual nature of this being as part of the contents the canzone intends to establish: a nature partially similar to that of the angel-intelligences.

However, a more complex thought penetrates here because praise in this canzone is grounded in the double identity of the lady. On one hand, she is an intellectual, heavenly being. The adjective "gentile," in its correspondence to "noble," further enhances her intellectual nature. On the other hand, she seems to be an earthly creature. The lady thus belongs to both the earth and the heavens, and it is in virtue of her duality that the sun during its diurnal rotation can see her as the most noble object of vision: "Non vede il sol che tutto il mondo gira / cosa tanto gentil, quanto 'n quell'ora / che luce nella parte ove dimora / la donna di cui dire amore mi face" (The sun that circles all the world sees nothing so gentle as at that time when it shines upon the place where dwells the lady of whom love makes me speak; 19–22).

A separate substance that is both heavenly and earthly is a new content that requires a further level of understanding. The reader first needs to be aware of the intellectual debates of the time and of the different answers put forth regarding human knowledge. Such lines of thought, however, do not furnish an exhaustive answer. The different elements that enter to create the discourse of the canzone have to be evaluated recalling what Dante wrote in his *De vulgari eloquentia*. There he defined the canzone as a "fascio" or bundle composed of many "fili" or threads. Within the canzone's "fascio," there are no doubt many contents, including the many lines of medieval thought that derive from philosophy, theology, and rhetoric.

Amor che ne la mente mi ragiona's philosophical contents are largely shaped by the eclectic thinking of Albertus Magnus. Albert assumes that the possible intellect can contemplate the agent intellect in life and as form – that is, as a separate substance. In addition, he assumes that the possible intellect is a separate being and a form given by God. This matches what we read in the two canzoni, thus strengthening the continuity between them.

Albert, however, is not the only thread in the canzone, *Amor che ne la mente mi ragiona*. Dante's "fascio" also includes filaments that come from what we indicate as a heterodox field. To be evaluated here is the following issue: What light does the synchronous debate shed on the representation of the gentle lady as an object of contemplation on the part of the heavenly intellects, God, and human beings? Aquinas informs his readers that this is a most controversial content.

In his *De unitate intellectus contra averroistas*, Aquinas writes that if one is the intellected object (*intellectum*) from the part of different beings this means that there is only one intellect. Aquinas here rejects this theory that he thinks is derived by Averroes. To combine beings of a different nature in the action of *intelligere*, Aquinas thinks, is implicitly to affirm that there is one intellect not just for all human beings but for all thinking beings.[3] This is one of the tracks we may follow in order to identify in the canzone a crucial content that is obscurely introduced. The topic enters in *Amor che ne la mente mi ragiona* in connection with the theory of the *verbum*, which, according to the Christian tradition, is in fact thought by God, the angels, and human beings. To retrace this content is of great importance because it shows that Dante is shaping his discourse in an effort to rethink an entire tradition in light of new controversial topics. One must not ignore that the theory of the oneness of the intellect was a content highly debated in Dante's time. Dante's most illustrious contemporaries, like Albert and Aquinas (among others), were coping with this challenging issue. Dante's true contribution is not his assent to such theory; rather, it is his ability to rethink the debated issue concerning the unity of intellectual knowledge in light of the theory of the *verbum*. The theme is announced in the canzone and will return in the prose section; it is, in fact, presented in the very first chapter of the doctrinal treatise. There the cognitive goal is immediately announced by way of the incipit from Aristotle's *Metaphysics*, which Dante proceeds to connect with the biblical "pan delli angeli" – that is, the *verbum*.

Looking at articles from the condemnations of 1270 and 1277, we will see in the following chapters that a few of them are related to the territory Dante opens up. For instance, the contemplation of a separate substance in mortal life is related to the field of prohibited beliefs. However, it is also true that Albert accepts partially some tenets derived from the thinking of the commentator. The contemplation in life of a separate substance on the part of the human being is one such tenet. He also agrees that such contemplation is the highest happiness the human being can reach in this life. Albert strongly rejected, however, the theory of the possible intellect as one – that is, he was opposed to the theory of the uniqueness of the intellect.

The question now arises: Does the invention of the gentle lady enter into a controversial heterodox field? Aquinas and Albert had both designated as erroneous the Averroistic theory of the intellect as one. We actually know that this was the main error that Greek-Arabic thought produced, as in the rereading of Averroes, and that was circulating in Europe. It is difficult to exclude the possibility that Dante was fascinated by some heterodox tenets. The *Convivio* shows, however, that he draws freely from the edifice of Aristotelianism, rethinking and reshaping crucial problematic issues linking Platonism and theology to the Aristotelian encyclopedia.

To speak about Dante's penchant for heterodoxy, we must clarify the meaning of the word itself. We do not accept, for instance, as has often been done, that heterodoxy necessarily opposes Aquinas, who is taken to be the champion of orthodoxy. We use the word aware that, in the face of the condemnations (especially that of 1277), many issues were assumed as heterodox that really were not. The condemnations require that we bring to our task as posthumous readers a historical awareness. That is, in the light of it we must make distinctions. That many contents were condemned because they were close to others that actually deserved to be condemned is well known today. It is, in fact, well known that certain contents that were condemned were part of the thinking of Albert and Aquinas.

There is no doubt that the true problematic issue, as medieval historians of philosophy have underlined, is the doctrine concealed in the theory of the unique intellect. The theory of an intellect that was unique, separate, and eternal, and as such proper to the whole of humankind, was linked, as Aquinas stresses, to the mortality of the individual soul and to the theory of the eternity of the world. It implicitly denies the biblical creation, as well as the value of individual moral choices. By proposing the *donna gentile* as a separate substance contemplated by God, angelic intelligences, and the human mind, the canzone introduced a "hot topic," in which the true invention was not so much the identity of the gentle lady but that of the mind that contemplates her.

The human mind can be defined in the canzone as a kind of mathematical "incognita" that the reader is called upon to detect. This unknown element, to be evaluated through the description of the *donna gentile*, is the logical subject of the canzone. All the different contents of the canzone converge in her. This is one of the true inventions of *Amor che ne la mente mi ragiona*. In a mix of philosophical and rhetorical ability, Dante employs tools already activated in his first poetic activity and in the *Vita nuova* and utilizes them to introduce new contents.

Augustine's *De doctrina christiana*, the notion of the difficult as beautiful and formative for the reader, the *ornatus difficilis*, and a strong awareness of the rhetorical language of figures preside over the invention of the *donna gentile*. Dante's use of *transumptio*, once recognized, is of great help here. Dante imposes names by using the technique of *modus transumendi*. This obliges the reader to complete the mosaic that the poet has organized. To grasp the identity of the human mind from that of the gentle lady requires study, as well as a reader who is able to work with both intuition and logic. Like Cavalcanti's "Donna me prega," but for different reasons, *Amor che ne la mente mi ragiona* is a turning point in the history of Western poetry.

Several notions, some of them derived from controversial, and in a few cases heterodox, contents that I will discuss in the section devoted to the commentaries, are useful in introducing the reader. One, shared by various thinkers, is that in separate beings the thinking being (the *intelligens*) and what is thought (*intellectum*) are one and the same thing: "intelligens and intellectus in separatis est idem." The identity of the gentle lady, whom the canzone clearly indicates as a separate substance, thus throws light on the identity of the mind that contemplates her. In addition, by recalling both Aquinas and Albert, we are directed to other crucial issues. The lady, we recall, is an object of contemplation on the part of God and heavenly intellects, from a community identified through a collective name, "gente," all sharing the same object of contemplation. This sheds light on the common attitude of different heterogeneous beings in the medieval hierarchy. Of course, the canzone merely suggests this idea, and it is the close reading of the treatise that will reveal what this attitude signifies.

In addition, because the gentle lady in the canzone is one or unique, even though many people gaze upon her, it is the collective name "gente" that suggests that Dante is considering a plurality – which the collective name refers to – as one. This would perhaps anticipate what we read in the *Monarchia*, where *humanitas* is the collective name for a thinking subject to be identified as the common possible intellect. If this analysis is correct, then Dante would be involved in perhaps exploring one of the most dangerous philosophical contents of his time, but in a way peculiar to him, namely, through the link that he introduces between the *donna gentile* and the notion of *verbum*. Understanding the canzone thus requires an evaluation not only of Dante's relation with contents assumed to be heterodox but also his attitude to rethink them and reorganize them in a new complex whole.

It should be noted that in the *Inferno*, Dante speaks of heresy, not heterodoxy. Canto 10 condemns heresy as a sin that is certainly linked to the Averroistic theory of intellect conceived as one. Dante concentrates here on the Epicureans – that is, followers of the philosophy of Epicurus who believed that the soul dies with the body. This theory has been related to Averroism, as it was criticized by Aquinas, who reasoned that Averroes's theory of the possible intellect thought as separate and one, implied that the individual soul dies with the body and that what endures eternally is the common intellectual soul. The canzone, to be sure, does not indicate at all that Dante is following such ideas. Nevertheless, the reader is invited to realize that the *donna gentile* – as eternal, separate, and one – suggests indirectly that the mind that contemplates her is also endowed with these same qualities.

Discussing the prose commentary, I will use texts by Albert and Boethius of Dacia's *De summo bono* in order to decode Dante's position. With these theories in mind, we come to see that Dante, through the love for the gentle lady, enters the area of intellectual happiness. This is confirmed when we consider how the word "intellect" is used in the canzone, where a distinction is made between a single thinking subject and one impersonal and no doubt plural subject. This content is reiterated in the prose chapters of the third treatise.

I will revisit these topics when I take up the prose section. In concluding this section, it is useful to emphasize that the canzone is deeply linked to Cavalcanti's canzone "Donna me prega." Dante's canzone quotes and echoes a crucial fragment of Cavalcanti's poem, but as a point of dialectical contradiction. Dante does not deny intellection to the individual. His idea about the human intellect shows his own unique way of considering it. The relation he suggests in the verse text between the *donna gentile* and the *-logos-verbum* – a relation the prose will confirm and intensify – testifies that Dante shapes an idea of human being intellect that is most personal.

He runs alongside the field of heterodoxy but the result is not heterodox at all. More than revealing Dante's conviction within the parameters of heterodox thinking, the canzone anticipates an intellectual attitude to rethink traditional contents in light of a new thinking. The writing appears to be an effort to compare and approach contents that are apparently distant from each other. The crucial result of the canzone is that the love for the *donna gentile* introduces a link between the theory of the intellect as one and the theory of the *verbum-logos*. The idea that human beings think together seems to be a point of long reflection for Dante.The *Convivio* opens to the *Monarchia* but it is not a continous line that drives the reader; on the contrary, Dante's thought is inscribed in a discontinous one.

The invention of the *donna gentile* is superb, not just because it is a new contribution to the debate about love and human knowledge, but because the love she inspires is considered as the shining forth of an inner essence. The true rhetorical intuition of the canzone lies in its use of *transumptio* as a logical and rhetorical mode that makes the language of poetry even more powerful. Dante seems to be aware of Boncompagno da Signa interpretation of *transumptio,* in which an Augustinian tenet works with others derived from the thirteenth century *Poetriae.* If, according to Boncompagno, in the figure of *transumptio* one thing is said and another must be understood, then in Dante's canzone, the thing to be understood is the nature of the mind that loves the gentle lady. The identity of the mind is the true centre of the canzone. Furthermore, poetry is revealed as the language most suited to pronounce these issues. Dante actually writes two commentaries, at least for the first two canzoni: one literal, the other allegorical. He assigns to the poetry of the thirteenth century the role that traditionally has been attributed to the great poems of antiquity and to the *sacra pagina.* It is the transumptive mode of both the literal and allegorical commentaries that, while confirming the philosophical nature of the canzone, introduces the political goal of the treatise. Poetry and poetics are linked. The link creates a political goal for poetry and for the prose that will comment on it, as our reading will attempt to trace.

2. Praise and Friendship: The Anagogical Sense

My reading of the third treatise starts by considering the relationship between the canzone *Amor che ne la mente mi ragiona* and the prose text that comments it. I do so in an attempt to verify whether the meanings

I have found in the canzone (Ardizzone 2011) and proposed as the thesis of a thought in progress are confirmed in the prose. I start by considering a few sections of the text. The suggested manifold relations require, on the reader's part, a mind able to activate a synchronous reading, in which the temporal sequence of the chapters is transformed into an intellectual simultaneity.

Let me underline at the outset that my reading proceeds through the elaboration of a few *suspiciones* – "suspicions" or suspected inferences – activated by many different contents that refer to synchronous debates of Dante's time. The canzoni, and the later *Convivio*, introduce the reader to many issues related to these debates. In my reading of the canzoni (Ardizzone 2011), I have traced a line of thought Dante has drawn while organizing the framework of his love for the gentle lady. I have also emphasized a content that lies at the centre of Dante's construction – that is, the problematic notion of the human intellect. My reading of the third treatise aims at establishing that it shows Dante's fascination with the notion of possible intellect thought of as common and separate, a notion derived from an Averroistic tenet that, however, Dante reshapes in a most personal way. What is important in this assumption is the tie the *Convivio* organizes between theories of knowing and a strong civil awarness. Dante's idea of happiness that conjugates the idea of intellectual knowledge with that of a political happiness opens up to a better understanding of the nature of the treatise and of the *Convivio* in general.

According to my reading, the construction of the theory of the intellect therefore lies at the centre of the *Convivio*. It paves the way to Dante's position in the *Monarchia*, which straightly enunciates the idea that the possible intellect is better actualized by the many. The construction of the theory of intellect was part of Dante's reflection since the time he was writing the first two canzoni, as Dante will commentate in the *Convivio*. The importance of social life as the natural status of the individual is part of this discussion. The correspondence between social life and intellectual life as naturally motivated seems to be a content that Dante strongly reflects on during his writing of the treatise.

Written in endecasyllables, structured in allusive language, and constructed on the *sub-intendue* or "implied meanings," the canzoni we call "dottrinali" were shaped largely on the use of the *ornatus difficilis* in an alliance of rhetoric and philosophy as the hallmark of Dante's innovative writing. This mode, which Dante confirms in the prose text and theoretically explains in *De vulgari eloquentia*, was first introduced in the *Vita nuova* (chapter 25). There, Dante anticipates that prose must be written like poetry, and that poetry furnishes the model for the writing of prose. The prose of the *Convivio* assumes in part as its model the language of poetry. Strategies of writing, for instance, are introduced as part of the *figurae* or barbarisms permitted to poets. Among these, we may list equivocal words or constructions and amphiboly as strategic tools that introduce a central meaning that is not explicitly given but needs to be inferred. To such strategies of writing there must correspond a strategy of reading. One such strategy can be activated if we assume as *habitus* the activity of *suspicio* or *suppositio*. I use this word to indicate the state of mind of the reader who, following Dante's discussion and its organization, elaborates a *suppositio* or *suspicio* of a meaning that the text itself produces, but in a way that is for the most part hidden. *Suspicio* belongs to a level of certitude that rhetorical argumentation produces. Aquinas uses this word *suspicio* in his *Proemium* to his commentary on Aristotle's *Posteriorum Analyticorum*. Here he is referring to rhetoric as part of the logic called "inventive," which he distinguishes from that of poetry and which deals with arguments whose premises produce *suspicio*, or the inclination to accept one position rather than its opposite.[4]

I start with the first chapter – in particular, the section in which we read that there is no better discourse about love than that which praises the beloved (III.1.4). Dante introduces the verb "commendare," a vernacularization of the Latin "commendare" (to celebrate or to honour) and links the theme of praise to friendship. Friendship, he writes, requires that difference be transformed into likeness. Dante here recalls Aristotle's *Nicomachean Ethics*: "si come dice il filosofo nel nono nell'amistade delle persone dissimili di stato conviene, a conservazione di quella, una proporzione essere intra loro, che la dissimilitudine a similitudine quasi reduca" (as the philosopher says in the ninth book of the *Ethics*, in a friendship of persons of unequal rank there must exist, in order to preserve it, a relation between them that in some way transforms the unlikeness into likeness; III.I.7). This is introduced in order to establish, through friendship, an anagogical content as the following passage clarifies:

> Per che io, considerando me minore che questa donna, e veggendo me beneficiato da lei,[proposi] di lei commendare secondo la mia facultade, la quale, se non simile è per sé, almeno la pronta volontade mostra ... e così si fa simile a quella di questa gentil donna.

> Therefore, considering myself inferior to this lady and finding myself benefited by her, I resolved to praise her according to the scope of my power, which, if it is not in itself similar to her, at least shows my eager desire. For if I were able to do more, I would do so. In this way, then, my power becomes similar to that of this gentle lady. (III. 1.9)

But the *Nicomachean Ethics* is rethought here in light of a tradition that goes beyond itself. To understand what is being said, the reader must enlarge his or her intellectual perspective by making the given meaning more inclusive. A few key words allow us to understand the nature of Dante's "new love." One belongs to the sphere of praise: the identity of the gentle lady becomes a focal point because she is the one to whom praise is given.

Aristotle's discussion of friendship, in which difference is transformed into likeness, because it is here connected with praise, introduces a tension that is both anagogical and linguistic. For Dante, praise in fact implies an intellectual dimension that characterizes the virtue of the woman and her excellence. Intellectual as well is the language that speaks about her. The continuity here is evident with the canzone *Amor che ne la mente mi ragiona* that Dante himself identifies with praise: "Dunque, se le mie rime avran difetto / ch'entreran nella loda di costei" (And so if fault is found to mar my verse which undertakes the praise of her; 14–15).

The identity of the *donna gentile* is confirmed as intellectual. Dante has shaped this identity ever since the first canzone, *Voi che 'ntendendo il terzo ciel movete*. He now reintroduces it through praise as a tool able to express the desire for that being the canzone has clearly set out to praise. Dante writes, "impresi dunque a lodare questa donna,e non come si convenisse,almeno innanzi quanto io potesse; e cominciai a dire: *Amor che ne la mente mi ragiona*" (I therefore undertook to praise this lady, and if not in a fitting manner, at least insofar as I was able; and I began by saying *Love, that speaks to me within my mind*; III.1.13).

Friendship is a relation between two human beings who, though separate, are spiritually connected. Friendship, however, which Aristotle links with praise in the *Nicomachean Ethics* (8.14.4) becomes more complex now. In fact, the old theme ("se le mie rime avran difetto / ch'entreran ne la loda di costei") – that is, the *modus laudis* of *Amor che ne la mente mi ragiona* – enters again, to which the commentary adds the Aristotelian reference. For Aristotle, friendship is part of civil life, and it is related to civil life in Cicero's *Lelius* or *De amicitia*, a work that the

Convivio has recalled in its second treatise as a text that Dante was reading after the death of Beatrice, and important in what he indicates as his conversion to philosophy.

If the friendship for the gentle woman is introduced in continuity with the contemplation, according to what we have read in the canzone, of a separate substance – a kind of contemplation that is close to that proposed in book 10 of the *Nicomachean Ethics* as the highest virtue and perfect form of happiness – our reading takes into consideration the possibility that the friendship for the gentle lady, linked to praise, could introduce, in the prose of the *Convivio*, a larger meaning, thus empowering what my reading of the canzone *Amor che ne la mente mi ragiona* has suggested. My reading of the canzone, in fact, has pointed out that the love for the *donna gentile* was lived as a form of contemplation by the mind of the character who says "I," but is shared by the human beings conceived as a community.

In the prose of III.1, friendship is introduced into a discourse which until now was expressed in terms of love, Dante was perhaps bringing on surface a line of reflection already active in the canzone. According to Aristotle, friendship is not just a private link; he indicates also the natural link among humans as friendship, and he assumes that the civil friendship is superior to private friendship (*Politics*, 1.1), while in the *Nicomachean Ethics*, friendship is the basic bond of state (8.1.4). The most interesting aspect to be understood, however, is the tie Dante establishes between friendship for the gentle lady and knowledge, suggesting that the notion of friendship penetrates to affect that of knowledge.

We have seen that the opening of the treatise confirms the gentle woman as an intellectual being. The vocabulary suggests this intellectual nature when we read that she is related to excellence and virtue: "eccellenza manifesta" (manifest excellence), "considerazione de la sua virtude" (consideration of her virtue), "intendimento de la sua grandissima virtude" (the understanding of her greatest virtue; II.1.12). The reader naturally wishes to be immediately aware of the nature of this virtue. The text, however, as we have noted, usually reveals its significance if we organize a reading in which the first level of meaning is considered only as a step towards a new meaning, as it results from the interaction of different forms of learning. The reader must activate a continuous transfer of meanings, which makes the contents of the text more powerful. Here, if we connect the field of "considerare" and "intendere" with that of virtue, we are led once again to evaluate the link between contemplation and Aristotle's ethical teaching. We cannot reach a meaning, however, unless we are aware of Dante's method, in which different cultural lines are brought together on the same page.

Consideration (from "consideranza"), although a key word in the field of mysticism, does not introduce here meanings related to this line of thought; rather, it launches the idea of the union of the human mind with a being that *Amor che ne la mente mi ragiona* has suggested as a separate substance, superior to the human being. This content renvoys us to the debate on knowledge, as it takes place in relation to the reading of Aristotle's philosophy. We cannot grasp the meaning of this treatise in fact without invoking Aristotle's *Nicomachean Ethics* in its relation to his *Metaphysics*, in particular book 12. In book 10 of the *Nicomachean Ethics*, in fact, the highest virtue is the intellectual virtue of contemplation (10.7.7) and such contemplation is described as similar to God's thinking activity that Aristotle introduces in 10.8. Dante structures here a level of what he indicates as the anagogical sense in the second treatise, which he explains as "sovrasenso," and as what "spiritualmente s'intende" (which is spiritually intended) that, as he writes, "per le cose significate significa delle superne cose dell'etternal gloria" (signifies by means of the things signified a part of the supernal things of eternal glory).[5] This sense occurs when the things signified bring a meaning, which sends us to the eternal superior things. No doubt that the *donna gentile* has to be understood as enclosing a spiritual meaning which sends the reader to celestial and eternal beings. The word "anagogical" derives from "anagogé," its meaning being what brings up, and in this sense it was used by Pseudo-Dyonisius as Roques (1966, 57) underlines: anagogia implies the function of lifting up as proper to the angelic orders. In this context has an anagogical function also the language of praise[6] that the canzone *Amor che ne la mente mi ragiona* has openly used following the line that has been inaugurated in "Donne ch'avete intelletto d'amore" and in the *Vita nuova,* and which the prose here reiterates.

The relation between what is indicated as the analogical sense and the *Donna gentile* as a separate substance (her excellence) to be praised – in which the language of praise is used in order to make similar what is not such – if read in light of the *Nicomachean Ethics* seems to repronounce and rethink in the Aristotelian language contents already thought and assimilated in a different context and perspective. Once more, the love for the gentle lady must therefore be read in light of the problematic issue of knowledge, with which the *Convivio* opens its first treatise: "Tutti gli uomini naturalmente desiderano di sapere" (all men by nature desire to know). It is also through knowledge that human beings fulfil their nature, which is both intellectual and political. That knowledge is a desire proper to all human beings implies a *de facto* community that the sharing of the same goal makes one. Such unity is a category most pervasive of Dante's reflection since the time of *Vita nuova*, as the language of praise manifests, because prayers, and praise as part of it, are expression of the unity of the people accomunated by such activity and lifted up in the contemplation of the One.[7] This is just a facet of the poet's pathway of reflection; as we will see, in many ways he will formulate the idea that a naturally founded unity is the basis for a political unity. Later in the *Convivio*, he will make use of the adjective "compagnevole" to express such natural basis that seems to translate Aristotle's "political" animal (IV.4.1). In the *Monarchia*, he will assert in a most essential way that the human intellectual potentiality can be better actualized by the entire human community. Summarizing what has been said, praise and friendship, if related to the being of the *donna gentile* as separate substance, open up a new way to read this section of the *Convivio*, in which ethics and knowledge seem to interact with a social-political awereness.[8]

In what follows, I select a few sections of the prose text in order to confirm my hypothesis regarding Dante's method and contents. The reader will remember that I have previously suggested such a method as a process of composition in which different tiles are organized to create an ensemble in which various contents enter. They are organized as blocks in which there is no break between the fields but rather continuity.

After the field of praise is introduced through the verb "commendare" (1.4; 1.9), we read that "intra dissimili amistà esser non possa" (for since there can be no friendship between those who are unalike). A fragment from Aristotle's *Nicomachean Ethics* is highly useful on this point: "Similitudo est per se causa amiciziae . . . factiva e conservativa" (Likeness is the cause that makes friendship and preserves it; 8.3). Love induces the author or, better, the character who says "I," to praise the lady: "Amore lo porta a dire e a lodare la donna" (Love brings him to say of and praise the lady; 1.4). The text quotes the *Nicomachean Ethics* to show that praise works as a form of language that introduces a proportion by which difference and unlikeness (*dissomiglianza*) are reduced to similarity. Then, the author shows his intention to reveal the quality and excellence of the woman who has changed his previous love for

Beatrice: "Ché per la sua eccellenza manifesta avere si può considerazione della sua vertude; e per lo 'ntendimento della sua grandissima vertù si può pensare ogni stabilitade d'animo essere a quella mutabile, e però me non giudicare lieve e non stabile" (For by her manifest excellence we can form some idea of her virtue; and by understanding her great virtue we can perceive how any steadfastness of mind is capable of being changed by it, and consequently how I might not be judged inconstant and unsteadfast; 1.12).

This section helps in understanding Dante's method, which, via Aristotle's *Nicomachean Ethics*, intends to establish a similitude in which, however, an intellectual difference does exist. The "facultade" (power) Dante introduces – "lei commendare secondo la mia facultade, la quale se non simile è per sé, almeno la pronta volontade mostra, che, se più potesse più farei" (I resolved to praise her according to the scope of my power, which, if it is not in itself similar to hers, at least shows my eager desire. For if I were able to do more, I would do so; 1.9) – shows the intellectual inferiority of the character who says "I" and underlines the intellectual excellence, which the *donna gentile* represents in the most excellent way.[9] This significance is established in the canzone *Amor che ne la mente mi ragiona* and stands in continuity with the central meaning of the first canzone, *Voi che 'ntendendo il terzo ciel movete*.

The field of speculation enters again when we read that Dante's eyes "ne l'abitaculo del suo amore fissamente miravano" (while mine were gazing intently on the dwelling of my love!; 1.3). If the eyes look at the mind, which is the *locus* of the intellectual vision of the gentle lady, what takes shape here is reflection or speculation. In addition, the author informs his reader that three reasons had urged him to speak about love: "tre ragioni m'informaro" (three reasons moved me). The first was "lo proprio amore di me medesimo" (one of which was my own love for myself; 1.5). The principle put forth here will continue to be important in Dante's work – that is, the natural love we have for ourselves, which is the foundation of all other forms of love: "lo quale è principio di tutti gli altri sì come vede ciascuno" (which is the beginning of all other loves, as anyone can see; 1.5). This is part of the series of speculative contents insofar as it implies reflection.

Intellectual virtue provides a centre of meaning structured through different elements that are dependent on different lines of thought. In the *Nicomachean Ethics*, 9.4.3, for instance, we read that self-love is part of our intellectual activity (the Greek word is *dianoetikou*), which, Aristotle affirms, is the true self of the human being. In his commentary on the *Nicomacheian Ethics* 9.4, Aquinas compares this activity of the human being to the divine being and explicitly refers to "revertere" (*revertendo ad cor suum*) as a form of meditation.[10] I must emphasize here, however, that this reflexive significance takes place in virtue of a link to a separate substance.The meaning of such a link is part of what will be discussed in the next sections. In the meantime, I want to underline that the canzone has already introduced this content. The relation between poetry and prose, which is crucial if we are to grasp the meaning of the prose discussion, is thus confirmed. This continuity suggests also that the virtue of the woman, her intellectual excellence, can be seen in light of the cosmological reference that the first canzone has introduced and the second has reiterated (Ardizzone 2011, 115–216; also chapter 2 of this book).

However, what is new in the prose text is the tie that connects cosmology, intellection, and ethics. The theme of friendship seems perfectly suited to link different fields. In addition, we may note that the literal sense is in itself allegorical and discloses also an anagogical sense, which Dante announced in the second treatise as part of the four senses of the *Convivio* (II.1).

3. Love as a Natural Being

The second chapter comments on the first verse of the canzone. It evaluates two things: (1) who the speaker is who reasons in the mind, and (2) the place in which he speaks or puts forth his reasoning – "chi è questo ragionatore ... e che è questo loco nel quale dico esso ragionare" (who this speaker is ... and the place in which he speaks). We read the following:

> Amore veramente pigliando e sottilmente considerando è unimento spirituale de l'anima e de la cosa amata. Al quale "unimento di sua propria natura l'anima corre tosto o tardi, secondo che è libera o impedita. E la ragione di questa naturalitade può essere questa: ciascuna *forma sostanziale* procede da la sua prima cagione, la quale è Iddio, sì come nel libro Di Cagioni è scritto,e non ricevono diversitade per quella che è semplicissima, ma per le secondarie cagioni e per la materia in che discende.

> Love, taken in its true sense and subtly considered, is nothing but the spiritual union of the soul and the thing which is loved, to which union the soul of its own nature hastens quickly or slowly according to whether it

is free or hindered. The reason for this natural tendency may be this: that every substantial form proceeds from its first cause, which is God, as is stated in the book *On Causes*, and these forms receive their diversity not from it, which is most simple, but from the secondary causes and from the matter into which it descends. (III.2.2–5).

In the same book,which treats of the infusion of divine goodness, the following words appear: "Onde nel medesimo libro si scrive, trattando della infusione della bontà divina: E fanno[si] diverse le bontadi e i doni per lo concorrimento della cosa che riceve" (And the goods and the gifts are made diverse by the participation of the thing which receives them; III.2.4).

Here Dante introduces a theme derived from the *Liber de causis*, in particular propositions 20 and 24, but is probably aware of Albert's reading of the book because he uses the expression "substantial form" as it derives from the first cause conceived as "dator formarum."[11] In Dante's text, the fragment that appears as a quotation from the *De causis* (propositions 20 and 24),[12] and which is linked to Alpetragius, helps us in getting a meaning: If every effect holds the nature of its cause, since our soul derives from the first cause, such a soul holds a divine nature:

Onde, con ciò sia cosa che ciascuno effetto ritegna della natura della sua cagione – sì come dice Alpetragio quando afferma che quello che è causato da corpo circulare *n'ha* in alcuno modo circulare essere – ciascuna forma ha essere della divina natura in alcuno modo: non che la divina natura sia divisa e comunicata in quelle, ma da quelle [è] participata, per lo modo quasi che la natura del sole è participata nell'altre stelle.

Consequently, since every effect retains part of the nature of its cause (as Alpetragius says when he affirms that what is caused by a circular body must in some way be circular), every form in some way partakes of the divine nature; not that the divine nature is divided and distributed to them, but that it is shared by them in almost the same way that the nature of the Sun is shared by the other stars. (III.2.5)

Dante adds:

Più una forma è nobile più tiene de la natura divina per cui l'anima umana che è forma nobilissima di queste che sotto il cielo sono generate, più riceve de la natura divina che alcun altra … E però ché naturalissimo è in

> Dio volere essere ... l'anima umana essere vuole naturalmente con tutto desiderio; e però che 'l suo essere dipende da Dio e per quello si conserva, naturalmente disia e vuole essere a Dio unita per fortificare il suo essere.

The nobler the form, the more it retains of this nature; consequently, the human soul, which is the noblest form of all those that are generated beneath the heavens, receives more of the divine nature than any other. And since the will to exist is most natural in God – because, as we read in the book cited above, "being is the first thing, and before that there is nothing" – the human soul by nature desires with all its will to exist; and since its being depends on God and is preserved by him, it naturally longs and desires to be united with God in order to strengthen its being. (III.2.5–8)

According to what we read, the desire to be is natural; God wants to be, and the human being wants to be. This to be in union with God is because the human being depends on Him and is preserved by Him. What is indicated as "natural" derives from God and is patterned on Him. The word "natural" applies to everything that manifests its own nature. We note that what is called soul or "anima," in its desire for the divine, is represented as in relation to a separate being derived from the divine. Love, in fact, is indicated as a union determined by the nature of a substantial form, which, since it is caused by God, tends towards the being it naturally loves (III.2.4). Love is a desire for union, and the will to exist is in fact described here as part of the Neoplatonic theory of "reditus." A "reditus" here takes place in virtue of love itself, as we read in the following passage:

> E questo unire è quello che noi dicemo amore, per lo quale si può conoscere quale è dentro l'anima, veggendo di fuori quelli che ama. Questo amore, cioè l'unimento della mia anima con questa gentil donna, nella quale della divina luce assai mi si mostrava, è quello ragionatore del quale io dico; poi che da lui continui pensieri nasceano, miranti ed essaminanti lo valore di questa donna che spiritualmente fatta era colla mia anima una cosa.

> This union is what we call love, whereby we are able to know the quality of the soul within by seeing outside it those things which it loves. This love, that is, the union of my mind with this gentle lady in whom so much of the divine light was revealed to me, is that ["ragionatore"] of whom I speak, for thoughts were continually being born of him that would gaze upon and ponder the worth of this lady who spiritually was made one with my soul. (III.2.9)

Here ends the first fragment of this exposition. We have understood that a substantial form derived from the first cause and participating in God's essence is given to human beings. Such form is substantial and participates in the divine essence. According to a general law, every form partakes of such essence and more according to its nobility; the human soul, because of its highest nobility, partakes more of God's nature. Because God naturally wants to be, the human soul also desires to be. Furthermore, because human beings depend on God and are preserved by Him, it is natural for the human soul to long to be united with God. Dante identifies love and interior reasoning. In this context, in which the substantial form is suggested as the essence of the human intellectual soul, the reader has to realize something more specific and important. In fact, that soul, because of participating in the divine essence, also partakes of the divine simplicity. God is the simplest essence (*semplicissima*), so that what differentiates souls, we read, must derive from the "cause seconde e dalla materia nella quale discende" (from the second causes and from the matter in which it penetrates; III.2.4). According to this passage, though sharing a simple formal being, human beings are diversified thanks to secondary causes and matter. The fact that our diversification takes place because of the cooperation of the angelic intelligences and through matter suggests a more specific meaning: it is the *sensitive* soul, not the intellective, that makes us different. Because human beings participate in God's simplicity, they share a simple intellectual form. Important in this passage is the introduced notion of God's simplicity,[13] a notion we read in Albert's *De causis*, in which what is simple is one, but also in Siger, who discusses it in his *Questiones in Metaphysicam* and identifies simplicity with oneness. According to the philosopher, what is simple excludes composition and is one. [14]

In this passage, we are told in addition that, because the soul participates in the divine nature, it is natural that the soul wills to exist, since this will necessarily exists in the nature of God. Because of this participation, the human soul desires to be united with God in order to become stronger. In fact, all the discussion seems to require from the reader an understanding of the notion of the human soul that derives from such passages: the text offers a pathway to this understanding. The fragments I have quoted are a crucial part of that path.

The second passage we must consider is the following: "E poiché ne le bontadi de la natura e de la ragione si mostra la divina, viene naturalmente che l'anima umana con quelle per via spirituale si unisce tanto tosto e più forte quanto quelle più gli appaiono perfette" (Because the divine goodness reveals itself in the goods of nature, it happens that the human soul naturally unites itself with them in a spiritual manner, more quickly and more strongly as they appear the more perfect; III.2.8–9).

This assertion is modulated on the Neoplatonic mystical tradition. Dante recalls *De causis*, but he does not forget Pseudo-Dionysius. The word "union" – *henosis* in Greek[15] – recalls the Neoplatonic field (Ardizzone 2011, chap. 4), but there are also traces of the medieval Pauline theory of speculation. Because of our love for God, we desire to be united with those beings that manifest Him. In the tradition of Saint Paul and Augustine – later interpreted, for instance, by the Victorins or by Bonaventure – the things that manifest God are mirrors and enigmas, or traces and "vestigia." We cannot know God in this life, but we may look for His image in the things He has made. The union introduced in the present context, however, is not part of the Pauline theory of speculation. Rather, "union" suggests a more specific meaning – namely, the union between the intellectual soul and the gentle lady in virtue of love. Clearly, the Pauline theory of speculation cannot explain this connection, since our tending towards God no longer takes place, as it does for Paul, through specula or mirrors that are in the world. The medieval modes of speculation are recalled and thus superseded, and a different kind of speculation is established. The language used is proper to the field of mysticism. This speculation is named in the text as "love." The identity of the *donna gentile* as given in the canzone helps the reader; in this text, it has been suggested that such a lady is a separate substance, an idea of God's thought – "costei pensò chi mosse l'universo" (v. 72) – and that she is eternal "però fu tal da etterno ordinata" (v. 54).[16]

Let us now consider the fragment quoted above: "Questo amore cioè l'unimento della mia anima con questa gentil donna, nella quale si mostra la luce divina è quello ragionatore del quale io dico, poi che da lui continui pensieri nasceano, miranti ed esaminanti lo valore di questa donna che spiritualmente fatta era con la mia anima una cosa" (III.2.9). In the condition described here, the soul is represented as united to the new woman. Love is the name of such union, and its activity is interior reasoning. From this love are born continuous thoughts, which contemplate and examine the value of such a woman, with whom the author's soul is united (III.2.9). The narrator's experience appears to be the prototype of that proper to the human being: his experience with the lady illustrates how human beings can know. This part of Dante's commentary confirms what we read in the canzone: that the union between the human mind and a separate substance allows the existence of the "ragionatore" responsible for interior speech. To think implies here the union with a separate being, and this being is an object of contemplation from the part of God.

The text clarifies that the place in which love generates reasoning is the mind and that the nature of this mind needs to be explained: "e però è da vedere che questa mente propriamente significa" (Thus we have to see what this word "mind" properly signifies). As already in the canzone, the love for the gentle lady imposes to consider the being of the mind that is able to contemplate her. However, in saying that it is the mind that is the heart of discussion, we gain no better understanding of it than before, and therefore we must see what this word "mind" properly signifies in the prose text (III.2.11).

4. On the Nature of the Human Mind

Actually, what is indicated as "mente" (mind) here implies a name of a relation in reasoning with the gentle lady. The name given to this relation is "love." The union between the mind and a separate form here is the meaning offered. The reader can easily reach such understanding if he or she is aware of the contents Dante has introduced in the canzone *Voi che 'ntendendo il terzo ciel movete* and, in particular, in what *Amor che ne la mente mi ragiona* has proposed in a very similar style.

The tautological nature of what is indicated as "mente" and as "love" is suggested because both exhibit a relational being. That is, love names the relation that unites the mind and the woman, where mind functions as the place in which love performs its operation of reasoning. We should observe that such unity (which, in line with the teaching of Aristotle, is that of the exemplary union of friendship) here recalls a Trinitarian relation, in which the relation between two beings implies a third being, who embodies the relation itself, and this third being is in this place called "love."

At this point, Dante begins a digression in which he discusses the nature of the human soul and its power. The discussion is clearly based on the Aristotelian notion of soul, and on the theory of the soul's functions – "vivere, sentire, ragionare" – in their inner correspondence with the three souls powers: vegetative, sensitive, and intellective . The rational soul is defined as the highest and noblest power. It participates in the divine nature as a sempiternal intelligence:

> E quella anima che tutte queste potenze comprende, [ed] è perfettissima di tutte l'altre, è l'anima umana, la quale colla nobilitade della potenza ultima, cioè ragione, participa della divina natura a guisa di sempiterna Intelligenza: però che l'anima è tanto in quella sovrana potenza nobilitata e dinudata da materia, che la divina luce, come in angelo, raggia in quella: e però è l'uomo divino animale dalli filosofi chiamato.

> The soul that comprehends all these powers, and the one that is the most perfect of them all, is the human soul, which, by the nobility of its highest power, that is, reason, participates in the divine nature as an everlasting intelligence. For the soul is so ennobled and divested of matter in this supreme power that the divine light shines in it as in an angel; and therefore man is called a divine living being by the philosophers. (III.2.14–15)

This definition, in which the human soul is said to be divine and to participate through reason in the divine being as a sempiternal intelligence, suggests that the gentle lady is the name used to express the intellectual nature of the human being, and the way in which such nature knows and actualizes itself. This is confirmed because the angelic intelligence is generally regarded as capable of seeing inside the mind of God, and therefore seeing the ideas in the mind of God.[17] According to such a theory, the fact that the *donna gentile* in the canzone is identified as a divine idea suggests that the human being has a similarity to the angel-intelligences' vision. The incipit of the *Convivio* introduced this idea through a biblical reference to the "bread of angels," which refers to speculation. This in fact accords with the reading of Augustine, who thinks that the bread of angels concerns the ideas in the mind of God that the angels are able to speculate.[18] In that context, however, the reference asserts that such contemplation is also possible for human beings. A line of reflection initiated in the second treatise continues here.

5. Mind as a Being of Relation

The union of the mind with the gentle lady thus establishes at least two things: one is the relational nature of our mind and its ability to contemplate a separate form, this form being assimilated to the divine being; the second, derived from the first, suggests the necessity of understanding the nature of the mind itself. In the canzone, our interpretation established that mind because the way in which it was depicted was suggested as performing the role of the possible intellect, and the gentle lady, we assumed, was the nomination for the agent intellect.

A question arises with respect to the nature of the gentle lady. If she is an intellectual being that is contemplated and seems to perform the role of Aristotle's active intellect, how do we have to consider the mind-intellect that contemplates her? Dante is introducing here in the prose text a discussion about knowledge and how the human mind knows, reiterating what he has introduced in the canzoni, and in particular, in *Amor che ne la mente mi ragiona*.

To address this question, we must first make a distinction in order to clarify what is meant here by the agent intellect. This lady cannot be assimilated with the agent intellect, as interpreted by Aquinas (*De anima*, III, L10). For him, in fact, the agent intellect is certainly a kind of participation in the divine being, but in our earthly life we cannot see or contemplate this intellect.

In this context, at first even more important, we must understand the notion of substantial form (III.2) that derives from God as the giver of forms (*dator formarum*). This treatise does not explain clearly what this form is in relation to the lady. We have seen that Dante uses the expression "substantial form" (III.2.2) and the verb "procede," or proceeds (3.2.4), which belongs to the area of Neoplatonism, and defines God as "first cause." He adds that every effect maintains the nature of its cause, and that every form has its being in the divine nature through participation in it, as the stars participate in the nature of the sun. The nobler the form, the more it participates in the divine. Consequently, the soul, which is the noblest form generated under the sky, receives more from the divine nature than any other (III.2.5–7).

Up to this point, then, and reading this fragment in light of the *De causis* (in particular, in Albert's commentary),[19] we may consider that God bestows a substantial form as light that flows down on the human soul.

In fact, in the first canzone, *Voi che 'ntendendo il terzo ciel movete*, we have read that a celestial spirit gifted with speech comes down from the heavens and is this spirit which generates the love for the new lady.

If we read Albert's commentary on the *Liber de causis* in light of Augustine, and in particular Augustine's commentary on the fragment of the Gospel of John, where wisdom (*sapientia*) is indicated as life and light, we may understand that this passage rethinks contents that Dante had already proposed in other linguistic forms. Here, participation in the divine takes place through the process of a form, or an infusion of the divine. By virtue of this infusion, the human soul is a noble being that longs to be united with God in order to become intellectually stronger. Dante identifies here as "substantial form" what proceeds from God. This expression occurs in the *De causis* more than once in Albert's commentary.[20] "Substantial form" in Dante's text seems to indicate the possible intellect given as a form and infused by God, according to Albert's theory, and that generates our turning towards God as the most perfect being.[21] The love for the woman, therefore, implies a form of reflection and a return to our origin, since she is one of those "bontadi" that are divine – that is, the separate substance to which the possible intellect tends. To this extent, the lady can be compared to the agent intellect, although the notion of the agent intellect still needs to be clarified. This notion, in addition, should provide, as we will see, the link, in Aristotelian terms, between the theory of knowledge and the field of ethics.

I underline that this prose passage is in fact the turning of a page, which takes place through the juxtaposition of different texts and themes that Dante places in continuity with one another. At the heart of the passage is the theory of human knowledge, which Dante offers here in a difficult context, linking knowledge and ethics.

The canzone, according to our reading, has suggested themes found in Albert and in other texts, but now the framework becomes more inclusive, and the Neoplatonic circle of "processio" and "reditus" creates a reference in which another equally powerful meaning is inserted. The concept of God as giver of forms, according to Albert in his commentary on the *Liber de causis* and in his synthesis of the Pseudo-Dionysian *De divinis nominibus*, seems to provide the content where Dante initially rests.[22] The process (*processio*) involves the return (*reditus*), which can take place as *henosis*, or union with a separate form. Dante's focus is on the natural character of such an impulse to return.

The concept of the intellectual soul is offered in the union of two beings that are represented as linked, one of which is a substantial form issuing from the divine, the other of which is the gentle lady. Dante seems to be thinking in terms of relations that create a horizontal path that crosses the traditional vertical reading. The reader must attend to this dual dimension in order to understand the dynamics within which the narrative is organized – that is, if he is to grasp how love produces a union that makes evident what the soul is like on the inside. We read in fact that "E dunque questo unire è quanto chiamiamo amore e da cui si mostra cosa è l'anima dentro veggendo di fuori quelli che ama" (This union is what we call love, whereby we are able to know the quality of the soul within by seeing outside it those things which it loves; III.2.9).

The tendency of the soul towards union with a being that we know is separate and divine is proposed in the text as able to make manifest the nature of the soul itself. The ontology of the human being is made evident in this love. In light of this, the reader is invited to deduce the soul's essence from that of the gentle lady. In other words, the being of the gentle lady may reveal the essence of the soul itself; the true centre of discussion is the nature of the being who loves, and that the love for the gentle lady makes manifest the ontology of the human being. The human being, as a participant in the process of intellection whose source and final goal is the divine, is part of the reagents that penetrate through the love for the gentle lady. However, it is the notion of substantial form, "simple" in itself and diversified in virtue of the concourse of the thing that receives it, that leads us to further synthesis: "Onde nel medesimo libro si scrive, trattando della infusione della bontà divina: 'E fanno[si] diverse le bontadi e i doni per lo concorrimento della cosa che riceve'" (Thus in the same book, in treating of the infusion of divine goodness, the following words appear: "And the goodnesses and the gifts are made diverse by the participation of the thing which receives them"; III.2.4).[23]

The love for the gentle lady personifies the human tendency towards the divine that lives in the intellectual soul. Love is the name of the unity of mind and woman, which are two entities but form one. In the fourth treatise, we will read that friendship creates a new being (love here appears to be the third, and is a new being). After reading this passage from the literal commentary, the reader once again must enter into a relational system. Love and the lady both involve a relational field that is indispensable and inseparable. This field, however, implies a triune relation involving the mind, the gentle lady, and the relation between the two. Such relation is called "love," and every member can be seen as one and triune at the same time.

The text that helps us to understand the meaning of this relation is from Augustine's *De trinitate* (1968, 8.9, 359). "Love, we read, supposes that who loves and that who is loved. Three things are at work here: the one who loves, what you love, and love itself. What, then, is love but a life that unites or that tends to unite two beings? Let us lift up with our soul. What loves the soul in a friend, if not the soul? So, here are three things: one who loves, that which is loved, and love itself." In relation to the passage of the treatise recalled, the three exponents are the gentle lady, the mind, and the name of the union, which is love. If this is true, however, what we must again observe is the Trinitarian relation that lives inside the human being – that is, the relation mentioned in the first part of this section. What is clear, in this context, is that the essence of this Trinity is realized in virtue of the contemplation of a being represented as external to the human realm. This idea was also present in the canzone.

Comparing these texts, we see that Dante returns to themes that were important for him at the beginning of his authorial work. He now repronounces them in light of other texts, where the strength of the new text is to establish a new content without defining it, but while building its role along different philosophical and theological lines. A method of comparison is introduced, and we may see not only that the Platonic-Christian tradition is one of its own reagents, but also that the old texts are reread through the filter of a mostly Aristotelian perspective. For instance, the love that speaks within is depicted on an Augustinan basis, but the author seems to rethink it in light of new philosophical perspectives.

We now return to the prose text to see how it organizes the concept of soul. Dante indicates at first the three powers of soul: "Dico adunque che lo Filosofo nel secondo dell'Anima, partendo le potenze di quella, dice che l'anima principalmente ha tre potenze, cioè vivere, sentire e ragionare" (I say then that in the second book of *On the Soul*, the Philosopher, in distinguishing its powers, asserts that the soul has three principal powers: namely life, sensation, and reason; III.2.11). He continues, "E quella anima che tutte queste potenze comprende, [ed] è perfettissima di tutte l'altre, è l'anima umana" (And the soul that includes all these powers, and is the most perfect of all others, is the human; III.2.14). In addition, he offers the following explanation of "mind," which he links with reason and defines as the highest and noblest part of the soul: "The human soul, with the nobility of its highest power, that is reason, participates in the divine nature in the guise of eternal intelligence, because the soul is so ennobled in that sovereign power and stripped from matter that the divine light, as an angel, in her rays, this is why man is called a divine animal by the philosophers." And so, he continues:

> In this most noble part of the soul there exist many powers, as the Philosopher says, especially in the third book of *On the Soul* where he observes that there exists a power in it that is called scientific, and one that is called ratiocinative or deliberative, and with it are found some powers – as Aristotle says in that same place – such as the inventive and the judicial. All these most noble powers, and the others within this excellent power, are called collectively by this name, the meaning of which we

desire to know: that is, mind. Thus, it is manifest that by mind is meant the highest and noblest part of the soul (III.2.14–16).[24]

6. Mind and Philosophy

Having established that "this mind is predicated only of man and of the divine substances" (III.2.17), Dante introduces a fragment that recalls Severinus Boethius:

> E che ciò fosse lo 'ntendimento, si vede: ché solamente dell'uomo e delle divine sustanze questa mente si predica, sì come per Boezio si puote apertamente vedere, che prima la predica delli uomini, ove dice alla Filosofia: "Tu e Dio, che nella mente [te] delli uomini mise"; poi la predica di Dio, quando dice a Dio: "Tutte le cose produci dallo superno essemplo, tu, bellissimo, bello mondo nella mente portante."
>
> That this was his meaning is obvious, for this mind is predicated only of man and of the divine substances, as may be clearly seen in Boethius, who predicates it first of men when he says to Philosophy: "You and God, who placed you in the minds of men," and then to God when he says to God: "You produce all things from the supernal exemplar, you, most beautiful, bearing in your mind the beautiful world." (III.2.17–8)

Here Dante is quoting two fragments from *De consolatione philosophiae*. Here is the original Latin of the first fragment: "Tu mihi et qui te sapientium mentem inseriut" (*De consolatione*, 1.4). That of the second – "tutte le cose produci da lo superno essemplo, tu, bellissimo,bello mondo ne la mente portante" – is the following: "tu cuncta superno ducis ab exemplo, pulchrum pulcherrimus ipse mundum mente gerens" (*De consolatione*, 3.9, v. 6–8).[25] The fragment of Severinus Boethius is also quoted by Albert in his commentary on *De causis*, where Severinus Boethius is cited twice.[26] It is also quoted by Aquinas in his *De ideis*, where he discusses the theory of ideas in the mind of God, a theory he confronts in this text, which is part of his *De veritate*.[27] These passages strongly suggest that Dante here quotes the *De consolatione* aware that it functioned as an *auctoritas* in the Middle Ages for the theory of ideas in the mind of God. He appropriates this *auctoritas*, but he does so, as we shall see, in order to give new meaning to an old content. For Dante, these fragments assume their own peculiar meaning because they enter as part of a discussion about the human mind. In the first quotation, the original Latin asserts that philosophy is in the mind of *sapientes*, whereas Dante uses just "uomini." However, it is the word "philosophy" here that leads to a fundamental and not previously emphasized content of the *Convivio*. As sometimes happens in Dante's doctrinal treatise, the reader is offered a meaning that can be understood only if he links fragments of the text with other, remote fragments. Here, in order to understand the meaning of the two fragments from *De consolatione*, the reader must fill a gap or, better, an empty space: he or she must first of all be aware of the existence of this gap and then indicate what can work as link between the first quotation and the second. In the first, we learn that philosophy is in the mind of human beings; in the second, that the archetypes for the things in the world exist in the mind of God. The logical subject in both passages is the *mind*.

If we remain at the first level of meaning, the two fragments from Severinus Boethius assert that mind belongs to both human beings and the divine being. Since the flatness of the assertion does not satisfy the reader, the first thing he should note is that Dante, by artfully linking the two fragments that in Severinus Boethius are far apart, focuses on the new term "philosophy." The shifting of the logical subject seems to be a required operation, a shifting that works as a tool in order to assess a meaning.[28] The focus is now philosophy. The first gap to be filled requires that we assume as problematic the meaning of the word "philosophy."

The link emerges once the reader applies the name "philosophy" to God's mind and its beauty. This *impositio nominis* is required if the reader is to grasp the complete meaning of the text. In light of this *impositio*, we see that philosophy, in accordance with the first fragment of Severinus Boethius, is in the human mind and, according to the second, is in the mind of God. By rereading the two fragments in the continuity in which they are organized, we may understand that the meaning of philosophy is bound to the theory of ideas in the mind of God, where God is represented as the most beautiful being. Indeed, beauty here is proposed in relation to the archetypes of the world that God bears in Himself, and which He produces (*gerens*) in His mind: "tutte le cose produci da lo superno essemplo, tu, bellissimo, bello mondo ne la mente portante" (You produce all things from the supernal exemplar, you, most beautiful, bearing in your mind the beautiful world). Because of this link, we may infer that it is necessary to give "philosophy" a meaning close to that offered in the description of God's mind – that is, the reader must fill another empty space. This suggests that the fragments from Severinus Boethius must be integrated into what Dante has written in the final part of the second treatise, where philosophy was indicated as the "daughter of God": "E così, in fine di questo secondo trattato, dico e affermo che la donna di cu' io innamorai appresso lo primo amore fu la bellissima e onestissima figlia dello Imperadore dell'universo, alla quale Pittagora puose nome Filosofia" (So at the end of this second book I assert and affirm that the lady of whom I was enamored after my first love was the most beautiful and honourable daughter of the Emperor of the universe, to whom Pythagoras gave the name of Philosophy; II.15.12). Philosophy as "daughter" implies, in turn, a begetting, something produced in the mind of God. This anticipates a content that we will find in the section devoted to the allegorical commentary on the second canzone, where philosophy is explained as the love for wisdom, the exemplar of which is God's thinking.[29] If philosophy is in the divine mind, then Dante's quotation from Severinus Boethius confirms that – because philosophy is also in the human mind – in some way, human mind also stands in relation to a form or idea.[30] The love for the gentle lady shows that human beings can have a living relationship with a separate form of divine origin. God here is not just the *dator formarum* but the eternal thinking being, the model of intellectual activity in which beauty and intelligence are one and the same. Philosophy, in other words, is in both the divine and the human mind. God's mind represents the "superno" example, on which the human mind is patterned. On the one hand, it is suggested that the human mind is similar to that of intelligences (*divine sostanze*), because it is able to contemplate God's ideas; on the other, when the discussion focuses on the human mind itself, we read about our similarity to the divine being, since philosophy is implanted in our minds. In virtue of philosophy, the beauty of God's mind is also implanted in us. This seems to be the pathway that Dante seeks to trace. Because God's mind is identified with philosophy in virtue of an activity both reflective and productive, the identity of God's thinking and philosophy works to delineate the notion of philosophy in reference to the human mind. Since the human mind is proposed in its relationship with an entity that is separate and divine, we may understand that philosophy deals with the mind conceived of as a thinking entity in union with a substance of divine origin. Mind and philosophy here appear to be equivalent – philosophy implies the activity of human and divine mind. The brief passage on philosophy thus acquires a strong significance: it introduces a new pathway that confirms our previous reading, as well as generates a new pathway which is in continuity with the previous one.

This circular organization of the meanings the *Convivio* proposes can be grasped if we activate a horizontal line of reading in which contents that are far apart combine to organize a central content. Thus, the notion of philosophy given in the allegorical commentary of the second treatise, where philosophy was defined as the daughter of God (II.15.12), brings a content that will run along different pathways with the purpose of an ultimate synthesis as it occurs in the final chapters of the allegorical commentary of this third treatise, starting from defining the name philosophy: "dire che è questo che si chiama Filosofia, cioè quello che questo nome significa" (to say what this thing is which is called philosophy – that is to say, what this name signifies; III.11.1). The definition that is given is the following: "Filosofia non è altro che amistanza a sapienza o vero a sapere: onde in alcuno modo si può dicere catuno filosofo, secondo lo naturale amore che in ciascuno genera lo disiderio di sapere" (Philosophy is nothing but "friendship for wisdom" or "for knowledge"; consequently, in a certain sense everyone can be called a "philosopher," according to the natural love which engenders in everyone the desire to know; III.11.7).

What seems evident is that philosophy and love for the gentle lady are different words that express the same content.

7. Philosophy as Eternal

Returning to the third treatise, we see, as a first meaning deriving from this passage in chapter 2, that philosophy, because it is in the mind of God, is suggested as being eternal, eternal being God's thinking. This, of course, is confirmed in the section of the allegorical commentary already quoted, in which we read that philosophy is proper to the divine essence in a way that is perfect and true as for an eternal marriage: "È adunque la divina filosofia della divina essenzia, però che in esso non può essere cosa alla sua essenzia aggiunta; ed è nobilissima, però che nobilissima è la essenzia divina; [ed] è in lui per modo perfetto e vero, quasi per etterno matrimonio" (Divine philosophy is therefore of the divine essence because in Him nothing can be added to His essence; and she is most noble because the divine essence is most noble; and she exists in Him in a true and perfect manner, as if by eternal marriage; III.12–13). However, we have read in the same above-quoted passage that philosophy is also in the mind of human beings. But how can we attribute the eternality of thinking or mind to a mortal being? It is true that, according to Christian teaching, the intellectual soul is eternal because it lasts forever, but Dante's discussion here has nothing to do with the survival of the soul after the death.

Philosophy is presented here as the product of an activity of the union of mind with a separate substance during our temporal life, a union Dante denotes as friendship, love, and now as philosophy. Dante introduces fragments from Severinus Boethius's *De consolatione* in order to generate a circle of related issues. One among these, it seems, is especially suited to the nature and meaning of philosophy. It is useful to relate Dante's brief but important quotations from Severinus Boethius to a debate that was active in Paris and was also occurring in Bologna. Philosophy was in fact at the centre of the intellectual debate of the late thirteenth century. The list of the articles condemned in Paris in 1277 starts with the following one: "Quod non est excellentior status quam vacare philosophiae" (The study of philosophy is the highest condition of life). There follows another proposition which states that philosophers are the only wise human beings: "Quod sapientes mundi sunt philosophy tantum" (Hissette 1977, proposition 1, 2, 15 and 18). Apparently, Dante does not take into consideration the *vacare in philosophia* as the highest occupation according to the Parisian debate. Philosophy is for him a divine activity. It belongs to the absolute thinking of God and implies the divine reflection and its production of archetypes. Proclus's *Elementa theologiae* (1987) called such thinking, which is God's creative thinking, *poiesis* – that is, someone whose activity is *poiesis*, who performs a thinking-productive activity.[31] Dante, who has no knowledge of Greek, seems, on the basis of Severinus Boethius, to introduce a similar concept. Philosophy is a divine activity and is therefore both contemplative and productive. Philosophy introduces the model of perfect knowledge. If God thinks, his thinking, like him, is eternal, and therefore the human mind, by engaging in philosophy, is capable of thinking a divine eternal being. Dante makes us also aware that this mind is shared by the divine substances (III.2.17), and he adds that "mente" is that excellent part of the soul that is "deitate." Furthermore, the canzone clearly says that the *donna gentile* is part of God's thought – "costei pensò chi mosse l'universo" (v. 72) – and also suggests that she is "eternal" because what God thinks is eternal like him.[32] This similarity urges the reader to desire to know more about the nature of the human mind insofar as this mind is proposed, in light of the parallel with God, as divine as well. The text, we have read, establishes that a substantial form comes from God and that the human mind, because of its origin and nature, loves the *donna gentile* because being a divine being, it longs for Him. We have been told that the love for the gentle lady manifests the nature of the lover – that is, that such love reveals the nature of the soul that loves. The inference here is that, since the gentle lady is a separate substance, the nature of the loving mind should be similarly separate and divine. In this context, it is helpful to recall again a content that was claimed by philosophers of different backgrounds. It asserts that in what is eternal and separate, *sciens* and *scitum* are coincident – that is, beings that are separate and eternal are able to contemplate separate and eternal entities.[33] This was also claimed by Albert[34] and Siger of Brabant.[35] I recall this issue because it implies that the mind, represented in union with the gentle lady through contemplation, is suggested also as an eternal and separate entity. The quotations from Severinus Boethius, however, suggest a more specific landscape, not only because the word "philosophy" is introduced but also because the meaning of philosophy reiterates indirectly a content that had been stressed in my previous reading of the canzone *Amor che ne la mente mi ragiona*, in which the discussion about human knowledge and the idea of intellect has been central. The thought of God and creation as a product of His thinking provide the grounding reference, but the meaning that can be inferred goes well beyond such reference. If human philosophy is modelled on God's philosophy, and God's philosophy is eternal, the question arises: Can the human mind that thinks this philosophy be conceived as eternal too? Moreover, does there exist a form of earthly human knowledge that can be eternal, and does this eternity suggest that the mind which thinks it is eternal and divine as well? Is philosophy an activity that takes place during a human being's earthly life? If so, then how is it possible to establish such content if the human being is mortal and his life has an end? In other words, if we enter in such a dimension of eternity, who is the thinking subject to whom such eternity can be applied?

Dante once more connects different lines of learning in order to compare and rethink them. For instance, in Severinus Boethius, too, we find that the human being is said to be divine by virtue of his rationality – "ut divinum merito rationis animal" (II.5) – although Dante does not explicitly refer to it. It is evident that Lady Philosophy – with whom Dante fell in love in his Florentine years, according to what we read in the second treatise when he recalls Pythagoras (II.15.12) as the inventor of the name "philosophy" – is constructed with a philological accuracy rooted in etymology: as we will read in the third treatise, philosophy is the love for *sophia*, or wisdom, that God has in his mind. In other words, the likeness with divine thinking means love for a separate substance that is coincident with the new lady as already introduced in the canzoni *Voi che 'ntendendo il terzo ciel movete* and *Amor che ne la mente mi ragiona*.

The third treatise, in the final allegorical commentary, will again furnish the etymology of "philosophy" and its sources but the reading of the canzoni is crucial for determining the sense of the prose text. In fact, the new lady in both canzoni is proposed as a being that is related to the celestial sphere. In particular, in the second canzone, *Amor che ne la mente mi ragiona*, we are told that she is contemplated by the celestial intelligences, God and the human being's mind. The prose confirms and reiterates such an interpretation. Such identity, more or less clear at this point, opens to a new field of inquiry. What I want to stress is that the love for the *donna gentile*, described as an activity of the human mind, has the goal of pushing the reader to understand the nature of the mind that is able to love and contemplate such a lady. The shifiting of the logical subject is required in order to understand. I have already underlined, in my reading of *Amor che ne la mente mi ragiona* that the love for the new lady imposes the difficulty of understanding the meaning of the word "mind." In that context, no clear traces were found of an Aristotelian theory. It is instead evident that the discourse on the soul, given in the prose of this chapter, is in part Aristotelian, and that "mind" renders the notion of the intellectual soul, and of its most noble activity of contemplation, of a separate substance. If this is true, then what Dante calls philosophy is the result of an *impositio nominis*, at first following Pythagoras as he is introduced in the second treatise (II.15.12). That is, he adopts the method of imposing a new name – "dico e affermo che la donna di cu' io innamorai appresso lo primo amore fu la bellissima e onestissima figlia dello Imperadore dell'universo, alla quale Pittagora puose nome Filosofia" – introducing a new context: philosophy is the daughter of God. Then he reiterates such a method, introducing in the third treatise the two fragments from Severinus Boethius's *De consolatione*, which I have quoted above. The recalling of Pythagoras for the name "philosophy" appears also in Aquinas' commentary on Aristotle's *Metaphysics*, which is an important reference, especially when it is linked to the quotation from Severinus Boethius.[36]

For Dante, in this context, philosophy is primarily a form of *transumptio*. It is active as *nominatio*, which includes a *pronominatio*, and appears to be closely related to what the philosophers called intellectual happiness. Apparently, philosophy here has nothing to do with a rational secular thinking and methodology, but deals only with the idea that the human being, as a divine animal, is entitled to have a knowledge of a separate entity. This notion of philosophy requires, therefore, a further discussion that runs parallel with the notion of mind or intellect.

8. More about Philosophy

Let us return briefly to Severinus Boethius. From the fragments quoted above, it follows that God and human beings are similar because of the activity their minds share, but God contemplates exemplars that He produces in His mind, and from which He creates all things (*in imagine formans*). I return to this fragment because I intend to show the link that it suggests between philosophy and intellectual happiness. In pointing out the human mind, it is important to establish whether, in some ways, this mind, investigated in these relations, can be regarded as eternal, too. That the fragment from Severinus Boethius holds a pivotal meaning is confirmed; in fact, continuing our reading, we note the following passage: "Onde si puote omai vedere che è mente: che è quella fine e preziosissima parte dell'anima che è *deitate*. E questo è il luogo dove dico che Amore ragiona de la mia donna" (So now we may see what is meant by mind, that distinguished and most precious part of the soul which is deity. This is the place in which I say Love speaks to me about my lady; III.2.19)

It appears that the union between the mind and the woman, who is suggested as a separate substance in the canzone's text, reiterates our likeness to the divine, whose thinking thinks his ideas and in which thought and eternal production are one and the same thing. However, the human mind, represented in union (indicated as love in the canzone) with an idea or a separate being, also suggests a likeness to the divine thinking. In light of it, the human mind appears to perform an activity of thinking when it contemplates an idea or separate being. God thinks His ideas *ab eterno* and in the canzone we read that the gentle lady is a divine idea ("costei penso Chi mosse l'Universo") and therefore eternal: "Però fu tal da eterno ordinata." The human intellect, in virtue of the union with the idea, or lady, reaches its own intellection. In light of the asserted likeness, this activity, it seems, should share in some way a form of eternity. But this meaning is not made explicit; *subtilitas* and close speech are peculiar to the *Convivio* in spite of the apparent explicative tone of the language. If philosophy (*philo-sophia*, according to the etymology furnished) is in the mind of human beings and also in the mind of God (*sophia* is the Greek word according to Aristotle's *Nicomachean Ethics* and *Metaphysics*, which in Latin is *sapientia*), then this word introduces us to a knowledge which, in the *Metaphysics*, is the science of eternal things.[37] *Philos* and *sophia*, as parts or components of philosophy, form a name that, according to latin grammarians like Priscianus, is "compositum." A scholar of logic, Petrus Hispanus, one of the *sapienti* Dante meets in his Paradise in the heaven of the sun, and celebrated for his twelve *libelli* (i.e., the *Summulae logicales*), lists such names as being part of equivocation and amphiboly. In the section Hispanus devotes to *Fallacies*, we read that equivocation takes place because a *nomen compositum* means many things, but if ithey are taken separately, they have only one meaning. If we thus reduce the *compositum* to its parts in order to determine the principal sense of the term, in this case, the parts do not have many meanings but only one (7.49). Hispanus stresses that in composite names it is the composition that is the cause of the plural meanings.[38] This fragment invites us to rethink the word "philosophy" as including many meanings, or as an equivocal term, according to what Dante himself suggests when he decides to explain it.[39]

We note that if two entities – love and wisdom – compose the name "philosophy," the word confirms a recurrent technique we may term relational. An example of such methodology is implicit in Dante's utilization of the word "love," as it occurs at first in the opening of *Amor che ne la mente mi ragiona*, which supplies a *de facto* link between the mind and the lady, a link reiterated in the prose and reintroduced through "amicizia" (friendship) as a new name for apparently the same being. This relational pathway also includes "mind," represented in its rational activity because it is united with the lady through love.

The parallel established by Severinus Boethius offers a stronger meaning because the divine ideas are eternal. That philosophy implies the knowledge of eternal things is a point on which Aristotle and his commentators agree. The brief passage on philosophy thus acquires a greater significance if we recall that in Aristotle's *Metaphysics* philosophy implies the knowledge of separate and eternal beings ("huius scientiae quae sapientiae dicitur proprium est considerare causas").[40] If we read chapter 1 in Aquinas's *Commentary*, we see that he introduces Pythagoras in order to set up the meaning of the word, in which the awareness of a *compositum* name, reduced to its simple elements and their unequivocal meaning, helps the reader:

> Notandum est quod cum prius nomine sapientiae uteretur, nunc ad nominem philosophiae se transfert … Pithagoras vocavit se philosophum id est amatorem sapientiae … ista non est scientia humana … est maxime divina … scientia divina dicitur quam deus habet … oportet quod sit de deo … talem scientia de deo et de primis causis. Deus habet … patet sit scientia non humana, sed divina.
>
> Now we must note that, while this science was first designated by the name wisdom, this was later changed to the name philosophy, since they mean the same thing … Pythagoras … called himself a philosopher, i.e., a lover of wisdom … But this science is not human but is the most divine … is said divine science because God has it and the science which is about divine matters is said to be divine. This science is about first causes and principles, it must be about God … it is evident that is a science not human but divine. (Thomas Aquinas, *In Metaphysicorum,* 1.1.2–3, pp. 15–17)

Sophia, in fact, from the Greek *sophia,* according to Aristotle, is the highest science. *Sophia* (*sapientia*) is at the same time science and intelligence of the most sublime things as they are naturally (*Nicomachean Ethics,* book 6).[41] This coincides with the knowledge of the eternal or separate substances of book 12 of the *Metaphysics.*[42] In this work, the word implies the highest knowledge that is that of causes and principles (separate substances). Aquinas and Siger (*Quaestiones in Metaphysicam*) agree about such meaning.[43] In any case, the word "philosophy," while confirming Dante's penchant for treating love as a relational being, seems to offer an answer to the problematic notion of human mind.

In the articles of condemnation (as they are usually understood), the word "philosophy" implied a rational learning different from that of faith. However, in light of what is proposed above, when Dante writes that he fell in love with philosophy, the meaning of this assertion cannot be taken for granted. The *Convivio* shows that its author was building the meaning of this word as a composite inlay.

Summarizing what I have said: in light of the above relation, the human mind is confirmed as a being able to think a separate substance. The human being is divine because his mind can contemplate an eternal substance. Thus the notion of the human mind proposes a problematic identity and appears to recall that of the possible intellect, which is actualized in the contemplation of the agent intellect as form, according to an idea that Albert adopts in his *De anima* (Nardi 1960b, 114–15; Ardizzone 2011, 202–3). It is not sufficient, however, to recall Albert's theory, since Dante's notion of philosophy seems to imply the concept of its eternity, and the concept of eternity here can be explained only by introducing the theory of the eternity of the intellect. What "eternity" means needs here to be explained, because eternity implies two different things: it is something that lasts forever, but also something that does not have a start. In this later meaning, of course, eternity opposes creation.

According to radical texts circulating in the thirteenth century, only separate beings are able to know other separate beings (Kuksewicz 1965, 236). This is a topic that Siger discusses in his *In tertium de Anima* and also in his commentary on *De causis*. Our question, however, deals with Dante's position. The doubt introduced through the quotation from Severinus Boethius obliges us to evaluate whether the text offers alternative suggestions. To explore this possibility, we must return to the notion of mind, or "mente," as it appears in the fragments quoted above. In chapter 2.15, Dante tells his readers that there are many virtues in this noblest part of the soul. One is scientific, another ratiocinative or deliberative, which includes powers such as the inventive and judicial (as Aristotle says in that same place). In relation to the scientific virtue in Aristotle's *Nicomachean Ethics,* the philosopher explains that this virtue has as the object of knowledge what exists necessarily. It is therefore eternal, for everything existing of absolute necessity is eternal, and what is eternal does not come into existence or perish. We have science when we have a conviction arrived at in a certain way, and when the first principles on which that conviction rests are known to us with certainty (*Nicomachean Ethics,* 6.3). This passage introduces intellectual virtues – that is, the virtues through which the mind can achieve the truth. The attainment of truth belongs to the intellectual activity of the soul. In Aristotle, the word used is *episteme* (*Nicomachean Ethics,* 6.3), which William of Moerbeke translates as *scientificum genus animae.*[44] *Sophia* is in its turn translated as *sapientia.* "Virtù scientifica," Dante recalls, is of course, an intellectual virtue, but if we read the *Nicomachean Ethics* 6.7, we see that Aristotle establishes in *sophia* or *philosophia* the intellectual virtue that supersedes scientific knowledge.[45] According to the philosopher, in fact, true knowledge is *sophia* (*Nicomachean Ethics,* book 6),[46] which is the result of scientific virtue (certain demonstration) and *nous* or intellect (the immediate apprehension of first principles). Aquinas, in his *In Ethicorum,* explains that "Postquam Philosophus determinavit de virtutibus intellectualis quae perficiunt intellectum circa ea quae sunt ex principiis hic determinat de virtutibus intellectualis perficientibus intellectum circa ipsa principia." According to both Aristotle and Aquinas, the perfect speculative science is philosophy. This is the science of the speculative intellect. Philosophy is the result of science (demonstration or deduction) and intelligence (the apprehension of first principles), and this will be the science of the first being (*Nicomachean Ethics*, 10.7).[47] As Aristotle writes, it is the science of the most sublime beings.[48]

If we compare this passage with the one in the *Convivio* III.2.17, which recalls Severinus Boethius's notion of philosophy, mind assumes a further meaning that confirms and enlarges that of Aristotle. It appears here in relation to Severinus Boethius that philosophy (*philo-sophia*) is in the mind of both God and human beings, and is coincident with the knowledge of eternal things identified with the ideas or divine substances. The Aristotelian notion is thus indirectly clarified through the method of comparison. Important here is the method Dante chooses in order to establish this content. This method links fields that are apparently distant – Severinus Boethius, Neoplatonism, and Aristotle's *Nicomachean Ethics* – in order to establish the divine status of the human mind. This method in chapter 2 thus works through the integration of a fragment of the *Nicomachean Ethics* with two fragments of Severinus Boethius's *De consolatione*. In this way, Dante introduces a thought that incorporates two different lines of thinking in order to establish a content much debated in Dante's time. The contemporaneous debate pronounces ancient contents; Dante seems interested in showing how much the ancient tradition is active in topics discussed and sometimes judged in his time to be heterodox. It seems that he wants to suggest that what is judged as heterodox is a product of an historical judgment, not an absolute truth. He reads Severinus Boethius in continuity with Aristotle, Aquinas, Albert, and perhaps Siger.

9. Reading with *Suspicio*

More clarity emerges when we attend to another fragment in chapter 2. Our focus has been the notion of philosophy as suggestive of the eternity of the human mind. In light of it, every section already examined works in detecting a meaning mostly doubtful: the eternity of human intellect and the chain of relations that this notion activates.

In light of such analysis, I will now start by reconsidering a fragment already quoted. If the fragments from Severinus Boethius have introduced a *suspicio* about the nature of the human mind in which philosophy is located on the model of God's mind, such *suspicio* may become stronger in light of the following passage, in which we read that "ciascuna forma sostanziale procede da Dio, e non ricevono diversitade per quella che è semplicissima, ma per le secondarie cagioni e per la materia in che discende" (Every substantial form proceeds from its first cause, which is God, as is stated in the book *On Causes*, and these forms receive their diversity not from it, which is most simple, but from the secondary causes and from the matter into which it descends; III.2.5). In the same book, he continues, in treating the infusion of divine goodness, is written the following: "And goodnesses and gifts are made diverse by the participation of the thing that receives them."[49] Then we read that "quello che è causato da corpo circulare dee in alcun modo circulare essere." Consequently, since every effect retains part of the nature of its cause (as Alpetragius says when he affirms that what is caused by a circular body must in some way be circular), every form in some way partakes of the divine nature, not because the divine nature is divided and distributed to them but because it is shared by them in almost the same way in which the nature of the sun is shared by the other stars.[50] Commentators on the *Convivio* here provide information about Alpetragius and his work *De Motibus*, and also quote passages from the anonymous *Liber de causis*. The central issue, however, belongs to the method Dante seeks to establish. To understand this method, we must examine the relation among the various fragments. It is evident, in fact, that if the substantial form is in itself "semplicissima," and if its diversity derives from the secondary causes and from the matter into which it descends, a *suspicio* or doubt takes place – that is, that the substantial form given by God can be one for all human beings. About this form we know also that it is natural for it to have a movement that is conversionary. The reason is that this movement is divine par excellence. The text has inserted this notion as well and suggests that the human mind is of divine nature, which means that it is a separate substance. Thus, if this is true, what has to be established is the identity of the thinking subject or mind. Such a mind could be identified with the possible intellect conceived as separate and eternal (eternal are the ideas in the mind of God). In addition, because this given form is defined "semplicissima," it could be suggested that, because it shares this property with its cause, who is God, and who is one and only one, this form is one for humankind taken as a whole. Siger, in his *Questiones in Metaphysicam*, commenting on book 5 of Aristotle's *Metaphysics*, had discussed the concept of *simplicitas*.[51] He identifies *simplicitas* with the being of the first cause: to be simple means to be not composed and to be one. One is not conceived merely as number but as principle. Accordingly, the one is indivisible. Siger also discusses the idea of oneness in the separate substances and declares that in such substances there is only one indivisible being that cannot be multiplied, a theory that Siger also takes up in his *In Tertium* (question 9). I recall these texts because Dante points out that the *simplicitas* of the giver of forms is also in the form given. This suggests a link with the idea that this *simplicitas* derives from the fact that what is one is able to give one. This is the view Siger proposes in his *Quaestiones in Metaphysicam* – as said – and in his *In Tertium* (but will reject in *Questiones de physica*, written years later). The notion of *simplicitas*, if rightly understood, is crucial to detecting Dante's position: If *simplicitas* introduces the notion of the human intellect as one – in this case, that is the unity of the intellect – Dante's position is not coincident with that of Albert. The nature of the being which the human mind contemplates, the *donna gentile*, in the framework the text organizes, in which our similitude to God's thinking is crucial, leads us to a most important content: the nature of the being that performs this activity of contemplating such a being – an activity that, as Aristotle says, is the science of the most sublime beings (*Nicomachean Ethics*, 6.7).[52] The eternal activity of God's philosophy, in this case, parallels the human mind's activity because the being of the intellect conceived as one is also eternal. Siger defines this intellect as being both eternal and created, while Dante affirms its divine philosophical activity, thus indirectly suggesting a parallel with the mind and the *philo-sophia* of God. This is probably the most important content of the third treatise of the *Convivio*, although it is mostly neglected; it is probably the content at which the unfinished *Convivio* is aimed in the first three treatises. In addition, Dante introduces another element that works, making the *suspicio* stronger; he writes, in fact, that the nature of what is desired reveals the nature of the being who desires, just as thinking and the thing that is thought are equal.

At 2.8, Dante says that it is possible to know the nature of the soul that loves by looking at the being that the soul loves: "si può conoscere quale è dentro l'anima, veggendo di fuori quelli che ama." Thus, if this being that the mind loves is separate and eternal – that is, according to the theory of eternity, a being ungenerated and incorruptible – this urges us to consider the nature of the human intellectual soul and mind, which, in loving, is united to and contemplates this separate and eternal being. We also know that this mind is a substantial form given by God, that it is extremely simple, and that it is diversified in virtue of the secondary causes and the matter that receives it. I will return to this principle later. Here, it is sufficient to say that, according to this teaching, what is one becomes plural according to the being, which receives it; that is, plurality is derived from what belongs to materiality. In terms of human cognition, we may say that it is the sensitive soul that allows our plurality. In addition, if we link this fragment with a fragment in Albert, which condemns the theory he attributes to "quidem philosophi" that what is one can contemplate only what is one, and the *donna gentile* is one,[53] then perhaps the peculiarity of what is here indicated as "mind" begins also to be delineated in relation to the being this mind contemplates. The simplicity shared by God and the form He gives are therefore of enormous importance, because this introduces another suspicion or doubt, which, if placed in continuity with the doubt about the eternity of philosophy, delineates, in a text deliberately given in a most fragmented way, a coherent line of contents. Dante's methodology relates different texts and lines of thinking from Aristotle's *Nicomachean Ethics* with an awareness of its link to the *Metaphysics*, the Neoplatonism of the theory of ideas, and archetypes in the mind of God, introduced through Severinus Boethius. Here, philosophy has the meaning of the intellectual activity that contemplates a divine idea. This allows us to compare such thinking or philosophical activity with the theories of intellectual happiness that were circulating in Dante's time. What takes form in our reading, therefore, is the justified *suspicio* or doubt that all these apparently scattered fragments create a coherent meaning: the eternity of philosophy seems to imply the eternity of the human mind, which is thought of as being both eternal and created (probably in line with Siger). This eternity of philosophy arises because eternal is the mind in which philosophy lives, that God's mind is eternal is well known, but eternity for the human mind implies not the individual mind but a universal mind that is one and everlasting. Philosophy, if attributed to the human mind, implies its eternity and such eternity sends us back to the highly problematic issue of a thinking entity – that is, one. This oneness, if read in light of the thinking of the commentator as retaken in the thirteenth century's so-called radical thought, is the only antecedent through which we may relate the two fragments from Severinus Boethius. This would imply that Dante, in an indirect way, is using ancient texts in the awareness of theories elaborated in more recent years and that have been condemned, in order to establish through the love for the gentle lady that the human mind is one for all human beings. It is therefore the simplicity of the form given by God that cooperates in opening here a thought offered in an oblique way, but which works to establish a crucial content: the form that human beings receive by God is one and eternal because it is in God, and is created because it was given to human beings (i.e., it is eternal and created). That this belief was part of a radical line of thinking we will further discuss by introducing texts that are part of the theory of intellectual happiness or the happiness of the mind.

However, if we use an Aristotelian terminology, the following question arises as it was put forth in my reading of the canzone: Because love implies that human minds contemplates the *donna gentile*, can this gentle lady be assimilated to Aristotle's agent intellect? If so, can the mind be assimilated to the possible intellect? In my explanation of the canzone's text, I first introduced the theory proposed by Albert, according to which the human possible intellect can contemplate the agent intellect as form. Then, in addition, certain lines of the canzone persuaded me to introduce tenets derived from Siger and his theory of the possible intellect (as exposed in his *In tertium*). In the canzoni, however, although Dante did not use an Aristotelian theory, the understanding of the theory of the agent intellect, which the text suggested, was crucial to my reading. I think that this theory is crucial in the commentary as well, where it is suggested rather than explicitly stated. Aquinas, in his commentary in book 3 of *De anima*, assumes that the agent intellect participates in the divine light as a separate substance but is not a separate substance. Therefore, it is not a Thomistic Aristotelianism that helps here, but rather an Aristotelianism related maybe to Albert (mixed with Neoplatonic elements). The peculiar inclination of Dante's position is suggested in passages like the following: "L'anima umana, che è forma nobilissima di queste che sotto il cielo sono generate" (The human soul that is the most intellectual among those that are created under the heaven). The superlative, "nobilissima," implies the supremacy of the intellectual. The similitude to the divine intelligences, as already underlined, suggests that the human intellect is actualized when united with a separate form.[54] This is in line with a theory that was active in Albert, whose positions were partially close to those of the Parisian philosophers. The French historian of medieval philosophy, Alain De Libera, has clarified this issue. His account recalls the important contribution of Nardi in order to show Albert's responsibility in establishing several contents close to a radical line of thinking. In fact, it is evident that Dante takes some contents that recall those of Aristotelianism from Albert. What is crucial to our understanding, however, is whether his basis (Dante's theory here) is that of Albert, or includes tenets more radical and derived from Averroes as mediated by the so-called radical Aristotelianism. Dante designates the object of such contemplative activity as the *donna gentile*, and the activity itself as philosophy. The subject that contemplates is indicated as mind, but the way in which this similitude of the divine mind and the human mind takes form requires careful consideration. The reason is that, through the fragments of Severinus Boethius about philosophy, it seems that the text is introducing an issue that coincides with the theory of intellectual happiness – that is, the discourse on the *summum bonum* (the highest good).

Dante here puts forth contents related to a debate that appears in documents from the last thirty years of the thirteenth century, although the debate draws on a more ancient tradition in order to witness the foundation of the present. It is clear that if we use the interpretive categories of Dante's time, we are in the area of the theory of intellectual happiness. This theory is built on a rereading of book 10 of the *Nicomachean Ethics*, as is testified for instance by Giacomo da Pistoia's *Quaestio de felicitate*. What interests us here is intellectual happiness, as it was discussed by a few commentators of Aristotle's *Nicomachean Ethics*. Among these commentators is Aquinas, who firmly distinguishes what we can know in this life and what in the other, and therefore what kind of happiness is reserved to this life. The latter is the temporal happiness Aquinas calls "imperfect beatitude." Dante recalls the definition of the human being as a "divine animal" (III.2.14). This definition refers to concepts in both Albert and the philosophers. Albert's *De anima* (1968) recalls, for instance, the philosophers who say that the human being has a divine operation because it is a caused being made in the likeness of the first cause (2.2, p. 21). It is also true that according to the philosophers, the intellect is regarded as divine. This was the position of Boethius of Dacia in his *De summo bono*. Albert, on this same point, recalls the philosophers and attributes the responsibility for their belief to the "Philosophus" (perhaps Avicenna) and to Algazel. The content he stigmatizes is the following: the intellectual soul is different in genus from the vegetative and sensitive soul, as it is a kind of divine genus, and the philosophers say that this alone is separated from the body as the eternal from the corruptible.[55] Albert condemns this theory; but what is Dante's position in relation to this passage? Dante draws on the thoughts of philosophers, and his position coincides with their horizon of thinking. Indeed, the theory of intellectual happiness that involves speculation and contemplation of separate substances in life finds its natural origin in the theory of the possible intellect, which, for Averroes and his followers, is unique, eternal, and separate. We should therefore place a strong distinction in the debate on happiness, as it was discussed by Aquinas in his commentary on the *Nicomachean Ethics*, and in a different way by Albert in his *Super ethicam*. Above all, we must distinguish the contents that were developed in the late thirteenth century by philosophers such as Boethius of Dacia, Giacomo da Pistoia, and Siger. (We have only a few pages of Siger's work on ethics, but his position can be inferred from other writing – for instance, his *In tertium*.)

Two points in Dante's text are worthy of special attention. It is true that the contemplation of separate substances during our earthly life is accepted by Albert. It is also true that this appears in Siger's *In Tertium*, and in the lost work *Tractatus de intellect*, handed down to us by the late testimony of Augustine Nifo. Both Albert and Siger believe that it is possible for humans in their earthly life to contemplate separate entities. In that belief, both differ from Aquinas, as was said above. We will see, however, that with respect to this common content, Albert and Siger stand apart from each other as well, and the cause of their difference is their different notions of the possible intellect. In any case, intellection here appears similar to the intellection which, according to Albert's *De anima*, is that of the speculative intellect. For Albert, this represents the possible intellect when it is linked in contemplation to a separate substance. What Dante is therefore focusing on is the speculative intellect, a human power that Albert explains in the following way: to live according to the speculative intellect is above human power. According to that intellect, he does not live as a human being, but according something divine that is in him: "Vivere igitur secundum intellectum speculativum supra hominem est. Secundum enim illum intellectum non vivit secundum quod homo est, sed vivit secundum quod aliquid divinum in ipso est" (*De anima*, 3.3.11). Of course, Albert asserts that the human mind, its possible intellect, can contemplate a separate substance. In such activity, the intellect is eternal and incorruptible and therefore able to contemplate an eternal being. However, the notion of eternity applied to the intellect in Albert is peculiar. He thinks that the possible intellect performs two functions in one: in one, it is perishable and takes place in its turning to phantasms; in the other, when it contemplates the agent intellect, it is eternal (eternal meaning, for Albert, "lasts forever"). Eternity, for him, does not touch on the theory of creation. In addition, Albert believes that every human being has his own possible intellect. He violently opposes the idea of the possible intellect as one for all human beings. Now our question is the following: Is there something in Dante's text that is *not* derived from Albert? What seems to be suggested here is that the eternity of philosophy implies the eternity of the mind in which such philosophical activity takes place; in this case, the intellect is indicated as mind, or "mente," a content that Dante does not derive from Albert.

Averroes, who is given the status of a "spirito magno" in Limbo, is without doubt a willed sign of Dante's independent judgment. Here, in this part of the *Convivio*, Dante draws from thinkers who represent a line of thinking close to what we call radical thought. In addition, if we compare this fragment from the *Convivio* with Albert's theory of the knowledge of separate substances in our mortal life, linking it to the debate on divine ideas as testified by the Parisian condemnation of 1277, we may infer that, according to Dante in this passage, the human being can know eternal beings in this life. The soul that performs this activity is the intellectual soul. We have seen that this idea was also accepted by Albert. But what remains to be seen is whether we are here in an area of thinking that could be identified as Albertine, or whether we must evaluate a line of thinking characterized as heterodox. In fact, it is the identification suggested between the thinking of the gentle lady and philosophy that creates *suspicio* or doubt. Nothing, however, can be affirmed with certainty at this point.

10. Intellectual Happiness and Philosophy

Intellectual happiness, as I use it, refers to a theory, which has been circulating since the late thirteenth century. It was derived from Aristotle's *Nicomachean Ethics* and was discussed by a few thinkers who, however, assumed different positions. According to such a theory, the human being can reach the perfect happiness in this life through his intellectual virtues.

A few articles condemned in Paris in 1277 are a document of the circulation of such a theory. The following condemned article, for instance, tells us that "Omne bonum quod homini possible est consistit in virtutibus intellectuales" (Every Good that is possible to human being consists in intellectual virtues). According to such a thesis, the good for a human being lies in his intellectual virtues, which are wisdom and philosophy (Hissette 1977, 263). Happiness as an intellectual goal was inspired by book 10 of the *Nicomachean Ethics;* it was retreaceble in many commentaries on ethics attributed to the thirteenth century and studied in the twentieth century by R.A. Gauthier and others. Medieval historians of philosophy have found the source of such a theory also in a work of Boethius of Dacia, *De summo bono*, and in other synchronous texts, which I will briefly introduce later.

Because the theory of intellectual happiness was a tenet of Aristole's ethics, the issue was confronted by thinkers like Aquinas and Albert in their comments on the *Nicomachean ethics*. As already mentioned, Aquinas asserts that it is impossibile in this life to reach such happiness; we cannot, he says, in our temporal state, contemplate separate substances. In fact, he distinguishes earthly from eternal happiness, whereas Albert thought that intellectual happiness can be reached during our mortal life (see Nardi 1960a, 114–15; Ardizzone 2011, 202–3). However, the circle of references in which Albert rooted his theory of intellectual happiness was different from that shared by philosophers like Boethius of Dacia and Giacomo of Pistoia. It is in them that the theory was clearly exposed and shaped on the idea that, during earthy life, it is possible to reach the intellectual contemplation of a divine being. In the *Nicomachean Ethics*, such contemplation was that of the wise man as a lover of *sophia*, or wisdom. However, Aristotle's ethics had to be linked with the thinking of the commentator in order to assess the radical theory of intellectual happiness. What has been read in Dante at this point does offer the picture of a sailing course, mapping the main error which the Greek-Arabic learning implanted in Europe in the thirteenth century – that is, the theory of the unicity of the human intellect. We proceed with such *suspicio*, which is difficult to transform into a certainty. If this is the case, however, we will see that in Dante, if this error is present, it has its own articulation. We know that Dante assumes this notion and elaborates it in a most personal way. Here his *Monarchia*, written years later, in which the possible intellect was conceived as one, and it was clearly said that the possible intellect actualizes itself though the multitude of human beings. We note that in the third treatise of the *Convivio*, the word "mind," as already said, indicates a being in an act in virtue of the contemplation of an entity which is eternal, incorruptible, separate, and one. Love, in the first verse of the canzone, introduced a relationship between two beings, and the interior reasoning indicated the link with an eternal substance – but on the part of what kind of entity? Moreover, what is the "amicizia" between the mind and the woman as introduced in chapter 1 of the third treatise? We must also consider that the canzone organizes its meanings by using a complex doctrinal language. The prose, which is apparently clear and mostly explicative, seems to create its own ground reference surreptitiously. The watchword was *to veil*; but how does Dante follow this path? Philosophy has not to be veiled, as Gauthier (1984) has pointed out; this was Siger's statement. In other philosophers, however, the discussion was conducted though a close and difficult speech. It is not a coincidence that the *Convivio* writes that the woman is veiled and what is veiled is the soul. This must be deciphered as a sort of sign of intelligence with the people Dante thought to be his readers. These readers, we are informed, were ignorant of Latin but, according to what we have read, had to be able to grasp strategies entrusted to the vocabulary and to the contexts Dante was organizing. They were required, it seems, to read and detect relationships, the meaning of which was not immediately evident on the page. The notion that this chapter 2 of the third treatise introduces, thanks to relations still to be better understood, is the nature of the human mind described as able to contemplate a separate substance. The reading given of the canzone seems confirmed up to this point, but, as we have seen, it builds on more texts. We have, as on a screen, the image of what the philosophers call intellectual happiness or the *summum bonum* (supreme good). Albert's position is confirmed, but probably something more specific, and maybe heterodox, enters. What remains open is whether and how the contents that were introduced in the canzone are taken up. The being able to contemplate eternal separate substances in life is the possible intellect. Albert's position is close to contents introduced by the Arabs and Averroes, but he reshapes them. He opposes the idea of the possible intellect as one; however, he does consider it unmixed and separated from the body. Giacomo takes a different position in his *Quaestio de felicitate*, which introduces the notion of intellectual happiness as the final result of a difficult path that may culminate in the contemplation of separate substances or God. This kind of contemplation is offered as proper to the possible intellect.[56] In Siger, this contemplation is available to us as a collective knowledge and just because the possible intellect is separate, eternal, and incorruptible. More difficult to grasp is the position of the *De summo bono* by Boethius of Dacia, assumed by some as to be a kind of manifesto of radical Aristotelianism.[57] Here is a fragment:

> Divinum autem in homine vocat intellectum; si enim in homine aliquid divinum est, dignum est quod hoc sit intellectus ... Cum enim intellectus primus sit maximae virtutis in intelligendo, *intelligibile* autem quod intellegit sit nobilissimum, quia suis ipsius essentia-quid enim nobilius potest intellectus divinus intelligere quam sit essentia divina? – ideo habet vitam voluptuosissimam.
>
> The human being intellect is called divinum, in fact if something divine is in the human being this is his intellect ... and because the first intellect is the highest intellectual being and the object that he intellects is the noblest, because is part of his essence,what can be more noble that the divine intellect can intelligere than his own essence? (*De summo bono* 1976, 370–1)

We may also note that Boethius of Dacia's philosophical rigour culminates in a goal that is theological, although his goal derives from book 10.7–8 of Aristotle's *Nicomachean Ethics*. Boethius of Dacia introduces a parallel between the happiness of the *intellectus primus* and that of the human being. Here is another fragment from his *De summo bono*:

> Unde ex hoc quod intellectus delectate intelligentem vult Philosophus in XI Metaphysicae quod intellectus primus vitam habet voluptuosissimam. Cum enim intellectus primus sit maximae virtutis in intelligendo intellegibile autem quod intelligit sit nobilissimum, quia sui ipsius essentia.
>
> According to the Philosopher in Book XII of the *Metaphysics*, the first intellect or God enjoys a life of pleasure. And because this intellect has as its greatest virtue the activity of intellection of an intelligible being, what he intellects is the most noble, because it is part of his essence. (*De summo bono* 1976, 370–1)

Boethius of Dacia explains that the human being is given as his *summum bonum* the contemplation of "universitatis entium quae sunt a primo principio et per hoc primi principii" – that is, of beings that derive from the first principle and therefore of the first principle itself: "Hoc enim est maius bonum quod homo a deo recipere potest et quod deus homini dare potest in hac vita" (This is the highest good that a human being can receive from God and which God can give him in this life;372). He continues:

Philosophus autem gustavit delectationem intellectualem in speculando veritates entium ... ideo philosophus vivit sicut homo innatus est vivere secundum ordinem naturalem, cum omnes virtutes in eo inferiores et actiones earum sint propter virtutes superiores et actiones earum et omnes universaliter propter virtutem supremam et actionem ultimam, quae est speculatio veritatis et delectatio in illa, et precipue veritatis primae, numquam enim satiatur appetitus sciendi, donec sciatur ens increatum. Quaestio enim de intellectu divino est naturaliter sciri desiderata ab omnis hominibus, ut dicit Commentator.

The philosopher tastes intellectual pleasure when he contemplates the truth of beings. He thus lives according to the natural order. In fact, his lower virtues and actions aim at higher virtues and actions, and all universally have as their goal the highest virtue and supreme and final action. This is the knowledge of the highest truth and the pleasure in contemplating this truth: the appetite for knowledge is never satisfied until it knows the uncreated being. The *quaestio* about the divine intellect is the natural knowledge of what is desired by all human beings, as the Commentator says. (*De summo bono* 1976, 377)[58]

This fragment introduces an eloquent presentation of intellectual happiness. Such happiness, coincident with the *summum bonum*, is the act of contemplating the separate substances or the first being that is the *ens increatum*, or God. We read also that it is proper to the philosopher to contemplate the truth of *entium*. This content obviously refers to Aristotle's *Metaphysics*, which introduces what in the Latin translation corresponds to philosophy. According to this *quaestio*, however, the reason why the philosopher can reach this knowledge or science is not given, nor is there a discussion about contemplation as possible for the intellect conceived as one. This lack is what the reader seeks when he tries to ascertain whether there is in the text a space or a meaning that is not yet understood. We read here that the *quaestio* about the divine intellect is the natural knowledge of what is desired by all human beings. Here emerges a kind of common good as a natural good.[59] According to theories derived from Averroes, it is the common possible intellect that can reach such perfection. In Boethius of Dacia, there is a passage that can be referred to as something related to such a theory: "Tunc sequitur quod summum bonum quod est homini possibilis, secundum intellectum speculativum, est cognitio veri in singulis et delectatio in eodem" (From this it follows that the highest good which is possible for the human being to reach according to his speculative intellect is the cognition of truth as it takes place in what is singular (one) and happiness in the same; 1976. 371). The expression *in singulis* means, I suggest, one and, in particular, one by one. It strongly suggests that cognition and delight are equal, and that both take place in what is one. *In singulis* implies thus that the speculative intellect is one –that is, singular in number. The Latin ablative in its plural form means that cognition (*veri*) and intellectual delight (*in eodem*) can take place between two single beings (although Wippel 1976 does not translate in this way). According to Averroistic tenets, these are the possible intellect thought as one, and the first being. As mentioned above, a different view is taken by Aquinas, for whom such happiness is impossible in this life. Boethius of Dacia assumes, however, and says clearly, that it belongs to this life and is reached by reason: "Qui enim perfectior est in beatitudine, quam in hac vita homini possibile esse per rationem scimus, ipse propinquior est beatitudini quam in vita futura o per fidem expectamus" (The one who is more perfect in blessedness, which we know to be possible for man through his reason, is himself closer to the blessedness that we expect in a future life or through faith; 1976, 372). Dante does not express a similar view. Rather, he says, as we read in the canzone, that the form which the human mind contemplates belongs to the divine, is thought by God, and is also contemplated by the intellects, which includes angelic intelligences, a concept he reiterates in the prose. This theory, to which I will return later, that is refuted by Aquinas in his criticism of Averroes in his *De unitate intellectus*, confirms that Dante's position is close to radical contents. Before concluding this section, however, I want go back to another text I have previously recalled on happiness written in the 1290s by a magister from Bologna, Giacomo da Pistoia. In his *Quaestio de felicitate*, Giacomo presents the issue of intellectual happiness as *summum bonum* and as a kind of intellectual pleasure that can be reached if the human being lives a pure intellectual life and has perfect control of his passions. Happiness (*felicitas*), we read, is an operation *optima et nobilissima* and is performed by an *optima et nobilissima virtute*. This virtue is *sapientia*. *Felicitas* consists, therefore, in something we share with God and consists in speculation, an operation proper to people who have intellect: "Et hoc dicit Aristotle in decimo ethicorum, quod felicitas consistit in speculari" (Happiness for intellectual beings is coincident with speculation; 1955, 448–50). Giacomo explains that this *intelligere* must be a *summum et nobilissimum intelligere* (the highest and most intellectual form of intellection), which must be exercised on the best and noblest intelligible; "Prima est quod sit alicuius optimi et nobilissimi intellegibilis." This operation must be continuous and belongs to the noblest virtue (451). What follows is most important; here Giacomo summarizes and further explains what he has said:

> Sunt ergo quattuor condiciones eius intelligere in quo consistit ultima felicitas hominis. Prima est quod sit nobilissimi intelligibilis, seconda quod sit continuum prout possible est homini, tertia est quod sit a nobilissima virtute, quarta quod sit in nobilissimo subiecto. Cum igitur nobilissimum intelligible sit substantia separata et inter substantias separatas ipse Deus, ut planum est omnibus intelligentibus in philosophia, et nobilissima virtus sit sapientia, ut dicitur sexto ethicorum, relinquitur quod felicitas nihil alius est quam continue sicut possibilis est homini intelligere substantias separas et precipue ipse deum.
>
> There are four conditions of the intellect in which the highest happiness consists. The first is an intellection of what is the most noble and intelligible; second, it must be continuous for the human being as far as possible; third, it must be an activity of the highest virtue; and fourth, it must be exercised in the most noble subject. Because the highest intelligible are separate substances (among them God himself), as is clear to all who have intellection in philosophy, and because the highest virtue is *sapientia.* According to book 6 of the *Ethics*, what remains is that happiness is nothing other than a continuous intellection of separate substances and of God himself, an intellection that is continuous, insofar as this is possible for human beings. (1955, 451–2)

In the next section, Giacomo further clarifies that it is the possible intellect which has the power of intellecting *substantias separatas* and God. Here the possible intellect is defined as a *genus novum materiae* (453). Happiness is presented as consisting in an intellectual virtue that performs the operation of contemplating a being separate and eternal on the part of the possible intellect, which also is a separate being. Crucial to this theory is the idea that the intellectual is separate from the vegetative and sensitive functions of human beings. The union occurs, according to Giacomo, through the *medium* as the natural tool able to link what is separate and which implies that in the human being there are a plurality of souls' functions. The similarity between Boethius of Dacia and Giacomo is well known, but my aim is to establish whether, and in what way, Dante participates in this thought. Giacomo states that sciences are a kind of training for reaching intellectual happiness. Thus, in order to prepare the intellect for speculative activity, it is necessary to activate its dispositions. This is possible through the sciences, which, in the order in which they are listed, comprise dialectic, rhetoric, mathematics, physics, and finally the science of beings that are separate from materiality and that are speculative, divine, and separate from matter. In them are the most noble of the things that are speculative: "speculabilia divina atque separate a materia qua sunt intelligibilium nobilissima." *Sapientia* here is the term for philosophy, as we find it in Aristotle's *Metaphysics*, and (as Giacomo recalls) in book 6 of the *Nicomachean Ethics*, a book referred to in my previous section, following Dante's indication. The coincidence between *sapientia* as an activity or operation performed by the possible intellect and its object of contemplation, which is a separate substance or God, implies that this operation is possible for a being that is also separate and defined as a *novus genus materiae*, according to the commentator, as Giacomo writes.

Going back to Dante, we see that this theory is of help in our attempt to understand the way in which "mind" (chapter 2) is suggested in his text and in light of the relations that have been activated. According to Giacomo, *sapientia* is the noblest virtue proper to the possible separate intellect, which, as described by the commentator, is one, eternal, and incorruptible (although Giacomo does not explicitly say so, but just that it is a "novum genus materiae"). Therefore, recalling philosophy as an activity shared by God's mind and by that of human beings (according to Severinus Boethius), Dante creates a frame of far-reaching references. The human mind is capable of contemplating the divine ideas, which are separate substances. It shares this activity with God and with the divine substances or intelligences. Thanks to the citation from Severinus Boethius, we enter into a context that offers a new element. It is not only (as we have noted) the notion of human mind proposed in the likeness of God's mind contemplating a separated substance. It is also this notion of philosophy in the mind of God that requires further investigation. Contemplation or philosophy on the part of God is suggested as eternal, once this is indicated as something shared by human beings, and this raises a problem. Eternal beings think only eternal things, and God has philosophy in his mind eternally, but how can human beings share this philosophy and its eternity? This problem was not introduced in the canzone in these terms. The eternity of the woman was clearly put forth because what God thinks (the lady was thought by God) is, like him, eternal. One line in particular was unequivocal: "costei penso chi mosse l'universo" (She is thought by him who set the heavens in motion; 72). Now again it is clearly suggested that philosophy is eternal. This is one of the topics of the *Convivio* that is never taken into consideration by his readers. In my reading, it emerges in virtue of Dante's methodology, which sometimes, in order to point out a precise source, looks at the relationships that Dante's discussion builds on the page.

What I intend to investigate is the following: Does the suggested notion of the eternity of philosophy told as in the mind of human beings leads us to the view that the intellect is one for all human beings? Dante works by organizing forms of syllogistic reasoning that are not perfectly structured. In this way, he pushes the mind of his reader to work through deductions. In our discussion of the canzone, we have already indicated a few contents crucial for setting such deductions. In my reading, it was the being of the lady that established the first level of meaning. From this, we deduced the significance of the word "mind" described as contemplating this woman. I have discussed these topics earlier. Now, however, the prose text offers a new content that should confirm what the canzone has already suggested – that is, the unity or oneness of the intellect. In the third treatise, however, a new meaning arises because philosophy, as it exists in the mind of God, is said to be in the minds of human beings as well. We cannot deduce much more from these fragments, but new studies on the so-called *introductiones* to philosophy are of help. To these texts, edited by Lafleur in 1988, we may add in particular a text of Bolognese origin published by Gianfranco Fioravanti in the early 1990s, "Sermones in lode della philosopfia e della logica a Bologna nella prima metà del xiv secolo," in which we read, "est autem sapientia divinarum humananrumque rerum a quibus hec res continentur, scientia cuius studium qui vituperat non sane intelligo quid cum laude hec" (172).[60] Fioravanti briefly discusses this text in his introduction and describes it as part of the texts in praise of philosophy that were circulating in Paris in the thirteenth century. The content of the sermons, which functioned as an introduction to university courses in the faculty of arts, share something with the discussion addressed in the *De Quaestio de felicitate* by Giacomo and in *De summo bono* by Boethius of Dacia (1976).

The similarity of the two texts consists in their establishing that the philosophical pathway through the sciences is a tool for reaching the highest science, or *sapienta*. This knowledge thus represents a conquest activated by our intellect. In the *sermo* of Matheus De Eugubio (edited by Fioravanti, 1992), philosophy is identified with the *sapientia* of the proverbs and with the *verbum* of the Gospel of John, in which we read, "Ego sum lux mundi" (I am the light of the world). In this context, Averroes's teaching is recalled and linked to the Bible (177). Philosophy's eternity seems therefore to be suggested because of the eternity of *sapientia* and of the Word. A few passages in the *sermo* are of interest. One in particular, in which philosophy is praised as being of divine origin, provides a description in which Cicero's *De officiis* is quoted in order to define philosophy, in particular *sapientia*. Here, we read that philosophy is wisdom of things divine and human in which such thing are contained, a science that has to be studied, that is not possible to rail against, and for which just praise is proper (Fioravanti in Buzzetti, Ferriani, and Tabarroni 1992, 172). Philosophy is divided into logic, physics, divine, and moral philosophy. Moral philosophy is divided into *monastica* when it teaches the *bene vivere* as *individuum* (how to live as an individual), *oeconomica* when it belongs to the family, and *politica* when it belongs to the life of the city. The first *scientia* is logic, and the commentator (*Averroes commentista*) is recalled. The Gospel of John is also used to establish the meaning of *philosophia rationalis*. After a discussion on physics, there follows a brief discussion of *scientia deitalis*, which is identified with *metaphysica* and *sapientia*. Recalling Seneca's *Litterae ad Lucilium*, *philosophia* is praised as being derived from God. In the final part, we read that, thanks to philosophy, we get an inestimable deity: "consequimur deitatem inextimabilem" (Fioravanti, 1992, p. 185). Then, recalling an unidentified Boethius on Seneca's *auctoritate*, he says: "hoc est unum quod mihi promittit philosophiam ut me Deo parem facet" (This is what to me philosophy promises: that I become similar to God). In this text of Matheus of Eugubio, who is an author listed as an Averroist in Kuksewicz's 1965 edition of Averroism in Bologna in the fourteenth century (Kuksewicz 1965, 226–45), this notion of philosophy can be linked to heterodoxy. A trace of this thinking can be found in the discussion about the human soul as part of physics, which suggests that the intellectual part, assimilated to that of the angels, is separate. The soul here is defined as being one in *substantia*; the name changes because the soul's *proprietates* are diverse. What is evident, however, is the knowledge of divine things on the part of philosophers. In this context, there is no indication of the main error – that is, the notion of the intellect as separate and one. The same Matheus wrote about this contemplation of divine things in the text published by Kuksewicz (1965). There, traces can be found of so-called monopsychism. However, it was a content that had to be researched through a close reading in order to be properly understood. In this text by Matheus, too, it seems that what we read has to suggest something that is not immediately understandable; it seems that we have a blank page, a space not yet filled, which seems to be the true centre of the text itself. Looking at these texts I have shortly introduced, it seems to be usual to discuss the framework in order to suggest the true centre of discussion – that is, the true nature of the intellect, a notion that only philosophers can detect. The discussion about happiness seems related to this issue, at least for Giacomo and Boethius of Dacia. Readers, however, must engage in their own intellectual work if this connection is to emerge. The praise of philosophy, like that of Matheus, shares crucial assertions with the teachings proposed by Giacomo and Boethius of Dacia. Another text can also be introduced before we conclude this section. This text was published by Fioravanti in 1991 in which some similarities with Boethius of Dacia and Giacomo are traceable:

> Intellectus humanum naturaliter inclinatur ad ens increatum quia intellectus (sciens) habet cognitionem de aliqua re, sciens rem istam habere aliam causam, naturaliter inclinatur ad istam causam rei quia non potest cognoscere rem nisi per causam, sed omnis res citra primum habet [causam] causam primam, ergo intellectus naturaliter inclinatur ad causam primam.
>
> The human intellect naturally inclines towards the knowledge of God. Because it has the power to know *per causam*, it has the inborn inclination to know this cause. But everything with the exception of the first being has a first cause thus the intellect naturally inclines toward the first cause. (Fioravanti 1991, 280–1)

The conclusion makes clearer the theory expressed above:

> Item homo non cognoscit Deum per virtutem sensitivam, sed per *effectum immediate dei qui est intellectus* et ideo cum intellectus sit impressio cui imprimatur Primum, per istam impressionem intelligit homo Primum, non autem per sensum et talis cognition forte est naturalis in intellectu hominis.

> The human being does not know God in virtue of his sensitive soul, but through the immediate effect of God that is his intellect, thus the intellect being an imprint in which is imprinted God, for such impression the human being knows God and not in virtue of his sensitive soul, and such cognition is natural to the human being intellect. (Fioravanti 1991)

This fragment eloquently explains the notion of *effects* and reintroduces the notion of *reditus* recalled above. The notion of "effectum immediate dei" recalls the theory that the immediate effect that comes from the One is just one. Because God has impressed in us the intellect, it is through this impression that the intellect, by virtue of its natural inclination, can know the first cause. What is of importance here is that the intellect is indicated as *effectum immediate dei*. Here, in fact, the author recalls a theory well known to the philosophers, a theory condemned in an article which, in Hissette (1977, 70–2), is listed as proposition 64: "Quod effectus immediatus a primo debet esse unus tantum et simillimus primo" (The immediate effect that comes out from the first being has to be One and the most similar to the first being). It is precisely this theory that makes the *Quaestio* interesting for us, since it addresses the theory of the intellect as the one that can reach the knowledge of God. This is, of course, a theory on which Siger, too, is involved. Hissette (1977) quotes two fragments by Siger on this point.[61] What matters for us is that the work seems to testify and confirm the link among the knowledge as it is announced at the beginning of the *Metaphysics* – that is, the theory of intellectual happiness with the oneness of the intellect. In light of this landscape of a debate, as testified by texts that Dante just partially may or may not have known, the author of the *Convivio* seems to assume his own position. According to him, it is not just the philosopher who can contemplate the separate substances or God.

He introduces, in fact, as already underlined, a variant in his quotation from Boethius. In addition, he offers his readers crucial tools in order to orient them. These tools are, at first, the brief passage in which he underlines the notion of the simplicity of the form given by God, a simplicity that is differentiated in virtue of the material being that receives it – that is, because the intellect is one, it is the sensitive soul that allows what is individual. Dante has his own way of thinking about this crucial content, but the notion of the simplicity of the form is offered here only as a trace of a thinking in progress.[62] The possible coincidence with a radical line of thinking is confirmed if we note another passage of *Convivio* in which the prose text conceals a concept that takes us back to Boethius of Dacia:

> L'anima umana che è forma nobilissima di queste che sotto il cielo sono generate ... l'anima umana essere vuole naturalmente con tutto desiderio; e però che il suo essere dipende da Dio e per quello si conserva, naturalmente disia e vuole essere a Dio unita per lo suo essere fortificare. E però che ne le bontadi de la natura si mostra la divina, ven[e] che naturalmente l'anima umana con quelle per via spirituale si unisce, tanto più tosto e tanto più forte quanto quelle più appaiono perfette.
>
> The human soul, which is the noblest form of all those that are generated beneath the heavens, receives more of the divine nature than any other. And since the will to exist is most consequently natural in God – because, as we read in the book cited above, "being is the first thing, and before that there is nothing," the human soul, which is the noblest form of all those that are generated beneath the heavens, receives more of the divine nature than any other. The human soul by nature desires with all its will to exist; and since its being depends on God and is preserved by Him, it naturally longs and desires to be united with God in order to strengthen its being. Because the divine goodness reveals itself in the goodnesses of nature, it happens that the human soul naturally unites itself with them in a spiritual manner, more quickly and more strongly as they appear the more perfect. (2.7–9)

This passage utilizes the mystical language but conceals a different theory; it echoes also the speculative theory of St. Paul but substitutes vision with union. The content of Paul's theory, however, is given a new goal. The gentle lady is a natural good, but "natural" here does not mean that she belongs to the world of physics. She is, on the contrary, a substance separate and intellectual. For this reason, the tendency towards union with her takes us back again to the discussion about contemplation of a being, the lady, who brings us closer to the first being or cause. "Natural" means that this tension is in agreement with the nature of the intellect, which is separate and simple, and therefore looks for what is separate and one. Thus the mystical Pauline echos in this text introduce meanings that are the opposite of those explicitly given in such a tradition. In St. Paul, for instance, we cannot have knowledge of God during our earthly life. In this life, we can know God only through mirrors and enigmas. In Dante's text, however, we may contemplate and thereby achieve the union with the lady, who partakes of God's essence. However, because she has been described as a separate substance and as a being that the divine thinks, we can infer that Dante uses covert speech similar to that of Boethius of Dacia in his *De summo bono,* or to that of the unknown author of the *Questiones in metaphisicam* (edited by Fioravanti, 1991) that I have quoted above.

Here is another quotation from Boethius of Dacia that is not so far from Dante's fragment quoted above:

> Ideo philosophus speculando entia causata,quae sunt in mondo, et naturae eorum et ordinem eorum ad invicem inducitur in speculationem altissimarum causarum rerum, quia cognitio effectuum est quedam manuductio in cognitionem suae causae,et cognoscens causae superiores et naturae earum esse tales, quod necesse est eas habere aliam causam, inducitur in cognitionem primae causae.
>
> The philosopher speculating on caused beings that are in the world, and on their nature and order, is induced to contemplate the highest causes of things. The reason is that the knowledge of effects is a pathway to the cognition of their causes. Moreover, the philosopher knows that causes and their natures necessarily lead to a knowledge of the highest or first cause. (1976, 375)

Here, however, the Pauline theory is recalled to be denied, because from the effects or caused beings the human being can reach knowledge of God in this life. Other elements may also cause wonder in the reader of this third treatise, especially if we go on to read the next chapter (chapter 3, which I discuss in the next section), which is strongly linked to this one and which makes more explicit what the discussion about philosophy seems to introduce, furtherly contributing to showing how Dante shapes his own participation in the general debate of the time. In light of it, the idea shared by many scholars that Dante has worked on the *Convivio,* and in particular on this part of the doctrinal treatise in Bologna, acquires more evidence. Bologna was, in fact, the centre of the doctrinal debate and masters in Bologna were Giacomo da Pistoia and other radical intellectuals.

11. The Honest (*Honestum*) as *Summum Bonum*

The third chapter of the third treatise requires another pause. Navigation here traverses an apparently calm but in fact treacherous stretch of water. The pervasive theme of his part of the treatise deals with the nature of human mind that is discussed in relation to the honest. Once more, our reading requires an understanding of Dante's writing strategy. This is accomplished by building the discourse on the human soul in a way that is almost allusive.

The chapter opens with a description of love as performing its own operation in the mind: "Non senza cagione dico che questo amore fa la sua operazione ne la mente, ma ragionevolmente si dice a dare a intendere quale amore è questo per lo loco nel quale adopera" (It is not without cause that I say that this love performs its operation in my mind, but with good reason, so that by telling of the place in which it operates we might understand what kind of love this is; III.3.1). Love is then discussed in relation to the theory of natural place, which is one of the *topoi* of Aristotle and Aristotelianism. Because everything has an inborn love specific to its nature, so that the simple bodies love the place natural to them, we see that the earth always tends and descends towards the centre, and fire has a tendency to ascend. In the same way, the human soul participates in many different natures and performs different functions. These are coincident with the Aristotelian division of the three souls' functions. In virtue of its intellectual nature, the soul tends towards the perfect and the honest: "li uomini hanno loro proprio amore a le perfette e oneste cose ... E però che l'uomo- avvegna che una sola sostanza sia tutta[sua] forma per la sua nobilitade – ha in se natura divina, queste cose [e] tutti questi amori puote avere, e tutti li ha." Here, it is said that the human soul participates in the hierarchy of natural beings and therefore participates in elements or simple bodies like air, water, fire, earth, and in mixed bodies such as minerals. It also participates in the life of plants because of the vegetative soul, and in the life of animals because of the sensitive soul. For his intellective soul, which is properly human or, better, angelic – that is, rational – the human being has his *proprium bonum* or proper good, towards which he tends. Because this tending implies natural desire, the human being has an inborn love of truth and virtue (III.2.5).

According to what we read in the *Nicomachean Ethics*, the good (*bonum*) is what all beings desire,[63] but the good (*bonum*) proper to the human being is indicated as the "honestum," and Dante's text reads that "l'uomo ha il suo proprio amore a le perfette e oneste cose" (men have their proper love for things that are perfect and honest; 3.5). From this angelic nature, "la quinta e ultima natura: vera umana o meglio angelica e cioè rationale" (by virtue of the fifth and last nature, namely the truly human or, to be more precise, the angelic nature, which is to say the rational, because of it, man has a love for truth and virtue, from which is born the true and perfect friendship that belongs to the honest, as the philosopher says in the eighth book of his *Ethics* when he discusses friendship; III.3.11). The human being's specific nature is rational, angelic, and has a name – that is, *mind* – "questa natura si chiama mente" (III.3.12). This association between the human and angelic nature is also traceable in a partially synchronous Latin work, *De vulgari eloquentia*, where the human rationality is linked with the search for the honest (*honestum*), "secundum quod rationale, honestum querit, in quo solus est, vel angelice sociatur nature" (because he is rational he searches the honest, in that he is alone, or better, he is associated with the angelic nature; 2.2.6).

In the *Vita nuova*, Dante introduced the adjective "honest," which I have proposed to read in relation to Augustine as intellectual beauty, or better, as an intelligible beauty, "honestatem voco intelligibilem pulchitudinem." This meaning may be confirmed in the fragment quoted above from the *De vulgari*. In this text, the relation with the angels suggests the common desire for, and tendency towards, God, who is the *bonum* proper to the angelic intelligences.In fact, starting with Cicero, who translated Plato's *kalon* as *honestum*, this word delineates what is beautiful as intellectual, or better, the intellectual as good and beautiful. The source of our reading was in Augustine, and in turn, his reading of Cicero. Along this track we find Albert, who, in his work on the *Divinis nominibus* by Pseudo-Dionysius, discusses the *honestum* as coincident with the good and the beautiful (*De bono et pulchro*).[64] In his commentary on the *Nicomachean Ethics*, Aquinas identifies the *bonum* with the *honestum* ("honestum quod est bonum simpliciter"). He regards the love for the *bonum-honestum* as a form of friendship, and because what is *bonum* is in itself perfect and desirable, and the true good for the human being is what is proper to him according to reason, the perfect friendship (which, according to the beginning of this treatise, makes of two one) assumes the form of love for what is good and honest, and so intellectual and intelligible.[65] Because we know that God being the absolute *bonum* is the model for this love, that in Him the beautiful and the good are coincident (*kalos kai agathos*), and that He is the absolute intellectual being, then, it seems that the human being, in his love for the gentle woman, participates in the angelic nature and, like the angels, experiences the same desire for the divine. In this love, therefore, he shows the possibility of contemplating something that belongs to the divine. If this is true, our tendency towards the *honestum* is a tendency towards the divine.[66]

This takes us back to the desire for knowledge, with which both the *Convivio* and Aristotle's *Metaphysics* start, and also back to intellectual happiness, which consists in the contemplation of the divine or something belonging to the divine. The honest here thus implies perfect friendship, which establishes an intellectual unity between two entities: the human mind and the gentle lady. How this love for the honest takes place depends, according to Dante, on our mind, which, we have been told, is angelic or rational. The angels, as is well known, have as the object of their desire only one being – God. The *Convivio* is grounded in this love, which it takes as its starting point, and indicates it, in a biblical trope, as "pane degli angeli." This angelic bread is the proper food for intellectual beings. It is the contemplation reserved to *i sapienti*. According to Augustine's commentary on the Gospel of John, however, the bread of angels is the *verbum* or *logos*, where *logos* is identical with the divine ideas, and the *verbum* is the idea of ideas.[67] Dante will reintroduce this content in his *Paradiso*, where Christ is identified as the divine idea ("quell'idea che partorisce amando il nostro sire," XIII.54). What is of note is that the gentle woman, because the friendship with her is perfect, is put forth here as being that perfect and honest thing that the human mind loves and towards which it always tends. We have here, therefore, a confirmation of the results of our reading of the canzone, because there the gentle lady was presented as a separate substance thought by God ("costei pensò chi mosse l'Universo," v. 72) and contemplated by intelligences ("ogn'Intelletto di lassu la mira," v. 23). The link we have underlined with the *De vulgari eloquentia* and the angelic contemplation of God suggests that the *honestum* in the treatise plays a crucial role formulated on the basis of intellectual happiness.

The relation between this part of the third treatise and the incipit of the *Convivio* returns if we consider that there the desire for knowing was related to the assertion that every being naturally inclines to its own perfection, which was regarded as the result of the being's first and proper nature, "la natura propria e sostanziale di ogni cose" (the nature that is proper and essential of every thing).[68] In the incipit, the human inclination towards perfection manifests itself as the desire to know, and science is said to be the highest perfection of our soul and the source of our happiness. Here, in this third treatise, the specific nature of the human being drives him to his own *bonum*, which is the honest. Dante seems to find his own way towards contributing to a field he entered when he wrote the two canzoni, and in particular, *Amor che ne la mente mi ragiona.*

It is evident that the author creates a circle of references in order to express his own content. A reference to the framework that he organizes may help in understanding Dante's own path. What belongs to the contemporaneous debate is rethought in light of the *auctores* of the past: the present has an ancient flavour. The importance of the honestum is built on this awareness. In Cicero's *De officiis,* the honestum was considered to be the *summum bonum.* There we read the expression *perfectum honestum,* or the perfect honest, a kind of honest which coincides with the *summum bonum* and is the thing towards which wise men tend. In fact, this object of desire on the part of the *sapientes* is the *honestum,* which is also the *summum bonum.*[69] According to Cicero, this *summum bonum* as *honestum* implies intellectual values and an intellectual good, and such good is a common good. Right (*ius*) appears to be the common good for human beings living in an organized political community (see Coleman 2000, 253). For Cicero, it is opposed to the *summum bonum* as *voluptas,* which was the Epicurean notion of the *summum bonum.* Dante, perhaps at this time, has already and importantly located *ius,* or "dirittura," in the mind of God. In the *De vulgari eloquentia,* he has indicated himself as *cantor rectitudinis* (rectum, right). Later, the *Monarchia* will clearly and powerfully establishes the *ius* in the mind of God. The same content we read in the canzone *Tre donne intorno al cor mi son venute,* certainly written in the years of exile, probably in the first years of it. The perfect friendship between the human mind and the *donna gentile* seems to herald a divine common good. For that, Dante seems to link Cicero and Aristotle, but in Boethius's *De consolatione,* God was the *summum bonum.* When Dante uses the expression "perfect friendship" (or friendship that approaches perfection and honesty), he seems to echo Cicero, not in order to overshadow the relation of perfect friendship between the mind and the gentle woman, but mostly because he intends to rethink the notion of the *honestum,* relating it to the *summum bonum.* He does not, however, openly enunciate it.

We know that *De summo bono* was the title of Boethius of Dacia's radical text on intellectual happiness, but Dante does not mention it. He introduces instead the word "honest" in a context in which he speaks of the natural friendship of the human mind with the gentle lady. He seems to organize a mosaic made of different tiles in order to put forth the perfect good for human beings. What is important here is an awareness of the synchronous debate and Dante's attempt to formulate his own answer. Up to this point, we have seen that the gentle lady is suggested as a separate substance thought by the divine and therefore part of the divine thinking. If the human being has a perfect friendship with this separate substance, then the love for this woman not only implies the contemplation of a separate substance in life but perhaps also covertly introduces a topic related to intellectual happiness; if the the honestum as it is present in "oneste e perfette cose" implies a divine common good, this confirms the *suspicio* of our reading. The theory of intellectual happiness, in fact, deals with the field of contemplation of God or perfect theoretical consideration in life.

We have underlined that this contemplation takes place through human intellectual virtue. In a thinking labelled as "radical," the intellect that can contemplate a separate being is separate, too. In addition, some philosophers have asserted that only that which is one can contemplate what is one. I have already recalled in my reading of *Amor che ne la mente mi ragiona* that Dante suggests a link though contemplation between the *donna gentile*, who is one, and the many included in the collective name "gente." Collective implies unity as plural, and "gente" is a name which implies the many (Ardizzone 2014). These are concepts that deal with a strong linguistic sense, and of this sense we may find a trace in Siger's *Questiones in Metaphysicam*. My aim here is to determine whether this suspicion or doubt, as it occurs in the canzone, is confirmed in what Dante indicates as a literal commentary. It is well known that this theory of the intellect as one was vehemently rejected by both Albert and Aquinas, and that this theory of the unity of intellect was responsible for a series of errors that led to the Parisian condemnations of 1270 and 1277. The theory was instead accepted by Siger, and, it seems, by Boethius of Dacia, according to my reading of his *De summo bono* and, in particular, of a specific passage as given above. The notion of soul that this chapter offers is not useful, however, in disclosing the concept of earthly or temporal intellectual happiness, which the theme of perfect friendship and the honest as *summum bonum* seems to contain.

I quote the following fragment from the Convivio: "Avegna che una sola sustanza sia, tutta fia[ta la]forma, per sua nobilitade, ha in sè[e] la natura d'ognuna [di]queste cose,tutti questi amori puote avere e li ha" (And since man – although his whole form consists of a single substance for its nobility – has in himself a divine nature, he has the power to possess these things and all these loves, and he does possess them all; III.3.5). This definition, according to Nardi , derives from Albert. In fact, it is difficult to establish the meaning of "una sola sostanza sia tutta sua forma." For the same reason, it cannot be said with certainty that its meaning coincides with the definition of soul given in *Purgatorio* 25, which is the prevalent reading. Its meaning seems to focus on the superiority of the intellectual soul. The sense seems to be that one single substance is the form of the human being towards which other souls have a tendency.[70] This is confirmed if related to what we read in the commentary section of the *Convivio* is indicated as allegorical. There the vegetative and sensitive soul are defined as "ancille" of the intellectual soul, "per che non per loro sono, ma *per altrui*" (since they do not exist for their own sake but for the sake of others; III.14.10). I will return to such issues later. For now, it is worth underlining that "per altrui" recalls a content present in two texts I have already introduced, texts that are part of the synchronous debate: one is the *De summo bono* by Boethius of Dacia, and the other the *Quaestio de felicitate* by Giacomo. In both treatises, the generative and sensitive souls are *propter intellectivam*.[71]

In the same treatise in allegorical commentary, Dante seems to share this meaning, too (14.11). He will, in fact, quote Aristotle's *Metaphysics*: "libera quella cosa che è per sua cagione e non per altrui" (is free what is for its own cause and not for the cause of something else). This leads to the conclusion that the intellectual soul alone is for itself or independent and is therefore said to be "domina," while the other souls are merely "ancille."[72] It is the *altrui*, however, that suggests (*"per se e non per altrui," per* as the equivalent of *propter* as final cause) their different nature – that is, between the vegetative, sensitive, and the intellectual. In this, however, no trace can be found of the main error. The important role, attributed here to the intellectual soul, is confirmed in light of the honest, which is associated with the perfect and intertwined with the notion of the soul quoted above. What appears important here is that "only one substance is its form," this recalls what we read in chapter two (3.2). There it was said that God gives the human being a substantial form that is simple – that is, a form that is one and is diversified by secondary causes and the matter into which it descends. As already emphasized, the text acquires its meaning in this context. The introduction of the "honest," in spite of the ambiguity regarding the definition of soul, works as a sign of the course to follow. What matters is not just the relationship between the human mind and a separate substance, but mainly the nature of the mind and the proposed simplicity and oneness of this substance. The discourse, however, also implies a reflection on the topic of friendship. What we read there is helpful. In fact, the perfect friendship that the text introduces and links to the honest must be seen in light of the fact that friendship is a kind of superior love and union between two beings: the human mind and the gentle lady. But how does this union take place? Dante himself explains it when he writes that love performs an operation in his mind.

12. Love as Operation

I return now to the link between love and operation, with which the third treatise starts. This link is one of the issues that help in the identification of a meticulous weaving. The map that is traced in such weaving reveals the cardinal points of the navigation. The coherence and precision of the text works by offering the reader the right direction and aim. This precision reveals itself where the term "love" is tied to operation and the place in which this operation is performed. Such operation, in fact, constitutes the logical subject of this passage: "Non senza cagione dico che questo amore ne la mente mia fa la sua *operazione*, ma ragionevolmente ciò si dice, a dare a intendere quale amore è questo per lo loco nel quale adopera" (It is not without cause that I say that this love performs its operation in my mind, but with good reason, so that by telling of the place in which it operates we might understand what kind of love this is; 3.1). In chapter 2, we saw that the place in which love has his reasoning of the lady is that part of the soul which is a goodness (*deitate*). We have also seen that "love" is a term denoting union, which here implies an operation, so that the relationship between the mind and the woman (also defined as friendship) is presented as an operation. The reader is urged to engage in deductive reasoning – in fact, it is the place in which love works that can show the kind of love that is at issue.

Actually, this passage recalls a topic that both Albert and Aquinas have stigmatized and that was prohibited in the condemnation of 1277. The reason for the refutation is explained by Aquinas: according to some philosophers, the intellect is not the act of the body; rather, the act takes place only in virtue of the operation performed once body and intellect are united. In this union, the intellect is united to the body as a mover because the intellect and body become one. The operation of intellect is thus attributed to the human being.[73] The *quidam* about whom Aquinas speaks is probably Siger, who proposes this theory in his *In tertium* and reiterates it in his *De anima intellective*. What Siger asserts is that the intellect is the act of the body in virtue of a union that is accidental. The intellect is therefore a separate being. This distinguishes Albert from Siger. In fact, for Albert, the intellect is separate but is also the act of the body, whereas for Siger it becomes incidentally the act of the body through an operation that is similar to that of the *nauta navis* – that is, of the sailor in relation to his ship. In other words, the intellect is accidentally the act of the body.

By going back to Dante's text, we may infer that the operation introduced here (in chapter 3) does not take into account the union between the body and gentle lady; rather, the union is that between the mind and the lady, "mind" meaning the rational activity of the human mind, here depicted in its accidental operational unity with the lady. What seems to be suggested is that this union is also accidental. Again, because the lady is a separate being, the question arises: What is the activity of this mind, and how does this accidental union with the lady work? In other words, what is this mind, which we have been told is divine, when it is not in relation to the lady, and when it does not perform the operation of contemplating her? No doubt Dante is here preparing the ground for what he will present as the discontinuous nature of the human mind: "guardare discontinuato" and "non sempre," as he will write in the *Convivio* (III.13.5–8). Such discontinuity, once understood, addresses the double nature of our possible intellect or mind and the double operation it performs. I have introduced the double nature of the possible intellect in my discussion of the canzone *Amor che ne la mente mi ragiona*, and shortly touched on it above. Here, however, in the prose text, it is necessary to determine whether what we have traced there is confirmed. This double nature and activity of the possible intellect is a topic on which Siger and Albert agree. In the vocabulary Dante uses, there is probably an echo of the debate, but it is rethought. Dante insinuates, through the term "operation," an accidentality that drives the reader to engage in the work of logical deduction. If there is an operation, and if this operation has a "quando" which temporally locates it – "quando amore fa della sua pace sentire" (when Love makes felt the peace he brings; v. 26) – then the field of accidentality implies that this mind, though divine, is also able to experience something different. More and more this love, union, and friendship for the gentle lady requires an understanding of the human mind's nature and essence. What, exactly, is this mind that is able to experience such love? The nature of the human mind again becomes the central point, a point concealed but powerfully suggested as the true centre of this part of Dante's treatise. According to Albert and Siger, the possible intellect performs two operations: one of them is aimed at the abstraction of the individual phanthoms, while the other aims at the contemplation of the agent intellect.[74]

This theme surfaces more clearly if we go back to the honest and the implied link between ethics and intellectual knowledge. I quote again the two fragments of the treatise in which the honest appears: "Li uomini hanno loro proprio amore a le perfette e oneste cose" (Men have their proper love for things that are perfectly virtuous; 3.5); and "E per la quinta e ultima natura,cioè vera umana o, meglio dicendo angelica, cioè razionale ha l'uomo amore a la veritade e a la virtude,e da questo amore nasce la vera e perfetta amistade, de l'onesto tratta, de la quale parla lo Filosofo ne l'ottavo de l'Etica, quando tratta de l'amistade" (By virtue of the fifth and last nature, namely the truly human or, to be more precise, the angelic nature, which is to say the rational, man has a love of truth and virtue; 3.11).

13. More about the *Honestum*

We must now evaluate the word "onesto" by relating it to the field of ethics. Earlier, I recalled that *honestum,* which Cicero introduced in order to translate *kalon* from the *Phaedrus* and which Augustine appropriates (question 30 of 83 questions). The word "honest" was later used by William of Moerbeke to translate *kalon*, associated with *bonum,* in his version of the *Nicomachean Ethics* (Vanier 1965, 258). In this work, William of Moerbeke translates the Greek word *kalon* as *bonum-honestum.* What takes place is that the honest-beautiful denotes not an aesthetic value but an intellectual one, or better, the honest indicates the coincidence of beauty and intelligence, and what is beautiful requires the work of intelligence in order to be understood. In fact, Augustine uses the word "intelligible" to denote not only an object that has an intellectual nature but also the work a subject must do in order to reach intellection: "Honestum voco intelligibilem pulchritudinem" (Honest I define as a beauty that is intelligible).[75]

Aquinas, in his commentary on Moerbeke's text, as already said, writes that friendship for the honest is a friendship for what is *bonum simpliciter* (*In Ethicorum* 8.1.3, 1563, 1565). In Albert's *Super ethicam,* we read that "honestum est bonum simpliciter omnibus et semper" (1987, 50, 67). In his commentary on the divine names, Albert discusses and reiterates the identity among *pulchrum, honestum,* and *bonum.* In this context, Cicero's *De officiis* is recalled, along with a fragment by Boethius. This fragment is the same as we have seen quoted by Dante at the end of the second chapter of this third treatise: "Boethius in libro de consolatione philosophiae, de Deo loquens, mundum mente gerens, pulcrum, pulcherrimus" (Boethius in his *De consolatione philosophiae,* talking about God having the world in his mind, beautiful, the most beautiful; *De divinis nominibus,* 88350). This passage confirms the relation in God between the beautiful and the intellectual, a relation proposed through Boethius. God's beauty here coincides with the fact that He is the perfect intellectual being in whom thinking and creation of the archetypes of the world are one and the same.

Albert's quotation from Cicero introduces the definition which makes coincident the good and the *honestum*: "videtur enim quod pulcrum sit idem quod honestum ... Utrumque enim diffinitur a Tullio,in principio de officiis ... ergo bonum et pulcrum sunt idem" (Beautiful and honest are one and the same thing. Both are defined by Cicero at the beginning of *De officiis* ... therefore the good and the beautiful are coincident beings; *De Divinis nominibus,* 88330). In his *Super ethicam,* Albert distinguishes two kinds of *bonum.*

As for Aquinas, the *bonum simpliciter,* or simple good, is that which coincides with the honest and is sought for its own sake. It is also the object of desire of the rational soul: "honestum est quod secundum se appetitur a rationali appetitu" (L.2, 1, 3, 274, p. 78). Dante, in the first passage, writes that human beings have "amore a le perfette e oneste cose" (love for the perfect and honest things). In Aquinas, that which perfects the nature of a thing is itself perfect (*Nicomachean Ethics,* 1.1). In Dante, however, it seems that the goal of the human being, because of his intellectual nature, is the love for the honest in the form of an honest (intellectual-intelligible) being. Therefore, his natural inclination, his love-friendship for the honest, coincides with his love for the *donna gentile,* whose identity is that of a separate – that is, intellectual – divine being. If the human being has as its *bonum-honestum* the contemplation of a separate substance as comes out from the second fragment, the field which is circumscribed in the juxtaposition between *bonum-honestum* and intellectual, while confirming the separate and divine being of the *donna gentile,* offers here a more specific insight into the notion of human mind and what is called intellectual happiness.

In Giacomo, intellectual happiness requires the contemplation performed by the possible intellect, a contemplation that must have as its object the highest intelligible – that is, separate substances or God. The similarity with this passage of Dante's text is confirmed because in Giacomo this contemplation is also presented as an operation performed by the possible intellect and coincident with its contemplation, as said above. Aquinas assumes that this kind of contemplation is possible only in the eternal life. According to Busnelli and Vandelli's commentary on the *Convivio*, Dante's expression "perfette e oneste cose" derives from the *bonum perfectum* that Aquinas utilizes in his commentary on Aristotle's *Nicomachean Ethics*: "quod felicitas est de numero honorabilium, eo quod est quoddam bonum perfectum" (happiness is part of the things worthy of honour; in fact, it is the perfect good; *Convivio*, 1964, vol. 1, 282–3). According to Aquinas, the good can be either absolute or relative, and it is only the *bonum perfectum* that confers happiness (*In ethicorum* 1.1.18). Aquinas's position is, however, very different from that of Dante. But if the theme of the honest is identified with the search for *bonum*, or perfect good – "le perfette e oneste cose" (3.5) – then the suggestion given by the two scholars works if the field of ethics is reconsidered in light of different approaches to the *bonum perfectum*. Aquinas uses this expression in his commentary on the *Nicomachean Ethics* but assumes that human beings cannot achieve the highest good in this life.

Dante's text says the opposite. The similarity, however, with Giacomo's intellectual happiness throws light on the nature of the mind that in Dante allows love's operation. In light of this reference, love seems to be coincident with intellectual happiness, which Dante's prose also calls friendship. It is helpful to recall that this expression, in its vernacular form, "buon perfecto," was also used by Cavalcanti in his major canzone, "Donna me prega." The reader who has a good memory will remember that "buon perfetto," ("bonum perfectum") in the canzone (v. 39), indicated the object of knowledge of the possible intellect, which is suggested as a separate being. Can "Le oneste e perfette cose" of Dante's *Convivio*, later reiterated as true and perfect friendship ("vera e perfetta amistade, de l'onesto tratta"), be associated with the "buon perfetto" of Cavalcanti's canzone? And can the *bonum perfectum* as thought by Aquinas be associated with Cavalcanti's "buon perfetto"? Certainly not. It is important to stress, however, that although they have the Aristotelian basis in common, they use and think of it in different ways. Discussing Cavalcanti's canzone, Nardi, in his study of Cavalcanti, has explained that the "buon perfetto" *bonum perfectum* derives from Aristotle's *Nicomachean Ethics* (I, c.5, 1097a28 – 1097b21) (*teleion agathon*). This is the good that is desired for its own sake and not as a means to another good. For Aristotle, the perfect good is the ultimate good of human life. To reach it is coincident with *eudaimonia*, or intellectual happiness (Nardi, 1985).

We may also note that Aquinas makes it coincident with happiness. It is worthy of mention that the good which is sought for its own sake, and which enters the topos of perfect friendship, fits the definition offered by Aristotle's Latin text. The perfect *bonum* as coincident with the peculiarities of the "honestum" in itself is opposed to the useful, according to Cicero's and Augustine's definition of the honest. The honest, however, as opposed to the useful, also refers us to Aristotle's *Metaphysics* and to the knowledge that is sought for its own sake. This is speculative science: "Nulla scientia in qua queritur ipsum scire propter seipsum, est scientia activa, sed speculativa, sed illa scientia quae sapientia est, vel philosophia dicitur est propter ipsum scire: ergo est speculativa et non active" (No science in which knowledge itself is sought for its own sake is a practical science, but a speculative one. But that science which is wisdom, or philosophy as it is called, exists for the sake of knowledge itself. Hence it is speculative and not practical; *In metaphysicorum* 1.3.53). This is the science that searches for the causes and principles of things. In the same way, "operation," which takes place in the mind, refers us to the *Metaphysics* too, since the operation of knowing is proper to the intellect: "Propria autem *operatio* hominis in quantum homo est intelligere. Per hoc enim ab omnibus aliis differt. Unde naturaliter desiderium hominis inclinatur ad intelligendum, et per consequens ad sciendum" (The operation that is proper to the human being because human is to have intellection. In this he is different from the other beings. Therefore it is natural that the human being desires to have intellection and thus to know; *In metaphysicorum* 1.1). In this fragment of the *Metaphysics* (which I cite in Aquinas's commentary), the implication is that what is proper to the human being and to his intellectual nature is the contemplation of a separate substance, in which contemplation, human happiness does consist. According to this view, it is natural for this intellectual nature to incline towards and take satisfaction in science (*scientia*).

In Aquinas' commentary on the *Metaphysics*, we read a fragment that explains the pathways that cross in the friendship for the *donna gentile*. The mind's friendship with a separate substance, indicated as a tendency towards the "perfette e oneste cose," thus moves us towards the theory of the *summum bonum*, which Aquinas exposes but does not believe is possible in our earthly life. Incidentally, we may observe that

Dante's discourse has, as its own centre, a content that Cavalcanti indicates as "consideranza." This activity is proper to the possible intellect. Cavalcanti, however, in "Donna me prega," considers this intellect a being for itself, and detached from the experience of love as it is experienced by the human being as an individual. Shortly said for Cavalcanti is the sensitive soul, which is the act of the body, the activity of consideration belonging to the intellect and having nothing to do with the individual knowledge, which is bounded to the sensitive soul (Ardizzone 2002, esp. chaps. 2 to 4).

According to Cavalcanti, the connection between the phantasms generated by the sensitive soul activity and the possible intellect does not imply that this sensitive soul has knowledge. Knowledge belongs to the separate possible intellect but not to the human being as an individual. In other words, Guido criticizes the Averroist tenet according to which, in the copulation of the possible intellect with phantasms, the individual has intellectual knowledge. According to him, this belongs only to the separate possible intellect. This criticism is in line with a radical text published by Maurice Giele (Ardizzone 2002, chap. 2). Cavalcanti therefore produces a break, and not a continuity, between the intellectual and sensitive soul. Cavalcanti is not in agreement with the theory of intellectual happiness proposed by Giacomo. It is on this theoretical basis that the human being is located in a world ruled by sensuality and physical pleasure. Dante reverses this theoretical construction. He, however, does not discuss "buon perfecto." He imposes a new name, or better, a new field of meaning. It is worth recalling that for Severinus Boethius happiness and the *summum bonum* coincided in God.[76] For Dante, according to our reading, the gentle lady is proposed not only as a separate being but also as being part of what God thinks. She is therefore a separate substance or idea, or *dea*.

In the second treatise, I introduced the discussion about the separate substances as evident in two texts written by Aquinas that I have taken into consideration: his commentary on the *Liber de causis*, and his treatise on the separate substances (*De substantiis separatis*). There, the cosmological order was insured because, in the hierarchy of intellectual beings, some beings were conceived as movers, others as only contemplating. The mind, represented as in love with the gentle lady in *Amor che ne la mente mi ragiona*, implied pure contemplation. Here, in the prose text, this contemplation is presented as an operation of the mind, or better, as an operation that takes place in the mind. Because the honest embodies the *summum bonum* or prefect good, and because this *summum bonum* is commonly assumed to be the highest good, it provides the context that allows the reader to understand Dante's position. This context is clearer in the light of the two fragments from Severinus Boethius, in which philosophy is said to be both in human minds and in God's mind. The love for *sapientia* is the love of separate beings, according to the *Metaphysics*. *Sapientia* or Sophia is also in the *Nicomachean Ethics* as the highest intellectual virtue.

The third treatise of the *Convivio,* in the allegorical commentary (14.11), will introduce the gentle woman as philosophy. It will show that philosophy, according to the definition found in the *Metaphysics*, deals with a love for a being that is for itself, which is the goal of metaphysics or "first philosophy." In virtue of such relations, we must emphasize that both Dante's *honestum* (related to perfection) and Cavalcanti's *buon perfetto* echo the *summum bonum* as discussed by Boethius of Dacia in his *De summo bono*. I quote once again a fragment of this text, which contains something of what Dante introduces as the *bonum proprium* to the intellectual nature of the human being:

> Cum in omni specie entis sit aliquod summum bonum possibile … oportet quod aliquod summum bonum sit homini possibile. Non dico summum bonum absolute, sed summum bonum sibi, bona enim possibilia homini finem habent nec procedunt in infinitum. Quid autem sit hoc summum bonum, quod est homini possibile per rationem investigamus. Summum bonum quod est homini possibile debetur sibi secundum optimam suam virtutem … Optima autem virtus hominis ratio et intellectus est … Ergo summum bonum quod est homini possibile debetur sibi secundum intellectum.

> Because every being has his own highest good it is necessary that the human being has his own possible highest good. I do not speak about an absolute highest good, but a good that is good for him, in fact the goods for the human beings are not infinite. We may investigate through reason which is this highest good possible for the human being. The highest Good possible for the human being is that which is given to him according to his best virtue … Because his best virtue is rationality and intellect thus the Highest Good for the human being is intellectual. (1976, 379)

The same expression is found in Giacomo ("Summum bonum qui est possibilis homini advenire") and also in Albert's *Super ethicam*. The nature of this love for the honest in Dante's fragment, revealed as the union of love and friendship ("in amicitia dissimilitudo a similitudo si reduca"), implies a relation with a gentle woman. This "donna" has been identified, starting with the canzone, as a separate being, superior to the mind, and suggested as being one. It is also suggested that she is eternal because she is part of God's eternal thinking.

This has been organized by introducing the angelic nature of the human being, whose intellectual nature seeks its satisfaction in what is proper to it, as we read; "accio che questa natura si chiama mente" (therefore this nature is called mind; 3.12). The human being seeks the divine or the divine ideas which are the object of the vision of the angelic intelligences. As already said, in *De vulgari eloquentia*, Dante had put forth as proper to the angels the love for the *honestum*, and this love the humans share with angels (II.2.6). In addition, identifies himself as pursuing the honest and identifies the honestum with rectitude, the basis of such identification being in Aristlotle's *Nicomachean Ethics*. Now he is assimilating the appetitive proper to human beings to this angelic love. This confirms the meaning of "perfette e oneste cose" as related to the *honestum* as coinciding with what belongs to the divine as divine ideas, or causes of things. In Boethius of Dacia (1976), the *summum bonum* was in fact coincident with the divine. Boethius calls both the human intellect and its object divine: "si enim in homine aliquid divinum est, dignum est quod hoc sit intellectus ... quid enim nobilius potest intellectus divinus intelligere quam sit essentia divina?" (if in the human being there is something divine, this is the intellect ... what more noble the intellect can understand than the divine essence?; 370–1).

Similar is the position of Giacomo and that of the praise of philosophy by Matheus. This resonates with what Dante attributes to the philosophers, who call the human being a divine animal, or "animal divino da li filosofi chiamato." Philosophical happiness is the central meaning of this passage, and it is patterned after the divine model. Just as the divine *intellectus primus* has *a divine intelligible* that is *sui ipsius essentia*, so too the human *intellectum*, called *divinum*, has the contemplation "cognitio universitatis entium quae sunt a primo principium et per hoc primi principii, sicut possibile est et delectatio in illo." The word "intelligible" in Boethius of Dacia resounds with the intelligible of Giacomo's *quaestio*. It also recalls the intelligible beauty of Augustin *question* 29, which Augustine, following Cicero, defined as *honestum*, as said above. In Boethius of Dacia's *De summo bono*, the word *honestum* does not appear, but his *summum bonum* seems to suggest the absolute intelligible as the highest good, which is decisive for the construction of the meaning of Dante's *honestum*. We have no proof that Dante read

Boethius of Dacia. It is more likely that Cavalcanti was aware of this line of thought, but Dante certainly read Cavalcanti and was perhaps his best reader.

However, if intellectual happiness is indeed the true meaning of this passage, here the adjectives "oneste" and "perfette" (attributed to "cose") render in Italian the *honestum perfectum* of Cicero's *De officiis* (3.11–15), which I quoted above and which must be related in turn to the perfect good or *bonum perfectum*. Also in Severinus Boethius, the perfect good was coincident with God and happiness: "Bonum esse deum ratio demonstrate ut perfectum quoque in eo bonum in esse convincat." He takes this idea from the Latin tradition but claims his own perspective. The *pulchrum* as intelligible and *honestum*, which we find in Augustine, has its apex here. The tendency towards the *honestum* implies a moral value that is coincident with the intellectual value. The friendship for the *donna gentile* implies an ethical value, in Cicero's *De amicitia*: there is no friendship without virtue and, as we read, if we suppose that virtue is the *summum bonum*, virtue is the basis of this friendship for the gentle lady, but this virtue is the intellectual virtue of book 10 of the *Nichomachean Ethics*. It is the identity of the *donna gentile* that reveals the meaning of such friendship. Boethius of Dacia clearly says that the speculative intellect has as its highest good the cognition of truth in what is singular, and happiness in the same: "summum bonum cognitio veri in singulis et delectatio in eodem." The *summum bonum*, which is possible for the human being's practical intellect is instead "operatio boni et delectatio in eodem." This delectation implies the practice of the right medium (*optos logos* N.E.6.1) to be chosen in every human action and the pleasure we take in it (*De summo bono*, 371). This short quotation from Boethius of Dacia shows a relation between intellectual knowledge, intellectual virtue, and moral life. It is because the human divine intellect contemplates the divine being that the practical intellect can accomplish the good.

Dante will return to this topic in the fourth treatise, but from a different perspective. Dante has used "oneste cose," relating it with the word "honestum" and, according to Cicero, *honestum* is coincident with "ius" and "ius" is coincident with the field of "drechura," or rightness. "Ius" represents a commong good.[77] The relationship between the *donna gentile* and the "perfette cose e oneste" implies the idea that what is highest as good has to be common. Dante takes this idea from Aristotle, in which the common good, the good of politics, is superior to the private good. However, such common good in politics implies the naturality of community, as the love for the *gentle lady* shows. Such love is not just an experience lived by the character who says "I," but is a common human experience. This is a very important aspect of this part of the *Convivio*.

The use of the word "friendship" that has been introduced in this treatise has thus to be rethought in light of Aristotle, who writes that friendship implies the political link, that it is the basis for the political *conviventia*.

Conclusion of Treatise Three, Part 1

In the third book of the *Convivio*, Dante traces in a few sections a kind of system based on a line of thoughts independent and parallel. In this treatise, I have identified essentially three of them: the given intellectual form as one for all human beings and made different through the sensitive soul; the eternity of philosophy, from which is suggested the eternity of the mind that thinks it; and the *summum bonum* as *honestum*. All such themes imply a natural relation among human beings. The friendship of the mind with the lady requires, in order to be understood, an exploration of the nature of the mind that is able to live such experience, and such experience, according to what we have read in the canzone *Amor che ne la mente mi ragiona*, belongs not just to the "I," but to a indefinite but plural being called "gente." Such a name, according to grammarians, is a collective name. It seems that it is the human collectivity that is able to contemplate such lady. Friendship as a natural relation between two beings, if it implies a plurality, suggests that a community is enclosed in such friendship. Such contemplation is also proper to the intellects as we have read in the canzone. Another nucleus that I have explored is the nature of the human mind.

Summarizing, the "perfette e oneste cose" leads us to the vision of the divine, according to a position close to that of Albert (and of Boethius of Dacia), who thinks that the human being can have this contemplation in his mortal life. The difference is that in Boethius of Dacia, this is a *cognitio veri* that takes place in the relationship between two single beings – that is, the subject that knows must be singular. The meaning of this obscure passage, in light of the theories then in circulation, seems to be clear: only a singular being has delectation in a singular being, "singular" here means one but implies the plurality of human beings sharing a single intellect. This last content is refuted by Albert, who, however, accepts that we may contemplate separate beings in our temporal life. This contemplation of the divine in this life and intellectual happiness are, as we know, denied by Aquinas.

I want to underline two contents here. The first is that the theory of intellectual happiness in life can be associated with different levels of error. The most serious and dangerous error derives from the theory of the uniqueness of the intellect, which is denied by both Albert and Aquinas but accepted by Siger and Boethius of Dacia, according to my reading (more difficult to ascertain is Giacomo's position). Of course, the theory of contemplation of separated substances in life, a theory accepted by Albert, is condemned, too, by the Parisian censorship. This error is less dangerous, however, and the reason for its condemnation derives from the fact that it is generally linked to the notion of the intellect conceived as separate, which, in many cases, leads to the theory of the intellect as one, a theory Albert firmly denies and condemns.

Another aspect to be emphasized is that in this context, and in particular, in the discussion about the honest, we have an example of Dante's method in the *Convivio*, which needs to be understood. Dante uses Aristotelian fragments. He uses the commentary of Aquinas as well, but he does not share Aquinas's position. From what has been said, it is clear that the discourse on the "honest," if read in relation to the *bonum perfectum* or *summum bonum*, introduces the theory of intellectual happiness. We must, however, have a clear idea of the different positions held by Dante and Cavalcanti and by those who embrace radical positions. Both Cavalcanti and Dante, at this time, seem to share some tenets of the theory of the possible intellect as separate and unique, but for Cavalcanti this doctrine shows the sensuous nature of the human being and the separate nature of the intellect. For this reason, the author of "Donna me prega" is critical of the main contents of the philosophical theory from which he draws. Cavalcanti appears to follow the radical view of a commentary on the *Anima* published by Giele. Cavalcanti's radical thought results in a materialistic vision of the human being. He celebrates the values of human individuality, values that are related to our sensual being and our power of imagination. Cavalcanti is a natural philosopher, and natural philosophers and medical doctors are his interlocutors and readers.

Beyond Cavalcanti's verses, there is a public of this kind, among them the medical doctor Dino del Garbo, who will write the most authoritative commentary on the canzone "Donna me prega." Cavalcanti organizes his major canzone as a natural *dimostramento*. The whole of his poetry displays this naturalistic point of view, in which the human body plays a central role (Ardizzone 2002). Different and opposite is Dante's position, which aligns itself with texts by Boethius of Dacia and Giacomo and which stresses the contemplation of a substance that is separate, eternal, single, and part of the divine thinking. In opposition to Cavalcanti, Dante seals the intellectual nature of the human being. He regards the human being almost as an angel and a divine being thanks to his intellect. The distance between a natural philosopher and a simple philosopher (a distinction which would require a longer discussion and which is testified in a fragment from Siger's *Questiones de Metaphysique*) may be of help in order to distinguish the different positions of Dante and Cavalcanti. These positions culminate in Cavalcanti's materialism and unbridled individualism, which Dante counteracts through the absolute importance of *intellectualitas* – that is part of what he indicates as "oneste e perfette cose": the *honestum*. In the *De vulgari eloquentia* II.6, the *honestum* was the proper object of the angelic contemplation. Dante there related the *honestum* to direction vountatis II.8. We find in the *Monarchia* I.11.3 *rectitudo*, which coincides with justice. Here in the *Convivio*, however, we see that, for Dante, the field of honest is related to the perfect intellect, to the exaltation of the divine nature of the human mind. This suggests a relation with the ethical and social contents of the *Convivio*, contents which, according to my reading, were already suggested in the canzone *Amor che ne la mente mi ragiona*, and on which the third treatise is openly organized.

Dante's assumption of the notion of the possible intellect as common to the human beings, a theory clearly manifested in his *Monarchia* and in a most personal way, has its gestation in the *Convivio*. This is an important thesis of this study, which, as we have seen, follows the development of Dante's thinking regarding the notion of human intellect. We must also take into account Dante's uncertainties and doubts. Such doubts, which begin to appear in in our analysis with the canzoni *Voi che 'ntendendo il terzo ciel movete* and *Amor che ne la mente mi ragiona*, will be reiterated in the prose text of the second and third treatise. They will result in a kind of *retractatio* that appears in the fourth treatise and will take the form of an opposition to materialism. This theme is extremely important. Dante no doubt thinks that a refutation of materialism is necessary in order to eliminate the dangerous contours to which the theory of human intellection he has introduced in an obscure way is linked. The problematic issue on which the fourth treatise opens is a clear demonstration of Dante's attempt to dissolve the dangerous, potentially heterodox sides of his discourse. Also in the canzone *Le dolci rime d'amor ch'io solia* was a sign of *retractatio*. It testifies to Dante's attempt to distinguish his position and to clarify the limits of his discourse. The opposition to materialism can be traced to the canzone *Le dolci rime d'amor ch'io solia*, and is also present in the canzone, *Doglia mi reca nello cor ardire*, and in *Poscia ch'amor del tutto m'ha lasciato* and *Tre donne intorno al cor mi son venute*. These texts confirm the importance of Dante's critique of materialism in the years of his exile.

I will briefly return to this line of thinking later when I comment on the fourth treatise of the *Convivio*. In this final part, I will shortly return to the third treatise and to its introduction of the honest in order to summarize my central meaning. My reconstruction suggests a line of thinking that links Dante's position to intellectual happiness. This theme, I have stressed, is present in Boethius of Dacia (*De summo bono*) and in Giacomo (*Quaestio de felicitate*), but is also present in Albert. It is certainly part of Siger's thinking (although we have only a small fragment of his *Ethics*). I have also clarified both what is common to these thinkers and what distinguishes them. This happiness is in fact central in Boethius of Dacia and in Giacomo, and is accepted by Siger and Albert; but their approach to this issue testifies to a different belief that involves a different perspective about the notion of human being. Comparing Boethius of Dacia's description of happiness in his *De summo bono* and Siger's theory of the possible intellect, and Giacomo's *quaestio* on happiness with Albert's *Super ethicam*, and Aquinas's position as it appears in his various writings, we may draw a conclusion.

The theory of intellectual happiness is part of the debate on the human intellect. This intellect is thought to be separate by all commentators, with the exception of Aquinas, and single by all, with the exception of Albert and Aquinas. The notion of the human soul, as it is defined in this treatise, is therefore essential if we are to understand the general discourse of the *Convivio* and its intended readers. The superiority of the intellectual soul is evident; the operation that love performs tells us that the natural operation proper to the human being is *intelligere* and that the human being tends to his own *perfectum bonum*. Referred to as "perfette oneste cose," this implies the contemplation on the part of the human mind of a separate entity which is part of God's thinking. As Dante proposes it, such happiness shares its object of contemplation with God and with the angelic intelligences. Happiness is the philosophical equivalent of what the canzone calls love. It is depicted as an activity coincident with reasoning which takes place in the mind of the one who says "I," and is a reasoning about the gentle lady. Other facets, however, are necessary to complete the set. In essence, the honest – that is, intellectual virtue – is absolute and coincides with the aim of the philosopher or the wise, according to Cicero, as mentioned before. For Dante, however, this virtue is regarded as belonging to all human beings. In addition, as the highest good, and as the beautiful – which has a moral as well as an intellectual value – it combines the content of the synchronous debate with other ancient authors.

Once again, the method that allows us to reconstruct the meaning emerges from taking different sets from ancient contents in order to create a new set. Here, the act of *auctor*, as Dante will discuss later, is necessary in order to confer *auctoritas*. Dante proceeds by collecting fragments from the Latin tradition. He juxtaposes ancient texts with less ancient ones, which he reads and redesigns in order to mirror the present. Intellectual freedom emerges as a result of the ability to rethink categories of relation. To this extent, the field of *honestum* is similar to a "highest good," or *summum bonum* or *bonum perfectum*. It is also possible to identify it with the "bread" the angels eat, and which human beings will also eat (as the biblical text indicates), the bread introduced in the first treatise of the *Convivio*. Augustine's comment on John reads that the bread of angels or *verbum* corresponds to the divine ideas that angels eagerly contemplate. In the same way, the love of knowledge with which the *Convivio* opens is the knowledge of the separate being that all human beings desire.

My reading has started to emphasize here the unity or commonality of human beings in this desire – and this no doubt was Dante's intent since *Amor che ne la mente mi ragiona*. Cicero acknowledges that, from one point of view, the pursuit of the *bonum honestum* is but a means for the realization of the common good, in which it finds its purpose and limit; this makes *honestum* a form of *utile*. Cicero, however, identifies *honestum* with the common good and *utile* with individual interest, whereas in Dante the notion of *honestum* implies, as we have seen, much more. The nature of the human intellect, as it emerges from this third treatise, is the point where the different directions investigated converge. In fact, the theory of happiness that this chapter introduces covertly requires that we assess more clearly the nature of the human intellect, which is able, it seems, in this part of the third treatise, to contemplate such a lady – a divine idea.

4 Community and Intellectual Happiness: The Invention of a Shifting Logical Subject

1. The Shifting of the Logical Subject: The One and the Many

In evaluating the comment (III.3.13) to lines 3 and 4 of the canzone, "move cose di lei meco sovente, / che lo 'ntelletto sovre'esse disvia" (awakens often thoughts of her such that my intellect is led astray by them), we may note that the verse is quoted here in a different version: "move sovente cose che fanno disviare l'intelletto" (often stirs thoughts that bewilder the intellect).[1] The lines are not explained, but the meaning is indirectly given by way of an important theme: the superiority of this lady who is above human reason.[2] We read:

> ... pero che li miei pensieri ragionando di lei molte volte voleano cose conchiudere di lei che io non le potea intendere e smarrivami, sì che quasi parea di fuori alienato ... E quest'è l'una ineffabilitade di quello che io per tema ho preso; e consequentemente narro l'altra, quando dico: "Lo suo parlar."

> ... and I say that it "often stirs thoughts that bewilder the intellect." I speak truly, for in speaking of her my thoughts many times desired to conclude things about her which I could not understand, and I was so bewildered that outwardly I seemed almost beside myself ... This is one ineffable aspect of what I have taken as my theme; and, subsequently, I speak of the other when I say *His speech.* (III.3.13–14)

Another meaningful fragment follows:

> E dico che li miei pensieri – che sono parlare d'Amore – "son[an si dolci"] che la mia 'anima, cioè lo mio l'affetto arde di potere ciò con la lingua

narrare; e perchè dire nol posso, dico che l'anima se ne lamenta dicendo: *lassa! ch'io non son possente.*

I say that my thoughts – which are the words of Love – "have such sweet sounds" that my soul, that is, my affection, burns to be able to tell of it with my tongue; and because I am not able to speak of it, I say that the soul therefore laments, saying *Alas, I lack the power.* (Ibid., 3.13–14)

In both passages, the woman's superiority is indicated as ineffable (ineffabilitate). This ineffability takes place in two different ways. One is coincident with an intellectual act that is rendered through reasoning: "di costei ragionando" (reasoning about her). Here, what is put forth as ineffability is something that cannot become a clear thought. This points to the identity of thinking and the interior word, which is important for Dante since the time of his first poetic productions and the *Vita nuova.* The other ineffability strengthens the first meaning and refers the reader to the relation between interior word and intellect: ("li miei pensieri – che sono parlare d'amore") as established, among the others, by Aquinas, who linked Augustinian and Aristotelian contents.[3] Moreover, it introduces the difficulty of transforming intellectual activity into a sensible linguistic sign. The text in fact uses the word "soul," *anima*, but specifies its meaning by explaining that soul here refers to affect (affetto), which in Aristotelian terms means that the reference is to the sensitive soul and its power to express thinking in a sensible alphabetical sign.

Actually, what is said here reveals two different levels. The first refers to the intellectual superiority of the woman, who is so superior that the interior word, which is the expression used to indicate the intellectual-cognitive act, remains interminate, that is, according to the Augustinian idea about the interior word, cannot reach its mental linguistic form.[4] The second level indicates the disproportion between the interior word and the sensible word; but the first ineffability, which suggests a cognitive insufficiency, guides the reader towards the nature of a separate entity and towards the relation of the lady's being with the divine being. This ineffability is, in fact, traceable to the Neoplatonic mystical tradition and therefore to the *De causis*, in which it is said that the first cause is ineffable.[5] This ineffability reveals the difficulty on the part of the human being's capacity to know such a separate and divine entity. Among the propositions condemned in 1277, Proposition 118 states that the agent itellect is a separate substance that is superior to the possible intellect and, according to its power, substance and operation, is separate from the body and is not the act of the body (Quod intellectus agens est quaedam substantia separata superior ad intellectum possibilem; et quod secundum substantiam potentiam et operatione est separatus a corpore, nec est forma corporis hominis) (Hissette 1977, 193). According to Siger of Brabant, the agent intellect was not in continuity with the human being and was identified with the first cause (Van Steenberghen 1977, 361).[6] The same position is evident in both Giacomo of Pistoia and Boethius of Dacia, as the fragments that I have quoted in chapter 3 testify.

In this passage, however, the reader may note that "dolce," sweet, is useful for rendering this high intellectual level. What sounds sweet is suggested as being the interior word, which is the result of the link between the mind and the lady. The identification of "pensieri," "parlare d'amore," and "dolce," while confirming the above-mentioned relation between the mind and the woman, suggests that many levels of the human being are interrelated in a linguistic act. Of course, in this passage there is a crucial antecedent to the notion of "dolce stil novo," as offered in *Purgatorio* 24 (49–63). This antecedent is in strong continuity with the notion of the interior word that Dante first established in his *Vita nuova*. The linguistic is conceived as an intellectual act, while the ineffability confirms the separate being of the gentle lady. Love, as metaphor, confirms the relational nature of human mind, as discussed above. Also, a part of this meaning is the word "alienato," which in Italian means to become something different, "aliud" or other. It implies the notion of the self and the possibility of becoming different from what this self usually is.

Briefly put, when the separate nature of the agent intellect is established, it indirectly brings together the theory of the interior word and the ineffability of the first cause. The difficulty of rendering in a sensible language the interior word is not therefore the only meaning that the reader must grasp. In Dante's Epistle XIII we can find an echo of it: "Multa per intellectum videmus quibus signa vocalia desunt," and here in this fragment we read: "E questa è l'altra ineffabilitade; cioè che la lingua non è, di quello che l'intelletto vede, compiutamente seguace" (This is the other ineffable aspect: that is, that the tongue cannot completely follow what the intellect perceives; 3.15). In any case, the field of ineffability bears traces of the *Liber de causis*, which asserts the ineffability of the first cause (proposition 5). In general, the ineffable of the mystical tradition here connotes the divine nature of the lady and the events she "moves" in the human being.

An interesting correlation is put forth: an interior word that is extremely sweet but that the soul (as affect) is unable to express. In the same way, the reasoning of the human mind is inferior to the being of this woman. The interior word is thinking. The Augustinian substrate creates a kind of weft. Once it becomes related to casuistic and Aristotelian learning, it allows Dante to depict the discourse on love as the human being's attempt at, and desire of, the cognition of the divine. But the identity of such knowing does not proceed in a straight line. On the one hand, we have read that the human mind is divine, but on the other, the human mind is not able to know this being or separate substance to which the mind is nevertheless united in love: "E veramente dico; però che li miei pensieri, di costei ragionando, molte fiate volevano cose conchiudere di lei, che *io* non le potea intendere, e smarrivami sì che quasi parea di fuori alienato" (And I say that it "often stirs thoughts that bewilder the intellect." I speak truly, for in speaking of her my thoughts many times desired to conclude things about her which I could not understand, and I was so bewildered that outwardly I seemed almost beside myself; 3.13).

It is evident, as previously said, that something superior to the human mind is introduced here. Yet that introduction seems to put forth an extremely important content, and Dante's uncertainties are probably part of the importance of what he intends to say. The word "alienato," read in relation to the "I" who would like to have cognition of the lady, suggests that this "I" is unable to reach so high an intellectual level. Since the verb used is "conchiudere," the meaning seems to be that an act of cognition on the part of the "I" cannot be actualized.

The commentary avoids giving an explanation of what the poetry has presented. Nor does the terminology offer any clarity: Aristotelian terms are used, but they are not sufficiently specific. The discourse about the *donna gentile* is a discussion about the power and limits of the human being. This separate substance must be related to the human soul's power or ability. The word "soul," here equated with "affect" (3.14) seems to express, as mentioned earlier, a function of the sensitive soul. The meaning of "che lo intelletto disvia" (v. 3) has not been given, but the field of alienation suggests that the lady generates a path that the "I" or human intellect cannot follow (disvia). This suggests that the intellect proper to the "I" usually follows a different path. Since the discussion is about knowledge, the estrangement from the self, as the sign of an extreme perturbation, requires a deeper understanding.

The fourth chapter will narrate the insufficiency of the "I." He who speaks must in fact give up many things regarding her (the lady), because he does not understand them. But the logical subject at 3.4.4 becomes poetry, more especially in the following verses that the "I" (narrator and character at once) writes: "*Pero se le mie rime avran difetto* escusomi di una colpa de la quale non deggio essere colpato, veggendo altri le mie parole essere minori che la dignitade di questa" (Then where it says, *And so if fault is found to mar my verse,* I excuse myself for a fault for which I should not be blamed, since others can see that my words are inferior to the dignity of this lady; 3.4.4). Here, the speech is subtle, elusive, and almost equivocal.

The gentle woman, who has been proposed by virtue of love in union with the human mind, is the expression of something high and perfect. We read in chapter 3 that, in virtue of his rational nature, the human being loves truth and virtue. From this love is born true and perfect friendship, a friendship that deals with the *honestum.* I have given above an explanation of the word "honest." Here, however, Dante seems to introduce something new. To understand this newness, we must clarify which is the knowledge proper to the human mind. This is one of the points that the third treatise does not clarify: the difficulty of the canzone returns at this point. The text seems to intend to divert the suspicious reader, and at the same time to refer the expert reader to a philosophical meaning. This comes from the ambiguity of the wording that plays subtly to postpone themes, scattering them throughout the text, not placing them where the reader would be allowed to reach a meaning. The reader's mind must be able to use his or her memory, and memory is of course intelligence because it establishes logical relations. Such relations will work only if the reader is able to see past the first level of meaning and go beyond the words themselves. An understanding takes place where a level of achieved significance does not arise as a point of arrival, but as a limit that constantly seeks to be violated. The strength that the prose of the *Convivio* organizes is done through the agglutination of different lines of thought. These are proposed as fields tangential to each other, which the prose text attempts to gather and express. If, in the second chapter, the human soul (reason) was said to participate in the divine nature in the guise of an eternal intelligence (III.2:14), the third chapter has introduced friendship (which makes one of two) with the honest. The "honest," as we have seen, implies the *pulchrum* as intelligible and an intellectual and moral value, which, in its association with the adjective "perfect," suggests an identification with the *summum bonum* as the highest intellectual value coinciding with the absolute *bonum* that Aquinas discusses in his commentary on Aristotle's *Nicomachean Ethics*, but that we also find in Boethius of Dacia and his *De summo bono*.

Now in the fourth chapter, the theme is human inadequacy. It is here that the text requires an adequate decoding device. In the third chapter, in fact, the whole discourse through the notion of mind, united in love and through an operation to the gentle lady, led us to discuss the notion of mind rethinking that given by Albert the Great, as we had traced it in our reading of the text of the canzone (see Ardizonne 2011, esp. chap. 4). Or, as in the paragraphs above, looking at the notion of intellect as conceived by Siger (the unity of possible and agent, which, however, perform different operations)[7] and introducing the discussion about intellectual happiness as active in a few texts involved in the debate of the late thirteenth and early fourteenth centuries.

In chapter 3 of the third treatise, we are told that the thoughts of the narrator are inferior to the being of this woman. In this declared insufficiency, we have noted that the word "soul" means "affection" (III.3.14), which leads us to think that the text is pointing to a meaning of "soul" that includes the sensitive. Therefore, the soul that complains and confesses her inability to tell what she hears and feels introduces the sensitive level of the human being, which appears to be disconnected from the intellectual level, as the reasoning of love takes place (as we read) in the intellectual soul. The gap between the inner word that is pure thinking and the sensible word seems to express here that a duality between the sensitive and the intellective is proper to the human being. This reiterates the duality introduced in the first canzone *Voi che'ntendendo il terzo ciel movete* and confirmed in our reading.

Chapter 4 continues on this track. I quote a fragment:

> Dico adunque che la *mia* insufficienza procede doppiamente, sì come doppiamente trascende l'altezza di costei, per lo modo che detto è. Ché a me convene lasciare per povertà d'intelletto molto di quello che è vero di lei, e che quasi nella *mia* mente raggia, la quale come corpo diafano riceve quello non terminando e questo dico in quella seguente particula E certo e mi conven lasciare in pria.

> I say then that my insufficiency derives from a twofold source, just as the grandeur of that lady is transcendent in a twofold manner, in the way that has been mentioned. For because of the poverty of my intellect, it is

necessary to leave aside much that is true about her and much that shines, as it were, into my mind, which like a transparent (diaphanous) body receives it without arresting it; and this I say in the following clause: *And surely I must leave aside*. (III.4.1–2)

We recall that previously it was said that the gentle lady is a separate substance. Now we see that the text, embracing positions acknowledged as orthodox, glosses the verses recalled and quoted in order to express the impossibility of knowing such a separate substance. The passage briefly recalls the theory of the diaphanous[8] in order to say that light, as it appears in a diaphanous body, penetrates the mind but does not terminate in it. This implies, according to the theory of diaphanous, that a vision of the separate substance fails to take place. That is, the mind is unable to contemplate such a separate being.[9]

Then the narration continues:

Poi quando dico *E di quel che s' intende* dico che non pur a quello che lo *mio intelletto* non sostiene, ma eziandio a quello che *io intendo* sufficiente non [sono] pero che la mia lingua non è di tanta facundia che dire potesse ciò che nel pensiero *mio* se ne ragiona; per che è da vedere che, a rispetto de la veritade, poco fia quello che dirà.

Then when I say *And of what is understood* I assert that my inability extends not only to what my intellect does not grasp but even to what I do understand, because my tongue lacks the eloquence to be able to express what is spoken of her in my thought. Consequently, it will be apparent that what I shall say concerning the truth will be quite little. (III.4.3)

This insufficiency links "mio intelletto" and "io" as the grammatical subjects of "intendo." The suggested insufficiency is reiterated later because of the expression "la debilitate de l'intelletto" (III.4.4) which is tied to "cortezza del nostro parlare che dal "pensiero è vinto." "Debilitate" recalls the word "imbecillitatem" of intellect, which Aquinas uses in his commentary on *De causis*. However, "debile" here probably signifies, more specifically, something that does not last. The theme cannot be labelled as simply Thomistic. This insufficiency reiterates the gap between the mental word and the sensible word, indirectly confirming the relation between intellection and the interior word. Here is the text: "La cortezza del nostro parlare lo quale per lo pensero è vinto sì che seguir lui non puote appieno" (The inadequacy of our power of speech, which is so overwhelmed by a thought that it cannot fully follow it; III.4.4). What follows reiterates the expression "s'intende" but in a different context. We read in fact that such ineffability results in praise of the lady, "ne la quale principalmente *s'intende*." Here is the full quotation: "E ciò resulta in grande loda di costei, se bene si guarda: nella quale principalmente *s'intende*. E quella orazione si può dire bene che vegna dalla fabbrica del rettorico, nel[la] quale ciascuna parte pone mano allo principale intent" (And this, upon close examination, brings great praise to her, which is my principal purpose; and that speech in which every part contributes to the principal purpose can properly be said to come from the workshop of the rhetorician; III.4.3). "S'intende" here, read in relation to what follows, has nothing to do with the meaning we have found in the first occurrence of "s'intende." In fact, it is generally understood and translated as "which is my principal purpose," a reading which is not wrong in light of what follows: "and that speech in which every part contributes to the principal purpose can properly be said to come from the workshop of the rhetorician."

The reader who is expecting an explanation that could confirm what he has previously understood searches in the impersonal form "s'intende" for a trace that would bring him or her back to the content that the text of the canzone has powerfully suggested (see Ardizzone 2011, 173–232). Actually, the way in which the comment is articulated indicates a methodology. Although there is not a single hint of the notion of intellect, the reader who is acquainted with philosophy finds materials on which to reflect. *S'intende* is recalled initially, as quoted above (III.4.3). It is then reiterated after the declaration that what he will say is a small portion of the truth, adding "ciò risulta in grande loda di costei, ne la quale principalmente *s'intende*." Here a level of meaning can be grasped if we read the first occurrence of *s'intende* as a desire for the gentle lady as shared by many, something towards which there is a tendency or desire. We note in fact that "s'intende" introduces an impersonal form of the verb "intendere." The verb *s'intende*, because it is impersonal, implies a meaning embodied in a grammatical form and in which the subject, because it is impersonal, may possibly be plural. In light of this, an important theme is suggested, and the lady, because she is proposed as a separate form, and the praise attributed to her is a proof of it, is the being in which an act of intellection takes place that perhaps involves a plurality of subjects.

If this is true, then "quello che lo *mio* intelletto non sostiene" (III.4.3) should refer to the inferiority of the individual intellect that is unable to have intellection of the gentle lady. Moreover, "*io* intendo" appears to refer to what the individual being, as individual, can understand in a limited way.

In Aristotelian terms, such ambiguities or equivocal speech appear to introduce the distinction between the possible intellect as proper to an individual and as limited in its capacity and the possible intellect, which is powerfully in act in virtue of the many. The *s'intende* appears, therefore, to refer to the experience of a possible intellect that is actualized in the virtue of many. The difference of meaning arises from the canzone, and the reading that it authorizes is evident. In the canzone we have singled out the trace of a deliberate ambiguity, which could be untied if we consider the word "intellect," which points to the different levels and functions of the human soul. Here we come upon an important hint: the possible intellect of the single human being also has intellection, "intende." It is, however, only in relation to the *donna gentile* that the *s'intende* takes place. In this way, the mind is actualized in an impersonal and perhaps collective tendency towards the gentle lady, who is one. Here, the plurality of the many that have intellection is put forth and overshadowed in a collective form that implies a collective act. A plural unity is the new content that drives us to the notion of the possible intellect and to its contemplation of a divine separate substance. Here, therefore, and beyond the love for the gentle lady, which is intellectual, Dante seems to put forth the idea of the possible intellect as powerfully belonging to the many.

If my analysis is correct, there returns here the *suspicio* that the text is introducing once more the notion of the intellect as an activity proper to the community of human beings, which of course implies the notion of the intellect as one or unique. This notion, as previously said, was the most disputed theses among those discussed in the main cultural centres in Europe and condemned in Paris in 1270 and 1277. In fact, the text seems to summon Dante's position in the *Monarchia*. In this work, in a way that is almost lapidary, it is said that the possible intellect is better actualized in the community of humanitas.[10] It seems that what is anticipated here is something of what will be made explicit in the *Monarchia*, namely, that intellection is in fact not denied to the individual; rather, it is said that the possible intellect can be reduced in act and will better actualize its power through the multitude of the human race.

Dante, here in the *Convivio*, introduces the issue by showing a point of view that since the beginning of the doctrinal treatise has its own peculiarities. The multitude is composed of many, but the individual is able to have his own intellection. Dante is far from the radical position of Cavalcanti, whose main canzone powerfully contributed to this radicalism. For Dante the individual in fact has intellection.

Homo intelligit opposes the radical *homo non intelligit*, the Parisian axiom according to which the individual as individual has no intellection (see Ardizzone 2002, esp. chap. 2). Dante's position is different: the possible intellect is more fully actualized by the multitude of human beings, as we read in *Monarchia*. It is in the "universitas" that the possible reaches its own power and, linking it to our present passage, that the "s'intende" takes its significance. The impersonal form suggests that the subject of this act of intellection can be plural, as I have observed earlier.

It is important to remember that the verb form *s'intende* was introduced by Guido Cavalcanti in his canzone *Donna me prega* ("ven da veduta forma che *s'intende*," 21), and that its correspondent form in Latin was "quae intelligitur" (Corti 1983, 23–4). Apparently, Cavalcanti used the form in an effort to further develop his radical ideology, and partly to criticize the most accredited contents of the radical thought.[11] Dante's position was different, as we have often stressed, but the *s'intende* seems to recall a topic at the centre of the synchronous debate. Dante uses the same expression, yet says something different. His meaning focuses on intellection as a collective experience, which makes such activity more powerful.

The shifting of the logical subject that this passage of the treatise introduces is thus the turning of a page. It designates a subject that is impersonal (because plural), and it is this subject that is both singular and universal, that is, it allows us to contemplate the gentle lady. In the establishment of such content, the love for the gentle lady seems to find its meaning and goal.

2. "La fabbrica del rettorico"

More should be said about this fragment of chapter 4 by considering what is indicated as "fabrica del rettorico." The meaning of the passage is clear: the *donna gentile* is something the I cannot describe because the poverty of his language. In addition, we read that this insufficiency constitutes a form of praise of the one who is the object of the most important act of intellection ("nella quale principalmente s'intende"). This is the principal purpose of the author's rhetorical construction. Dante links two different meanings in one expression: "E ciò resulta in grande loda di costei, se bene si guarda: nella quale principalmente *s'intende*.

E quella orazione si può dire bene che vegna dalla fabbrica del rettorico, nel[la] quale ciascuna parte pone mano allo principale intento" (And this, upon close examination, brings great praise to her, on whom takes place essentially the act of intellection ["nella quale principalmente s'intende"], and that speech in which every part contributes to the principal purpose can properly be said to come from the workshop of the rhetorician; III.4.3). Evidently, he introduces the ambiguity in order to express a supplementary new meaning: the "principale intento" in fact leads the reader to link the meaning of the first impersonal form "nella quale principalmente s'intende" to the "principale intento." Actually, "intendere," if related to "intento," means two things: an act of intellection, and something towards which there is a tendency, such as an intent or a goal. Dante has used a similar double meaning in the canzone *Voi che' ntendendo il terzo ciel movete.* There, the verb "intendere" (intendendo) implied both intellection and a desire and tendency towards God, from that arose the movement of the heavens (*Convivio* II).

Here, the second meaning, intent or goal, is not detached from the first, a fact to which the careful reader is alerted. The recalled fabrique (construct) of the rhetorician suggests that the meaning enclosed in *s'intende* aims at something and reminds us what Brunetto Latini underlines in his *Tresor* (1968, 3, 4, 645): What is said or written, we read, without "contesa," that is, arguing or fighting does not belong to rhetoric. Therefore, if rhetoric implies a fighting, then to recall rhetoric authorizes us to see in the difficult speech a goal. Here, in this passage, to reiterate that the *donna gentile* is the central purpose of the work could sound redundant because the reader at this point is perfectly aware of such a goal. But such redundancy can be justified if we evaluate its purpose. The recalled rhetoric construct opens the field of "contesa" or opposition. A new space seems to be delineated, that of the sub-intendue, which must be read in what is said and in what is opposed, without being expressed. We may guess that the field that the text opposes or confronts is related to a debate about the nature of the human intellect, which Dante discusses in what he calls love and friendship for the *donna gentile.* The new content that our reading has indicated is the identity of the subject that can contemplate her, a subject that is impersonal and thereby plural, since it is enclosed in the impersonal form of the verb *s'intende.* In this context, the recalled praise indirectly works in addition to underline that the gentle lady belongs to the sphere of intellectual beings, according to what Dante introduced in his first canzone *Donne ch'avete* (Ardizzone 2011, 39–53).

In general, we may say that this part of chapter 4 is constructed to underline the importance of *s'intende*. This verbal form returns, in its impersonal form, in the final part of the chapter in its non-ambiguous meaning "to understand": "E così omai *s'intenda* la prima parte di questa canzone che corre omai per mano" (And this is the sense that has to be understood of the first principal part of the canzone, which is at hand). This reiteration is not casual but rather functions as a tool given to the reader to help his or her difficult interpretative task. The "fabbrica" of the rhetorician thus seems to link rhetoric and dialectic, according to a tradition that conceives this art as part of logic, that is, as part of an enlarged Aristotelian *Organon*, a tradition retaken by Aquinas and widely circulating in the thirteenth century.

Continuing our main discussion (i.e., the nature of our intellectual activity in the same chapter III.4.9), we may say that our limitation is attributed to our imagination. This faculty conditions the activity of the intellect, which cannot rise to things like the contemplation of separate substances:

> Dico che nostro intelletto per difetto della virtù dalla quale trae quello ch'el vede che è virtù organica, cioè la fantasia non puote a certe cose salire-però che la fantasia nol puote aiutare, che non ha lo di che-sì come sono le sustanze partite da matera; de le quali se alcuna "considerazione" avere potemo intendere non le potemo, nè comprendere perfettamente.

> Returning then to the subject, I say that our intellect, by defect of that faculty from which it draws what it perceives, which is an organic power, namely the fantasy, cannot rise to certain things (because the fantasy cannot assist it, since it lacks the means), such as the substances separate from matter. And, if we are able to have any concept of these substances, we can nevertheless neither apprehend nor comprehend them perfectly. (III.4.9)

Here, Dante adds that the universal nature or God "volle privarci in questa vita di questa conoscenza": Man is not to be blamed for this, for as I say he was not the maker of this defect; rather universal nature was, that is, God, who willed that in this life we be deprived of that light (III.4.10). This passage seems to be a concession to orthodox theories, but it contradicts what we have read before. This contradiction can be explained if we seek to determine the logical subject which is, in this case, phantasy or imagination. In order to find a meaning, we may assume that the reference is to intellect, to the operation of the possible intellect. This operation here, according to the double function of the possible intellect, is presumably the operation of knowing abstract forms. No mention is made of the other operation of the possibile intellect, which, as was previously said, consists in the contemplation of separate substances. This double activity of the possible intellect is crucial to Dante's theory of human knowledge. I have traced this theory as a content already indicated in the canzone. This theory is shared by both Siger and Albert the Great, who believe that the intellect can accomplish two different cognitive functions: abstracting the forms generated by the imagination, and knowing separate substances (*In tertium*, question 15, 59; *De Anima*, 3.2.19, 205–6).

In light of this double activity, this passage of the treatise takes on a new meaning. In fact, it seems quite clear that the imagination's role belongs to the action of the possible intellect in its conversion to phantasms. In this operation, proper to the human individual, he does not know the separate substances. Although Dante has introduced in the canzone the contemplation of a being that is in many different ways assimilated to a separate substance, now he seems to deny it and to say that it is not possible: "sustanze partite da materia, de le quali se alcuna considerazione potemo avere, intendere non le potemo, né comprendere perfettamente" (such as the substances separate from matter, and if we are able to have any concept of these substances, we can nevertheless neither apprehend nor comprehend them perfectly; III.4.9–10). It appears that Dante here is embracing the classical position assumed by Aquinas. I have pointed out, however, that in the field of "intendere" there is a distinction between what the "I," "intende," as a singular subject he understands and what a plural and collective subject understands (*s'intende*). This marks a line that distinguishes an "I" as a singular subject from a subject that is impersonal and probably collective. Therefore, "io intendo" (III.4.3) is both consonant with and opposed to the "si intende" (III.4.3). This interpretation, which is able to evoke a *suspicio* in the reader, is confirmed by the following fragment: "si che se la *mia* considerazione mi trasportava in parte dove la fantasia venia meno a lo intelletto, se *io* non la potea intendere non sono *io* da biasimare" (consequently, if *my* contemplation has transported me ito a region where my fantasy has failed my intellect, If I was unable to understand her, I am not to be blamed; III.4.11).

We have already noted that the verb "considerare" (to be with stars, cum sidera) holds a specific meaning in the field of speculation, because it implies the knowledge of celestial or separate beings (see Freccero 1986, 226, 310–11n9; Ardizzone 2002, 112). In light of this word, a break seems to be exhibited between the experience of imagination and that of consideration or thought. It must not be forgetten that the break belongs to the individual, the "I," whose imaginative activity is unable to reach this intellectual activity. We as readers are interested in understanding what such activity of consideration implies, but nothing more is said. We can only assume that a weak form of consideration or thought is allowed to the *I*, and that in this activity, imagination is of no help and plays no part. We note that the impersonal form appears when the discourse implies intellection as in the following passage: "Massimamente là dove il pensiero nasce da amore, perchè quivi più che altrove l'anima *s'ingegna*." This passage reiterates that the thinking generated by this kind of love represents the highest possible level of human intellection.

We should note the strategy behind inserting the expression "nostro intelletto," which Aquinas applies to the individual human intellect and Siger instead to the unique intellect in a discussion apparently aimed at establishing from the part of Dante an orthodox position. I return to this important passage:

> Dico che *nostro* intelletto, per difetto de la virtù da cui trae quello ch' el vede, che è virtù organica, cioè la fantasia non puote salire a certe cose pero che la fantasia nol puote aiutare che non ha lo di che- si come sono le sostanze partite da materia; de le quali se alcuna considerazione avere potemo, intendere non le potemo nè comprendere perfettamente.
>
> I say that *our* intellect, by defect of that faculty from which it draws what it perceives, which is an organic power, namely the fantasy, cannot rise to certain things (because the fantasy cannot assist it, since it lacks the means), such as the substances separate from matter. And, if we are able to *have any concept* of these substances, we can nevertheless neither apprehend nor comprehend them perfectly. (III.4.9)[12]

No doubt the text is obscure, and beyond the apparent clarity it seems that a kind of *trobar clus* is transferred in prose. Some fragments are introduced, it seems, with the aim of clarification, but they are dispersed throughout the text.

The reader is partially lost because he cannot link what he has read until now with the new fragment. The passage that follows actually seems to confirm our reading. The word "considerazione," from the

Latin "consideratio," implies in the Middle Ages, as said above, a speculative knowledge. In light of this meaning, we may assert, in precise terms, that his imagination cannot follow his consideration, and that this has a meaning, only if is understood that it refers to the break between the sensible knowledge and that related to the intellective, that is reiterated. "Consideranza" implies the contemplation of a separated substance, but this contemplation does not belong to the human being's sensitive soul. If "consideranza" implies the contemplation of a separate substance, imagination has no power in it. In this case, the notion of the possible intellect and its double operation (one related to the vision and union with the abstract forms and the other of contemplation of the agent intellect, established by both Albert the Great and Siger of Brabante) helps the reader to catch a glimpse of meaning. If we follow this trace, then the ego ("I") who cannot understand the gentle lady seems to reiterate the inability of the individual to contemplate the separate form. It seems also in the fragment that follows that Dante insists on the theme of the interior word and the inability to express his thinking in sensible language, but actually he is introducing another important content in which he distinguishes between the "pensiero nostro" that reaches the "perfect intellect" and the "pensiero nostro" that does not. The ambiguity in the use of "nostro" is reiterated: "Dunque, se 'l pensiero *nostro*, non solamente quello che a perfetto intelletto non vène, ma eziandio quello che a perfetto intelletto *si* termina, è vincente del parlare, non semo noi da biasimare, però che non semo di ciò fattori" (Therefore if our thought surpasses our speech – not only that which does not reach perfect intellect [understanding] but also that which results in perfect intellect [understanding] – we are not to blame, because it is not of our doing; III.4.12). This distinction, which is in itself interesting for testifying a double cognitive activity, is introducing the expression "perfetto intelletto." This perfect intellect, while reiterating the meaning the text was assigning to the honest, also recalls the expression "buon perfetto" (perfect good), which Cavalcanti used in his major canzone: "da buon perfetto tort'è per sorte" (it is diverted from the perfect good) with the meaning of the highest intellection as that performed by the possible intellect (Nardi 1985, 102). I underline that the expression "nostro intelletto" remains ambiguous.

I now return to the double operation of the possible intellect, which appears with uncertainty but is confirmed in another passage. When the reader confronts the canzone's text that the prose is quoting with the explanation it offers about the different operations of the possible intellect, he is directed to understand the nature of what has been presented as love for the gentle lady.

As we have noted, Dante has put forth a relation between the activity of imagination and that of poetry when commenting on the following verses of the canzone: "Pero, se le mie rime avran difetto / ch'entreran ne la loda di costei, / di ciò si biasimi il debole ["debile" as read in De Robertis 2005] intelletto / e 'l parlar nostro che non ha valore / di *ritrar* tutto ciò che dice amore" (vv. 4.13).

At the centre of the discourse is the activity of imagination. The "debile" intellect seems to be coincident with this activity. Its weakness suggests that here the activity of the possible intellect is linked to imagination, which is also indicated as the passive intellect. Related to this intellect is the human imaginative power, which represents the part of the soul that will die, according to all thinkers. In this sense, the adjective "debile" (De Robertis 2005), which refers to something that does not last, works much more than "debole" (weak) to take us back to the Aristotelian area. In the commentary on the above verses, we find a further meaning if we note that the prose seems to rethink and put forth in a different perspective what has been written earlier in the canzone: "Tornando adunque al proposito, dico che nostro intelletto per difetto de la virtù da la quale *trae* quello ch'el vede,che è virtù organica,cioè la fantasia, non puote a certe cose salire ..." (Returning then to the subject, I say that our intellect, by defect of that faculty from which it draws what it perceives, which is an organic power, namely, the fantasy, cannot rise to certain things [because the fantasy cannot assist it]; III.4.9).

Actually, "trae" (draws) is not the same as "ritrar" (portray) (v. 18). In the canzone, the focus was on the disproportion between imagination and poetic speech, on the one hand, and the interior intellectual word of love, on the other. In the above quoted passage, however, imagination seems to introduce, in the link with "trae," the first form of abstraction that the imagination makes of the sensible visible form. The *ritrar* in the canzone perhaps implied the difficulty of "figurare," that is, of rendering in rhetorical-poetic forms the internal discourse of love. This seemingly small change is the sign of a thinking offered in a subtle way – a subtlety that can be determined again in light of the double function of the possible intellect.

The human being defined as "divino animale" (divine animal) in the second chapter of this treatise seems to be contrasted with what is written here, but only if we remain at a superficial level of reading. Dante works by using rhetorical-logical tools. The shifting of the subject is used once more with the purpose of introducing meaning. In the same way, recalling the imagination as responsible for our cognitive limit seems to embody a strategic endeavour.

Going back to the metaphor of diaphanous, introduced above (III.4.2), and according to what we have been told about the impossibility of reaching knowledge, we must ask: Who is the subject of this not knowing? It would be difficult to identify the subject with the divine animal, as the philosophers say (III.2.14). But, if the logical subject is the possible intellect, then the discourse matches what was previously understood. In fact, if we recall what was already said about the "perfect intellect," we see that the text repeats the impersonal form in reference to the possibility of reaching the perfect intellect: "Dunque se 'l pensiero nostro non solamente quello che a *perfetto intelletto* non viene, ma eziandio quello che a *perfetto intelletto* ***si*** termina, è vincente del parlare non semo noi da biasimare, però che non semo di ciò fattori" (Therefore, if our thought surpasses our speech – not only that which does not reach perfect understanding but also that which results in perfect understanding – we are not to blame, because it is not of our doing; III.4.12).

What appears here is a distinction between two ways of referring to the intellect. One is called "perfect," in which thinking seems to reach its end. The other presents a thinking that does not. The expression "perfect intellect" (perfetto intelletto) may derive, as already quoted, from Albert and his *De anima* in the first part of this treatise. But, according to Albert's *Super Etica*, such perfect intellect is called divine and also "lucidus," while in his *De anima* the adjective "perfectus" is referred to as the "intellectus adeptus." There is no doubt that that sense is hidden here, but the meaning can be reached in the distinction between the two functions that converge in the word "intelletto." One indicates the possible intellect when it does not reach the perfect intellect and therefore does not see God or separate substances, or both. This is the possible intellect in relation to the sensitive soul. The other is the divine intellect and its contemplation of the divine being. Therefore, when we read that our intellect, because of the defect on the part of the virtue through which it abstracts everything that it sees, that is, the imagination, cannot rise to the level of some things because imagination cannot help him (III.4.9), we see that Dante is introducing not only the relation between vision and imagination but also the impossibility of rising up to the highest knowing ("non puote a certe cose salire"). This refers to the knowing of the possibile intellect in its link with imagination or passive intellect.

The double nature and activity of the possible intellect, a content common to both Albert and Siger, is the tool to be used in understanding this passage. As Siger writes, the possible intellect has a double function. When it is turned to the agent, it has a continous intellection and is eternal and separate both in its operation and substance. But it is merely possible when it turns to the phantasms. Although it is eternal in its substance, in this operation is corruptible and coniunctus.[13] In light of Siger, the fragment I have quoted from the third treatise perhaps should be referred to the conversion "ad phantasmata" of the possible intellect of which, of course, the activity of imagination is part.[14]

Dante's position in this chapter seems to emerge by way of cautions. Once more the discussion about the possible intellect takes us back to Siger. Here is what Siger writes about when he writes about "intellectus noster" in question 14:[15] "Commentator solvit: intellectus copulatur humanae speciei, et intellectus copulatur huic individuo humanae speciei. Et intellectus copulatio humanae speciei essentialior est quam copulatio quae est huic individuo" (The commentator has resolved in this way: the intellect is connected to the human species and is connected to the individual human being. The coniunctio with the human species is more essential than that with the specific individual).

In Dante's *Monarchia* we read that the possible intellect is better actualized by the whole of humanity than by the individual.[16] This seems to be very close to Siger's position. The content in Siger is related to the core of his theory, which assumes that the human race is eternal, along with its intellect: "propter hoc quod humana species aeterna est et quia intellectus qui ei copulatur aeternus est" (because of it the human species is eternal and eternal is the intellect that is coniunctus to such human species) (*Quaestiones in Tertium*, question 14, 52).

Dante does not follow this theory in its most dangerous contents but rather opposes it in many different ways. In any case, the *donna gentile* is proposed as a separate substance and eternal as a content that takes form in many ways and from different passages. What we are reading in this part of the treatise suggests the attempt to introduce a plurality of human beings linked in a common activity of intellection. Another fragment of Siger is helpful for understanding the role that imagination plays in relation to the possible intellect:

> Unde in natura huius intellectus non est quod ipse copuletur huic individuo, sed in natura eius est quod sit in potentia ad intentiones imaginatas cuiuscumque hominis: et cum ipsi sint omnes eiusdem rationis, propter hoc

> intellectus, unus ex se existens, essentialiter *unitur sive copulatur humanae speciei, sicut accidentaliter se habet ad intentiones imaginatas huic individuo.*
>
> Therefore, in the nature of this intellect there is not an act of conjunction with the individual human being; rather, this intellect is potentially in relation to the imaginative species of every human being. And because human beings share the same rationality, the intellect, being one and separate, is conjoined in its essence to the whole of the human species, but as an accident it joins with the imaginative species of an individual human being. (*Quaestiones in Tertium,* question 14, 52)

Dante's aim at introducing the idea of an act of understanding common to "humanitas" (as he will write in *Monarchia*) draws in a most personal way from such thinking. Beyond the love-friendship for the *donna gentile,* what takes shape, is the problematic issue of the nature and identity of the human mind, which is capable of contemplating such a *donna gentile.* This identity seems to be plural and one at the same time. A plurality that is also one enters as the new subject – and introduces a new sense of history. The one-to-one relationship is established, the intellectual unity of human beings that takes place in time confronts the eternal One and becomes a new subject of history. A word will be important in *Monarchia*: *humanitas,* a word that includes a content that is stigmatized as the article n.124 of the 1277 condemnation shows because – we read – it (*humanitas*) implies a unity of reason.[17] In the becoming of the meaning of this word from its Latin-Roman background to Dante's age, perhaps the beginning of a new era is announced.

Going back to our chapter, we see that the language is mostly allusive and cryptic. In the light of it, we may ask if the text is borrowing the method of some philosophers, that of using allusive or veiled speech. We have noted Dante's allusive speech in the second treatise as a tool to establish a new content in harmony with the new field he was introducing. Here, however, the strategy is different because the text apparently both affirms and denies the same thing. In fact, the thought that reaches the "intelletto perfetto" (III.4.12) (as he writes) seems to express the possibility of human "consideratio" and therefore of knowing and of union with a separate substance, according to what the first two chapters have testified, but which according to this chapter, is impossible. Such ambiguity is perhaps strategic. It may also be the sign of an uncertainty – an indication of a problematic confirmation of a crucial content that the author is attempting to circumscribe. We know that human thinking can reach the perfect intellect or it cannot. We have introduced as a key the double nature of the possible intellect and its discontinuity in the contemplation of the agent in virtue of its relation with phantasms. To repeat what I quoted earlier can be of help:

> Dico che nostro intelletto, per difetto de la vertù da la quale *trae* quello ch'el vede,che è virtù organica,cioè la fantasia non puote a certe cose salire-però che la fantasia nol puote aiutare che non ha lo di che- sì come sono le sustanze partite da materia de le quali se alcuna considerazione avere potemo, intendere non le potemo
>
> I say that our intellect, by defect of that faculty from which it draws what it perceives, which is an organic power, namely the fantasy, cannot rise to certain things (because the fantasy cannot assist it, since it lacks the means), such as the substances separate from matter. And, if we are able to have any concept of these substances, we can nevertheless neither apprehend nor comprehend them perfectly. (III.4.9)

To clarify his point, he adds: "Si che se la mia *considerazione* mi trasportava in parte dove la fantasia venia meno a l'intelletto, se *io* non la potea intendere non sono *io* da biasimare" (Consequently if *my* contemplation has transported me to a region where my fantasy has failed my intellect, I am not to blame for being unable to understand; III.4.11).

It seems that pointing out the limits of the knowledge tied to imagination merely indicates a weakness. But the real meaning emerges if we recall that the field of *considerazione* is conceived not in continuity with imagination but as the contemplation of a separate being, on the part of a subject that performs a different function. The I (*io*) appears to be able to perform two operations. One of them is consideration, an operation that drives the intellect far from imagination. Here, the weakness of the I seems to be different from his consideration. The activity of the imagination is confirmed as being unable to contemplate the lady. This is an activity of the I, who, nevertheless, in his consideration is brought very far from imagination. Also, the term "intelletto," which can be "perfetto" or "non perfetto," has the goal of establishing the existence of a potentiality that can be perfected or not. This, however, suggests an ambiguity, which requires the following clarification:

> *Dico che se difetto fia ne le mie rime*, cioè ne le mie parole che a trattare di costei sono ordinate, di cio è da biasimare la debilitate de lo intelletto e la

> cortezza del nostro parlare, lo quale per lo pensero è vinto, si che seguire lui non puote a pieno, massimamente li dove lo pensiero nasce da amore, perchè quivi l'anima profondamente più che altrove s'ingegna.
>
> Then where it says *And so if fault is found to mar my verse,* I excuse myself for a fault for which I should not be blamed, since others can see that my words are inferior to the dignity of this lady. And I say that if fault is found to mar my verse – that is, in my words which are arranged to treat of her – the blame is due to the weakness of the intellect and the inadequacy of our power of speech, which is so overwhelmed by a thought that it cannot fully follow it, especially where the thought springs from love, because then the soul is stirred in a more profound manner than at other times. (III.4.4)

The meaning of this passage emerges only if we refer the "debile" intellect as the possible in his conversion to the individual phantasms. In this case, it is evident that "thought" in its part overshadows the intellectual experience, and that "love" is the conjunction and vision of a separate form on the part of possibile intellect.

Human nature is proposed here as a dual being, but this is enunciated with a deliberate ambiguity. In his *Summulae logicales,* Peter Hispanus, whom Dante will recall in his *Paradiso,* defines the *equivocatio* in terms that allow us to understand the nature of the ambiguity. We have equivocation, he writes, when different definitions of things are united in a name that is the same. And "the fallacy of equivocatio is the deceit caused in us by the inability to distinguish the different definitions which are in the same name" (*Summulae logicales* 7, 28). In other words, the term "intellect" is strongly charged with ambiguity.

Recalling a fragment quoted earlier, we know that Dante uses the ambiguity inherent in the theory of the diaphanous in order to say that the intellectual soul is illuminated but does not see the light of the separate substance. This fragment compels us to recall what was said earlier: that the agent intellect is a separate substance superior to the human being, and that the individual human being does not know this separate substance. Since the possible intellect in relation to the sensitive soul performs an operation that is assumed to be mortal, although in itself the intellect is eternal, in this operation it is inferior to the separate divine substance. This is what we read in Siger's question 13: "Utrum intellectus possibilis agentem intelligat" (If the possible intellect has intellection of the agent intellect).[18] This is the answer as given in the fragment quoted in the note and in which we read that the possible intellect has the power of having intellection of the agent intellect, but in this action it is not in continuity with us. The rational soul is considered a separate substance. It includes both the possibile and the agent intellect. But the possible intellect alone knows the agent and in this operation is not in continuity with us as individual human beings.[19]

It is not difficult, comparing this part of chapter 4 with the canzone, to find a radical line of thinking with a certain amount of ease. In the prose text, this line is sometimes confirmed and sometimes denied. The text proceeds in a cryptic way, and the reader wishes to know at this point whether a human being in this life can know the separate substance. From the first three chapters it seems that the answer is positive. This answer is at first rejected, but then reaffirmed in a most complex perspective in chapter 4. In other words, the author of *Convivio* embraces the same ambiguity typical of the intellectual milieu of the philosophers of his age, as texts like Boethius of Dacia and Giacomo testify. The text, therefore, imposes a double pathway but in an equivocal way. It appears that it seeks to establish a strategic knot that will focus the reader's attention but it seems to have a sophismatic nature. It is not a true sophism but rather, for the most part, a form of veiled or hidden speech. According to Peter Hispanus (1972), it is part of the sophismatic procedure to confute what has been previously said. This kind of sophism is called *redargutio* and is one of five sophisms (*Summulae logicales* 7.13). Equivocatio and amphibolie are part of sophism as well. According to the medieval logician, a discourse is amphibolous when it uses the same terms and words to signify different things (*Summulae logicales* 7.45–9).

3. Intellection as Proper to *Humanitas*: A Political Issue

In light of the condemnations and of the debates to which the prohibited articles testify, hidden speech could nevertheless be decoded, at least in part. From the text of the condemnation of 1277, we know that the discourse on imagination generated suspicion in the censor because it was deeply related to theories of the unique intellect. This content may be understood by relating it to the great central problem introduced by Arabic thought, in particular that of the commentator who assumed that the possible intellect was separate and unique for all human beings. This thinking, typical of the most radical positions, was refuted not just by Tempier and Bonaventure but also, and most strongly, by Aquinas and Albert. There is no doubt, however, that Siger, who was influenced by Albert, followed this radical theory in his early work. Earlier, I recalled Dante's *Monarchia,* which testifies that for Dante the possibile intellect performs its operation better when it is actualized by the (multitude) of human beings ("necesse est multitudinem esse in humano genere, per quam quidem tota potentia hec actuetur"; there must needs be a vast number of individual people in the human race, through whom the whole of this potentiality can be actualized; *Monarchia* 1.3.8). Regarding this aspect of Dante's *Monarchia,* Gilson has underlined that this thinking is not linked in *Monarchia* to what this theory includes in the field of Averroism (E. Gilson, 1972, 167–72). Such observation is also useful for understanding Dante's position in the *Convivio.* In Dante, the suggested echoes of theory of the intellect as separate and common to a multitude does not imply that the individual has no knowledge or that the individual soul is mortal.

In *Monarchia,* Dante will express his thought clearly: the possible intellect belongs to the multitude of human beings, a view that supports his concepts of *universitas* and *humanitas.* We may note that both words are used in *Monarchia* and that his concept of *humanitas* is similar to the one put forth in a prohibited proposition introduced earlier. Here is the proposition, according to the text given by Hissette: "Quod humanitas non est forma rei, sed rationis" (Humanity is not a form of a thing but of reason) (Hissette 1977, proposition 124, 201). According to the censors, the meaning of this proposition, as Hissette explains, derives from its link to the notion of the possible unique intellect, but the source has not been indentified. This proposition suggests that the concept of *humanitas* in the *Monarchia* is part of the notion of the possibile intellect conceived as enclosing a plural logical subject that becomes one. This may also be in part why Dante also uses the word *universitas.*

The discussion of the possible intellect in this work is certainly not incidental, but is rather an aspect to be discussed in the correspondence Dante introduces between God as the One, the *Monarch* as one, and the Intellect as one, where one is both a number and a principle. That this is not incidental, but on the contrary, it is of the structure is made stronger in light of the meaning that the *Convivio* offers us.

Actually, the cognitive problem introduced with the invention of the *donna gentile* – starting with the canzoni, the *Convivio* commentates, and the love for philosophy which has the same cognitive nature – aims (in the link which the text establishes between ethics and metaphysics) at establishing a content that includes a socio-political value. The notion of a possible intellect in the *Convivio* must be seen in its peculiar relation to ethics and politics.

This actually is enclosed in the third treatise in the discussion about the *honestum*, as I have proposed. It returns in a different form in the fourth treatise. The complex genesis of this idea in Dante, which probably dates from his first years of intellectual engagement in Florence, is not extraneous to the values he had introduced with his love for Beatrice, who was certainly a transumptive way to introduce incarnation in history. Because of this, Beatrice included the awarness of the *logos-verbum*, which the incarnation brought into time along with a new sense of *communitas* naturally identified and unified because of the *logos*. The Lamentations of Jeremiah that are introduced in the *Vita nuova* and the recalled letter to the princes of the earth for the death of Beatrice are signs of a great perturbation that her disappearance creates. Two concepts crucial in the Christian tradition are at work: the *logos-verbum* and the Catholic universality. Quoting Jeremiah, Dante presents the city of Florence as a widow, but the city's borders are extended and suggested as coinciding with that of the earth. This seems to be the first fragment of a socio-political awareness as it enters in the *Vita nuova* (chapter 30). No doubt, *De vulgari eloquentia* bears strong traces of a political awareness. The vernacular as a language based on a pre-natural language common to all people suggests the awarness of a community linked by the common linguistic act that the vernacular manifests. But now, in the *Convivio*, many new authors and texts enter to strengthen this line of thinking. For instance, the *Nicomachean Ethics* here offers Dante the perspective he needs. The earthly happiness that is the goal of the *Ethics* according to Aristotle takes place in the social life of an organized community. In *Politics*, Aristotle identifies the community with the state – the polis (*Politics* 1.1). Because the human being is a political animal, his happiness takes place in the community. Community is natural, and the state is natural, too (*Politics* 1.2; *Ethics* 1). Aristotle's commentators, like Thomas and Albert, follow this view.

But in Dante, if the possible intellect is common to the *humanitas* or to the *universitas*, not only does such an intellect need a community or better the community in order to actualize itself but also human beings are able to realize an intellectual perfection because they constitute a *societas*. Human happiness makes evident the essence of individual human beings, because their intellect is common. It guarantees in the *conviventia* the actualization of the goal of *humanitas*. This means that philosophical happiness implies a community, a plurality of human beings who, because of community, are conceived as being plural and one at once. The political unity is natural and is, moreover, the expression of a natural intellectual unity. Dante will take into account the small communities, starting by evaluating the essential link between two human beings as it takes place in love, and then considering families, villages, and so on in order to establish the natural base of *communitas* (*Convivio* IV.4; *Monarchia* 1.3; 1.5). The perfect life is the actualization of our intellect, which includes the life of the individual as part of a community. A thinking emerges from that in which the civil forms of *conviventia* are the result of a natural need. Dante will start in the fourth treatise of the *Convivio* to recall such forms of aggregations as natural. The link that Aristotle's *Nicomachean Ethics* makes between friendship, as a natural form of unity, and other forms of aggregations implicitly suggests that friendship becomes a category of relevance. The friendship for the *donna gentile* must be rethought from this perspective; in fact, in the canzone, she was proposed as the one loved by many. The love for her, because this love is for a separate substance, brings together human beings and angelic intelligences. It was therefore a way of introducing a superior principle of unity, in which the cosmological order was the expression of a superior intellectual love and desire, one which human and superhuman beings may share. An earthly happiness based on the common intellection seems to be interwined with the love for the *donna gentile* as a divine separate being. Such love manifests human beings into community and manifests a one out of many. The love for the *donna gentile* implies that the human *communitas* is united in this love.

The *Convivio* proposes that a common intellectual structure is the natural basis for the political *cumviventia*, an expression of a will that is naturally grounded in the human being. In the allegorical commentary to this treatise, we will find the vernacular word *convivenza* as something proper to humans. Human happiness cannot be merely individual. We have already underlined that Aristotle's *Nicomachean Ethics* was linked to his *Politics* – a connection to which both Albert and Aquinas subscribed. Brunetto Latini in the *Tresor* started his section devoted to ethics by discussing the government of the city: "Dou government de la cite." He asserted that "li ars qui enseigne la citè governer est principal et soveraine et dame de toutes ars, por ce que desoz lui sont contenues maintes honorables ars, si come est rethoriques et la scientia de fere ost et de governer sa mesnee" (The art that teaches the government of the city is the most important and the lady of all arts under it are other honourable arts such as rhetoric and the science of organizing an army and that of the government of the people) (Latini 2007, II.3, 334). According to Brunetto, the art that shows how to govern the city is the most important of all arts. Politics is a noble art because it gives order and purpose to all the arts over which politics presides. The accomplishement and goal of politics is the accomplishment and goal of all other arts.

In this formulation, Brunetto was mostly indebted to Cicero, but no doubt also to the Arabic philosopher Alfarabi. Politics as the most important science was a crucial content of Alfarabi's philosophy. We may retrace this content in Alfarbi's work that was highly diffused in Western culture, *De enumeratione scientiarum* (Enumeration of the sciences), a work that Mahdi through his scholarship has allowed us to rethink Alfarabi as being influential in Europe before Aristotle's *Politics* was known; that is, before the year 1260.[20] In Brunetto's *Tresor*, politics is proposed, as we have seen, as the most important science. Also in *La rettorica*, it appears that the practical sciences (ethics, economics, politics) are most important. Politics in particular is said to be a very important science, since it is made, as we read, by things that are done and made and therefore linked to arts and disciplines (magisterii) that are made in the city "in città si fanno," and to things said "n detti," that is, to grammar, dialectic, and rhetoric.

The influence of Alfarabi's thought may be due to the mediation of Dominicus Gundissalinus (1903). In any case, the Ciceronian basis appears to have been supported by Brunetto's knowledge of new texts as they derive from his experience and contacts in Spain and in France. It seems that here, during Brunetto's exile in France, some introductions to philosophy may testify to the diffusion of both Alfarabi and Gundissalinus (Lafleur 1988). In Alfarabi, who was a reader of Plato's *Republica*, the philosopher's duty was not detached from his political duty. Brunetto, by making ethics a discipline subordinated to politics, was in fact suggesting that the philosophical happiness described in the *Nicomachean Ethics* was related to politics. But for Dante, according to the organization of the sciences in *Convivio* II, the link he establishes between ethics and metaphysics derives from the Aristotelian teaching. The goal of *Ethics* 10 is intellectual contemplation during earthly life (see Fioravanti 2014). Dante introduces the *donna gentile* in order to discuss this issue. His answer includes a link between ethics and politics. If the *donna gentile* is the highest good, this good can be reached only in the context of the human community.

It is the thinking of the commentator, as filtered through the thirteenth-century translation and debates, that offers Dante a new awareness of Aristotle's *Nicomachean Ethics* and of the *Honestum*, assumed to be coincident with the *summum bonum,* because it is the common good (as I discussed in an earlier section of this study). The later awareness of Dante's *Monarchia* is the result of a process that passes through this content. The link that Dante (following Aristotle's *Ethics* and Cicero) creates between *honestum* and rationality and *honestum* and *Directio voluntatis* in the *De vulgari eloquenti* (2.2.6–8) is the basis for understanding the *honestum* as it returns in this treatise. I also introduced the link between intellection and *communitas* as important for Dante as starting from the time he wrote the canzoni *Voi che 'ntendendo il terzo ciel movete* and *Amor che ne la mente mi ragiona.* Brunetto certainly played a role in Dante's evolution. This is well known, and Dante will ackowledge it in canto 15 of his *Inferno.* The *Convivio* bears strong traces of Brunetto's teaching, which forms part of Dante's attention to politics. Here, I wish only to recall that Brunetto in his *Tresor* used an Arabic-Alexandrine summary of the *Nicomachean Ethics,* which Hermann the German translated into Latin in Toledo, which was a centre of translations from Arabic into Latin in the twelfth century. This was the same translation that, in turn, was translated into Italian by Taddeo Alderotto, the physician from Bologna whom Dante denigrates for his "laida traduzione" (bad translation). Brunetto translated this text into French, and it is this translation that appears in his *Tresor.*[21]

But to go back to the link between ethics and politics, the tenet that ethics had its natural link with politics was mostly Aristotelean in origin. For Aristotle, the highest good was not that of the individual. Rather, he considered the common good of a nation or state to be more noble and divine. It is here that ethics is indicated as having politics as its goal, where politics is defined as "scientia architectonica" (*Nicomachean Ethics* 1, 2, 8, 1094b7–12). In addition, we read at the very beinning of the *Nicomachean Ethics* that the knowledge of the supreme good is of great importance for our behaviour in life. In Dante, it seems that the divine animal of the *Convivio* is put forth as the complement of man as a political animal. The link, of course, is Aristotle's *Ethics* but rethought in light of the current debate on human intellectual happiness.[22] This reflection forms the basis of Dante's future work on the *Monarchia.* The *Convivio* confirms itself as a crucial step in Dante's reflection and progressive awareness. A political goal is an important part of Dante discussion about the *donna gentile.* And here, I use the adjective "political" to indicate earthly values proper to a human being naturally living in the community and reaching his goal within and because of such community.

The making of the notion of *humanitas* seems to be in progress in the *Convivio.* What the "I" as a single human being understands is proposed as inferior to what the collectivity understands. Such collectivity, in the passages quoted above, is introduced through an impersonal verb ("s'intende"). The word "form" used in relation to the unity of reason of *humanitas* in the above-quoted prohibited proposition of 1277 was understood by the censor as implying the notion of intellect conceived as a shared unity. On this basis, the speech about *humanitas* implied not just notions derived from classical culture but a new content, a new awareness of the natural unity of human beings joined together by the common search for earthly intellectual happiness. For Dante, this intellectual goal is the basis for the political well-being that takes place in the *conviventia*. Gauthier, in his 1948 essay "Trois commentaires 'averroistes' sur L'Ethique à Nicomaque," touches on the relation between intellectual happiness and politics that is suggested in the area of radical thinking. Happiness, he writes, is at once ethical, intellectual, and political (288).

4. More Philosophical Contents

If we return to the above section on the imagination and compare it with what we read in Hissette (1977), we see why the discourse on the imagination as imperfect aroused the suspicion of the censor, according to what I have introduced there. Related to the imagination, and reported as suspect speech, is proposition 146. This proposition informs us that humans can have an intellection that can be more or less good, and that this depends on the passive intellect, which is said to be a sensitive power. The censor condemns this content and believes it is derived from the idea that there is only one intellect in all human beings, or in all souls, that is, that what distinguishes our thoughts would be in the different images and phantasms as produced by imagination.

Here is the text of proposition 146: "Quod nos peius aut melius intelligimus, hoc provenit ab intellectu passivo, quae dicit esse potentiam sensitiva. Error quia hoc ponit unum intellectum in omnibus, aut aequalitatem in omnibus animabus" (The fact that we may have a better or worse level of intellection derives from the passive intellect, which is said to be a sensitive power. This is an error because this establishes that there is just one intellect in all human beings, or equality in all souls) (Hissette 1977, 225).

In the passage of the treatise that we have examined, this thought is not present, but the word used for the imagination and intellect – *debile* – is perfectly legitimate. This appears to suggest that wherever a distinction is introduced between intellect "perfetto" and its opposite, as different kinds of beings related to different realities, a content is suggested that confirms something we already noted in the commentary of the first canzone *Voi che'ntendendo il terzo ciel movete.* There, according to the explanation given in the prose, it was impossible for the character who says "I" to turn his head back by virtue of the new woman. This distinction expresses actually an opposition, that is, a break between the two functions of the human being: the sensitive and the intellective. This view belongs to a thinking labelled as heterodox in the thirteenth century and is attributed to the philosophers (Van Steenberghen 1991, 334–6).

In the third treatise, however, the author appears to contradict what he has introduced. Here, the human intellect is defined as a divine being (III.2). While we have seen this content to be denied, in our reconstruction it is indirectly confirmed. The sense one has, as already said, is that Dante is trying to introduce something that is important, but it is declined in a speech that sounds repetitive. By virtue of the terminology alone, there are two intellects or intellectual functions that are active in the human being. One is the intellect that humans share with intelligences. Dante has given this function a shape with the invention of the love for the gentle woman, who is in fact "mirata" by the intelligences ("Ogn' intelletto di lassù la mira") and receives the divine light. The second is intellect that does not get the perfect intellection and is connected with the passive faculty or fantasy. The text does not say more, but it is useful to remember that this content led to the condemnation of a suspected theory in the list. This is article 122 in Hissette's work: "Quod ex sensitivo et intellectivo in homine non fit unum per essentiam, nisi sicut ex intelligentia et orbe, hoc est unum per operationem" (The sensitive and intellectual in the human being does not make an essencial unity. What is possible to have is an operational unity as that of the intellectual motor and the heaven) (1977, 198).

Proposition 121 finds an echo in Dante's fragment because it distinguishes what belongs to the material of a human being from what is intellectual. In proposition 121 we read: "Quod nulla forma ab extrinseco veniens potest facere unum cum materia. Quod enim separabile est, cum eo quod est corruptibile unum non facit" (No form which comes in from the external can be united with matter. What is separate cannot create a unity with what is corruptible) (Hissette 1977, 197).

Chapter 4 of the third treatise appears mostly to distinguish the corruptible from the separate and intellectual. Imagination as part of the corruptible because a function of the sensitive soul was part of Aristotle's thought and of Aristotelianism in general. For Albert the Great, for instance, the sensitive and intellectual souls, though different, form a unity. This view was criticized by Siger. According to him, the vegetative, sensitive, and intellectual do not form a unity or, as he says, they form a unity that is not simple but composite. According to Siger, the intellect is a virtue rooted in a form that is not material; it comes *ab extrinseco*. The vegetative and sensitive parts of the soul are rooted in a material substance. This implies that what is intellectual is not rooted in a simple soul with vegetative and sensitive alone, but is rooted along with them in a soul that is composite (*In tertium*, question 1, 2–3).

We now turn to a fragment from Albert's *De unitate intellectus*, in which Albert refutes the error that assumes that the *intellectus adeptus* (as he calls it) is separate and unique. He traces the error back to Averroes. Albert, who on many occasions is fascinated by the Commentator, in this case opposes him in a most radical way. This opposition is part of a content he takes to task in order to unmask it. His writing on *De Unitate intellectus* is in fact a strong denunciation of the theory of the intellect conceived as one.[23] Albert uses fragments of Averroes's *De anima* in order to refute this content. In doing so, he offers elements that are helpful in our effort to recognize the contexts of Dante's discussion.

According to this theory, Albert explains, every mover that is separate is unique and cannot be mutiplied, for the virtue through which is linked to what it moves. He then observes that, according to Averroes and his followers, the intellectual soul is part of this kind of beings. The mover is separate in the way that the pilot of the ship, "nauta navis," is not linked to the individuals but is separate from them. The intellectual soul is similarly separate; it remains unique and for itself, and does not multiply itself.

There follows a fragment that is worthy of quotation in its original Latin. It helps to decode what we have already emphasized in our reading of the text of the canzone. Here, in fact, the gentle lady is described as being one. Both intellects and the human beings gaze at her, since she is a separate form. But the contemplation of the latter is intermittent or discontinuous, as suggested by the adverb "quando." This content, which is elliptical in the canzone, will become clearer in the allegorical section of the third treatise, where Dante introduces the word "discontinuo" as a definition of the human beings kind of intellection.

What is important for us is a fragment in which Albert cites Averroes, who asserts that everything that receives a form that is one, and is not multiplied in many human beings, is unique in all of them. In this way, he continues, the possible intellect receives the intelligible form, as has been said. Therefore, the possible intellect is one in all human beings. The received form is enumerated by the number of subjects that receives it. If the received being is in all beings one, it is necessary that the recipient in them be one. Here is Albert's fragment:

> Quidquid recipit formam, quae est una, non multiplicata in multis hominibus, in quibus est ipsum est unum in omnibus illis. Intellectus possibilis sic recipit formam intelligibilem ut dictum est. Igitur intellectus possibilis est unus in omnibus illis in quibus est forma intellectualis. Probatur autem prima pars primae ex hoc, quod forma recepta numeratur per numerum subiecti recipientis. Et ideo si receptum in omnibus vel multis est unum, oportet, quod recipiens in eisdem sit unum et idem.
>
> What receives a form,that is one, and is not multiplied in many human beings is one in all.The possible intellect in this way receives the intelligible form as has been said.Thus the possible intellect is one in all in which is intellectual form. This is proved in the very first part; a form that is received is numerated from the subjects that receive it. Thus, if what is received in many is one, it is necessary that what receives is one. (*De Unitate*, 12)

According to what Albert explains, and seeks to refute, Averroes says that whatever receives an intelligible form that is one, is one. In light of this, we may deduce that *if what is given is one, it is received as one, and what receives is one.* Going back to the first chapters of this treatise, we may recall that one was the given form, and the form was defined as *simplicissima* (the most simple) because *semplicissimo* was the giver. In addition, we have discussed, as Dante writes, that our differences derive from what is material, which individualizes us.

Siger's *In tertium* is extremely helpful in understanding Dante's position. According to the philosopher, the intellect is "simplex" and "intrasmutabilis." It is made, "factus," by the Causa Prima, immediate and is "unum et factum aeternum" (one and eternal) (question 4). That the material was responsible for what is called "principium individuationis" was a tenet suggested at the beginning of the third treatise (III.1.3). This principle is used by both Siger and Aquinas but with different aims. For Aquinas, what individuates is the body, the material, and for that reason Aquinas asserts that the intellect is the form of the body. In other words, every human body has its own intellect. For Siger, on the contrary, what makes us individuals is the activity of imagination. Because the intellect is one, what individuates are the so-called *intentiones imaginatas*.[24]

In order to better understand Dante's discourse, another content derived from Siger can be of help. This is the notion of intellect as coeternal with the first cause. According to Siger, this intellect is "extrinsecus" not "generabilis" and therefore incorruptible and separate (*In tertium*, question 4). In question 8, we read that it is *indivisible* and therefore cannot establish its substance in pluribus but "potest *informare* plura," that is, to give its form to many or to move many (verum est quod indivisibile non potest esse vel situari secundum suam substantiam in pluribus, bene tamen potest informare plura vel movere plura) (*In tertium*, 25). In addition, according to the philosopher of Brabant, the possible intellect is one in substance with the agent. Siger does not say whether the intellect given from the first cause is the possible or the agent intellect; he calls it simply intellect. Then he distinguishes the two functions of this simple being: the possible and the agent.

There is, however, a crucial observation made by Albert the Great to which I want to return. This observation, which I have recalled above, reminds the reader what the love for the gentle lady means in terms of cognition. Because the gentle woman is one, according to what Albert recalls in order to stigmatize and oppose it, that which contemplates her – that is, the mind – should also be one. The *Convivio* discusses this issue indirectly, but it nevertheless offers the tools that make the issue recognizable. The following chapters (5 and 6) of the treatise confirm our reading and establish once more, and in an indirect way, the topic of intellection as central. The text introduces a new topic: the sun and what the sun sees in its circular movement around the earth.

The Ptolemaic-Aristotelian theory of the cosmos here comes into play. The *donna gentile* is projected once more into a cosmological framework. The earth is immobile at the centre of the cosmos, while the sun circles around it. Prosopopeia works here to give, not voice or speech to an inanimate being, but vision. The sun, an inanimate being, is proposed as endowed with the ability to see.

5. In Navigation: What the Sun Sees

Chapter 5 introduces the sun and its circular movement in order to comment on the verse "il sol che tutto il mondo gira." We read that the sun enlightens the "world," a term that Dante clarifies in the following passage: "per mondo non intendo tutto il corpo dell'universo, ma solamente questa parte del mare e de la terra" (I say that by the term "world" I do not here mean the whole body of the universe but only the part which consists of land and sea). In the poetry, the passage reads: "Non vede il sol, che tutto 'l mondo gira / cosa tanto gentil *quanto 'n quell'ora* / che luce nella parte ove dimora / la donna di cui dire Amore mi face" (The sun that circles all the world. Sees nothing so gentle as at that time when it shines upon the place where dwells the lady of whom love makes me speak). The text here introduces crucial cosmological information, to this which the discussion of chapter 5 is devoted. In the sixth chapter, another digression is introduced with a discussion about time.

We continue our reading following our main theme. We see that the lady, until now indicated as a separate substance, is now identified, according to the canzone verses, as something belonging to the earthly world. We have information here about the sun. It accomplishes a complete cycle, and its circling implies a going and returning to the initial point in virtue of a complete circuit or annual revolution:

> Nel precedente capitolo è mostrato per che modo lo sole gira; sì che omai si puote procedere a dimostrare la sentenza della parte alla quale s'intende. Dico adunque che in questa parte prima comincio a commendare questa donna per comparazione all' altre cose; e dico che ' l sole, girando lo mondo, non vede alcuna cosa così gentile come costei: per che segue che questa sia, secondo le parole, gentilissima di tutte le cose che 'l sole allumina.

> In the preceding chapter, it has been shown in what manner the sun makes its revolution, so that now we may proceed to explain the meaning of the part with which we are concerned. I say then that in this part, I begin first to praise this lady in comparison to other things; and I say that the sun, circling the world, sees nothing so noble as she, from which it follows that she is, according to these words, the noblest of all the things on which the sun shines. (III.6.1)

If we read this passage in relation to the allegorical commentary, we understand that the circling implies thinking. The sun in its movement circulates and, representing the sensible image of God – ("Nullo sensibile in tutto lo mondo è più degno di farsi essemplo di Dio che 'l sole"; Nothing in the universe perceptible by the senses is more worthy to be made the symbol of God than the sun; III.12.7) – is the sensible form of God's reflexive activity which is offered through a circular thinking: "Dico adunque che Dio, che tutto intende (ché suo "girare" è suo "intendere") (I say, then, that God, whose understanding embraces everything [for His "circling" is His "understanding"], sees nothing so noble as He sees when He gazes upon the place where this Philosophy dwells; III.12). "Ché, avegna che Dio, esso medesimo mirando, veggia insiememente tutto, in quanto la distinzione delle cose è in lui per [lo] modo che lo effetto è nella cagione" (For although God, gazing upon Himself, sees all things collectively, yet He sees them discretely insofar as the discreteness of things exists in Him in such manner that the effect exists within the cause). The God who intends and thinks himself as represented in the image of the sun proposes the divine thinking as circular, as exemplified in the sensible world. The sun is not only the sensible image of the divine being but also the moving image of his reflexive thinking. Its circular movement represents the idea of eternal reflection, but the sun is also the figure of time.

Such reflection in the allegorical commentary also introduces the link between God's thinking and creation as an act of reflection that is at once creation. God sees in Himself the ideas, that is, the archetypes of things. Therefore, thinking and creating are one and the same operation. This divine thinking, which reshapes the ancient Platonic theory of the contemplation of ideas on the part of the demiurge, establishes creation as generated from a thinking that produces the idea-archetypes. But here, in this part, creation is not clearly mentioned. God appears as the first cause. Here, because of the perfection and circular motion of such thinking, we read that the cosmos receives in every part the same amount of light and shadow: "Per che vedere si puote che per lo divino provedimento lo mondo è si ordinato che, volta la spera del sole e tornata a uno punto questa palla dove noi siamo, in ciascuna parte di sè riceve tanto tempo di luce quanto di tenebra" (Thus we may now see that by divine provision the world is so ordered that when the sphere of the sun has revolved and returned to its starting place this globe on which we dwell receives in every place an equal time of light and darkness; III.5.21). If the circling of the sun manifests a thinking that is divine and inscribed in the cosmos, the order of the cosmos manifests an intellect. The gentle lady is linked to this thinking, and in fact the sun does not in its circling see a thing more gentle than her: "gentilissima di tutte le cose che il sole illumina" (III.6.1). But if the sun represents a thinking that is both divine and eternal, the sun would be the sensible moving sign of eternity. Plato said that time is the moving image of eternity. This idea implied for him the eternity of time. What matters here derives from the fact that the sun in its circling "sees" the gentle lady. That is, the sun sees a being that has been depicted as an eternal being. Moreover, since world means earth and sea, this eternal being is not only heavenly but also earthly.

The text in prose suggests a link between these contents. In the allegorical commentary, "vede" is explained as "enlightens." Another verse in the canzone is hard to decipher: "Costei pensò chi mosse l'universo." Does "mosse" here mean that God, in thinking the idea of the *donna gentile,* moved in the sense of creating the universe? Dante's commentary does not offer a clear explanation. Thomas Aquinas, for example, denies that "to move" means "to create" (*Summa contra gentile* Ii.16; *Summa theologiae* 1.45.a2). Of course, the lady is suggested as eternal, but this eternal being is also earthly. Here, eternity is not that of archetypes in the mind of God. Rather, the sun is suggested as being eternal because the divine thought is eternal. And if "vede" means "he sees" in the literal sense, and "enlightens" in the allegorical commentary, both seem to suggest the theme of the eternity of the lady but in an indirect way. There also enters the theme of the eternity of the world. What God sees must be eternal because in eternal beings nothing can change, including vision. Siger, in the first quaestio of his *In tertium,* underlines that change implies transmutation, which does not take place in an eternal separate being. What God thinks is no doubt eternal, like him. In the same way that the sun in its circling the world sees the lady, God's thinking sees her. The divine is the model, and the sun is his examplar.

Giles of Rome cites, as one of the errors of philosophers, that the sun is conceived as being eternal. This content is introduced indirectly as part of the idea that the only eternal movement is the circular one, because only the circular is continous. Since the circular movement is that of the heavens, they may be eternal along with the sun. For Aristotle, time is eternal as well (Giles of Rome 1944).

The discourse about the sun contains a further significance that strengthens what has already been discussed. In reference to the sun, Aquinas informs us that according to "quidam" the sun would be a way of indicating the agent intellect. He says also that, according to this theory, the agent intellect is God, and that the notion of a unique intellect is accepted by many, recalling that Plato believed that there is only one intellect, one and separate, and compared it to the sun, which is one but is received by many (*De unitate intellectus contra Averroistas* 4, 83). A twentieth-century medieval scholar, R. Gauthier, informs us that Averroes thought that, just as there is one sun, there is also one intellect, and that the sun was the image of the unique possible intellect (Gauthier 1948, 284).

Albert, too, used the metaphor of the sun in his *De unitate*, but in a different mode, and Dante quotes Albert's *De intellectu et intelligibile* in the fouth treatise of *Convivio*. According to heterodox theories that I have quoted above as referred to by Albert the Great, only what is one can contemplate what is one. The gentle lady in the *Convivio* is one. She appears to represent a form that is unique, intelligible, and eternal. The way in which Dante depicts her is similar to what Aquinas recalls in order to condemn it in his *De unitate*.

If this is true, a meaning here would be that the sun, which sees the woman, implies that the possible intellect (according to Averroes, as recalled by Gauthier 1948) sees the lady, that is, contemplates the agent. In the allegorical commentary, the sun is identified with God, who in his reflexive thinking sees his idea or gentle lady. This would suggest the way in which the possible knows the agent or itself. Gauthier offers a confirmation of such interpretation when he writes that the sun was identified by Averroes with the possible intellect. Following Gauthier, the meaning here would be that the possible intellect identified with the Sun-God sees the woman because of his reflexive thinking. The sun contemplates the lady, and its circling implies a self-reflexive thinking. Its movement implies the cognition that the possible has of the agent. This interpretation would shed light on the nature of the human possible intellect and its self-reflexive cognitive operation, which takes place because it is one in substance with the agent intellect, as Siger explains. But the meaning is also that this *donna gentile* belongs not only to eternity but also to earth and time. This would confirm our reading of *amore* as a reflexive principle, as proposed in the canzone, which takes place in the mind, because only in this way can a separate substance know. Dante calls "spirito celestiale" the spirit that has generated such love. It comes from the heavens and from light, and because of this the spirit has tension towards God. This fragment about the sun becomes crucial for interpreting the meaning of the love for the gentle lady and the methodology Dante uses to pronounce it. It is the identity of the lady that throws light on the identity of the human intellect. It is no doubt an invention in which Dante's transumptive rhetoric is at its highest level.

Through a deductive reading, we may approach the meaning of this love. In the same way, we may know the human being's ontology by looking at the beloved, as we read in the third treatise. The love for the *donna gentile* throws light on the ontology of the lover, and because the lover is the mind, the human mind becomes the true subject of the inquiry. If the *donna gentile* is a name for a separate substance that is divine, eternal, and intelligible, the mind that loves her should hold the same attributes.

For such content it is useful to read some sections of Siger's *In tertium*. Here both the agent and the possible intellects derive from the first cause. Because in separate beings *sciens and scitum* are one and the same (a theory we find also in Aquinas), reflexive knowledge implies both the possible and the agent intellects, the possible in the act of conversion to the agent, or self-reflection. Dante calls "mind" a separate being, whose thinking implies the contemplation of the divine being. In light of the condemned propositions recalled above, it seems possible to reach a meaning. We proceed now to the next chapters (III.6) in order to complete our exploration into the making of the theory of intellect by attempting to retrace the philosophical contexts to which Dante links it.

The chapter starts with a return to praise as part of the literary commentary. This praise, we read, is made by comparing the lady to other things. The lady is defined as "gentilissima" and the most excellent being that the sun illuminates:

> Dico adunque che in questa parte prima comincio a commendare questa donna per comparazione all'altre cose; e dico che 'l sole, girando lo mondo, non vede alcuna cosa così gentile come costei: per che segue che questa sia, secondo le parole, gentilissima di tutte le cose che 'l sole allumina.
>
> I say then that in this part I begin first to praise this lady in comparison to other things; and I say that the sun, circling the world, sees nothing so noble as she, from which it follows that she is, according to these words, the noblest of all the things on which the sun shines. (III.6.1)

We must here examine more closely the double identity of the lady – whether she is eternal and so in the heavens as well as on earth.

Again, Dante uses praise when he recalls a line from the canzone, underlining that the praise is only for her: *"Ogn' Intelletto di lassù la mira"* (*Every intelligence admires her from above*; III.6.3): "le intelligenze del cielo – writes – la mirano e anche la gente di qua giù gentile pensano di costei *quando* più hanno ciò che li diletta" (I say that the intelligences of heaven see her and that those who are noble down here think of her when they must have that which delights them; III.6.4). The vision of the *donna gentile* is proper to the intelligences, and we know that they contemplate the divine ideas and therefore eternal beings, a content Dante reiterates here, as we shall see.

But human beings also think of her, and the adjective "gentile" ("gente ... gentile"; people ... gentle) enters here to qualify the people who think of her. They are, like the lady, gentle. But as *gentile* as applied to the lady implies an intellectual separate being, this adjective used for the *gente* is another way to alert the reader that a correspondence is suggested between the plural subject that thinks the lady and the lady herself. We know that to think means to see with the mind. We will read that this thinking takes form with discontinuity. Such discontinuity is coincident with the limits of the human mind's speculation or intellectual happiness. I will return to this later. What matters here is the collective name "gente," which is used to speak about human contemplation. The word "gente" here seems to anticipate the *humanitas* and *universitas* of the *Monarchia*. The many human beings that are able to better actualize the possible intellect seem to be overshadowed in the use of "gente" as a community that participates in the contemplation of the *donna gentile*. This would suggest that it is a kind of knowing proper to the community and that can be reached as a community. If a community contemplates together, then what Dante seems to be introducing is a subject that is plural and one at the same time. That this could be related to a knowledge that takes place "indivisive," as Jandun and before him Siger proposed, is the element that has to be evaluated, an element of great importance that cannot, however, be anticipated.

I now follow Dante's text step by step. In the next paragraph, Dante once more recalls the *Liber de causis* and explains that the intelligences have knowledge of what is above and below them in the hierarchy of beings. What is above, they know as cause, and what is below, as effect: "E poiche Dio è universalissima cagione di tutte le cose, conoscendo Lui, tutte le cose conosce secondo lo modo della intelligenza" (And because God is the most universal cause of all things, by knowing Him the intelligence knows all things, according to the way the intelligence knows; III.6). The conclusion is as follows: "Hence all the intelligences know the human form insofar as it is determined by intention within the divine mind" (III.6.5).

The intelligences know God because they know all things in the mind of God and know them according to the way the intelligences know. That is, they see the archetypes of things in the mind of God, and they see in the mind of God the human form (idea, species) because it is regulated through "intentio" ("per intenzione regolata ne la divina mente").

The term "intenzione" is synonymous here with "species" or "forma" or "idea," according to a vocabulary recalled earlier (Michaud-Quantin 1974). Regulated or "regolata" refers us to the divine idea as the rule or model (Pepin 1994). The theory of ideas in the mind of God is reintroduced here to underline the role of the celestial movers.

Because the intelligences know the human form in the mind of God, they are the most special cause of it and of every generated form (III.6.5). This fragment delineates a path full of knots. The author challenges his reader to recognize them. Certainly, the creation through the intelligences is suggested, but it is not enunciated. The verb "generata" introduces the philosophical theory of generation and corruption that takes place through the influence of the heavens. This philosophical theory does not exclude creation, and the "specialissima cagione" should introduce the theory of creation, which takes place with the cooperation of the secondary causes.[25] This is a prelude to what Dante will explain in the fourth treatise. What is important here is the suggested unity of the archetype and its differentiation through matter, to which the reference to generation seems to refer. If this is true, it would reiterate in a different way the same so-called *principium individuationis*, which was recalled above.

In the meantime, there now seems to take shape a new content, which Aquinas has pointed out in his refutation. If both the intelligences and human beings gaze at the gentle lady, then there is only one thought or object that is thought or only one intelligible for both the intelligences and human beings (*De unitate intellectus*, proposition105). But because God thinks the *donna gentile* in his reflexive thinking, this object of thought is not just participated in by intelligences and human beings but by God as well. This thinking reiterates what was first of all in the canzone where the *donna gentile* was part of God's thinking: "Costei penso Chi mosse l'universo." What Aquinas has stigmatized is confirmed and strengthened here. This throws light on the identity of the subject involved in such contemplation.

The gentle lady represents the intellectual soul as a separate being and as an archetype in the mind of God. She is eternal and unique, but her contemplation is shared by many, or belongs to the thinking of the community of human beings ("gente … gentile"; people … gentle).

The text here inserts a detail of great importance if the love contemplation for the lady unites the human beings, what is individual in the human being derives from and is related to the human being's materiality, that is, his sensitive soul. I have above recalled the so-called *principium individuationis*. This principle is derived from Averroes's theory of the unique possible intellect, which sought to establish the cognitive differences among human beings. Such differences, according to the commentator, derive from the phantasms created by the individuals. This *principium* comes into play, as we will see, when Dante uses the verb "individuare." I quote what Dante writes about it and how he intertwines it with the discourse about the intelligences: "E se essa umana forma, essemplata e individuata, non è perfetta, non è manco dello detto essemplo, ma della materia la quale individua" (And if the human form is not perfect when reproduced in individual beings, it is not the fault of the exemplar but of the material which furnishes individuality; III.6.6–7).

The form given is perfect and one, as it is in the mind of God. If this form, once it is "esemplata e individuate," lacks perfection at this stage, this is not caused by the form itself but by the matter that makes it individual. The discourse on the intelligences and their role in the creation is therefore intertwined with another content, which refers us to a prohibited issue, which, in the field of Aristoteleanism, is derived from the idea that the intellect is one for all humanity. The meaning here is that what is individual in the human being derives from his activity of imagination, which is part of the sensitive soul and therefore of the human being's materiality. This individuality is recalled, in fact, in order to ensure the individual in a thinking that is conceived as common. Then the text recalls an important line of the canzone: "E quella gente che qui s'innamora" (25). Again, we find the collective name "gente," "people," which confirms this line of thinking.

If people (a collective name) reach the greatest delight when they find this lady in their thoughts, the focus of discourse implies perfection as it is reached by a plurality of people, who together as a collectivity contemplate the lady as a unique separate eternal being, which human beings may have in their thoughts when they have what makes them happy. This happiness is coincident, in Dante's language, with the peace of love. It is the perfection for which human beings thirst and which is naturally possible for them.

I quote:

> Dove è da sapere che ciascuna cosa massimamente desidera la sua perfezione, e in quella si queta ogni suo desiderio, e per quella ogni cosa è desiderata. E questo è quello desiderio che sempre ne fa parere ogni dilettazione manca: ché nulla dilettazione è sì grande in questa vita che all'anima nostra possa [sì] tòrre la sete, che sempre lo desiderio *che detto*

> *è non rimagna nel pensiero.* E però che questa è veramente quella perfezione, dico che quella gente che qua giù maggiore diletto riceve quando più hanno di pace, allora rimane questa ne' loro pensieri, per questa, dico, tanto essere perfetta quanto sommamente essere puote la umana essenzia.
>
> To confirm this, I add by way of saying *And those down here who are in love.* Here it should be known that each thing most of all desires its own perfection, and in this it satisfies all of its desires, and for the sake of this each thing is desired. It is this desire that always makes every delight seem defective to us, for no delight in this life is so great as to be able to take away the thirst such that the desire just mentioned does not still remain in our thoughts. Since this lady is indeed that perfection, I say that those who here below receive the greatest delight when they are most at peace find this lady then in their thoughts, because she is, I affirm, as supremely perfect as the human essence can be. (III.6.7)

The human intellect reaches its perfection when it contemplates "questa," the lady, whose being and essence have been previously clarified. If, according to the definition given, she is the "essemplo intenzionale che de la umana essentia è ne la mente divina," she is, as an archetype, the intention or form or species or idea in the mind of God. Indeed, if both intellectual beings and human beings gaze upon her, it is easy to deduce that the form on which pure intellectual beings and humans gaze is one. This happens because she is in the mind of God and is contemplated by Him. I quote again a fragment discussed above:

> Però quando dico: *Ogni Intelletto di là su la mira,* non voglio altro dire se non ch'ella è così fatta come l'essemplo intenzionale che della umana essenzia è nella divina mente e, per quella, *in tut*te l'altre, massimamente in quelle menti angeliche che fabricano col cielo queste cose di qua giuso.
>
> Therefore when I say *Every intelligence admires her from above,* I mean only that she is created as the intentional exemplar of the human essence which is in the divine mind, and hence in all other minds, above all in these angelic minds which along with the heavens fashion these things here below. (III.6.6)

If we link this content to the line of thought called intellectual happiness, a meaning emerges. Intellectual happiness implies the contemplation of a separate substance that is at once separate and eternal.

The intellects that contemplate her, I am suggesting, include the human possibile intellect, which is also separate, eternal, and unique. We recall again Albert's theory, which asserts that what is one can only be received by what is one, and that only what is eternal and separate can receive what is eternal and separate. It is in this light that the belief in one common intellect associated with what makes individual the human being becomes the tile that completes the mosaic that the text has organized. In light of this mosaic, we read the verb "individuata" (and "individua"): "E se essa forma, essemplata e individuata, non è perfetta, non è manco de lo detto essemplo, ma de la materia la quale individua" (And if the human form is not perfect when reproduced in individual beings, it is not the fault of the exemplar but of the material which furnishes individuality; III.6.6). This passage indicates that the human being is an individual in virtue of matter, along with the generative and sensitive functions of the soul, which are individual and belong to the individual, while the intellective is one.

Imperfection belongs to matter insofar as it is corporeal. Such thinking, which is treaceble to Averroes's *De anima*, is also present in Siger.[26] In light of these references, it is difficult to avoid the conclusion that Dante, in fact, followed some tenets of the radical thinking of his age. What is more, however, is the way he organizes such thought and the tools he uses: grammar, logic, and rhetoric work together to establish philosophical contents. His rhetoric is a construction that implies the awareness of a controversy. His ornaments are subtle and difficult. The notion of "ornatus" includes a double meaning, a construction that is difficult to penetrate and, for that reason, is beautiful.

This content is indirectly reiterated in the so-called allegorical commentary in III.13.7, where he writes that human contemplation is "discontinuata," discontinuous, or takes place "non sempre." He concludes: "E così si vede come questa è donna primieramente di Dio e secondariamente dell'altre intelligenze separate per continuo sguardare; e appresso dell'umana intelligenza per riguardare discontinuato" (So we can see how this lady exists primarily in God and secondarily in the other separate intelligences, through their continuous contemplation of her, and afterwards in the human intelligence through its discontinuous contemplation of her; III.13.7). Such discontinuity depends, according to our reading, on the two different operations of the possible intellect. This is a content that Albert and Siger share but build on different assumptions (as explained above), since they derive it from their different positions on the nature of the possible intellect.

Dante here establishes that the human intellect has its own relation to the intellectual divine archetype. Unlike the intelligences and angels, who are able to speculate always, the human intelligence contemplates this lady discontinually or intermittently.

Paradiso 29 is of help in our reconstruction. Dante reiterates our difference from the angel-intelligences, to whom canti 28–9 are devoted. The angels, we read, do not have their vision "interciso de novo obietto," nor do they need to remember. The human being, on the contrary, holds a vision that is discontinuous: "il vedere interciso de novo obietto." The intelligences, as we may interpret this line, contemplate eternal beings or the divine ideas always, while human beings do so only sometimes. Proper to our intellect are two different operations: the abstraction of phantasms and the contemplation of the agent (as a self-reflexive operation). In *Monarchia*, Dante will reiterate that the angels have an intellectual activity "sine interpolation," that is, without break, ceaselessly (I.3.7). The double activity of the possible human intellect, which, according to Albert and Siger, can perform two different operations and is able to contemplate both the abstract forms and the separate forms, seems to be confirmed. But an essential distinction creates a break between the two operations. This is a different notion of the possible intellect, which is one and common for Siger, and plural and individual for Albert. The notion of "continous" appears in Aristotle's *Metaphysics*, where one and continous are both identified (5.1016a). This helps us in understanding the meaning of the adjective "discontinuous" in Dante's sense. Its meaning by way of deduction is that it is opposed to the continous. The definition of "continuous," on which both Thomas and Siger agree, is thus helpful. Aquinas writes that "quedam dicuntur unum esse natura continuitatis, idest essendo continua" (Some people say that the nature of continuity is one because it is continous; *In duodecim libros metaphysicorum* 5.1.7, 849), and Siger says that the continous is that which is *unum*: "dicitur aliquid unum quia continous, et continuitas est eius unitas, quod patet" (Something is continous because it is one and continuity is its unity; *Questions sur la Metaphysique* 5, 339). This is similar to Albert's position in his *Metaphysica*. Thus, the word "discontinuous" in Dante introduces, in a most synthetic way, the double activity of the human intellect. It implies a duality that takes us back to its different nature as it is manifested in the double operations of the possible intellect – eternal in its contemplation of the agent, mortal in its operation of "conversionem ad phantasmata" (*De anima* 3.2.19,10–33, 206). This notion is crucial to our understanding of Dante's discussion of human knowledge.

"Discontinous" is the function that manifests the essence. It implies a methodology based on a deduction, and that imposes a new name, "discontinuous." The meaning of this term implies time, as Dante himself indicates through his first explanation of "quando": "non sempre." Discontinous and "non sempre" qualify the power and limits of human intellectual power. Because of this discontinuity our natural thirst cannot be fulfilled, since intellectual happiness requires continuity (Aristotle's *Nicomachean Ethics*, X.VII.3). This is a central tenet in Giacomo da Pistoia's *Questio de felicitate* and Boethius of Dacia's *De summo bono*. By introducing the word "discontinuato," Dante was aware that the term encompassed a meaning that can be immediately understood by the philosophers and intellectuals who were dealing with issues like intellectual happiness and the field of references it encloses. It is because of discontinuity that the human being is different from the intelligences. The discontinous implies the accidentality of the activity of intellection on the part of possible intellect, an intellect that according to Albert has two functions and "intelligit aliquando et aliquando non, hoc ideo est quia movetur ab phantasmatibus, qui sunt potential intelligibilia et ideo non semper actu movent" (the possible intellect has an intellection discontinous and this happens because of the panthoms which are potentially intelligibles and not always in act; *De anima* 3.2.19,10–33).[27]

Before concluding, and in order to confirm what has been said, I wish to evaluate a term that appears in this chapter and that introduces the area of perfection. The occurrences are noteworthy: "ciascuna cosa massimamente desidera la sua perfezione" (each thing most of all desires its own perfection; III.6.7); "E pero che questa è veramente quella perfezione" (Since this lady is indeed that perfection; III.6.8); "allora rimane questa nei loro pensieri, dico tanto essere perfetta quanto puote l'umana essentia" (I say that those who here below receive the greatest delight when they are most at peace find this lady then in their thoughts, because she is, I affirm, as supremely perfect as the human essence can be; III.6.8); "mostro che non solamente questa donna è perfettissima ne la umana generazione, ma più che perfettissima" (I show that not only is this lady the most perfect in the realm of human beings, but perfect more than most in that she receives more of the divine goodness than what is due to man; III.6.9); "Onde dico qui che esso Dio, che da l'essere a costei, per caritade de la sua perfezione infonde in essa de la sua bontade oltre li termini del debito de la nostra natura" (I say here that God Himself, who gives being to her for the love of her perfection, infuses a part of His goodness in her beyond the limits of what is due to our nature; III.6.10); "E così [si] pruova, per questa apparenza, che è oltre lo debito della natura nostra (la quale in lei è perfettissima, come detto è di sopra) questa donna da Dio beneficiata e fatta nobile cosa" (Thus outward appearance provides proof that this lady has been endowed and ennobled by God beyond what is due to our nature, which as has been said above is most perfect in her; III.6.13).

Such perfection recalls the perfect intellect we have already touched on in our discussion. Because of it, intellection seems to be the goal of the insistence on the term perfection, an intellection that seems to be shared by the "gente."

What is interesting here is the strategy Dante uses to link the gentle lady to the area of *verbum*. Her double essence, which is both earthly and divine, as Dante points out, recalls the double nature of the *verbum* as both divine and incarnate. This area is clearly linked to the discourse on intellectual happiness and the perfection that implies the intellectual perfection that can be reached in virtue of speculation of a separate substance in this earthly life. It is coincident with the speculation of this lady, so that the perfect intellect is in act because of its union with a substance that is predicated as being one and separate. The notion of a perfect intellect seems to be the equivalent of that of perfect friendship between the human mind and the lady that this treatise has introduced as a link between two excellent beings. It is this friendship that Aristotle defines as a political link, which the love for the *donna gentile* includes. This love reveals the natural basis of human *conviventia*. This experience is common to human beings or "gente." The subject who thinks is the mind. The nature of this subject has been investigated in our discussion because this mind is the true subject of Dante's discussion in the third treatise of *Convivio*.

The notion of perfection implies that of the intellect. The "ben perfetto" of Guido Cavalcanti in "Donna me prega" was that good ("ben") reached by the possibile intellect in its activity of "consideranza" (consideration) (Nardi 1985, 102; Ardizzone 2002, 112). Cavalcanti, however, denied that such experience lived by the possible intellect could be an experience of the individual. He ascribed to him the sensitive soul as the perfection of the body and its act. He denied intellectual perfection and happiness to the human being. This position linked him to a radical and extreme idea, which seems close to that of an anonymous commentary on the *De anima* published by Maurice Giele.[28] Dante, on the contrary, aims at such happiness. The two friends both confront a heterodox and radical line of thought but from two opposite perspectives. The exaltation of the human being as a sensitive being is the result of Cavalcanti's position, a position that Dante strongly condemms in canto 10 of *Inferno*, assimilating his belief to that of Epicureans and emphasizing the materialism on which this theory draws.

According to Dante in the *Convivio*, intellectual perfection is proper to human beings, but only in a discontinous way. Such perfection is reached by the separate and common intellect. In addition, if the object of contemplation of this intellect is the "donna gentile," and the lady is a divine idea or form or intention, then the lady too is eternal, along with the possible intellect that contemplates her. The theses condemned in Paris testify to how dangerous this theory was considered to be for the Christian faith.

6. The *Verbum* and the Intellect

The different blocks of thinking are, however, here welded together. The gentle lady, who is the object of the vision of different beings (God, heavenly intellects, human minds), is in chapter 6 suggested as in relation to what in the theological–philosophical tradition is called *verbum*. In the following passage, this content enters because the knowledge of the divine ideas in the mind of God on the part of the angels-intelligences is coincident with their vision of the *verbum*: "E però che Dio è universalissima cagione di tutte le cose, conoscendo Lui, tutte le cose conosce sì secondo lo modo de la Intelligenza" (And because God is the most universal cause of all things, by knowing Him, it knows all things, according to the measure of its intelligence; III.6).[29] It is crucial here to understand that the logical subject of this passage is the intelligences, who know the *verbum*. The *Convivio* did start introducing a line of thinking, which the opening of Aristotle's *Metaphysics* strongly announces, and a few lines below, it introduces the image of the "pan degli angeli," a quotation from Psalm 77, in which "pan degli angeli" and *verbum* or *logos* are coincident, according to what Augustine says about this passage in his commentary on the Gospel of John (*In Evangilium Johannis*, Om.13.4). As I noted in my introduction to this book, since its beginning, the *Convivio* has attempted to create an inner relation between the aim of knowledge in the *Metaphysics* and the knowledge of the biblical angels, an approach that anticipates a crucial content of the *Convivio*. In fact, it is similar to what is discussed in *Metaphysics*, namely, the desire to know separate substances or, according to Aquinas's commentary, the causes of things. The knowledge of the angels, who are full of desire for the "pan degli angeli," is aimed at the *verbum*, and *verbum*, according to Augustine, is equal to God's ideas, which are the archetypes or models of things. But what enters here is more specific and new. The attempt is to think, in terms of a relation of similitude, the notion of *verbum* and that of the possible intellect. The possible intellect as unique presides over and motivates this approach. In the same way that the intelligences contemplate the lady, human beings contemplate her.

The *logos-verbum* as a common principle of human rationality presides overmany passages and meanings of the subsequent chapters of this treatise and penetrates the very notion of philosophy, a notion the allegorical commentary will focus on in the final chapters of the treatise. The praise of philosophy that Dante organizes is part of what we will discuss. As we have seen, praise has played an important role in the *Vita nova* and in the first two canzoni on which the *Convivio* will later comment, and which I have evaluated in a recent work (Ardizzone 2011). This background forms the basis that will allow us to reach a deeper level of understanding.

Since the writing of the canzoni, the founding dimension was the intellectual. As we will see in the allegorical section, the gentle lady will be called "lady of the intellect whose name is philosophy" or "donna del lo 'ntelletto che filosofia si chiama" (I say that this lady is that lady of the intellect who is called Philosophy; III.11.1). A few sections of the literal commentary actually were anticipating contents that are proposed again in the allegorical section. The notion of the *verbum* is so cardinal that the three strata – poetry, literal commentary, and the allegorical section – all organize, in relation to the intellectual dimension, an important content that is present in both the literal and allegorical levels.

In chapter 7, we read the following description of Christ: "Colui che fu crocifisso … creò la nostra ragione e volle che fosse minore del suo potere" (He who was crucified – who created our reason and willed it to be less than his power; III.7.16). Here "nostra ragione" appears to be identical with logos. *Ratio*, in fact, is one of the terms used as being synonymous with *logos* and as a way to translate it.[30] Here, it is the *verbum incarnatum* that has created our reason. Reason is the way of enunciating the *logos-verbum* that human beings share as a common logical linguistic identity. The emphasis on the adjective *nostro* stresses the commonality of the activity of reasoning. The descent of the Holy Spirit upon the apostles is no doubt useful in understanding this passage.

There follows an important fragment in which the gentle lady is defined as eternal: "E però ultimamente dico che *'da' etterno* cioè etternalmente, fu ordinata ne la mente di Dio" (Therefore, I say, lastly, that by eternity [that is, eternally], she was ordained in the mind of God; III.7.17). In a quotation from *Proverbs*, by way of commenting on a line of the canzone, it is suggested that the gentle lady is identical to *sapientia*, which has existed from eternity in the mind of God and helps human beings to have faith and to believe in miracles. The link between the biblical *sapientia* and the *logos-verbum* that existed since the beginning, that is, *ab eterno* in the mind of God, according to the Gospel of John, reiterates the eternity of the lady.[31]

The concept of the eternity of *verbum* allows us to link the discussion about the gentle lady not only to the separate substances but also to the divine ideas that are coincident, according to Augustine, with the divine *verbum*. These contents create a kind of inlay in which, rather than a tendency to enclose some issues of the intellectual debate of the time, there seems to be a tendency to rethink them by seeking to create, or establish, intellectual *loci* in which philosophical and theological contents can be put in relation. A fragment of interest occurs once we find the gentle lady indicated as a model. If we examine the commentary on the line "gentile è in donna ciò che in lei si trova" (gentle is in woman what is found in her; v. 49), we read that "manifesto esempio rendo a le donne, nel quale mirando possano [se]far parere gentili" (where I present a manifest example to women, by gazing upon which they may make themselves, by following it, appear gentle; III.7.14–15).

The use of "women," here, while recalling again the ladies of the *Vita nuova*, probably refers to the human soul's functions that look at the gentle lady, because they look at the intellectual soul as the final cause. This content is introduced in the literal commentary, but the model is proposed here as useful for all people ("narro come ella è utile a tutte le genti"). The addition is quite interesting when we read that "l'aspetto suo aiuta la fede" (III.7.15–16); and because "aspetto" derives from the Latin *aspicio* (to see), the intellectual vision of the lady is predicated as able to help faith. Again, there seems to be the attempt to rethink two opposite ways of knowledge: intellectual vision corroborates faith, which leads to believing in miracles.

We note again that crucial topics of the discourse about Beatrice in the *Vita nuova* are used to describe the gentle lady. We are, of course, in the field of Christology, which is circumscribed in various ways. The gentle lady is at once earthly and heavenly, as Beatrice was (Ardizzone 2011, esp. chaps. 1 and 2). But now Christology is organized in relation to philosophical ingredients. Such philosophy rethinks theology in light of the new field of the thirteenth-century Aristotelianism, along with its Neoplatonist contents.

Chapter 8 introduces, with clarity, the theme of earthly happiness: "E dico che ne lo suo aspetto appariscono cose le quali dimostrano de piaceri di Paradiso" (And I say that in her vision appear things that reveal some of the delights of Paradise; III.8.5). But an addition is essential when the text specifies that the happiness in Paradise is perpetual, a thing that does not happen here: "è perpetua cosa che qui non può essere" (the happiness of Paradise that is everlasting, which this cannot be for anyone; III.8.4–6). The discontinous nature of our intellection is confirmed. In addition, we see that the gentle lady is identified with a kind of happiness, which recalls the intellectual happiness of the *Nicomachean Ethics*. In this work, the highest happiness is reached in a contemplation like that of God in life, as we read in book 10. Of course, here this happiness is both recalled and denied because of its discontinuity. But such discontinuity must be related to the notion of the possible intellect and its mode of intellection, as introduced above. The intellection that the *Convivio* will define as proper to the human being is "discontinuous," and such discontinuity seems to be identical with that of the possible intellect itself, as it is thought by both Albert and Siger.

What must be underlined again is the balance Dante seeks to establish between philosophical happiness and biblical truth. The equivalence between the gentle lady and *sapientia* underlines her eternity. Consider the following quotation from Ecclesiastes (1:3; 3:22): "La sapienza di Dio, precedente tutte le cose, chi cercava?" (Who has sought out the wisdom of God that goes before all things?; III.8.2). The eternity of *sapientia*, and thus of *verbum*, confirms the eternity of the gentle lady and throws light on her identity. Once more, it is confirmed that the vision of her anticipates the pleasures of Paradise. During our life, this pleasure is not perfect, but accords with our human possibilities; that is, this happiness is discontinous:

> E dico che nello suo aspetto apariscono cose le quali dimostrano de' piaceri *di Paradiso; ed intra li altri di quelli*, lo più nobile, e quello che è frutto e fine di tutti li altri, si è contentarsi, e questo si è essere beato; e questo piacere è veramente, avegna che per altro modo, nell'aspetto di costei. Ché, guardando costei, la gente si contenta, tanto dolcemente ciba la sua bellezza li occhi de' riguardatori; ma per altro modo che per lo contentare

in Paradiso, [ché lo contentare in Paradiso] è perpetuo, che non può ad alcuno essere questo.

And I say that in her countenance appear things which reveal some of the delights of Paradise. Among them the most noble and the one that is established as the end of all of the others is to achieve happiness, and this is the same as to be blessed. This delight is truly found in the vision of this lady, although in another way; for, by gazing upon her, people become happy, so sweetly does her beauty feed the eyes of those who behold her, although in another way than by the happiness of Paradise that is everlasting, which this cannot be for anyone. (III.8.5)

This of course must be connected with the "discontinous" that was stressed earlier as a key word in the comprehension of the meaning of the human love for the *donna gentile*. As already said, as opposed to the the continous, the discontinous implies not just intermittency but also the evaluation of two diverse objects of speculation and the nature of the being that speculates on them. The mixing of materiality and intellectuality, of what is corporeal and sensitive and of what is intellectual, that is, the interior word that is purely intellectual, and the word that takes a sensible form, or possesses sensual impulses – all of these draw a profile of the human individual as a being who is in a precarious balance between the intellectual and the corporeal, a being whose nature is at once individualistic and socially inclined and on which the *civitas* is built. *Convivio* 4.4 will introduce the political *conviventia* as the natural good and *Monarchia* I.3–5 will identify the associative impulse as an origin that is both biological and intellectual (see Ardizzone 2013). Dante will compare the human being to the horizon as a being on the border between time and eternity (*Monarchia* 3.15.3).

At line 15, Dante introduces the term "effect":

Poi quando dico: *Sua bieltà piove fiammelle di foco*, ricorro a ritrattare del suo effetto, poi che di lei trattare interamente non si può. Onde è da sapere che di tutte quelle cose che lo 'ntelletto nostro vincono, sì che non può vedere quello che sono, convenevolissimo trattare [è] per li loro *effetti*: onde di Dio e delle sustanze separate e della prima materia, così trattando, potemo avere alcuna conoscenza.

Then when I say *Her beauty rains down little flames of fire,* I undertake to describe beauty's effect, since it is impossible to describe the beauty

> itself completely. Here we must know that all those things which surpass our intellect, so that it cannot perceive what they are, are most suitably described by means of their effects; and thus by approaching God, the separate substances, and the first matter in this way, we can gain some understanding of them. (III.8.15)

At line 22, the gloss to the verse 54 – "costei pensò Chi mosse l'universo" (in which the one who moves is God) – confirms once more the line we have retraced. Ideas are divine thoughts. The lady is the effect of such thinking, and the word "effect" is introduced again: "per dare a intendere che per divino proponimento la natura cotale effetto produsse" (to make it understood that nature produced such an effect by divine intention).

The text then introduces praise, indicating that this refers to the *donna gentile's* body. It is evident from the context that this praise of her body is nothing else than a transposed way of indicating the being of the lady, once related to human knowledge, so that human beings, through the contemplation of the lady (effect), are able to reach God. This word "effect" recalls Boethius of Dacia's *De summo bono,* a text that I have quoted above. And at the begininning of the chapter, that is indicated as allegorical *expositio,* a crucial *impositio nominis* is made, and the lady becomes "donna de l'intelletto che filosofia si chiama" (lady of the intellect who is called Philosophy; III.11.1). Here, the importance of naming is evident. Book 4 of *Metaphysics* is recalled as we read that "diffinizione è quella ragione che il nome significa" (a definition is that conception which a name signifies), and Dante adds that "conoscere la cosa sia sapere quello che ella è, in sé considerata e per tutte le sue cose" (to know a thing means to understand what it is, considered in itself and with respect to all of its causes; III.11.1). He then proceeds to explain what the name "philosophy" means: philosophy is defined as love for *sapientia* and he writes: "li seguitatori di scienza prima di Pitagora erano chiamati non filosofi ma sapienti" (before him those who sought knowledge were not called philosophers but wise men. Pythagoras was not a philosopher but just a lover of wisdom; after this everyone dedicated to wisdom was called a "lover of wisdom," for *philos* in Greek means the same as "lover" in Latin, and so we say *philos* for lover and *sophia* for wisdom from which we can perceive that these two words make up the name "philosopher," meaning "lover of wisdom," which, we might note, is not a term of arrogance but of humility (III.11.5).

The sources of this highly diffused etymology are various. Dante offers the Greek etymology, then says that the two words *philos* and *sophos* are the two words that make up the name *philosophos*, and philosophy, he adds, is a term of humility: "d'umiltà è vocabolo" (III.11.6). Philosophy is a word that implies an act. The philosopher is therefore "vocabolo del suo proprio atto," a "lover of wisdom." The further level of awareness that the allegorical commentary offers juxtaposes the love for philosophy as proper to the human being with that proper to God. It also evaluates the love on the part of the angels for God's wisdom (*sapienza*).

The text reiterates contents already introduced. Earlier I stressed that love, ever since the canzone, was the element expressing the relation between the mind and the lady. Love was the third element that defined the kind of relation. In this link, mind appeared as a relational being. A significant kind of tautology was introduced, since "love" and "mind" were both words that implied a relation. In her turn, the lady was suggested as an archetype in the mind of God. Now we are informed that philosophy is the word of God's own action, that is, the love of wisdom: *sapienza*. Philosophy is the result of a link between the two. We are informed about such mutual and exchanging relations of love. In fact, the philosopher loves every part of wisdom in the same way that *sapientia* loves the philosopher (III.11.12).

We must note here that the meaning of the word *sapientia* is simple and complex at once. Divine wisdom implies God's reflection on and contemplation of His ideas. There is no doubt that, according to Aristotle's *Metaphysics*, God thinks Himself, and *sophia* is the knowledge of what is eternal and necessary, and therefore of separate substances or God. But in the biblical tradition, *sapientia* is identified with the *verbum*. Dante quotes biblical sources in an attempt to rethink the two different traditions, the philosophical and the theological, as different but not as excluding each other. The most important aspect is that he does not intend to reach a synthesis juxtaposing the two fields; instead, he wants to expose them in their naked truth. They remain close but not unified. Rather than offering an identification, this method brings them together on the same page by suggesting the awareness of two traditions considering and confronting each other. In this context, to know through God's effect implies a new way to designate the *verbum*. God's essence remains unknown. We may know his *verbum*, that is, his manifestations.

It is worth emphasizing here that the allegorical commentary reiterates what we already saw in the early chapters of this third treatise, namely, that philosophy in this context appears to be eternal. That is, what is reiterated here was already introduced in the third treatise through the quotation from Severinus Boethius, and philosophy again seems to be a proper activity for both God and human beings. The concept of philosophy built on God's contemplation of his ideas, that is, of his *verbum*, becomes the model of contemplation for angels and humans: both share the contemplation of the same being, however in a different mode. The object of this thinking is eternal, and so the subject that thinks it should also be eternal.

In a new paragraph we read that philosophy is coincident with intellectual activity. Its form consists of a divine love for the intellect: "Filosofia … in sè considerata ha per subbietto lo 'ntendere, e per forma uno quasi divino amore a lo 'ntelletto" (Philosophy is in itself intellection, its form is an almost divine love for the intellect; III.11.13). Philosophy has as its own goal of true happiness, which can be reached through the contemplation of truth, and whose goal is the "vera felicitàde che per contemplazione de la veritade s'acquista" (III.11.14). Following Aristotle, the *Nicomachean Ethics* is linked here to the contents of the *Metaphysics*.

Then the text introduces the highest sciences: "le scienze nelle quali … la Filosofia termina la sua vista." These are natural science, ethics, and metaphysics. This last science is identified as first philosophy because in this science is the highest knowledge. Here, the text makes clear that the gentle lady must first be indentified with philosophy. Worthy of emphasis here is the hierarchy that Dante establishes. This apparently violates what was said about the hierarchy of sciences in the second treatise. There, metaphysics was recalled and inserted after the physics, whereas here metaphysics holds the meaning of first philosophy and is located above ethics. This meaning includes that, as first philosophy, it is coincident with the science of the principles of things, which is the goal of the intellectual virtues of the *Nicomachean Ethics* (book 10.6.8–7.9).

Aquinas, in his *Proemium* to *Metaphysics*, distinguishes between metaphysics as the science of the being as being, and theology as science of God – of separate substances and of beings that can be objects of consideration. This seems to be the text Dante uses as his reference. Aquinas defines theology according to its object of study: it is the study of separate substances and of biblical theology.[32] The name "first philosophy," we read, means that this science considers the first causes of things. The identification of philosophy as love for wisdom, whose paradigm is in

God and His contemplation, has already been anticipated above (III.2). Severinus Boethius was recalled there. Now it returns in a more complex framework. Because of the relationship between *sapientia* and the ideas in the mind of God, and metaphysics as the science of essences and of principles of things, which for Aquinas are coincident with the archetypes or ideas in the mind of God, the human mind is confirmed as able to contemplate an eternal being. But because only what is eternal can contemplate eternal beings, a teaching generally accepted, such correlation confirms the suspicion (*suspicio*) that has methodologically informed our reading. As I have proposed, love, as a being of relation between the mind and the lady, was the phenomenal being of the separate nature of the mind itself. We know, as the text clarifies, that such contemplation is not continous. That is, it is discontinuous. Dante has also introduced the word *gente* (people) as the collective name for a thinking subject, suggesting in a few passages an awareness of the theory of the possible intellect as a being shared by the many. But the allegorical commentary does not encourage the reader to follow this line of thinking. In fact, the plurality of human beings also experiences the intermittency of such speculation.

The possible result of our reading, therefore, seems at this point to be delineated. The subject that lives the experience of the intermittent intellectual knowledge is the same possible intellect in its double operation of conversion to phantasms and of contemplation of the agent intellect lady. This thinking entity seems to be one and plural at once. That is, the thinking subject is proposed as plural. I have indicated the few passages in which the text suggests that the "I," as a single subject, is confined to a knowledge determined by his imagination. More than this, it is not possible to establish. The shifting of the logical subject, according to what I have underlined in the previous chapter offers the key to our interpretation.

The reader is asked to follow a pathway that is always in progress, where every relation is organized in a way in which a content already expressed is presented again but in a new perspective, which may modify the antecedent or may confirm it, but in a difficult way that needs to be understood.

In chapter 12, Dante initiates the discussion about God, who is considered a spiritual intelligible sun: "sole spirituale e intelligibile" (III.12 6). God has intellection of everything because his circling is equal to his understanding (III.12. 11). This passage is close to what we read in Aquinas's *De veritate* (the section on *De scientia dei*, especially article 2).

God sees no more gentle a thing than when he looks at the place in which such philosophy exists.

The meaning of this phrase is evident in light of what follows. We understand, in fact, that the place in which God sees the lady (philosophy) is his mind. This introduces God's reflexive thought. Below is the quotation in which we understand that God, in circling, contemplates his own thought, his own *verbum* or *sapientia*, with which Lady Philosophy is identified. Such circular thinking is reflexive, and God's self-return is perfect and complete according to the *De causis* proposition 15 (Aquinas, *Super librum De causis expositio*, 25). But in this thinking, which is self-reflexive, the divine mind sees philosophy, and to see means to think and implies the production of archetypes or models of things. Here is the text: "Che avegna che Dio, esso medesimo mirando veggia insiememente tutto, in quanto la distinzione de le cose è in lui per lo modo che *lo effetto è* ne la cagione, vede quelle distinte" (For although God, gazing upon Himself, sees all things collectively, yet He sees them discretely insofar as the discreteness of things exists in him in such manner that the effect exists within the cause; III.12.11). And, we read, God sees philosophy in Himself. This is the most noble being because it is for himself. He here sees this most noble of things absolutely, insofar as He sees her perfectly in Himself and in His essence (III.12.12).

What we read here is the attempt to establish a likeness between divine thought and human thought. Philosophy is defined as "un amoroso uso di sapienza." Understanding this passage is ardous. But, if we read it in the field of Trinitarian relations, we may once more see that the verbal universe can be linked to that of action. This action takes place through a relation and through wisdom, as God's love gives form to creation. In fact, we read that "amoroso uso di sapienza viene detto essere massimamente in Dio in quanto in lui è somma sapienza, sommo amore e sommo *atto*, che non puo essere altrove se non in quanto da esso procede [processio]" (philosophy is a loving use of the wisdom which exists in the greatest measure in God, since supreme wisdom, supreme love, and supreme act are found in Him, for it could not exist elsewhere, except insofar as it proceeds from Him; III.12.14). After that, it is said that "per che dire si può che Dio non vede cioè non intende cosa alcuna tanto gentile quanto questa, dico 'cosa alcuna' in questo l'altre cose vede e distingue, come detto è veggendosi essere cagione di tutto" (thus it may be said that God sees [i.e., understands] nothing so noble as she is. I say "nothing" since He sees and distinguishes all other things, as said above, by seeing Himself as the cause of being in all things; III.12.14). A line culminates here that we have traced and that identifies philosophy and ideas in the mind of God, *sapientia* or *logos-verbum*. The *donna-gentile philosophia* is coincident with the *verbum* and the "pan delli angeli" introduced in the first treatise. The subject of Dante's discourse thus establishes a kind of contemplation that is accessible to human beings, though in an imperfect way. It is imperfect in humans, but perfect in God.

Our model is the divine thinking. God thus provides the paradigm of a thinking that is attributed also to the intelligences and, as we shall see better, to the human beings. It is stressed that in God this activity of philosophy, being part of his essence, is perfect as a kind of eternal marriage. In the other intelligences, however, it is active but to a less perfect degree. In any case, in looking at her aspect, that is, seeing her in the act of speculation, they are satisfied. The reflexive activity of God, as said above, is the model.

God sees in himself this Lady Philosophy, the noblest thing, and in the most perfect way. The knowledge of God is at once reflexive and eternal. From this knowledge proceeds the knowledge of the angels-intelligences and that of humans. This content implies the field of eternity. Divine thinking and philosophy are both eternal. Eternal is the contemplation of the intelligences that are able to see the eternal being. In chapter 13, such contemplation enters in a programmatic way, as we read that we have to investigate in what way she (Lady Philosophy) is in the caused intelligences. This is the verse Dante comments on: "Ogn'intelleto di lassù la mira." He recalls the celestial intelligences that see her and that are mirrored in her. By excluding the rebellious angels, Dante reiterates that in order to philosophize, it is necessary to love. Then the text enters into human speculation, where we read that philosophy is not perfect in the human mind. It is anticipated that in this last part of the treatise Dante will speak only about "human philosophy." He distinguishes human contemplation from that of angel-intelligences. Philosophy comes into human intelligences. In fact, those who have love here feel her in their thoughts, but this does not take place with continuity (*non sempre*) but only when love makes them feel her peace.

If, however, the reflexive activity of God is causative and the angels intelligences participate in it by looking at the models that are in the mind of God, then by using them they make ("fabbricano") with the heavens, the things of the world. If this is true, the question arises: What does human philosophy allow? Dante in the *Monarchia* will write that from speculation or philosophy there arises *action*.

Of course the angelic model is crucial: such thinking is reflexive. Also the love for the *donna gentile* in human beings appears to be the result of reflection. That is, speculation implies a reflexive principle. It seems that the conversion of the human being takes place in virtue of a separate substance. If we use the notion of the possible intellect as identical in substance with the agent, according to an idea that is shared by Albert and Siger, then the love for the *donna gentile* would be the natural love that the possible intellects nourishes for the agent and that takes place through reflection.[33] It is thus evident that the allegorical commentary intends to make God the model of human intellectual behaviour. That God's thinking is the model of human highest activity that is speculation is content that we find in Aristotle's *Nicomacheian Ethics* 10.8.7, and is coincident with the highest form of earthly happiness.

Now we start to focus on what distinguishes human speculation. Earlier I stressed the peculiarity of such contemplation on the part of humans, so that what distinguishes it belongs to its discontinuity. As we read in chapter 13, this means that human beings have a potentiality that is not always actualized. What actualizes such potentiality is called love, that is, the union between the mind and the gentle lady. It is this love that allows us to feel her peace. The human being that "sees" this lady must be called "philosopher." And at chapter 13.11, it is reiterated that love is a form of philosophy and is manifest in the use of wisdom ("ne l'uso de la sapienza"). From this derives the contemplation of the "mirabili bellezze" that is happiness ("contentamento").

There follows a fragment in which Dante explains that not all human beings have this happiness, but only those who love wisdom and have disdain for the goods that other people master. In fact, we read that some human beings follow their senses more than their reason. These people do not love this lady because they cannot have any apprehension of her (III.13.4–5). It seems that here Dante is following the teaching of the philosophers who assert that philosophy is a *habitus* that has as its result the contemplation of a separate being (see, for instance, Giacomo da Pistoia, *Quaestio de felicitate*, or Boethius of Dacia, *De summo bono*).

Chapter 14 stresses again the identity between such love and speculation: "Sì come detto di sopra Filosofia per subbietto materiale qui ha la sapienza e per forma ha amore, e per composto de l'uno e de l'altro, l'uso di speculazione" (Philosophy here has wisdom as her material subject, love as her form, and the exercise of speculation as the combination of the one and the other; III.14.1–3). Commenting on the verse: "In lei discende la Virtù divina" (57) he writes that: "discender la virtude di una cosa in un altra non è che ridurre quella in sua similitudine ... così dico Dio questo amore a sua similitudine reduce" (Here we must observe that the descent of virtue from one thing into another is nothing but the causing of the latter to take on the likeness of the former ... So I say that God causes this love to take on His own likeness to the extent that it is possible for it to resemble him; III.14.2–3). This implies that the *sapienza* in which this love takes place is eternal: "la sapienza, nella quale questo amore fere, etterna è" (III.14.6–7). Then Dante notes that the divine virtue in human beings descends in the same way as it does in the angels: "e pero è manifesto che la divina virtu [a guisa che] in angelo in questo amore ne li uomini discende" (It is therefore evident that the divine power descends by this love into men just as it does into the angels; III.14.9).

For the *donna gentile*, we read, must be understood as the noble soul, "d'ingegno."[34] This soul is free in her reason, while the other souls are her servants. This love in its turn has as its place of activity *sapienza*, who is the mother of everything (III.15.15). Again, the text touches on the theory of *logos*. The phrase "di tutto madre" (mother of everything) seems to echo the theory of the *verbum* through which all things were made in the Gospel of John. This confirms that here the *donna gentile* is not just a divine idea, but the idea of the ideas.

For those who are are hunting for Dante's heterodoxy, we may note that this part of the third treatise seems to be the closest to radical positions. In fact, chapter 14 first draws an important distinction – "Dio pinge la sua virtu in cose per modo di diritto raggio e in altre riflesso" (God instils His power into things by means of direct radiance or by means of reflected light; III.14.4) – and then goes on to say, "la divina virtu senza mezzo questo amore tragge a sua similitudine" (I say therefore that without mediation the divine power draws this love into resemblance with itself; III.14.3–6). "E cosi come lo divino amore è tutto eterno cosi conviene che sia eterno lo suo obietto e perciò eterne le cose che ama e cosi face a questo amore amare che la sapienza nel quale questo amore fere eterna è" (Since divine love is in all respects eternal, so its object must of necessity be eternal, so that those things which it loves are eternal; and in the same way, He makes this love enact its loving, for wisdom, on which this love strikes, is eternal; III.14.6–7).

The meaning here is evident, as it reiterates contents already introduced: the human being participates in the vision of the *verbum* (idea) in the same way that the angels-intelligences do. This love is, in fact, the love that God has for His wisdom and is therefore eternal, as is the divine being. The three texts that are recalled here are Ecclesiastes, Proverbs, and the Gospel of John. The eternity of wisdom is reiterated and is based on the Old and New Testaments. What takes place confirms a method that has been introduced. A philosophical content that in the thirteenth century is stigmatized and is filtered through the theological tradition. The human being, like the intelligences, participates in the vision of a substance that is separate and eternal. Aquinas discloses the perspective that seems to be delineated here and refuted: there exists a unique being that is contemplated by the all-intellectual beings, and such being belongs to, indeed is identical with, the divine being (*De unitate intellectus*, 102–4). Crucial here is the notion of eternity that is being expressed: the eternity of philosophy is made clear, and the eternity of philosophy implies an eternal thinking.

The opening of *Convivio* – "Tutti li uomini desiderano naturalmente di sapere" (All men naturally desire to have knowledge), which in Averroes's commentary on the *Metaphysics* implied the knowledge of God – culminates here. The introduction of the "Atene celestiali" seems to be a further attempt to link philosophy and biblical theological tradition. Philosophy is linked to heaven, and the three theological virtues of faith, hope, and charity lead us upward to a heavenly Athens, in which a kind of *concordia* seems to be established among the three main philosophical schools of the antiquity, now pacified in the light of a superior truth. This happens, we read, thanks to the art of God, which is identified with eternal truth. As far as I know, this is the first time that the *Convivio* attemps to unify the divergent traditions. Athens, as the city of philosophy and of philosophical tradition, is transferred to the heavens, and the theological virtues are responsible for a kind of philosophy guided by charity.[35]

In the next chapter, which comments on the line "Cose appariscono nello suo aspetto" (55), Dante reiterates that gazing upon this lady, upon her eyes, gives the highest pleasure of beatitude that anticipates the highest good (*bonum*) of Paradise. The word *sapienza* enters charged with a meaning that links it to metaphysics. We saw in the previous chapter that Dante praised the lady in one of her components, that is, love. Now the praise will be for the other component – wisdom. The word *sapienza*, which is taken from the theological field, now encloses a reference to Aristotle's *Metaphysics*. The highest pleasure in this life, we read, is in the activity of contemplating the eyes and the smile of *sapienza*. The language uses rhetorical figures in order to establish the possibility of contemplating both the *truth* and the *persuasiveness* of metaphysics. Here, it is also declared that since the human being desires such contemplation, and in this operation can be satisfied, this desire, once satisfied, is the only way to reach human perfection, which depends on the perfection of our reason. Moreover, all our operations and sensations are aimed at the perfection of reason. Only reason is for itself and does not aim at anything else. It is in such perfection of reason that the human being reaches happiness.

Clearly, the reference here is Aristotle's *Nicomachean Ethics* and the true happiness that human beings can reach. At this point, Dante introduces a quotation from the Book of Wisdom, in which philosophy is compared to the "candore of the eternal light and the mirror without spot of God's majesty." That is *philosophia* or *sapientia*. However, here again, Dante reiterates an issue that was introduced earlier. What is said can be easily summarized by a commentary to the verse, "Elle soverchian nostro intelletto" (v. 59), in which "Elle" refers to the things that anticipate the pleasures of Paradise here on the earth and that are seen in Lady Philosophy's aspect. The canzone stated that the "I" cannot "mirar fiso" (61), that is (as I read it), not in a straight way and probably, in light of what the commentary has said, not continuously. Yet here, in this final chapter of the third treatise, the verse is quoted in order to return to the same issue that had been discussed above in chapter 14. We read that the subject who speaks cannot say much about such things because they are superior to the human being. These things, because of their superiority, dazzle (*abbagliano*) our intellect. In fact, it is assumed that there exists some things that our intellect cannot look at. These are God, eternity, and prime matter. We believe that they exist, but we may not understand them for what they are, that is, in their essence. We may approach this knowledge only *via negationis*.

This appears to flatly contradict what was said before this point. But perhaps it does not. In fact, Dante reiterates that we can see these things (*che certissimamente si veggiono*), which confirms what we have read in this treatise. The next section reiterates that the human being desires to know what is in his nature to know, and he cannot know "Dio quale esso è," that is, the divine substance. In fact, this knowledge is not desired to be known by the human being. That God cannot be known in His essence is a tenet that is discussed in a commentary on the *Anima* published by Van Steenbergen (Giele, Van Steenberghen, and Bazán 1971).

My reading here is that the contradiction is more apparent than real. A distinction must be made between seeing God and knowing God in His essence. Falzone (2010), in his study, helps to explain this passage, as does Fioravanti (2014). Falzone discusses the issue in light of the debate of the time and distinguishes between the vision of God and the knowledge of his essence. He observes that this last knowledge also does not belong to the angels-intelligences.[36]

The conclusion of this chapter produces a kind of enlargement on the theme of contemplation which appears to deny what was said until now. In fact, the text announces a form of happiness that is indicated as secondary in relation to the earlier one. It is true that the human being cannot know God in his essence. But now the beauty of *sapienza* is assimilated into philosophy and identified with moral virtues, and happiness is not that of book 10 of the *Nicomachean Ethics*. Instead, people are urged to look at Lady Philosophy in that part of her that is called moral philosophy, where philosophy-*sapientia* shows herself as a model of humility. The pathway of the *logos-verbum* is once more the driving content. In fact, Lady Philosophy is identified with *sapienza* because she is the mother of every principle and of every movement. She is the origin of the world and of the movement of the heavens.

The assimilation between philosophy and the *logos-verbum* almost marks the end of the treatise. Its final paragraph explains the adjectves Dante has used in the canzone, where he called the lady *fera* and *disdegnosa*. These were due, respectively, to his inability to *understand* her persuasions and to *perceive* her demonstrations.

In this way the third treatise reaches its end – with Dante's engagement with human knowledge and its limits and powers. The pronouncement in the field of theology contains themes taken from a thinking that was in part condemned and close to heretical positions, as was evident perhaps and above all to Dante himself. The fourth book of *Convivio* will contain a kind *retractatio* that starts with the canzone *Le dolci rime d'amor ch'io solia* and continues in some parts of the prose text. The main contents that show Dante's new positions are, in the prose, the problematic issue he introduces about the origin of prime matter. The first is whether matter is thought and willed by God ("se la materia degli elementi era da Dio intesa"). The second is the theory according to which intellect contains in itself all the forms. The third is the reduction of virtues to the moral virtues, with no mention of the intellectual virtues.

The introduction of the concept of *persona*, as we find it initially in the canzone *Le dolci rime rime d'amor ch'io solia*, eliminates any doubt about his position regarding the possible intellect as something common to or shared by human beings. My reading stops here because the new idea about intellect dissolves the relationship between intellection and politics that is the true invention of Dante's *Convivio*. This invention presides over his *Monarchia* but draws from sources and contents he introduces also in his *De vulgare eloquentia*. From what Dante deletes or denies, either directly or indirectly, emerges a need to free himself from tenets linked to an area and line of thinking that he decides to remove. The relation between the *donna gentile-philosophia* and the *logos-verbum-sapientia* are part of a rethinking that distinguishes Dante's position. In this rethinking, a major role has been played by the idea that human community derives from an intellectual power that is common. Enunciating this content in the language of the biblical tradition, Dante did not intend to use the theory of the double truth but the theory of one truth entrusted to different linguistic formulations. The utilization of the figures of *nominatio* and *pronominatio* that strongly mark the *Convivio* shows that the poet as giver of names is able to create a world of relations and suggestions that may work to build the mind of the readers. That Dante in the *Convivio* is aimed at the construction of a new reader is a content I have previously introduced. In what follows I will briefly discuss the identity of such readers by assuming that the most vital part of the *Convivio* is in its attempt to identify and link an intellectual and political happiness.

The teaching of Aristotle's *Nicomachean Ethics*, in which the two forms of happiness are proposed, should be a text of great importance. However, in my reading, Dante's awareness should also derive from his idea of the common intellect (which Dante compares with the commonality of human *logos*) as de facto realizing a political community that is naturally linked by its intellectuality. The idea of a universal Monarchy in Dante seems to stem from such slowly matured reflection.

7. Politics and Speculation: A Conclusion of the First Three Treatises

Because of this connection, the *Convivio* requires, first of all, an understanding of the identity of the reader or readers to whom the work is addressed. To what extent can people who do not know Latin and to whom Dante devotes his vernacular treatise, according to his own words, understand the subtleties that pervade such a work? We must suppose that there existed a group of people, perhaps laity, to whom such intricacies could sound quite familiar. But if this is true, where and when did this happen? Imbach (2003) has discussed the importance of this issue, but his discussion remains generic. It does not focus on or discuss where, that is, in which cities, a group of laity or groups among the laity were so well formed that they could be designated as ideal readers.[37] Dante's *Convivio* implies, or should imply, the existence of its readers, yet it is difficult to think of them as concentrated in one place or one city.

It is now commonly accepted that Dante wrote the *Convivio* in Bologna, where, no doubt, ideal readers could be found because philosophy and philosophical contents were at stake there. However, it is crucial to acknowledge that the prose of the *Convivio*, grounded in the language of poetry, according to what we have read initially in *Vita nuova* and in *De vulgari eloquentia* (i.e, that poetry is the model that prose has to follow), creates its own reader. Such a reader should be able to detect the difficulties of the vernacular prose because he is equipped with philosophy and poetry, rhetoric and poetics. Above all, he should be able to evaluate the importance of having access to the Latin contents that the text offers in translation. The treatise has to be seen in the context of the rise of a new public and a new society of individuals, among whom the *Convivio* finds its ideal readers. This public creates an ideal "city" that does not coincide with any one city in the usual sense. Its *communitas* identifies itself at first in what it reads. Dante seems to appeal to, and to anticipate in some ways, the intellectuals of humanism who are able to read both poetry and philosophy, but who are also concerned with aspects of moral philosophy that collaborate in establishing the civic stature of a human being. The goal of an ideal city that presides over Dante's ideal city will be the universal kingdom of Monarchy, an imperial universal city that the fourth book of *Convivio* begins to draw.

It is here that the superior unity of poets – intellectuals that *De vulgari eloquentia* has delineated as an ideal body that connects scattered limbs – seems to preside over the first treatises. Intellectual unity faces the linguistic poetic unity. It suggests a methodology of thinking *communitas* as a de facto unity that is not located in or coincident with a space or place.

Dante's intellectual predisposition was different when he wrote the first two canzoni. The reading of the first two canzoni has shown that many contents that are present in the commentary were already traceable in the poems, which Dante wrote in his Florentine years. At that time we may suppose that his interlocutors were the philosophantes he recalls in *Convivio* but also the poets of his circle, among them Guido Cavalcanti. The prose text continues the pathway of the canzoni. Evolution and continuity mark the making of the *Convivio*. There is no doubt that Dante's visits to new cities and getting to know new societies persuaded him about the opportunity to create new cultural tools for a new society, even though he was not necessarily in direct contact with these new groups. That this new society includes the merchant class is not far from the truth, but Dante did not conceive his work for them.[38] People who do not know Latin and work for the city or for the family are part of the world of politics and economy. The *Convivio* no doubt was intended to give to such groups an awareness of a human being's nature and goals, but the treatise does not conform itself to the cultural and intellectual level of such a milieu. In any case, Dante's ideal readers take their shape in time, and their identity is in continuous evolution, as is the *Convivio* itself. Dante's travels to the north of Italy, his living for two years in Verona, and the fact that he was visiting different cities during his exile are, of course, important. Bologna and the north of Italy, Verona in particular, seem to play a major role. Padua, for instance, probably played a role too in the *Convivio*. Padua at the time Dante was travelling in the north was not just the city of Pietro d'Abano or Marsilio da Padova. It was the place where Lovato Lovati and Alberto Mussato lived. Both were contemporaries of Dante and both were part of the Padua's pre-humanists: Lovati was a judge and Mussato was involved in politics (Skinner 1978, 35–41).

There is historical background that, if better known, would explain what the first chapter of the treatise announces: the human being's universal desire to know. This universality is the true subject of the treatise. Such *universitas* is Dante's true interlocutor, a community delimited and defined here by its desire to know.

The human being defined as a divine animal, according to the philosophers (III.2), exudes a kind of pre-humanistic fragrance. Of course, this permeates the text and can indicate Dante's path, but it is not this anticipation of humanism that offers the meaning of what Dante is seeking to introduce here. As a part of the *universitas*, the *Convivio*'s reader remains a part of the ideal but at the same time is still largely shaped by the culture of Dante's first Florentine interlocutors.

An aspect of newness in the *Convivio* derives from the evident importance given to the field of ethics, which is not taken in isolation but rather in its relation with other Aristotelian works, in particular the *Politics* and *Metaphysics*. Crucial in this work is the concept of virtue, which, according to Aristotle's *Nicomachean Ethics*, is divided into the moral and the intellectual. What E. Gilson, in *Dante e la philosophie* (1972), has seen as the primacy of ethics needs to be rethought.

The fact that the goal of ethics is happiness modelled on metaphysics or first philosophy is crucially important. This is because the final goal of ethics is God's thinking. Dante presents two kinds of virtues: the intellectual (III.3) and the moral. The latter is briefly introduced in the last section of the third treatise. It is this double pathway through which Aristole offers a new awareness of what ethics implies in response to the political and contemplative nature of the human being.

I previously underlined that the *Convivio* cannot be read as a kind of cultural digest. Of course, Dante offers an encyclopedic learning written in the vernacular that the prose develops chapter by chapter, but in particular in the second and mostly in the third treatise, a main content takes form, a content in which it is the notion of human intellect that is central. This notion announces in Dante not just an issue related to knowledge but also an awareness of what belongs to our common or political life. What emerges is the interaction between intellection and politics, two issues that are usually considered unrelated. The *Convivio* seems to establish, thanks to the love for the gentle lady, that there indeed exists a natural community that the love for her makes manifest. The peculiarities of such love are crucial in order to express the natural bond that creates a *communitas*. People are naturally linked because the object they love and that which their mind contemplates is one. The construction of the One in Dante more as principle (*principium*) than as number starts here. The one as principle implies our origin from the One and our final cause as one. Unity implies the world of civic *conviventia* as a unity that Dante regards as natural, and an inner bond relates what is natural to what is divine. The importance of Aristotle's *Ethics* for the *Convivio* is better understood in light of the link Dante establishes between human *conviventia* and intellection. The idea of an intellection that takes place or actualizes itself better in the whole human being's *universitas* creates a de facto natural unity. In Dante, the contemplation of the gentle lady is proper to the "gente," the people. The Empire will be the right juridical political organization for this natural unity.

Earlier in this study, I discussed the importance of intellectual happiness in the *Convivio*, and I linked this content to Dante's appropriation of a thinking that he derives from Averroes's theory of the intellect, which, however, he reshapes in his own way, following in part Albert and in part Siger. He is probably aware of the debate about intellectual happiness as testified by Giacomo da Pistoia, Boethius of Dacia, and others. But it has also been my claim that Dante's idea about intellectual happiness implies a community that contemplates together and that intellectual happiness was coincident with a political happiness shared because the thinking subject was one. This theory actually was not part of any tenet traceable to one particular work. Dante's idea seems to spring from the links he establishes among different sources. One of these may be found in the link he establishes between the theory of intellection and the contents of ethics.

Brunetto's *Tresor*, in particular the section devoted to Aristotle's *Ethics* (*Tresor*, book 2), is one of the works on which Dante draws. This work is recalled in the meeting of the pilgrim in the realm of shades with the maestro that takes place in the circle of sodomites under the rain of fire (*Inferno* 15). In *Tresor*, politics is proposed as the most important science, and rhetoric is part of politics. But following Aristotle, politics is associated with ethics. In fact, in the section of *Tresor* devoted to the *Nicomachean Ethics*, the importance of political life and of civil friendship is stressed. When Dante meets Brunetto in canto 15.85, he praises him for having taught him "come l'uom s'etterna." That is, Brunetto is recognized as someone who taught him how a human being becomes eternal.

This statement has prompted a debate among readers. Actually, such an issue can be understood if we read it in the context of the *Nicomachean Ethics*. In this case, such eternity in *Inferno* 15 could be derived from the fact that Dante first read Aristotle's ethics in Brunetto' *Tresor*, which captured the true goal of ethical virtues. Such virtues ruled by the right mean create the basis for the action of human beings in society but also work for the development of wisdom, that is, the highest ethical activity of contemplation. Whether this is true or not, such interpretation[39] of Brunetto's philosophy was coincident with the Aristotelian sciences. Philosophy also implied the activity of the lover of wisdom. According to Aristotle, moral virtues pave the way for intellectual contemplation, which is coincident with happiness. The idea that social happiness built on ethical or moral virtues leads to intellectual happiness was actually part of Aristotle's teaching in his *Nicomachean Ethics*. It is the right mean that allows for ethical behaviour, which is crucial for both the common life of the community and the development of the individual. It is this right mean, a kind of higher moderation, that allows application and study, which are formative and which create the basis for the process towards the highest theoretical knowledge. This is an activity that Aristotle conceived as similar to God's activity of reflection or pure thinking. Thus, recalling Brunetto's role as important for teaching him how the human being can make himself eternal, in Dante's words, would imply an acknowledgment of his debt to Brunetto for introducing him to contents of great importance as they derive from the *Nicomachean Ethics*. They are important in the *Convivio* but will also return in his

Monarchia, which Dante writes in the last years of his life. In the verb "etterna" (*Inferno* 15.85), Dante thus recalls Aristotelian *theoria* or contemplation, an issue he will not abandon, primarily because of its link to political well-being and human life.

What I wish to stress is that Dante's main line of thinking derives from the *Nicomachean Ethics*, a work Dante started to read probably in Brunetto's *Tresor*, and later in the commentaries by Albert and Aquinas. It is often stressed that the *Ethics* is important insasmuch as it presides over the *Convivio*'s fourth treatise. It is my point here that this work presides over the organization of other sections of *Convivio* as well, and that the fourth treatise actually develops a final section of the third, in which the *Ethics* is recalled when it is said that there is an intellectual contemplation and "secondariamente," the happiness that derives from the moral virtues (III.14).

Aristotle himself declares at the beginning of his *Ethics* that the aim of ethics is to establish what is good for the human being. He points out that to know this goal is useful in life. He also explains that politics and ethics as part of politics have as their goal not just knowledge but action: it is not enough to know what virtue is, it is necessary that we practise it (1103b25–29 and 1179a 35–b3). As Verbecke (1983) has pointed out, Aristotle does not look at offering a science of customs or behaviours but rather offers a philosophical reflection about the true value of the human being. His goal is to establish the principles of moral philosophy. He thinks that human activity is aimed at a good, and that such good has to be a supreme or highest good, which he identifies with happiness from the very beginning of book 1 of the *Nicomachean Ethics* (1096a10). Such good implies deliberate choice and its realization (1178a35). Aristotle distinguishes between true happiness and apparent happiness; then he eliminates pleasure, which leads to a bestial life. There is a natural desire in all men, but in order to be truly happy, it is necessary that men know where to find true happiness. Then they must tend freely to it. In books 2 and 3 of the *Nicomachean Ethics*, a propos of the nature of virtue, he shows that virtue consists in a deliberate choice and is reached through and in the exercise of virtue. There is a natural tension towards an achievement and final perfection. Because the virtuous activity is not given but gained, the desire for happiness provides the end and gives rules to all our activities (1097a20–21). We practise courage, moderation, intelligence, and all the virtues because we want to be happy, and we trust that we will be happy thanks to them (1097b1–b6).

If there is an agreement among human beings about the name of the highest ultimate goal, Aristotle puts out as problematic the effort to establish what the true nature of happiness is. This problem is related to another: that of determining the true nature of the human being. To this true nature there corresponds the true good. And because the true good in the human being must correspond to what is specific to him, and this is his reason, the true good must be an activity, indeed the best activity. Happines (*eudaimonia*) enters as an *energeia*. In books 8 and 9, Aristotle considers the goal of happiness in the context of discussing friendship. Communality becomes responsible for a shared happiness. Friendship is considered as a private thing, but is also linked to the political nature of the human being and to the *koinonia* of goods. Here, it is the enlargement of happiness in light of a commonality, and friendship is considered as the link that unifies the city.

The *concordia* among human beings is similar to friendship. It is thus the highest condition of the sublunar world because it is friendship that unifies the world. This peculiarity in Aristotle is, however, linked to another, in which it is said that the true friendship is that which takes place between the contemplatives and those who work for the common good of the city. Two principles seem to preside, God and the city, over true friendship. In fact, friendship implies virtue, and the goal of virtue is in the common good, whether as immanent or separate (1155a23–25). This double nature of ethics is based on moral and intellectual virtues. But the political also seems to be a field of reflection for Dante. We have underlined above how the theme of perfect friendship that in Aristotle was between the *aristoi* was tied in Dante to a method in which ethical values implied a social awareness. Aristotle suggested, but did not define, the relation between the highest contemplation of the *Ethics* and political life (Vanier 1965, 406). In the *Convivio* there returns as fundamental the contemplation of a divine separate substance. This is described in the third treatise as friendship between the human mind and the lady. According to our reading, this included a tendency that was suggested but not openly stated regarding the notion of intellection conceived as common. In order to reveal a crucial centre of meaning, I have focused on the notion of mind. I have attempted to show, starting with my reading of the canzone, that intellect in this sense is the core of the discussion.

An issue of importance that the discussion about the *donna gentile* has raised must be read in its inner link with the notion of the mind itself, proposed as a being able to contemplate the gentle lady/separate substance. It requires on the part of the reader the ability to grasp its identity as that being a separate substance too endowed with the same oneness of the separate substance it contemplates in the *Convivio* named *donna gentile.*

In this we have suggested that intellectual happiness implied a common happiness and the natural being of humans in their *communitas.* This kind of thinking is first put forth in the *Convivio.* The canto of Charles Martel in *Paradiso* 8 will return to this issue. It will reveal the importance of friendship in its tie to love and what friendship means in the political context. The mode in which it works for the community and social life is openly recalled when the Aristotelian human being is referred to as *cive.* As previously said, this shows Dante's attempt to create a line in which perfect intellection is thought in relation to a community. This follows Aristotle, who says that perfect happiness cannot be that of the individual but that of a community. Cicero, too, in *De officiis* thinks that the *summum bonum* is the common good. In this sense, a strong continuity is established between the second and third treatises of the *Convivio.* That Dante derives this glimpse about the relation between perfect contemplation and the sense of community from the *Ethics* is made stronger in light of the theory of the common intellection that Dante seems to embrace here. Gauthier, in his *Trois commentaires* (1948) on Aristotle's *Ethics,* has touched on this issue when he observes that happiness is at once intellectual and political.

We should probably rethink this perspective not only in Dante's *Convivio* and its writing but also in the *Monarchia.* In light of Aristotle, the civic *conviventia* and *humanitas* or *universitas* did find a natural link in the idea that perfect contemplation belongs to a community. The intellectual unity of human beings becomes the natural basis for the human *conviventia.* In light of it, the *polis* enlarges its walls. It is the Empire conceived as coincident with the world – the true political organization for the common intellect. People think together and their link, before being political, is intellectual. Maybe this is the true meaning of the love for the gentle lady. In the *Convivio,* Dante introduces the theory of *logos-verbum* by establishing a kind of continuity with the notion of intellect, as it is repronounced in the word "philosophy."

We have traced such a line of thinking in this treatise by underlining the theme of perfect friendship and by showing its internal tie with the honest and its background. We have also shown how Dante constructs continuity with what he indicates as the "perfect intellect." In the *De vulgari eloquentia* he wrote that we share the love for the honest with the angels, and we know that the angels' love is for God, or better the *verbum*. These relations are part of what has brought me to propose that the love for the *donna gentile* is, for Dante, a way of introducing a topic that was very important to him since his Florentine years. In a way that is very personal, he proposes the idea that his true subject is the thinking of a community being both intellectually and politically motivated. In this he confronts contents that are at once ethical and civil, or, in Aristotelian terms, ethical and political.

In conclusion, I wish to underline an aspect that sheds light not just on the contents of the *Convivio* but also on its method. The two works that the *Convivio* recalls as the two books that Dante was reading after the death of Beatrice were both strongly related to philosophy. As Dante informs us about it, the two texts were of course far from radical thinking, but he uses them in order to introduce nuances of a radical thinking. Classical texts are read with the ear for the contemporaneous. In fact, our reading has underlined that it is through one of these texts (Boethius, *De consolatione philosophiae*) that first enters the love for philosophy and the eternity of philosophy. To this is related the friendship for a separate being coincident with the *summum bonum*, the love for the *honestum* as the *bonum perfectum*. All these are part of the general framework. Dante opposes his notion of *bonum perfectum* to that of Cavalcanti. What he opposes is Cavalcanti's idea that the human being is relegated to the life of the senses, because the sensitive soul is the act of the body. Opposing Cavalcanti but also embracing a position of doubt with respect to what is defined orthodoxy, Dante attempts to think in terms of *communitas*, *civitas*, collectivity. The human being regarded as an angel opposes the human being as a merely sensuous being. The love for the *donna gentile* heralds a turning point. Her identity – which is intellectual, separate, thought by God, and therefore eternal – shows the true intellectual nature of the human being who loves and intellects her. It suggests a complex idea about human intellection as being in some ways related to the notion of the intellect as one or common, an idea that nevertheless in Dante diverges from the field of true herodox thinking.

One other point I would like to underline is the correlation between true wisdom or philosophy and friendship that is stressed in treatise 3, in particular civil friendship, as it appears in the following paragraph:

> E sì *come* fine dell'amistade vera è la buona dile[tta]zione che procede dal convivere secondo l'umanitade propiamente, cioè secondo ragione, sì come pare sentire Aristotile nel nono dell'Etica; così fine della Filosofia è quella

> eccellentissima dile[tta]zione che non pate alcuna intermissione o vero difetto, cioè vera felicitade che per contemplazione della veritade s'acquista.

> And just as the end of true friendship is delight in what is good, which proceeds from living together according to what is proper to humanity [i.e., according to reason, as Aristotle seems to hold in the ninth book of the *Ethics*], so the end of philosophy is that most excellent delight which suffers no cessation or imperfection, namely, true happiness, which is acquired through the contemplation of truth. (III.11.14)

In a most veiled speech, a kind of equation can be established: If friendship's goal is the *diletto* or pleasure derived from *conviventia* (according to what is proper to humanity, and according to human reason), in the same way the end of philosophy is that most excellent delectation which has no intermission or defect, that is the true happiness that we may reach through the contemplation of truth.

The equation shows that a third element would no doubt be of help in detecting an inner link in the two delectations. We recall that at the beginning of the third treatise friendship was established between the mind and the lady. If this mind is not individual but common, as I have suggested, the principle of happiness in contemplation involves the principle of a plural unity or community that reaches at once the *diletto* of *conviventia* and the *diletto* of intellectual knowledge. In Aristotle, *conviventia* (*Nicomachean Ethics* 9. 9.1170 b 5–17) in fact implies civic life as a natural life for the political human being. According to the philosopher, the happiness of a society is superior to that of an individual.

What appears in the passage quoted above is the equivalence of the two *diletti*. It seems that Dante is seeking to relate ethics and knowledge by linking a content considered in the thirteenth century as heterodox (intellectual happiness in life) to a political one. This is probably the most original aspect of the *Convivio*.

This reading would require also a rereading of the fourth treatise along with that of the *Monarchia* and of some parts of the *Commedia*. But this exploration opens a new field that is not possible to fully discuss in this book. In the next and final chapter, I will summarize the topics that Dante introduces in the canzone *Le dolci rime d'amor ch'io solia* and in its commentary. The discontinuity between the third and fourth treatise that marks the *Convivio* is the first aspect that will be confronted.

5 Syllogism and Censura: The Moralization of Nobility and the Decline of Intellectual and Political Aristocracy

1. Continuity and Discontinuity: Introducing the Canzone: *Le dolci rime d'amor ch'io solia*

The last treatise of *Convivio* was written, like the others, during Dante's exile and perhaps after the years he was living in the north of Italy, between 1302 and 1306. The treatise is conceived as a commentary on the canzone *Le dolci rime d'amor ch'io solia*. Both the canzone and the prose section introduce new themes and new interests. Scholars agree that the canzone belongs to the Florentine years. Maria Corti, however, in light of the canzone's organization and syllogistic reasoning, has proposed that its composition should be located close to the years of the writing of the commentary (Corti 1983, 144–5).

My reading of the last part of the *Convivio* will introduce the main contents of the canzone and its commentary, emphasizing the discontinuity of its themes when juxtaposed with those of the first three treatises. The reader who expects a further development of what is discussed in the previous treatises will be disappointed. Discontinuity marks the link between the first three treatises and the fourth. This discontinuity is determined by the entrance of a new main topic that focuses on the theory of true nobility. Dante indicates this as the "valore, / per lo qual veramente omo è gentile" (vv. 12–13).

This study has put forth a thematic reading of the *Convivio*, tracing an organic line of thought aimed at establishing the notion of human beings as defined by their intellect. In the fourth treatise, this line of thought seems to vanish. The discontinuity is especially evident between treatises three and four. The reasons for this, on our reading, are extremely important because they confirm the results of our exploration. In this section, I will map a few contents of the last treatise that offer the reader a sense for the new themes that emerge in the canzone and in the prose text and which are determinants for the discontinuity mentioned above.

The *suspicio* that governs my mapping is that the treatise and the canzone strongly aim at organizing and reshaping the contents that were the foci of the previous treatises. Dante announces his turning of the page at the very opening of the canzone *Le dolci rime d'amor ch'io solia.* He will speak no more, he says, of love, because the proud and scornful manner of the lady has barred his access to his customary mode of speech. The new theme will instead be nobility, based not on ancient privileges and wealth but rather on virtue. This virtue is the result of a gift, given by God, which coincides with our ability to choose the *mean* (*mezzo*) in matters pertaining to moral action. Dante names this divine gift *grazia*, an appellation that again confirms the importance of *transumptio* as a rhetorical methodology of the *ornatus difficilis,* which is not discontinued. *Grazia*, a new name for the intellectual power that God bestows on us, introduces the reshaping mentioned above. This reshaping includes the notion of the human intellect, which in the fourth treatise is different from that of intellect as it was organized in the previous treatises.

A form of what I indicate as reshaping was first announced in the final part of the canzone *Amor che ne la mente mi ragiona.* In fact, the canzone at line 76 recalls another text in which the lady was defined as *fera* and *disdegnosa*. This recalling emphasizes the discord between the canzone *Amor che ne la mente mi ragiona*, which depicts the lady as humble, and the ballad, *Voi che sapete ragionar d'amore* (De Robertis 2005, 228–31), in which the adjectives *fera* (v. 43) and *disdegnosa* (v. 3) portray her in a very different light. The latter description arouses uncertainty and doubts. The uncertainty reappears even more clearly in the prose-commentary to the canzone, in the third treatise, and, as we have noted, at the beginning of the third canzone, *Le dolci rime d'amor ch'io solia.* The initial section of the fourth treatise (as we shall see) returns to this theme but develops on its basis a new line and direction.

Reading the canzone *Le dolci rime d'amor ch'io solia*, we see that the major theme of the previous canzoni fades away. The model is no longer that of intellectual contemplation. The love-contemplation of the *donna gentile*, displayed as an intellectual goal shared by humans and heavenly intelligences, finds no place in the last treatise of the *Convivio.* A new tension arises in which an historical notion is superseded by an historical attempt: the criticism of nobility based on ancient privilege and wealth marks the entrance of a theme of great importance in Dante's age. In fact, the criticism of riches in the canzone is part of a larger issue that includes the criticism of materialism. Dante is dealing with new themes that indirectly work to reshape the thought he has previously proposed. A new type of prose takes form, in which two synchronous operations are active. The writing implies both an erasing and a reshaping. Dante tends, in the treatise, to use syllogistic reasoning, clearly aiming at demonstration. He thus signals a break and a new beginning. The *donna gentile* almost disappears and is simply identified with philosophy, the very meaning of which is rethought in light of new contents.

The poem, and above all, the treatise thus organize a kind of *retractatio*. I use this word in Augustine's sense, giving it the same meaning and goal the Bishop of Hippo gave it in a later work (*Retractationes*), in which he claimed to act as a censor of what he had asserted in his earlier work (see his "Prologue"). Because of this *retractatio*, a new field enters. Although we may give it different names, Dante introduces an Aristotelian terminology to define it, which he derives from the *Nicomachean Ethics*. The new section no doubt aims at eliminating features that could be related to a radical thinking. Contents that were retraceable in the second and third treatises of the *Convivio* are discussed again in the fourth treatise, but with a different approach and perspective. Here we need to know more about Dante's exile, and about the years of composition of the last treatise, in order to better understand the reasons for his new attitude.

We know that 1306 concluded the two years he spent in Verona (Petrocchi), and it is also probable that in those years he visited Padua, a city in which Aristotelianism, in its radical declinations, was prominent. During and even before his exile, Dante spent a period in Bologna. Both Padua and Bologna were centres well known for an Aristotelian-Averroistic tradition that was already established. We do not know which people Dante met there. We may speculate about his frequenting the Capitolare Library in Verona, or about the Bolognese group of radical thinkers he should have met before. Padua, of course, was the city that was home to a famous thinker suspected of heresy, Pietro d'Abano. These meetings, for Dante, no doubt gave rise to a new field of reflection (assuming they in fact took place) and allowed him to proceed in an unexpected direction. We may surmise that the more he understood this new line of thinking, the more he attempted to detach himself from it as potentially threatening. Moreover, if we recall that the writing of the *Convivio* came to an end between 1307 and 1308, the new element that no doubt played a key role in this interruption was the writing of the *Commedia*. Indeed, the fourth treatise in many ways foreshadows Dante's poem.

My study in this concluding section will underline how Dante organizes his new line of thinking, and why a kind of *retractatio* drives him to act, as mentioned above, as his own censor and critic. The new canzone openly marks a new beginning or palinode. Both in the poem and later in the prose, as stated above, the text openly indicates a break between the first three treatises and the fourth, thereby implying a new perspective. This perspective must be investigated by comparing several themes in the last treatise with those of the second and third.

Dante appears no longer to be interested in the contents he previously embraced. It seems to mark the end of a season of great engagement and of brilliant (and tormented) intellectual enterprises. Political-social endeavour now becomes evident. The text no longer reiterates the idea of the love for the *donna gentile* as the unifying principle for an intellectual community. Dante instead organizes a new framework that introduces the historical institution of Empire, which, since the beginning, is charged with the goal of producing earthly happiness. The idea of a common intellection does not appear, suggesting that he was bracketing this theme. As is well known, this notion will reappear in the *Monarchia*, the political treatise devoted to Empire, in which the notion of the possible intellect as better actualized by the world community is clearly enunciated. In this last Latin treatise, Empire will create the political organization that allows the actualization of the possible intellect.

The love for the *donna gentile* that the tormented pages of treatises two and three of the *Convivio* were discussing and suggesting as creating a *de facto* intellectual community, according to our reading, now appears to be the basic antecedent of a greater political unity that will be discussed later. In light of this, political community appears to be natural. Natural, too, is the idea that the possible intellect is better actualized by the whole human community than by the isolated individual. Human beings think best when they think together. This issue is foundational and is not to be superseded in the reflection on Empire.

To find a trace of the quest for a unifying principle, we must go back to the *De vulgari eloquentia*. In this work, the unifying principle was in the *volgare illustre* as created by different poets in their works. It gave form to an ideal court – that is, an ideal centre as a point or a unifying principle. This ideal court was put forth in the awareness that a real one was absent. However, the idea of a superior kind of unity was a quest active in the *De vulgari eloquentia,* which identified the vernacular as the natural, and therefore, universal language. Dante here discusses the vernacular *lingua del sì,* though it is implicit that a vernacular form is proper to all languages. The vernacular appears to be the primary form of language that human beings learn from their nurse. Dante thinks of it in terms of continuity and similitude with the mental word (*verbum-logos*), a word that Anselm, on an Augustinian basis, defined as universal (*Monologion* II.10).

In the first treatise of the *Convivio,* the vernacular identified a new public of potential readers that the barley bread (that is a learning offered in the vernacular) will feed. The *donna gentile* of the canzone *Voi ch 'intendendo il terzo ciel movete* was conceived in the Florentine years at the time of Dante's meeting with Charles Martel. This canzone contains what may be the first intuition of the need for a unifying principle, in which the highest form of speculation and the field of ethics were thought of as related. Following the years in which he wrote the canzone *Amor che ne la mente mi ragiona,* a quest for a superior principle begins to take shape, a principle that Dante organizes by rethinking old biblical contents together with a Stoic-Augustinian line in light of a new Aristotelian and Neoplatonic thought. These contents merge into a new idea: the true contemplation of a separate substance or divine idea in life as a cognitive experience that is possible for human beings only when united in a superior kind of speculation.

This idea was conceived in a personal way and began to take shape in the milieu of the Florentine years, in which the canzoni were written. Two influences were at work here: on the one hand, after the death of Beatrice, Dante attended the convents and engaged in the philosophical debates recalled in the *Convivio* II.12; on the other, there was his friendship and progressively dialectical relation with Guido Cavalcanti, the prestigious radical interpreter of heterodox contents that were circulating in Paris, Bologna, and Florence. These included Giacomo da Pistoia's *Questio de felicitate* (see Kristeller 1955; Zavattero 2005), which we know was dedicated to Cavalcanti. In this philosophical field, Dante introduces a political issue. A politically balanced life as the prerequisite for intellectual happiness was present in the thought of Arabic thinkers like Alfarabi. In Gauthier (1948, 227), we find quoted a text in which philosophic activity was also related to the common good conceived as political.[1]

In Dante's *Convivio*, according to my reading, there emerges the idea that speculation or perfect intellectual knowledge is the result of a communal thinking. As discussed above, the basis of this reflection was probably Aristotle's *Nicomachean Ethics*, which is closely related to politics. Aristotle's *Politics* it seems entered Dante's life in the years he was writing the *De vulgari eloquentia* (Tavoni 2011). In the *Politics*, Aristotle proposes a natural bond among human beings, a natural unity of thinking, or *logos*, as linked to the organization of the *polis*. Dante, as we have seen, seems to formulate his idea about speculation by looking at philosophical theories and rethinking them in light of the theory of *logos-verbum*. He enters into this reflection first in the canzone *Amor che ne la mente mi ragiona*, and later in the prose section of the third treatise of the *Convivio*. Both philosophical and theological documents cooperate for him on this issue, albeit through different linguistic forms and theoretical bases. Going back to the palinodic mode introduced with the canzone *Le dolci rime d'amor ch'io solia* of the last treatise, we note that the fourth treatise opens by touching on the theory of the origin of prime matter, a content that is introduced in relation to the perception of philosophy as something dangerous and destructive. It seems that the new section of the doctrinal treatise must, right from the start, erase any connection with a thinking that might prove threatening. This theory in the philosophy of Aristotle, as well as in that of Averroes, was related to the theory of the eternity of the world. The theory played a decisive role in the construction of Averroes's system, and in particular, his conception of the common unique intellect. By touching on this problematic issue of the origin of the matter and shaping it in relation to God's thinking – thereby suggesting a dangerous doubt implicit in the theory itself, but at the same time opposing it as something that should be related to the divine creative thought – Dante detaches his position from the Aristotelian-Averroistic line. In the third treatise, the theory of human intellect suggested as common was not associated with an Averroistic position (yet perhaps was influenced by it). Dante was discussing human intellectual knowledge in his own way. Similarly, the opening of the fourth treatise shows Dante's attempt to trace his own line and position.

The discussion of the origin of prime matter (which is, of course, a philosophical topic), by revealing a threatening manifestation of Lady Philosophy, implies in the prose a general rethinking. A kind of *retractatio* takes place that is understandable in light of a careful reading of the first three treatises, in particular the third. The fourth treatise of the *Convivio* changes its focus and perspective and does not continue the themes we have previously retraced. However, we may speak of a continuity if we take into account that it seems organized in order to modify, or eventually refute, the previously introduced contents.

The fourth treatise shows that his palinode is an attempt to change the perspective introduced in the first three treatises. Dante's uncertainty and doubts were evident in his writing, and since the canzone *Amor che ne la mente mi ragiona*. In our reading, this canzone introduced topics partly related to a heterodox field. Moreover, in the last stanza of this canzone, the lady started to appear threatening. In the prose treatise, written many years later, it was philosophy that appeared to threaten the character that says "I." In this sense, there is a narrative continuity between the final part of the third treatise and the beginning of the fourth, because such uncertainty and doubts are reiterated at first in the canzone *Le dolci rime d'amor ch'io solia* in virtue of "atti disdegnosi e feri / che nella donna mia / sono appariti" (5–7). These doubts suggest a problematic continuity that will result in a discontinuity.

In its opening (1.8), the prose section of the fourth treatise tells the reader that philosophy has transmuted its sweet *sembianti*, especially when Dante was investigating whether the prime matter of elements was the effect of God's intellect:

> Perché, con ciò fosse cosa che questa mia donna un poco li suoi dolci sembianti transmutasse a me, massimamente in quelle parti dove io mirava, e cercava se la prima materia delli elementi era da Dio intesa – per la qual cosa un poco dal frequentare lo suo aspetto mi sostenni.
>
> Since this lady of mine had somewhat altered the tenderness of her looks at me, especially in those features at which I would gaze when seeking to learn whether the primal matter of the elements was contained within God's mind – for which reason I refrained for a time from coming into the presence of her countenance. (V.1.8)

The narrative consistency, however, which links the final part of *Amor che ne la mente mi ragiona*, the beginning of *Le dolci rime d'amor ch'io solia*, and a section of the first chapter of the fourth treatise, aims at establishing a philosophical discontinuity. By indicating philosophy as something threatening, the author seems to attempt to introduce a clarification of issues related to what he had previously discussed. He engages in a kind of *distinguo*, in which he begins to track the borders of his discussion to delimit a territory not coincident with the previous one.

At the very beginning of the fourth treatise, we read that Dante, in virtue of the love for the lady, begins to despise errors: "Li errori della gente abominava e dispregiava, non per infamia o vituperio delli erranti, ma delli errori" (I sought, as far as I was able, to scorn and despise the errors of mankind, not to defame or denigrate those who err, but rather their errors; IV.1.5).

The main subject is now truth, and the author conforms himself to truth by loving and hating according to the lady's true essence. Dante now uses the word *errore*. The worst error is *malizia*, which will be a central topic of his *Inferno*. One of the most dangerous errors is that human goodness is implanted in us by nature, such goodness being coincident with what should be named nobility: "Questo è l'errore dell'umana bontade in quanto in noi è dalla natura seminata e che 'nobilitade' chiamare si dee" (This is the error concerning human goodness insofar as it is sown in us by nature, and which should be called "nobility"; IV.1.6–7). This error is badly and falsely considered, and of course what is condemned is the historical notion of nobility. *Subtilitas* is recalled here as a tool that can help us better understand what follows from this error.

After that, Dante touches upon the doubt about the theory of the origin of prime matter, which, however, he does not discuss. He then enters into the theme of what constitutes true nobility. It is here, we are told, that the lady changes her appearance. The reason is that the question of prime matter – whether it is intellected or willed or actualized by God, that which guides the character who says "I" – would interrupt Dante's philosophical speculation and would introduce a new perspective. The reader is thus alerted that a link may be established between the theory of true nobility and the doubt about the origin of prime matter. Dante tells his reader that it is because he wanted to cry out to those who were treading this evil path that he started to write the canzone *Le dolci rime d'amor ch'io solia*. He writes so that they might correct their errors and return to the true path.

My suggestion, which is the result of my reading of the first three treatises, is that this link can be seen as including a kind of *retractatio*. That the narrative continuity is aimed at a philosophical discontinuity is a preliminary matter of fact. Scholars who do not acknowledge this discontinuity base their interpretation on their reading of the second and third treatise. It has been my hint, along with the following preliminary one, that their interpretation, in its turn, depends on the widespread custom among scholars of not reading the canzoni in relation to their commentaries, a relation on which the *Convivio* is clearly organized, as I have discussed throughout this book.

A methodology of *suspicio* is at stake here in my reading. The first *suspicio* to take form is the following: that a link can be found between the criticism of wealth as a foundation for the historical notion of nobility and the doubt or inquiry regarding the origin of prime matter. The prose stresses this criticism, which becomes pervasive, and suggests a continuity between the criticism of materialism and the doubt-filled inquiry about the origin of prime matter. As we know, the text does not discuss the theory itself; however, the implications of the theory are understandable. The attempt here seems to be to eliminate the side effects to which the discourse about the *donna gentile* and philosophy could be related. One of these just mentioned as paradoxical is the theory of the eternity of the world, which denies the theological doctrine of creation. Both theories are in fact linked to the Averroistic theory of the intellect based on the assumption of the eternity of the human species and on the mortality of the individual soul, according to the reading of Averroes as opposed by Aquinas and others. The theory of the eternity of the world, which was discussed in Dante's time by philosophers like Siger of Brabant, Boethius of Dacia, and Aquinas himself, contributes to our understanding of the general picture of Dante's doubts regarding the origin of matter.

In what follows I will discuss two topics, nobility and the possible intellect, as they enter both in the canzone and in the prose of the fourth treatise. I start by briefly introducing the canzone *Le dolci rime d'amor ch'io solia*.

2. Towards a New Society: The True Nobility and the Criticism of Riches

The canzone *Le dolci rime d'amor ch'io solia* opens by signalling a break with what Dante had previously written. It announces a new type of poetry that employs a kind of rhyme that Dante calls *aspra e sottile*. He presents this as a new mode of writing that is opposed to his previous mode, which he characterizes in the opening of the canzone as "sweet" and centred on "love." He informs his readers that he has devised this poetry by searching for it in his thoughts (*cercare nei miei pensieri*).[2]

The verb *cercar* must be read in relation to *trobar* or *invenire*. It suggests that the invention here, in the classical rhetorical meaning of the thing to be found, derives from the mind's inner power of thinking. However, the first of the seven stanzas, together with a *congedo* that forms the scheme of this canzone, takes us back in part to Dante's previous mode of writing in order to refute it. The announced break with the past is evident, even though the canzone includes the attempt to reshape in a new perspective contents already established in the first two canzoni on which the *Convivio* has commented. Traditionally, the date of composition of *Le dolci rime d'amor ch'io solia* has been assumed to be that of the Florentine years and close to the composition of the first two – that is, around 1294. This date fits with the critique of the theory of nobility that is the focus of Dante's text in an ideal relationship with *Gli ordinamenti di giustizia* of Giano della Bella of 1293. As said above, Corti, in her *La felicità mentale* (1983), has proposed a different date, mainly on the basis of Dante's syllogistic language. She proposes that its composition should be placed later, closer to the writing of the third treatise. The impossibility of establishing the date of this poem with certainty allows, however, the reader to exploit its chronological fluidity in order to assess its complex meaning.

The canzone is organized as a medieval *quaestio*, which initially puts forth a thesis that is coincident with a refutation or *pars destruens*, after which will follow the *pars construens*, or antithesis. The fact that an eminent jurist, Bartolo of Sassoferrato, in the 1340s, commented on this canzone has drawn attention to the historical theme of nobility (Borsa 2007). My reading here will focus on the first part of the text and on what the canzone refutes, namely, the idea of nobility based on ancient privilege, material wealth, and refined or "gentle" customs of life. The canzone, in opposing this traditional idea, introduces a new idea that relates nobility to virtue. This virtue is the result of a gift given by God, a gift named nobility and also *grazia*, which produces and inspires virtue. Virtue, here, is coincident with the Aristotelian ethical mean (*mezzo*) that allows human beings to shun excess by choosing the median between two extremes. The excess as something natural to the human being that the gift of *grazia* allows him to control, driving him to the choice of the mean, is a notion that must be pointed out. In the prose section, Dante will explain this notion of the mean, without, however, mentioning the reason why human beings are inclined to extremes or excesses. In fact, the theory of the right mean in Aristotle's *Nicomachean Ethics* worked to counteract the natural passions to which human behaviour is subjected. The Aristotelian moral virtues were shaped on the idea that morality implies control and free will. Our inclination to the extremes is explained in the prose commentary, although it is touched on in the canzone. That human nature has a material component on which our passions depend and which is their origin, is a field that Dante confronted since the years in which he was writing a few poems which entered in the *Vita nuova* and the *Vita nuova* itself.[3]

Dante will return to this topic later, but this canzone shows that he now starts by seeking to create a new referential framework. In this section, I intend to point out how the criticism of materiality and materialism[4] go together in the canzone, and how they preside over the section that deals with refutation and also with the construction of a new paradigm that parallels and opposes the model that is refuted. I will consider how, in the first part of the canzone, Dante criticizes the concept of nobility and focuses on a critique of material goods. The link that unifies the two different sections of the canzone, which my readings stress, opens up a new interpretation of the text and, more importantly, of Dante's future work. I anticipate my reading and the thesis to be proposed as follows. The focus of the canzone is socio-political. Its core is the individuation of what creates social discrimination on the one hand and the individual's wrong belief that affects society on the other. Dante's analysis offers an answer in which the roots of the problem are located in a unifying principle – that is, in our natural inclination to materiality and materialism. I will also consider that in the initial prose section, Dante will introduce a short but extremely important appeal to the problematic issue of matter and its origin – "se la prima matera delli elementi era da Dio intesa" (IV.1.8) – relating this issue to his break with philosophy. My reading emphasizes the existence of a link between this doubt about the ontology of matter and the false values that the canzone refutes, and proposes that the prose radicalizes and motivates in a philosophical perspective the criticism active in the first section of the canzone. This confirms and must be understood in light of our reading of the previous treatises of the *Convivio* and of Dante's desire, in the fourth, to clarify his position. To individuate the borders inside which he encloses his reflection on the nature of human intellect is part of what I will attempt to in this part of my study.

3. A Philosophical Doubt and the Criticism of Materialism: Time and Logic

At the centre here is the complex medieval theory of the origin of matter, a debated issue the prose text mentions as a problematic one, and which we may understand in its centrality by linking the canzone to this particular prose passage. I offer as a thesis that at the centre of the canzone there is the criticism of nobility in its inner link with that of materiality and materialism. This continues to be a problematic issue that is confirmed in the first part of the prose text, written many years later. It is on this basis that Dante's ontological problem of evil begins to take shape. In fact, the discussion about matter can also be fruitfully related to Dante's future work, most especially the *Commedia*.

Going back to the canzone, now that the sweetness of style is removed, we must evaluate the *aspro* and *sottile*. *Aspro* is opposed to the sweet, and *sottile* introduces the *difficilis*. But the *difficilis* here is coincident with the practice of syllogism (Aquinas 1955). *Aspro*, which De Robertis (2005) explains as technical according to what we read in the *De vulgari eloquentia*, is coincident with the polysyllabic and seems to return to the vocabulary that is able to introduce the topics at stake. However, the fact that *aspro* and *difficilis* appear in a canzone with a socio-political nature is an original aspect of Dante's work. In fact, Dante seeks to reduce different elements *ad unum*. This works as a kind of subtext that rules the text and aims at organizing a unifying principle that is basic in both the *pars construens* and the *pars destruens*. This is the critique of materiality. The logical weaving is no doubt given and exhibited, and the reader must be aware of the socio-political issues and the logical rhetorical apparatus of this.[5] In fact, the *refutatio* is part of both logic and rhetoric.

Since the *Vita nuova* (and later, in the canzoni *Voi ch 'ntendendo il terzo ciel movete* and *Amor che ne la mente mi ragiona*), Dante had introduced the adjective *gentile* in a way that problematized its meaning. Of course, as he himself writes, he is indebted for this to Guinizzelli's canzone *Al cor gentile*, a treatise in verses on love and *gentilezza* as intellectual. This text was important to Dante, since in the *Vita nuova*, as well as in the first two canzoni of the *Convivio*, here the *donna gentile* radicalizes in philosophical terms contents of Guinizzelli, mostly using the Neoplatonic and Aristotelian learning that thirteenth century *philosophantes* were linking.

In *Voi ch 'ntendendo il terzo ciel movete*, in fact, the adjective *gentile* attributed to the angel-intelligences (v. 5) connoted a network of ties suggesting a relationship between the minds of the angelic intelligences, the movement of the heavens, and the human mind that conceives the new love for the woman. Later in *Amor che ne la mente mi ragiona*, the new lady is suggested as *gentile*. Now, in *Le dolci rime d'amor ch'io solia*, *gentilezza* as nobility becomes a category in itself and something to be understood. The conclusion in the canzone will be that nobility is the friend of the lady identified with philosophy: "io vo parlando de l'amica vostra" (v. 144).

This canzone, which is written in *rima aspra* for its sound and technicality and with subtlety according to the sentence of the words, proceeds with arguments and disputations. The announced break in *Le dolci rime d'amor ch'io solia* is said to be derived from something threatening that has appeared in the deeds of the *donna*. These actions have prevented the author from continuing the usual sweet style he had used in his discussion about love. In this context, a new word, *valore* (v. 12), is introduced. It is trisyllabic and technical at once, and points to value in light of which one may say that a man is gentle – that is, noble. The reader does not receive any further information about the reason for the lady's threatening aspect, but the prose section will reiterate that something has created a short circuit, which the prose will link to the question about the origin of matter. The reader of the poem is therefore left with a space to be filled in order to get the reason of the "atti feri e disdegnosi che ne la donna mia sono appariti" (the proud and scornful manner that my lady bears; vv. 5–7), the true sense of the change that is announced, and the new poetry the canzone is inaugurating.

The question is this: In what way is the diversion assumed? As an opposition to the past way, or as a continuation that seeks to correct or reshape issues that the author assumes to be dangerous? In reading the canzone, the reader will be once more driven by *suspicio*, which will work in understanding the text while looking for a meaning to be understood, and which could explain both the reasons of the break with the old way of writing and, first of all, the acts *disdegnosi* and *feri* that have appeared in the lady.

The relationship between true nobility and ethics is at the basis of the *inventio* of the canzone. This relationship, in turn, can be established only if the false idea and judgment regarding *gentilezza* is refuted. After that, the canzone will build the new meaning of *gentilezza* and its origin and signs. It is in this second part that the canzone will introduce ethics.

A continuity of *Le dolci rime d'amor ch'io solia* with the canzone *Amor che ne la mente mi ragiona* is evident in this text, where we read that in another poem the lady was described as *fera* and *disdegnosa*. The other text was (as stated above) the ballad *Voi che sapete ragionar d'amore*. It is evident that the canzone maintains some doubts expressed in that *ballata* and that it also reiterates its peculiar terminology; *fero* (fierce) reappears at line 85 of *Amor che ne la mente mi ragiona*: "sì che mi par fero" (it appears to me so fierce).

For all these reasons, which are more than a simple diversion, the reader who works within this relational field is inclined to think that the canzone, while emending the error about nobility, also seeks to emend other errors that the author himself may have made, perhaps a dangerous meaning that his previous two canzoni should have suggested, or something from which such a meaning could be inferred Alternatively, perhaps he intends to reshape rather than simply emend something he had introduced in them. That the vocabulary (*feri* and *disdegnosi*) he uses appears in Cavalcanti's canzone "Donna me prega" (love in this text is defined as *fero*) and in Dante's reference in *Inferno* 10 to Cavalcanti's behaviour (*disdegno*), adds further contents to the grounding of *suspicio*.

We start by considering that the canzone, in confronting the notion of *gentilezza*, identified with nobility, organizes a critique of the historical notion of nobility. It apparently eliminates *gentilezza* as intellectual, which Dante had introduced in *Voi ch 'ntendendo il terzo ciel movete* and in *Amor che ne la mente mi ragiona* and whose paradigm is that of separate substances. Now, in the third treatise, nobility is a divine gift given to the individual, in which the harmony between soul and body emerges as the human being's natural predisposition to grace. Because the adjective *gentile* was qualifying the being of the *donna* as related to the field of *gentilezza* in the first two canzoni, it is suggested that the discussion about nobility works also towards redefining nobility and the identity of the lady. If this is true, then the canzone implies a re-writing with the purpose of reshaping certain contents. A reader who is aware of the meanings of the two previous canzoni on which the *Convivio* comments is immediately conscious of this enterprise. Not only is *gentilezza* now grounded in a divine gift, but also the notion of virtue as an intellectual aim, implicit in the first two canzoni, is refuted. Now ethics consists in the moral virtues, and from these virtues the Aristotelian theory of the right medium enters. Teodolinda Barolini (2014) has recently written an essay on the Aristotelian mean that is extremely suggestive and scientifically exhaustive. I will refer to this study for what belongs to moral virtue. My reading of the canzone, however, will focus on a different issue that can be traced as part of the criticism of the notion of nobility rooted in wealth and materialism.

The first topic the canzone refutes is the false and vile judgment of those who think that the criterion for judging *gentilezza* is wealth: "riprovando 'l giudicio falso e vile / di quei che voglion che di gentilezza / sia principio ricchezza" (vv. 15–17). Here, *principio* (principle) means origin and criterion of judgment. Dante's method introduces speculation before starting the discussion of nobility, at line 18, where he calls as a witness the lord who dwells in the eyes of the lady. The meaning here is that speculation anticipates action, where action is coincident with the content expressed in poetry. Poetry, conceived as part of civil discourse, an idea that is active in an influential line of thought in the thirteenth century, is thus part of politics, which is an architectonic art, according to Brunetto, Alfarabi, and Aristotle, and which is the most important science according to the first two.

If the canzone was written in the years of the *Ordinamenti di giustizia* of Giano della Bella (1293), these are close to the years in which Dante is just entering the political arena (1296), and this may be related as well to this canzone. What emerges is a political-social use of speculation that leads to practical activity. The logical dialectical discourse shapes poetry, and poetry is written as a call to action: "My song against-the-erring-ones, go forth ..."

Speculation and praxis are related. This reiterates what we have read in the canzone *Voi ch 'ntendendo il terzo ciel movete,* where the angels were able to move the heavens because of their divine speculation. The idea that human beings too are able to speculate permeates the first two canzoni. The way in which such speculation takes place is part of the meanings the canzoni introduce, and in them a political endeavour must be evaluated, which, in light of the third, becomes more evident. Here, in this third canzone, the human ability to speculate is related to the meaning of his love for philosophy. This speculation, it is suggested, allows him to act through poetry. The envoi informs his readers that the canzone is written to oppose the *erranti* – that is, those who are responsible for a false idea about nobility. Poetry may influence other human beings: *poiesis* and *praxis* are related. The link should be operative in the life of the city or politics. Brunetto, in his *Tresor,* while proposing politics as an architectonic science, writes that this science contains both things said and things done – words and actions. Politics as an architectonic science has a command of other sciences. According to the definition Aristotle offers in his *Metaphysics* at A 2 982a16–17, politics has under it practical and linguistic sciences. In this way, we may trace Dante's awareness of a socio-political goal given to this canzone. What cannot escape is a kind of ideological *militanza* that powerfully contributes to shape the text: "Contra gli erranti mia tu te n'andrai" (My song against-the-erring-ones, go forth; v. 141).

The second stanza of the canzone (lines 21–40) refutes the error of defining nobility with ancestral possessions and refined customs of life: "che fosse antica possession d'avere con reggimenti belli." In the third stanza, this refutation starts to run in parallel with a cognitive issue. The parallel is established to show that, in the same way, defining a human being as animated wood utters no truth and is a speech that is incomplete: "Chi diffinisce: Omo è legno animato, prima dice non vero, e dopo 'l falso parla non intero." In the same way, Frederick II, when he defines nobility with anciently held possessions and refined manners – "d'averi con reggimenti belli" – on the one hand establishes a false thing, and on the other, proceeds with defect because wealth cannot give or take out *gentilezza*, because the possessions of their own nature are vile.

Gentilezza and material wealth differ in nature, and the vileness of wealth is manifested because, however vast its accumulation may be, it can give no peace, and the right and true human being does not care to hold or to lose riches. In this discussion, nobility is detached from material value and also from refined manners, insofar as these depend on inherited wealth and are considered formally vitiated by false conventions.

Gentilezza is not a privilege of birth, or a privilege determined by an inherited tradition, nor is it a privilege determined by beautiful manners as the result of ancestral riches. The text announces at lines 12–13 that its goal will be to establish the meaning of *valore* in relation to *gentilezza*: "e dirò del valore, / per lo qual veramente omo è gentile" (I'll speak about the value which makes a person truly noble). For this reason, the canzone organizes a logical sequence. Its result is a kind of reasoning structured in a parasyllogistic way (a kind of imperfect syllogism).

Here is the first of them, as traditionally formulated and thus refuted: *gentilezza* is a value, old riches are a value, *gentilezza* is ancestral riches.

What follows here is opposed and shaped again as a parasyllogistic reasoning, and opens a new problematic territory:

> *Gentilezza* is a value, riches are vile, and *gentilezza* is not the possession of wealth.

The meaning here is not just that *gentilezza* is not coincident with material wealth, but more importantly and powerfully, that value, or *valore*, and wealth are opposites. What is material and what is of value are disconnected. What takes form here is also the concept of value as a field of reflection. *Valore* (value) has nothing to do with the material in this canzone. The change that is introduced belongs first of all to the area of mental associations that are disconnected, and it is here that the parasyllogistic texture works. The vocabulary is a grounds for cultivated attention. *Valore* in Guinizzelli was also power as energy – "Al cor gentil reimpaira sempre amor" (13). Now, the text attempts to open a new relational field for *valore*. The dissimilitude that is established between true nobility and riches works in light of the natural similitude between the image that we create inside our mind when we want to make a *figura* and the fact that this *figura*, before being expressed, must already be in the mind. This natural innate link (similitude) cannot be established between *gentilezza* and riches. They are naturally diverse and cannot have any kind of relation, as a stream that runs far from a tower cannot be influenced by the far tower. Here distance introduces non-reconciliation, or natural dissimilitude (52–5).

It is interesting that the devaluation of riches is attributed, among the others, to the fact that they are rooted in instability (*indiscreto avenimento*); in fact, their imperfection may be observed first in the lack of discretion and in the accidentality in their appropriation – that is, they are rooted in time, change, and the accidental (IV.11.4). True nobility, on the contrary, is a divine gift and is thus substantial; that is, it belongs in the category of substance. It is natural and, as such, part of the individual to whom it is given. The accidental is opposed to what is essential. Moreover, the roots and phenomenology of materiality are in time. In their structural imperfection, riches can be numerically infinite but do not give peace: "ché, quantunque collette / non posson quietar, ma dan più cura" (for however great they are, they bring no peace, but rather grief; vv. 57–8). Riches are vile and imperfect, and the latter adjective is explained in relation to the fact that they do not give peace because the desire for them is always increasing and has no end (IV.12.4). Here Dante announces what the *Monarchia* will indicate as *avaritia* and what the *Inferno* will identify as the insatiable hunger of the she-wolf. What should be stressed here is the dimension of infinity that penetrates inside time, a time that, according to the Christian tradition, starts with creation and has a finite dimension. This infinity, which belongs to the field of materiality and materialism that Dante introduces as part of what is defective, should be understood in relation to the field of materiality itself.

The basic meaning of the canzone lies, we said, in the link between the socio-political field of nobility and the ethical field of virtue. Both are confronted in relation to the criticism of materialism, and from different perspectives. The vice implicit in materialism is figured as a desire that has no limits, and this matches Aristotle's theory of matter as the principle of all infinite potentiality. The vice in the field of ethics is considered an excess peculiar to the human being's materiality. The idea of God as *metron* occurs in *divinis nominibus* of Pseudo-Dionysus, who defines measure as a *misura* with which to measure. This may be in relation to the gift of grace that is given by God and that allows us to choose the mean, which is coincident with *misura* (Barolini 2014). This, as Aristotle explains, is the point of a segment on which a hypothetical rope would fall straight. This is the right (*orthos*, in Greek) *medium* or mean between two equally distant points. The field of ethics is shaped on this notion that implicitly recalls the concept of *misura*, as peculiar to God and to the divine gift shared by those who are able to choose the right medium.

Going back to the text of the canzone, in the third stanza, time enters as a dimension to be evaluated. Here the positive dimension of time appears to be that of change as a becoming that includes the educational process. The text organizes an opposition that points out a logical contradiction. Time implies movement and becoming. In the discussion of nobility, those who do not accept that a villain may become *gentile* deny this dimension. Nobility for them is a privilege of birth. It is here that Dante shows how much they fall in a logical contradiction. In fact, they accept temporal becoming for what they see as *antiche ricchezze*. Here, the temporal dimension of ancient riches generates, in fact, (according to them) the coming to be of good manners. Because of this, a dimension of value is attributed to riches insofar as they create a tradition of *reggimenti belli*, which are part of high educational standards. The axis of this discussion is temporal becoming, which, in the same way that it can create good manners, should allow someone born from a father who is not noble to become gentle. From this contradiction is deduced a third argument: If we do not accept the change implicit in becoming, we must hold that we are, since the beginning, all noble or all villain, because we derive from the same unique human being (i.e., Adam), unless we want to argue that there is not a first human being, but from eternity many human beings – that is, "che non fosse ad uom cominciamento" (that mankind had no origin; v. 71).

Here, the logical subject is still the becoming of time, to which creation is related. The issue, however, seems to introduce a bigger topic: that of the eternity of human genus, of course presented as paradoxical and, however, recalled. Because the eternity of the human species is denied and we all derive from a first man, we are equal in birth. It is therefore wrong to define as "gentle" someone who can say, "I am the son or niece of someone who is worthy": "ed è tanto durata / la così falsa oppinïon tra nui,/ che l'uom chiama colui / omo gentil, che può dicere: 'Io fui / nepote' o 'figlio di cotal valente,'/ benché sia da nïente" (And so ingrained has this false view become among us that one calls another noble if he can say "I am the son, or grandson, of such and such a famous man," despite his lack of worth; vv. 32–7).

The Italian word here is *valente* (someone of value), which is part of the area of value that is criticized. Both *valore* – "e dirò del valore/ per lo quale veramente omo è gentile" (I'll speak about the value which makes a person truly noble; vv. 12–13) – and *valente*, in light of this logical-historical analysis, appear to define a mobile semantic area. They are the new relations in which these words are used which, reversing the traditional point of view and reorganizing the meaning of vocabulary through new relationships, powerfully contribute to grounding human excellence.

To better understand how the text organizes a weaving of different threads in order to unify them, we return to the second stanza. We see that here the text links "false" with an incomplete speech by way of two examples: "Chi difinisce 'omo è legno animato,' / prima dice non vero, e dopo il falso parla non intero; / ma più forse non vede. / Similmente fu chi tenne impero / in diffinire errato, / ché prima puose il falso e d'altro lato / con difetto procede (He who claims "Man is a living tree" first says what isn't true and, having said what's false, leaves much unsaid; but possibly he sees no deeper. The ruler of the Empire likewise erred by making such a claim, for first he claims that which is false and then proceeds, moreover, defectively; vv. 41–8).

In the definition of "man" as "a living tree" – *omo* as *legno animato* – to speak partially means to speak falsely, for what belongs to nobility to proceed with a defect implies a relation between things naturally different. In the definition of the human being, the false is coincident with the *non intero*, or the partial, because the above-quoted proposition does not take into account the third – that is, the intellectual – function of the human soul. In this definition, the human being, according to the Aristotelian definition, is reduced to the material dimension of the vegetative and sensitive soul. In the discussion about nobility, what is opposed is the identification of excellence with the field of material things. Both oppose materialism, but this opposition is the result of two different considerations, which may be complementary. The first is the assumption that the human essence is material; the other assumes that human excellence is related to or dependent on material values. They are the prelude to a third emergence of materialism to be opposed and that is related to the position of those who deny that "fosse ad uom cominciamento" (v. 71), that is, those who think that the human species is eternal, but this thread is not unravelled.

While the responsibility given to Frederick II may anticipate the accusation of Epicureanism of *Inferno* 10, in the *Monarchia,* Dante will later correctly attribute this theory about nobility to Aristotle (the *Monarchia* was written after *Inferno* 10). It is also true that the assertion "omo è legno animato" (man is an animated tree; v. 41) recalls Cavalcanti's discussion of the ontology of love, together with those who celebrated the material essence of the human being and only this. The link suggested between Frederick II and Cavalcanti seems to anticipate contents of *Inferno* 10. Materialism appears to be, in its very nature, protean. The fields in which it occurs are different (socio-political, cognitive), but only one is the root of what is false and defective: the importance given to materiality or the material as value. What will emerge is that the antidote to materialism should work in both fields – that is, socio-political and cognitive. Here, however, an element is felt as missed, namely, the ontological notion of which is materiality and on which materialism is based.

I mentioned above that it is possible to establish for this canzone 1293 as a *post quem* date for the reshaping of the theory of nobility of Giano della Bella and his *Ordinamenti di giustizia.* The analysis and condemnation of materialism, however, cannot be detached from Dante's frequenting the Florentine convents. Franciscan poverty, as well as the preaching and thought of Pietro Giovanni Olivi, is either responsible for or, at least, influences this deep opposition. The discussion of nobility thus goes far beyond the social endeavour in Dante and attempts to introduce a larger issue, in which nobility and the discussion of the true essence of the human being open fields of relations that need to be understood.

Summarizing, we may see that what is refuted is the result of many tiles in a mosaic organized by those who, in the canzone, are identified as *errantes*:

> If *gentilezza* implies antiquity, and antiquity implies time, and time implies mutability, from this derives that the notion of nobility, rooted in time and becoming, according to the definition attributed to Frederick II, is not just a privilege of birth but also an historical category targeted erroneously as value.

The paradox of this reasoning is the following: If *gentilezza* is made by old possessions and ancient customs of life, its value is built on the temporal dimension, a dimension that is at the same time denied when it is said that it is impossible for a villain to become a noble. In fact, time implies becoming and transformation. The fourth stanza shows the false reasoning: "Né voglion che vil uom gentil divegna, / né di vil padre scenda / nazion che per gentil già mai s'intenda: / questo è da lor confesso; / onde lor ragion par che sé offenda / in tanto [in] quanto assegna/che tempo a gentilezza si convegna, / diffinendo con esso" (Nor will they grant that one born base may yet be noble, nor that a low-born father's progeny be ever thought to qualify as noble; for this is what they claim. And so their argument, it seems, negates itself insofar as it asserts that time is a prerequisite of nobility, defining it according to this rule; vv. 61–8). It is this implicit contradiction that shows the fallacy of their reasoning and its false nature.

The logic of contraries, which defines contradiction as an opposition which is absolute (Peter Hisponus, *Summulae logicales* 5.27),[6] impels the reader to the reasoning that is constructed here.

This way of reasoning touches upon a controversial topic, as in the debate that placed in doubt the notion of the first man and the Judaeo-Christian theory of creation – a theory in the thirteenth century targeted in the light of the philosophy of Aristotle and some of his readers, who assumed that the world is eternal. In the late thirteenth century, both Siger of Brabant and Boethius of Dacia did in fact write on the eternity of the world. Aquinas, too, participated in the debate, to which several of the articles condemned in Paris in 1270 and 1277 are related.

The complexity that the canzone organizes is embodied in a chain of deductions that relate a socio-political issue to problems of a cognitive nature. This is confirmed when it is said that to assume that human beings are eternal – "ritenere non fosse ad om cominciamento" – would be a position opposed to the Christian faith and so must be refuted – "ma ciò io non consento." But this I do not grant (v. 72).

This is the reasoning: If we derive as humans from a first man, and if we deny change and mutability, we are all base or all noble, unless we want to say that the human genus is eternal. But Dante does not agree with it. Of course, at issue here is the notion of time. If it is related to the denial of creation and thus to the eternity of time, then, if the world is eternal, time is also eternal. Creation in Christian culture also marks the beginning of time. The world is created not in time, but with time (Augustine). In this context, another question thus takes on a form that is not explicit: If we do not believe in the creation, then what is the origin of the human being? Is he son of the sun and of the man, as Aristotle says? If this is accepted, a materialistic principle presides over the world and the human being. Dante opposes this point of view. He will organize his answer in the prose text. What is accepted is the notion of creation and the origin of the individual human being's soul in the re-reading of Albert's theory and the mixing of embryology, Aristotle, and theological tenets. As for what belongs to the canzone, however, the doubt about the creation of the first man is recalled as a paradox. In a discussion aimed at refuting materialism, however, it is suggested that the canzone is aware that materialism is a pervasive category with many facets in the synchronous philosophical debate. However, when it says that *gentilezza* is a gift given by God, there is an implicit theological reflection. The prose text will introduce, through a question, a key problem that for many reasons is related to the discussion of nobility in its inner link with the criticism of riches. In this, the problematic issue that suggests evil as related to materialism seems to be organized. The doubt is expressed in *Convivio* IV.1. Whether the prime matter was willed or intellected by God – "Se la prima materia delli elementi era da Dio intesa" – is a question put forth in relation to philosophy, and her threatening aspect suggests that it takes form as result of contents Dante was dealing with since the first two canzoni and their commentaries.

In our construction, the meaning arises from the empty spaces of contents that his poetry suggested and that were enclosed sometimes in an implicit way in his prose discussion of the first three treatises. I summarize in three hypothetical propositions his deductive, parasyllogistic reasoning:

1. If *gentilezza* is a value and ancient wealth is a value, *gentilezza* is ancient wealth.
2. On the contrary: If *gentilezza* is a value and riches are vile, *gentilezza* is not wealth.
3. In addition: If *gentilezza* is ancient wealth with good manners (as erroneously said), and antiquity implies time, *gentilezza* implies a becoming.

In light of this becoming, we should accept that a villain can become a noble. It further follows from what was said above that each of us is noble or each base, or also that mankind had no starting origin. But this I do not grant, nor do they either, if they are Christian ("Ancor, segue di ciò che innanzi ho messo, / che siàn tutti gentili o ver villani / o che non fosse ad uom cominciamento; / ma ciò io non consento, / néd ellino altressì, se son cristiani!"; vv. 69–73). Indeed, if there is creation and thus a first man, if we deny a becoming, we are all noble or all base because we all derive from the first man. At line 78 the canzone, after having enunciated the refutation (*riprovo*) – "Per che a 'ntelletti sani / è manifesto i lor diri esser vani; / e io così per falsi li riprovo, / e da lor mi rimovo" (Thus it is clear to every mind that is sound that what they say lacks sense, and hence I claim their words are false, and so dissociate myself from them; vv. 74–7) – introduces the *pars costruens*, in which its author will say what true *gentilezza* is, from what it derives, and what signs manifest it. The key meaning is that to a materialistic principle is opposed the main content of ethics: virtue. Within this field, he reconstructs the principle of value, implicitly denying that materiality is a value and that it presides over the origin of the human being.

4. Happiness as Moral Virtue

For Aristotle, ethics presides over the choice and establishment of the rule of self-control. This is, as stated in the *Nicomachean Ethics*, a chosen habit which occupies the mean alone: "abito eligente / lo qual dimora in mezzo solamente" (vv. 86–7). This is coincident with the right medium and is opposed to the materialism coincident with our inclination to the excess that is naturally a part of, but only a part of, our human nature. The first line of the fifth stanza introduces the word "virtue" (v. 81), thereby suggesting a link to value, from which derives the fact that moral virtue is a value. Having erased every connection to the field of materiality, this *habitus* derives from a gift that God has given to us. This gift, because it allows us to make a balanced choice, implies that the rational component of human beings is what defines them.

Here, what makes the human being happy is identified with moral virtue. This will be confirmed in the prose section. What is also confirmed is that nobility and virtue derive from a third element: both are in fact manifestations of the ontology of the human being. This ontology is constructed by opposing materiality and materialism, and establishing the notion of true nobility; its name is *grazia* and its divine origin is clearly asserted because it is a gift from God: "Ché solo Iddio all'anima la dona / che vede in sua persona / perfettamente star: sì ch'ad alquanti / ch'è 'l seme di felicità, si acosta, / messo da Dio nell'anima ben posta" (For God alone bestows it on that soul which he perceives dwells perfectly within its person; and so, as some perceive, within the soul that's properly disposed. It is the seed of happiness, instilled by God; vv. 116–20).

That virtue is identical with the practice of the mean, and that the control of passion opposes materiality, must be read in light of the medieval theory of passion and its link with the theory of matter, as traced by Aristotle and his readers. Matter in itself is an excess, since it is the absolute potential as opposed to the actual. According to the philosopher, matter is like the womb that has an infinite appetite for being acted upon.[7] Thus what seems to take form is that the right medium is coincident with the rational choice, which allows human beings to oppose the inclination to the vice that derives from our materialism.

While the right medium is the way to control our materiality, or our inclination to the excess of passion, a confrontation or a parallel seems to be established between the materiality of possessions and that of the passions. The seeds of the problem of evil, as Dante will present them in the *Commedia*, seem to be implanted here. The question, then, that leads to doubt as a method in order to discover the truth – that is, "se la prima materia degli elementi era da Dio intesa" (if the prime matter of elements has been willed and or intellected by God) – correctly understood, means the following: If matter has been created by God, is its form in the mind of God? If this is true, then materiality is in God's command and will. The fourth treatise of the *Convivio*, however, exposes only the doubt about the origin of matter, not the solution. This problem is so difficult and dangerous that Dante tells his readers that because of it he has interrupted his philosophical search.

The reasons why Dante left the *Convivio* unfinished are suggested here. It is the problem of evil that determines what Freccero (1986, 1–28) has importantly seen as the failure, or better the shipwreck, of Dante's *Convivio*. For Freccero, this failure originates in the arrogance of the philosopher, a content on which we should return in the future. But now, rather than focus on the arrogance of the philosopher, we will only touch here on the apparent result of Dante's philosophical doubts and uncertainties that, at this point, dramatically open up a new field to be explored. It is in the poetry of the *Commedia* that Dante starts to give form to the problem of evil and its ontology. The *Inferno*, in its organization, is first of all the dramatization of the problem of evil and its ontological and historical roots. The fourth treatise of the *Convivio* suggests that Dante's doubts about matter originate in part from his condemnation of materialism, whose roots are related to the theory of matter. The last treatise suggests a parallel between the infinite desire of prime matter to be acted upon (matter being the absolute potentiality that always seeks its actualization) and the infinite desire for material goods as active in *avaritia*, which cannot be satisfied (IV.12). The roots of materialism are in matter; philosophically considered, matter is an infinite potentiality that looks for its actualization.

A continuity should be established here between the *Convivio* and the *Inferno*, which, in its first canto, indicates in the she-wolf's hunger an appetite that cannot be satisfied (1.49–50), and which in *Purgatorio* 20.10–12 is clearly the *figura* of *avaritia*. This is a line that continues in the *Monarchia* as well. The fourth treatise of the *Convivio* establishes that *avarizia* or the endless amassing of goods is dangerous for social life, and the *Monarchia* states that this opposes *iustitia*: "iustitiae maxime contrariatur cupiditas" (Justice highly opposes cupidity; 1.11.11). Dante's source here is book 5 of Aristotle's *Nicomachean Ethics*, which is devoted to justice. This idea is no doubt related to the reflection that this section of the *Convivio* organizes, in which Dante lists many *auctores* in order to support his condemnation of *avaritia*. It is an issue of great importance in the general economy of Dante's reflection that we unfortunately cannot discuss here. What can be said now is that the fourth treatise of the *Convivio* suggests that *avaritia* has its roots in the medieval Aristotelian theory of matter, since infinite potentiality is an excess and the ontological origin of evil. At the beginning of the *Inferno*, Dante is lost in a dark wood – what Plotinus and Augustine call "the region of Otherness." According to the Platonic and Neoplatonic tradition, this forest (*silva* in Latin) could be a transumptive way to introduce the theme of matter, the realm of matter, in its relation to evil, *hyle* being the original Greek form whose meaning is matter and which is translated as the Latin word *silva*.[8]

In summary, the fourth treatise makes comprehensible the pathway that drives Dante to exercise a kind of *censura* about what he has written in the previous treatises, and such *censura* seems mostly focused on remaking the discourse about human intellect. Such remaking, it has to be understood, is the beginning of a powerful rethinking. Dante introduces as his aim the fight "contra gli erranti." This aim drives his discussion of nobility. Reading the canzone, we may easily understand that the word "nobility" is the correlative of the intellect that God bestows on human beings. The ways of this bestowing are explained in the prose section, but the canzone requires an initial basic understanding of why the discussion of nobility is linked to a quotation from

Aquinas' *Summa contra gentiles*, and what the main topic is that is confronted here.

As previously said, Barolini (2014), in her rereading of the canzone, has stressed that the true heart of the discussion is *misura*. She confronts the Aristotelian weaving of the canzone and attends to the details of the Aristotelian theory of moral virtues. Having explored all these elements, she understands something of importance: Dante focuses on measure as the origin and result of the intellectual nobility of the human race. In this sense (going back to the canzone), when we read that nobility is the friend of the *donna gentile* (vv. 143–6), we understand in light of our previous discourse that friendship marks the relation between human intellect and the *donna gentile*. Thus, when in the prose section he tells his readers that after having lived and being involved in an intellectual crisis that gives rise to a break in his philosophical search he writes the canzone *Le dolci rime d'amor ch'io solia*, we may understand that the doubt about the origin of matter is in some dialectical way related to the right mean or *misura*, at focus in the canzone. The reader should be aware that materiality rooted in excess is counteracted by Dante's attempt to oppose what is beyond measure with that which is ruled by measure.

Dante opposes Cavalcanti's main assertion in "Donna me prega," that love is *oltre misura* – "oltre mesura di natura torna (44). His canzone *Donne ch'avete*[9] is a trace that testifies to his awareness" (44) of the meaning of this verse. In Dante's canzone, *misura* is an inner rule given to nature by God, one of whose names is *misura* (*metron*). Here in *Le dolci rime d'amor ch'io solia* the right medium as measure is a rule that regulates our moral behaviour. What is condemned and refuted in this framework is the excess. What must therefore be understood is the link with the doubt about the prime matter of the elements, as the prose of *Convivio* 4.1 introduces. In my reading, the text suggests a link between such doubt and Dante's previous discourse about his love for the *donna gentile* as confronted in the first three treatises of the *Convivio* (especially the second and third) using a covert speech.

In my reading, in fact, these treatises contain a discussion of the nature of human intellect shaped in a highly rhetorical way, which, because of it, needs to be detected. The fourth treatise eliminates the problematic issue of the love-contemplation of the *donna gentile*. Dante, however, returns here to discuss human mind, but his discussion has a different perspective. The intellect now no longer seeks to contemplate the *donna gentile*. We are told that it has in itself potentially the forms it needs (IV.21.5).

This new perspective, once it is related to the doubt about the origin of matter, tells us something very important. I have stressed that the peculiarities of intellection in the third treatise show some heterodox inclinations in which the idea that the intellect is common is assumed, but in a perspective in which the Aristotelian radical penchant has no space. What must be understood, however, is that in its Averroistic formulation the theory of common intellect is related to that of matter. In the Averroistic frame, the eternity of matter implies eternal generation: the individual provided with the sensitive soul is just a mortal being, because in this theory the human race is eternal but the individual disappears. The intellect in its eternity is not part of this dynamic, but the individual can have only a momentary link with this intellect that, for its part, copulates with the human race (its phantasms) eternally. According to this theory, in the human being taken only as individual, nothing is eternal: what is eternal is the common intellect that is, however, separate and detached from the individual.

The theory of *copulatio* and how a *continuatio* can be established between the individual sensitive soul and the common intellect is basic in this line of thought, a thought of which Cavalcanti's "Donna me prega" is a document. Belonging to Dante's time is a text dedicated – and thus we assume well known – to Cavalcanti and possibly to Dante – namely, the *Quaestio de felicitate* by Giacomo da Pistoia, which shows how the individual can be linked to the common intellect. True happiness, we are told, is continuous, but this continuity in the Averroistic frame is not of the individual, but of the common possible intellect. Left to a material life and dimension, the individual's sensitive soul, in this theory, is under the rule of matter as an infinite desire to be acted upon; matter being passive, the human being is subjected to passions and infinite desire. Cavalcanti was the poet who has dramatized in his verses this human condition, assigning to his canzone "Donna me prega" the establishment of its ontological origin in the medieval theory of matter (Ardizzone 2002). Dante is indebted partially to Cavalcanti when he depicts the passion of love in canto 5 of the *Inferno*, but a great part of the entire canticle is ruled by the excess determined by human materiality when this is not balanced by the measure provided by the intellectual choice. According to Averroes, intellection is an activity performed by the possible intellect, assumed to be a separate being, accidentally copulating with the individual's phantoms. In light of it, the individual is left to materiality because, as an individual, mostly ruled by the sensitive soul's appetites, he lacks as individual the rationality that allows him to oppose materiality.

Going back to the fourth treatise, if we evaluate the notion of *misura* as basic, a link must be established between the poetry and the prose section. The reason is that *misura* (or *mezura*) tacitly opposes *oltre misura* ("Donna me prega"; 44). This is a peculiarity of matter, which, being an infinite eternal potentiality, has no measure. The relation between the eternity of matter and the eternity of the world has probably played a part in Dante's reflection and tormented doubt about the origin of prime matter. What my reading of the first three treatises has introduced, however, seems to be rethought and reshaped in the fourth. Dante activates a new perspective focusing, since the canzone, on the intellectual as a divine gift bestowed to the individual and named *grazia*. It is such a gift that allows human beings to choose the right medium. My point here is that establishing the canon of "medium," which is coincident with the election of the practice of moral virtues, Dante abandons his previous discourse on intellectual happiness, as in treatise three. Now, happiness is guaranteed by the practice of the right medium. The aim of perfect intellection is no longer the focus of treatise, and the love for the *donna gentile* no longer aims at establishing the possible intellect that looks for the knowledge of a divine idea.

The prose will shortly clarify that the human individual intellect is potentially endowed with all the intellectual forms – that is, it has no need to search for its form. In this way ends the love for the *donna gentile* as conceived and discussed in treatises two and three of the *Convivio*.

The theory of intellect in the fourth treatise is new and important; it suggests that a link can be established between the doubt regarding the origin of matter and the new way to discuss intellection, in which the doubt itself works to open a pathway to a general rethinking. In fact, it is at first the canzone *Le dolci rime d'amor ch'io solia* that shows that Dante changes his focus. I have traced a pathway in which the theory of nobility was related to a larger discussion of time and change, only touching on the paradox about the eternity of the human species. I also stressed the internal relation between the theory of the right medium, or *misura*, and that of matter, the latter introducing the excess as the ontology of matter, an excess proper also to the desire of material goods or *cupiditas* of avarice.

These elements, connected as they are, indicate a relational field that is very important for the meaning of the treatise itself. In this perspective, a relation should be evaluated between the theory of matter as touched in the prose (IV.1.8) and that of the intellect as organized in a most complex way in the second and third treatise. Dante's refraining for a time from coming into the presence of her countenance, while living, as it were, in her absence, indicates a field of tension determined precisely by the doubt about the origin of matter. In fact, in relation to it the lady has altered the tenderness of her looks at him, especially when he was seeking to know whether the prime matter of the elements was *intelletta* or willed by God, or both. It is in this context that Dante begins to consider the theory of true nobility. This relational field that my reading points out suggests that Dante was reconsidering his first approach to the theory of intellection as proposed in the second and third treatises, introducing in the canzone a new name, *grazia*, later reshaping the notion of intellect in light of it. In this reshaping, the relational field works if we evaluate the inner link between *medietas* and *misura*, as opposed to matter and excess, as manifestations of its eternity.

It is perhaps the work of Bonaventure that helped Dante evaluate how dangerous the philosophical thought related to this theory can be. For Bonaventure, the theory of intellect as common and thus eternal is intimately connected with that of the eternity of the world. If the world is eternal, matter is, of course, also eternal. Bonaventure also discusses the eternity of the human species: If we consider that the world is eternal, then we must accept that from eternity there were many human beings. And if the world is eternal, then the human intellect must be eternal as well (Petagine 2009, 265–79). Dante, as my reading has proposed, did not accept the Averroistic theory of intellect. However, in the light of a totally new perspective, of eradicating the errors as derived from the *errantes*, he may have started to eradicate, and thus reshape, aspects and contents previously discussed that could be seen by readers as close to the errors. Because of this, he activates a kind of *retractatio* in which he acts as a censor; such censorship works in creating a new context, and it is in this context that the new enunciated theory of intellect must be seen. The theory of nobility he shapes opposes the *errantes*, but the error does not belong just to the social field; rather, it is intertwined with different lines of thought, as I have proposed above.

This discussion, however, goes beyond the scope of this book. I will therefore limit my discourse by briefly examining the discourse about intellection in the fourth treatise, since it seems to record a changing perspective.

Scholars like Fioravanti (2014), who do not recognize this shift in perspective, must be evaluated in light of the fact that his reading of the first three treatises does not imply a theory of intellection formulated in the ways I have indicated above.[10] In the last section of this chapter, I will try to indicate how Dante establishes his new perspective.

I start by stressing a passage of the canzone in which the introduction of the word *persona* represents an attempt to evaluate how much and in which way *persona* includes a detachment from the previous contents. We will see that this detachment includes a new idea of happiness – new, that is, compared with the idea of happiness as given in the third treatise, where happiness was intellectual. Now, happiness is the result not of intellectual virtues but of moral virtue. What takes place is the moralization of human happiness. Nobility – that is, our intellectual nature – allows us to remain inside the borders of the right medium. This detachment includes, above all, the discussion of the human intellect. I will shortly consider this issue in this final part of my study, in an attempt to show how it seems to oppose an idea of human being that is ruled by excess, material desires, materiality, and an immoderate desire of goods. The notion of *cupiditas* as embracing different kinds of desires, all motivated by the material component of human beings, begins to take shape here.

In the canzone, at lines 114–20, we read that *gentilezza* or nobility is a divine gift from which our virtue derives. In other words, nobility is not coincident with virtue, but derives from *grazia*, which is a natural, endowed gift that allows for ethical behaviour. Dante's position is clear: "ch'elli son quasi dei / quei c'han tal grazia fuor di tutti rei; / ché solo Iddio all'anima la dona / che vede in sua persona / perfettamente star: sì ch'ad alquanti / ch'è 'l seme di felicità, si acosta, / messo da Dio nell'anima ben posta" (For they are almost gods who have such grace without a spot of vice. For God alone bestows it on that soul which he perceives dwells perfectly within its person; and so, as some perceive, it is the seed of happiness, instilled by God).

This gift is thus given to those predisposed to it. The passage quoted above contains the word *persona*. At first, Dante's statement sounds strange, since it seems to replace an historical privilege with one based on nature.

However, this passage perhaps holds the key to something important.

Nobility derives from God, who gives grace to those souls he sees well placed in their *persona*. It is this word that offers a clue. According to Severinus Boethius, who took the term from the theory of the Trinity and gave its definition, *persona* is linked to what is personal and individual – that is, "singularis: nusquam in universalibus persona dici potest, sed in singularibus tantum atque in individuis." It is not correct to use *persona* in reference to universal things, since the word applies only to things that are singular and belong to individuals.[11] Boethius stresses that *persona* belongs to the individual as a rational being: "naturae rationabilis individua substantia" (an individual substance of rational nature). Aquinas, on the trace of Boethius, writes that "persona ... significat singulare in rationalibus substantiis" (person means singular in rational substances). Thus *persona* implies an individual rational being in which what is individual is coincident with what is rational, and this is implicit in the word "persona" itself. It should also be noted that *persona* is related to soul and to corporeality. In relation to *persona*, we may note that *persona* and *anima* are related. What penetrates here is a principle that connects what is individual with what is rational and corporeal at once. The word "persona" encompasses all these meanings and implicitly opposes Dante's discussion as authored in the second and third treatises.

In the prose section, the conversation about nobility follows a discussion that was anticipated in the third canzone (114–20). Nobility is a gift given by God to the soul that is perfectly suited to the person. It is not the seed of happiness for all people, but only for those whose souls are properly located in the body (see Falzone 2010, 81–93). This theory reverses and changes the perspective Dante has organized in the third treatise, in which happiness consists in the contemplation of the lady. This was an intellectual happiness, and what the text (both the canzone and the prose) suggested in a most enigmatic way was that this happiness is the result of a collective knowledge. We will see that *grazia* allows an ethical happiness – that is, a happiness which is coincident with the practice of moral virtues. It is also true that the text is not always consistent. Nevertheless, earthly happiness was assumed to be identical with this contemplation, and the doubtful attitude was related to the fact that Dante, in the third treatise, was inconsistent in attributing this power to the human being. The fourth treatise introduces Empire as the political institution rooted in the historical goal of ensuring human happiness. The individual human being cannot by himself satisfy his needs; he is a social or political animal, and because of this, it is in society that he is at his best and fulfills his potentiality (IV.4.2). Here Dante initiates a discussion of the first forms of human associations and small communities. Gradually, he establishes the origin of cities, always with the aim of human satisfaction. He then discusses the goal and highest good of the human being. Following a part of Aristotle's *Nicomachean Ethics*, he conceives this goal as moral or ethical, where morality is coincident with choosing and following the *mean*. Grace creates in us a habit of making right choices, and the goal of the human being is moral virtue. Virtue is a *habitus* (*abito eligente*) that consists in our capacity for right choice or, more precisely, in our capacity to establish ourselves in the mean position between two mutually opposed extremes. Because nobility, as we read, is perfection of all things in their own nature – "perfezione di tutte le cose in propria natura" – such perfection derives from one principle, namely, the *habitus* of right choice, or the choice of the right mean.

There follows the list of the eleven virtues organized as the practice of *medietas*. What most interests us here is that happiness is defined as "operazione secondo virtute in vita perfetta" (operation according to virtue in a perfect life; IV.17.8). It is easy to see that happiness based on moral virtues is different, and the opposite of the happiness Dante was searching for in the third treatise, where happiness was the result of the intellectual, rather than moral, virtues. This is a theme of great importance for Dante, and on such distinction will be shaped the character of Ulysses in *Inferno* 26. In the third treatise, intellectual virtues aimed at the intellectual happiness of contemplating the gentle lady. This happiness, which was coincident with philosophy as a divine activity, was proposed in the third treatise as an activity shared by separate substances, God, and human beings. The latter, however, can partake of intellection only in a discontinuous way. The *gentilezza* of the *donna gentile* was intellectual. Perhaps one of its models were the noble substances of the *Liber de causis*. There, intellectuality and nobility were one and the same thing. According to Aristotle, Dante says, there are in fact two forms of happiness: one intellectual and contemplative, the other related to the life of moral action. Only if our morally active life reaches happiness are we able to achieve contemplative happiness (IV.17.9).

At this point, Dante poses a question: Why, if contemplative happiness is more excellent than the happiness based on moral action, do the moral virtues come before the intellectual? The explanation offered is that this hierarchy derives from the fact that people understand moral virtues better than the intellectual ones, but this explanation does not actually explain so much.

In summary, in treatise four, virtue derives from nobility; nobility is given by God and is a divine infusion (IV.20.7). This nobility is the seed of human happiness, and virtue is the habit of exercising right choice.

Another important topic is related to the discussion of human intellect as it is reshaped in the fourth treatise. In an explicit mode, it changes what the previous treatise has introduced. Here we read that every human being receives his own intellect from God. Fundamental to this claim is the following addition: the possible intellect "potenzialmente in se adduce tutte le forme che sono nel suo produttore" (the possible intellect has in itself potentially the forms that are in its creator). This is different from what we read in the second treatise, and especially the third, regarding the meaning that the love for the *donna gentile* introduces and represents. There we were told that the lady is a separate form or idea to be contemplated, and that this contemplation for human beings is *discontinuous*. But, as noted above, Dante was not consistent. In fact, such contemplation – the contemplation of a separate form in our earthly life – was also, in the same treatise, apparently denied. Here in the fourth treatise, the forms that are in God are potentially in the human possible intellect. The result is that the *donna gentile*, described as a divine idea that the possible intellect seeks to contemplate in life, no longer plays a role. This may be why the commentary does not at all discuss the *donna gentile*.

From this, another modification follows: the highest intellectual virtue is no longer that which is modelled on a contemplation similar to that proper to God – that is, God's way of contemplation – as established in book 10 of Aristotle's *Nicomachean Ethics*. In fact, the theory of contemplation in general is modified. At first (IV.22.12), we read that in our mind we have a practical and a contemplative activity. Again it is established that contemplation is superior to practical activity. But virtue is here identified with the practice of the *honestum* related to prudence, temperance, fortitude, and justice. The adverb *onestamente* assumed in relation to its Latin form, *honestum,* if compared to the meaning established in the third treatise, and in the *De vulgari eloquentia*, as well as in the *Vita nuova*, can be assumed as a word belonging to the field of mobile semantics.[12] Even more striking, however, is the explanation given of contemplation. Rather than dealing with contemplation as given in book 10 of the *Nicomachean Ethics*, Dante goes back to the Pauline-Augustinian theory of contemplation, according to which humans cannot see God in this life but contemplate him only in his reflections or mirrors – that is, in the works of creation. Our beatitude is determined by our seed. Perfect speculation in life is impossible, and we must rest content with contemplating God's effects. This is reiterated at IV.23 with a quotation from the Gospel of Mark. A purely active life as predicated by the three sects (Epicureans, Stoics, and Peripatetics) is dismissed. It is part of what belongs to the "monimento" (sepulcher), which, in the Gospel, represents what is *ricettacolo* – that is, receptive of the corruptible. We read that beatitude is not in the morally active life; rather, it is contemplation that is the most spiritual divine activity, which, however, we cannot reach in this life, because we cannot in our earthly lives reach God. According to this crucial passage, the reason is not that God is beyond us but that He is before us: "li precederà in Galilea." Contemplation is confirmed as supreme, but it is different from the contemplation that Dante had established in the third treatise and on which the love for the *donna gentile* was founded.

In light of this result, and from a brief comparison between the construction set up in the second and third treatises on the one hand, and the fourth on the other, we are invited to conclude that when Dante speaks out against the *errantes*, he wishes to emend also what he assumed to be his own errors, or what could be seen as errors. In any case, the doubts and uncertainties expressed in the *Convivio* show that its author was aware that, in his discourse and in his fascination for the *donna gentile*, he was embracing contents that tended towards heterodox issues. Dante returns to the roots of the Western tradition. He assumes Platonic and Aristotelian contents and links them with theological contents, but rethinks them through a healthy transfusion that results in a new perspective. The *Convivio* is the product of long application and study. In it a new idea of the human being takes form, in which new trends determine Dante's method of revisiting the old contents and revitalizing them in light of the most recent and new.

In the fourth treatise, there occurs a reshaping that dismisses many crucial facets previously accepted. The treatise leads to the *Commedia*, a work that implies a different perspective and attitude, and which stresses even more strongly the need to be free from errors. The political dimension that was implicitly included in the discussion of the first treatises in this last part is evident and coincides with the creation of Empire. The human being is defined for the first time as a social-political animal (*compagnevole*), whose happiness is possible within this institution. The third treatise, according to our reading, attempted a more arduous aim: for human beings, intellectual happiness coincides with social happiness. Earthly happiness is both social and intellectual. In the fourth treatise, however, there emerges a new idea: namely, that human beings need an individual who guarantees that the natural human goal is fulfilled. This special individual will be defined at greater length in the *Monarchia*. This work is responsible for the idea that the organization of and responsibility for civic life and happiness is trusted to a single human being. Finally, an issue to be touched on is the following. The *Monarchia*, which Dante wrote during his exile and certainly after the final treatise of *Convivio*, is the only work that introduces, and very briefly touches on, the possible intellect as one and common and as better actualized by the whole human community. The text also recalls Averroes. This notion of the common possible intellect appears to be linked to Dante's theory of Empire, insofar as it represents the most natural political organization based on a community of thought.

The question in the *Monarchia* is put forth with clarity: "Quid est finis totius humanae civilitatis?" (What is the goal of human society as a whole?; 1.3). The answer is unequivocal. There is an operation proper to all human beings: namely, the apprehensive being of the possible intellect. To fulfil this potentiality is the goal of human beings. Thus the *Monarchia* makes programmatic the principle and rule of the One. The *Monarchia*, according to what we read, in fact implies, first of all, the principle of the One, or the One as principle and goal. In the light of this principle, political life and intellectual life are related and in fact coincide, and political unity appears to be the natural historical condition of a *de facto* natural intellectual unity. Dante's reader might think that this perspective would be anticipated in the fourth treatise of the *Convivio*, which was written before the political treatise, and that it would be possible to establish a continuity between the last section of vernacular doctrinal and the Latin political treatises. However, this direct continuity cannot be established. In fact, reading the fourth treatise, in the section devoted to the intellect, we see that the text offers a discussion of the intellect that has nothing to do with the theory of the contemplation of a separate form which is one (the *donna gentile* was presented as one and a separate substance or divine idea in the third treatise), or with the possible intellect conceived as able to actualize a common activity of thinking, as *Monarchia* 1 proposes. In the fourth treatise of the *Convivio*, the intellect is something given by God: it is *grazia*. The crucial point, however, is how Dante discusses individuation. It seems that he organizes individuation in a way that cannot allow any doubt. It is no longer bodily events, which could include senses and imagination, that mark the individual, a theory that (as I emphasized in the third chapter) left space for doubt about the common and separate nature of the intellect; rather, it is the father's seed and the mother's menses:

> E però dico che quando l'umano seme cade nel suo recettaculo, cioè nella matrice, esso porta seco la vertù dell'anima generativa e la vertù del cielo e la vertù delli elementi legati, cioè la complessione; [e] matura e dispone

> la materia alla vertù formativa, la quale diede l'anima [del] generante; e la vertù formativa prepara li organi alla vertù celestiale, che produce della potenza del seme l'anima in vita.
>
> Therefore I say that when the seed of man falls into its receptacle, namely the matrix, it carries with it the virtue of the generative soul, and the virtue of heaven, and the virtue of the combined elements, namely temperament. It matures and disposes the material to receive the formative virtue given by the soul of the generator, and the formative virtue prepares the organs to receive the celestial virtue, which brings the soul from the potentiality of the seed into life. (IV.21.4)

It is on this individual soul that infused grace is bestowed, and here the intellect is no doubt the form of body: "La quale, incontanente produtta, riceve dalla vertù del motore del cielo lo intelletto possibile; lo quale potenzialmente in sé adduce tutte le forme universali, secondo che sono nel suo produttore, e tanto meno quanto più dilungato dalla prima Intelligenza è" (As soon as it is produced it receives from the virtue of the celestial mover the possible intellect, which draws into itself in potentiality all of the universal forms as they are found in its maker, to an ever lesser degree the more it is removed from the primal Intelligence; IV.21.5) (Nardi 1960a, 22–48; 1985, 206–24).[13] A careful reader will note that an intellectual unifying principle persists, insofar as the intellect derives from God. The embryological diversities among human beings, however, are basic and responsible for an idea of intellect that belongs to the individual, and so is individual. The idea that God inspires in the human being the intellectual soul implies once more that what is intellectual in human beings derives from the same unique source. This is another way of stating that human beings share a unique intellectual principle. The intellectual as a divine gift is proper to all human beings, but is strongly individualized in the prose that I have quoted above.

This idea of a common and universal thinking, for Dante, is so important that the *Monarchia* introduces the possible intellect as a potentiality that can be actualized only in the collective. Dante recalls Averroes[14] no doubt because he wants his meaning to be perfectly clear. The possible intellect actualizes itself better in the human community. Dante seems to think that the intellectual unity of human beings is something of great importance. He does not shape it in light of the Averroistic philosophy but rather uses it as a point of reference. The third treatise of the *Convivio* proposed that it is possible to think this notion of a common intellect in light of the notion of *verbum-logos* and biblical *sapientia*. This attention to the *verbum-logos* as foundational for the community (mostly in the Augustinian formulation) was, since Dante's youth, a point of cultivated attention: the death of Beatrice was a public loss that involved the city – not only Florence, but the world city – as we see when, in the beginning of chapter 30 of the *Vita nuova*, Dante quotes Jeremiah's *Lamentations*. Later, the canzone *Amor che ne la mente mi ragiona* was still linking intellection and the interior word. This introduces for the first time the idea of a group of people that the shared love-intellection of the unique *donna gentile* manifests as a community that is one, while also composed of many human beings.

It is extremely important in our reading that the reformulation of the theory of the intellect is organized in the treatise that opens by introducing the doubt about the origin of matter, which Dante touches at the beginning of the prose section. To consider matter in relation to God – willed, created, or actualized by God expressed as a doubt – opens one of the great debates active in Dante's time. The importance of this debate has been underlined by Nardi (1985, 197–206). This should probably be seen in light of the theories of the ideas in the mind of God and, in the case of *intesa*, would have had as first meaning that of *intellecta*, and thus would probably imply that matter could be created. A parallel is suggested, in the fourth treatise, between the appetite for riches, which chapters 11–13 characterizes as without end, and the peculiar indefiniteness of prime matter. As an infinite quest for actualization that corresponds to an immoderate desire inscribed in physics, physics and its laws preside over the corporeal component of the human being, according to Aristotle and Aristotelianism. Dante seems to be aware of the synchronous debate on matter – a debate that started with Plato, was reshaped by Aristotle, was discussed by Plotinus and Augustine, and was continued in Averroes, Peter John Olivi, and Aquinas, among others. Bonaventure shows how the theory of matter as eternal, in its link with the theory of the eternity of the world, is fatally tied to that of the intellect conceived of as one and common. However, if matter is God's creation, then it is part of the world harmony of human beings in their relation to God. Olivi's teaching and lectures, active in the Franciscan Convent of Santa Croce in Florence in Dante's time, were maybe responsible for the link between the theory of matter and the condemnation of materialism, to which is opposed poverty, as *Inferno* 1 proposes.

The *Monarchia* will reintroduce materialism as an infinite appetite for goods, which the monarch will oversee. The most interesting aspect here is that his being free from avarice or immoderate desires for goods derives from the fact that he already possesses everything and therefore has no desires. Materialism is confirmed as part of the human ontology, and politics must be realistically based on this awareness. The *Monarchia* will openly reintroduce the possible intellect as a potentiality that human beings may actualize as *humanitas*. In the fourth chapter of this study, I informed the reader that this word, *humanitas*, refers to a prohibited proposition discussed in Hissette's work on the 1277 Parisian condemnations (1977, article 124, 201).

Our reading has underlined how Dante, in various ways and since his Florentine years, had formulated the idea that human beings think best when they think together. Perhaps during the time that he was still working on the *Convivio*, he thought that introducing a doubt about prime matter would make manifest how his position was far from the theory of intellect in some way associated with an Averroistic line. In light of this, we may deduce that in his love for the *donna gentile*, as discussed in the second and third treatises the *Convivio*, perhaps entered intellectual temptations inclined to encompass heterodox nuances that the fourth attempted to eliminate. Dante's position here is clear: he does not intend to leave any doubt about his idea on the human being and his way of intellection. He rejects the Averroistic position. At the same time, however, encompassing a different tradition, he holds that human beings can and should think together. The *Monarchia* will unambiguously introduce the possible intellect as better actualized by human community. Dante here appears free from every conditioning fear; he speaks with clarity, and his speech does not conceal any heterodox penchant. Such freedom in the *Monarchia* can be explained perhaps in relation to his writing of *Purgatorio* and *Paradiso*. An interlinear relation does exist between the *Monarchia* and this writing, while the fourth treatise of the *Convivio*, in our reading, postulates and prefigures one of the reasons for Dante's writing of the *Inferno*.

To complete this study, the evaluation of one point remains: the importance Dante gives to the moral virtues as a pathway to happiness in this life. Practice of the right mean based on the moral virtues and *continentia* suggest that Dante is changing the perspective that was active in the second and third treatises of the *Convivio*. This is confirmed when we consider the mobile semantics of the field of *honestum*, which, in the last treatise, seems to lose its meaning as something linked to beauty as an intellectual activity. We may thus hypothesize that in the fourth treatise Dante is attempting to close what has been the subject of his discussion in the second and third treatises. The choice of *medietas* marks the end of the intellectual challenge. The love for the gentle lady presented as a divine idea was also an attempt to ascend to the ways of the cosmos. The human being seems to be naturally and strongly inclined towards this end because there is, in human nature, according to the *Convivio*, something divine.

The turning of the page of the fourth treatise is therefore the end of a heroic ideal and the opening of another ideal: that of Empire. Looking at the canzoni, we may say that the style of the first two canzoni was the tragic; it was high and sublime (*De vulgari* II.2), because it was intellectual. Love was coincident with the intellectual life and the intellectual virtues. This was, in fact, not just a literary-philosophical project but also a project for a way of life. It was an aristocratic project in which the aristocracy was reinterpreted as intellectual.

A book widely diffused and commented on in the thirteenth century, the *Liber de causis* circulated the idea that noble and intellectual were coincident because true nobility meant having proximity to the divine being, who was the *intellectualitas* itself. Thus the *Liber de causis*, a textbook then at the University of Paris, was imposing a different idea about nobility in the same years in which the crisis of the nobility was evident and widely recognized.

In the Neoplatonic hierarchy of intellectual beings, a new concept of nobility takes shape, supercedes nobility of birth, and throws it into crisis. But for Dante the end of the construction of the true nobility as intellectual runs parallel with the historical crisis of nobility of birth. The palinode of the canzone *Le dolci rime d'amor ch'io solia* thus celebrates two different ends. One is that of the nobility of birth as a privilege derived from family, ancient riches, and good manners. The other is that of an intellectual aristocracy. The notion of virtue or excellence remains, but the new excellence rewards the grace that allows us to stay within the mean. Moral virtues impose their supremacy, and the decline of nobility of birth is more or less synchronous in Dante's work with the historical decline of the supremacy of intellectual virtues and intellectual aristocracy.

Conclusion

Reading as the Angels Read has started its investigation by taking into consideration the statement that Dante introduces in the first line of the *Convivio*, where he cites the opening of Aristotle's *Metaphysics* – "Tutti gli uomini naturalmente desiderano di sapere" (all men by nature desire to know) – and has explored whether, and in what way, this desire can be satisfied. According to Aquinas, this aspiration, interpreted as the desire to know God, cannot be fulfilled in this life. Dante fashions his own complex answer by developing a personal and suggestive pathway in which this desire cannot be fulfilled by the individual human being but perhaps by a plural subject that can in this life reach the contemplation of a separate substance or a divine idea, which is to say that this subject can know God. This divine idea, in the text called *donna gentile*, is the protagonist of an abstract philosophical narration that focuses on the human attempt to enjoy this superior knowledge, which is coincident with the knowledge of God. This intellectual operation is related to the quest for what the philosophers of the thirteenth century called "intellectual happiness." Dante confronts this issue in various ways in the *Convivio*, in particular in the third treatise, when he discusses the nature of the human mind. According to the interpretation put forth in my study, Dante's answer is concealed in a highly organized, rhetorical way.

Because it is an earthly happiness, it implies a *bios theoretikos*. Dante seems to think that this dimension is proper to the community that the love for the *donna gentile* indicates. This is the beginning of a link between speculation and political reality. It is worth noting that, in suggesting this activity as proper to a community, Dante was perhaps rethinking a tenet of Aristotle's *Nicomachean Ethics* and *Politics*, where social happiness was more important than that of the individual. However, the Averroistic theory of intellection and happiness no doubt helped him to clarify his position.

Dante, we must note, does not embrace an Averroistic tenet and does not accept, as already said, the materialistic counterpart of this theory as in Averroes and his followers. The fact that human contemplation is *discontinuata* implies that such intellectual activity is conceived in terms completely different from those related to the theory of intellectual happiness. The third treatise shows that this idea of a common intellection, by introducing a subject that is impersonal and may be plural, results, on my reading, in a community of human beings who share the same object of love-contemplation, this object being a divine idea or a separate substance. This is also presented again in a different framework in the final section of the third treatise in an attempt to link the idea of intellection as common with the philosophical Christian theory of the *logos-verbum*.

A careful reading of the doctrinal treatise suggests that the evolution of this idea in Dante is the antecedent of what he will call *universitas* or *humanitas* in the *Monarchia*. The chronology of writing is important in this development, and the Latin political treatise should be read, in part, as the culmination of this line of thought. This development of the idea of a subject, that is one and plural at once, suggested as able to contemplate the *donna gentile*, identified as a divine idea, is a relevant part of my study.

In the *Convivio*, Dante locates this subject not just in the community of philosophers but in the human community that will be coincident in the *Monarchia* with the *universitas* of human beings ruled by the emperor or ruler. This *universitas* is coincident with the entire human community.

Both in the canzone *Amor che ne la mente mi ragiona* and in the prose section that comments on it, Dante establishes a subject that is plural and one and introduces a vocabulary in which a collective name, *gente*, enters. The prose section makes this more powerful by introducing an impersonal verbal form. In this way, it creates a grammatical-rhetorical mechanism that the reader must collaborate with in order to open. This content must be understood in relation to a social awareness that is present in the doctrinal work, a social awareness that is related not just to Dante's knowledge of Aristotle's *Politics*, as evident in the fourth treatise. It derives perhaps also from Dante's reading of works that are related to the *Politics* but were also in circulation before the diffusion of the Latin version of Aristotle's work.

Taking into account a few obscure passages of the second and third treatises of the *Convivio*, along with some contents of the treatise on the vernacular (*De vulgari eloquentia*), the reader is alerted that, since the *De vulgari eloquentia*, Dante has been attempting to create an ideal *typus* (Spitzer 1976) of language that corresponds to an ideal *societas*, identified by the creation and use of a poetic language that he calls *volgare illustre*. In the same way, he identifies a court that is dispersed and yet unified, since the poetic body is one.

In this, a sense of an ideal unity composed of many can be established that is in continuity with the idea that what is one can be rethought as being one and plural at once, and composed of many people linked through a common purpose, or through their participation in something common. The *De vulgari eloquentia* shows a political awareness of both poetry and language that takes as its model the Sicilian court and looks towards the creation of a new *koine* as result of a new *koinonia*, or community, that the use of the *volgare illustre* allows to identify. While the *koine* of the *volgare illustre* is built by poets, the *koine* of the *Convivio* is much larger. It virtually tends to identify a new social community whose members, although they do not know Latin but only the vernacular, are inclined towards knowledge as a common human attitude. Priscian's grammar, which underlines a series of words that are singular but express a plurality of things or people, can be recalled for the word *gente*, which Dante introduces to describe a plurality of individuals sharing some peculiarities that make them a unity in relation to their activity of intellection and goals.

This sense of a higher unity may be rethought in light of new social realities that were arising in the twelfth and thirteenth centuries. Membership in a community is part of the culture of the Middle Ages. This creates social groups united by a shared activity. Groups such as *hansa*, guilds, and the corporations of arts typically have a legal status. We may speculate that Dante's intuition of a community, in which the unity is composed of a many, parallels a notion we may indicate as *persona morale* (moral persona). This derives from the *Digestum*, as part of the Justinian codex and its glossators, a field of law that can be traced also in the *Decretum Gratiani* (Michaud-Quantin 1974). An example of this moral *persona*, which is not an actual person, was emerging in the twelfth century as an object of study. According to Pope Innocent IV, for example, *collectivitas* is a *fictiva persona* (*fingitur una persona*), and such *collectivitas* is an intellectual name (Michaud-Quantin 1974, 207). This analysis brings us very close to an article that was part of the 219 propositions prohibited in

Paris in 1277 and which stigmatized the word *humanitas*, because, as we read, "Humanitas non est forma rei, sed rationis" (*humanitas* does not express the form of a thing, but of reason; proposition 124 in Hissette 1977, 201). Hissette assumes that the article is prohibited because *humanitas* appears to be related to the notion of the unique intellect.

It is well known that before the discovery of Aristotle's *Politics* the basis of political teaching was in canonical and civil right. In this we may perceive a direction of Dante's thought that he may have developed in the years of his exile in Bologna and also in the cities of Veneto, like Verona and perhaps Padua.

In these cities, the study of the Justinian Codex was extremely important. In Padua in particular, a class of notaries was studying this text and its glossators along with Cicero's *De finibus* (Witt 2000). We know that Dante spent two years in Verona (1302–4) and was in Verona again from 1304 to 1306 (or perhaps 1305). He may also have been in Padua as well, if we believe that he met with Giotto di Bondone while he was working in the Cappella Scrovegni (Petrocchi). It is worth noting that if the notion of *persona morale* is suggested in the *De vulgari eloquentia* as a *fictiva* unity of a court dispersed and unified in light of the *volgare illustre*, in roughly the same years, Dante identifies a larger community in the people who know only the vernacular as a potential new public that the *Convivio* would help to educate.

The fourth book of the *Convivio* bears evident traces of Aristotle's *Politics*. Dante's vocabulary, however, shows an awareness that derives from life experiences and readings that go beyond Aristotle. From the activity of notaries, legal scholars, and readers of the codex, and from that of doctors in law, Dante developed an awareness of entities that his travels and stays in the north helped him to evaluate. The canonical right and the civil right gave great importance to associative phenomena that were active in social life and, in some cases, they were also part of what Gratian's *Decretum* indicated as local customs (Ardizzone 2013). The fourth treatise of the *Convivio*, as well as the *Monarchia*, bears traces of these.

An attention to ideal intellectual groups that create a *de facto* community may be considered the antecedent of the human community as a subject that embodies the view that human beings think better when they think together. This notion will enter, we said, in the *Monarchia*, where words like *universitas* and *humanitas* represent an awareness that now reaches its apex. *Universitas* is the human ensemble, but it cannot be detached here from the notion of Empire as the political-legal entity that makes human beings an organized unity.

That the Empire is the result of small social entities that start with family, as Dante writes, must now be rethought in light of the fact that, for Dante, these social groups included communities that were legally organized as the result of local customs. The fourth treatise of the *Convivio*, and later the *Monarchia*, introduces a word that belongs to the north: *vicinia*, an assembly of *vicini* (neighbours) that can have a legal character (Ardizzone 2013). In the *Convivio*, Dante starts by circumscribing this collective dimension. For instance, his first word is a quotation from the *Metaphysics* of Aristotle: *Tutti* (*Omnes homines*). The work of reading helps to detect the sense of community in evolution that lives within the *Convivio* as part of a political endeavour. The unity of people who contemplate the *donna gentile*, and whom Dante indicates as *gente*, is an example of a virtuous society grounded in intellectual activity. For Dante, an intellectual link superior to the individual seems to empower individual contemplation in a collective contemplation. This is evident in the third treatise, where philosophical contemplation is established as proper to all human beings.

The fourth treatise will introduce the tenet taken directly or indirectly from the *Politics* – that is, that of the human being as a political animal. Of great importance is the parallel Dante activates between the ontological intellectual essence of the living being and his political essence. This is something that was traced to some extent in Alfarabi, but Dante did not know Alfarabi's *Città virtuosa*, which contains this theory. As mentioned above, Dante starts to shape this idea in his Florentine years, but it is the *Convivio* that organizes the idea in a more concrete way. The notion of the human mind is part of this construction. The human being, to whom (in the fourth treatise) is given the grace or nobility of intellect as something individual and common at once, is a crucial issue of the *Convivio*. In the fourth treatise, this emerges in the canzone *Le dolci rime d'amor ch'io solia*, when Dante indirectly reiterates that human beings share an intellectual activity bestowed by God and thus the intrinsic unity of the human intellectual activity. That this unity is not intended in Averroistic terms appears clearly from the discussion of the possible intellect in the prose of the fourth treatise, where the possible intellect is, for the first time, openly recalled and proposed in terms that dissolve every heterodox temptation or *suspicio*. These heterodox fields contribute to shape Dante's position in the treatise three of *Convivio*. Dante, however, seems to be the first to regard the human being as a universal subject without devaluing his individuality.

It is important to recall that, for Aristotle, politics is an architectonic science. In his *Metaphysics*, Aristotle defines the word "architectonic" because metaphysics is also an architectonic science. At A, 2, 982a16–17, he explains that a science is architectonic when it has command of the other sciences and is superior to them. It is the science that knows the goal according to which everything must be done or made. This goal is the common good and, in general, the best end in the natural order. The science that speculates on first principles and first causes is *sophia*, which is also an architectonic science. Politics, as an architectonic science, has under it practical and linguistic sciences (Brunetto speaks of things made and things said). The good of the city, here, is more important than the individual good. The third treatise of the *Convivio* seems to link the *summum bonum* with the common good conceived as an intellectual and shared good. Here Dante probably draws on Cicero and derives his idea from the field of Aristotelianism, and perhaps also from Remigio de Girolami.

In the system of the sciences of the *Convivio*, ethics, which is located before theology, should include, on the model of Aristotle, politics. Politics, in Dante, is thus part of philosophy. But philosophy is the study of causes and principles, while politics does not deal with this. The first things for politics do not belong to the origin of things. Political science looks at human life with an eye to what is better for the human being as a citizen. For Aristotle, however, as well as for Dante, the end of politics is not politics itself. Both thinkers are aware that the final goal of political life is not reached through politics but rather through a life devoted to contemplation and philosophy. Because of it, the link between ethics and politics drives to theology.

Statesmen or experts in politics can lead human beings to happiness, but this is a Platonic idea. In the *Convivio*, the idea seems to be that politics and ethics lead to metaphysics, because the contemplation of the *donna gentile* is considered the apex of a noetic endeavour. Aristotle, in book 10 of the *Nicomachean Ethics*, sees in contemplation an activity that makes human beings similar to God, but in Aquinas' commentary, contemplation implies a divine contemplation that human beings cannot reach in this life. For Dante, such contemplation belongs, however imperfectly, to the earthy life. However, his position is offered in a way that is difficult to understand, and what he introduces in his vernacular treatise is extremely important: the highest intellectual activity cannot be reached by the individual alone, but is the result of a community of living beings who think together. *Communitas* seems to enter as a new subject of history.

Ethics and politics belong to earthly life and work as a kind of introduction to metaphysics. The *Convivio,* which introduces the cosmological discourse as ruled by an intellectual desire and goal, offers this as a model for the human being's earthly life. The angel-intelligences, who share the contemplation of the absolute good, impose a new paradigm to the world of time. It manifests *in primis* a *de facto* celestial community or society. This perspective shows the importance of contemplation as the antecedent of praxis. The angel-intelligences are able to move the heavens because they are able to contemplate the perfect good or *summum bonum* – that is, God.

That the goal of the work as a whole is contemplation conceived as linked to praxis confirms the educational project of the *Convivio*. The language of the *Convivio* serves this goal. Dante uses the vernacular but does so in a way that makes it difficult; his language is clear and plain in the first three treatises, and syllogistic in the fourth. Such language educates human beings in the new learning introduced by the diffusion of Greek-Arabic thought, which Dante confronts and rethinks in light of the theological-Platonic tradition, thereby creating a philosophical discourse that includes theology rethought in light of philosophy. Neoplatonism, Aristotle and Aristotelianism, and the biblical Christian tradition are part of what the *Convivio* offers to its readers as an educational project, in that the rhetorical level is crucial and is part of the work's political endeavour. Through the continuous use of rhetorical subtleties disseminated in every chapter, the author seeks to establish a cooperative effort with the reader. This suggests that the formation of the reader is part of politics, just as rhetoric is part of politics. Both are related to the sciences of civil discourse, according to a line that encloses Alfarabi, Dominicus Gundissalinus, and Brunetto.

As noted above, the rhetorical organization of the *Convivio* is part of its political construction. The work includes an educational goal, perhaps devoted to the formation of a new emerging class of politicians. In the first treatise, Dante speaks of "baroni," or noble people, and includes also women as potential readers of his vernacular prose (I.9.5). But the ideal reader of the *Convivio* cannot be identified with and limited to them. To establish his identity, we must go beyond the already existing reader. We must think of someone yet to be made, a reader who is educated in the very act of reading the work itself. The vernacular treatise postulates a future reader who will be aware of the culture that the poet anticipates.

In the first treatise, Dante announces that he will write in a high style in order to give "gravezza" to his text (I.4.13). Actually, the *Convivio* develops a kind of communication that is peculiar to the work. Written in a style that is at once plain and obscure, it creates the reader's intellectual behaviour and awareness.

A paradox lies at the basis of this writing. The clarity of the exposition leads the reader to search for a further meaning that takes form in the relations that the text activates, without however explaining them. There is thus a further meaning that the text urges us to recognize. Perhaps the first level was shaped for the majority of readers, whereas the deeper meaning, which needs to be detected, was addressed only to a few. In any case, the reader must collaborate to complete the meaning that is suggested but not explicitly given. This happens, for example, with the passage on the natural desire to know which belongs to everyone – a desire, we should note, that cannot be fulfilled, however, unless we know together. According to this interpretation, the *Convivio*'s tormented drafting can be considered the antecedent of the discourse about the possible intellect that is established in the *Monarchia* 1. The fact that the second and third treatises of the *Convivio* suggest an idea about the possible intellect that the fourth treatise does not confirm, and which, however, the *Monarchia* retakes and clearly establishes, remains an open question and a most mysterious aspect of the relation between the vernacular doctrinal treatise and the political Latin work.

Notes

1. Introducing a Cosmic Intellectual Dimension

1 For more on the first canzone, see Ardizzone (2011, chap. 3, 115–72).
2 The text of the canzoni is that of Domenico De Robertis's monumental edition of *Rime* (2002) and reproduced in his recent annotated edition (2005).
3 According to Hugh of Saint Victor, *Didascalicon* 5.2, it is necessary that in the sacred scripture we do not try to find history, allegory, or tropology at each step but that rather we place things in their context as reason requires. Often in fact it is possible to find in the same literal context various meanings together as the truth of a story suggests a mystical meaning by virtue of allegory and at the same time shows through tropology how we should act.
4 The explanation provided by De Robertis is tautological, see note 1 to the text of the canzone in Vasoli, *Convivio* (1988, 92). De Robertis nonetheless updated his interpretation in his recent edition of *Rime* (2005, 22).
5 The interior reasoning is part of Dante's crucial discourse on the interior word that he introduces as early as the *Vita nuova* and his first poems. For a short introduction to such theory, see the Arens article on Augustine, "Verbum cordis" (1980).
6 The commentary indicating the relationship between the Thrones, the object of their contemplation – which in the Trinitarian structure, it will be seen, is the Holy Spirit – and rhetoric also involves a relationship between rhetoric and divine justice which is manifested in the Thrones. This relationship opens up to consideration not just the one between rhetoric and the Holy Spirit, but also between rhetoric and justice, which brings us back to something that Boncompagno da Signa had already elaborated when he wrote that rhetoric is the pupil of the two civil and canon laws,

therefore irreparably binding it to law, for Dante, the historical form of divine justice. (Law in the mind of God according to the doctrine of ideas widely patronized in the Middle Ages as will be said and testified to furthermore by a work like the *Monologium* of Anselm d'Aosta and Thomas Aquinas' *Summa theologica*, human law as the historical realization of lex Divina. Dante's *Monarchia* 2.2.4–5 proposes law as a divine idea. On law and right, see the canzone *Tre donne intorno al cor.*) "Voi che 'ntendendo" is recalled in *Paradiso* 8, the heaven of Venus, in the canto of Carlo Martello. But justice in the Aristotelian century is part of politics and politics is intertwined with ethics. Rhetoric as *ars politica* is found in Brunetto Latini's *Tresor* and his Ciceronian model. But for the importance of politics the model could be also in Alfarabi, in his *De scientiis*, widely circulating in Europe by way of synthesis and translation. The link between the canzone and rhetoric as established by the commentary suggests the political nature of the treatise.

7 In canto 10 of the *Inferno*, the "cui" (whom) would seem to render the tension towards Beatrice as high in the terms already singled out in the canzone *Donne ch'avete*. I believe that the ambiguity of the "cui" is meant to also link Virgil and Beatrice to suggest the notion of tragic (as intellectual and sublime) that Dante had elaborated in the *De vulgari* but to which the *Convivio* also contributes, together alluding to the nature of his own poetry in opposition to that of Guido.

8 With regard to praise and its link with tropes, see also Chenu (1999, 119) who calls them *transnominatio* (but I think of *transumptiones*) and the mention of the tropes (105).

9 The vocative case and the exhortative verb are, for human beings, characterized as modes of a language of ascension. In Gregory the Great, God uses the imperative when he addresses the angels and the biblical example is put forward of when he asks the angels to destroy the Tower of Babel. According to Bonaventure's *Sententiae* the angel-creatures and human beings use the vocative-exhortative in addressing God. Augustine talks about the vocative case as perfect form. These modes are built upon syntactic, optative, desiderative, or exhortative forms; the vocative case was typical furthermore of the praise also in Jacopone's "Donna del paradiso" ("Lady of heaven"), for example, and prayers also use the vocative, for example, the Salve regina, the Paternoster, or Francis's praise of the creatures (Cantico di Frate Sole). But even a text of mystical theology like that of Dionysius used the same mode. And this mode recurs in the Psalms. In Origen's *De oratione*, prayer is associated with invocation; see Origen, *La preghiera* (1997 42–3).

10 De Robertis (1988, 2005) traces the genealogy of the opening and recalls Cavalcanti, "Voi che per li occhi" and "I' prego voi," up to the *Vita nuova*, and *Rime*, "O voi che per la via d'Amor passate," "Voi che savete ragionar d'amore," and "O dolci rime che parlando andate."

11 If the *Convivio* introduces a method this is the speculative method, of which praise is a part. The praise that returns in the second canzone makes its own linguistic and anagogical mode explicit.

12 For angel-intelligences influencing human beings, see Albertus Magnus, *Super Dyonisium de caelesti hierarchia* (1993), 69, 80–4: "Dicimus quod deus est fons totius intellectualis luminis, unde si homines, qui sunt ultimi in hoc genere debent illuminari, hoc erit agentibus angelis, qui sunt medii virtute luminis divini, quo et ipsi illuminati sunt, sine quo nihil intellegi potest" (We say that God is the source of every intellectual light, thus if men, who are the last one in such genus have to be illuminated, it will take place through the action of angels, because they have the power to mediate the divine light. They are in fact illuminated and without it nothing can be understood).

13 On this I quote a fragment again from Albertus Magnus, *Super Dyonisium de caelesti hierarchia* (1993): "Motus enim caeli compositus est ex virtute spirituali quae est dirigens ad finem quem sortitur a motore, scilicet intelligentia, et iterum ex virtute corporali, quam habet ex ipso mobili, sicut etiam est in actione animae virtus eius et virtus naturae. Unde secundum quod motus attingit corpus, quod est istrumentum animae, anima accipit illuminationem spiritualem ex motu propter virtutem spiritualem, quae est in ipso [...] et huius modi dicunt esse influentiam intelligentiae in animas nostras tali continuitate" (The movement of the heaven is made by a spiritual virtue that has a goal derived from a motor, that is, intelligence and also from the body's virtue that derives from the heaven, in the same way it happens in the action of the soul. Thus when the body, which is the instrument of the soul gets its movement, the soul receives a spiritual illumination from the movement that is caused by a spiritual virtue that is in it, in the same way is said takes place the influence of an intellectual being in our soul in virtue of such continuity; 67). This position seems to be close to those condemned, see Hissette (1977), proposition 76: "Quod intelligentia motrix caeli influit in animam rationalem sicut corpus caeli influit in animum humanum" (The intellectual motor of heaven is influent in a rational soul in the same way a heaven body has influence on the human soul) (136). In Albert we find the theory that not all the angels-intelligences move the orbits and not all are joined to motion (67, 82–3, from the commentary on the angelic hierarchy).

14 Litt (1963) writes that Thomas Aquinas considers that the heavenly spheres are moved by created spirits to be solid and certain doctrine. Must these mover spirits be conceived as beings distinct from the spheres or as their substantial forms in such a way as to construct living beings with them? Aquinas hesitates and, rather, is brought to reject this opinion. In any case, what interests us here is the intellectual nature of the influence as it is exercised by the mover spirits. Litt refers to the *Contra gentiles* and summarizes Aquinas's thought: the fact that heavenly bodies are moved by spirits serves as the premise for proving that mover spirits direct heavenly bodies and, by consequence, inferior bodies towards their ends, or for proving that the substantial forms of inferior bodies derive from the species intellegibiles that exist in the mover spirits. Further on (107), Litt recalls a fragment of Aquinas's *De spiritualibus creaturis* where it is asserted that the finality of this movement, and the finality of the mover spirit in its motor activity, cannot be but an abstract intelligible good, that is, separate from matter and in view of which the intelligent substance exercises its motor activity towards the aim of reaching, through this activity, resemblance to that separate intelligible good and in order to reveal in act what is virtually contained in that intelligible good and especially the fulfillment of the number of the elect, which seems to be the finality of all things (99–109).

15 The *De causis* was a diffuse work and among the prescribed books in thirteenth-century curricula studiorum in Paris. See Van Steenbergen (1991, 115). Its diffusion is also testified to by the various commentaries, among which are those of Albertus Magnus, Thomas Aquinas, and Siger de Brabant.

16 Well fitting here is Vasoli's (1988) note that cites a passage of Albertus Magnus's *Metaphysics* (11, tr. 2, 33): "Ex dictis autem iam fere intelligitur, quid sit modus intelligendi istarum substantiarium. Non enim intelligunt ens causatum nisi per modum illum qui sunt causae ipsius" (From what has been said, it is possible to understand which is the way in which such substances have intelligence, that is, have intellection of the caused being because they are the cause of it.) ("Ens causatum" is to be verified and read in context, that is, what is caused is the movement of heaven.) Yet, in this passage of Convivio, the terms "intendono," "understand," and "operation" are to be considered. Dante seems to suggest that there is an intrinsic relation between his way to love the Donna gentile and the intellectual operation of the angels who understand by way of intellect (intelligere) and that in that and only in that move the heavenly body and, that is, in operation. This was Siger's position, which he utilized in order to illustrate the

resemblance between human beings' intellect and the angel-intelligences. Thomas Aquinas recalls this theory in the *De unitate* (2000) in order to criticize it (66–9). Hissette (1977) recalls it in commentary on propositions 73 and 132 and discusses it in relation to Siger. In Van Steenberghen's *Maitre Siger de Brabant* (1977), we find it recalled again in relation to Siger (343–4). In any case, to recall intellection in relation to operation would imply that the unity between the angel and heaven is not substantial but operational. In this, as regards the human soul, an evident error would come together in what would only in the operation be unity between the intellect and the body.

17 "Utrum animae superiores caelestes imprimant in animas nostras intellectivas." Siger sustains that influence occurs by virtue of an alteration that the heavenly orb inspires in our body. "Est tamen attendendum quod orbis immediate non imprimit in animam intellectivam, sed per alterationem quam inducit in nostro corpore causat in nobis quorundam intellectum et appetitum" (It should be understood that the movement of heaven does not cause alteration in an intellectual soul, it is only in virtue of an alteration which it impels in our body that it causes in us a kind of intellection and desire). Furthermore, in *Les Queastiones super librum De Causis,* the heavenly souls are suggested as being eternal (Siger 1972b, question 25, 100–2). On this see question 13, "Utrum Intelligentia sit in aeternitate et aeternitate parificetur" (If an intellectual being is in eternity and is eternal), which sees on one hand the exposition of philosophical thought – eternity not only of the intelligences but also of the heavens – and on the other hand the attempt at a "conciliation" with the authority of the Christian faith (Siger 1972b, 63–7).

18 Siger refers here to the thought of the anonymous author of the *De causis*: "Auctor hic dicens in littera animas superiores influere in animas inferiores suas bonitates" (The author here asserts that the superior soul allows its goodness penetrate in the inferior souls). In relation to this, the following fragment, already quoted above, has to be read: "orbis immediate non imprimit in animam intellectivam, sed per alterationem quam inducit in nostro corpore causat in nobis quorundam intellectum et appetitum" (the movement of a heaven does not cause directly an alteration in an intellectual soul, but it is in virtue of an alteration it impels in our body that it causes in us a kind of intellection and desire). (Siger 1972b, question 25, 100–2)

19 Litt (1963) refers to Thomas Aquinas, *De veritate catholicae Fidei contra errores infidelium seu Summa contra Gentiles*, and summarizes the content of the article: heavenly bodies have influence over bodily effects, but not directly over the spiritual acts of human beings. The conclusion states that the heavenly body acts like a body according to corporeal power; but this action only regards bodies since the instrument of the spiritual agent does

not act through spiritual power but this occurs through corporeal power (129).

20 Thomas Aquinas in the *De magistro* writes that the intelligences can influence the imagination (*De magistro,* article 3, 1965).The question is the following: If human beings can be instructed by an angel, Aquinas answers that the angel can form some species in imagination which can be formed stimulating the bodily organ. Aquinas variously debates the type of influence the angel can exercise on the human being.

21 The *Liber de causis,* proposition 1, states: "Omnis causa primaria plus est influens super causatum suum quam causa secunda universalis"; and Thomas Aquinas comments: "Quod est quia causa universalis prima agit in causatum causae secundae, antequam agat in ipsum causa universalis secunda quae sequitur ipsam" (Every primary cause has an influence on what it causes that is superior to that of an universal secondary cause) (This is so because the universal primary cause acts on the effect of the secondary cause before the universal secondary cause, which follows it [the primary cause] acts on the same thing).

22 See his articles "La langue, le vocabulaire" and "Spiritus" in Chenu, *Studi di lessicografia filosofica medievale* (2001, 143–5, 171–94).

23 The intelligences as separate substances that move the heavens are already in Aristotle's *Metaphysics*, book 12, and also in *De causis*, proposition 3 (Aquinas's commentary), and in Proclus, proposition 201 (Dodds 1992). But in Aristotle these separate substances are immobile; in Proclus, self-moving; in Dionysius, who identifies them as angelic hierarchies, they have a triple and spiral movement. See preceding notes.

24 See Aquinas, *Summa contra gentiles*, 3.24, as cited by Litt (1963, 197): "Si autem corpus caeleste a substantia intellectuali movetur ut ostensum est motus autem corporis caelestis [...] procedant ex intentione substantiae intelligentis [...] sunt igitur formae et motus inferiorum corporum a substantia intellectuali causatae et intentae sicut a principali agente, a corpore vero caelesti sicut ab instrumento" (If the celestial body is moved by an intellectual substance as it has been explained, the movement of a celestial body [which proceed from an intention of an intellectual substance [...] thus the forms and movements of inferior bodies are caused from the intent of an intellectual substance that acts as the first agent, and from a celestial body as an instrument).

25 "Intendere" (to understand) and also as "to have influence" is found in the *De causis*, proposition 48, but includes the relation with the first cause: "Et Intelligentiae primae influunt super intelligentias secundas bonitates quas recipiunt a causa prima, et intendunt bonitates in eis usquaequo

consecuntur ultimam earum" (And the first intellectual beings influence the second intellectual beings the goodness that is received from the first cause and *intendunt* [influence] goodness in them until they reach the lowest). It is canto 8 of *Paradiso* that recalls the first verse of the canzone reaffirming this theory and, that is, that the intelligences influence because they mediate the first cause or divine being.

26 See Dondaine's always important *Le corpus Dionyisien a de L'Université de Paris* (1953), as well as Weisheipl's "The Celestial Movers" (1961) and Dales's "The De-animation of the Heavens in the Middle Ages" (1980).

27 See Albertus Magnus, *De natura et origine animae* (1976, p. 17): "Ex his autem quae dicta sunt clarum est qualiter haec anima sola perfecta est et nobilis eo quod tres habet operationes, divinam videlicet et intellectualem et animalem. Divinam quidem in formas faciendo tam intelligibiles [...] Intellectualem autem habet in intelligendo et in intellectu reflectendo se super ipsam. Animalem autem habet in animando eo quod ipsa est forma hominis" (From what has been said, it is evident why this soul is the only one that is perfect and noble in so far it has three operations: divine, intellectual, and animal. It is divine because it makes the forms intelligible [...] Intellectual because it has intellection and reflection upon itself. Animal because it animates, in fact, it is the form of human beings).

28 Thomas Aquinas, in the commentary on proposition 3, underscores the identity between noble soul and divine soul recalling Proclus's proposition 201, and he then explains that their divine being is tied to the intelligences' capability of participating in the separate forms. "Sciendum est quod Plato posuit universales rerum formas separatas per se subsistens [...] ideo omnes huiusmodi formas sic subsistens deos vocabat nam hoc nomen deus universalem quandam providentiam et causalitatem importat [...] et quia per speciem intelligibilem, sub ordine deorum, idest predictarum formarum, posuerunt, ordinem, intellectum qui partecipant ordines praedictas ad hoc quod sint intelligentes, inter quas formas est etiam intellectus universales" (We have to know that Plato establishes that the forms of the things are separate universal substances ... thus such substantial forms he called gods and this name god includes a universal providence and causality ... and under the order of gods, that is of the above said forms he establishes the order of intellects who participates in the above said forms because they are intelligent beings and among such forms there is also the universal intellect). That which brings us back to the canzone is in the passage in which after having led the essence of intellectuality back to participation in the divine: "oportet ergo dicere quo a prima causa a qua

habet essentiam habet enim intellectualitem" (we have to say that from the first cause from which has its essence it has also the intellectual being), he refers then to Dionysius and Aristotle (*Metaphysics*) in which, as is well known, the theory of Platonic ideas is critiqued. Aquinas then concludes this part by saying: "Aliquo tamen modo potest hoc habere veritatem, si referatur non ad naturam intellectualem, sed ad formas intellegibiles quas animae intellectivae recipiunt per operationem intelligentiarum; unde et Dionysius dicit IV capitulo De divinis nominibus quod animas per angelos fiunt partecipes illuminationum a deo emanantium" (We may get a truth if we refer not to the intellectual nature, but to the intelligible forms that the intellectual souls receive through the operation of intelligences, therefore the Pseudo-Dionysius says in chapter 4 of the divine names that the souls through the angels participate in the illuminations which proceed from God). (*Super Librum de causis exposition*, 2002, 17–24)

29 "Omnia autem viventia suipsorum motiva sunt propter vitam primam. Omnia autem cognitiva cognitione participant propter intellectum primum" (All living beings move themselves because of the first life.In fact, all cognitive beings participate in cognition because of the first intellect). (Aquinas, *Super Librum de causis expositio*, 2002, 101)

30 "Omnis sciens scit essentiam suam, ergo est rediens ad essentiam suam reditione completa" (Every being who knows knows its essence, thus it returns to its essence with a full circular movement). (Aquinas, *Super Librum de causis expositio*, 2002, 88)

31 For the Greek text, I use Proclus, *The Elements of Theology* (1992), proposition 15 (to be seen in relation to 16 and 17; and the note on pages 202–3). In Proclus (1987), Morbecca's (William of Moerbeke) translation of the term is "conversivum" ("Omne quod ad se ipsum conversivum est incorporeum est; Omne ad se ipsum conversivum habet substantiam separabilem ab omni corpore; Omne se ipsum movens primo ad se ipsum est conversivum" (everything that is able to return to itself is without body; every being who is able to return to himself has a substance that is possible to separate from any body; everything that is able at first to move towards itself is able to have a circular motion; propositions 11–12, 15, 16, 17). In *Super Librum de causis expositio,* in the commentary on proposition 15, Aquinas reproduces fragments of Proclus's text from Morbecca's translation (88–92). Proposition 15 will be important in the concept of science that the *Convivio* organizes, and to which we will return.

32 "Secundum hoc ergo platonici ponebant quod id quod est ipsum esse est causa existendi omnibus, id autem quod est ipsa vita est causa vivendi omnibus, id autem quod est ipsa intelligentia est causa intelligendi

omnibus; unde Proclus dicit XVIII propositione sui libri: omne derivans esse allis, ipsum prime est hoc quod tradit recipientibus derivationem" (Platonists establish that the being is the cause of the exsistence of all things, in fact the being is life itself and the cause of life for all beings, and is also intelligence and thus the cause of intelligence of all beings; therefore Proclus says in proposition 18 of his book that everything that derives from others is what gives to the receivers their derivative being) (Aquinas, *Super Librum de causis expositio*, 2002, 22). Chapters 4 and 5 of Pseudo-Dionysius's *De divinis nominibus* dealt with similar subjects; in Aquinas's commentary on the *De divinis nominibus*, for example, "angel" was rendered also as "messenger" because it announced the divine essence, participates in his image and thus makes manifest the being of the divine; thus the angels who are good make manifest the light of the divine which is hidden to us. In 4.1.18 of the *De divinis nominibus*, the concept of likeness was explained through the image of the mirror given by Dionysius; mirror, then, because it receives the divine image and is also capable of displaying it.

33 Corti, in *La felicità mentale* (1983, 116), reads the first verse of *Voi che 'ntendendo il terzo ciel movete* by assimilating it into Nardi's discourse on matter. But the citation that Corti quotes from Nardi when he cites Bonaventure is just a fragment. This changes meaning in Corti's adaptation. See Nardi, *Dante e la cultura medioevale* (1985), 198 et seq., for Bonaventure's citation; for the word "collatione" in Bonaventure's text, see Chenu, *Studi di lessicografia filosofica medievale* (2001, 67–8); "collectio," from which comes "collatio." In any case, Corti proposes that "intendendo" means to make the shift from "potentia" to act, which could also work in this context. What cannot be left out of consideration is that to understand the divine by way of intellect (intelligere) is characteristic of the angelic intelligences and that moving the heavens is tied to the intellection of the divine. In the *Convivio*, the heavens are declared to be passive, unlike in *Paradiso* where they have power and act.

34 For proposition 3: "Ipsa est exemplum, id est imago, virtutis superioris, id est divinae" (It is the example, that is, the image of a superior virtue that is divine) (Aquinas, *Super Librum de causis*, 2002, 21), see the Pseudo-Dionysius, *De divinis nominibus*, Thomas Aquinas's commentary (4.7).

35 It would seem possible to retrace a sign of determinism here even it if does not seem to be the main point towards which the canzone aims. In any case, in proposition 76, as reproduced by Hissette (1977, 136; see note 13 above in which I quote proposition 76), a parallel is put forth between the intellectual influence of the intelligences on human intelligence and that of heaven on the human body. Aquinas is clearly against an influence of the heavens on the human intellectual act. See Litt (1963, 201–3) who cites

a series of Thomistic texts. Aquinas is also perplexed about the influence of the intelligences on human intelligence because he sees in it a form of limitation on human liberty. See the *De veritate* as recalled above in note 19. But he agrees on the angels as mediators of divine light; see, for example, the *De divinis nominibus* ("animas per angelos fiunt partecipes illuminationum a deo emanantium"; the souls through the angels participate of the illuminations emanated from God) as recalled in the commentary on the *De causis* (24).

36 Hamesse, "Spiritus chez les auteurs philosophiques" (1984, 163–5). In this article, "spirito" is also in reference to the angelic intelligences. See also in the same volume Busa, "De voce spiritus in operibus S. Thomae Aquinatis" (1984), especially the paragraph where the meaning of "angelo" as "spirito" is pointed out. De Robertis's (2005) note does not explain it, and so a fundamental level of comprehension of this text escapes him and his readers.

37 Lonergan (1967, 196) attributes the idea that "in all intellects there is a procession of inner word" to Thomas Aquinas, *Summa theologica*, question 27, article 1c.

38 See Chenu, *Studi di lessicografia*, the part on the spirit (171–232, 218 in particular), and "La langue, le vocabulaire" (144).

39 See Dronke's (1986) and Aquinas's (1992b, 1997) commentary on Boethius's *De trinitate*. In Aquinas (1992b), see the discussion about the knowledge of physics (279), and then see the discussion on the knowledge of that which is not possible to abstract since it is separate (292, 334, 338, 340).

40 The relation between word and inner vision and imagination as something free of the senses and intellectual in nature is useful for explaining parts of the *Vita nuova*, like chapters 24 and 25.

41 If we read canto 10 and the passage tied to the "disdegno" ("cui Guido vostro ebbe a disdegno" (63)) and the "cui" that ambiguously suggests a bond between Virgil and Beatrice with this awareness, what emerges is that it is the intellectual dimension that constitutes a rift between Dante and Cavalcanti. While it confirms the relationship between intellectual and tragic, this introduces us to the revisitation of the Virgilian tragic by Dante that in him takes shape through what the *De vulgari* calls "honestum." The "honestum" that introduces the relationship between intellectual beauty and moral beauty will be the object of discourse later on.

42 However, it is a novelty indebted to Cavalcanti if we consider that the lady about whom "Donna me prega" begins could have been natural philosophy as was intuited and proposed by Corti, but called into

question by Contini in his review of *La felicità mentale* in Corriere della Sera (now in G. Contini, 1988). The donna gentile opposed to natural philosophy and of which the *De anima* is part, according to a thought characteristic of Aristotle and Aristotelianism, finds the opposing dimension in the intellectual.

43 "Quod ipsa (anima rationalis) non est actus alicuius corporis nec est forma corporalis, neque virtus operans in corpore. Propter quod impossibile est, quod per aliquas qualitates aut formas, quae in semine sunt, educatur de semine, sed cum intellectus separatus sit primus motor in natura [...] anima rationalis est similitudo lucis intellectus agentis in generatione" (The rational soul is not the act of a body, it is not a corporeal form, or a virtue active in the body. Because of it is impossible that it is derived from the seed according to the qualities and forms that are in the seed, but because the separate intellect is the first motor in nature ... the ratonal soul is in its generation the image of the light of the agent intellect). (Albertus Magnus, *De natura et origine animae* I.5.12, 75–85 [1976])

44 "Ex dictis autem elucescit, quod in sexto decimo scientiae De Animalibus libro diximus, quod intellectus in animae rationalis natura ingreditur in conceptum ab extrinseco ... quia educit eum de luce sua e non de aliquo materialium principiorum" (From what has been said it is clear what we said in the book 16 of the book of animals that the intellect penetrates in the rational soul and is conceived from an external source, because [the agent intellect] takes it from its own light and not from a material principle). (Albertus Magnus, *De natura et origine animae* 1976, 1.13, 25–31)

45 "Oportet autem scire, quod ... in homine inchoatio vegetativi est in materia...et inchoatio sensibilis est in vegetativo et inchoatio rationalis est in sensitivo ... Sed quia nihil horum fit nisi per virtutem intellectus et non ex materia aliqua efficitur, ideo terminus esse hominis ad similitudinem intellectus primi, qui divinus est" (It is necessary to know that in the human being the generation of the vegetative soul is in matter and the generation of the sensitive soul is in the vegetative soul and that of the rational in the sensitive soul. And because all these happen thanks to the virtue of the intellect, and not of matter, thus the goal of the human being is his likeness to the first intellect, which is divine). (Albertus Magnus, *De natura et origine animae* 1976, 1.13, 82–92)

46 "Et ideo compositio nulla est in anima per rationem formae et materiae, [...] Sed melius dicitur esse intellectualis natura composita ex eo quod est de sua natura intellectuale et ex quo est perfectio intellectus. Ex intellectu enim possibili, [...] est natura intellectualis id quod est, sed ex agente est perfectio ipsius secundum esse intellectuale in actu, [...] talis igitur est

animae compositio" (Thus in the soul there is not a composition according to matter and form ... but it is better to say that the intellectual nature is composed from what is in its own nature intellectual and from what is the perfection of the intellect. The possible intellect is what is in itself intellectual, but in the agent intellect we have its perfection because it is intellectual in act, this is the composition of the soul). (Albertus Magnus, *De natura et origine animae* I.8.17.15–28 [1976])

47 "Cum enim anima sit 'resultatio quaedam lucis intelligentiae' separatae erunt in ipsa duo necessaria quorum unum est forma lucis, et alterum est id in quo lux recipitur et stat … ab hoc esse animae fluunt duae virtutes, quarum una est intellectus agens, qui causatur ab ipsa luce recepta, et alia est intellectus possibilis qui causatur ab eo in quo lux recipitur" (The soul being the result of the light of a separate intelligence has in iself two beings. One is the form of light and the other is the recipient of light and in which light stays … From this being of the soul derive two virtues, one is the agent intellect which is caused by the light received, and the other is the possible intellect that is caused by the being in which light is received). (Albertus Magnus, *De anima* 3.2.18.45–49 [1968, 205])

48 About this issue, see Albert Magnus, *De anima* 3.3.11 (1968, 221), where we read that the possibile intellect has the property of contemplating the agent intellect as forma. See also Nardi (1960a, 103–17) who has underlined this content, and de Libera (1990a, 242–6).

49 For the importance of Augustine in Albert the Great's philosophical theory of intellect, see Fuhrer (1991).

50 Albert opposes variously this theory of the unicity of human intellect; he devotes his treatise *De unitate intellectus* to this subject (1975).

51 "La nominatio" is one of the figures that Geoffrey of Vinsauf (*Poetria nova*) includes inside the complex figure of "transumptio," which he identifies as *ornatus difficilis*. See Faral (1962, 221–31). For more about such complex figures, see Purcell (1987, 281–6). Purcell unfortunally has no knowledge of the *Rhetorica* of Boncompagno da Signa and of its important discussion devoted to *transumptio* (see Boncompagno da Signa, *Rhetorica novissima*, 1896, 281–6).

52 Augustine, in book 4.7.15 of *De doctrina christiana* (1970), underlines that in the Bible many tropes are difficult to understand – the more difficult they are, the sweeter they are, and once they are opened by the reader, they in fact *dulcescunt*.

53 That the difficult is allowed to climb towards the divine was also in Alain de Lille (*Regulae* P.L.210) and had already been an important Augustinian point (Augustine, *De Trinitate* 4.8.22, and *De doctrina christiana* 4.7.15).

For Boethius, since God is an intellectual being, the discourse about Him can be nothing but intellectual (*De Trinitate*). Intellectual implies a climbing towards the divine. See Aquinas's introduction to the *Analytics*: the difficult is an exercise towards the divine. The syllogism in fact is a way of climbing. Consider that Alain de Lille indicates the enthymeme that is known as a truncated syllogism, as "mente interna" (internal mind) (the enthymeme, as is known, is also part of rhetoric). But the resumption of this line is also testified to variously both by Buoncompagno's *Retorica nuovissima* (1898) and by various *Poetriae*. For more about this, see Ardizzone (2011, 14–22 and 88–96).

54 No doubt, that the line that Dante opposes is the line Cavalcanti has activated in his canzone "Donna me prega." Boccaccio seems to be aware of the two different and opposite lines that Cavalcanti and Dante have activated. Such awareness can be retraced variously.

55 "Però che l'uno era soccorso dalla parte [della vista] dinanzi continuamente, e l'altro dalla parte della memoria di dietro; e lo soccorso dinanzi ciascuno die crescea, che far non potea l'altro, comen[dan]te quella, che impediva in alcuno modo a dare indietro il volto; per che a me parve sì mirabile, e anche duro a sofferire, che io nol potei sostenere" (For the one was continually reinforced by the part of the memory in front, and the other by the part of the memory in back; and the support in front, being that which hindered me from turning my gaze in any way backward, increased with each day, which the other could not do; hence it seemed to me so wonderful and also so hard to endure that I could not bear it). (*Convivio* II.2.4)

56 I follow Ageno's text; the integration offered by G. Inglese does not seem acceptable to me: "L'uno era soccorso da la parte della [memoria] davanti." That of Ageno is instead acceptable: "L'uno era soccorso dalla parte [della vista] dinanzi continuamente."

57 Ageno gives a variation: "Comen[dan]te quella" (70).

58 Here is the text of the Epistle III to Cino: "Utrum de passione in passionem possit anima transformari: de passione in passionem dico secundum eandem potentiam et obiecta diversa numero sed non specie [...] Redditur ecce sermo Calliopeus inferius, quo sententialiter canitur, quamquam transumptive more poetico signetur intentum, amorem huius posse torpescere atque denique interire, nec non huius, quod corruptio unius generatio sit alterius, in anima reformari [...] omnis namque potentia que post corruptionem unius actus non deperit, naturaliter reservatur in alium: ergo potentie sensitive, manente organo, per corruptionem unius actus non depereunt, et naturaliter reservantur in alium. Cum igitur potentia

concupiscibilis, que sedes amoris est, sit potentia sensitiva, manifestum est post corruptionem unius passionis qua in actum reducitur, in alium reservatur" (Whether the soul can pass from passion to passion; that is to say, from one passion to another, the nature of the passion remaining the same, but the objects being different, not in kind, but in identity … Behold, there is given below a discourse in the diction of Calliope, wherein the Muse declares in set phrase [though, as poets use, the meaning is conveyed under a figure] that love for one object may languish and finally die away, and that (inasmuch as the corruption of one thing is the begetting of another) love for a second may take shape in the soul. And the truth of this, although it is proved by experience, may be confirmed by reason and authority. For every faculty which is not destroyed after the consummation of one act is naturally reserved for another. Consequently, the faculties of sense, if the organ survives, are not destroyed by the consummation of one act but are naturally reserved for another Since, then, the appetitive faculty, which is the seat of love, is a faculty of sense, it is manifest that after the exhaustion of the passion by which it was brought into operation it is reserved for another; Epistole 532–5).

59 The angel-intelligences as mediators of God or secondary causes exercise their power on what is living and on those things that are subjected to their action. Albert the Great in his *De causis et processu universitatis* (1993) writes that "vita est actus ab ente quieto" (life is an act that flows from the quiet being) 26.63; "vita secundum actum sive vivere est motus et processum" (life according to its action or living is movement and process)148.3.80; at 27.51, "esse vivere intelligere actus continui sunt qui sunt in fieri a primo ente et a prima vita et a primo intellectivo exerciti" (being, living, and understanding are continous acts they are in becoming and derive from the first being and from the first intellectual activity); and at 151.12, we read "omne esse est ab ente primo et omnis vita a vita prima et omni scientia intellectiva ab intellectu primo" (every being derives from the the first being,and every life from the first life and every intellectual science from the first intellect … The intellect is given to what is living).

60 See, additionally, Lindberg (1978): the heavens exercise their influence on animate and inanimate bodies (288).

61 See Bianchi (1997, 106–10); see Ardizzone (2002, chap. 2) for more about sophisms as instructive as utilized by Cavalcanti in "Donna me prega."

62 For *integumentum*, see Chenu (2001), 165–9.

63 The English translation is that of Hollander and Hollander (2007).

64 The theory on the internal senses of Arab-Jewish origin was circulating in the culture of Dante's time; see Woolfson (1935). For what belongs

to memory, see Carruthers and Ziolkowski (2003), who have collected a series of primary sources.

65 I will introduce *suspicio* as a rhetorical-logic figure in the next treatise.

66 In the *De anima* (3.427B), Aristotle introduces imagination as sensation and judgment on sensation. And imagination (beyond every metaphorical sense) is a process through which an image is generated inside of us (the corresponding Greek words are *phantasma* and the verb *gignomai* [*gignestai*]). Imagination does not happen apart from sensation, that is, it includes sensation. Therefore, imagination is a movement produced by an operation sensation. Sight is the key or most important sense, as Aristotle points out when he writes about the relationship between imagination and vision: imagination (*phantasia*) comes from *phos* (light), because without light there is no vision. And, with no vision, therefore, there is no imagination (*De anima* 3.3.427a–429a).

67 See Meyeroff, ed., *The Book of the Ten Treatises on the Eye, Ascribed to Hunain Ibn Is-Haq* (1928, 17–18). The second treatise deals with the nature and function of the brain and reads: "The act of thinking is affected by the brain itself. Thinking involves three things, the imaginative faculty, reflection and recollection. Imagination lies in the anterior part of the brain, reflection in the Middle Part and Recollection in the Posterior Part." The explanation of the activity of the psychic or animal spirit follows, whose origin derives from the vital spirit that is born in the heart (the exact terminology of the *Vita nuova*). From the heart, two arteries ascend that arrive at the brain and divide into branches similar to a network. The vital or animal spirit circulates in this network until it is made rare and refined. And then it passes from the arteries to the two anterior cavities of the brain where additional refinement is undergone and from there to the central cavity where it is further refined and then to the posterior cavity by means of a channel that exists between the two cavities. But this channel is not always open; rather, in its medulla, there is something like a worm that blocks it until nature decides to admit the vital spirit into the posterior cavity. When it decides, it removes the structure similar to that of a worm and it admits the spirit deciding the amount that can pass. So, through the spirit that is in the posterior cavity the movement and activity of remembrance ("recollection") happens, through the spirit that is in the anterior part of the brain the activity of observation and imagination happens, and through the spirit that is in the middle part of the brain reflection happens. The brain must be cold; heat is contrary to the activity of thought. In the introduction by Meyeroff, it emerges how this text was attributed to the famous Constantine the African. This explanation was common; see the collected

textual resources in Carruthers and Ziolkowski (2003), in particular the section on Albertus Magnus and Thomas Aquinas.

68 What is important in this writing is that there is a part in which is introduced the possible infinities that God thinking contains in Himself. See question 7 and see the introduction (63). This knowledge is possible by way of ecstatic intuition reserved for the world of the possible (and only for the person provided with grace).

69 "Haec autem sensibilia exteriora sunt quae primo ingrediuntur in animam per portas quinque sensuum; intrant, inquam, non per substantias, sed per similitudines suas, primo generatas in medio et de medio in organo et de organo exteriori in interiori et de hoc in potentiam apprehensivam, et sic generatio speciei in medio et de medio in organo et conversio potentiae apprehensivae super illam facit apprehensionem omnium eorum quae exterius anima apprehendit" (As far as the three kinds of things are concerned, this whole sensible world enters into the human soul through "apprehension." The external sensibles, however, are what first enter the soul through the five doors of the senses. They enter, I say, not through their substance, but through their similitudes. These are first generated in the medium, and from the medium are generated in the organ and pass from the external organ into the internal, and from there into the apprehensive power. And thus the generation of the [sensible] species in the medium and from the medium into the organ and the reaction of the apprehensive power to it [the species] produce the apprehension of all those things which the soul apprehends from without). (*Itinerarium*, 2.4; 516)

70 "Si enim diiudicatio habet fieri per rationem abstrahente a loco, tempore et mutabilitate, ac per hoc a dimensione, successione et transmutatione, per rationem immutabilem et incircumscriptibilem et interninabilem, nihil autem est omnino immutabile, incircumscriptibile et interminanbile nisi quod est aeternum; omne autem quod est aeternum, est deus, vel in Deo: si ergo omnia, quaecumque certius diiudicamus per huiusmodi rationem diiudicamus, patet quod ipse est ratio omnium rerum et regula infallibilis et lux veritatis, in qua cuncta relucent infallibiliter [...] et intellectualiter. Et ideo leges illae per quas iudicamus certitudinaliter de omnibus sensibilibus, in nostram considerationem venientibus; cum sint infallibiles et indubitabiles intellectui apprehendentis, sint indelebiles a memoria recolentis tamquam semper praesentes, sint irrefragabiles et indiiudicabiles intellectui iudicantis, quia, ut dicit Augustinus, "nullus de eis iudicat, sed per illas"; necesse est, eas esse incommutabiles et incorruptibiles, tamquam necessarias [...] intellectuales et incorporea non factas, sed increatas, aeternaliter existentes in arte aeterna, a qua, per quam et secundum quam formantur

formosa omnia; et ideo nec certitudinaliter iudicari possunt nisi per illam que non tantum fuit forma cuncta producens, verum etiam cuncta conservans et distinguens tamquam ens in omnibus formam tenens et regula dirigens, et per quam diiudicat mens nostra cuncta quae per sensus intrant in ipsam" (By a more excellent and immediate way we are led by judgment into seeing eternal truths more surely. For if judgment comes about through the reason's abstracting from place, time, and change, and therefore from dimension, succession, and transmutation, by the immutable, illimitable, and endless reason, and if there is nothing immutable, inimitable, and endless except the eternal, then all which is eternal is God or is in God. If, then, all things of which we have more certain judgments are judged by this mode of reasoning, it is clear that this is the reason of all things and the infallible rule and light of truth, in which all things shine forth infallibly, indestructibly, indubitably, irrefragably, unquestionably, unchangeably, boundlessly, endlessly, indivisibly, and intellectually. And therefore those laws by which we make certain judgments concerning all sensible things which come into our consideration – since they [the laws] are infallible and indubitable rules of the apprehending intellect – are indelibly stored up in the memory as if always present, are irrefragable and unquestionable rules of the judging intellect. By a more excellent and immediate way are we led by judgment into seeing eternal truths more surely. And this is so because, as Augustine says [Lib. Arb., II, ch. 4], no one judges these things except by these rules. It must thus be true that they are incommutable and incorruptible since they are necessary, and boundless since they are inimitable, endless since eternal. Therefore they must be indivisible since intellectual and incorporeal, not made but uncreated, eternally existing in eternal art, by which, through which, and in accordance with which all things that have a form are formed. Neither, therefore, can we judge with certainty except through that which was not only the form producing all things but also the preserver of all and the distinguisher of all, as the being who preserves the form in all things, the directing rule by which our mind judges all things which enter into it through the senses). (*Itinerarium*, 2.9; 520–2)

71 I give here the Latin text: "Ex secunda apparet, quod ipsa [memoria] non solum habet ab exteriori formari per phantasmata, verum etiam a superiori suscipiendo et in se habendo simplices formas, quae non possunt introire per portas sensuum et sensibilium phantasias. Ex tertia habetur quod ipsa habet lucem incommutabilem sibi praesentem, in qua meminit invariabilium veritatum." (*Itinerarium*, 2.9; 530)

72 I give here the English translation: "From memory is generated the intelligence as its own offspring. We have in fact intellection when the likeness

that is in memory penetrates in the intellect, which is the verb, therefore from memory and intellect is generated love as the link between them. Thus the generative mind, the word, and love are in the soul." (*Itinerarium* 3.5; 534)

2. Loving a Divine Idea

1 This fundamental passage of Aristotle's *Metaphysics*, a passage obviously commented on by both Aquinas and Albert, is quoted from *Aristotle Latinus*. That God thinks only Himself was among the propositions condemned in 1277. See Hissette (1977), proposition 13 (37): "Quod deus non cognoscit alia a se." Obviously the basis in Aristotle is that God thinks only Himself as is readable, in book 12 of the *Metaphysics*, but according to Hissette at the basis of this condemnation there is Siger. In any case, with regard to the *Convivio*, the indirect question that appears in book 4 is whether God understands, by way of intellect, the first matter. This is linked to divine knowledge and the theory of ideas if we read the *Summa theologica* 1.15 a 1–3 entitled *Quaestio de ideis* where it is discussed whether God knows the first matter (article 3).

2 The tract on the separate substances (*De substantiis separatis*, 1969) is an essential point of reference for understanding the plot of the subtexts on which the discourse is organized, which links the angelic intelligences with the ideas in the divine mind and which is to be read in relation to the brief discussion on the number of separate substances that the *Convivio* faces in the second book. Thomas, in the opening to his tract, examines first the opinion of the ancients and of Plato and then that of Aristotle, trying to consider on what the two opinions agree and disagree.At the end of chapter 14, he synthesizes what was already expounded thus: "Et ita, si sit sic in Deo quod suus intellectus non sit sua intelligentia, et aliquid aliud intelligat; non erit sua intelligentia optima, quia non erit optimi intelligibilis. Relinquitur ergo quod se ipsum intelligat, cum ipse sit nobilissimum entium. Patet igitur praedicta verba philosophi diligenter consideranti, quod non est intentio eius excludere a Deo simpliciter aliarum rerum cognitionem, sed quod non intelliget alia a se quasi participando ea, ut per ea fiat intelligens, sicut fit in quocumque intellectu cuius substantia non est suum intelligere. Intelligit autem omnia alia a se intelligendo se ipsum, inquantum ipsius esse est universale et fontale principium omnis esse, et suum intelligere quaedam universalis radix intelligendi, omnem intelligentiam comprehendens. Inferiores vero intellectus separati, quos Angelos dicimus, intelligunt quidem se ipsos singuli per suam essentiam, alia vero

intelligunt secundum quidem Platonicas positiones per participationem formarum intelligibilium separatarum, quas deos vocabant, ut supra dictum est; secundum Aristotilis vero principia partim quidem per suam essentiam, partim vero per participationem ipsius primi intelligibilis, quod est Deus, a quo et esse et intelligere participant" (And so if it be thus in the case of God, that His intellect is not His understanding and that He understands something else, then, His understanding will not be the best because it will not have the best intelligible object. It remains, therefore, since He is the noblest of things, that He understands Himself. It is therefore apparent to anyone who considers carefully the above words of the Philosopher, that it is not his intention to exclude absolutely from God a knowledge of other things, but rather, that God does not understand other things through themselves as participating in them in order that He then may become understanding through them; as happens in the case of any intellect whose substance is not its understanding. He rather understands all things other than Himself by understanding Himself, inasmuch as His being is the universal and fontal source of all being and His understanding is the universal root of understanding encompassing all understanding. The lower separate intellects, however, that we call angels, understand themselves in each case through their essence, but according to the Platonists' position, they understand other things by participating in the separate intelligible forms that they call gods, as we have said. According to Aristotle's principles, they understand other things partly through their essence and partly through a participation in the first intelligible, who is God, from whom they participate in both being and understanding).

3 In Epistle 13, in fact, we read that the Empyrean persists in everlasting calm and it is to all things as the formative is to the formable, which is to say acting as cause. And since every causative force is a ray emanating from the first cause which is God, it is clear that the heaven that has more force of cause takes more of His light. "Propter quod sciendum quod illum coelum est celum supremum, continens corpora universa et a nullo contentum, intra quod omnia corpora movetur ipso in sempiterna quiete permanens et a nulla corporali substantia virtutem recipiens. Et dicitus Empyreum, quod est idem quod celum igne sui ardoris flagrans [...] ergo se habet ad omnia sicut formativum ad formabile quod est se habere per modum cause. Et cum omnis vis causandi sit radium quidam influens a prima causa que Deus est, manifestum est quod illum celum quod magis habet rationem cause, magis de luce divina recipit" (For which reason you must know that that heaven is the highest heaven, containing all bodies, and contained by none, within which all bodies move [while it remains in

eternal quiet], and receiving power from no corporeal substance. And it is called *empyreum*, which is the same as fiery heaven or flaming with heat; [...] thus it is related to all as the formative to the formable, which means to be related by way of cause. And since all causative power is a kind of ray flowing from the first cause, which is God, it is obvious that that heaven which has the greatest degree of cause receives more of the divine light). The Empyrean as the heaven of calm is in Thomas Aquinas, *Summa theologica* 1.66 a 3. And the abovecited passage of the *Convivio*, book 2, depends perhaps on this passage: "ita coelum empyreum habet influentiam super corpora quae moventur, licet ipsum non moveatur. Et propter hoc potest dici quod influit in primum coelum quod movetur, non aliquid transiens et adveniens per motum, sed aliquid fixum et stabilem; puta virtutem continenti et causandi, vel aliquid huiusmodi ad dignitatem pertinens" (thus the Empyrean has influence on the body that are moved, however it is not moved.And because of it it is possible to say that has influence on the first heaven that is moved, not something that is changing and happening, but something that is stable and without movement, for instance the virtue of containing and causing, or something of this kind and belonging to dignity).

4 The English translations here are those of Hollander and Hollander (2007).

5 "Si etenim perspicaciter consideramus quid cum loquimur intendamus, patet quod nichil aliud quam nostre mentis enucleare aliis conceptum. Cum igitur angeli ad pandendas gloriosas eorum conceptiones habeant promptissimam atque ineffabilem sufficientiam intellectus, qua vel alter alteri totaliter innotescit per se, vel saltim per illud fulgentissimum Speculum in quo cuncti representantur pulcerrimi atque avidissimi speculantur, nullo signo locutionis indiguisse videntur" (Now, if we wish to define with precision what our intention is when we speak, it is clearly nothing other than to expound to others the concepts formed in our minds. Therefore, since the angels have, in order to communicate their own glorious conceptions, a ready and ineffable sufficiency of intellect – through which either they make themselves, in themselves, completely known to each other, or, at least, are reflected, in the fullness of their beauty and ardour, by that resplendent mirror which retains an image of all of them – they seem not to have needed signs to represent speech).

6 In this text, drafted around 1272 and which Saffrey holds had been written contemporaneously with the commentary on the *De causis*, Thomas Aquinas takes up a theory that he attributes to Plato and he institutes a cosmic hierarchy for participation in the One: "[Plato] Sub hoc autem uno [Deus] diversos ordines participantium et participatorum instituebat

in substantiis a materia separatis: quos quidem ordines deos secundos esse dicebat, quasi quasdam unitates secundas post primam simplicem unitatem. Rursus, quia sicut omnes aliae species participant uno, ita etiam oportet quod intellectus, ad hoc quod intelligat, participet entium speciebus. Ideo sicut sub summo Deo, qui est unitas prima, simplex et imparticipata, sunt aliae rerum species quasi unitates secundae et dii secundi; ita sub ordine harum specierum sive unitatum ponebat ordinem intellectuum separatorum, qui participant supradictas species ad hoc quod sint intelligentes in actu: inter quos tanto unusquisque est superior, quanto propinquior est primo intellectui, qui plenam habet participationem specierum, sicut et in diis sive unitatibus tanto unusquisque est superior, quanto perfectius participat unitate prima. Separando autem intellectus a diis, non excludebat quin dii essent intelligentes; sed volebat quod superintellectualiter intelligerent, non quidem quasi participantes aliquas species, sed per se ipsos; ita tamen quod nullus eorum esset bonus et unum nisi per participationem primi unius et boni. Rursus, quia animas quasdam intelligentes videmus; non autem convenit hoc animae ex eo quod est anima (alioquin sequeretur quod omnis anima esset intelligens, et quod anima secundum totum id quod est, esset intelligens) ponebat ulterius, quod sub ordine intellectuum separatorum esset ordo animarum; quarum quaedam, superiores videlicet, participant intellectuali virtute, infimae vero ab hac virtute deficiunt. Rursus, quia corpora videntur non per se moveri nisi sint animata, hoc ipsum quod est per se moveri, ponebat corporibus accidere inquantum participabant animam: nam illa corpora quae ab animae participatione deficiunt, non moventur nisi ab alio. Unde ponebat animabus proprium esse quod se ipsas moverent secundum se ipsas. Sic igitur sub ordine animarum ponebat ordinem corporum; ita tamen quod supremum corporum, scilicet primum caelum, quod primo motu movetur, participat motum a suprema anima, et sic deinceps usque ad infimum caelestium corporum. Sic igitur patet quo inter nos et summum Deum quatuor ordines ponebant: scilicet deorum secundorum, intellectuum separatorum, animarum caelestium, et Daemonum bonorum seu malorum. Quae si vera essent, omnes huiusmodi medii ordines apud nos Angelorum nomine censerentur. Nam et Daemones in sacra Scriptura Angeli nominatur, ipsae etiam animae caelestium corporum, si tamen sint animata, inter Angelos sunt connumerandae, ut Augustinus definit in Enchiridion" (Under this One, he established among the substances separate from matter diverse orders of participating and participated beings, all of which orders he called secondary gods, as being unities below the first simple unity. Again, inasmuch as all forms participate in the One, the intellect likewise must participate in the forms of things in order to have understanding. Therefore, just as under the highest God, who is the prime unity, simple and unparticipated, other forms of things exist as secondary unities and gods; so, under the order of these forms or unities, he posited an order of separate intellects, which participate in the above-mentioned forms in order to have actual understanding. Among these intellects, an intellect is higher according as it is nearer to the first intellect which has full participation in the forms; just as among the gods or unities, that one is higher which shares more perfectly in the first unity. Although Plato distinguished between the gods and the intellects, he did not mean to imply that the gods could not have understanding. It was his desire, rather, that they should understand in a supra-intellectual manner; that is, instead of understanding by participating in certain forms, they should have understanding through themselves, with the proviso that every one of them was good and one only through participating in the first One and Good. Again, because we see that certain souls possess understanding which, however, does not befit a soul by the fact that it is a soul, otherwise it would follow that every soul is an intellect and that it would he intelligent in its whole nature, he further posited that under the order of the separate intellects, there was an order of souls, the nobler of which participate in intellectual power, while the lowest of them are lacking in it. Again, because bodies do not seem to be capable of moving themselves unless they have a soul, Plato held that self-motion belongs to bodies insofar as they participate in soul, since those bodies lacking in this participation, are not moved, unless they are moved by another. Whence he considered it to be an essential property of souls that they move themselves. In this way, below the order of souls, Plato posited the order of bodies, but in such a manner that the highest of the bodies, namely, the first heavens, which is moved by its own motion, receives motion from the highest soul, and so on to the very lowest of the heavenly bodies. Below these, furthermore, the Platonists placed immortal bodies, namely, aëreal or ethereal bodies, which participate eternally in soul. Some of these they considered to be altogether independent of earthly bodies and these they said to be bodies of demons; others became entombed in earthly bodies, which is the case with human souls. For they did not believe that this earthly human body which we touch and see, participates immediately in the soul; rather, there is another nobler body belonging to the soul, incorruptible and everlasting, even as the soul itself is incorruptible in such wise that the soul with its everlasting and invisible body is in this grosser body not as a form in matter but as a sailor in a ship. And just as they said that some men were good and others wicked, so too, with the demons. But the heavenly souls, the separate intellects and all the gods, they said were all good. In this way, therefore, between us and the highest God, it is clear that they posited four orders, namely, that of the secondary gods, that of the separate intellects, that of the heavenly souls, and that of the good or wicked demons. If all these things were true, then all these intermediate orders would be called by us 'angels,' for Sacred Scripture refers to the demons themselves as angels. The souls themselves of the heavenly bodies, on the assumption that these are animated, should also be numbered among the angels, as Augustine determines in the *Enchiridion*). (*De Substantiis separatis* 1969, 1)

7 "Unde relinquitur quod primum mobile appetit primum movens appetitu intellectuali. Ex quo potest concludi, quod primum mobile sit appetens et intelligens. Et cum nihil moveatur nisi corpus, potest concludi, quod primum mobile sit corpus animatum anima intellectuali. Non autem solum primum mobile, quod est primum caelum, movetur motu aeterno, sed etiamo omnes inferiores orbes caelestium corporum: unde et unumquodque caelestium corporum animatum est propria anima, et unumquodque habet suum appetibile separatum, quod est proprius finis sui motus. Sic igitur sunt multae substantiae separatae nullis penitus unitae corporibus. Sunt etiam multae intellectuales substantiae caelestibus corporibus unitae" (The first movable, therefore, seeks the first mover with an intellectual appetite and from this it can be inferred that the first movable is appetitive and intelligent. And since only a body is moved, we may infer that the first movable is a body animated by an intellectual soul. But the prime movable, namely the first heavens, is not the only one moved with an eternal motion; but also all the lesser spheres of the heavenly bodies likewise are. Therefore each of the heavenly bodies is animated by its own soul and each has its own separate appetible object which is the proper end of its motion). (Thomas Aquinas, *De substantiis separatis* 1969, 2)

8 Thomas Aquinas, in the commentary on the *Metaphysics* (12, 1.10 2589), notes: "Sed tamen primum non est necessarium, scilicet quod omnis substantia immaterialis et impassibilis sit finis alicuius motus caelestis. Potest enim dici quod sunt aliquae substantiate separatae altiores, quam ut sint proportionatae quasi fines caelestibus motis; quod ponere non est inconveniens. Non enim substantia immateriales sunt propter corporalia, sed magis e converso" (Yet the first assumption is not necessary, namely, that every immaterial and immutable substance is the end of some celestial motion. For it can be said that there are separate substances too high to be proportioned to the celestial motions as their ends. And this is not an absurd supposition. For immaterial substances do not exist for the sake

of corporeal things but rather the other way around). (*In Duodecim libros Metaphysicorum Aristotelis expositio* XII, 2589)

9 "Sic igitur secundum Aristotelis positionem, inter nos et summum Deum non ponitur nisi duplex ordo intellectualium substantiarum: scilicet substantiae separatae, quae sunt fines caelestium motuum; et animae orbium, quae sunt moventes per appetitum et desiderium. Haec autem Aristotelis positio certior quidem videtur, eo quod non multum recedit ab his quae sunt manifesta secundum sensum" (Thus, according to the position of Aristotle, between us and the highest God, there exists only a twofold order of intellectual substances, namely, the separate substances which are the ends of the heavenly motions, and the souls of the spheres, which move through appetite and desire. Now this position of Aristotle seems to be surer because it does not depart greatly from that which is evident according to sense). (Aquinas, *De substantiis separatis* 1969, 2.10)

10 "Unde numerus et virtus et dispositio immaterialium substantiarum ex numero caelestium motuum sufficienter apprehendi non potest" (In view of this, the number, power, and disposition of immaterial substances cannot be adequately grasped from the number of heavenly movements). (Aquinas, *De substantiis separatis* 1969, 2.12)

11 "Non est autem necessarium quod proximus finis supremi caeli sit suprema substantia immaterialis, quae est summus Deus; sed magis probabile est ut inter primam immaterialem substantiam et corpus caeleste sint multi ordines immaterialium substantiarum, quarum inferior ordinetur ad superiorem sicut ad finem, et ad infimam earum ordinetur corpus caeleste sicut ad finem proximum. Oportet enim unamquamque rem esse proportionatam quodammodo suo proximo fini. Unde propter distantiam maximam primae immaterialis substantiae ad substantiam corpoream quamcumque, non est probabile quod corporalis substantia ordinetur ad supremam substantiam sicut ad proximum finem" (And the proximate end of the highest heavens is not necessarily the highest immaterial substance which is the all-high God, but it is more probable that there are many orders of immaterial substances between the first immaterial substance and the heavenly body. The lower of these immaterial substances is ordered to the higher as to an end and a heavenly body is ordered to the lowest of these as to its proximate end. For each thing must in some way be proportioned to its proximate end. Accordingly, because of the greatest possible distance between the first immaterial substance and any corporeal substance, it is not probable that a corporeal substance should be ordered to the highest substance as to its proximate end). (Aquinas, *De substantiis separatis* 1969, 2.13)

12 "Unde etiam Avicenna posuit, causam primam non esse immediatum finem alicuius caelestium motuum, sed quamdam intelligentiam primam. Et idem etiam potest dici de inferioribus motibus caelestium corporum. Et ideo non est necessarium quod non sint plures immateriales substantiae quam sit numerus caelestium motuum" (Hence even Avicenna posited that the immediate end of any of the heavenly movements was not the first cause but a certain first intelligence; and the same can likewise be said of the lower motions of the heavenly bodies. Hence that there should not be more immaterial substances than the number of heavenly motions is not a necessary fact). (Aquinas, *De substantiis separatis* 1969, 2.14)

13 "Superiores autem intellectus Angelorum, species intelligibiles participant vel ab ideis secundum Platonicos, vel a prima substantia, quae Deus est, secundum quod est consequens ad positiones Aristotelis, et sicut se rei veritas habet. Species autem intelligibilis intellectus divini, per quam omnia cognoscit, non est aliud quam eius substantia, quae est etiam suum intelligere, ut supra probatum est per verba philosophi. Unde relinquitur quod intellectu divino nihil aliud sit altius, per quod perficiatur; sed ab ipso intellectu divino tanquam ab altiori proveniunt species intelligibiles ad intellectus Angelorum; ad intellectum autem humanum a sensibilibus rebus per actionem intellectus agentis" (The highest intellects of the angels, however, receive intelligible species either from the Ideas – according to the Platonists – or from the first substance, which is God – according to that which follows from Aristotle's position and what is in reality true. The intelligible species of the divine intellect, however, through which it knows all things, is nothing other than his substance, which is likewise his understanding as was proved above through the words of the philosopher. Hence it remains that in the case of the divine intellect there is nothing nobler through which it is perfected; but from the divine intellect itself as from a higher source, intelligible species come to the intellects of the angels; whereas to the human intellect, intelligible species come from sensible things through the action of the agent intellect). (Aquinas, *De substantiis separatis* 1969, 16.82)

14 I introduce now a fragment from Bonaventure's *Collationes in Hexaemeron* 21.27 (394) because it can be helpful in understanding the uncertainty of this passage. Dante in fact inclines towards a division of tasks in the hierarchy because it serves him to establish the existence of separate substances. Bonaventure, in turn, postulates within the Dionysian order a division of tasks but which is put into effect within the angelic sphere: "Triplex est enim genus vitae in coelo et in terra, scilicet actuosae, otiosae, et ex utaque permixtae. Actuosa respondet operationi, otiosa, scientiae;

permixta ordini. Ideo sunt activi, contemplativi ex utroque permixti" (The genus of life in heaven and earth is of three types, or active or idle, or made by both. Those that are active have operation, those idle have science, those mixed are part of a hierarchy or order).

15 For comparisons with Pseudo-Dionysius, see Roques (1996, 38–43).

16 Consider Aquinas's commentary on John, which cites Augustine, Lectio 8 Catena in Io, chapter 1, 1.8: "Dixerat in ipso vita erat [...], unde dicitur et vita erat lux hominum; quasi dicat: lux ista non est sensibilis, sed intellectualis, illuminans ipsam animam. Augustinus super Ioannem. Ex ipsa enim vita illuminantur homines, pecora non illuminantur, quia non habent rationales mentes, quae possint videre sapientam; homo autem factus ad imaginem Dei, habet rationalem mentem, per quam possit percipere sapientiam. Ergo illa vita per quam facta sunt omnia, lux est, et non quorumcumque animalium, sed hominum" (Said that in him was *vita, et vita* is not different from the verb [...] and thus says that *vita* was the light of human beings in that saying that this light is not sensibile, but intellectual, enlightning the soul itself).

17 The discourse on the contemplation of the angels and the trinitarian relationship should be rethought, then, in the perspective of an infinity of separate substances put in charge of contemplation and an internal transmission between contemplating and moving, between contemplating beings and other moving ones. Actually, Pseudo-Dionysius does not introduce separate substances acting as movers; the function of the angels in his text is purely contemplative. So the two chapters seem to draw two different lines of thought that are close to each other, at least as far as this point is concerned.

18 See Wippel (1993, 36–7, 46–8).

19 See chapters 14 and 16 of the *De substantiis separatis* and, in particular, the passage of chapter 16 cited in note 11 above; see also note 13.

20 For the Latin tradition, see Gersh (1986).

21 For the relationship between separate substances and divine ideas, the source cannot be in Albertus Magnus's *Metaphysics* 11.2 because there Albertus speaks in a generic way about "quaedam divinae substantiae." Rather, it is Aquinas who introduces in *Metaphysics* 12, Lectio 10 2588, a subject that is similar to what will be explained in his *De substantiis separatis*.

22 This seems confirmed when Dante writes that it seems confirmed by the poets and is shown in the many names (II.4.6–7). The discourse on the separate forms as species is in *De causis*, in Albertus Magnus the word "idea" appears in his *De causis*, but also and mostly he uses "forms" or "separate substances." In the *De causis* in Aquinas's commentary on proposition 3,

we find "called deos the first forms separated because they are separated and universals thus in this way divine intellects, divine souls and divine bodies they called according to the influence that they exercise on the inferior." Aquinas then recalls Dionysius's position (*In librum de causis*, 2002, 20). See also the entry "Tommaso d'Aquino" in the *Enciclopedia Dantesca*.

23 On this basis, the reading of chapter 13 of this book is to be reconsidered. The explanation provided by Vasoli does not mean much.

24 It is to be underscored again that where he faces the problem of the number of these substances, the first text on which Dante depends is the Aristotelian one: *Metaphysics* 12. What is to be discussed instead is the commentary from which he draws it. What matters to us in particular is the withdrawal from the Lambda book 12, for Aquinas, after the translation of book K by William of Moerbeke, 11 of the *Metaphysics*. Book 12 was, in fact, book 11 for Albertus Magnus who uses a text that preceeds the translation of K.

25 See the *Hierarchia* in the translation of John Scotus Eriugena, for example, Migne, *PL* vol. 122, the chapter entitled "Quod significat nominatione angelorum." The names express their relationship with the divine being.

26 "Sed est quaestio de nostro intellecto, qui coniunctus est magnitudini sensibilium [...] eo quod non *accipit nisi formas abstractas a magnitudine,* utrum *unquam contingat ipsum intelligere aliquod sic separatorum a magnitudine vel non.* Si enim contingit ipsum *intelligere separata* tunc *non semper* accipit a phantasmatibus et a magnitudine, sed *coniungitur intelligentiae separatae* danti forma intellegibiles. Quod duobus modis esse potest, quod scilicet coniungatur ei sicut efficienti tantum formas intellegibiles in nobis aut quod coniungatur ei sicut efficienti et formae et si isto secundo modo esset coniunctus noster materialis intellectus agenti intelligentias separato, tunc hoc esset maior felicitas et divinitas quedam quam intellectus humanus consequi posset" (This is a question about our intellect that is connected to the the sensibile things, [...] and does not accept forms if they are not separated from what is big. If it could happen that this intellect receives forms that are sometimes separated and sometimes not. If in fact it happens that this intellect has intellection of separate beings this means that it does not allways receives forms from panthasms and things that have a measure; rather, it means that it connects to a separate form that offers intellegibles forms.This could happen in two ways: that it makes intelligibile forms in us or that it works as an efficient form; in this second case it would be that our material intellect is connected to the agent and separated, this then would be the highest happines and divine condition that the human intellect could reach). (Albertus Magnus, *De anima* 1968, 3.3.6, 214)

27 In the *Convivio*, Dante refers to the passage of *Metaphysics* 12 which cites the fact that they are called gods (12.8 1074a 38-b). But reading Aquinas's commentary on the *De causis*, it does not escape that "deos" is used by Aquinas in order to explain proposition 3 of the *De causis*. Essentially, in the *De causis* there are intermediate creator beings. Dionysius eliminates them and leads them back to God. Dante seems to erect the *donna gentile* as divine thought and God as *dator formarum*. Avicenna, taken up by Albert, helps us to understand her identity. The *donna* is treated both as a divine idea and as a separate being or substance. Further on in the third book she will also be said to be eternal and suggested as a creative being, and in Aquinas we find the theory of the divine ideas as creators. See Wippel (1993, 4–6).

28 Siger's response recalls the twelfth book of the *Metaphysics*; here it is in synthesis: at the end it is worthwhile that according to the Platonic way there are some intelligences that are not ordered to motion but are only intelligent and speculating the essence of divine goodness. But also the Aristotelian way is not refused (see Siger 1972b, 96).

29 "Animae caelestes sunt sub ordine intelligentiarum; quare videtur quod inter primum principium et intelligentias partecipantes perfectiones quae sunt in primo principio, per modum motus explicantes eas in materia, principium motus existentes, erunt intelligentiae partecipantes perfectiones entium quae sunt in primo principio per modum intellegibilem, contemplantes solum, non ad motum ordinatae, cum ordo rerum naturalium non procedat ex dissimilbus ad dissimilia sed ex similibus ad similia: ut primo sint rerum perfectiones, *dii quidam per se existentes et ideae platonicae*, secundo intelligentiae partecipantes eas per modum intellegibilem; tertio intelligentiae magis a natura primarum perfectionum recedentes, eas per motus partecipantes, fines lationum quae in caelestibus existentes" (Celestial souls are under the order of the intellectual souls, thus it is possible to see that between the first principle and the intellectual being participating in the perfections that are in First Principle, are beings which activate such perfections in matter through the movement ; there are other intellectual beings who participate in the perfections of being that are in primo principio in virtue of contemplation and are not ordered to movement, in fact the order of natural things does not proceed from things that are different but from things that are similar. We have at first the things that are the most perfect: Gods and Platonic ideas. Then intelligent beings who participate in them through contemplation, and then those most far from perfection and that participate per modum of motion). (Siger 1972b, 95–6).

30 For the importance of Plato and his Parmenides in the Pseudo-Dyonisius, see the second volume of Turner and Corrigan (2010), the section devoted to the Pseudo-Dionysius.

31 "Pater est in se et in filio et in filio et in spiritu sancto, et filius est in Pater in se et in spiritu sancto, et spiritus sanctus est in Pater et in Filio et in se secundum rationem circumincessionis, quae notat identitatem cum distinctionem" (The Father is in himself and in the Sun and in the holy spirit, and the sun is in the Father in himself and the holy spirit; and the holy Spirit is in the Father in the Sun and in himself according to an order of circular procession, this implies identity and distinction). (21.2)

32 Foster, in his article "Tommaso d'Aquino" in the *Enciclopedia Dantesca*, dates this relationship between the angels and the Trinity back to Bonaventure's *Collationes in Hexaemeron*.

33 For the identification between ideas and gods in Thomas Aquinas, see D'Ancona Costa (1995, 242), and the relative appropriate citation from the *De causis* in note 69 of that text.

34 For the relationships between the *De causis* and Proclus and Dionysius, see Saffrey (1990).

35 Here is the fragment from the *De causis* that is useful to understand: "Ideo omnes huiusmodi formas sicut subsistentes deos vocabat" (All these forms because substances were called gods). (Thomas Aquinas 2002, 18)

36 D'Ancona Costa (1995, 133 and ff).

37 This theory of the identity between "ens intelligens" and "quod intelligitur" in the separate beings ("quod actus intelligendi et quod intelligitur in separatis sit idem") is a theory that texts ascribed to Bolognese Averroism date back to the commentator. See Kuksewicz (1965), and in particular Matheus De Eugubio, "Utrum actus intelligendi, quo intelligentia intelligit deum, sit idem cum deo" (235–9).

38 It was Siger who linked the theory of the single intellect to that of the separate substances of causistic ascendancy. I quote some passages, then, from question 9 of the *In Tertium*: "Consequenter queritur qualiter intellectus nobis copulatur utrum scilicet sit unus intellectus in omnibus, non numeratus numeratione hominum, vel sit intellectus plurificatus et numeratus secundum numeratione hominum" (The question is in which way the intellect is connected to us, and if there is only one intellect that is not numbered according to the number of human beings, or if there are a plurality of intellects numbered according to the number of human beings). Siger's answer reports that there is a single intellect and he adds that "nulla forma immaterialis, una in specie, est multiplicata secundum

numerum. Sed intellectus est forma immaterialis una in specie. Ergo non est multa in numero" (Immaterial form that is one in its species can be mutiplied according to the laws of number). He then recalls Averroes's position which holds that the intellect is single because for Averroes it is not a power of the body; if that were so it would number the same as the number of bodies. He continues going back to the theory of the heavenly movers in order to assert that in the same way that the heavenly movers are multiplied according to the number of spheres, the intellect could be multiplied according to the number of human bodies. But the point he insists on is that being immaterial and separate, the intellect can link itself with the various imagined species or "intentiones imaginatas" and it is numbered only through these intentions. Further on he recalls the movers again in order to say that "[u] nus motor non debet habere nisi unum mobile, verum est de motoribus qui habent mobile incorruptibile; intellectus autem habet mobile corruptibile, propter quod debet habere plura mobilia" (a motor that is one has to have just one mobile; this is true of those motors who have an incorruptible mobile.The intellect has a corruptible mobile, thus is has to have many mobiles). The sense of this assertion is clear: the heavens are here held to be incorruptible while the body's phantasms are corruptible just as the so-called passive intellect is held to be corruptible by Siger but not only by Siger. The relationship that is opened up is the following: the intellect, because multiplied, is corruptible, but in itself it is one and eternal. The more moderate *De anima intellectiva* also returns to the single intellect. In chapter 7 it is asked: "Utrum anima intellectiva multiplicetur multiplicatione corporum humanorum" (If the intellectual soul is made plural according to the plurality of human bodies); and the answer is given here with much caution. On one hand, it is asserted that the intellectual soul is multiplied according to the multitude of human bodies, then against it Siger seems to quote only the thesis of some philosophers – "aliqui philosophi contrarium senserunt et per viam philosophae contrarium videtur" (a few philosophers thought in a different way and following a philosophical approach) – and so a nature that is separate from matter is not multiplied by the multiplication of matter itself. The intellectual soul is separate from matter. Further on he adds: "Omnis igitur forma per se sub sistens, non habens esse materiale de sui ratione est individuata, et cum nihil individuatum possit esse commune pluribus, nulla forma liberatum esse habens a materia, potest esse communis pluribus individuis; ita quod, secundum hoc in qualibet specie separatarum intelligentiarum a materia non est nisi una numero intelligentia in qua consenserunt omnes philosophi" (Every substancial form that has not materiality is individual, and what is individual cannot be common,forms that are free from materiality can not be common to many individuals, thus in every species of separate intelligent beings we have just one intellectual being, on that agree all the philosophers). (*De anima intellectiva* 7, 102). Question 12 is also recalled for the perspective in which it is put forth that intelligence has its being from the first cause – "sic a causa prima semper est esse intelligentiae" – and there is no before and after in that being since the first cause made it not through *trasmutatione* because nothing proceeds from that cause through transmutation. But its being, that of the intelligence, is always from the first cause: "sed semper ex causa prima esse eius invenitur." But the context in which the meaning of that discoursing is placed is to be understood where it is asserted that that opinion, that is, the eternity of the intelligence, was necessary in Aristotle because he postulated that heavenly motion was "sempiternum, continuum et unum" (eternal continous and one). For this reason, both the moved and the movers were, according to Aristotle, eternal and he adds, "ita quod intentionem suam de causa prima et aliis intelligentiis fundat Aristoteles super eternitatem motus caelestis, sicut apparet duodecimo metaphysicae" (Aristotle bases his idea about the first cause and other intellectual beings on the eternity of the celestial movement as it appears for his *Metaphysics*, book 12). Siger, however, also keeps "auctoritas fidei christianae" (authority of Christian faith) in mind and adds that according to faith, intelligence is not eternal and even though there is no demonstration of this, he is nonetheless with faith.

39 On the relationship between Pseudo-Dionysius and Proclus, Saffrey's (1990) essays "Un lien objective entre le Pseudo-Denys et Proclus" (227–34) and "Nouveaux liens objectifs entre le Pseudo-Denys et Proclus" (235–48) are fundamental. See also Beierwaltes (2000, 49–97).

40 Strabismus is a visual problem in which the eyes are not aligned properly and point in different directions.

41 When, in chapter 13, we will read with regard to science and the similitude instituted with the heavens we will learn that "E la terza similitudini si è lo inducere perfezione ne le disposte cose. De la quale induzione, quanto a la prima perfezione, cioè de la generazione sustanziale, tutti li filosofi concordano che li cieli siano cagione, avvegna che diversamente questo pongano: quali da li motori, sì come Plato, Avicenna e Algazel; quali da

esse stelle" (The third similarity is that they bring about perfection in things disposed to receive it. All philosophers agree that the heavens are the causes which bring about the first perfection, that is, the generation of substances, even though they give different accounts of how this effect is produced by them. [Some say that it is brought about by the beings which move the heavens; this is the opinion of Plato, Avicenna and Algazel. Others say that it is brought about by the stars themselves]; II.13.5). What is important here is the generation of substances and so the "ens per se stans" that is given to human beings through angelic mediation and that here would indicate the possibile intellect that inspires him to look at a lady and so to contemplate a substance that in becoming reveals itself to be separate. This means that the "ens per se stans" is, in human beings, a form given by the external, originating from the divine through angelic mediation. The science here is, instead, second perfection. Whoever believes that the first perfection comes from the influence of the heavens on the heat of the seed proposes a material idea of human beings.

42 See the *Liber de causis* in Siger's (1972b) commentary, in particular Marlasca's introduction.

43 See Fioravanti (2014).

44 This principle governed the interpretation of the *Convivio* from Busnelli and Vandelli's commentary to Foster's research and in part to Nardi's and Gilson's studies which follow that standard. A critical discourse on the method held by Dante, which also involves an awareness of the one adopted by his readers, allows us to reconsider those interpretations and crystallizations.

45 This is part of the questions attributed to Matheus De Eugubio, who was active when Dante was already dead, but by recalling it I mean to underscore the possible continuity of a theme: "Utrum omnes homines naturaliter scire desiderant" (If all men desire naturally to know) (Kuksewicz 1965, 282–4).

46 On this provenance, see D'Ancona Costa (1995, esp. 121–38).

47 I quote below the full text of the proem to Aquinas's *Metaphysics,* which proposes subjects that are also found in his commentary on Boethius's *De trinitate*. Aquinas distinguishes metaphysics as divine science and theology from the metaphysics as the science of the causes and principles, and he conceives metaphysics as first philosophy and as the science of the first being: "Sicut docet philosophus in politicis suis, quando aliqua plura ordinantur ad unum, oportet unum eorum esse regulans, sive regens, et alia regulata, sive recta. Quod quidem patet in unione animae et corporis; nam anima naturaliter imperat, et corpus obedit. Similiter etiam inter

animae vires: irascibilis enim et concupiscibilis naturali ordine per rationem reguntur. *Omnes autem scientiae et artes ordinantur in unum, scilicet ad hominis perfectionem, quae est eius beatitudo.* Unde necesse est, quod una earum sit aliarum omnium rectrix, quae *nomen sapientiae* recte vindicat. Nam sapientis est alios ordinare. Quae autem sit haec scientia, et circa qualia, considerari potest, si diligenter respiciatur quomodo est aliquis idoneus ad regendum. Sicut enim, ut in libro praedicto philosophus dicit, homines intellectu vigentes, naturaliter aliorum rectores et domini sunt: homines vero qui sunt robusti corpore, intellectu vero deficientes, sunt naturaliter servi: *ita scientia debet esse naturaliter aliarum regulatrix, quae maxime intellectualis est. Haec autem est, quae circa maxime intelligibilia versatur.* Maxime autem intelligibilia tripliciter accipere possumus. Primo quidem ex ordine intelligendi. Nam ex quibus intellectus certitudinem accipit, videntur esse intelligibilia magis. *Unde, cum certitudo scientiae per intellectum acquiratur ex causis, causarum cognitio maxime intellectualis esse videtur. Unde et illa scientia, quae primas causas considerat, videtur esse maxime aliarum regulatrix.* Secundo ex comparatione intellectus ad sensum. Nam, cum sensus sit cognitio particularium, intellectus per hoc ab ipso differre videtur, quod universalia comprehendit. *Unde et illa scientia maxime est intellectualis, quae circa principia maxime universalia versatur. Quae quidem sunt ens, et ea quae consequuntur ens, ut unum et multa, potentia et actus.* Huiusmodi autem non debent omnino indeterminata remanere, cum sine his completa congitio de his, quae sunt propria alicui generi vel speciei, haberi non possit. Nec iterum in una aliqua particulari scientia tractari debent: quia cum his unumquodque genus entium ad sui cognitionem indigeat, pari ratione in qualibet particulari scientia tractarentur. *Unde restat quod in una communi scientia huiusmodi tractentur; quae cum maxime intellectualis sit, est aliarum regulatrix.* Tertio ex ipsa cognitione intellectus. *Nam cum unaquaeque res ex hoc ipso vim intellectivam habeat, quod est a materia immunis, oportet illa esse maxime intelligibilia, quae sunt maxime a materia separata.* Intelligibile enim et intellectum oportet proportionata esse, et unius generis, *cum intellectus et intelligibile in actu sint unum.* Ea vero sunt maxime a materia separata, quae non tantum a signata materia abstrahunt, *sicut formae naturales in universali acceptae, de quibus tractat scientia naturalis,* sed omnino a materia sensibili. *Et non solum secundum rationem, sicut mathematica, sed etiam secundum esse, sicut Deus et intelligentiae.* Unde scientia, quae de istis rebus considerat, maxime videtur esse intellectualis, et aliarum princeps sive domina. Haec autem triplex consideratio, non diversis, sed uni scientiae attribui debet. Nam praedictae substantiae separatae sunt universales et primae causae essendi. Eiusdem autem scientiae est considerare causas proprias alicuius generis et genus ipsum: sicut naturalis considerat principia corporis naturalis. Unde oportet quod ad eamdem scientiam pertineat considerare substantias separatas, et ens commune, quod est genus, cuius sunt praedictae substantiae communes et universales causae. *Ex quo apparet, quod quamvis ista scientia praedicta tria consideret, non tamen considerat quodlibet eorum ut subiectum, sed ipsum solum ens commune. Hoc enim est subiectum in scientia, cuius causas et passiones quaerimus, non autem ipsae causae alicuius generis quaesiti. Nam cognitio causarum alicuius generis, est finis ad quem consideratio scientiae pertingit. Quamvis autem subiectum huius scientiae sit ens commune, dicitur tamen tota de his quae sunt separata a materia secundum esse et rationem.* Quia secundum esse et rationem separari dicuntur, non solum illa quae nunquam in materia esse possunt, sicut Deus et intellectuales substantiae, sed etiam illa quae possunt sine materia esse, sicut ens commune. Hoc tamen non contingeret, si a materia secundum esse dependerent. *Secundum igitur tria praedicta, ex quibus perfectio huius scientiae attenditur, sortitur tria nomina. Dicitur enim scientia divina sive theologia, inquantum praedictas substantias considerat. Metaphysica, inquantum considerat ens et ea quae consequuntur ipsum. Haec enim transphysica inveniuntur in via resolutionis, sicut magis communia post minus communia. Dicitur autem prima philosophia, inquantum primas rerum causas considerat.* Sic igitur patet quid sit subiectum huius scientiae, et qualiter se habeat ad alias scientias, et quo nomine nominetur.

(When several things are ordained to one thing, one of them must rule or govern and the rest be ruled or governed, as the philosopher teaches in the *Politics*. This is evident in the union of soul and body, for the soul naturally commands and the body obeys. The same thing is true of the soul's powers, for the concupiscible and irascible appetites are ruled in a natural order by reason. Now all the sciences and arts are ordained to one thing, namely, to man's perfection, which is happiness. Hence one of these sciences and arts must be the mistress of all the others, and this rightly lays claim to the name *wisdom*; for it is the office of the wise man to direct others. We can discover which science this is and the sort of things with which it deals by carefully examining the qualities of a good ruler; for just as men of superior intelligence are naturally the rulers and masters of others, whereas those of great physical strength and little intelligence are naturally slaves, as the philosopher says in the aforementioned book in a similar way that science which is intellectual in the highest degree should be naturally the ruler of the others. This science is the one which treats of the most intelligible objects. Now the phrase "most intelligible objects" can be understood in three ways. First, from the viewpoint of the order of knowing; for those things from which the intellect derives certitude seem to be more intelligible. Therefore, since the certitude of science is acquired by the intellect knowing causes, a knowledge of causes seems to be intellectual in the highest degree. Hence that science which considers first causes also seems to be the ruler of the others in the highest degree. Second, this phrase can be understood by comparing the intellect with the senses; for while sensory perception is a knowledge of particulars, the intellect seems to differ from sense by reason of the fact that it comprehends universals. Hence that science is pre-eminently intellectual which deals with the most universal principles. These principles are being and those things which naturally accompany being, such as unity and plurality, potency and act. Now such principles should not remain entirely undetermined, since without them complete knowledge of the principles which are proper to any genus or species cannot be had. Nor again should they be dealt with in any one particular science, for, since a knowledge of each class of beings stands in need if such principles, they would with equal reason be investigated in every particular science. It follows, then, that such principles should be treated by one common science, which, since it is intellectual in the highest degree, is the mistress of the others. Third, this phrase can be understood from the viewpoint of the intellect's own knowledge. For since each thing has intellective power by virtue of being free from matter, those things must be intelligible in the highest degree which are altogether separate, from matter. For the intellect and the intelligible object must be proportionate to each other and must belong to the same genus, since the intellect and the intelligible object are one in act. Now those things are separate from matter in the highest degree which abstract not only from signate matter [as the natural forms taken universally of which the philosophy of nature treats] but from sensible matter altogether; and these are separate from matter not only in their intelligible constitution [*ratio*], as the objects of mathematics, but also in being [*esse*], as God and the intelligences. Therefore the science which considers such things seems to be the most intellectual and the ruler or mistress of the others. Now this threefold consideration should be assigned to one and the same science and not to different sciences, because the aforementioned separate substances are the universal and first causes of being. Moreover, it pertains to one and the same science to consider both the proper causes of some genus and the genus itself; for example, the philosophy of nature considers the principles of a natural body. Therefore, it must be the office of one and the same science to consider the separate substances and being in general [ens commune], which is the genus of which the aforementioned substances are the common and universal causes. From this it is evident that, although this science [metaphysics or first philosophy] studies the three things mentioned above, it does not investigate any one of them as its subject, but only being in general. For the subject of a science is the genus whose causes and properties we seek, and not the causes themselves of the particular genus studied; for a knowledge of the causes of some genus is the goal to which the investigation of a science attains. Now although the subject of this science is being in general, the whole of it is predicated of those things which are separate from matter both in their intelligible constitution and in being. For it is not only those things which can never exist in matter that are said to be separate from matter in their intelligible constitution and being, such as God and the intellectual substances, but also those which can exist without matter, as being in general. This could not be the case, however, if their being depended on matter. Herefore, in accordance with the three things mentioned above from which this science derives its perfection, three names arise. It is called divine science or theology inasmuch as it considers the aforementioned substances. It is called *metaphysics* inasmuch as it considers being and the attributes which naturally accompany being [*for things which transcend the physical order are* discovered by the process of analysis, as the more common are discovered after the less common]. It is called first philosophy inasmuch as it considers the first causes of things. Therefore, it is evident what the subject of this science is, and how it is related to the other sciences, and by what names it is designated).

48 In Bonaventure, every science is the result of an illumination that derives from God and to which corresponds the *reductio artium ad theologian* as the return of science to *sapientia*. See Maierù (2001).

49 This is a fragment from Aquinas's commentary: "Unde corpus celeste quod movetur non est in momento aeternitatis, sed in momento temporis. Et praeterea motus non est actio eius quod movetur sed magis passio: est autem actio moventis [...] Principium autem motus est anima, ut in II propositione habitum est. Quia ergo anima nobilis secundum se est immobilis actio autem eius est motus, consequens est ut anima secundum suam substantiam sit in momento aeternitatis, eius vero actio est in tempore; intelligentiae vero et substantia et actio est in momento aeternitatis" (Thus the heavenly body that is moved is not in eternity but in time. In addition the movement is not an action of what is moved, but a passion, it is in fact an action of what moves. The source of movement is the soul, as we said in proposition 2. The noble soul is in itself without movement, its action is

movement, therefore according to its substance the soul is in eternity, but its action is in time. But the intelligences are in eternity, according to their substance and action). (Thomas Aquinas 2002, 141–2)

50 "Ergo ex dictis, ipsae, scilicet caelestes essentiae, sunt factae primo et multipliciter, ut dictum est, in partecipatione dei, et per hoc etiam sunt primo manifestatrices divinae occulationis, idest divini occulti, et propterea … cognominatione angelica super omnia alia nomina, eo quod edunt, idest recipiunt quodam conatu ut manifestatam divinam illuminationem in seipsas et per se deferunt in nos manifestationes ... Angelus enim nuntius dicitur propter nuntiandi nobis officium (From what has been said, the celestial substances are made at first and in various ways to participate in the divine being, they make manifest therefore the secret being of the divine, and because of it are the names of angels more important than the other names because they receive a power to manifest divine illuminations that they send to us as his manifestations … The angel, in fact, is the messenger because it announces our duty to us).

51 Philosophical practice is part of the condemned propositions. Proposition 56, "Quod substantiae separatae per suum intellectum creant res" (Separate substances create things through their intellect) (Hissette 1977, 110), is linked to the Neoplatonic theory of creation through intermediaries that Nardi already held was followed by Dante. Heresy manifests against a God, single creator and origin, writes Hissette. Siger comments on the *De causis* when explaining proposition 13 of the *De causis*, which deals with the noble soul, that is, the soul of heavenly bodies, the noble soul, that is, *anima caeli*. Siger teaches that it knows the intelligible realities through the representation that it has of them (through *modum imaginis*). But it has knowledge of the world of generation and corruption because it is the ideal model that it causes through the mediation of heavenly bodies: "Anima caeli per intellectum causat res sensibiles generabiles et corruptibiles cum per intellectum coelum moveat, quo mediante sensibilia causat" (The soul of heaven causes things sensible because it moves though its intellect of the heaven, and through it causes sensible things) (Siger's [1972b] commentary on the *De causis*, ed. Marlasca, 18–20, as cited in Hissette 1977, 111). And again: "Dicendum est quod species intelligibiles existentes in intelligentia naturam habent imaginis, non tamen imaginis a rebus causatae, sed a causa prima et quod etiam quaedam illarum specierum naturam habent exemplarium in quantum intelligentia per scientia est istorum inferiorum causa" (Siger 1972b, 162, 145–9, as cited in Hissette 1977, 111). But this last is also Aquinas's position: the intelligences as second causes. Proposition 61: "Quod cum intelligentia sit plena formis,

imprimit illas formas in materiam per corpora caelestia tamquam per instrumenta." Heavenly bodies are considered as instruments of intelligence, having intelligible species of things it possesses an informing causality that is exercised on the matter of the sublunar world. Hissette (1977) explains that the theory is not exactly orthodox, even if it does not affirm that creation develops an aspect of the Platonic theory of emanation (115). This is in part Dante's thesis in the canzone of this book. Thesis 62: "Quod materia inferior obedit substantiae spirituali" (Inferior matter obeys the spiritual substances.) It is an error if one understands through intellect (*intellige*) simply or according to every transmutation. According to Hissette (1977) matter is subjected to the intelligences, the censors cannot deny it but they cannot accept an absolute dependence, it would be the triumph of determinism if neither God nor the will of humans could avoid that influence. Siger, *De causis* (1972b): whether the intelligent substances imprint the intellectual soul.

52 In closing, it is worth underscoring that both the theme of the angel-intelligences and that of the divine ideas were part of the Parisian debate that, as is known, had seen the condemnation of 219 propositions. There is no doubt that the subjects of the *Convivio* participated in the more advanced debate. It is known that some positions accepted by Aquinas were among those condemned in Paris in 1277 (Weisheipl 1994, 338–9). The discourse on the angel-intelligences was clearly a complex and burning theme and the *De causis*, a text read at the University of Paris, in the thirteenth century was actually a text of dangerous content. The premises for sending the notion of creation as conceived on biblical and Christian bases into crisis were in this work, and the theories on the eternity of the world, among others, came from Aristotle and his readers. As is known, Aquinas himself did not feel up to asserting with certainty the theory of creation from nothing. The *Convivio* suggests a relationship between the central discourse on human knowledge and the one on creation, indirectly suggested through traces spread throughout the text. The fourth book will open with the problem of creation that is faced in a key subject of thought of Aristotelian-Platonic derivation: the origin of the first matter. Some propositions condemned in 1277 are given here that can account for the uneven terrain on which Dante's position is or is near or is in contradiction with. Let us start with propositions 50 and 52, which are close to what we previously discussed: "Quod si esset aliqua substantia separata quae non moveret aliquod corpus in hoc mundo sensibili, non clauderetur in universo" (That if there were a separate substance that does not move anything in this sensible world it would not be included in the universe; prop.

50); "Quod substantiae separate, eo quod habent unum appetitum, non mutantur in opere" (That the separate substances do not change in their operation since their appetite is single; prop. 52). It is unquestionable that the theme of the intelligences was one of those threads of great contestation; the theme of their eternity is correlated to their identity. For example, in proposition 38, we read that they are eternal and so not created (Hissette 1977, 76) and the debate is reconstructed looking also at the propositions that Hissette numbers as 39, 40, and 41. Essentially, what is separate is eternal and coeternal with the first principle: "Quod ommnia separata coeterna sunt primo principio" (39). The reasons, Hissette (1977) explains, are in propositions 40 and 41, and in fact what does not have matter is eternal (40) and the separate substances, since they do not have matter, are eternal (41). The theses are incompatible with the Christian doctrine that teaches the creation of the world and the intelligences. The thesis of the eternity of the intelligences, Hissette (1977) writes, is familiar to Siger who defends the *doctrine des philosophes* in the *Quaestiones in Metaphysicam* (1983) where Siger writes that everything that is not created, not generated is everlasting: "intentio aristotelis est omne ingenitum esse sempiternum" (cited in Hissette 1977, 79, commentary on the proposition). In this Siger, Hissette (1977) writes, expounds Aristotle's doctrine. And in the *De anima intellectiva* (5), he writes that the intellectual soul is eternal and separate from other powers of the soul, as the eternal is separate from the corruptible. The soul is eternal in the past as in the future and so Hissette cites from the *Liber de causis* in Siger's commentary: "ex hos sequitur quod intelligentia est sine principio et sine fine" (from it derives that an intellectual being is without a beginning and end). But alongside what we considered a proposition to reconsider is proposition 42, and 43 more specifically, for the intelligences and separate substances: "Quod quia intelligentiae non habent materiam. Deus non posset facere plures eiusdem speciei" (Because the intellectual beings have not materiality, God cannot create many of the same species) (Hissette 1977, 82). The variety of individuals within the same species is not possible except by means of matter. It is contradictory to affirm that God multiplies the individuals of one species without matter. God cannot create a great number of immaterial intelligences of the same species. The thesis is received as an attack on divine power. But the sense of this proposition regards the intellectual soul, single for the entire human species. It is what we saw that Siger posed as a problem in his commentary on the *De causis*. Does Dante, in formulating the thesis of the ideas in the mind of God, seem at least in part to escape that problematic of their eternity, that is not created? No, rather he concealed the eternity and the heterodox position through the theory of the ideas in the divine mind and making the *donna gentile* a divine idea and a separate substance, he aligned himself with the condemned positions where he went on to sustain that human beings were capable of contemplating the new lady. The idea that the intellectual soul is a compound being that is realized in the vision of a separate substance falls within the lines of the heterodox, but Dante uses Albertus Magnus's text and in this text intellection is held to be separate. Dante suggests the *coniunctio* without recalling it with clarity and postulates the intellectual essence of human beings not proceeding from the vegetative and sensible. It is Albert's position, and it is also true that Siger depends on Albert and that Albert, for some of his subjects, refers to Averroes.

3. Reading with *Suspicio*

1 In the prose of *Convivio* II, Dante explained the verb "udire" (to listen) that he has introduced in the canzone *Voi che 'ntendendo* as "intendere con l'intelletto" (to understand with intellect).

2 I have discussed the theme of praise in Dante and the medieval tradition in *Dante* (Ardizzone 2011, chaps. 1 and 2).

3 "Si unum intellectum tunc erit unus intellectus … Ergo secundum eorum rationem simpliciter concludere possumus quod sit unum intellectum tantum et non solum unum intellectum ab omnis hominibus" (This if the intellect is one … thus according to their reasoning we may conclude that there is just one intellect and not one just for the human beings). (Aquinas, *De unitate intellectus* 1976, 102–3)

4 I quote a fragment of Aquinas's text: "Rationis processui deservit alia pars Logicae quae dicitur *inventiva*. Nam inventio non semper est cum certitudo ... quandoque vere non fit complete fides vel opinio sed suspicio quedam quia non totaliter declinatur ad una partem contradictionis, licet magis inclinetur in hanc quam in illam et ad hoc ordinatur Rhetorica (Another part of logic needs to be discussed that is called inventive. In fact invention is is not always with certainty … sometime it does not take place with certainty or opinion but *suspicio* because it does not incline in full to one part of contradiction, but, it is inclined more to that and not to the other, and to this end is ordered Rhetorica). (*In Posteriorum Analyticorum* 1955, Proemium, 148)

5 "Lo quarto senso si chiama anagogico, cioè sovrasenso; e questo è quando spiritualmente si spone una scrittura, la quale ancora [che sia vera] eziandio nel senso litterale, per le cose significate significa delle superne

cose dell'etternal gloria: sì come vedere si può in quello canto del Profeta che dice che nell'uscita del popolo d'Israel d'Egitto Giudea è fatta santa e libera: che avegna essere vero secondo la lettera sia manifesto, non meno è vero quello che spiritualmente s'intende, cioè che nell'uscita dell'anima dal peccato, essa sia fatta santa e libera in sua potestate" (The fourth sense is called anagogical, that is to say, beyond the senses; and this occurs when a scripture is expounded in a spiritual sense which, although it is true also in the literal sense, signifies by means of the things signified a part of the supernal things of eternal glory, as may be seen in the song of the prophet which says that when the people of Israel went out of Egypt, Judea was made whole and free). (*Convivio* II.1.6)

6 For a discussion about praise in Dante, see Ardizzone (2011, 39–114) and Roques (1966, 225–6).

7 In the work of the Pseudo-Dyonisius – as Roques (1966) underlines – praise and prayers are identical (223–6).

8 In Aristotle's *Nicomachean Ethics,* all human associations are considered parts of the state and community is assumed to be the essence of friendship (8.9.1–4).

9 What the gentle lady means has been introduced in our reading of the canzone *Voi che 'ntendendo.* Dante will commentate on this in the second treatise of *Convivio.* The angel-intelligences as mediators of God or secondary causes exercise their power on what is living.and on those things that are subjected to their action. According to Augustine commentator of the John's Gospel, the verbum-logos is coincident with the Divine Sapientia and life is the divine idea. (See Augustine's commentary to John's Gospel in *In Evangilium Johannis* 1.9 and 1.16–17).

10 "... et dicit quod virtuosus maxime vult vivere seipsum et conservari in esse, et precipue quantum ad illam animam partem cui inest sapientia ... Ideo unusquisque vult se esse in quantum conservatur id quod ipse est. Id autem quod maxime conservatur idem in suo esse est Deus ... Deo autem maxime sumus similes secundum intellectum, qui est incorruptibilis et immutabilis ... Et dicit quod virtuosus maxime vult convivere sibi ipsi, scilicet revertendo ad cor suum et secum meditando" (and he says that the virtuous man desires to live and to preserve himself, especially that part of soul to which wisdom belongs. Thus everybody desires to be to preserve what he is in himself. The One who preserve himself in his being is God ... we are similor to God because our intellect, which is incorruptible and immutable ... And he says that the virtuous man wants to live with himself going back to his own heart and meditating). (Aquinas, *In Ethicorum, 1805–1808,* 1964a)

11 Albertus Magnus, *De causis et processu* (1993), takes from the Platonic tradition the idea of God as "dator formarum": "Plato formas posuit in lumine datoris formarum existentes" (Plato put forms in the light which is the giver of the forms that exist) (43, 63). For the *Liber de causis*, see the introduction by Pattin in *Le Liber de causis* (n.d.), édition etablie a l'aide de 90 manuscripts.

12 Proposition 20, p. 157: "Prima enim bonitas influit bonitates supra res omnes influxione una ... unaqueque rerum recipit ex illa influxione secundum modum suae virtutis et sui esse" (The first goodness flows goodness on the all things in virtue of one flowing and every thing receives such flowing according to its virtue and its being); and proposition 24, p. 179: "Et diversitas quidem receptionis non fit ex Causa prima, sed propter recipiens" (And the diversity of reception does not depend from the first cause but because of the recipient). See the comment by Thomas Aquinas to proposition 24: "Causa prima est in rebus diversimode ... non autem omnes res recipiunt eodem modo actionem causae primae ... recipiunt eam multipliciter scilicet secundum suae substantiae" (The first cause is in things in different ways ... in fact things receive in different ways the action of the first cause, they receive it according to their substance). (*Expositiones super librum de causis*, 120–1)

13 "Causa prima non potest esse nisi una" (The first cause can be just One) (*De causis et processu universitatis a prima causa*, 63.5); "Ab uno simplici non est nisi unum ab Aristotle scribitur ... et ab Alpharabio et ab Avicenna et Averroe suscipitur et explanatur" (From a one that is simple derives just one, writes Aristotle, and this is taken by Alpharabi, Avicenna, and Averroes and is explained) (13.69). "A simplici non est nisi unum simplex" (From what is simple can derive just a simple one) (100.28); "impossibile est ab uno et eodem simplici duo esse secundum ordinem naturae" (it is impossible that from the one and simple derive two according to the order of nature) (108.17).

14 "... primum et proprie necessarium sit simplex ... quia ex pluribus entis in actu non fit unum" (what is first and necessary is simple ... because from many beings in act can not derive one). (Siger, *Quaestiones in Metaphysicam*, 1983, 5, questions 15 and 16, 334–5)

15 For *henosis* (union), see the book that De Andia has devoted to it: *Henosis: L'union a Dieu Chez Denys L'Areopagite* (1997, esp. 23–4).

16 For the vision of the divine ideas by the angels, see Augustine, *In Evangelium Joannis, Omelia* 1.9–13 and 13.4; and Aquinas, *De cognitione angelorum* in *De veritate*, question 8.

17 Dante introduces the bread of angels in the opening of *Convivio*, which, according to Augustine, is the *logos-verbum* coincident with the divine

ideas that the angels desire to eat. See *In evangelium Johannis, Omelia* 1.9–13 and 13.4. Augustine identifies divine ideas and *logos* in his *De diversis questionibus*, question 46. Nardi (1944, 47–51), in the section in which he discusses the bread of angels as in *Convivio* I, does not take into account this Augustinian theory which appears to be essential for a correct understanding of the *Convivio*.

18 See note 9.

19 Here I quote two fragments from Albert, *De causis* (1995): "corpora naturalia sine anima exixtentia formas habent se continentes quae non habent a materia, quod formae substantiales sunt sed potius a coelo, quod primum formale corpus est" (natural bodies that have no soul have forms which do not derive from matter, in fact substantial forms derive from the Heaven which is the first formal body) (154.62–65); "corpus caeleste quod est quasi instrumentum animae, ad formam substantialem non moveret, nisi informaretur conceptu animae, qui conceptus agentis intelligentiae est" (the celestial body, which is almost the instrument of the soul, would not move toward the substantial form, if it is not informed by the the concept of the soul, this is the concept of the acting intelligent being) (185.3–6).

20 Aquinas in *Super librum de Causis* (2002), comments on proposition 28: "Omnis substantia stans per essentiam suam est simplex et non dividitur" (every substance being for it own essence is simple and is not divided) explains that "videtur quod simplex et impartibile est idem subiecto … simplex autem dicitur aliquid per privationem compositionis,quia scilicet non est ex multis compositum" (what is simple is one and the same thing with what can not be divided … simple in fact is said of something that is lacking of composition, that is, it is not composed by many things) (131–2). For his part, Siger in *Les quaestiones super Librum de causis* (1972b) writes that "dicendum est quod forma substantialis uniscuisque rei simplex est,non composita ex formis diversis (We have to stress that the substancial form of every thing is simple and not composed) (47–8).

21 De Libera (1990a, 102): "God is the giver of forms and every form is a ray of the First intelligence or first cause." The idea that in God are the archetypes of things recurs in Albert's *De causis*. See, for instance, the following quotations: "omnis forma sicut in archetipo est in motore primo" (every form is in the the first motor as in the archetype) (12.71 and 37.16). The field related to the word "idea" espresses the same principle as it proceeds from the first light. See for instance the following fragment at 85.25: "lumen … primi agentis vehit formas ideales in omnem rerum multitudinem" (the light of the fist agent sends the ideal forms in the multitude of all things).

22 "The reason for this natural tendency may be this: that every substantial form proceeds from its first cause, which is God, as is stated in the book *On Causes*, and these forms receive their diversity not from it, which is most simple, but from the secondary causes and from the matter into which it descends. Thus in the same book, in treating of the infusion of divine goodness, the following words appear: And the goodnesses and the gifts are made diverse by the participation of the thing which receives them" (*Convivio* III.2.4).

23 De Libera (1990a, 104) writes that the analogical divine communication implies also an internal ability of assimilation. God's communication to creatures can not be thought withouth our conversion of created beings to God … theophany draws a double movement of descent and ascent.

24 In Aristotle's *Nicomachean Ethics*, there are five virtues that allow the knowledge of truth: *tecne* (art), *episteme* (science), *pronesis* (prudence), *sophia*, and *nous* (the intuitive intelligence and rational intuition). *Sophia* combines intelligence and scientific knowledge.

25 The original Latin of the first fragment, "Tu e dio che nella mente (te) delli uomini mise" (You and God, who placed you in the minds of men), is the following: "Tu mihi et, qui te sapientium mentibus inseriut, deus" (*De consolatione* 1.4.8); and that of the second, "Tutte le cose produci da lo superno essemplo, tu, bellissimo, bello mondo ne la mente portante" (You produce all things from the supernal exemplar, you, most beautiful, bearing in your mind the beautiful world), is the following: "Tu cuncta superno ducis ab exemplo, pulchrum pulcherrimus ipse mundum mente gerens" (*De consolatione* 3.9.vv. 6–8).

26 *De causis* 2.1.1, 60, and 2a.4A.3, 158.

27 *De veritate* question 3.1.6.

28 Logical subject is the subject of a sentence that expresses the actual agent of an expressed or implied action (as *father* in "it is your father speaking"), or it is the thing about which something is otherwise predicated (as *to do right* in "it is sometimes hard to do right") – called also *real subject* and distinguished from the *grammatical subject*).

29 "Ché se a memoria si reduce ciò che detto è di sopra, filosofia è uno amoroso uso di sapienza, lo quale massimamente è in Dio, però che in lui è somma sapienza e sommo amore e sommo atto: che non può essere altrove se non in quanto da esso procede. È adunque la divina filosofia della divina essenzia, però che in esso non può essere cosa alla sua essenzia aggiunta; ed è nobilissima, però che nobilissima è la essenzia divina; [ed] è in lui per modo perfetto e vero, quasi per etterno matrimonio" (For if we recall what has been said above, Philosophy is a loving use of the wisdom

which exists in the greatest measure in God, since supreme wisdom, supreme love, and supreme actuality are found in him; for it could not exist elsewhere, except insofar as it proceeds from him. Divine Philosophy is therefore of the divine essence because in him nothing can be added to his essence; and she is most noble because the divine essence is most noble; and she exists in him in a true and perfect manner, as if by eternal marriage; III.12.12–13).

30 The allegorical commentary of the third treatise will confirm the link between philosophy and the ideas in the mind of God: "Dico adunque che Dio, che tutto intende (ché suo 'girare' è suo 'intendere'), non vede tanto gentil cosa quanto elli vede quando mira là dove è questa Filosofia. Ché, avegna che Dio, esso medesimo mirando, veggia insiememente tutto, in quanto la distinzione delle cose è in lui per [lo] modo che lo effetto è nella cagione, vede quelle distinte. Vede adunque questa nobilissima di tutte assolutamente, in quanto perfettissima in sé la vede e in sua essenzia" (I say, then, that God, whose understanding embraces everything (for his "circling" is his "understanding"), sees nothing so noble as he sees when he gazes upon the place where this Philosophy dwells. For although God, gazing upon Himself, sees all things collectively, yet he sees them discretely insofar as the discreteness of things exists in Him in such manner that the effect exists within the cause. He sees then this most noble of things absolutely, insofar as He sees her perfectly in Himself and in His essence; III.12.11–12).

31 Proclus, *The Elements of Theology*, prop. 174, p. 153.

32 About the eternity of the lady in *Amor che ne la mente mi ragiona,* see the last chapter in Ardizzone (2011).

33 See for instance, Thomas Aquinas in *Super Librum De causis*: "Intelligens et intellectum in intellectibus separatis sunt simul in quantum scilicet secundum substantiam suam non solum sunt intellectus sed intelligibiles" (The intellectual being and what is intellected in the intellects that are separated are at once, in fact according to their substance they are not only intellectual beings but also intellegibles) (prop. 13, p. 83).

34 "… quando intelligentia intelligit quamcumque rem tunc intelligens et id quo intelligit unum et idem sunt in una re et simul,et similiter id quod intelligitur" (when an intellectual being has intelligence of a thing then the intellectual being and what is intellected are one and the same thing and at the same time). (*Albertus Magnus,* 1993, 2.2.32, p. 125)

35 "Aristoteles in hoc tertio dicit quod in his quae sunt sine materia est idem intellectus et quod intelligitur … intelligentia quidquid intelligit, intelligit per rationem intelligendi suam substantiam. Et hoc sentit Aristoteles in

hoc tertio cum dicit in separatis a materia idem est sciens et scitum" (Aristotle says in book third of on soul that in those beings who are without matter the intellectual being and what is intellected are the same … An intellectual being whatever he intellects, intellects in order to understand his own substance. Aristotle is of the same opinion in this Tertium when he says that in the beings that separated from matter the being who knows and what he knows are one and the same thing). (Siger, *Quaestiones in Tertium De Anima* 1972a, proposition 17, pp. 61 and 63)

36 That God thinks Himself is in Aristotle's *Metaphysics;* Aquinas's comment on *Methaphysicorum* (1.1.15) while stressing that Aristotle eliminated the exemplaria of things or models recalls however "illa ratio," according to which "non removet divinam scientiam esse rerum ommnium exemplarem" (that reason which does not remove the idea that the divine science is the model of all things).

37 Aquinas *In Metaphysicorum* 1.1.3: "Alio modo, ut demonstret specialiter istam philosophiam, sive sapientiam, quae est circa altissimas causas; quia inter causas altissimas etiam est finalis causa, ut supra dictum est. Unde oportet, quod haec scientia consideret ultimum et universalem finem omnium. Et sic omnes aliae scientiae in eam ordinantur sicut in finem; unde sola ista maxime propter se est ... Illa scientia est maxime honorabilis, quae est maxime divina, sicut etiam Deus honorabilior est rebus omnibus: sed ista scientia est maxime divina: ergo est honorabilissima. Minor sic probatur. Aliqua scientia dicitur esse divina dupliciter; et haec sola scientia utroque modo divina dicitur. Uno modo scientia divina dicitur quam Deus habet. Alio modo, quia est de rebus divinis. Quod autem haec sola habeat utrumque, est manifestum; quia, cum haec scientia sit de primis causis et principiis, oportet quod sit de Deo; quia Deus hoc modo intelligitur ab omnibus, ut de numero causarum existens, et ut quoddam principium rerum. Item talem scientiam, quae est de Deo et de primis causis, aut solus Deus habet, aut si non solus, ipse tamen maxime habet. Solus quidem habet secundum perfectam comprehensionem. Maxime vero habet, inquantum suo modo etiam ab hominibus habetur, licet ab eis non ut possessio habeatur, sed sicut aliquid ab eo mutuatum" (Understood in another way, the expression may specifically indicate this philosophy or wisdom which deals with the highest causes; for the final cause is also one of the highest causes, as was stated above. Therefore, this science must consider the highest and universal end of all things. And, in this way, all the other sciences are subordinated to it as an end. Hence only this science exists in the highest degree for itself … That science which is most divine is most honourable, just as God Himself is also the most honourable of

all things. But this science is the most divine, and is therefore the most honourable. The minor premise is proved in this way: a science is said to be divine in two ways, and only this science is said to be divine in both ways. First, the science which God has is said to be divine; and second, the science which is about divine matters is said to be divine. But it is evident that only this science meets both of these requirements, because, since this science is about first causes and principles, it must be about God; for God is understood in this way by all inasmuch as He is one of the causes and a principle of things. Again, such a science which is about God and first causes, either God alone has or, if not He alone, at least He has it in the highest degree. Indeed, He alone has it in a perfectly comprehensive way. And He has it in the highest degree inasmuch as it is also had by men in their own way, although it is not had by them as a human possession, but as something borrowed from Him). However, for Aquinas, this science does not belong to human beings: "ergo predicata scientia non est humana possessio."

38 Petrus Hispanus (1972, 7.49).

39 Isidoro, *Etymologiae*, writes that "philosophia" philosophy derives from philos-sophos; see 2.24.

40 Aquinas, *In Metaphysicorum* 1.1.

41 In book 10 of the *Nicomachean Ethics* such knowledge is identified with theory. This is part of the discussion about *eudemonia*, or happiness, that is built on action, but this action derives from ethics and dianoethics (rational) virtues. Dianoethics as described in book 6, such virtues culminate in *sapientia*. It is theory or contemplation the highest activity of the intellect. This contemplation is proper to God, who is the thought of thought. For such contemplation, the human being becomes more similar to his principle (book 10.8.6–8).

42 Aquinas, *In Metaphysicorum* 1.1.3: as quoted abote in note 37.

43 See Siger, *Quaestiones in Metaphysicam* (1983, 2, p. 31): "ad quam scientiam pertinet cognition veritatis … ad philosophiam pertinet cognition veritatis … philosophia maxime est scientia veritatis… quae scientia intelligatur per Philosophiam … per eam sapientia intelligitur unde nec est quaecumque scientia,sed quae de primis causis considerat … scientia quae ad magis causam accedit magis est sapientia,magis autem causae sunt universaliores causae,que sunt entis causae" (to this science belongs the cognition of truth,to philosophy belongs the cognition of truth, philosophy is at the highest the science of truth … this science is understandable through philosophy … this is wisdom, and is not whatever science but that science which considers the first causes, the science which more has access to a

superior cause is wisdom, the causes that are more universal are the causes of beings).

44 This is a fragment from Moerbeke's translation: "*scientificum,* hoc autem ratiocinativum" (scientific, this is rational). Aquinas in his commentary explains: "Supponitur ergo quod pars rationalis dividitur in duas. Una quidem est per quam speculamur illa entia, scilicet necessaria, quorum principia non possunt aliter se habere. Alia pars autem per quam speculamur contingentia . . . ad obiecta quae differunt genere necesse est quod diversa genera partium animae adaptentur. Manifestum est autem quod contingens et necessarium differunt genere sicut habetur de corruptibili et incorruptibili decimo *Metaphysicorum.* Relinquitur ergo quod sit diversum genus partium animae rationalis quo cognoscit necessaria et contingentia ... Partibus animae inest cognitio secundum quod habent similitudinem quamdam ad res cognitas ... in quantum quaelibet potentia animae secundum suam proprietatem est proportionata ad talia cognoscenda ... imponit nomina predictis partibus … *una quidem quae speculatur necessaria potest dici scientificum genus animae,quia de necessariis est scientia*" (It is assumed that the rational part is divided in two. One is that through which we speculate those beings that are necessary. Their principles being what they are and which cannot be in a different way. The other part is that through which we speculate things that are contigent. In such operations are involved two different parts of the soul. In order to consider different genres of things it is necessary to adapt different parts of soul. In such operations he says are involved different parts of soul it is evident that what is contingent and what is necessary are genres different as the corruptible and the incorruptible in *Metaphysics* 10. From this derives that is different the genus of rational soul through which we know what is necessary and what is contingent. To the different parts of the soul is proper a cognition that has a certain similitude with the things we know … every power of the soul according to its property is made with proportion in order to know such things … and names are given to such parts. One of them belongs to the rational soul: *That which speculates things that are necessary is said scientific genus of the soul because of the necessary things we have science*). (*In Ethicorum* 6.1.1)

45 Gauthier (1958, 104–7).

46 "Ad sapientem pertinet quod habeat demonstrationem de aliquibus rebus,idest de primis causis entium; principia autem sunt indimostrabilia ut dictum est. Sapientia simpliciter est certissima inter omnes scientias, in quantum scilicet attingit ad prima principia entium, quae secundum se sunt notissima, quamvis aliqua illarum scilicet immaterialia, sint minus nota" (It belongs to the philosopher to have a demonstrative knowledge of some things, that is, of the first causes of things; however, it has been

said that of the principles there is no demonstration. Wisdom is the most certain of sciences because it reaches the first principles of things which are in itself well known; however, those which are immaterial are less well known). (Aquinas, *In Ethicorum,* Lectio 6)

47 See note 41.

48 Gauthier (1968, 106); see also *Nicomachean Ethics* 6.7.1141.16–19 and 11416.1–4.

49 "Onde nel medesimo libro si scrive, trattando della infusione della bontà divina: E fanno[si] diverse le bontadi e i doni per lo concorrimento della cosa che riceve" (Thus in the same book, in treating of the infusion of divine goodness, the following words appear: "And the goodnesses and the gifts are made diverse by the participation of the thing which receives them"). (*Convivio* III.2.5)

50 "Onde, con ciò sia cosa che ciascuno effetto ritegna della natura della sua cagione – sì come dice Alpetragio quando afferma che quello che è causato da corpo circulare *n'ha* in alcuno modo circulare essere –, ciascuna forma ha essere della divina natura in alcuno modo: non che la divina natura sia divisa e comunicata in quelle, ma da quelle [è] participata, per lo modo quasi che la natura del sole è participata nell'altre stelle. E quanto la forma è più nobile, tanto più di questa natura tiene: onde l'anima umana, che è forma nobilissima di queste che sotto lo cielo sono generate, più riceve della natura divina" (Consequently, since every effect retains part of the nature of its cause – as Alpetragius says when he affirms that what is caused by a circular body must in some way be circular – every form in some way partakes of the divine nature; not that the divine nature is divided and distributed to them, but that it is shared by them in almost the same way that the nature of the sun is shared by the other stars.The nobler the form, the more it retains of this nature; consequently the human soul, which is the noblest form of all those that are generated beneath the heavens, receives more of the divine nature than any other). (*Convivio* III.2.5–6)

51 See above note 14.

52 Gauthier (1958, 106).

53 Albert the Great, *De unitate* (1975, 12, pp. 8–18).

54 In chapter 1, I have underlined this issue and its relation to the Aquinas treatise on *De substantiis separatis.*

55 "Animam intellectualem genus alterum animae esse a vegetabili et sensibili, et quia divinum genus animae est, dicunt hoc solum separari a corpore sicut perpetuum a corruptibile" (The intellectual soul has a genus that is different from that of a vegetative and sensitive soul, and because it is a divine genus of the soul, they say that just this soul is separate from

the body in the same way as what is eternal is separate from the corruptible). (Albertus Magnus, *De natura et origine animae*, 1976, 21)

56 Giacomo da Pistoia, *Quaestio de felicitate* (in Kristeller 1955). Ardizzone (2002) compares Giacomo's *Quaestio* with Cavalcanti's theory of love and knowledge in "Donna me prega." A critical edition of the *Quaestio* is now available, see Zavattero (2005).

57 This interpretation is shared by Van Steenberghen (1977) and Hissette (1977). Wippel accepts partially such interpretation. See his introduction to Boethius of Dacia, *On the Supreme Good, On the Eternity of the World, On Dreams* (1976, 1–23).

58 Boethius of Dacia, *De summo bono*. The fragments translations are mine. I have compared them with Wippel's translation in Boethius of Dacia, *On the Supreme Good* (1976).

59 See also Siger, *Quaestiones sur la Metaphysique* (1948, 36–7).

60 Buzzetti, Ferriani, and Tabarroni (1992, 165–76).

61 De Libera (1991a) observes that proposition 64 derives from assertions included in the works of Avicenna, Al Gazel, and Averroes, although its content is commonly attributed to Aristotle.

62 We will see that in the allegorical commentary Dante will make a crucial addition when he writes that this love is made by God, "senza mezzo" or similar to Him: "Dico adunque che la divina virtue senza mezzo questo amore tragge a sua similitudine" (I say that divine virtue such love without medium such love makes similar to Him; III.14.6), that is, immediate. We note that *immediate* – according to the text I have quoted above and the condemned articles – does not consider the intelligences as mediator or secondary causes.

63 See, for instance, *Nicomachean Ethics* 1.1.1: "Omnis ars, et omnis doctrina similiter autem et actus et electio, bonum quoddam appetere videntur" (Every art and every doctrine in the same act and choice appear to desire something good).

64 Augustine, *De diversis quaestionibus octuaginta tribus* (30): "Honestatem voco intelligibilem pulchritudinem."

65 "Una est amicitia propter honestum, quod est bonum simpliciter ... amicita honesti quod est bonum simpliciter, cui primo et per se competit ratio amicitae" (Just one is friendship for the honest … friendship of the honest, which is simply the good, to which belongs the reason of friendship). (*In Ethicorum* 8.1.3.1563, 1565)

66 "Nam bonum dicitur aliquid secundum quod est in se perfectum et appetibile ... sed verum bonum hominis hic dicitur quod ei convenit secundum rationem ... philosophari est bonum simplicter" (It is in fact said that what is

good is something that in itself is perfect and desirable … but the true good of a human being here is said what is proper to him according rationality, to deal with philosophy is simply the good). (*In Ethicorum* 8.1.2.1552–1553).

67 Augustine, *In Evangelium Johannis* 13.4.

68 In his commentary, Vasoli (1988) summarizes the debate on this passage between Busnelli-Vandelli and Nardi (320–2). According to Busnelli-Vandelli, here Dante uses Aquinas's theory of the soul. In such reading, however, they refer themselves to a different version of the text. I quote the text as given in their edition: "E pero che l'uomo avvegna che una sola sustanza sia tutta [sua] forma, per la sua nobilitade" (Thus in the human being his form is just one substance). Nardi, who was using Dante's edition of 1921, was reading this passage in light of Albert's *De natura et origine animae* 1.6. Nardi, in *Saggi di filosofia dantesca* (1930, 341–80), quotes a fragment from Albert's *De origine et natura animae* 1.6: "Amplius iam patet qualiter inter omnes naturales formas anima intellectualis verius forma est, eo quod est magis separata et nobilior omnibus, eo quod colligit in se omnes alias sicut potentias, quae sunt esse vivere, sentire, moveri secundum locum et intelligere" (It is evident that among all natural forms the intellectual soul is the true form, because it is more separate and more noble and in itself collects the others as powers, these are: to be; to live; to feel, to have movement, and to have intellection).

69 "Nam, sive honestum solum bonum est, ut Stoicis placet, sive, quod honestum est, id ita summum bonum est" (For whether the honest [moral goodness] is the only good as the Stoics believe, whether, because honest is the highest good) (Cicero, *De Officiis* 3.iII.11); "Atque illud quidem honestum, quod proprie vereque dicitur,id in sapientibus est solis neque a virtute divelli unquam potest; in iis autem, in quibus sapientia perfecta non est, ipsum illud quidem perfectum honestum nullo modo, similitudines Honesti esse possunt" (And yet the honest in the true and proper sense of the term, is the exclusive possession of the wise and can never be separated from virtue, but those who have not perfect wisdom cannot have the perfect honest, but only a semblance of it) (ibid., 3.IiI.13–14).

70 "Nam sicut omnes virtutes inferiores, quae sunt in homine, naturaliter sunt propter virtutem supremam, nutritiva enim est propter sensitivam ... Sensitiva enim est propter intellectivam" (In fact all the inferior virtues that are in the human being are naturally disposed toward the supreme virtue, vegetative is in fact in function of sensitive soul … Sensitive soul is in function of intellectual soul). (*De summo bono,* 373)

71 I quote here the two fragments useful to establish such content: "Preterea sicut anima sensitiva est propter intellectivam, ita bonum sensitive est

propter bonum intellective ... appetitum intellectivum qui proprium est humanum" (In addition as the sensitive soul is in function of the intellectual soul, in the same way the sensible good is in function of the intellectual good ... intellectual appetite is what is proper to the human being). (Giacomo, *Quaestio de felicitate*, 446)

72 Siger (1972a, 3) discusses in the beginning of his *Quaestiones in Tertium De Anima*, the problematic issue of the difference between the intellect and the other levels of the human soul. This is his conclusion: "Dicendum enim quod intellectivum non radicatur in eadem anima simplici cum vegetativo et sensitivo, sicut vegetativum et sensitivum radicantur in eadem simplici, sed radicatur cum ipsis in eadem anima composita. Unde cum intellectus simplex sit, cum advenit, tum in suo adventu unitur vegetativo et sensitivo, et sic ipsa non faciunt unam simplicem, sed compositam. Per hoc patet ad illud quod dicit Averroes quod Aristoteles opinatur vegetativum, sensitivum, intellectivum esse unam animam in subiecto. Verum est: unam compositam, non autem unam simplicem" (It has to be said that the intellectual soul is not located in the same simple soul together with the vegetative and sensitive, in the same way vegetative and sensitive are located in the same simple soul, it is located with them but in a soul that is not simple but made of more things or composit and not one simple).

73 "Quidam vero videntes quod secundum viam Averrois sustineri non potest quod hic homo intelligat, in aliam diverterunt viam, et dicunt quod intellectus unitur corpori ut motor; et sic, in quantum ex corpore et intellectu fit unum, ut ex movente et moto, intellectus est pars huius hominis; et ideo operatio intellectus attribuitur huic homini, sicut operatio oculi, quae est videre, attribuitur huic homine" (A few philosophers, who have understood that according to Averroes it was impossible to assert that in this way the human being has intellection, have taken a different direction. They say that the intellect is connected to the body as a motor, and in this way, because the body and intellect make one, as make one the mover and movement, the intellect is part of this human being and the operation of intellect is attributed to this human being, in the same way the operation of vision is attributed to this human being. (Aquinas, *De unitate intellectus*, 39)

74 Here is a fragment from Albertus *De anima* 3.3.11: "Quod cum intellectus possibilis duas habet operationes quarum una est facera intellecta denudando ea a materia et altera intellecta intelligere et discernere" (The possible intellect has two operations one is to make intellectual things abstracting them from matter and the other is to have intelligence of intellectual things and to distinguish them). And here is what Siger writes in two different passages of his *In Tertium* (1972a, question 14): "Dico ergo

quod ad intelligere nostrum requiritur receptio intelligibilium abstractorum universalium ... et etiam abstractio eorumdem cum prius fuerunt intentiones imaginatas" (Thus I say that for our intellectual knowledge is required to receive the abstract intelligible universal beings ... and also the abstraction of those we were before forms of imagination). See also Van Steenberghen (1977, 344–5).

75 Augustine, *De diversis quaestionibus*, question 30 (*Patrologia Latina*, vol. 40, 1841).

76 "Id etiam sui substantia summum esse bonum verissima ratione concluserim ... Igitur, inquit, eum esse ipsam beatitudinem necesse est confiteri ... Atqui et beatitudinem et deum summum bonum esse colligimus; quare necesse est summam esse beatitudinem,quae sit summa divinitas" (Therefore I would conclude with the truest reasoning, that which is the principle of all things is also in its substance the highest good ... But we have granted that the highst good is happiness,therefore it must be confessed that happiness is itself God). (*De consolatione III*, 10)

77 See note 69 where I quote Cicero.

4. Community and Intellectual Happiness

1 For the difference between the text of canzoni and the text as quoted in the prose, see De Robertis (2005, 18.)

2 Proposition 118: "Quod intellectus agens est quaedam substantia separata superior ad intellectum possibilem; et quod secundum substantiam potentiam et operatione est separatus a corpore, nec est forma corporis hominis" (Intellect agent is a separate substance superior to the possible intellect, according to its substance, power, and operation it is separate from body, and is not the form of human being body). According to Hissette (1977, 193–4), this theory condemns a thesis proposed by Siger. The text to which Hissette refers to is Siger, *De intellectu*, a text that we know just through the reconstruction by Agostino Nifo. See Nardi, *Sigieri di Brabante nel pensiero del Rinascimento* (1945).

3 Hammesse in "Ratio dans l'oevre de Saint Bonaventure" (1994, 167–8) retraces the relationship between the agent intellect and the Augustinian light as it takes place in Bonaventura who makes a synthesis of Augustine and Aristotle.

4 About the Augustinian theory of interior word, see Arens (1980).

5 *De causis*, proposition 5: "Causa prima superior est omni narratione. Et non deficiunt linguae a narratione eius nisi propter narrationem esse ipsum, quoniam ipsa est supra omnem causam et non narratur nisi per

causas secundas quae illuminantur a lumine causae primae" (The first cause is superior to every narration, such narration is impossibile because of the nature of narration itself, in fact, the first cause is above every cause and can be told only through the second causes which are enlightened by the light of the first cause).

6 Siger writes: "Noster intellectus respicit causam primam tamquam suam causam (Our intellect contemplates the first cause as its cause). In this work, Siger identifies the possible and agent intellect as being one). (*In tertium*, question 17, 64)

7 See note 6 above, and Hissette (1977, 193–4).

8 The basis of the theory of diaphanous in the thirtheenth century is in Aristotle's *On the Soul [De anima]*, II.

9 The methaphor of diaphanous that derives from Aristotle's theory of vision is utilized in the thirteenth century to discuss not just vision but also knowledge. I have analyzed this word in Ardizzone (2002, chap. 2).

10 "Patet igitur quod ultimum de potentia ipsius humanitatis est potentia sive virtus intellectiva. Et quia potentia ista per unum hominem seu per aliquam particularium comunitatum superius distinctarum tota simul in actum reduci non potest, necesse est multitudinem esse in humano genere, per quam quidem tota potentia hec actuetetur" (It is thus clear that the highest potentiality of mankind is his intellectual potentiality or faculty. And since that potentiality cannot be fully actualized all at once in any one individual or in any one of the particular social groupings enumerated above, there must needs be a vast number of individual people in the human race, through whom the whole of this potentiality can be actualized). (*Monarchia* 1.3.7–8)

11 "Quae intelligitur" (i.e., "che s'intende") in Guido Cavalcanti's canzone *Donna me prega* (21) implies that the subject in the activity of intellection is not the individual. The break between the individual "I" who lives inside the sphere of sensibility and the possibile intelect in which takes form a superior kind of knowledge brought Cavalcanti in the canzone to conclude that the intellection is not proper to individual as individual. This text thus can be related to the positions of those who thought that the possible intellect is not the act of the body. Cavalcanti, in fact, seems to agree with those philosophers who assumed that the sensitive soul is the act of the body. See Ardizzone (2002) and its bibliography.

12 *Questiones anonime in De anima* edited by F. Van Steenberghen (in Giele, Van Steenberghen, Bazán, *Trois Commentaires* [1971]) refers to the same theory in question 21: "Intentio aristotelis est quod intellectus coniunctus corpori intelligit substantias separatas:quia ut dicitur decimo ethicorum,

ultima felicitas in hac vita consistit in cognitione substantie primae.Sed quod possumus habere cognitionem essentialem de eis,non credo quod sit de intentione Aristotelis" (It is Aristotle's idea that the intellect connected to the body has intellection of separate substances in fact this is said in book 10 of *Ethics*. The highest happiness in this life lies in the cognition of separate substances. But I don't believe that Aristotle thinks that we may have a substantial knowlwdge of them) (340).

13 I quote a fragment from Siger in which the double function of the possible intellect is enunciated: "unde possibilis per conversionem ad agentem intelligit semper et est aeternus et separatus quantum ad hanc operationem sicut quantum ad suam substantiam; sed ipse possibilis per conversionem ad phantasmata, licet quantum ad substantiam suam sit aeternus et separatus, tamen quantum ad operationem corruptibilis est et coniunctus" (thus the possible intellect in its conversion to the agent has a continous intellection and is eternal and separate for what belongs to this operation and its substance, but the possible in its conversion to the phantasms, however it is in its substance eternal and separate, in relation to this operation is corruptible and linked to the body). (*Quaestiones in Tertium De Anima*, question 15, 59)

14 In the same question 16 of the *In Tertium*, Siger writes: "et dico ad hoc quod intellectus agens de phantasmatibus facit actu intelligibilia per abstractionem, in hoc quod facit formas materiales sine materiis (I say that the agent intellect makes intelligible beings in act through abstraction because it deprives material forms of matter). (*Quaestiones in Tertium De Anima*, 60)

15 The title of the question is the following: "Utrum ad hoc quod intellectus noster intelligat exigantur species receptae in intellectu possibile" (If in order that our intellect has intelligence, it is necessary that it receives forms in the possible intellect). (*Quaestiones in Tertium*, 46)

16 See above note 10 for the quotation.

17 "Quod humanitas inon est forma rei, sed rationis" (Humanitas is not a form of a thing but of reason) (Hissette 1977, article 124, 201).

18 "Dico quod Intellectus noster possibilis intellectum agentem potest intelligere, sed secundum actionem istam non continuatur nobis ... Unde intellectus possibilis per conversionem eius ad agentem, neque aliquando intelligit, aliquando non intelligit, sed semper" (I say that our possible intellect can have intellection of the agent intellect, but in this action it does not continue with us … Thus our possible intellect in its conversion to the agent has not a discontinous but a continous intellection). (*In Tertium*, question 13, 43–5)

19 Siger writes: "Intellectus possibilis non continuatur nobis nisi per intentiones imaginatas ... Quia igitur neque intellectus possibilis nec intellectus agens nobis copulatur nisi per intentiones imaginatas, intellectus autem possibilis agentem non intelligit per intentiones, *propter hoc dico quod intellectus possibilis ipsum potest et limpide potest intueri, cum sit in substantia idem cum ipso, sed secundum istam actionem nobis non continuatur*. Et propter hoc conclusive infertur quod intellectus non esset actus corporis secundum suam substantiam, sed solum per suam operationem" (The possible intellect continues with us just through the forms of imagination ... Both the agents intellect and the possible have a continuity with us through the forms of imagination. *Because of it I say that the possible intellect can know intimately the agent because in its substance is one and the same with it, but in this action it does not have a continuity with us*. Thus it is possible to deduce that the intellect for what belongs to its essence is not the form of the body but just according to its operation). (*In Tertium*, 13, 45–6)

20 In his article "Science, Philosophy, and Religion" (1976) and in his book *Alfarabi and the Foundation of Islamic Political Thought* (2001), Madhi has demonstrated that Alfarabi's political thought in Western culture spread through book 5 of *De enumeratione*. His study thus implies a strong criticism on the theory that assumes that the political thought of this philosopher did not have a role in Europe in the Middle Ages. Recent works, like Burns's *Medieval Political Thought* (2007), which does not recognize any role that Alfarabi may have played in political thought, are not trustworthy as a source on this issue.

21 For more about Brunetto and his knowledge of the Arabic culture propitiated by his trip to the court of Alphonse X, king of Castille, in his role as ambassador, see Holloway (1990). This is, however, a study that in many instances takes for granted contents that need to be demonstrated. For a discussion of a possibile relation between Alfarabi and Dante about the structure of the science in *Convivio*, see Maierù (2003).

22 In *De bono communi*, 1301–2, Remigio De Girolami appears to be close to Dante's position: "Ex quo sequitur idem quod prius, quia comune bonum maiorem assimilationem habet cum Deo quam bonum particulare privatum, tum quia Deus comuniter appetitur ab omnibus, sicut dictum est, tum quia comuniter omnia sunt in ipso, idest perfectiones omnium creaturarum ... Ex dictis itaque manifeste colligitur quod tanto quis plus habet de participatione divinitatis quanto plus habet de amore comunitatis; et ideo Philosophus in I Ethicorum bene coniunxit maiorem divinitatem cum maiori amore comunitatis" (From it derives that, because the common good is more similar to God than a private good,thus because

God is desired from many, as already said, because all things are in Him, i.e., the perfections of creatures ... from what has been said we may conclude that what more participate of divinity is what more loves community. In fact the philosopher in the first ethicorum linked a divine condition with the love for community).

23 The way in which Albert recalls many theories in order to oppose them is useful to recognize contents related to the debate. In the following fragment from *De Unitate intellectus*, for instance, he recalls Avempace and his Epistle about the way in which the separate intellect is linked through continuation with that of the human being: "Dicit autem sic: Omne separatum ab aliquo respiciens aliquid post se, quod movet sicut motor separabilis ab illo, est unum apud se nec multiplicatur nisi virtute, qua continuatur cum illo quod movet. Veritas huius propositionibus probatur ex omnibus motoribus caeli separatis et ex omnibus motoribus civitatum et communitatum (He says that: everything that is separate from something that contemplates after it, that moves as a motor separable by it, is one in itself and does multiply only for the virtue that is in continuity with the being that moves. The truth of such assertion is proved by the separate motors of heavens and by the motors of cities and communities). (*De Unitate*, 11 in XV problematibus, 1975)

24 Sigier discusses this content in his *In Tertium*, question 9. Petagine (2009, 146) briefly discusses this issue in relation to Siger. For Aquinas's position, see Petagine (2009, 100–3).

25 Thomas Aquinas in his commentary to proposition 3 of *Liber de causis* (2002, 22) accepts that the intelligences participate in the causative activity of the first cause. Aquinas's basis is the Augustinian *Questio de ideis* that he links to Artistotle's *Metaphysics*. In his commentary to book 12 of *Metaphysics*, he identifies the ideas with the divine thinking; the ideas are models that God utilizes in his creative activity and this is their causative activity. In the distinction 36 he quotes Anselm's *Monologium*: "Unde creaturae secundum hoc quod in deo sunt non sunt aliud a deo: quia creaturae in deo sunt creatrix essentia,ut dicit Anselmus" (Therefore creatures because are in God are not different from God, because creatures in God are creative essence, as Anselm says); "Sunt enim in Deo per suam similitudinem: ipsa autem essentia divina similitudo est omnium eorum quae a deo sunt" (Are thus in God in virtue of similitude: Divine essence is in fact likeness of all things that derive from God) (*Monologium* c. 34). Dante uses "intenzione," and Aquinas in his *De veritate* discusses "intentio" (16). According to Aquinas, an idea is a form that is imitated by something else as the result of

an *intentio* from the part of an agent who determines a goal. It is here that Aquinas introduces a discussion about the possibles that God's mind should contemplate (23). For more on the ideas in the mind of God, see Wippel (1993). No doubt that Aquinas draws from the text of Pseudo-Dionysius's *De Divinis nominibus* 5: "Exemplaria autem esse dici in Deo existentium rationes substantificas et singulariter preexistentes" (Models are said to be in God forms essential of the things that exist and which, as singular things, have a prior existence). This is a fragment of his commentary (249): "Postquam Dionysius ostenditi deum esse causam omnium entium secundum proprias naturas, his determinat de exemplaribus rerum … primo enim ostendit quae sunt rerum exemplaria" (Dionysius after having explained that God is the cause of all beings according to their own nature, establishes the archetypes of things … at first he explains what are the models of things). (Aquinas, *In librum Beati Dionysii* De Divinis nominibus *expositiones*)

26 "Intellectus ... cum unus sit in sua substantia,immo provenit ista diversitas ex parte intentiones imaginatas … sed diversae intentiones imaginatae sunt causa diversitatis intellectorum diversis hominibus" (Intellect being one in its essence, its diversity derives from the forms of imagination … but the different forms of imagination are the cause of the diversity of intellects of the various human beings) (Siger, *In Tertium*, 56–7). For Aquinas's discussion about individuation, see Petagine (2009, 146). Siger draws from Aquinas, but in order to oppose him. Aquinas thinks that what makes a human being individual is his body of which the intellect is its form. Siger instead uses this idea to show that what individuates is the body because the intellect is common and one.

27 The nature of the human intellect and the double operation of the possible is a content common to Siger and Albert and seems to be the basis from which Dante draws his idea. For Siger's position, see Van Steenberghen (1977, 339–45).

28 This position seems to be close with that of Siger, when *In Tertium* he underlines that the intellection belongs to the *coniunctus*, which is made by the abstract form in its link to the possible intellect; that is, it is not the individual sensitive form which enters into relationship with the possible intellect in the act of *coniunctio* but the abstract form, thanks to the action performed by the agent intellect that abstracts the form making the link between the form and the intellect possible. According to Siger, such possible intellect has another operation – that of contemplating the agent intellect – and this takes place with continuity. However, the individual human being has knowledge of the first operation of the possible intellect and not

of the other. Dante's position does partially coincide with Siger's. This treatise has testified that his focus has been the contemplation of a separate substance as possible to the human mind. What emerges is a personal point of view that utilizes philosophical tools but reinterprets them. So his position seems not to be a synthesis of Albert's and Siger's. The human being as individual has no knowledge of the agent intellect as a separate form (which is instead Albert's position) – but the possible intellect as common and of course separate has such knowledge. Dante's logical subject is the human mind and its link with the gentle lady implies knowledge. At first in the canzone and then in the prose text, he distinguishes what he as an individual can know and what he can't, but he concentrates on the common knowledge. *Communitas* is a field of great importance in Dante's age and we can trace the use of this notion in Dante's vocabulary, which testifies to its importance, for instance by the appearance of words like "gente" and "conviventia" in *Convivio* IV, and *humanitas* in *Monarchia*. But the area that has to be evaluated before this is the area of *verbum* or *logos*.

29 Pepin, "La Doctrine augustinienne des Rationes Aeternae, affinités origines" (1994, 47–68).

30 The word *verbum*, through which God has created all things, is a translation of the Greek *logos*. Such *logos* is eternal. A passage of the Augustine commentary on the Gospel of John remarks that everything has been made through Him, as Augustine writes: "the human being has been made through the verb" (*In Evangilium* 1.13). See Pepin (1994, 47–68).

31 For Augustine, the ideas are the divine thought, and they are coeternal to his eternity. See Homily 2.2 of his comment to the Gospel of John. The opening "In principium erat verbum" (at the beginning was the Word) is explained giving to "in principio" the meaning of from eternity (*In Evangilium Joannis*).

32 "Secundum igitur tria praedicta, ex quibus perfectio huius scientiae attenditur, sortitur tria nomina. Dicitur enim scientia divina sive theologia, inquantum praedictas substantias considerat. Metaphysica, inquantum considerat ens et ea quae consequuntur ipsum. Haec enim transphysica inveniuntur in via resolutionis, sicut magis communia post minus communia. Dicitur autem prima philosophia, inquantum primas rerum causas considerat. Sic igitur patet quid sit subiectum huius scientiae, et qualiter se habeat ad alias scientias, et quo nomine nominetur" (Therefore, in accordance with the three things mentioned above from which this science derives its perfection, three names arise. It is called divine science or theology inasmuch as it considers the aforementioned substances. It is called

metaphysics inasmuch as it considers being and the attributes which naturally accompany being [for things which transcend the physical order are discovered by the process of analysis, as the more common are discovered after the less common]. And it is called first philosophy inasmuch as it considers the first causes of things. Therefore, it is evident what the subject of this science is, and how it is related to the other sciences, and by what names it is designated). (Aquinas, *Proemium* to *In Metaphysicorum*)

33 De Libera (1990a) points out that this thinking is in Albert. This thinking is also in Siger who, however, modifies it, as I have noted above in the second section of this chapter where I quote Siger, *In Tertium*. Nardi (1960b, 114–15) makes a most important contribution to establishing such a line of thinking.

34 The meaning of this word is difficult. If it derives from *in-genitum* it means both something that is created but also that is un-created; in Hissette (1977, 79) we read that, according to Siger, "ingenitum esse sempiternum" (what is uncreated is eternal).

35 On this passage, the best contribution is that of Fioravanti (2008).

36 Falzone (2010) has the best discussion of this passage of *Convivio*; Fioravanti (2014) discusses the same topic.

37 Barolini (2009) stresses the partial knowledge we have of Dante's years of exile.

38 I am not in agreement with Albert Ascoli (2008, 20–30).

39 John Freccero, for instance, deeply disagrees with such interpretation. (Freccero, in conversation with the author.)

5. Syllogism and Censura

1 Gauthier notes that, following Aristotle, the philosopher of the integral Aristotelianism thinks that the best contemplative life is inside the community and not outside the community. The philosopher cannot detach himself from human society (Gauthier 1948, 293).

2 The opening confirms that the *Le dolci rime* of the past were shaped on the authority of the interior word mostly thought in Augustinian terms. See Ardizzone (2011, chaps. 1 and 2).

3 See Ardizzone (2011, 53–63) where I point out that the canzone *Donne ch'avete intelletto d'amore* delineates the meaning of "non for misura" (v. 48) as a clear reference and opposition to Cavalcanti "oltra misura" ("Donna me prega," v. 44). For Cavalcanti's "oltre misura" as related and derived from the medieval theory of matter, see Ardizzone (2002, 70–86 and 94–102).

4 "Materialism," as I use this word, implies the criterion that links values and materiality or assumes as a value something that is material. Thus

"materialism" is coincident with the importance given to material things, as determined by our material component. In this sense "materialism" and "materiality" are strongly connected, and "materiality" is determined by the laws of matter that represent a power that may influence human behaviour.

5 In Ciceronian rhetoric, the parts of a speech (*partes orationis*) are the *exordium* or opening; the *narratio* or statement of facts; the *divisio* or *partitio,* that is, the statement of the point at issue and exposition of what the orator proposes to prove; the *confirmatio* or exposition of arguments; the *confutatio* or refutation of one's opponent's arguments; and, finally, the *conclusio* or peroration. This sixfold division is that given in *De Inventione* and *Ad Herrenium*, but Cicero tells us that some are divided into four or five or even seven parts, and Quintilian regards *partitio* as contained in the third part, which he calls *probatio*, proof, and thus is left with a total of five. See Clarke and Berry (1996).

6 "Contradictio is oppositio cuius secundum se non est medium, inter esse enim et non esse non est medium" (Contradiction is a kind of opposition that is absolute in which there is not a mediation, in fact between what is and what is not there is not a meeting point). (Petrus Hispanus, *Summulae logicales*, 5.27)

7 For the medieval theory of matter in its inner link with passion, see Ardizzone (2002, chap. 4).

8 For matter, *hyle* in Greek and *silva* in its Latin translation, Dante's roots should be in Isidorus of Sevilla, *Etimologiae*, and in Augustine, *De Natura boni*. Augustine discusses matter in his *Confessions* 12.6.6.1–2, but here he does not use the word "silva." The word is largely used by Calcidius in his commentary on Plato's *Timeus*, who devotes a chapter to discuss *silva* as matter. See Van Winden (1965).

9 In *Donne ch'avete*, Dante in relation to Beatrice writes that she is "non for misura: ell'è quanto di ben po far Natura" (she is not beyond measure / she is what nature can make of good). I have discussed this text in *Il Paradigma intellettuale* (Ardizzone 2011, 39–52).

10 I refer here to Floravanti's new edition of *Convivio* (2014a) and, in particular, to his introduction as well as to his note to the fourth treatise.

11 "Quocirca si persona in solis substantiis est atque in his rationalibus substantiaque omnis natura est nec in universalibus sed in individuis constat repaerta personae est definitio naturae rationabilis individua substantia" (Therefore if a person belongs to substances alone, and these are rational, and if every substance exists not only in universals but in individuals also, we have found the definition of person: the individual substance of

rational nature) (Severinus Boethius, *Contra Eutychen*, 3. *Opuscola sacra*, 85). In *Summa theologiae*, Thomas Aquinas uses Boethius's discourse offering a similar definition: "Et ideo in praedicta definitione personae ponitur substantia individua in quantum significat singulare in genere substantiae: additur autem rationalis naturae, in quantum significat singulare in rationalibus substantiis" (Thus in an already stated definition it is established as an individual substance and this means singular in the genus of substance. It is also added that it is of a rational nature because it means that it is singular in rational substances). (*Summa theologiae* 1.2.29.1)

12 Corti, *La felicità mentale* (1983, 38–60), introduces and discusses such expression.

13 Paola Ureni (2010, 2014) speaks about this theory in relation to *Purgatorio*, c. 25, in which this theory is again discussed. See also Gragnolati (2005).

14 In the recent edition of *Monarchia* (2014d, edited by Chiesa and Tabarroni), the editors speak about the possibility that the fragment recalling Averroes in *Monarchy* 1.3.9 is an interpolation.

Bibliography

Texts by Dante

Alighieri Dante. 1932. *La Vita nuova di Dante Alighieri*. Edited by M. Barbi. Società Dantesca Italiana. Florence: Bemporad.

–. 1964. *Il Convivio*. Edited by G.Busnelli-G.Vandelli. 2 vols. Firenze: Le Monier.

–. 1966. *Il Convivio*. Edited by M.Simonelli. Bologna: Patron.

–. 1966–7. *La Commedia secondo l'antica vulgata*. Edited by G. Petrocchi. 4 vols. Milan: Mondadori.

–. 1967. *Dante's Lyrical Poetry*. Edited by K. Foster and P. Boyde. 2 vols. Oxford: Clarendon Press.

–. 1979. *De vulgari eloquentia*. Edited by Pier Vincenzo Mengaldo. In *Opere minori*. Vol. 2.

–. 1979. *Epistole*. Edited by A. Frugoni and G. Brugnoli. In *Opere minori*. Vol. 2.

–. 1979. *Monarchia*. Edited by B. Nardi. In *Opere minori*. Vol. 2. Milan-Naples: Ricciardi.

–. 1980. *Rime*. Edited by G. Contini. Turin: Einaudi.

–. 1984. *Vita nuova*. Edited by D. De Robertis. In *Opere minori*. Vol. 1, part 1. Milano-Napoli: Ricciardi.

–. 1988. *Convivio*. Edited by C. Vasoli and D. De Robertis. In *Opere minori*. Vols. 1–2.

–. 1990. *Dante's Il Convivio (The Banquet)*. Edited and translated by Richard H. Lansing. New York: Garland.

–. 1995. *Convivio*. Edited by F.A. Brambilla. Società Dantesca Italiana. 3 vols. Florence: Le Lettere.

–. 1996. *Vita nuova*. Edited by G. Gorni. Turin: Einaudi.

–. 2000. *Inferno, Purgatorio, Paradiso*. A verse translation by J. Hollander and R. Hollander. Introduction and notes by R. Hollander. New York: Doubleday.
–. 2001. *Dantis Alegherii Comedia*. Edited by F. Sanguineti. 3 vols. Florence: Edizioni del Galluzzo.
–. 2002. *Rime*. Edited by D. De Robertis. Società Dantesca Italiana. 3 vols. Florence: Le Lettere.
–. 2005. *Rime*. Edited with commentary by D. De Robertis. Florence: Edizioni del Galluzzo.
–. 2004. *Convivio*. Edited by Giorgio Inglese. Milano: Rizzoli.
–. 2009. *Rime giovanili e della Vita nuova*. Edited by T. Barolini, notes by M. Gragnolati. Milan: Rizzoli.
–. 2011. *De vulgari eloquentia*. Edited by Mirko Tavoni. In *Opere*. Vol. 1. Milan: Mondadori, 2011.
–. 2014a. *Convivio*. Edited by G. Fioravanti. In Dante, *Opere*. Vol 2. Milan: Mondatori.
–. 2014b. *Dante's Lyric Poetry: Poems of Youth and of the Vita Nuova*. Edited and with commentary by Teodolinda Barolini, with original translations of Dante's poems by Richard Lansing. Translation of Barolini commentary by Andrew Frisardi. Toronto: Toronto University Press.
–. 2014c. *Monarchia*. Edited by D. Quaglioni. In Dante, *Opere*. Vol 2. Milan: Mondatori.
–. 2014d. *Monarchia*. Edited by P. Chiesa and A.Tabarroni, with the collaboration of D. Ellero. Rome: Salerno.

Primary Sources

Alanus De Insulis. 1855. *Opera Omnia*. In *Patrologia Latina*. Vol. 210.
–. 1981. *Regulae caelestis iuris*. Edited by N.M. Haring. *Archives d' histoire doctrinaleet litteraire du Moyen Age* 48: 97–226.
Albertus Magnus. 1964. *Metaphysica*. Edited by B. Geyer. In *Opera Omnia*. Vol. 15. Münster in Westfalorum: Aschendorff.
–. 1968. *De anima*. Edited by C. Stroick. In *Opera Omnia*, Vol. 7, part 1. Münster in Westfalorum: Aschendorff.
–. 1975. *De unitate intellectus*. Edited by A. Hufnagel. In *Opera Omnia*. Vol. 17, part 1. Münster in Westfalorum: Aschendorff.
–. 1976. *De Natura et origine animae rationalis*. Edited by B. Geyser. In *Opera Omnia*. Vol. 12. Münster in Westfalorum: Aschendorff.
–. 1980. *Summa de bono*. Edited by T. Hunt. In *Opera Omnia*. Vol. 28. Münster in Westfalorum: Aschendorff.

–. 1987. *Super ethica. Commentum et quaestiones*. Edited by W. Kubel. In *Opera Omnia*. Vol. 14, part 1.2. Münster in Westfalorum: Aschendorff.

–. 1993. *Super Dionysium de caelesti hierarchia*. Edited by P. Simon and W. Kubel. In *Opera Omnia*. Vol. 36, part 1. Münster in Westfalorum: Aschendorff.

–. 1993. *De causis et processu universitatis a prima causa*. Edited by W. Fauser. In *Opera Omnia*. Vol. 17, part 2.

Alfarabi. 1932. *Catalogo de la ciencias*. Edited by A. Gonzales Palencia. Madrid: Imprenta E. Mestre.

Anselm. 1968. *Monologion*. In *Opera Omnia*. Vol. 1. Edited by F. S. Schmitt. Stuttgart-Bad Canstatt: Frommann Verlag.

Aristotle. 1926. *Nicomachean Ethics*. Edited and translated by H. Rackham. Loeb Classical Library. Cambridge, MA: Harvard University Press, and London: William Heinemann.

–. 1933. *Metaphysics*. Edited and translated by H. Tredennick. 2 vols. Loeb Classical Library. Cambridge, MA: Harvard University Press, and London: William Heinemann.

–. 1936. *On the Soul* [*De anima*], *Parva naturalia*, *On Breath*. Edited and translated by W.S. Hett. Cambridge, MA: Harvard University Press, and London: William Heinemann.

–. 1942. *Generation of Animals*. Edited and translated by A.L. Peck. Loeb Classical Library. Cambridge, MA: Harvard University Press, and London: William Heinemann.

–. 1982. *De generatione et corruptione*. Translated and with notes by C.J.F. Williams. Oxford: Clarendon Press.

–. 1955. *On Sophistical Refutations. On Coming to Be and Passing Away*. Edited and translated by E.S. Forster. Cambridge, MA: Harvard University Press, and London: William Heinemann.

–. 1990. *Politics*. Edited and translated by H. Rackham. Loeb Classical Library. Cambridge, MA: Harvard University Press, and London: William Heinemann.

Augustine. 1841. *In Evangelium Ioannis tractatus centum viginti quatuor*. In *Patrologia Latina*. Vol. 35.

. 1841. *De diversis quaestionibus octuaginta tribus*. In *Patrologia Latina*. Vol. 40.

–. 1841. *Enarrationes in Psalmos*. In *Patrologia Latina*. Vol. 36.

–. 1845. *Sermones*. In *Patrologia Latina*. Vol. 38.

–. 1848. *Retractationes*. Book 2. In *Patrologia latina*.Vol. 32.

–. 1962. *De doctrina christiana*. Corpus Christianorum: Series Latina. Vol. 28. Thurnhout: Brepols.

–. 1968. *De trinitate*. Corpus Christianorum: Series Latina. Vol. 50–50A. Thurnhout: Brepols.

–. 1970. *Contra academicos, De Beata vita, De Ordine, De Magistro, De Libero arbitrio*. Corpus Christianorum: Series Latina. Vol. 12. Thurnhout: Brepols.
–. 2000. *L'istruzione cristiana*. Edited by M. Simonetti. Fondazione Lorenzo Valla. Milan: Mondadori, 2000.
–. 2001. *Commento ai Salmi*. Edited by M. Simonetti. Milan: Mondadori.
–. 2002. *Confessioni*. Edited by J. Fontainer, M. Cristiani, J. Guirau, L.F. Pizzolato, M. Simonetti, and P. Siniscalco. Translated by G. Chiarini. 5 vols. Fondazione Lorenzo Valla. Milan: Mondadori.
Averroes. 1953. *Commentarium magnum in Aristotelis De anima libros*. Edited by F. Stuart Crawford. Cambridge, MA: Medieval Academy of America.
Biblia Sacra Vulgatae Editionis. 1995. Edited by A. Colalunga and L. Turrado. Rome: Edizioni San Paolo.
Bird, Otto. 1941. "The Canzone d'Amore of Cavalcanti According to the Commentary of Dino del Garbo: Text and Commentary." *Mediaeval Studies* 2: 150–203; *Mediaeval Studies* 3: 117–60.
Boethius, S. 1877. *Commentarii in librum Aristotelis peri hermeneias*. 2 vols. Edited by Carolus Meiser. Lipsiae: B.G. Teubneri.
–. 1968. *The Theological Tractates* and *The Consolation of Philosophy*. Translated by H.F. Stewart, E.K. Rand, and S.J. Tester. New ed. Cambridge, MA: Harvard University Press.
Boethius of Dacia. 1976. *Topica, Opuscola* (*De Aeternitate mundi, De Summo bono, De Somniis*). Edited by N.J. Green Pedersen and J. Pinborg. Vol. 7, part 2. Copenhagen: Gad.
–. 1987. *On the Supreme Good, On the Eternity of the World, On Dreams*. Translated and with an introduction by J. Wippel. Toronto: Pontifical Institute of Medieval Studies.
Bonaventure. 1882–1902. *Breviloquium*. In *Opera Omnia*. Vol. 2. Ad Claras Aquas: Quaracchi.
–. 1882–1902. *Collationes in Hexaemeron*. In *Opera Omnia*. Vol. 3. Ad Claras Aquas: Quaracchi.
–. 1882–1902. *Commentarius in Quattuor libros Sententiarum*. In *Opera Omnia*. Vol. 1. Ad Claras Aquas: Quaracchi.
–. 1993a. *De Reductione artium ad theologiam*. In *Opuscoli Teologici*. Vol. 1. Rome: Città nuova editrice.
–. 1993b. *Quaestiones disputatae de scientia Christi*. In *Opuscoli Teologici*. Vol. 1. Rome: Città nuova editrice.
–. 1993c. *Itinerarium mentis in Deum*. In *Opuscoli Teologici*. Vol. 1. Rome: Città nuova editrice.
Boncompagno da Signa. 1896. *Rhetorica novissima*. Edited by A. Gaudenzi. Bologna.

Buzzetti, D., M. Ferriani, and A. Tabarroni, eds. 1992. *L'insegnamento della logica a Bologna nel xiv secolo.* Bologna: Istituto per la Storia dell'Università di Bologna.

Calcidius. 2003. *Commentario al* Timeo *di Platone.* Edited by C. Moreschini. Milan: Bompiani.

Cavalcanti, Guido. 1986. *Rime con le Rime di Iacopo Cavalcanti.* Edited by D. De Robertis. Turin: Einaudi.

Cicero. 1923a. *De amicitia.* Edited by W.A. Falconer. Loeb Classical Library. Cambridge, MA: Harvard University Press, and London: William Heinemann.

–. 1923b. *De senectute.* Edited by William Armistead Falconer. Loeb Classical Library. Cambridge, MA: Harvard University Press, and London: William Heinemann.

–. 1998. *De Inventione.* Edited by M. Greco. Lecce: Congedo editore.

–. 2001. *De officiis. On Ends.* Edited by J. Henderso. Loeb Classical Library. Cambridge, MA: Harvard University Press, and London: William Heinemann.

Contini, G., ed. 1964. *Poeti del Duecento.* Milan-Naples: Mondadori-Ricciardi.

De Girolami, R. 1302. *De bono communi.* Bibl. Naz. di Firenze. *Conv. soppr.* C 4.940 (1315-1316 ca.), ff. 97ra-106rb.

Denifle, Henri, and A. Chatelain. 1899/1964. *Chartularium Universitatis Parisiensis.* Vol. 1. 1899. Reprint, Brussels: Culture et Civilisation.

Dominicus Gundissalinus. 1903. *De divisione philosophiae.* Edited by L. Baur. Beitrage Zur Geshichte des philosophie des Mittelalters, n. 4, Münster.

Dionysius the Areopagite [pseudo]. 1853. *Patrologia Latina.* Translated by Johannes Scotus Eriugena. Vol. 122.

–. 1958. *La hierarchie celeste.* Introduction by R. Roques. Edited by G. Heil. Translated and notes by M. De Gandillac. Paris: Editions du Cerf.

–. 1981. *Tutte le opere.* Edited by P. Scazzoso and E. Bellini. 2 vols. Milan: Centro di Ricerche di Metafisica, Università Cattolica.

Dumeige, G. 1955. *Ives,* "Epitre a Severin sur la charite," *and Richard de Saint-Victor,* "Le Quatre degrés de la violente charité." Paris: Vrin.

Faral, E. 1962. *Les artes poétiques de xii et du xiii siécles. Recherches et documents sur la technique litteraire du Moyen Age.* Paris: Champion.

Fioravanti, G. 1991. "Desiderio di sapere e vita filosofica nelle Questioni sulla Metafisica del ms. 1386, Universitätsbibliothek Leipzig." In *Historia Philosophiae Medii Aevi,* 271–83. Edited by B. Mojsisch and O. Pluta. Amsterdam: B.R. Gruner.

–. 1992. "Sermones in lode della filosofia e della logica a Bologna nella prima metà del xiv secolo." In *La logica a Bologna.* Edited by D. Buzzetti, M. Ferriani, and A. Tabarroni. Bologna: Presso l'Istituto per la Storia dell'Università.

Gauthier, R.A. 1948. "Trois commentaires 'Averroistes' sur l'Etique a Nicomaque." *Archives d'histoire doctrinale et litteraire du Moyen Age* 16: 187–336.

–. 1984. "Notes sur Siger de Brabant, ii, Siger en 1272–1275. Aubry de Reims et la scissions de Normands." *Revue des Sciences Philosophiques et Theologiques* 68: 29–48.

Giele, Maurice, Fernand Van Steenberghen, and Bernard Bazán, eds. 1971. *Trois commentaires anonymes sur le Traité de l'âme d'Aristote.* Louvain: Publications Universitaires, and Paris: Beatrice- Nauwelaerts.

Giles of Rome [Egidio Romano]. 1944. *Errores philosophorum.* Edited by J. Koch. Translated by J.O. Riedl. Milwaukee, WI: Marquette University Press.

Guinizzelli, Guido. 2002. *Rime.* Edited by P. Rossi. Turin: Einaudi, 2002.

Hissette, Roland. 1977. *Enquete sur les 219 articles condamnès a Paris le 7 Mars 1277.* Paris: Publications Universitaires, Vander Oyez, S.A.

Hugh of St. Victor. 1939. *Didascalicon. De studio legendi.* Edited by C.H. Buttimer. Washington, DC: Catholic University Press

Isidore of Seville. 2004. *Etimologie o Origini.* Edited by A. Valastro Canale. 2 vols. Turin: Unione Tipografica Torinese.

Kristeller, Paul Oskar. 1955. "A Philosophical Treatise from Bologna Dedicated to Guido Cavalcanti: Magister Jacobus de Pistorio and His 'Questio de Felicitate.'" In *Medioevo e Rinascimento: Studi in onore di Bruno Nardi,* vol. 1, 425–63. Florence: Sansoni.

Kuksewicz, Z. 1965. *Averroisme Bolonais au xiv siècle. Edition des textes.* Wroclaw-Warsaw-Krakow: Ossolineum, Editions de l'Academie Polonaise des Sciences.

Lafleur, C. 1988. *Quatre introductions a la philosophie au xiiie siecle. Textes critiques et etude historique.* Paris: Vrin.

Latini, Brunetto. 1968. *La rettorica.* Edited by F. Maggini. Introduction by C. Segre. Florence: Le Monnier.

–. *Tresor.* 2007. Edited by P.G. Beltrami, P. Squillacioti, P. Torri, and S. Zatteroni. Turin: Einaudi.

Le Liber de causis. n.d. Edition etablie a l'aide de 90 manuscripts. Introduction and notes by A.Pattin. Leuven: Uitgave vanTijdschrift vor filosofie.

Marchesi, Concetto. 1903. "Il compendio volgare dell'Etica Aristotelica e le fonti del VI libro del 'Tresor.'" *Giornale storico della letteratura italiana* 42: 1–74.

Meyeroff, M., ed. 1928. *The Book of the Ten Treatises on the Eye, Ascribed to Hunain Ibn Is-Haq (809–877 AD).* Cairo: Government Press.

Migne, J.P., ed. 1844–1855. *Patrologiae cursus completus.* Series Latina. Paris: Apud Garnier.

Origene. 1997. *La preghiera.* Roma: Citta nuova.

Petrus Hispanus. 1972. *Tractatus called afterwards Summule logicales*. Edited by L.M. De Rijk. Assen: Van Gorcum,

Piché, D., and C. Lafleur, eds. and trans. 1999. *La Condamnation parisienne de 1277. Texte latin, traduction, introduction et commentaire*. Paris: Vrin.

Pseudo-Aristotle. 2001. *The Book of Causes: Liber de causis*. Edited by Dennis J. Brand. Translated by Bernardo Carlos Bezan. Lewiston, NY: Niagara University Press.

Proclus. 1987. *Elementatio theologica*. Translated by Guillelmo de Morbecca (William of Moerbeke). Leuven: Leuven University Press.

–. 1992. *The Elements of Theology*. Edited by E.R. Dodds. Oxford: Clarendon Press.

Richard of Saint Victor. 1845. *Opera, Pars Prima*. In *Patrologia Latina*. Vol. 196.

Siger of Brabant. 1948. *Questions sur la métaphysique*. Edited by C.A. Graiff. Louvain: Edition de L'Institute Superiéur de Philosophie.

–. 1972a. *Quaestiones in Tertium De Anima. De Anima intellectiva. De Aeternitate mundi*. Edited by B. Bazan. Louvain: Editions Universitaires Beatrice Nauwelaerts.

–. 1972b. *Les quaestiones super Librum de causis*. Edited by A. Marlasca. Louvain: Editions Universitaires Beatrice Nauwelaerts.

–. 1974. *Ecrits de logique, de morale, et de physique*. Edited by B.C. Bazan. Louvain: Publ. Univ.-B. Nauwelaerts.

–. 1983. *Quaestiones in Metaphysicam*. Edited by A. Maurer. Louvain-la-Neuve. Belgium: Institute Superier de Philosophie.

Thomas Aquinas. 1950. *In librum Beati Dionysii* De Divinis nominibus *expositio*. Edited by C. Pera, P. Caramello, and C. Mazzantini. Turin: Marietti.

–. 1953a. *Catena aurea in quatuor Evangelia*, ii, *Expositio in Ioannem*. Edited by A. Guarienti. Turin: Marietti.

–. 1953b. *Super Epistolam ad Colossenses lectura*. Edited by R. Cai. Turin: Marietti.

–. 1955. *In Aristotelis libros Peri Hermeneias et Posteriorum Analyticorum expositio*. Edited by R.M. Spiazzi. Rome: Marietti.

–. 1959. *In Aristotelis librum* De Anima *Commentarium*. Edited by A.M. Pirotta. Turin: Marietti.

–. 1961a. *Liber de veritate catholicae Fidei contra errores infidelium seu Summa contra Gentiles*. Edited by P. Marc, C. Pera, and P. Caramello. Vol. 2. Turin: Marietti.

–. 1961b. *Commentary on the Metaphysics of Aristotle*. Translated by J.P. Rowan. 2 vols. Chicago: H. Regnery.

–. 1964a. *In Decem Libros Ethicorum Aristotelis ad Nichomacum expositio*. Edited by R.M. Spiazzi. Rome: Marietti.

–.1964b. *In Duodecim libros Metaphysicorum Aristotelis expositio*. Edited by M.R. Cathala and R.M. Spiazzi. Rome: Marietti.

–. 1965. *De Magistro.* Edited by T. Gregory Roma: Armando.
–. 1969. *De Substantiis separatis.* In *Opera Omnia.* Vol. 49. Rome: Ad Sanctae Sabinae.
–. 1971. *Sententia libri politicorum.* In *Opera Omnia.* Vol. 48. Rome: Ad Sanctae Sabinae.
–. 1976. *De unitate intellectus contra Averroistas.* In *Opera Omnia.* Vol. 43. Rome: Editori di San Tommaso.
–. 1988. *Summa theologiae.* Milan: Edizioni San Paolo.
–. 1992a. *Expositio libri Boetii* De Ebdomadibus. In *Opera Omnia.* Vol. 50. Rome: Editions du Cerf.
–. 1992b. *Super Boetium* De Trinitate. In *Opera Omnia.* Vol. 50. Rome: Editions du Cerf.
–. 1997. *Commenti a Boezio. Super Boetium* De Trinitate. *Expositio Libri Boetii* De Ebdomadibus. Edited by P. Porro. Milan: Rusconi.
–. 2000. *Unità dell' intelletto.* Introduction, translation, and commentary by A. Ghisalberti. Milan: Bompiani.
–. 2002. *Super Librum de causis expositio.* Edited by H.D. Saffrey. Paris: Vrin.
–. 2005. *Sulla verità.* Edited by. F. Fiorentino. Milan: Bompiani.
–. 2007. *Commentary on Aristotle's Politics.* Translated by R.J. Regan. Cambridge, MA: Hackett Publishing.

Critical Sources Cited or Consulted

Anichini, F. 2009. *Voices of the Body. Liminal Grammar in Guido Cavalcanti's Rime.* Munich: Martin Medenbauer.
Ardizzone, M.L. 1997. "Guido Guinizzelli's 'Al cor gentil': A Notary in Search of Written Laws." *Modern Philology* 94: 455–74.
–. 2002. *Guido Cavalcanti: The Other Middle Ages.* Toronto: Toronto University Press.
–, ed. 2003. *Guido Cavalcanti tra i suoi lettori.* Florence: Cadmo.
–. 2006. *Guido Cavalcanti. L'altro Medioevo.* Florence: Cadmo.
–. 2011. *Dante. Il paradigma intellettuale. Un'inventio degli anni fiorentini.* Florence: Olschki.
–. 2013a. "The Small Medieval Community and Its Role in Dante's Political Thought." *Dante Studies* 131**: 00–00.**
–. 2013b. "Verbum valet plurimum: Tracing a Fragment of Dante's Poetics." *Italica* 90, no. 3: 319–42.
–. 2014. *Dante and Heterodoxy: The Temptations of Thirteenth-Century Radical Thought.* Edited and with an introduction by M.L. Ardizzone.Conclusion by Teodolinda Barolini. Newcastle upon Tyne, UK: Cambridge Scholars Press.

–. Forthcoming. "Ne la selva erronea":Dante's Quaestio about Nobility. The Criticism of Materialism as a Pathway to the Inferno." In F. Maier, ed., *Convivio: A Radical Work*. Edited by F. Maier.
Arduini, B. 2008. "Assigning the 'Pieces' of Dante's *Convivio*: The Compiler's Notes in the Earliest Extant Copy." *Textual Cultures* 3, no. 2: 1–12.
–. 2010. "Le implicazioni del *Convivio* nel corpus dantesco." *Medioevo letterario d'Italia* 6: 89–116.
–. 2012. "Il ruolo di Boccaccio e di Marsilio Ficino nella tradizione del *Convivio* di Dante." In *Boccaccio in America. Proceedings of the 2010 International Boccaccio Conference at The University of Massachusetts Amherst*. Edited by Michael Papio and Elsa Filosa, 95–103. Ravenna: Longo.
Arens, H. 1980. "Verbum cordis. Zur Sprachphilosophie des Mittelalters." *Historiographia linguistica* 7: 13–27.
Ascoli, A.R. 2008. *Dante and the Making of a Modern Author*. Cambridge: Cambridge University Press.
Azzetta, L. 2005. "La tradizione del Convivio negli antichi commenti alla commedia: Andrea Lancia, L'Ottimo Commento, e Pietro Alighieri." *Rivista di Studi Danteschi* 5, no. 1: 3–34.
–. 2009. "Tra i più antichi lettori del 'Convivio'Ser Alberto della Piagentina notaio e cultore di Dante." *Rivista di Studi Danteschi* 9, no. 1: 57–91.
Badawi, A. 1987. *La Transmission de la philosophie grecque au monde arabe*. Paris: Vrin.
Baranski, Z. 2004. "Il *Convivio* e la poesia, problemi di definizione." In *Contesti della* Commedia. *Lectura Dantis Fridericiana*. Edited by F. Tateo and D.M. Pegorari, 9–64. Bari: Palomar.
Barolini, T. 1984. *Dante's Poets: Textuality and Truth in the Comedy*. Princeton, NJ: Princeton University Press.
–. 2006. *Dante and the Origins of Italian Literary Culture*. New York: Fordham University Press.
–. 2009. "'Only Historicize': History, Material Culture (Food, Clothes, Books), and the Future of Dante Studies." *Dante Studies* 127: 37–54.
–. 2012. "Sociology of the Brigata Gendered Groups in Dante, Forese, Folgore, Boccaccio – From 'Guido, i' vorrei' to Griselda." *Italian Studies* 67, no. 1: 4–22.
–. 2014. "Aristotle's Mezzo, Courtly Misura and Dante's Canzone *Le dolci rime*: Humanism, Ethics and Social Anxiety." In *Dante and the Greeks*. Edited by J. Ziolkowski. Cambridge, MA: Harvard University Press.
Beierwaltes, W. 1990. *Proclo. I fondamenti della sua metafisica*. Introduction by G. Reale and translated by N. Scotti. Milan: Vita e Pensiero.
–. 1995. *Agostino e il neoplatonismo cristiano*. Milan: Vita e Pensiero.
–. 2000. *Platonismo nel Cristianesimo*. Milan: Vita e Pensiero.

Bettetini, M., and F.D. Paparella, eds. 2005. *La felicità nel medioevo*. Louvain-la-Neuve, Belgium: Fédération Internationale des Instituts d'Études Mediévales.
Bianchi, L. 1990. *Il vescovo e i filosofi.La condanna parigina del 1277 e l'evoluzione dell'aristotelismo scolastico*. Bergamo: Lubrica.
–, ed. 1997. *La filosofia nelle università. Secoli XIII–XIV*. Florence: La Nuova Italia.
–. 2005. "Felicità intellettuale. 'Ascetismo' e 'Arabismo' nota sul *De summo bono* di Boezio di Dacia." In *La felicità nel medioevo*. Edited by M. Bettetini and F.D. Papaparella, 13–34. Louvain-la-Neuve, Belgium: Fédération Internationale des Instituts d'Études Mediévales.
–. 2008. *Pour une histoire de la "double verite."* Paris: Vrin.
–. 2013. "Noli comedere panem philosophorum inutiliter.Dante Alighieri e John de Jandun on Philosophical Bread." *Tijdschrift voor filosofie* 75: 335–55.
–. 2015. "L'averroismo di Dante : qualche osservazione critica." *Le Tre Corone. Rivista internazionale di studi su Dante. Petrarca,Boccaccio. II*. 71–110.
Bianchi, M., and M. Fattori, eds. 1984. *Spiritus IV: Colloquio internazionale del lessico intellettuale europeo*. Rome: Edizioni dell'Ateneo.
–, eds. 1994. *Ratio VII: Colloquio internazionale del lessico intellettuale europeo*. Florence: Olschki.
Brenet, J.B. 2006. "Organisation politique et théorie de l'intellect chez Dante et Averroès." *Rivista di Filosofia Neoscolastica*, 98: 467–87.
Burns, J.H., ed. 2007. *Medieval Political Thought, c. 350–1450*. Cambridge: Cambridge University Press.
Bursill-Hall, G.L. 1975. "Some Notes on the Grammatical Theory of Boethius of Dacia." In *History of Linguistic Thought and Contemporary Linguistics*. Edited by H. Parret, 164–88. New York: Walter De Gruyter.
Busa, R. 1984. "De voce spiritus in operibus S. Thomae Aquinatis." In *Spiritus IV: Colloquio internazionale del lessico intellettuale europeo*. Edited by Marta Fattori and Massimo Bianchi, 174–89. Rome: Edizioni dell'Ateneo
Campanini, M. 2005. "Felicità e politica in Alfarabi e Avempace (Ibn Bajjah)." In *La felicità nel medioevo*. Edited by M. Bettetini and F.D. Paparella, 297–312. Louvain-la-Neuve, Belgium: Fédération Internationale des Instituts d'Études Mediévales.
Carpi, Umberto. 2004. *La nobiltà di Dante*. 2 vols. Florence: Polistampa.
Carruthers, M. 1998. *The Craft of Thought: Meditation, Rhetoric, and the Making of Images, 400–1200*. Cambridge: Cambridge University Press.
–. 2006. "Sweetness." *Speculum* 81, no. 4: 999–1013.

Carruthers, M., and J. Ziolkowski. 2003. *The Medieval Craft of Memory: An Anthology of Texts and Pictures*. Philadelphia: University of Pennsylvania Press.
Cassell, A.E. 2004. *The Monarchy Controversy*. Washington, DC: The Catholic University of America Press.
Chenu, M.D. 1995. *La teologia come scienza nel xiii secolo*. Milan: Jaca Book.
–. 1999. *La teologia nel xii secolo*. Edited by P. Vian. Milan: Jaca Book.
–. 2001. *Studi di lessicografia filosofica medievale*. Florence: Olschki.
Cherchi, P. 2004. *L'onestade e l'onesto raccontare del Decameron*. Florence: Cadmo.
Clarke, M.L., and D.H. Berry. 1996. *Rhetoric at Rome: A Historical Survey*. New York: Routledge.
Coccia, E. 2005. *La Trasparenza delle immagini*. Milan: Mondadori.
Coleman, J. 2000. *A History of Political Thought from Ancient Greece to Early Christianity*. Cambridge, MA: Blackwell.
Contini, G. 1970. *Varianti e altra linguistica. Una raccolta di saggi (1938–1968)*. Turin: Einaudi.
–. 1988. *Ultimi esercizi ed elzeviri*. Torino: Einaudi.
Cook, E. 2001. "The Figure of Enigma. Rhetoric, History, Poetry." *Rhetorica* 19, no. 4: 349–78.
Corti, M. 1981. *Dante a un nuovo crocevia*. Florence: Libreria Commissionaria Sansoni.
–. 1983. *La felicità mentale. Nuove prospettive per Cavalcanti e Dante*. Turin: Einaudi.
–. 2003. *Scritti su Cavalcanti e Dante. La felicità mentale, Percorsi dell'invenzione e altri saggi*. Turin: Einaudi.
Cox, V., and J.O. Ward, eds. 2006. *The Rhetoric of Cicero in Its Medieval and Early Renaissance Commentary Tradition*. Boston: Brill.
Curtius, E.R. 1990. *European Literature and the Latin Middle Ages*. Princeton, NJ: Princeton University Press.
Dahan, G., and I. Rosier Catach, eds. 1998. *La rhetorique d'Aristote. Traditions et Commentaires de l'antiquitè au XVIIe siècle*. Paris: Vrin.
Dales, R.C. 1980. "The De-animation of the Heavens in the Middle Ages." *Journal of the History of Ideas* 41, no. 4: 531–50.
D'Ancona Costa, C. 1995. *Recherches sur le Liber de causis*. Paris: Vrin.
Dauphinais, M., and M. Levering, eds. 2007. *Aquinas the Augustinian*. Washington, DC: The Catholic University of America Press.
Davis, C.T. 1963. "Early Collection of Books of S. Croce in Florence." *Proceedings of the American Philosophical Society* 108: 399–414.
–. 1984. *Dante's Italy and Other Essays*. Philadelphia: University of Pennsylvania Press.

–. 1988. *L'Italia di Dante*. Bologna: Il Mulino.

De Andia, Y. 1997. *Henosis: L'union a Dieu Chez Denys L'Areopagite*. Leiden, Netherlands: Brill Academic Publishers.

de Libera, A. 1990a. *Albert le Grand et la philosophie*. Paris: Vrin.

–. 1990b. "Albert Le Grand et Thomas D'Aquin Interpretes du *Liber de causis*." *Revue des sciences philosophiques et theologiques* 74, no. 3: 347–78.

–. 1991a. "La letter su le Principe de l'Univers e le condamnations Parisienses de 1277." In *Historia Philosophiae Medii Aevi*. Edited by B. Mojsisch and O. Pluta, 540–59. Amsterdam: B.R. Gruner.

–. 1991b. *Penser au Moyen Age*. Paris: Editions du Seuil.

–. 1999. *Storia della filosofia medievale*. Milan: Jaca Book.

De Rijk, L.M. 1962. *Logica modernorum. A Contribution to the History of Early Terministic Logic*. Vol. 1. Assen, Netherlands: Van Gorcum, and Comp. N.V., Prakke and Prakke.

De Robertis, D. 2001. *Dal primo all'ultimo Dante*. Florence: Le Lettere.

Dillon, J. 1996. *The Middle Platonists, 80 B.C. to A.D. 220*. Ithaca, NY: Cornell University Press.

Di Martino, C. 2008. *Ratio particularis. Doctrine de sens internes d'Avicenne a Thomas Aquinas*. Paris: Vrin.

Dondaine, H.F. 1953. *Le Corpus dionysien de l'Université de Paris au xiii siècle*. Rome: Edizioni di Storia e letteratura.

D'Onofrio, G., ed. 1996. *Storia della teologia nel Medioevo*. 3 vols. Casale Monferrato, Italy: Edizioni Piemme.

Doolan, G.T. 2008. *Aquinas on the Divine Ideas*. Washington, DC: The Catholic University Press.

Dronke, P. 1986. *Dante and the Medieval Latin Traditions*. Cambridge: Cambridge University Press.

–. 1997. *Dante's Second Love: The Originality and the Context of the Convivio*. Exeter, UK: Society for Italian Studies.

Emery, G. 2007. "Trinitarian Theology as Spiritual Exercise in Augustine and Aquinas." In *Aquinas the Augustinian*. Edited by Michael Dauphinais, Barry David, and Matthew Levering, 1–40. Washington, DC: Catholic University of America Press.

Enciclopedia Dantesca. 1970–9. 6 vols. Roma: Istituto dell'Enciclopedia Italiana.

Facoltà di Lettere e Filosofia dell'Università di Bologna, ed. 1967. *Dante e Bologna ai tempi di Dante*. Bologna: Commissione per i Testi di Lingua.

Falzone, P. 2010. *Desiderio della scienza e desiderio di Dio nel Convivio di Dante*. Bologna: Il Mulino.

Fattori, M., and M. Bianchi, eds. 1984. *Spiritus IV: Colloquio internazionale del lessico intellettuale europeo*. Rome: Edizioni dell'Ateneo.

–. 1994. *Ratio VII: Colloquio internazionale del lessico intellettuale europeo.* Firenze: Olschki.

Fioravanti, G. 2001. "Dante e Alberto Magno." In *Il pensiero filosofico e teologico di Dante Alighieri*. Edited by A. Ghisalberti, 93–102. Milan: Vita e Pensiero.

–. 2005. "La Felicità intellettuale: Storiografia e precisazioni." In *La felicità nel medioevo*. Edited by M. Bettetini and F.D. Papaparella, 1–12. Louvain-la-Neuve, Belgium: Fédération Internationale des Instituts d'Études Mediévales.

–. 2008. "'Le Atene celestiali.' Nota a Convivio III xiv 15." In *Per perscrutationem philosophicam. Neue Perspektiven der mittelalterliche Forschung*. Edited by A. Beccarisi, R. Imbach, and P. Porro, 216–23. Hamburg: Meiner Verlag.

–. 2014. "A Natural Desire Can Be Fulfilled in a Purely Natural Manner: The Heresy of Dante." In *Dante and Heterodoxy: The Temptations of Thirteenth-Century Radical Thought*. Edited and with an introduction by M.L. Ardizzone, 35–46. Newcastle upon Tyne, UK: Cambridge Scholars Press.

Fontanier, J.M. 1998. "*Honestum* = to kalon. Sur la pretendue equivalence *honestum* = to kalon; l'exemple d'Augustin." *Revue des sciences philosophiques et theologiques* 82, no. 3: 445–51.

Forti, F. 1967. "La Transumptio nei dettatori bolognesi e in Dante." In *Dante e Bologna ai tempi di Dante*. Edited by Facoltà di Lettere e Filosofia dell'Università di Bologna, 126–49. Bologna: Commissione per i Testi di Lingua.

Foster, K. 1970–9. "Tommaso D'Aquino." *Enciclopedia Dantesca*. Vol. 5. Roma: Istituto Enciclopedia Italiana.

Freccero, J. 1986. *Dante: The Poetics of Conversion*. Introduction by R. Jacoff. Cambridge, MA: Harvard University Press.

–. 1987. *La poetica della conversione*. Bologna: Il Mulino.

Fuhrer, M.L. 1991. "The Contemplative Function of the Agent Intellect in the Psychology of Albert the Great." In *Historia Philosophiae Medii Aevi*. Edited by B. Mojsisch and O. Pluta, 305–19. Amsterdam: B.R. Gruner.

Gragnolati, E. 2005. *Experiencing the Afterlife. Soul and Body in Dante and Medieval Culture*. Notre Dame, IN: Notre Dame University Press.

Gargan, Luciano. 2012. "Biblioteche bolognesi al tempo di Dante. Libri di logica, filosofia e medicina." *Aevum* 86: 667–90.

Gauthier, R.A. 1948. "Trois commentaires 'averroistes' sur L'Ethique à Nicomaque." *Archives d'Histoire Doctrinale et Littéraire du Moyen Age* 16: 187–336.

–. 1951. *Magnanimité. L'ideal de la grandeur dans la philosophie paienne et dans la théologie chrétienne*. Paris: Vrin.

–. 1958. *La morale d'Aristote*. Paris: Presses Universitaires de France.

Gersh, S. 1986. *Middle Platonism and Neoplatonism*. 2 vols. Notre Dame, IN: University of Notre Dame Press.

Ghisalberti, A., ed. 2001. *Il pensiero filosofico e teologico di Dante Alighieri*. Milan: Vita e Pensiero.

Gilson, E. 1972. *Dante et la philosophie*. Paris: Vrin.

–. 1974. "A la recherche de l'Empyrée." In *Dante et Béatrice: Études dantesque*, 67–77. Paris: Vrin.

–. 2007. *Dante and Philosophy*. Translated by David Moore. Grand Rapids, MI: Gilson Press.

Gilson, S.A. 2009. "Reading the *Convivio* from Trecento Florence to Dante's Cinquecento Commentators." *Italian Studies* 64, no. 2: 266–95.

Giunta, C. 2002. *Versi a un destinatario. Saggio sulla poesia italiana del Medioevo*. Bologna: Il Mulino.

Glorieu, P. 1971. *La facultè del arts et ses maitres au XIII siècle*. Paris: Vrin.

Goris, H. 2007. *Theology and Theory of Word in Aquinas. Understanding Augustine Innovating Aristotle*. In *Aquinas the Augustinian*. Edited by M. Dauphinais and M. Levering, 63–78. Washington, DC: The Catholic University of America Press.

Gorni, G. 2001. *Dante prima della Commedia*. Florence: Cadmo.

Grabmann, M. 1980. *Storia del metodo scolastico*. 2 vols. Florence: La Nuova Italia.

Gragnolati, M. 2005. *Experiencing the Afterlife: Soul and Body in Dante and Medieval Culture*. Notre Dame, IN: Notre Dame University Press.

Hadot, P. 2005. *Esercizi spirituali e filosofia antica*. Edited and with an introduction by A.I. Davidson. Turin, Italy: Einaudi.

Haldane, J. 1992. "Aquinas and the Active Intellect." *Philosophy* 67: 199–210.

Hamesse, J. 1984. "Spiritus chez les auteurs philosophiques." In *Spiritus IV: Colloquio internazionale del lessico intellettuale europeo*. Edited by M. Fattori and M. Bianchi, 164–85. Rome: Edizioni dell'Ateneo.

–. 1994. "Ratio dans l'oevre de Saint Bonaventure." In *Ratio VII: Colloquio internazionale del lessico intellettuale europeo*. Edited by M. Fattori and M. Bianchi. Florence: Olschki.

Holloway, J.B. 1990. "The Road through Roncesvalles: Alfonsine Formation of Brunetto Latini and Dante-Diplomacy and Literature." In *Emperor of Culture: Alfonso X the Learned of Castile and His Thirteenth-Century Renaissance*. Edited by R.I. Burns, 109–23. Philadelphia: University of Pennsylvania Press.

Hymes, D., ed. 1974. *Studies in the History of Linguistics*. Bloomington: Indiana University Press.

Imbach, R. 2003. *Dante, la filosofia e i laici*. Milan: Marietti.

Jaeger, W. 1966. *Cristianesimo primitivo e Paideia greca*. Florence: La Nuova Italia.

Koerner, H., J. Niederehe, and R.H. Robins, eds. 2000. *Studies in Medieval Linguistic Thought*. Amsterdam: J. Benjamins.

Kretzmann, N., A. Kenny, and J. Pinborg. 1982. *The Cambridge History of Later Medieval Philosophy: From the Rediscovery of Aristotle to the Disintegration of Scholasticism, 1100–1600*. Cambridge: Cambridge University Press.

Le Goff, J. 1985. *Gli intellettuali nel Medioevo*. Milan: Mondadori.

Lindberg, David C., ed. 1978. *Science in the Middle Ages*. Chicago: University of Chicago Press.

Litt, T. 1963. *Les corps célestes dans l'univers de Saint Thomas Aquinas*. Paris: Publications Universitaires Beatrice Nauwelaerts.

Lonergan, B.J. 1967. *Word and Idea in Aquinas*. Edited by D.B. Burrell. Notre Dame, IN: University of Notre Dame Press.

Lottin, O.D. 1948. *Psycologie et morale aux xii et xiii siècles*. Vol. 2. Edited by J. Duculot. Louvain, Belgium: Abbaye du Mont César.

Mahdi, M. 1976. "Science, Philosophy and Religion in Alfarabi's *Enumeration of the Sciences*." In *The Cultural Context of Medieval Learning*. Edited with an introduction by J.E. Murdoch and E.D. Sylla, 113–47. Boston: Dordrecht.

–. 2001. *Alfarabi and the Foundation of Islamic Political Thought*. Chicago: University of Chicago Press.

Maierù, A. 1972. *Terminologia logica della tarda scolastica*. Rome: Edizioni dell'Ateneo.

–. 2001. *La struttura del sapere*. In *Storia della scienza*. Edited by S. Petruccioli, 263–85. Rome: Treccani.

–. 2003. "La logica nell'età di Cavalcanti." In *Guido Cavalcanti tra i suoi lettori*. Edited by M.L. Ardizzone, 27–50. Florence: Cadmo.

Mann, W.E. 2005. "Anselm on the Trinity." In *The Cambridge Companion to Anselm*. Edited by B. Davis and B. Leftow, 257–78. Cambridge: Cambridge University Press.

Marti, M. 1962. *Realismo Dantesco e altri studi*. Milan-Naples: Ricciardi.

–. 1965. "Vita e morte della presunta doppia redazione della *Vita nuova*." *Rivista di cultura classica e medioevale* 7: 657–69.

Mazzotta, G. 1993. *Dante's Vision and the Circle of Knowledge*. Princeton, NJ: Princeton University Press.

Michaud-Quantin, P. 1970. *Universitas. Expressions du Mouvement Communautaire dans le Moyen Age Latin*. Paris: Vrin.

–. 1974a. Le champs semantiques de *species*.Tradition latine et tradution du grec. In *Etudes sur le vocabulaire philosophique du Moyen Age. Lessico Intellettuale Europeo*. Vol. 5, 113-50. Rome: Edizioni dell'Ateneo.

–. 1974b. "Nouvelles precisions sur les philosophantes." In *Etudes sur le vocabulaire philosophique du Moyen Age. Lessico Intellettuale Europeo.* Vol. 5, 103–11. Rome: Edizioni dell'Ateneo.

Mojsisch, B., and O. Pluta, eds. 1991. *Historia Philosophiae Medii Aevi.* 2 vols. Amsterdam: B.R. Gruner.

Moreschini, C. 2004. *Storia della filosofia patristica.* Brescia: Morcelliana.

Murdoch, J.E., and E.D. Sylla. 1973. *The Cultural Context of Medieval Learning.* Boston: D. Reidel.

Nani-Suarez, T. 2002. *Les anges et la philosophie.* Paris: Vrin.

Nardi, B. 1930. *Saggi di filosofia dantesca.* Milan: Società anonima editrice Dante Alighieri.

–. 1944. *Nel mondo di Dante.* Rome: Edizioni di Storia e Letteratura.

–. 1945. *Sigieri di Brabante nel pensiero del Rinascimento.* Rome: Edizioni italiane.

–. 1960a. *Studi di filosofia medievale.* Rome: Edizioni di Storia e Letteratura.

–. 1960b. "Alberto Magno e San Tommaso." In *Studi di filosofia medieval,* 103–17. Rome: Edizioni di Storia e Letteratura.

–. 1960c. *Dal "Convivio" alla "Commedia": Sei saggi danteschi.* Rome: Istituto Storico per il Medio Evo.

–. 1985a. "L'averroismo del 'primo amico di Dante.'" In *Dante e la cultura medievale,* 81–108. Rome: Laterza.

–. 1985b. *Dante e la cultura medievale.* Rome: Laterza.

Nencioni, G. 1967. "Dante e la retorica." In *Dante e Bologna ai tempi di Dante.* Edited by Facoltà di Lettere e Filosofia dell'Università di Bologna, 91–122. Bologna: Commissione per i testi di lingua.

Parret, H., ed. 1976. *History of Linguistic Thought and Contemporary Linguistics.* New York: Walter De Gruyter.

Pasnau, R. 1997. *Theories of Cognition in the Later Middle Ages.* Cambridge: Cambridge University Press.

Pepin, J. 1994. "La Doctrine augustinienne des Rationes Aeternae, affinités origines." In *Ratio VII: Colloquio internazionale del lessico intellettuale europeo* Edited by M. Bianchi and M. Fattori, 47–68. Florence: Olschki.

Petagine, A. 2009. *Aristotelismo difficile. L'intelletto umano nella prospettiva di Alberto Magno, Tommaso D'Aquino e Sigieri di Brabante.* Milan: Vita and Pensiero.

Petrocchi, G. 1983. *Vita di Dante.* Rome: Laterza.

Picone, M., ed. 1994. *L'Enciclopedismo medievale.* Ravenna: Longo.

Pohlenz, M. 1978. *La Stoa.* 2 vols. Florence: La Nuova Italia.

Porro, P. 2010. "Tra il 'Convivio' e la 'Commedia.' Dante e il 'forte dubitare' intorno al desiderio naturale di conoscere le sostanze separate." In *1308: Eine Topographie historischer Gleichzeitigkeit.* Edited by A. Speer and D. Wirmer, 631–59. New York: Walter De Gruyter.

–. 2012. "'Avegna che pochi, per male camminare, compiano la giornata.' L'ideale della felicità filosofica e i suoi limiti nel Convivio dantesco." *Freiburger Zeitschrift für Philosophie und Theologie* 59, no. 2: 389–406.

Purcell, W. 1987. "Transsumptio: A Rhetorical Doctrine of the Thirteenth Century." *Rhetorica* 5, no. 4: 369–411.

Quinn, J.F. 1973. *The Historical Constitution of St. Bonaventure's Philosophy.* Toronto: Pontifical Institute of Medieval Studies Publications.

Roques, R. 1996. *L'Universo dionisiano. Struttura gerarchica del mondo secondo ps. Dionigi Areopagita.* Milan: Vita and Pensiero.

Rosier, I., ed. 1988a. *L'Héritage des grammairiens latins, de l'Antiquité aux Lumières. Actes du colloque de Chantilly 2–4 septembre 1987.* Louvain, Belgium: Peeters.

–. 1988b. "Le Traitement spéculatif des constructions figurées au treizième siècle." In *L'héritage des grammairiens latins, de l'Antiquité aux Lumières. Actes du colloque de Chantilly 2–4 septembre 1987.* Edited by I. Rosier, 181–204. Louvain, Belgium: Peeters.

Rovighi, S.V. 1967. "Le 'disputazioni de li filosofanti.'" In *Dante e Bologna ai tempi di Dante*, ed. Facoltà di Lettere e Filosofia dell'Università di Bologna, 179–82. Bologna: Commissione per i Testi di Lingua.

–. 2006. *Storia della filosofia medievale. Dalla patristica al secolo xiv.* Edited by P. Rossi. Milan: Vita and Pensiero.

Ruello, F. 1963. *Les "Noms divins" et leurs raisons selon Albert le Grand commentateur du "De Divinis nominibus."* Paris: Vrin.

Saffrey, H.D. 1990. *Recherches sur le néoplatonisme après Plotin.* Paris: Vrin.

Scott, J.A. 1995. "The Unfinished *Convivio* as a Pathway to the *Commedia.*" *Dante Studies* 113: 31–56.

Skinner, Q. 1978. *The Foundations of Modern Political Thought.* Vol. 1: *The Renaissance.* Cambridge: Cambridge University Press.

Spitzer, L. 1976. *Studi Italiani.* Edited by C. Scarpati. Milan: Vita e pensiero.

Tanturli, C. 2003. "L'edizione critica delle *Rime* e il libro delle canzoni di Dante." *Studi Danteschi* 68: 251–66.

Trentman, J.A. 1974. "Speculative Grammar and Transformational Grammar: A Comparison of Philosophical Presuppositions." In *Studies in the History of Linguistics.* Edited by D. Hymes. Bloomington: Indiana University Press.

Tunberg, T.O. 1986. "What is Boncompagno's newest Rhetoric?" *Traditio* 42: 299–334.

Turner, J.D., and K. Corrigan, eds. 2010. *Plato's Parmenides and Its Heritage.* 2 vols. Atlanta, GA: Society of Biblical Literature.

Ureni, P. 2010. "Human Generation, Memory and Poetic Creation: From the *Purgatorio* to the *Paradiso.*" *Quaderni di Italianistica* 21, no. 2: 9–35.

–. 2014. "Medicine and Radical Thought: A Possible Galenic Presence." In *Dante and Heterodoxy: The Temptations of Thirteenth-Century Radical Thought.* Edited and with an introduction by M.L. Ardizzone, 225–41. Newcastle upon Tyne, UK: Cambridge Scholars Press.

Vallat, P. 2004. *Farabi et l'ecole d'Alexandrie. Des premisses de la connaissance a la philosophie politique.* Paris: Vrin.

Van Steenberghen, F. 1977. *Maitre Siger de Brabant.* Louvain, Belgium: Publications Universitaires, Vander Oyez, S.A.

–. 1980. *Thomas Aquinas and Radical Aristotelianism.* Washington, DC: The Catholic University of America Press.

–. 1991. *La philosophie au xiiie siecle.* Louvain, Belgium: Editions Peters.

Van Winden, J.C.M. 1965. *Calcidius on Mattter: His Doctrine and Sources: A Chapter in the History of Platonism.* Leiden, Netherlands: E.J. Brill.

Vanier, Jean. 1965. *Le Bonheur: Principe et fin de la morale aristotélicienne.* Paris: Desclée De Brouwer.

Verbecke, G. 1983. *The Presence of Stoicism in Medieval Thought.* Washington, DC: The Catholic University of America Press.

Weisheipl, J.A. 1961. "The Celestial Movers in Medieval Physics." *The Thomist* 24: 286–326.

–. 1994. *Tommaso D'Aquino. Vita Pensiero Opere.* Milan: Jaca Book.

Wippel, J.F. 1993. *Thomas Aquinas on the Divine Ideas.* Toronto: Pontifical Institute of Mediaeval Studies.

Witt, R.G. 2000. *In the Footsteps of the Ancients: The Origins of Humanism from Lovato to Bruni.* Boston: Brill.

Woolfson, H.A. 1935. "The Internal Senses in Latin, Arabic and Hebrew Philosophical Texts." *Harvard Theological Review* 28: 69–133.

–. 1948. *Philo: Foundations of Religious Philosophy in Judaism, Christianity, and Islam.* Cambridge, MA: Harvard University Press.

Zambelli, P. 1992. "Le stelle 'sorde e mute' ed i loro 'motori' alle origini della scienza moderna? Un case-study storiografico." In *Historia Philosophiae Medii Aevi.* Edited by B. Mojsisch and O. Pluta, 1099–117. Amsterdam: B.R. Gruner.

Zavattero, I. 2005. "La 'Quaestio de felicitate' di Giacomo da Pistoia. Una tentativa di interpretazione alla luce dell'edizione critica del testo." In *La felicità nel medioevo.* Edited by M. Bettetini and F. Paparella, 335–410. Louvain-la-Neuve, Belgium: Fédération Internationale des Instituts d'Études Médiévales.

Index